Communications in Computer and Information Science   **1210**

Commenced Publication in 2007
Founding and Former Series Editors:
Simone Diniz Junqueira Barbosa, Phoebe Chen, Alfredo Cuzzocrea,
Xiaoyong Du, Orhun Kara, Ting Liu, Krishna M. Sivalingam,
Dominik Ślęzak, Takashi Washio, Xiaokang Yang, and Junsong Yuan

More information about this series at http://www.springer.com/series/7899

Yuan Tian · Tinghuai Ma ·
Muhammad Khurram Khan (Eds.)

Big Data and Security

First International Conference, ICBDS 2019
Nanjing, China, December 20–22, 2019
Revised Selected Papers

 Springer

Editors
Yuan Tian 🆔
Nanjing Institute of Technology
Nanjing, China

Muhammad Khurram Khan 🆔
King Saud University
Riyadh, Saudi Arabia

Tinghuai Ma 🆔
Nanjing University of Information Science
and Technology
Nanjing, China

ISSN 1865-0929   ISSN 1865-0937   (electronic)
Communications in Computer and Information Science
ISBN 978-981-15-7529-7   ISBN 978-981-15-7530-3   (eBook)
https://doi.org/10.1007/978-981-15-7530-3

This Springer imprint is published by the registered company Springer Nature Singapore Pte Ltd.
The registered company address is: 152 Beach Road, #21-01/04 Gateway East, Singapore 189721,
Singapore

Preface

This volume contains the papers from the First International Conference on Big Data and Security (ICBDS 2019). The event was held in Nanjing, China, and was organized by Nanjing Institute of Technology, Oulu University, King Saud University, Curtin University, JiangSu Computer Society, Nanjing University of Posts and Telecommunications, and IEEE Broadcast Technology Society.

ICBDS 2019 brings experts and researchers together from all over the world to discuss the current status and potential ways to address security and privacy regarding the use of Big Data systems. Big Data systems are complex and heterogeneous. Due to its extraordinary scale and the integration of different technologies, new security and privacy issues are introduced and must be properly addressed. The ongoing digitalization of the business world is putting companies and users at risk of cyber attacks more than ever before. Big Data analysis has the potential to offer protection against these attacks. Participation in workshops on specific topics of the conference is expected to achieve progress, global networking in transferring, and exchanging ideas.

The selected papers come from researchers based in several countries including China, Australia, Finland, Saudi Arabia, the UAE, and Pakistan. The highly diversified audience gave us the opportunity to achieve a good level of understanding of the mutual needs, requirements, and technical means available in this field of research. The topics presented in the first edition of this event include the following fields connected to Big Data: Security in Blockchain, IoT Security, Security in Cloud and Fog Computing, Artificial Intelligence/Machine Learning Security, Cybersecurity, and Privacy. We received 251 submissions and accepted 49 papers. All the accepted papers were peer reviewed by three qualified reviewers chosen from our Technical Program Committee based on their qualifications and experience.

The proceedings editors wish to thank the dedicated Scientific Committee members and all the other reviewers for their efforts and contributions. We also thank Springer for their trust and for publishing the proceedings of ICBDS 2019.

May 2020

Tinghuai Ma
Çetin Kaya Koç
Yi Pan
Muhammad Khurram Khan
Markku Oivo
Yuan Tian

Organization

Honorary Chairs

Guojun Shi   Nanjing Institute of Technology, China
Jinfei Shi   Nanjing Institute of Technology, China

General Chairs

Tinghuai Ma   Nanjing University of Information Science
           and Technology, China
Yi Pan   Georgia State University, USA
Muhammad Khurram Khan King Saud University, Saudi Arabia
Markku Oivo   University of Oulu, Finland
Yuan Tian   Nanjing Institute of Technology, China

Technical Program Chairs

Victor S. Sheng   University of Central Arkansas, USA
Zhaoqing Pan   Nanjing University of Information Science
           and Technology, China

Technical Program Committee Members

Eui-Nam Huh   Kyung Hee University, South Korea
Teemu Karvonen   University of Oulu, Finland
Heba Abdullataif Kurdi   Massachusetts Institute of Technology, USA
Omar Alfandi   Zayed University, UAE
Dongxue Liang   Tsing Hua University, China
Mohammed Al-Dhelaan   King Saud University, Saudi Arabia
Päivi Raulamo-Jurvanen   University of Oulu, Finland
Zeeshan Pervez   University of the West of Scotland, UK
Adil Mehmood Khan   Innopolis University, Russia
Wajahat Ali Khan   Kyung Hee University, South Korea
Qiaolin Ye   Nanjing Forestry University, China
Pertti Karhapää   University of Oulu, Finland
Farkhund Iqbal   Zayed University, UAE
Muhammad Ovais Ahmad   Karlstad University, Sweden
Lejun Zhang   Yangzhou University, China
Linshan Shen   Harbin Engineering University, China
Ghada Al-Hudhud   King Saud University, Saudi Arabia
Lei Han   Nanjing Institute of Technology, China
Tang Xin   University of International Relations, China

Zeeshan Pervez	University of West of Scotland, UK
Mznah Al Rodhaan	King Saud University, Saudi Arabia
Zhenjian Yao	Huazhong University of Science and Technology, China
Thant Zin Oo	Kyung Hee University, South Korea
Mohammad Rawashdeh	University of Central Missouri, USA
Alia Alabdulkarim	King Saud University, Saudi Arabia
Elina Annanperä	University of Oulu, Finland
Soha Zaghloul Mekki	King Saud University, Saudi Arabia
Basmah Alotibi	King Saud University, Saudi Arabia
Mariya Muneeb	King Saud University, Saudi Arabia
Maryam hajakbari	Islamic Azad University, Iran
Miada Murad	King Saud University, Saudi Arabia
Pilar Rodríguez	Technical University of Madrid, Spain
Zhiwei Wang	Hebei Normal University, China
Rand. J	Shaqra University, Saudi Arabia
Jiagao Wu	Nanjing University of Posts and Telecommunications, China
Mohammad Mehedi Hassan	King Saud University, Saudi Arabia
Weipeng Jing	Northeast Forestry University, China
Yu Zhang	Harbin Institute of Technology, China
Nguyen H. Tran	The University of Sydney, Australia
Hang Chen	Nanjing Institute of Technology, China
Sarah alkharji	King Saud University, Saudi Arabia
Chunguo Li	Southeast University, China
Xiaohua Huang	University of Oulu, Finland
Babar Shah	Zayed University, UAE
Tianyang Zhou	State Key Laboratory of Mathematical Engineering and Advanced Computing, China
Manal Hazazi	King Saud University, Saudi Arabia
Jiagao Wu	Nanjing University of Posts and Telecommunications, China
Markus Kelanti	University of Oulu, Finland
Amiya Kumar Tripathy	Edith Cowan University, Australia
Shaoyong Guo	Beijing University of Posts and Telecommunications, China
Shadan AlHamed	King Saud University, Saudi Arabia
Cunjie Cao	Hainan University, China
Linfeng Liu	Nanjing University of Posts and Telecommunications, China
Chunliang Yang	China Mobile IoT Company Limited, China
Patrick Hung	University of Ontario Institute of Technology, Canada
Xinjian Zhao	State Grid Nanjing Power Supply Company, China
Sungyoung Lee	Kyung Hee University, South Korea
Zhengyu Chen	Jinling Institute of Technology, China

Jian Zhou	Nanjing University of Posts and Telecommunications, China
Pasi Kuvaja	University of Oulu, Finland
Xiao Xue	Tianjin University, China
Jianguo Sun	Harbin Engineering University, China
Farkhund Iqbal	Zayed University, UAE
Zilong Jin	Nanjing University of Information Science and Technology, China
Susheela Dahiya	University of Petroleum & Energy Studies, India
Ming Pang	Harbin Engineering University, China
Yuanfeng Jin	Yanbian University, China
Maram Al-Shablan	King Saud University, Saudi Arabia
Kejia Chen	Nanjing University of Posts and Telecommunications, China
Valentina Lenarduzzi	University of Tampere, Finland
Davide Taibi	University of Tampere, Finland
Jinghua Ding	Sungkyunkwan University, South Korea
Xuesong Yin	Nanjing Institute of Technology, China
Qiang Ma	King Saud University, Saudi Arabia
Tero Päivärinta	University of Oulu, Finland
Shiwen Hu	Accelor Ltd., USA
Manar Hosny	King Saud University, Saudi Arabia
Lei Cui	Chinese Academy of Sciences, China
Yonghua Gong	Nanjing University of Posts and Telecommunications, China
Kashif Saleem	King Saud University, Saudi Arabia
Xiaojian Ding	Nanjing University of Finance and Economics, China
Irfan Mohiuddin	King Saud University, Saudi Arabia
Ming Su	Beijing University of Posts and Telecommunications, China
Yunyun Wang	Nanjing University of Posts and Telecommunications, China
Abdullah Al-Dhelaan	King Saud University, Saudi Arabia

Workshop Chairs

Jiande Zhang	Nanjing Institute of Technology, China
Ning Ye	Nanjing Forestry University, China
Asad Masood Khattak	Zayed University, UAE

Publication Chair

Vidyasagar Potdar	Curtin University, Australia

Organization Chairs

Chenrong Huang	Nanjing Institute of Technology, China
Bangjun Nie	Nanjing Institute of Technology, China
Xianyun Li	Nanjing Institute of Technology, China
Jianhua Chen	Nanjing Institute of Technology, China
Wenlong Shao	Nanjing Institute of Technology, China
Kari Liukkunen	University of Oulu, Finland

Organization Committee Members

Wei Huang	Nanjing Institute of Technology, China
Pilar Rodriguez Gonzalez	University of Oulu, Finland
Jalal Al Muhtadi	King Saud University, Saudi Arabia
Geng Yang	Nanjing University of Posts and Telecommunications, China
Qiaolin Ye	Nanjing Forestry University, China
Pertti Karhapää	University of Oulu, Finland
Lei Han	Nanjing Institute of Technology, China
Yong Zhu	Jingling Institute of Technology, China
Päivi Raulamo-Jurvanen	University of Oulu, Finland
Bin Xie	Hebei Normal University, China
Dawei Li	Nanjing Institute of Technology, China
Jingrong Chen	Nanjing Institute of Technology, China
Thant Zin Oo	Kyung Hee University, South Korea
Shoubao Su	Jiangsu Key Laboratory of Data Science and Smart Software, China
Alia Alabdulkarim	King Saud University, Saudi Arabia
Juanjuan Cheng	Nanjing Institute of Technology, China
Xiao Wu	White Matrix Co, Ltd., China
Rand. J	Shaqra University, Saudi Arabia
Hang Chen	Nanjing Institute of Technology, China
Jiagao Wu	Nanjing University of Posts and Telecommunications, China

Contents

Big Data

Blockchain and Internet of Things

Security in Cloud and Fog Computing

Artificial Intelligence/Machine Learning Security

Cybersecurity and Privacy

An Efficient Lattice-Based IBE Scheme Using Combined Public Key

Yanfeng Shi[1(✉)], Shuo Qiu[2], and Jiqiang Liu[3]

[1] School of Computer Engineering, Nanjing Institute of Technology, Nanjing, China
shiyf@njit.edu.cn
[2] Jinling Institute of Technology, Nanjing, China
shuoqiu@jit.edu.cn
[3] Beijing Jiaotong University, Beijing, China
jqliu@bjtu.edu.cn

Abstract. Lattice-based Identity-based encryption (IBE) can both simplify certificate management and resist quantum attack in the real world. Combined Public Key (CPK) technology can be used to enhance the efficiency of IBE schemes. In this paper, we use CPK to construct a more efficient lattice-based IBE scheme based on a variant of learning with errors (LWE) problem, by avoiding complex trapdoor generation algorithm and preimage sampling algorithm required by the existing lattice-based IBE schemes from LWE. Its storage cost is also lower. We show that our IBE scheme is semantically secure against an adaptive chosen plaintext attack (CPA) from all probabilistic polynomial time adversaries in the random oracle model.

Keywords: Identity-based encryption · Discrete Gaussian distribution · Learning with errors · Combined public key

1 Introduction

Compared with regular public key cryptosystems, identity-based encryption (IBE) which is proposed by Shamir simplifies certificate management [13]. In an IBE scheme, the sender can encrypt messages using the identity of the receiver as the public key. So the receiver don't require to show his/her public key certification to the sender. The first efficient IBE scheme is presented by Boneh and Franklin. It is based on bilinear maps [3].

However, traditional IBE based on IFP, DLP, ECDLP and their derivants such as CDH and BDH, will face on the threat of quantum computing. Lattice-based cryptography is one of the most important Post-quantum cryptography. Firstly, as Daniele Micciancio and Oded Regev's show, there is no polynomial time quantum algorithm that approximates lattice problems to within polynomial factors [11]. So lattice problems are even hard for quantum and subexponential-time adversary. Secondly, compared with modular exponentiation, lattice operations are more efficient.

© Springer Nature Singapore Pte Ltd. 2020
Y. Tian et al. (Eds.): ICBDS 2019, CCIS 1210, pp. 3–16, 2020.
https://doi.org/10.1007/978-981-15-7530-3_1

In 2008, Craig Gentry et al., proposed an IBE scheme based on a lattice problem-learning with errors (LWE) problem and proved its security against IND-ID-CPA in the random oracle model [5]. Also, more constructions for lattice-based IBE have been put forward [1,2,14,16–18]. But the existing lattice-based ibe schemes from LWE are not efficient enough, especially in Setup and Extract phase. Because these schemes require trapdoor generation algorithm and preimage sampling algorithm. The most efficient trapdoor generation and preimage sampling algorithms are present by Micciancio et al. [10] and improved by Ye et al. with the implicit extension method [17]. However, their solutions need $O(n^3)$ times of multiplication and addition, which are still not practical enough.

In this paper, we take advantage of combined public keys (CPK) to present a more efficient lattice-based IBE. In our IBE scheme, Setup and Extract is much more efficient than the existing lattice-based IBE constructions by avoiding the complex trapdoor generation and preimage sampling algorithm. It only needs $O(n^3/\log n)$ additions of vectors, which is parallelizable. Moreover, the storage cost is much lower because the Private Key Generator (PKG) doesn't require to storage large-scale keys but only little-scale key "seeds". For balance, the scheme sacrifices the length of public key.

Then we analyze its security under a variant of LWE (learning with errors) assumption (which is Equivalent to standard LWE assumption) in the random oracle model and prove that it is semantically secure against IND-ID-CPA.

The rest of paper is organized as follows. In Sect. 2, we introduce some preliminaries, such as IBE, LWE-assumption, and so on. In Sect. 3, we propose a variant of LWE-assumption. Section 4 is our construction of IND-ID-CPA secure lattice-based IBE using CPK.

2   Preliminaries

2.1   Combined Public Key

Combined public key (CPK)is a new technology that can be used in key management. It is presented by Nan [15] and used in varies systems [7,8]. It can be used to enhance the efficiency of IBE scheme and retrench the storage space.

In CPK technology, there are two key matrixes-a private key matrix and a public key matrix. The public key and private key for each ID can be computed through a mapping algorithm and the key matrixes [15].

In this paper, our construction takes the advantage of the combined property of key pairs in CPK technology.

Supposing there is a public key matrix $(y_1, y_2, ..., y_{n'})$, the corresponding private key matrix $(x_1, ..., x_{n'})$, where $y_i = f(x_i)$, and a collision-resistant mapping function $h(\cdot) : \{0, 1\}^* \to \{0, 1\}^{n'}$. Therefore, the public key and private key can be calculated by mapping function and key matrixes. That is to say if a user's identity is id, the hash value is computed by equation $h(id) = h_1, ..., h_{n'}$. So the user's public key is $y_{id} = \sum\limits_{i=1}^{n'} y_i h_i$ and private key $x_{id} = \sum\limits_{i=1}^{n'} h_i x_i$, where $y_{id} = f(x_{id})$.

In this paper, we adapt this technology to lattice-based cryptography and use it to construct more efficient and secure lattice IBE schemes.

2.2 Identity-Based Encryption (IBE)

An identity-based encryption scheme consists of four algorithms: Setup, Extract, Encrypt, Decrypt.

Setup: This non-deterministic algorithm generates system parameters denoted by PP, and a master key. The system parameter is public whereas only the Private key Generator (PKG) knows the master key.

Extract: This algorithm extracts a private key corresponding to a given identity using the master key.

Encrypt: It encrypts messages for a given identity with system parameters.

Decrypt: It decrypts ciphertext using the private key.

2.3 IND-ID-CPA

In general, the standard IBE security model which is defined in [4]is the indistinguishability of ciphertexts under an adaptive chosen-plaintext and chosen-identity attack (IND-ID-CPA).

We consider the IND-ID-CPA game played between a challenger and an adversary.

Setup. The challenger runs Setup (1^λ), and generates PP (the system parameters) and the master private key. Then it gives PP to the adversary and keeps the master key secret.

Phase 1. The adversary can issue queries $q_1, q_2, , ..., q_l$ with an identity $<ID_i>$. The challenger responds with the corresponding private key. Of course, each query q_i may depend on the knowledge of the challenger's responses to $q_1, q_2, ..., q_{i-1}$.

Challenge. The adversary sends the challenger an identity ID which he did not request the private key in Phase 1, and two messages-M_0 and M_1. The challenger picks a random bit $\sigma \in \{0, 1\}$ and encrypts M_σ by computing C = Encrypt (PP, ID, M_σ). Then it sends C as the challenge to the adversary.

Phase 2. The adversary repeats the Phase 1 with the restriction that the adversary can't request a private key for the target identity ID.

Guess. Finally, the adversary outputs a guess $\sigma' \in \{0, 1\}$. The adversary wins if and only if $\sigma' = \sigma$.

The advantage of the adversary in attacking an IBE scheme is defined as $Pr^{adv} = |Pr[\sigma' = \sigma] - 1/2|$.

Definition 1 *(IND-ID-CPA secure). An IBE scheme is (k, ε)-semantically secure against an adaptive chosen plaintext attack if all probabilistic polynomial time (PPT) adversaries making at most k private key queries can get at most ε advantage in breaking the scheme [3].*

2.4   Statistically Distance

Suppose X and Y are two random variables are chosen from a finite set Ω. The statistical distance is defined as

$$\Delta(X;Y) = \frac{1}{2} \sum_{t \in \Omega} |Pr[X = t] - Pr[Y = t]|$$

If $\Delta(X(\lambda); Y(\lambda))$ is a negligible function of λ, then X and Y are statistically close [1].

2.5   Lattices

An n-dimensional lattice is the set of all integer linear combinations of some linearly independent vectors $b_1, ..., b_m \in \mathbb{R}^n$. where $b_1, ..., b_m$ are called basic vectors.

The n-dimensional lattice of rank m is defined as:

$$\Lambda = L(B) = \{y \in \mathbb{R}^n \; s.t. \exists s \in \mathbb{Z}^m, y = Bs = \sum_{i=1}^{m} s_i b_i\}$$

Obviously, L is contained in $\mathbb{Z}^m$. In our schemes, we mainly use the special lattice $\mathbb{Z}^m$ [5].

2.6   Discrete Gaussians

Let L be a subset of $\mathbb{Z}^m$, c is a vector, and $r \in \mathbb{R}$ is a positive parameter, then we have following definitions:

$\rho_{r,c}(x) = exp(-\pi \frac{\|x-c\|^2}{r^2})$, where $\|\cdot\|$ implicitly represent Euclidean l_2 norm: This is a Gaussian-shaped function on $\mathbb{R}^m$ whose mean is 0 and variance is r^2;

$\rho_{r,c}(L) = \sum_{x \in L} \rho_{r,c}(x)$: This function represents the sum of $\rho_{r,c}$ over L.

According to above two definitions, the discrete Gaussian distribution over L with parameter r and c is defined as follows:

$$\forall \tilde{x} \in L, D_{L,r,c}(\tilde{x}) = \frac{\rho_{r,c}(\tilde{x})}{\rho_{r,c}(L)}.$$

In the following sections, we will use a special discrete Gaussian distribution $D_{\mathbb{Z}^m, r}$, i.e. $L = \mathbb{Z}^m$ and $c = 0$.

Now we introduce SampleD algorithm that can sample from a discrete Gaussian over any lattice.

For example, taking some n-dimensional basis $B \in \mathbb{Z}^{n \times m}$, a sufficient large Gaussian parameter r and a mean $c \in \mathbb{R}^n$, it can output a sample from (a distribution close to)$D_{L(B),r,c}$. In the following section, we can generate a value chosen from $D_{\mathbb{Z}^m, r}$ by running SampleD [5].

2.7 Decision-LWE Hardness Assumption

Decision Learning with errors (Decision-LWE) problem is a variant of LWE problem. It is as hard as LWE problem [12]. In this section, we introduce the Decision-LWE problem and its hardness assumption.

Definition 2 *(Distribution $\bar{\Psi}_\alpha$). Consider a real parameter $\alpha = \alpha(n) \in (0,1)$ and a prime q. $x \in \mathbb{R}$, $\lceil x \rfloor = \lfloor x + 1/2 \rfloor$ denotes a nearest integer to x. Denote by $\mathbb{T} = \mathbb{R}/\mathbb{Z}$ the group of reals [0, 1) with mod 1 addition. Ψ_α denotes a distribution over $\mathbb{T}$ of a normal variable with mean 0 and standard deviation $\alpha/\sqrt{2\pi}$ then reduced modulo 1. $\bar{\Psi}_\alpha$ denotes the discrete distribution over $\mathbb{Z}_q$ of the random variable $\lceil qX \rfloor \bmod q$ where the random variable $X \in \mathbb{T}$ is chosen from distribution Ψ_α [1].*

We denote $\bar{\Psi}_\alpha$ by χ_α or χ.

According to [6,9,12], we can redescribe the definition of Decision-LWE problem as follows.

Definition 3 *(Decision $-$ $LWE_{q,\alpha}(DLWE_{q,\alpha})$ problem). Consider a positive integer n, an arbitrary integer $m \leq poly(n)$, a prime modulus $q \leq poly(n)$, and a distribution $\bar{\Psi}_\alpha(\chi)$ over $\mathbb{Z}_q$, all public. The challenger randomly chooses a matrix $A \in \mathbb{Z}_q^{n \times m}$, a secret vector $s \in \mathbb{Z}_q^n$, and a bit $\tau \in \{0,1\}$, uniformly and independently. If $\tau = 1$ it outputs the tuple $(A, A^T s + x) \in \mathbb{Z}_q^{n \times m} \times \mathbb{Z}_q^m$, where x is chosen from χ^m; Otherwise, it outputs the tuple $(A, d) \in \mathbb{Z}_q^{n \times m} \times \mathbb{Z}_q^m$, where d is uniformly and randomly chosen from $\mathbb{Z}^m$. Then the adversary outputs a guess τ' of τ. (all operations are performed in $\mathbb{Z}_q$.)*

The advantage of adversary in solving the $DLWE_{q,\alpha}$ problem is defined as [12]

$$Pr^{adv}(DLWE_{q,\alpha}) = |Pr[\tau' = \tau] - \frac{1}{2}|$$

DLWE Assumption: $DLWE_{q,\alpha}$ assumption holds if for any PPT adversary, the advantage of solving the $DLWE_{q,\alpha}$ problem.

For the certain parameters q and noise distributions $\bar{\Psi}_\alpha$ (denoted by χ) such that $\alpha \cdot q > 2\sqrt{n}$, $DLWE_{q,\alpha}$ problem is hard under a quantum reduction [12]. That is to say, $DLWE_{q,\alpha}$ assumption holds even for quantum PPT adversary.

Theorem 1. *Let n be a positive integer and q be a prime, and $m \geq 2n \lg q$. Then for all but a $2q^{-n}$ fraction of all $A \in \mathbb{Z}_q^{n \times m}$ and for any $r \geq \omega(\sqrt{\log m})$, the distribution of the syndrome $u = Ae \bmod q$ is statistically close to uniform over $\mathbb{Z}^n$, where $\omega(\cdot)$ is a function defined as: if $g(n) = \omega(f(n))$, then increment speed of $g(n)$ is faster than any $cf(n)(c > 1)$ and $e \leftarrow D_{\mathbb{Z}^m,r}$ [11].*

3 A Variant of LWE Assumption

In Sect. 2.7, we have showed that for certain q and α, $DLWE_{q,\alpha}$ is a hard problem. For convenience to our construction, in this section, we present a variant of $LWE_{q,\alpha}$ problem and prove it is as hard as the $DLWE_{q,\alpha}$ problem.

Definition 4 *(Twins − Decision − $LWE_{q,m,n,r,\alpha}$ ($TDLWE_{q,m,n,r,\alpha}$) problem).*
Consider a positive integer n, a arbitrary integer $m \leq poly(n)$, a prime modulus $q \leq poly(n)$, and a distribution $\bar{\Psi}_\alpha(\chi)$ over $\mathbb{Z}_q$, all public. Then the challenger randomly and uniformly chooses a matrix $A \in \mathbb{Z}_q^{n \times m}$ and a secret vector $s' \in \mathbb{Z}_q^n$, and randomly chooses a vector e' from discrete Gaussian distribution $D_{\mathbb{Z}^m,r}$. Then the challenger picks a bit $\tau \in \{0,1\}$ uniformly and independently. If $\tau = 1$ it outputs the tuple $(A, Ae', A^T s' + x', e'^T A^T s' + x) \in \mathbb{Z}_q^{n \times m} \times \mathbb{Z}_q^n \times \mathbb{Z}_q^m \times \mathbb{Z}_q$, where x' is chosen from χ^m and x is chosen from χ; otherwise, it outputs the tuple $(A, Ae', A^T s' + x', d) \in \mathbb{Z}_q^{n \times m} \times \mathbb{Z}_q^n \times \mathbb{Z}_q^m \times \mathbb{Z}_q$, where x' is chosen from χ^m and d is randomly and uniformly chosen from $\mathbb{Z}_q$. Then the adversary outputs a guess τ' of τ. (all operations are performed in $\mathbb{Z}_q$.)

We define the advantage of adversary solving the $TDLWE_{q,m,n,r,\alpha}$ as

$$Pr^{adv}(TDLWE_{q,m,n,r,\alpha}) = |Pr[\tau' = \tau] - \frac{1}{2}|$$

.

TDLWE Assumption: $TDLWE_{q,m,n,r,\alpha}$ assumption holds if for any PPT adversary, the advantage of solving the $TDLWE_{q,m,n,r,\alpha}$ problem.

In the following parts, we discuss the relationship between $DLWE_{q,\alpha}$ assumption and $TDLWE_{q,m,n,r,\alpha}$ assumption. Here, we adjust our parameters q, m, n, r, α so that the $DLWE_{q,\alpha}$ problem is a hard problem under a quantum reduction and Ae' is statistically close to uniform over $\mathbb{Z}_q^n$, where $e' \leftarrow D_{\mathbb{Z}^m,r}$.

Theorem 2. *For certain q, m, n, r, α, where $m \geq 2n \lg q, r \geq \omega(\sqrt{\log m})$, if $DLWE_{q,\alpha}$ assumption holds, then $TDLWE_{q,m,n,r,\alpha}$ assumption holds too.*

Proof. According to Theorem 1, for certain $m \geq 2n \lg q, r \geq \omega(\sqrt{\log m})$, Ae' is statistically close to uniform B. So TDLWE assumption tuple $(A, Ae', A^T s' + x', e'^T A^T s' + x)$ is equivalent to $(A, B, A^T s' + x', B^T s' + x)$. Also, if $DLWE_{q,\alpha}$ assumption holds, TDLWE assumption tuple $(A, Ae', A^T s' + x', e'^T A^T s' + x)$ can be replaced by $(A, B, C, B^T s' + x)$, with C is uniformly and randomly chosen from $\mathbb{Z}_q^m$. A and C is independent with $(B, B^T s' + x)$, which is equal to DLWE assumption.

4   A Lattice-Based IBE Scheme Using Combined Public Key

In Sect. 3, we proposed a variant of LWE problem-TDLWE problem and analyzed its hardness. In this section, we will construct a lattice IBE scheme using CPK based on TDLWE problem and analyze its security under TDLWE assumption in the next section.

4.1 Scheme Construction

Setup(1^λ) On input a security parameter λ, set the parameters q, n, m, r, α as specified as Sect. 4.2. Choose a common matrix $A \in \mathbb{Z}_q^{n \times m}$ uniformly at random. All operations are performed over $\mathbb{Z}_q$. Then choose n' secret vectors $e_i (i = 1, 2, ..., n')$ from the discrete Gaussian at random $D_{\mathbb{Z}^m, r}$.

Then the master private key is

$$E = (e_1, e_2, ..., e_{n'}),$$

and the public key is

$$U = (u_1, u_2, ..., u_{n'}), \text{where } u_i = Ae_i.$$

Additionally, choose a cryptographic hash function $H : \{0, 1\}^* \rightarrow \{0, 1\}^{n'}$. Then make $PP = (A, U, n', H, q)$ public.

Extract(PP, E, id) Suppose that h_i is the ith bit of $H(id)$, $i = 1, 2, ..., n'$ output

$e_{id} = \sum\limits_{i=1}^{n'} h_i e_i.$

Encrypt(PP, id, b) On input public parameters PP, an identity id, and a bit $b \in \{0, 1\}$, do:

1. Check whether this is the first time to encrypt a message under this id. If it is, construct $u_{id} = \sum\limits_{i=1}^{n'} h_i u_i = \sum\limits_{i=1}^{n'} Ah_i e_i = Ae_{id} \in \mathbb{Z}_q^n$.
2. To encrypt a bit $b \in \{0, 1\}$, choose $s \leftarrow \mathbb{Z}_q^n$ uniformly and compute $p = A^T s + x \in \mathbb{Z}_q^m$, where $x \leftarrow \chi^m$. Output the ciphertext as $C = (c_1, c_2) = (p, u_{id}^T s + \bar{x} + b\lfloor q/2 \rfloor) \in \mathbb{Z}_q^m \times \mathbb{Z}_q$, where $\bar{x} \leftarrow \chi$.

Decrypt(PP, e_{id}, C) On input public parameters PP, a private key e_{id} and a ciphertext $C = (c_1, c_2)$, do: compute $b' = c_2 - e_{id}^T c_1 \in \mathbb{Z}_q$. Output 0 if b' is closer to 0 than to $\lfloor q/2 \rfloor$ modulo q, otherwise output 1.

4.2 Parameters

Ref.Craig Gentry, Chris Perkert and Vinod Vaikuntanathan's show about parameters, we let $q \geq 5r\sqrt{n'}(m+1), \alpha \leq 1/(r\sqrt{n'(m+1)}) \cdot \omega(\sqrt{\log n})$,$q \cdot \alpha > 2\sqrt{n}$, $m \geq 2n \lg q$ and $r \geq \omega(\sqrt{\log m})$ [5]. According to Theorem 1, in this case the distribution of public keys u_{id} is statistically close to uniform over $\mathbb{Z}_q^n$ and $TDLWE_{q,m,n,r,\alpha}$ assumption holds. Also, we can show that the receiver can decrypt the ciphertext correctly with private key in next section.

4.3   Completeness

The correctness is analogous to [5]. Since the linear combination of the independent normal variables is also a normal variable, $e_{id} = \sum_{i=1}^{n'} h_i e_i$ is equally chosen from $D_{\mathbb{Z}^m, r'}$, where $r' = \sqrt{\sum_{i=1}^{n'} h_i r^2} \leq \sqrt{n'} r \leq \frac{q}{5(m+1)}$.

Then the Decrypt algorithm computes $c_2 - e_{id}^T c_1 = \bar{x} - e_{id}^T x + b\lfloor q/2 \rfloor = \bar{x} - e_{id}^T x + b\lfloor q/2 \rfloor$, so it outputs b if $\bar{x} - e_{id}^T x$ is at distance at most $q/5$ from 0 [5]. We can represent $\bar{x} - e_{id}^T x$ as $x'^T \tilde{e}_{id} = x'^T \begin{pmatrix} 1 \\ -e_{id} \end{pmatrix}$, where $x' \leftarrow \chi^{m+1}$.

According to the feature of Gaussian distribution, $\|\tilde{e}_{id}\| = \sqrt{1 + \|e_{id}\|^2} \leq \sqrt{1 + r'^2 m} \leq r'\sqrt{m+1}$(with overwhelming probability) [5], by definition of χ, $x'_i = \lfloor q \cdot y_i \rceil \bmod q$, $\| x' - qy \| \leq \sqrt{(\frac{1}{2})^2(m+1)} = \sqrt{m+1}/2$. By Cauchy-Schwarz inequality, $|(x' - qy)^T \tilde{e}_{id}|$ is at most $r'(m+1)/2 \leq \frac{q}{5(m+1)}(\frac{m+1}{2}) \leq q/10$ and $|x'^T \tilde{e}_{id}| \leq |(x' - qy)^T \tilde{e}_{id}| + q|y^T \tilde{e}_{id}|$.

$y^T \tilde{e}_{id}$ is a normal variable whose mean 0 and standard deviation $\|\tilde{e}_{id}\| \alpha \leq r'\sqrt{m+1}\alpha \leq \sqrt{n'}\sqrt{m+1}\alpha < 1/\omega(\sqrt{\log n})$. By the tail inequality on normal variables, $|y^T \tilde{e}_{id}| > 1/10$ is with negligible probability.

So $|x'^T \tilde{e}_{id}| \leq |(x' - qy)^T \tilde{e}_{id}| + q|y^T \tilde{e}_{id}| \leq q/10 + q/10 = q/5$, that is to say, $\bar{x} - e_{id}^T x$ is at distance at most $q/5$ from 0(mod q).

4.4   Efficiency

Our construction is much efficient by avoiding much complex trapdoor generation algorithm and preimage sampling algorithm. Specifically, according to Sect. 4.2, we can set $q \approx n^3$ and $n' = O(n^3/\log n)$. In Setup of our construction, it only needs to run SampleD algorithm to produce n' samples from $D_{\mathbb{Z}^m, r}$ just one time. However, in [1,5], and [17], they must run complex trapdoor generation algorithm to generate master public parameters and master secret key(msk). Moveover, in Extract phase, our construction only needs $n'/2$ additions of vectors on average for each id, which is parallelizable, while in [5] and [1] they require preimage sampling algorithm with process of orthogonalization and projection in time $O(m^2)$ times the representation length (in bit) of $(msk, H(id))$ for each id, and in [17], they need $O(n^3)$ times of multiplication and addition for each id.

Furthermore, because of the low computing cost of private key and public key. PKG doesn't require to storage large-scale keys but only little-scale key "seeds".

4.5   Multi-bit Encryption

As same as [1,5], we can reuse the same ephemeral encryption randomness s to encrypt multiple bits message. Suppose we encrypt a K-bit message, if we use the same ephemeral $s \in \mathbb{Z}_q^n$ throughout, then the total size of ciphertext is $2m + 1 \times K = 2m + K$ elements of $\mathbb{Z}_q$.

4.6 Security Analysis

According to Sect. 3, we suppose $TDLWE_{q,m,n,r,\alpha}$ problem is hard for certain parameters. In this section, we analyze the security of the above scheme under $TDLWE_{q,m,n,r,\alpha}$ assumption.

Theorem 3. *The above scheme is (k, ε)-semantically secure against IND-ID-CPA under the $\varepsilon(1-1/e-2^{k-n'})/2-TDLWE_{q,m,n,r,\alpha}$ assumption in the random oracle model.*

Analyze: Suppose there exists a probabilistic polynomial time (PPT) adversary $\mathfrak{A}$ who can make at most k queries and get at least ε advantage in the IND-ID-CPA game. Then if we can construct a PPT simulator $\mathfrak{B}$ which plays $TDLWE_{q,m,n,r,\alpha}$ game with the challenger and plays IND-ID-CPA game with $\mathfrak{A}$ can get at least $\varepsilon(1 - 1/e - 2^{k-n'})/2$ advantage to guess τ given $(A, B = Ae', C = A^T s' + x', Z)$ by the challenger in $TDLWE_{q,m,n,r,\alpha}$ game, then the theorem is correct.

We assume: In $TDLWE_{q,m,n,r,\alpha}$ game,

if $\tau = 1$ then $Z = e'^T A^T s' + x$, where x is chosen from the error distribution χ_α; else if $\tau = 0$ then $Z = d$, where d is randomly chosen from $\mathbb{Z}_q$.

In the following parts, we first detail the simulator $\mathfrak{B}$ and the IND-ID-CPA game, and then show $\mathfrak{B}$'s advantage of guessing τ.

Setup. The simulator $\mathfrak{B}$ randomly chooses k n'-dimensional binary vectors $V_i = (h_{1i}, h_{2i}, ..., h_{n'i})^T, i = 1, 2, ..., k$, where each V_i is chosen uniformly and independently. $\mathfrak{B}$ also needs to choose n' vectors $v_1, v_2, ..., v_{n'}$ from $D_{\mathbb{Z}^m,r}$ independently.

Then $\mathfrak{B}$ chooses one of tuples $(w_1, w_2, ..., w_{n'})$, $w_i \in \mathbb{Z}$ so that

$$(w_1, w_2, ..., w_{n'}) \begin{pmatrix} h_{11} & h_{12} & \cdots & h_{1k} \\ h_{21} & h_{22} & \cdots & h_{2k} \\ \vdots & \vdots & \ddots & \vdots \\ h_{n'1} & h_{n'2} & \cdots & h_{n'k} \end{pmatrix} = 0.$$

Then set the public key $U = (u_1, u_2, ..., u_{n'})$, where $u_i = w_i B + Av_i$. Here we ensure $\sqrt{(\sum w_i)^2 + 1} r \leq \frac{q}{5(m+1)}$ so that the distribution of e_i and e_{id} is as same as the above IBE scheme.

Obviously, the corresponding private key is $E = (e_1, e_2, ..., e_{n'})$, where $e_i = w_i e' + v_i$.

The simulator $\mathfrak{B}$ sends the parameters (q, U, n', H, A) to $\mathfrak{A}$.

Random Oracle Queries. In the random oracle model, we allows the adversary $\mathfrak{A}$ to get hash values by making queries to the random oracle H. In IND-ID-CPA game between $\mathfrak{A}$ and $\mathfrak{B}$, $\mathfrak{B}$ may answer random oracle queries from $\mathfrak{A}$ at most q_H times, where q_H is the polynomial upper bound of the number of H-queries. $\mathfrak{B}$ selects $V_H \in \{1, 2, ..., q_H\}$ such that $|V_H| = k$. Without loss of generality, we can assume that the set of identities in private key extraction queries is a subset of the set of identities in H-queries. Due to deal with the queries, $\mathfrak{B}$ maintains a list of $<ID_i, H(ID_i), \xi_i>$, where ID_i is an identity of user, $\xi_i \in \{0, 1\}$ is assigned when $\mathfrak{B}$ responds to the query. We denote this list of tuples by H-list which is initially empty. When $\mathfrak{A}$ makes a query $<ID_i>$, $\mathfrak{B}$ answers it as follows:

If the query $<ID_i>$ is already in the H-list, then $\mathfrak{B}$ returns the $H(ID_i)$ directly.

If the query $<ID_i>$ is the $i'th$ new query to the random oracle and $i' \in V_H$, suppose that i' is the $i''th$ smallest element in V_H, then $\mathfrak{B}$ sets $H(ID_i) = h_{1i''}...h_{n'i''}$ and $\xi_i = 1$; then $\mathfrak{B}$ returns $H(ID_i)$ and records the tuple $<ID_i, H(ID_i), \xi_i>$ in H-list.

If the query $<ID_i>$ is the $i'th$ new query to the random oracle and $i' \notin V_H$, $\mathfrak{B}$ randomly chooses a binary string $h_{1j}h_{2j}...h_{n'j} \in \{0, 1\}^{n'}$ which is not in H-list, then sets $H(ID_i) = h_{1j}h_{2j}...h_{n'j}$ and $\xi_i = 0$. At last, $\mathfrak{B}$ returns $H(ID_i)$ and records the tuple $<ID_i, H(ID_i), \xi_i>$ in H-list.

Phase 1. In this phase, $\mathfrak{A}$ may make different private key extraction queries $<ID_1>, <ID_2>, ..., <ID_l>$ where $l \leq k$, for each query $<ID_i>(i = 1, 2, ..., l)$ $\mathfrak{B}$ answers as follows:

(1) If ID_i appears in H-list and $\xi_i = 1$, $\mathfrak{B}$ computes $e_{ID_i} = \sum_{l=1}^{n'} h_{li} v_l$, where h_{li} is the lth bit of the recorded value $H(ID_i)$ and returns e_{ID_i}.

The e_{ID_i} is valid because $e_{ID_i} = \sum_{1}^{n'} h_{li} e_l = \sum_{l=1}^{n'} h_{li}(w_l e' + v_l) = e' \sum_{l=1}^{n'} h_{li} w_l + \sum_{l=1}^{n'} h_{li} v_l = \sum_{l=1}^{n'} h_{li} v_l$.

(2) If ID_i appears in H-list and $\xi_i \neq 1$ or ID_i doesn't appear in H-list and all the V_j created in Setup phase have been used in replying the previous queries, then $\mathfrak{B}$ restarts the IND-ID-CPA game. Of course, $\mathfrak{B}$ must re-choose the set $V_H \in \{1, 2, ..., q_H\}$ in the restarted game. However, we must notice that $\mathfrak{B}$ can restart the game at most $C_{q_H}^k - 1$ times. If the times of restarting exceeds $C_{q_H}^k - 1$, $\mathfrak{B}$ aborts and outputs an uniformly random bit as τ'.

(3) If ID_i doesn't appear in H-list then $\mathfrak{B}$ makes a query $<ID_i>$ to Random Oracle and generates a new record in H-list. If $\xi_i = 1$ then $\mathfrak{B}$ computes $e_{ID_i} = \sum_{l=1}^{n'} h_{li} v_l$; else if $\xi_i = 0$ then does the same as (2).

Challenge. $\mathfrak{A}$ chooses an identity ID^* which has not appeared in the private key extraction queries, and sends $(ID^*, b_0 = 0, b_1 = 1)$ to $\mathfrak{B}$. $\mathfrak{B}$ makes a query to Random Oracle to get a binary string $h_1^* h_2^* ... h_{n'}^* \in \{0,1\}^{n'}$. If the binary vector $V^* = (h_1^*, h_2^*, ..., h_{n'}^*)^T$ is a linear combination of $V_i(i = 1, 2, ..., k)$, then $\mathfrak{B}$ aborts and outputs an uniformly random bit as τ'; Otherwise, $\mathfrak{B}$ computes

$w = \sum_{i=1}^{n'} h_i^* w_i, v = \sum_{i=1}^{n'} h_i^* v_i$. and $u_{ID^*} = wB + Av = A(we' + v)$. The simulator $\mathfrak{B}$ picks $\sigma \in \{0,1\}$ uniformly and randomly. Then $\mathfrak{B}$ computes

$\quad C^* = (c_1^*, c_2^*) = (C, wZ + v^T C + b_\sigma \lfloor \frac{q}{2} \rfloor)$ and sends it to adversary $\mathfrak{A}$ as the challenge.

Phase 2. The adversary $\mathfrak{A}$ continues to access to random oracle and issues private key extraction queries $<ID_{l+1}>, <ID_{l+2}>, ..., <ID_{\tilde{k}}>$ where $\tilde{k} \leq k$.

Note that $\mathfrak{A}$ can't make a query $<ID^*>$ to simulator $\mathfrak{B}$ directly. And $\mathfrak{B}$ answers the queries as same as Phase 1.

Guess. The adversary $\mathfrak{A}$ outputs the guess σ' of σ. If $\sigma' = \sigma$ then $\tau' = 1$; Otherwise $\tau' = 0$.

Then we begin to analyze the security of the scheme.

In the following parts, first, we consider the advantage of simulator $\mathfrak{B}$ when the event *abort* doesn't happen. And then we analyze the probability *abort* happens.

Claim. when the event *abort* doesn't happen, the advantage of $\mathfrak{B}$ is at least $\frac{1}{2}\varepsilon$.

Proof.

(1) If $\tau = 1$, i.e. $Z = e'^T A^T s' + x$, $C^* = (C, wZ + v^T C + b_\sigma \lfloor \frac{q}{2} \rfloor) = (A^T s' + x', [A(we' + v)]^T s' + b_\sigma \lfloor \frac{q}{2} \rfloor - wx - v^T x')$

We analyze $c_2^* - (we' + v)c_1^* = [A(we' + v)]^T s' + b_\sigma \lfloor \frac{q}{2} \rfloor - wx - v^T x' - (we' + v)^T (A^T s' + x') = wx - we'x' + b_\sigma \lfloor \frac{q}{2} \rfloor$. We can obtain $wx - we'x'$ is at most $w(r(m+1)/2) \leq \sqrt{(\sum w_i)^2 + 1}(r(m+1)/2) \leq q/10$ away from $q/10$ similar to Sect. 4.3.

So C^* is equal to the ciphertext in real IBE scheme.

As we assume, the advantage of adversary $\mathfrak{A}$ of breaking the real IBE scheme is ε, i.e.
$\quad |Pr[\sigma = \sigma' | \tau = 1 \wedge \overline{abort}]| = \frac{1}{2} + \varepsilon$

(2) Else if $\tau = 0$, i.e. $Z = d$ then C^* is a random element of $\mathbb{Z}_q$.

In this case, $|Pr[\sigma \neq \sigma' | \tau = 0 \wedge \overline{abort}]| = \frac{1}{2}$.

So the advantage of simulator $\mathfrak{B}$ is

$$|Pr[\tau = \tau'|\overline{abort}] - \frac{1}{2}|$$

$$= |Pr[\tau = 1 \bigwedge \tau' = 1|\overline{abort}] + Pr[\tau = 0 \bigwedge \tau' = 0|\overline{abort}] - \frac{1}{2}|$$

$$= |Pr[\tau = 1 \bigwedge \sigma = \sigma'|\overline{abort}] + Pr[\tau = 0 \bigwedge \sigma \neq \sigma'|\overline{abort}] - \frac{1}{2}|$$

$$= |Pr[\sigma = \sigma'|\tau = 1 \bigwedge \overline{abort}]Pr[\tau = 1|\overline{abort}] + Pr[\sigma \neq \sigma'|\tau = 0 \bigwedge \overline{abort}]Pr[\tau = 0|\overline{abort}] - \frac{1}{2}|$$

$$\geq \frac{1}{2}(\varepsilon + \frac{1}{2}) + \frac{1}{2}\frac{1}{2} - \frac{1}{2}$$

$$= \frac{1}{2}\varepsilon$$

However, in the IND-ID-CPA game, the event *abort* maybe happen. So we need to analyze the probabilities of *abort*. Obliviously, there are two reasons will cause $\mathfrak{B}$ aborting. (1) The times of restarting the game exceeds $C_{q_H}^k - 1$ in Phase 1 or Phase 2; (2) The binary vector $V^* = (V_1^*, ..., V_{n'}^*)^T$ is a linear combination of $V_i (i = 1, 2, ..., k)$ in the Challenge phase.

Claim. The simulator $\mathfrak{B}$ aborts for reason (1) with the probability at most $\frac{1}{e}$.

Proof. For our choice of V_H, the probability that a private key extraction query causing restarting of the IND-ID-Game is at most $1 - \frac{1}{C_{q_H}^k}$. For convenience, we let $t = \frac{1}{C_{q_H}^k}$. The simulator can restart at most $1/t$ times, so the probability that t choices of V_H all lead to restarting is at most $(1 - t)^{1/t} \approx \frac{1}{e}$. So, the simulator $\mathfrak{B}$ aborts for the reason (1) with the probability at most $\frac{1}{e}$.

Claim. The simulator $\mathfrak{B}$ aborts for reason (2) with the probability at most $2^{k-n'}$.

Proof. We construct a matrix $M_{n'k} = (V_1, V_2, ..., V_k)$, where $k < n'$. The rank of $M_{n'k}$ is $k' \leq k$. So, there exist k' rows of $M_{n'k}$ are linearly independent. We suppose the first k' rows of $M_{n'k}$ are linearly independent. Let $M_{k'k'}$ denote a matrix which has k' linearly independent vectors consisting of the k' linearly independent elements of V_i. Let V_i' be the k'-dimensional vector consisting of the first k' elements of V_i. So there are at most $2^{k'}$ choices of $V^{*'}$ which is a linear combination of combination of $V_i'(i = 1, 2, ..., k)$, and $2^{k'} \leq 2^k$. Since there are $2^{n'}$ n'-dimensional binary vectors in total. Consequently, the probability that $\mathfrak{B}$ aborts for reason (2) is at most $\frac{2^k}{2^{n'}}$.

So, combining two above claims, the probability that simulator $\mathfrak{B}$ aborts is at most $\frac{1}{e} + 2^{k-n'}$. The advantage of the PPT simulator to solve the $TDLWE_{q,m,n,r,\alpha}$ problem is at least $\frac{\varepsilon}{2}(1 - \frac{1}{e} - 2^{k-n'})$. So far, Theorem 3 is proved completely.

5   Conclusion

In this paper, we proposed a much more efficient lattice-based IBE scheme using the Combined Public Key and proved its security against IND-ID-CPA in the random oracle model under the $TDLWE_{q,m,n,r,\alpha}$ assumption. It would be an interesting open question whether we can design a lattice-based IBE scheme using CPK which is secure under IND-ID-CCA. And another open problem is whether we can improve our constructions to adapt to ideal lattices.

Acknowledgment. This work was supported by the Scientific Research Foundation of Nanjing Institute of Technology (YKJ201980), Program for Scientific Research Foundation for Talented Scholars of Jinling Institute of Technology (JIT-B-201726), Program for Beijing Key Laboratory (40184042) and Natural science research projects of universities (19KJB520033).

References

1. Agrawal, S., Boneh, D., Boyen, X.: Efficient lattice (H)IBE in the standard model. In: Gilbert, H. (ed.) EUROCRYPT 2010. LNCS, vol. 6110, pp. 553–572. Springer, Heidelberg (2010). https://doi.org/10.1007/978-3-642-13190-5_28
2. Bert, P., Fouque, P.-A., Roux-Langlois, A., Sabt, M.: Practical implementation of Ring-SIS/LWE based signature and IBE. In: Lange, T., Steinwandt, R. (eds.) PQCrypto 2018. LNCS, vol. 10786, pp. 271–291. Springer, Cham (2018). https://doi.org/10.1007/978-3-319-79063-3_13
3. Boneh, D., Franklin, M.: Identity-based encryption from the Weil pairing. In: Kilian, J. (ed.) CRYPTO 2001. LNCS, vol. 2139, pp. 213–229. Springer, Heidelberg (2001). https://doi.org/10.1007/3-540-44647-8_13
4. Fujisaki, E., Okamoto, T.: Secure integration of asymmetric and symmetric encryption schemes. J. Cryptol. **26**(1), 80–101 (2013)
5. Gentry, C., Peikert, C., Vaikuntanathan, V.: Trapdoors for hard lattices and new cryptographic constructions. In: Proceedings of the fortieth annual ACM symposium on Theory of computing, pp. 197–206. ACM (2008)
6. Gordon, S.D., Katz, J., Vaikuntanathan, V.: A group signature scheme from lattice assumptions. In: Abe, M. (ed.) ASIACRYPT 2010. LNCS, vol. 6477, pp. 395–412. Springer, Heidelberg (2010). https://doi.org/10.1007/978-3-642-17373-8_23
7. Hong, J., Liu, B., Sun, Q., Li, F.: A combined public-key scheme in the case of attribute-based for wireless body area networks. Wirel. Netw. **25**(2), 845–859 (2017). https://doi.org/10.1007/s11276-017-1597-8
8. Meng, H., Chen, Z., Hu, J., Guan, Z.: Establish the intrinsic binding in naming space for future internet using combined public key. In: Proceedings of the 11th International Conference on Future Internet Technologies, pp. 62–68. ACM (2016)
9. Micciancio, D.: Lattice-based cryptography. In: Encyclopedia of Cryptography and Security, pp. 713–715 (2011)
10. Micciancio, D., Peikert, C.: Trapdoors for lattices: simpler, tighter, faster, smaller. In: Pointcheval, D., Johansson, T. (eds.) EUROCRYPT 2012. LNCS, vol. 7237, pp. 700–718. Springer, Heidelberg (2012). https://doi.org/10.1007/978-3-642-29011-4_41
11. Micciancio, D., Regev, O.: Worst-case to average-case reductions based on Gaussian measures. SIAM J. Comput. **37**(1), 267–302 (2007)
12. Regev, O.: On lattices, learning with errors, random linear codes, and cryptography. J. ACM (JACM) **56**(6), 34 (2009)
13. Shamir, A.: Identity-based cryptosystems and signature schemes. In: Blakley, G.R., Chaum, D. (eds.) CRYPTO 1984. LNCS, vol. 196, pp. 47–53. Springer, Heidelberg (1985). https://doi.org/10.1007/3-540-39568-7_5

14. Takayasu, A., Watanabe, Y.: Lattice-based revocable identity-based encryption with bounded Decryption Key Exposure Resistance. In: Pieprzyk, J., Suriadi, S. (eds.) ACISP 2017. LNCS, vol. 10342, pp. 184–204. Springer, Cham (2017). https://doi.org/10.1007/978-3-319-60055-0_10

15. Tang, W., Nan, X., Chen, Z.: Combined public key cryptosystem. In: Proceedings of International Conference on Software, Telecommunications and Computer Networks (SoftCOM04) (2004)

16. Yamada, S.: Adaptively secure identity-based encryption from lattices with asymptotically shorter public parameters. In: Fischlin, M., Coron, J.-S. (eds.) EURO-CRYPT 2016. LNCS, vol. 9666, pp. 32–62. Springer, Heidelberg (2016). https://doi.org/10.1007/978-3-662-49896-5_2

17. Ye, Q., Hu, M., Gao, W., Tang, Y.: A novel hierarchical identity-based encryption scheme from lattices. In: Sun, X., Pan, Z., Bertino, E. (eds.) ICCCS 2018. LNCS, vol. 11065, pp. 412–422. Springer, Cham (2018). https://doi.org/10.1007/978-3-030-00012-7_38

18. Zhang, L., Wu, Q.: Adaptively secure hierarchical identity-based encryption over lattice. In: Yan, Z., Molva, R., Mazurczyk, W., Kantola, R. (eds.) NSS 2017. LNCS, vol. 10394, pp. 46–58. Springer, Cham (2017). https://doi.org/10.1007/978-3-319-64701-2_4

A Novel Location Privacy Protection Scheme with Generative Adversarial Network

Wenxi Wang[1], Weilong Zhang[1], Zhang Jin[2], Keyan Sun[2], Runlin Zou[2], Chenrong Huang[1], and Yuan Tian[1(✉)]

[1] School of Computer Engineering, Nanjing Institute of Technology, Nanjing, China
ytian@njit.edu.cn
[2] School of International Education, Nanjing Institute of Technology, Nanjing, China

Abstract. With the booming development of technology and location tracking, location-based services (*LBSs*) are widely used in mobile phone applications. According to *LBS*, we can know the location information of relatives at any time, search the surrounding hospitals, restaurants and so on. Moreover, the police can use the LBS to catch escaped prisoners. Generally speaking, *LBS* brings a lot of convenience to our life and keep our lives safe. However, there are also hidden threats to *LBS*. Many criminals use *LBS* to steal location information to track or analyze the preferences of their victims to promote their products. This kind of harassment will affect people's normal life. It may threaten the location privacy of users. What more serious is it may damage the life and property of users who use an unsafe location system on the internet. To protect the location privacy of users more efficiently, we come up with a new model that includes the traditional model of location privacy and generative-adversarial net (GANs). As we all know generative-adversarial net (GANs) can generate fake data that is closed to real data. Therefore, we use the generative-adversarial net (GANs) to generate a cloaking region (CR) (as same as real location and attacker cannot perceive its false) so that it protects users' location privacy more efficiently. In our simulation, we generate the cloaking region (CR) in generative-adversarial net (GANs) by the eigenvalues of the initial location. Hence, the cloaking region (CR) we generated is harder to detect than others. But we cannot get details of the eigenvalues and it is bounded to the range of cloaking region (CR) now. We hope we can deal with these problems someday in the future.

Keywords: Location-Based Services (*LBSs*) · Cloaking Region (*CR*) · *GANs*

1 Introduction

With the rapid development of information network technology and the widespread of mobile intelligent terminals, the era of big data is developing rapidly. However, any types of data have dual properties, both privacy and value, therefore, the explosion of data has brought enormous benefits and challenges to our society. This makes some services in mobile intelligent terminals or Internet provides us with convenience while

© Springer Nature Singapore Pte Ltd. 2020
Y. Tian et al. (Eds.): ICBDS 2019, CCIS 1210, pp. 17–27, 2020.
https://doi.org/10.1007/978-981-15-7530-3_2

threatening our daily life. Such as location-based services (LBS) [1] not only bring us better service experience but also pose a serious threat [2] to users' location privacy.

Nowadays, many researchers use position dummies (false locations) [3], K-anonymity [4] and mix zones [5] to protect user's location privacy. They make position dummies to create false locations so that location trackers cannot identify which location is true or not. They also use K-anonymity and mix zones to conceal the true location.

In this method of hiding privacy protection, it is often simply to consider nearby poi types, ignoring much other useful information, resulting in failure to use more regional context information [6, 10] as input parameters in the process of generating CR. This way of not fully considering the context information of the surrounding area, due to the lack of conditions, often leads to the occurrence of the CR deviation, affecting the user's quality of service, so that the user's expectations are not well achieved.

To be specific, these researchers are limited to the assumption of adversarial knowledge. As we shall explain below, an adversary can gain information about a sensitive attribute, as long as she has information about the global distribution of this attribute. This assumption generalizes the specific background and homogeneity attacks used ways above. Another problem with the above methods, in general, is that they effectively assume all attributes to be categorical.

For the above problems, we will use GAN as the basic model for generating CR, taking the user's real location information and context information near its real location as input to the generator. In the next step, the generator returns the generated CR according to the internal generation function and generates the anti-network model to use the output of the generator as the input of the discriminator, which is no exception here.

However, we don't just use this CR as the only parameter. In our new model, the context information of the surrounding area will also be used as the input of the discriminator. The discriminator will use these two parameters to guess the user's "reallocation", which constitutes a traditional game problem. The loss function is calculated by judging the cross-entropy of the generator and discriminator results, thereby optimizing the neural network once and for all. The GaCR algorithm design framework is shown in Fig. 1.

In this model, we assumed the attacker model of the service provider and challenged it to generate the most secure CR: We use the cloaking region (CR) to expand a sensitive point into a range so that all points in the range can be sensitive. We use CR to achieve position ambiguity too. However, if a CR is generated at random, a service provider will exclude some locations for having a low probability of being the user's location. Moreover, if the time difference between multiple queries [7] is small enough such that the service provider can guess with high confidence that all the CR were generated from the same location, then it can find a smaller region containing the user's location. Now some attackers have proposed using maximum speed and time to calculate the distance to determine where a sensitive spot is. Therefore, we use velocity-based attacks to avoid these problems. Velocity-based attacks cannot be attacked based on the speed difference method to narrow the scope. When an attacker determines the range of sensitive points based on speed and time, we limited his scope to the identified CR, so that every point could be sensitive. To make the location information more closely protected, we assumed that the attacker model would fight against the generated CR and then generate the most secure CR. We use generative-adversarial net (GANs) to generate the most secure CR.

The remainder of this paper is organized as follows. The relevant related work about GAN and clocking method is described in Sect. 2 before introducing the concept of the combination of Generative Adversarial Networks and Cloaking Region in Sect. 3. Section 4 introduces the experimental results and analysis followed by conclusion and future work in Sect. 5.

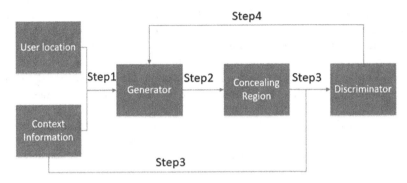

Fig. 1. GaCR *frame diagram*

2   Related Work

Location privacy has been a subject of active research in recent years and many excellent achievements were achieved. In this section, we discuss research results closely related to our work.

2.1   GAN

GAN was proposed by Goodfellow et al. [28] In 2014. It has a set of adversarial neural networks that include discriminator network and generator network to find a point of Nash equilibrium through a method like the zero-sum game. When the discriminator network can't discriminate where this data comes from, we can consider that the generator network could generate real data. It is very useful to make some fake figures which are close to the real figure.

In the original GAN, it faced many problems such as the data which the generator generated is unable to converge, and there was no theory to prove that a Nash equilibrium point can always be found.

There are many ways to address these problems. Arjovsky et al. [24] proposed Wasserstein GAN to solve the problem of disappearing training gradients. W-GAN uses Earth-Mover to measure the distance between real data and generated data. But the discriminator network can discriminate some very complex sample, it is easy to cause overfitting. Qi [25] uses Loss-sensitive GAN(LS-GAN) to limit the modeling capabilities of the model. It will minimize the objective function to get the loss function is limited to classes that satisfy Lipschitz continuity functions. The author also makes the analyses of gradient disappears.

DCGAN replaces the fully connected layer with the Deconvolution layer to enhance the effect in the task of generating images [11]. Many studies proposed that using semi-supervised methods will greatly improve the generation quality, so CGAN proposed a GAN with conditional constraints [12] and introduced a new variable in the GAN to guide the generation process. In this way, information needs to be labeled during the generation process.

Info GAN [13] does not need to be labeled to introduce mutual information, and it has a certain explanation for the behavior of this GAN. To improve the training speed of GAN, DC-GAN [14, 29]uses BN (Batch normalization) technology to standardize its input, and WN (Weight normalization) [15] can also speed up the training. This method normalizes the weight of the neural network, and experiments prove that it has a better effect than BN. Also, SN (Special normalization) [16] can also greatly improve the generation effect. Another way to improve the training effect is to integrate multiple models [17, 18].

Ada GAN [19] trains multiple models in sequence through multiple Ada Boost algorithms. The previous unfinished one will be enlarged. Weights, and finally the resulting model will be derived. LAP-GAN [20] optimizes the GAN model by stacking multiple layers of different adversarial networks.

2.2   Clocking Method

A useful privacy protection method is to generate a new fake user location every time the user updates the location [21]. This method determines its effectiveness because of its rationality. The method in [22] can automatically calculate the next location the user will arrive from the current location. In Kido et al. [26, 27], the querying user discloses one or more fake locations to the server. However, these locations could still fall within sensitive areas.

The K-anonymity [29] method is used to protect location privacy, and the K user locations are grouped into an anonymous set, so that even if the attacker obtains the specific location of each user, the attacker cannot determine the real query request user from the K users. To the extent that the purpose of protecting the privacy of the user's location is achieved. However, the increase of K may maximize the invisible area, and the response time is delayed due to the processing overhead on the server side. Therefore, maximizing the invisible area may reduce the quality of the query service provided by the LBS application. The focus of all their approaches is on protecting user identity, not location [8].

However, it also faces the problem of failure in sensitive locations. The issue of CR effectiveness is considered in the article [23], which considers how to protect the privacy of users in the case of responding to multiple attacks.

Whereas, Ran failed to fully consider the detailed location information of the user's location. This article will use the technology of combining adversarial network and cloaking region to fully consider the particularity of the user's location for targeted privacy protection. We use generative adversarial network to learn how to make a best cloaking region to cover user's location. In this method, we can protect users' privacy.

3   GaCR (Generative Adversarial Networks and Cloaking Region)

3.1   Generative Adversarial Networks and Cloaking Region

By acquiring the real position of the user U, all POIs within a certain range near the user are obtained. In this paper, the points of interest in the vicinity of the user are numbered. In the process of encoding, the importance degree of the user's privacy protection needs is sequentially labeled regarding the interest points (in order from the high degree of influence to the low degree of influence), and the level number and interest point category are constructed. For the comparison table is shown in Table 1, and this serial number is also used as one of the characteristic values of the generator.

Table 1. Comparison Table

No	Type
22	Accommodation services
21	Government agencies and social organizations
...	...
15	Incorporated business
...	...
2	Auto repair
1	Street furniture

We abstracts many feature items $F = \{f1, f2, ..., fn\}$ from the user's real position and interest points, which are used as input to the generator. To improve the training speed of the generator and prevent the training result from over-fitting, this paper uses mutual information to screen the important data. As shown in Formula 1.

$$I(Y;X) = \sum_{y_i \in Y} \sum_{x_i \in X} P(x_i = X, y_i = Y) \log_2 \frac{P(x_i = X, y_i = Y)}{P(x_i = X)P(y_i = Y)} \qquad (1)$$

Where X represents a feature and Y represents a feature class. X and Y either appear or do not appear. $P(x_i = X)$ represents the probability of occurrence of x_i, $P(y_i = Y)$ represents the probability of occurrence of y_i, and $P(x_i = X, y_i = Y)$ represents the joint probability. Through this method, it is possible to screen out features that contribute greatly to the generation of the confrontation network. According to the feature and the user's real position L, a plurality of false points are generated to form a hidden area CR, as shown in Fig. 3.

After the discriminator accepts the CR, it will judge based on the feature values possessed by each point. Each time, it is judged whether a point belongs to a half which is closer to the true coordinates, so that the judgment is made a plurality of times, and finally the real position L' of the user is accurately found. By comparing the real position L of the generator with the cross-entropy of the position L' obtained by the discriminator, we obtain the loss function of the generator and the discriminator, and the loss function of the generator is as in Eq. 2.

The loss function of the discriminator is as shown in Eq. 3.

$$\min_G V(D,G) = \min_G \left(E_{x \sim P_{data}}[\log(1 - D(G(Z)))] \right) \tag{2}$$

$$\max_D V(D,G) = \max_D \left(E_{x \sim P_{data}}[\log(G(x))] + E_{x \sim P_{data}}[\log(1 - D(G(Z)))] \right) \tag{3}$$

3.2   CR Privacy Leak

When a user has a good CR, it is possible to expose privacy when moving [30].

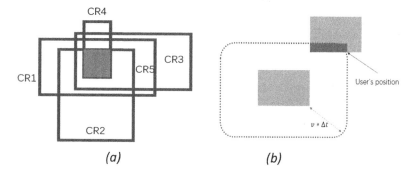

Fig. 2. Possible attacks

As shown in Fig. 2(a), when the CRs of the protection users overlap, the attacker can infer that the user is highly likely to overlap in the CR. To avoid this, make sure that the two CRs do not overlap, we use Eq. 4. D_{pp} is the Euclidean distance between CRa and CRb. v is the maximum speed of the user. t_r is the maximum time the user submits the next time.

$$\frac{d_{pp}(A,B)}{v} \leq t_r - t_A \tag{4}$$

As shown in Fig. 2(b), when the attacker obtains the maximum speed of the user, the farthest area that the user can reach can be inferred, and the overlap of the farthest area with the next CR is the location of the user. We use two CR distances between the Haussdorf to prevent this, as in Eq. 5.

$$d_H(X, Y) = \max\left\{\sup_{x \in X} \inf_{y \in Y} d(x, y), \sup_{y \in Y} \inf\ x \in X\ d(x, y)\right\} \leq \delta t \cdot v \quad (5)$$

$d(x, y)$ is the distance between two *CRs*.

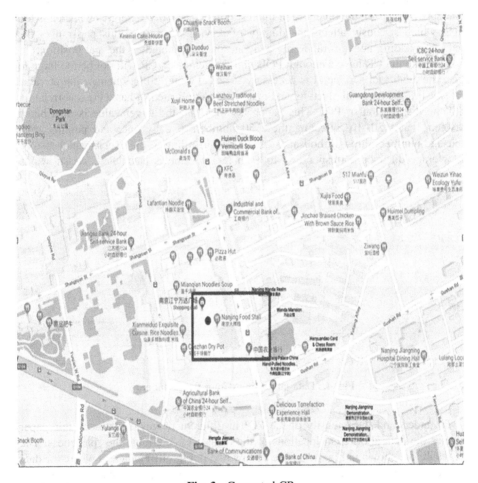

Fig. 3. Generated CR

4 Simulation

The data used for algorithm testing comes from the competition system of Peking University, which includes data from June 16, 2017, to August 13, 2017. It contains 221,100 national POI data. Since the original data table contains more fields, such as labels and coordinates, it has a more detailed description of the POI. Therefore, this paper first filters the feature fields we need through mutual information.

For large data sets, the concentration of POIs in a unit area is so different that there are hundreds of POIs in a commercial block, and the number of uninhabited areas is very small.

To ensure the overall quality of the service, this paper needs to make a rough assessment of the data set. For areas with a high degree of POI concentration, we choose to use detailed context information as the condition for generating CR. On the contrary, those areas with relatively low POI, if the same strategy is adopted, the generator will ensure the diversity of interest points. Sexually generated CR area is too large, which seriously affects the quality of service. Therefore, this paper uses the method of adding noise to randomly generate the area including the real position.

To make the CR have a enough POIs and the generated CR will not be too large to affect the quality of service, it is necessary to select a target POI quantity target value that satisfies the regional diversity and is not too complicated. It has a great correlation with the distribution of POI. This paper assumes that the target value is distributed between 1 and 50. By selecting these 50 numbers one by one, and passing each thousand numbers through thousands of cycles, according to the experimental results, the average distance corresponding to each target value is calculated. As shown in Fig. 4(a).

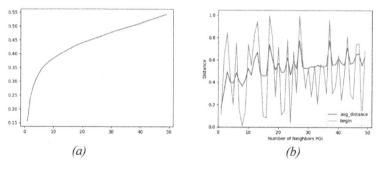

Fig. 4. Data processing (Color figure online)

To understand the intensity of the POI in different ranges of datasets, this paper samples the data at different locations of the dataset to determine the sparseness. The test results are shown in Fig. 4(b). The yellow line in Fig. 4(b) indicates where the data sample is in the entire data set, and when the value is small, it indicates that the data sample is in front of the data set. Conversely, it indicates that the data is sampled at a position behind the data set.

As can be seen from the figure, the location of the sample will affect the intensity of the POI. From the figure, the selected position is positively correlated with the intensity of the POI, and it is concluded that the POI concentration in the first half of the data set is relatively high. Therefore, in the training, the first half of the data set is selected as the training data, which can improve the training effect based on the background knowledge generator. If the selected location is negatively correlated with the intensity of the POI, the POI concentration in the second half of the dataset is relatively high. If the selected location does not have much correlation with the POI intensity, the overall POI of the dataset is dense. The degree distribution is relatively average.

The effect of the experiment is judged by the loss function of the generator and the discriminator, and the result is shown in Fig. 5. The loss function of the generator and discriminator is calculated from its cross-entropy.

Through the loss function, the accuracy of the training model can be known. D_loss consists of Dreal_loss and Dfake_loss. The former indicates the accuracy of judging the true data, that is, the discriminator distinguishes whether a certain point in the CR is the accuracy of the half closer to the real position. The latter is the accuracy of judging that it is not half the distance of the real position. The same is true for generators. From this, we can evaluate the quality of the model training.

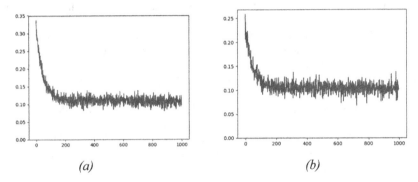

Fig. 5. Loss function

5 Conclusion and Future Work

In this paper, we use based cloaking region (CR) to determine the range of sensitive points. This approach allows us to guarantee privacy from numerous inference attacks. We also rely on knowledge about maximum velocity to pinpoint the exact user coordinates within a cloaking region (CR) to avoid attackers according to maximum velocity and time to narrow the range. Finally, we assumed the attacker model of the service provider and use GANs to challenge it to generate the most secure CR. Later we provide relevant algorithms and go to simulate.

At this stage, we take the type and quantity of POI as the characteristics. In future research, the potential effects of the more concrete details of POI ought to be considered, like the numbers of trees near protectors plays an important role in the process of generating region. Another point is that there exist some limitations in the shape and scope of the CR.

We hope that in the future work, we can use the improved Generative Adversarial Network and the advanced technology to generate irregular and small CR to improve the service quality. Finally, it will be interesting to compare our approach to a context-free notion of privacy such as DP.

References

1. Siddieq., A., Nurhaida., I.: Mobile application of BTS tower search build upon location based service (LBS). Library Hi Tech News **36**(3), 1–6 (2019)
2. Damiani., M.L., Bertino., E., Silvestri., C.: The PROBE framework for the personalized cloaking of private locations. Trans. Data Priv. **3**(2), 123–148 (2010)
3. Kapoor., T., Altenhof., W., Wang., Q., Howard., A.: Injury potential of a three-year-old hybrid III dummy in forward and rearward facing positions under CMVSS 208 testing conditions. Accid. Anal. Prev. **38**, 786–800 (2006)
4. Zhou, C.L., MA, C.G., Yang, S.T.: Location privacy-preserving method for LBS continuous KNN query in road networks. J. Comput. Res. Dev. **52**(11), 2628–2644 (2015). https://doi.org/10.7544/issn1000-1239.2015.20140532
5. Lu, R., Lin, X., Luan, TH., et al. Pseudonym changing at social spots: an effective strategy for location privacy in VANETs. IEEE Trans. Veh. Technol. **61**(1), 86–9 (2012). https://doi.org/10.1109/tvt.2011.2162864
6. Peng., T., Liu., Q., Wang., G.: Enhanced location privacy preserving scheme in location-based services. IEEE Syst. J. **11**(1), 219–230 (2014)
7. Liao, D., Huang, X., Anand, V., Sun, G., Yu, H.: k-DLCA: An efficient approach for location privacy preservation in location-based services. In: 2016 IEEE International Conference on Communications (ICC), pp. 1–6, May 2016
8. Arjovsky, M., Chintala, S., Bottou, L.: Wasserstein GAN. arXiv preprint arXiv:1701.07875 (2017)
9. Qi, G.J.: Loss-sensitive generative adversarial networks on Lipschitz densities. arXiv preprint arXiv:1701.06264 (2017)
10. Radford, A., Metz, L., Chintala, S.: Unsupervised representation learning with deep convolutional generative adversarial networks. arXiv preprint arXiv:1511.06434 (2015)
11. Mirza, M., Osindero, S., Conditional generative adversarial nets. arXiv preprint arXiv:1411.1784 (2014)
12. Rebollo-Monedero, D., Forne, J., Domingo-Ferrer, J.: From t-closeness-like privacy to postrandomization via information theory. IEEE Trans. Knowl. Data Eng. **22**(11), 1623–1636 (2010). https://doi.org/10.1109/tkde.2009.190. ISSN 1041-4347
13. Chen, X., Duan, Y., Houthooft, R., Schulman, J., Sutskever, I., Abbeel, P.: Infogan: interpretable representation learning by information maximizing generative adversarial nets. In: Proceedings of the 30th Conference on Neural Information Processing Systems, Barcelona, Spain, NIPS, pp. 2172−2180 (2016)
14. Ioffe, S., Szegedy, C.: Batch normalization: accelerating deep network training by reducing internal covariate shift. In: Proceedings of the 32nd International Conference on Machine Learning, Lille, France, pp. 448−456. PMLR (2015)
15. Salimans, T., Kingma, D.P.: Weight normalization: a simple reparameterization to accelerate training of deep neural networks. In: Proceedings of the 30th Conference on Neural Information Processing Systems, NIPS, Barcelona, Spain, pp. 901−909 (2016)
16. Miyato, T., Kataoka, T., Koyama, M., Yoshida, Y.: Spectral normalization for generative adversarial networks. arXiv preprint arXiv:1802.05957 (2018)
17. Dietterich., T.G.: Ensemble methods in machine learning. In: Kittler., J., Roli., F. (eds.) MCS 2000. LNCS, vol. 1857, pp. 1–15. Springer, Heidelberg (2000). https://doi.org/10.1007/3-540-45014-9_1
18. Zhou., Z.H., Wu., J.X., Tang., W.: Ensembling neural networks: many could be better than all. Artif. Intell. **137**(1), 239–263 (2002)

19. Tolstikhin, I., Gelly, S., Bousquet, O., Simon-Gabriel, C.J., Sch¨olkopf, B.: AdaGAN: boosting generative models. arXiv preprint arXiv:1701.02386 (2017)
20. Denton, E., Chintala, S., Szlam, A., Fergus, R.: Deep generative image models using a Laplacian pyramid of adversarial networks. In: Proceedings of the 29th Annual Conference on Neural Information Processing Systems, Montreal, Canada, pp. 1486−1494. Curran Associates, Inc., (2015)
21. Lecun., Y., Bottou., L., Bengio., Y., Haffner., P.: Gradient-based learning applied to document recognition. Proc. IEEE **86**(11), 2278–2324 (1998)
22. Kido, H., Yanagisawa, Y., Satoh, T.: An anonymous communication technique using dummies for location-based services. In: Krumm, J. (ed.) Proceedings of International Conference on Pervasive Services (ICPS 2005), pp. 88–97 (2005)
23. Yiu, M.L., Jensen, C.S., Huang, X., Lu, H.: SpaceTwist: managing the trade-offsamong location privacy, query performance, and query accuracy in mobile services. In: Proceedings of IEEE International Conference on Data Engineering (ICDE 2008) (2008)
24. Shokri, R., Troncoso, C., Diaz, C., Freudiger, J., Hubaux, J.P.: Unraveling an old cloak: K-anonymity for location privacy. In: Proceedings of ACM Workshop on Privacy in the Electronic Society (2010)
25. Hinton., G., Deng., L., Yu., D., Dahl., G.E., Mohamed., A.R., Jaitly., N., et al.: Deep neural networks for acoustic modeling in speech recognition: the shared views of four research groups. IEEE Signal Process. Mag. **29**(6), 82–97 (2012)
26. Ghinita, G., Kalnis, P., Khoshgozaran, A., et al.: Private queries in location based services: anonymizers are not necessary. In: Proceedings of the 2008 ACM SIGMOD International Conference on Management of Data, New York, pp. 121–132. ACM (2008)
27. Ghinita., G., Damiani., M.L., Silvestri., C., Bertino., E.: Protecting against velocity-based, proximity-based, and external event attacks in locationcentric social networks. ACM Trans. Spatial Algorithms Syst. **2**(2), 8:1–8:36 (2016)
28. Goodfellow, I.: Generative adversarial nets. In: Proceedings of the 2014 Conference on Advances in Neural Information Processing Systems 27. Montreal, Canada, pp. 2672−2680. Curran Associates, Inc., (2014)
29. Bengio., Y.: Learning deep architectures for AI. Found. Trends Mach. Learni. **2**(1), 1–127 (2009)
30. Liccardi, I., Abdul-Rahman, A., Chen, M.: I know where you live: inferring details of people's lives by visualizing publicly shared location data. In: Proceedings of the 2016 CHI Conference on Human Factors in Computing Systems, pp. 1–12. ACM (2016)

Security, Safety and Privacy Issues of Unmanned Aerial Vehicle Systems

Najla Al-nabhan[✉]

Computer Science Department, King Saud University, Riyadh, Saudi Arabia
nalnabhan@ksu.edu.sa

Abstract. The impressive growth and advancement of Unmanned Aerial Vehicles (UAVs)-enabled solutions and systems has motivated their employment in variety of applications ranging from military and security to surveillance, entertainment, business, and media. In most of these applications, UAVs were employed to tackle critical operations. Most of operations require more reliable solutions in order to ensure operating UAVs safely. Unfortunately, UAV systems are vulnerable for many types of security threats. In this paper, we discuss and analyze the security issues of UAVs systems. It also examines the safety, security, privacy and regulatory issues associated with integration into the national airspace and conclude with some recommendations.

Keywords: UAVs · Unmanned Aerial Vehicles · Security · Privacy · Cyber-physical attack · Hacking · Trust

1 Introduction

Unmanned Aerial Vehicles (UAVs) are expected to play an important role in future aerospace and defense applications. The early development history of UAVs was started before 1960, when armed conflict required looking for new technologies. However, when these conflicts ended interest in developing pilotless vehicles has waned. After World War I, attention then turned to adding remote control ability. In the 1990's, research focused on enabling the unmanned vehicles to stay airborne for periods over 24 h and above 50,000 feet by using new materials in the construction of the craft to make them lighter and stronger, and on harnessing solar power to propel the aircraft for indefinite periods of time [1–3].

UAVs have numerous uses beyond military applications. UAVs have been employed to perform many operations such as offensive, commercial, surveillance and other civilian missions. As they exclude the risk factors involved in manned vehicles, UAVs can be employed to tackle hazardous missions such underground mines and caves, military training, disaster relief and search and rescue. They can by also employed to monitor gas leakage, weather, forest fires, and pipelines in factories. UAVs also have a variety of business applications. Recently, UAVs were utilized to deliver packages to customers in less than 30 min [1–3].

Besides their various advantages and applications, UAVs are vulnerable to many types of attack. UAVs are equipped with many types of sensors that allow them to perform their missions and maneuvers safely. Since all information critical to the

© Springer Nature Singapore Pte Ltd. 2020
Y. Tian et al. (Eds.): ICBDS 2019, CCIS 1210, pp. 28–39, 2020.
https://doi.org/10.1007/978-981-15-7530-3_3

mission is sent through wireless communication channels, the need to secure these channels is one of the most important design, development and performance considerations. Moreover, as there is no pilot to monitor the activities in some situations, it is well-understood that loss of control over these systems to adversaries due to lack of security is a potential threat to national security. Moreover, there are several issues related to the integration of UAVs into unsegregated airspace which necessitate significant research and to explore and address issues related to their safety, security and privacy [1–3].

In this paper various security threats to a UAV system are presented and discussed. The rest of this paper is organized as follows; next section provides the required background to understand UAV threats. It discusses the architecture, applications requirements, more communication model. Section 3 discusses threats and the existing approaches for securing UAV systems and improving their privacy and safety. In Sect. 4 we conclude with some final remarks.

2   An Overview of Unmanned Aerial Vehicles Architecture, Applications, and Design Considerations

UAVs is considered as complex systems that combine a diverse set of hardware and software components. This section discusses the architecture, applications, and requirements.

2.1   General Overview of UAVs Architecture

UAV architectures represent system-of-systems. Therefore, their design is required to well-integrate these components in a way that allows UAVs to meet their performance requirements.

Mainly, UAV systems consist of three main elements, as shown in Fig. 1. The first element is the unmanned aircraft which contains: an airframe, a propulsion system, a flight controller, a precision navigation system, and a sense and avoid system.

The second component is the ground control station (GCS) which represents an on-land facility that provides the capabilities for human operators to control and/or monitor UAVs during their operations. GCSs vary in size according to the type and mission of the drone.

The third component is communication data link. The data link refers to the wireless link used to carry control information between the drone and the GCS. The adopted communication link depends on the UAV operation range. Drone missions are categorized according to their distance from the GCS into Line-of-sight (LOS) missions where control signals can be sent and received via direct radio waves, and Beyond line-of-sight (BLOS) missions where the drone is controlled via satellite communications or a relaying aircraft which can be a drone itself [4, 5].

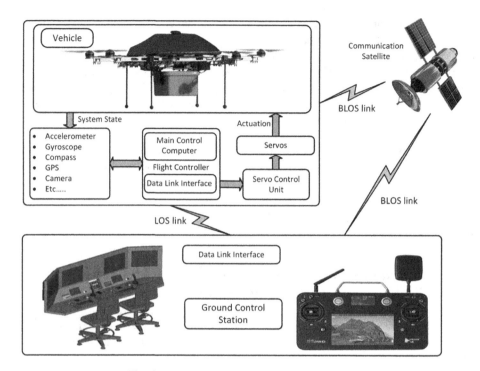

Fig. 1. General architecture for UAV systems.

Modeling a UAV from the communication network perspective has been discussed in Javaid et al. [4, 5], detailing communication among various modules. There are several information flows between an UAV and its environment, as shown in Fig. 2. The two most important operational connections are 1) the bidirectional information flow between the communications system and the ground control station (GCS) and 2) the information flow from the environment to the sensors. However, additional influences between the environment and the UAV must be considered. These influences are the changes of the attitude of the UAV induced by the avionics, the result of weapons on the environment and the influence of the environment on the communication links.

The links are diverging in reliability and receptive to manipulation in different ways. While the reliability of sensors and system components are mostly investigated during system design, the consideration of the receptiveness of a sensor or system component to manipulation is not common. The key to unauthorized control of an UAV is knowledge of the receptiveness of the system components to manipulation. To avoid third parties to take advantage of this knowledge, the receptiveness must be considered during system design [6].

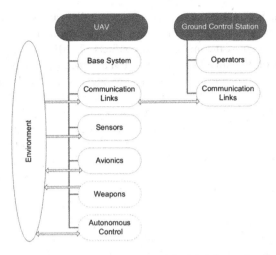

Fig. 2. Extended UAV component model with information flow [6].

2.2 Applications of UAVs

UAVs were successfully used in 3D modeling, industrial inspection of solar parks, wind parks, power lines, engines and plants, and industrial parks. They were also used in offshore oil, gas and power plants and utilities, bridge inspection, visual structure assessment and monitoring, inspection and survey of structures. Additionally, there were also used in aerial images & photography: Advertising photography, product photography, real estate photography, landscape photography, up to 360° spherical panoramas, Point-of-Interest (POI) imaging and Circle-of-Interest (COI) imaging. In media, UAVs were used for aerial movies and videography: Image, advertising and product spots, music clips, sport and extreme sports footage. In monitoring applications, UAVs were employed for condition-analysis and target-analysis to document construction sites, structural monitoring, sound barrier and wall monitoring, excavation documentation, plant and wildlife preservation and conservation, or any kind of first-responder activities in crisis regions.

In Addition, there are many UAV-based remote sensing systems for mapping and surveying, UAV-based precision agriculture for crop, soil and irrigation monitoring, UAV-based structural analysis, UAV-based documentation with aerial imaging, UAVs as first responders in accident, fire or crisis, UAV-based flight dynamics and control theory research, flight automation and reproduction, computer vision and SLAM research. UAV -based swarming intelligence and networking.

2.3 Challenges and Design Considerations

UAVs can be remotely controlled or fly autonomously through software-controlled flight plans in their embedded systems, working in conjunction with onboard sensors and GPS. Remote control is considered to be the centralized mode. Operating UAVs in the free-flight mode is possible but it creates many conflicts and safety concerns in non-segregated airspace. Ensuring air-traffic safety requires the ability to detect and avoid unexpected events, such as incoming flight conflicts [7–10].

The integration of unmanned aircraft into civil airspace is a complex issue. One key question is whether unmanned aircraft can operate just as safely as their manned counterparts. The absence of a human pilot in unmanned aircraft automatically points to a deficiency that is the lack of an inherent see- and-avoid capability [11].

In order to ensure the operational safety, technological innovations must enable a UAV's operator to detect other aircraft to avoid midair collisions within the current and next generation air traffic control systems. The lack of standard training procedures requires regulatory attention to guarantee operators are competent and international regulations must be uniform to encourage UAS expansion.

Communication is key in UAV applications. Modern solutions enable constant communications between the UAV and ground control station, as well as provide a datalink for transmitting UAV-captured information, including image and video files. UAVs are also starting to deliver critical communications at the edge of the battlefield, helping deploy Long-Term Evolution (LTE) networks in even remote locations.

To guarantee the security of unmanned aerial systems, exploitable weaknesses in civilian GPS technology and operational frequencies must be eliminated through the introduction of new or existing technologies in the most cost-effective manner.

The potential for Fourth Amendment privacy violations and the need to develop comprehensive privacy policies must be addressed to protect United States' citizens from unrestricted law enforcement and surveillance activity.

UAVs technological challenges include conflict detection and resolution, which aims at developing a capability for UAVs to detect, sense, and avoid other aircraft; addressing communications and physical security vulnerabilities; improving UAV reliability; and improving human factors considerations in UAV design. A lack of regulations for UASs limits their operations and leads to a lack of airspace for UAV testing and evaluation and a lack of data that would aid in setting standards.

Despite their benefits, UAVs are prone to attacks as they are equipped with numerous on-board sensors to gather data and this exposes them to various vulnerabilities. More precisely, in the absence of manual control, an attacker can gain access to sensitive sensory data and feed fraudulent information to the UAV. As a result, it can be reprogrammed to an undesirable effect and this can cause irreversible damage. This paper provides a general overview of current hacking methods, and defense and trust strategies to overcome cyberattacks on UAVs.

To further highlight the importance of the requirement of developing new methods to avoid any intrusion, a hacking procedure is implemented on a commercially available UAV and its severe results are demonstrated. It is shown that the hacker can make irreparable damage and take complete control over the UAV by compromising the communication link between the operator and UAV and uses Robot Operating System-based tools to alter the flight path.

3 Security, Privacy and Safety Approaches for UAV Systems

3.1 Threat and Vulnerability Models

A survey on security modeling of autonomous systems was presented in [4]. It discusses the history of automation and the various approaches of autonomy to get a deeper understanding of the scope of automation in these systems. It also highlights significant research done toward the study of security in some widely researched systems both in the industry as well as academia. A threat modeling for identifying and understanding the threats is presented in Fig. 3. They analyzed each part of the system for a different aspect of security by following the CIA model (Confidentiality, Integrity, Availability) lays the foundation for researchers to identify certain attacks [3, 4].

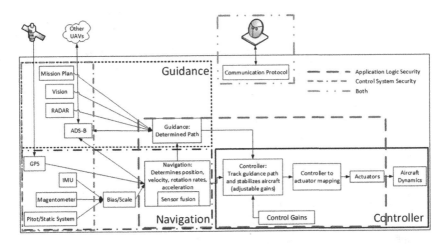

Fig. 3. UAVs threat model.

A Taxonomy of attacks on autonomous systems is presented in Fig. 4. The attack types include: Jamming, Spoofing, Flooding, Side-channel Attack, Stealthy Deception Attack, Sensor input spoofing. Jamming caused by intentional interference, e.g., GPS Jamming. Spoofing means masquerading as a legitimate source. For example, GPS Spoofing Flooding of packets thereby overloading the host.

Side-channel Attack is attack based on the extra information gained by the physical analysis. Stealthy Deception Attack means tampering system component or data. Sensor input spoofing tries to manipulate environment to form implicit control channel. Their major effects on autonomous systems include loss or corruption of packets disrupting communication, gaining an unauthorized access to the system, information, loss of communication through network congestion, leakage of sensitive information without exploiting any flaw or weakness in the components, and mislead the system to take undesirable action [3].

In [12], authors explored security vulnerabilities of UAVs. Their demo proves that professional UAVs are not strongly resilient to security threats by finding security gaps of a professional UAV that are used for critical operations by police forces around the world. We demonstrate how one can exploit the identified security vulnerabilities, perform a Man-in-the-Middle attack, and inject control commands to interact with the compromised UAV. They also proposed appropriate countermeasures to help improving the security and resilience of professional UAVs. Another paper that describes the most critical aspects of security and the safety of drones, the interruption of privacy, benefits that the drone offers to human environments, as well as the challenges of drones in health and industries was presented in [13].

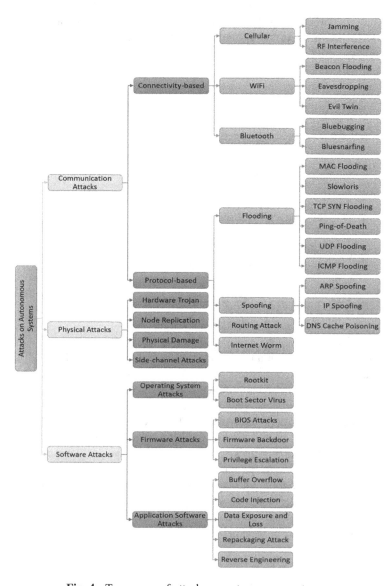

Fig. 4. Taxonomy of attacks on autonomous systems.

3.2 Security of Military Applications

The use of drones in military services has increased to a large extent. Drones are boon for our society, but they attract hackers who try to hack the drones. A hacked drone is not necessarily be captured, hackers can just tap the camera of the drone and can take out some very important information of any warzone or any area under surveillance. In 2009 some Iraqi militants were able to get access of the drone footage, which gave them a lot of information about the military intelligence.

As UAVs are being used for spying and warfare, they become vulnerable to be hacked and used for malicious purposes. There are also security loopholes in this technology like the radio waves which can be exploited by the rivals and can cause a large amount of destruction or loss of data. An Intelligent approach for UAV and Drone Privacy Security Using Blockchain Methodology was presented in [14]. As blockchain is a highly secured technology as it uses private key cryptography and peer to peer network, their methodology incorporates this technology in transmitting signals from controller to drone or UAV. It improves security and connectivity. Employing blockchain to secure UAVs is interesting since blockchain has many security advantages. It is immutable That something is unchanging over time or is unable to be changed which means that once data has been written to a blockchain no one, not even the system administrator can change it. Furthermore, blockchain is not governed by single authority rather all the members have the complete information of the blockchain.

Another group of researchers developed a threat model for smart device ground control station (a portable hand-held ground control stations for UAVs) that allows soldiers to pilot UAVs in the battlefield. The key components addressed in the model are attack motivation, vulnerabilities in these systems, cybersecurity threats, and mitigation steps in case of attacks on these devices [15]. They presented a risk analysis summary of threats and their impact based on hardware, software, communication network, and human errors. Similar discussion based on policies to defend against CIA threats in the context of unmanned autonomous systems has been done along with threat modeling and risk analysis using the STRIDE approach. Some software products like Microsoft Threat Modeling Tool and Threat- Modeler automate threat modeling, with the latter offering more sophisticated features [15, 16].

3.3 Physical-Layer Security

A general overview of hacking methods, defense and trust strategies to overcome cyber- physical attacks on UAVs was presented in [17]. It highlights the importance of the requirement of developing new methods to avoid any intrusion, a hacking procedure is implemented on a commercially available UAV and its severe results are demonstrated. It is shown that the hacker can make irreparable damage and take complete control over the UAV by compromising the communication link between the operator and UAV and uses Robot Operating System-based tools to alter the flight path.

Reference [18] addresses the issue of physical-layer security in a UAV communication system, where a UAV sends confidential information to a legitimate receiver in the presence of a potential eavesdropper which are both on the ground. We aim to maximize the secrecy rate of the system by jointly optimizing the UAV's trajectory and transmit power over a finite horizon. They exploit the mobility of the UAV in this paper to enhance the secrecy rate via a new trajectory design. Although the formulated problem is non-convex and challenging to solve, we propose an iterative algorithm to solve the problem efficiently, based on the block coordinate descent and successive convex optimization methods. Specifically, the UAV's transmit power and trajectory are each optimized with the other fixed in an alternating manner until convergence. Numerical results show that the proposed algorithm significantly improves the secrecy rate of the UAV communication system, as compared to benchmark schemes without transmit power control or trajectory optimization [18].

Reference [19] design and evaluates security framework for multilevel ad hoc wireless networks with unmanned aerial vehicles (UAV-MBN) that suits battlefields, the framework adapts to the contingent damages on the network infrastructure. The presented security framework for UAV-MBN networks suits hostile environments such as battlefields. The design adapts to the dynamical infrastructure changes of the network, depending on the availability of UAVs. Centralized design is employed with UAVs to achieve efficiency and flexibility when a theater is operating in infrastructure mode. In the scenarios in which the UAV is destroyed by enemies, the system switches to infrastructureless mode in which distributed security function sharing is applied to maintain comparable certification services and intrusion detection.

3.4 Collision Detection and Avoidance

Conflict is defined as a situation in which two or more UAVs experience a loss of minimum distance separation. Conflict detection and resolution (CDR) aims at efficiently and effectively obtaining safe separation between multiple UAVs. Automating CDR can improve the safety and robustness of the system, as flight control will be autonomously managed and adapted to the environmental changes instead on relying on a remote, central controller to coordinate and control UAVs [7–10].

CDR consists of two core functionalities: conflict detection (CD) and conflict resolution (CR). In UAVs context, CD and CR operations are often designed separately before they are integrated together in a later phase [20]. CD uses flight-state information from the surrounding UAVs to detect and report the expected future conflicts. Once a conflict is detected, a CR mechanism is invoked to address conflict by determining how, and which maneuvers should be performed to avoid the detected conflicts [7].

Integrating UAVs into a non-segregated airspace requires efficient CDR mechanism to save resources, maximize reliability, and ensure the safe operation of multiple UAVs. Conflict detection and resolution typically refers to a mechanism in which conflict detection performance affects resolution and vice versa. The existing UAVs CDR mechanisms suffers from a number of issues, including: considering uncertainties, handling multiple conflicts, lack of coordination, high computational requirements, robustness to failure or performance degradation, consideration of environmental hazards, and certification requirements [10].

Yang et al. [21] proposed a cooperative, centralized solution in which CDR is formalized as a nonlinear optimization to minimize maneuver costs. Their strategy is two-layer in and uses stochastic parallel gradient descent (SPGD) and an interior-point algorithm. To coordinate multiple UAVs in flight, the CR mechanism was designed with cooperative heading control, and the airspace was assumed to be composed of sectors and managed by an air-traffic controller (ATC).

Sislak et al. [22] proposed a pairwise, cooperative, decentralized approach. In their paper, the authors presented peer-to-peer processes for CD and collision avoidance. In addition, two cooperative, negotiation-based CR algorithms were discussed: the iterative, peer-to-peer collision avoidance (IPPCA) algorithm and the multiparty collision avoidance (MPCA) algorithm.

Conflict resolution for a multiple-UAV system based on graph theory is proposed by Yang et al. [23], who presented a short-term CDR problem found with cooperative heading control in fixed-wing UAVs. The paper described some cases (i.e., during take-off/ascent and descent/approach) in which UAVs may fly at different altitude levels. This problem was resolved through several cooperative, nonlinear optimization methods performed in two-dimensional space, then extended to three-dimensional space. Two layered algorithms—the SPGD method and the sequential quadratic programming (SQP) algorithm—were used to achieve nonlinear optimization.

As proposed by Park [24], UAV maneuvers can be made based on the predicted movement direction of conflicting UAVs. This paper focuses on en route UAV collision avoidance, and the UAVs are assumed to be connected to the ADS-B database for information exchange. The author calculated the point of closest approach (PCA) to detect the worst conflict that could occur between two UAVs and followed the "vector-sharing resolution" logic to resolve the conflict.

Omer [25] proposed a mixed-integer linear modeling approach that adjusts velocity and heading maneuvers in a predefined trajectory, based on space discretization. The author focused on defining the key points of the planned trajectories, including the intersecting points.

4   Conclusion

The risk assessment of UAVs is a complex task consisting of vulnerability and threat analysis and is additionally dependent on mission details. To ensure that UAVs are safe and secure to be used by humans, new approaches toward cybersecurity and autonomy are needed. The research community in this area lacks algorithmic solutions to address: uncertainties in modeling, security of autonomous systems from malicious attacks, accomplishing higher goals through cooperation and collaboration.

Autonomy is a dynamic property of UAVs that allow them to adapt to varying unknown situations, depending on the mission complexity. We need a resilient system that performs well over its lifetime. Though we are moving ahead toward an autonomous future, there are many research challenges that researches have to face. The existing UAVs CDR mechanisms suffers from a number of issues, including considering uncertainties, handling multiple conflicts, lack of coordination, high computational requirements, robustness to failure or performance degradation, consideration of environmental hazards, and certification requirements.

References

1. Carr, E.B.: Unmanned aerial vehicles: examining the safety, security, privacy and regulatory issues of integration into US airspace, National Centre for Policy Analysis (NCPA) (2013)
2. Solodov, A., Williams, A., Al Hanaei, S., et al.: Analyzing the threat of unmanned aerial vehicles (UAV) to nuclear facilities. Secur. J. **31**, 305–324 (2018). https://doi.org/10.1057/s41284-017-0102-5
3. Jahan, F., Sun, W.Q., Niyaz, Q., Alam, M.: Security modeling of autonomous systems: a survey. ACM Comput. Surv. **52**, 1–34 (2019)
4. Altawy, R., Youssef, A.M.: Security, privacy, and safety aspects of civilian drones: a survey. ACM Trans. Cyber Phys. Syst. **1**, 1–25 (2016). https://doi.org/10.1145/3001836
5. Javaid, A.Y., Sun, W., Alam, M., Devabhaktuni, V.K.: Cyber security threat analysis and modeling of an unmanned aerial vehicle system (2012). https://doi.org/10.1109/ths.2012.6459914
6. Hartmann, K., Steup, C.: The vulnerability of UAVs to cyber attacks—an approach to the risk assessment. In: Podins, K., Stinissen, J., Maybaum, M., (eds.) 2013 5th International Conference on Cyber Conflict (cycon) (2013)
7. Mahjri, I., Dhraief, A., Belghith, A., AlMogren, A.: SLIDE: a straight line conflict detection and alerting algorithm for multiple unmanned aerial vehicles. IEEE Trans. Mobile Comput. (TMC) **17**(5), 1190–1203 (2018)
8. Yang, J., Yin, D., Shen, L., Cheng, Q., Xie, X.: Cooperative deconflicting heading maneuvers applied to unmanned aerial vehicles in non-segregated airspace. J. Intell. Rob. Syst. **92**(1), 187–201 (2018). https://doi.org/10.1007/s10846-017-0766-4
9. Wollkind, S., Valasek, J., Ioerger, T.R.: Automated conflict resolution for air traffic management using cooperative multiagent negotiation. In: Proceedings AIAA Guidance, Navigation, and Control Conference and Exhibit Providence, Rhode Island (2004)
10. Kuchar, J.K., Yang, L.C.: A review of conflict detection and resolution modeling methods. IEEE Trans. Intell. Transp. Syst. **1**(4), 179–189 (2000)
11. Lai, J.S., Ford, J.J., Mejías, L.F., O'Shea, P.J., Walker, R.A.: See and avoid using onboard computer vision. In: Angelov, P. (ed.) Sense and avoid in UAS: research and applications. Wiley, West Sussex (2012)
12. Rodday, M., de Schmidt, R.O., Pras, A.: Exploring security vulnerabilities of unmanned aerial vehicles. In: NOMS 2016–2016 IEEE/IFIP Network Operations and Management Symposium, Istanbul, pp. 993–994 (2016)
13. Javaid, Y., Sun, W., Devabhaktuni, V.K., Alam, M.: Cyber security threat analysis and modeling of an unmanned aerial vehicle system. In: 2012 IEEE Conference on Technologies for Homeland Security (HST), Waltham, MA, pp. 585–590 (2012)
14. Rana, T., Shankar, A., Sultan, M.K., Patan, R., Balusamy, B.: An intelligent approach for uav and drone privacy security using blockchain methodology. In: 2019 9th International Conference on Cloud Computing, Data Science & Engineering (Confluence), Noida, India, pp. 162–167 (2019)
15. Mansfield, K., Eveleigh, T., Holzer, T.H., Sarkani, S.: Unmanned aerial vehicle smart device ground control station cyber security threat model. In: 2013 IEEE International Conference on Technologies for Homeland Security (HST), Waltham, MA, pp. 722–728 (2013)
16. Ya dereli, E., Gemci, C., Aktaş, A.Z.: A study on cyber-security of autonomous and unmanned vehicles. J. Defense Model. Simul. Appl. Methodol. Technol. **12**, 369–381 (2015). https://doi.org/10.1177/1548512915575803

17. Rani, C., Modares, H., Sriram, R., Mikulski, D., Lewis, F.L.: Security of unmanned aerial vehicle systems against cyber-physical attacks. J. Defense Model. Simul. Appl. Methodol. Technol. **13**, 331–342 (2015). https://doi.org/10.1177/1548512915617252
18. Zhang, G., Wu, Q., Cui, M., Zhang, R.: Securing UAV communications via trajectory optimization. In: GLOBECOM 2017–2017 IEEE Global Communications Conference, Singapore, pp. 1–6 (2017)
19. Kong, J., Luo, H., Xu, K.D., Gu, L.L., Gerla, M., Lu, S.: Adaptive security for multilevel ad hoc networks. Wireless Commun. Mobile Comput. **2**(5), 533–547 (2002)
20. Fan, L., Tang, J., Ling, Y., Liu, G., Li, B.: Novel conflict resolution model for multi- UAV based on CPN and 4D trajectories. Asian J. Control **18**(2), 721–732 (2016)
21. Yang, J., Yin, D., Cheng, Q., Xie, X.: Two-layer optimization to cooperative conflict detection and resolution for UAVs. In Proceedings IEEE Conference on Intelligent Transportation Systems, pp. 2072–2077 (2015)
22. Šišlák, D., Volf, P., Houček, M.: Agent-based cooperative decentralized airplane- collision avoidance. IEEE Trans. Intell. Transp. Syst. **12**(1), 36–45 (2011)
23. Bekmezci, I., Sahingoz, O.K., Temel, S.: Flying Ad-Hoc networks (FANETs) a survey. Ad-Hoc Netw. **11**(3), 1254–1270 (2013)
24. Park, J.W., Oh, H.D., Tahk, M.J.: UAV collision avoidance based on geometric approach. In: Proceedings of the SICE Annual Conference, pp. 2122–2126 (2008)
25. Omer, J.: A space-discretized mixed-integer linear model for air-conflict resolution with speed and heading maneuvers. Comput. Oper. Res. **58**, 75–86 (2015)

A Trust Model for Evaluating Trust and Centrality Based on Entropy Weight Method in Social Commerce

Yonghua Gong and Lei Chen[(✉)]

School of Management, Nanjing University of Posts and Telecommunications, Nanjing, China
{gongyh2008, zlermay}@163.com

Abstract. Trust of the nodes plays an important role in users' purchase decisions and trusted nodes can influence other nodes in the social commerce. The evaluation and prediction of users' trustworthiness is also of great importance for social commerce marketing and promotion. However, analysis of trust and detection of what factors influence trust between users need investigation. This paper proposes a trust model and divides trust into direct trust and indirect trust which presented in the form of familiarity trust, similarity trust, prestige trust and ability trust. The respective weights of four attributes are calculated through entropy weight method. Different centrality approaches such as Eigenvector Centrality, PageRank and Katz Centrality are used to find influential nodes. We found similarity and prestige is relatively more important than familiarity and ability trust in users' connections. Besides, there is a strong linear relationship between user nodes' trust and their centrality.

Keywords: Trust model · Trust evaluation · Social commerce · Entropy weight method · Centrality

1 Introduction

A large number of users are gathered on the social commerce platform, and a large amount of user-generated content is continuously generated spontaneously for information exchange. Users participate in comments and share products to form a close communication group or virtual community, thus transforming the way of communication, which makes difference between social commerce and traditional e-commerce. Different users have difference in their cultural, personal and educational characteristics and have different relationships with other users [1]. Likewise, the users' participation in social commerce varies from person to person. For example, some users are more active and have a higher reputation on the platform, thus having a greater impact on other users. Their opinions and behaviors motivate other users to follow them and adapt to their preferences.

The importance of trust was pointed out in everyday life [2]. Moreover, people decide whether or not to respond to the information provided, and only truly consume the information they trust [3]. In the context of social commerce, trust as an essential

© Springer Nature Singapore Pte Ltd. 2020
Y. Tian et al. (Eds.): ICBDS 2019, CCIS 1210, pp. 40–50, 2020.
https://doi.org/10.1007/978-981-15-7530-3_4

prerequisite for verifying the authenticity of information, especially for user-generated content (UGC) in social commerce, factors must be understood that influence trust in the collaborative environment to ensure the value of the user-generated content, which has significant effects on the use of information. Trust has different interpretations in different fields, such as psychology, sociology, communication, marketing, and computer science [4]. Trust is a multidimensional metric which measures trustor's confidence in trustee's behavior. In the context of this article, trust is the connection between two users, the authenticity of commodity or UGC in which user a has confidence in user b's behavior if and only if a has certainty that b carries out all expected activities that do not abuse the given security strategy [5].

The trust between users and users and the trust of users in the social commerce platform are important factors that affect users' use of the platform. For example, trust between users can have a strong impact on user interaction, which can result in the exchange of high-quality content, while the user's trust in the social commerce platform will affect the usage rate and order quantity of the platform, and directly link the survival of the platform. The trust between users is also affected by many factors. For example, user A often encounters such situations where he/she receives a friend application from an anonymous user B who has not had a trading experience, and receive a friend application from user C that recommended from A's familiar friend. In general, user A will accept the latter's friend application which is C's friend application. In such situation, the familiarity between users can affect trust. In addition, the recommendation of a user who has high reputation in social commerce is easily accepted by other users, which indicates that reputation has an impact on user trust to a certain extent. Therefore, the research questions studied in this paper are: What are the metric attributes of trust? How do these metric attributes relate to each other to form a holistic trust? The work of this paper focuses on the network structure analysis of the selected real-world datasets, and proposes the applicable trust model in a targeted manner to achieve direct trust calculation and indirect trust calculation, and to give the relationship and weight between the various attributes of trust based on real-world data sets. Then three centrality approaches such as Eigenvector Centrality, PageRank and Katz Centrality are used to investigate the relationship between nodes' trust and centrality.

2   Related Work

Trust which increases information seeking which in turn increases familiarity with the platform and the sense of social presence is vital in social commerce due to the salient role of peer-generated contents, and eventually increases the purchase intentions [6]. Due to the important role in social commerce, there are lots of researches in trust model.

Two combination strategies were proposed to find the top-k trusted neighbors, considering two factors including semantic information of individual users and topology information of social network. The similarity between users was calculated based on different weighted interest topics and trust propagation ability of each node was evaluated according to the topology information. However, due to the presentation of users' interests were presented in the form of comments or ratings, the techniques for similarity analysis need to be advanced in future [7]. A model developed investigated the relationship of trust and influence of nodes, the model used global and local structure information to evaluate the influence of a node, including closeness centrality, Betweenness, Eigenvector, PageRank, etc. The research highlights the relationship between variables at both the network and the community level. However, every trust attribute was set to the same weight and not dynamically adaptable to the data set [8]. [9] proposed a model for the evaluation of authenticity of UGC based on three dimensions: stability, credibility and quality. The model measured trust in Genius as a collaborative environment and positive correlation between the trust degree and the number of edits could be seen. Lastly, research found that trust plays an important role as a bridge between information quality and information usage. The limitation was that UGC must go through user review process before it could be classified by the trust model. [10] pointed out that most research on trust prediction focused on users' history of interactions in evaluating the reputation of other users, service providers and the research suffered from malicious or inconsistent recommendations, then a global trust calculation model that made use of recommendations made by trust entities in weighing users' ratings was proposed. The trust entities gained higher reputation and their weight got larger compared to others. [11] considered each individual user's specific recommendation situation into recommender system due to existing methods just only focused on a one-size-fit-all trade-off strategy, an adaptive trust-aware model was proposed based on a new trust calculation developed using a user-item bipartite network. But the model is time-consuming to obtain set of parameters in accord with an expected goal.

3   Proposed Trust Model

Let $G = (U, E)$ is a weighted trust network, where U represents set of vertices, i.e. user nodes in network, E represents set of arcs between them and each vertex u has arcs, where (u_i, u_j) represents trust relationship between user u_i and user u_j, and $T(u_i, u_j)$ represents the trust value of (u_i, u_j). The Fig. 1 below shows the trust network diagram, the nodes from A to G on the graph represents the users and the directed arcs between users are the trust relationships. For example, node G points to node A and the weight of arcs is 0.6, that is the trust value from G to A is 0.6.

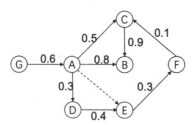

Fig. 1. Trust network diagram.

3.1 Direct Trust Calculation

In this model, direct trust is composed of two trust values that are calculated for each user in the trust network, including relationship trust and similarity trust.

Familiarity Trust. The lack of face-to-face interactions could result in users' suspicion of truthfulness in online exchanges while trade with familiar people other than anonymous people will improve users' purchase intentions. The enhancement of experience with exchange entities could reduce the uncertainty. Users' relationships that are presented in the form of connections and interactions play an important role in the behavior of users. On the other hand, users are often influenced by the set of trusted friends.

The familiarity between users can be calculated by the connections or friends that they have in common. A larger value means the users have more familiarity which shows they can build more valid trust relationships between them. The familiarity trust of users is defined as follows:

$$Fam(i,f) = \frac{F(i) \cap F(f)}{F(i) \cup F(f)} \tag{1}$$

Here $F(i)$ is the friends of user i. The friends of user i denotes that the links or arcs between i and other users exist in the trust network.

Similarity Trust. Users that have similar preferences tend to show interest in the same items and trust relationships probably exist between themselves. That is to say, users mostly trust others having similar attributes. In social commerce, the similarity between users usually come in the form of buying the same products or provide the same ratings for items. In our research, the user's rating of the item is used to measure the user's rating similarity to the item. The similarity trust of users is defined as follows:

$$Sim(u_i, u_j) = \frac{\sum\limits_{k \in E_{u_i,u_j}} r_{u_i,k} \cdot r_{u_j,k}}{\sqrt{\sum\limits_{k \in E_{u_i,u_j}} r_{u_i,k}^2} \sqrt{\sum\limits_{k \in E_{u_i,u_j}} r_{u_j,k}^2}} \tag{2}$$

Where k is the item that user u_i and u_j have rated and $r_{u_i,k}$ is the rating that user u_i marked to item k, E_{u_i,u_j} denotes the set of items both u_i and u_j have rated.

3.2 Indirect Trust Calculation

Indirect trust is expressed as global trust and the evaluation of users throughout the trust network is considered while indirect trust is calculated at the local trust level. Indirect trust shows the reliability and the credit history of the users in the social commerce network.

Ability Trust. Ability trust is an important indicator to measure the influence of users' recommendation information, the recommendation information of users with higher ability trust directly affects the purchasing decisions of other users. The user's ability trust is calculated by the recommendation accuracy rate. Because the recommendation accuracy rate can't directly be calculated by numerical indicators in social commerce, the difference between the user and other users' ratings on a certain product can reflect the user's recommendation accuracy on the product to a certain extent. The ability trust of users is defined as follows:

$$Abi(u_i) = \frac{\sum\limits_{k \in E_{u_i}} \sum\limits_{u \in U_k} N \left(\left| r_{u_i,k} - r_{u,k} \right| < \varepsilon \right)}{\sum\limits_{k \in E_{u_i}} \left\| U_k \right\|} \tag{3}$$

Where U_k represents the set of users who have an experience about item k, and ε is a predefined error tolerance threshold. $r_{u_i,k}$ is the rating that user u_i marked to item k and E_{u_i} denotes the set of items u_i has rated.

Prestige Trust. The user who has a higher reputation or more popular in social commerce is that we called opinion leader, prestige trust could be a representative of it, it comes in the form of in-degree of a node. In the real-world dataset we adopted, the in-degree of a node can be calculated by the directed arcs from other user nodes to this particular node, the final result is the proportion of these directed arcs to all potential directed arcs to this particular node. The prestige trust of users is defined as follows:

$$Pre(u_i) = \frac{Indegree(u_i)}{n - 1} \tag{4}$$

Where $Indegree(u_i)$ represents the directed arcs that point to user node u_i, and n denotes the amount of nodes is n in trust network.

The trust value of user node u_i is composed of both direct trust $DT(u_i)$ and indirect trust $IT(u_i)$, $DT(u_i)$ is calculated by using Eq. (1) and Eq. (2) while $IT(u_i)$ is calculated by using Eq. (3) and Eq. (4). The weight of each trust attribute is set to balance the component each attribute in trust value.

$$T(u_j) = a.Fam(u_i, u_j) + b.Sim(u_i, u_j) + c.Abi(u_j) + d.Pre(u_j) \tag{5}$$

Due to the nature of the environment in which trust is calculated and the particular needs of users, the importance of every attribute is different when evaluating users' trust. So we do not allocate the same fix weightage to each of trust attribute. The value of a, b, c, and d is calculated by entropy weight method and vary from user to user according to the dataset in the next section.

3.3   Influence Identification

Eigenvector Centrality. In this centrality measure, the connections to high-scoring user nodes contribute more to the score of the user node than links to low-scoring user nodes. Based on this consideration, all of the user nodes are assigned to respective values. The centrality of a user is a function of all the centrality of the users that linked to this user. The Eigenvector Centrality of user can be defined as:

$$EC_{u_i} = \frac{1}{\lambda} \sum_{u_j \in F(u_i)} EC_{u_j} = \frac{1}{\lambda} \sum_{u_j \in G} A(u_i, u_j) \cdot EC_{u_j} \tag{6}$$

For a given network graph $G = (U, E)$, let $A(u_i, u_j)$ be the adjacency matrix of graph $G = (U, E)$, $A(u_i, u_j) = 1$ if u_i is linked to u_j and $A(u_i, u_j) = 0$ otherwise. $F(u_i)$ represents the neighbors of u_i, λ is a constant.

PageRank. The PageRank of user node is the sum of contributions from its incoming links, and this sum depends on the PageRank of source user node. The votes of a user are determined by the importance of all users directed to this particular user, one link equals to a vote. PageRank is a variant of the Eigenvector Centrality measure.

$$PG(u_i) = \frac{1 - d}{N} + d \sum_{u_j \in M(u_i)} \frac{PG(u_j)}{Outdegree(u_j)} \tag{7}$$

Where $M(u_i)$ is the set of users that link to u_i, $Outdegree(u_j)$ is the out-degree of u_j, damping factor d is normally set to 0.85, and N is the set of all users in social network.

Local Structure Centrality. Due to the number of neighbors of a user can affect its spreading ability, Local Structure Centrality considers the structure of the nearest and next nearest neighbors of a user. Besides this, the topological connections among neighbors are also investigated.

$$CLS(u_j) = \sum_{u_i \in F_1(u_j)} \left(\alpha \cdot S(u_i) + (1 - \alpha) \cdot \sum_{u_i \in F_2(u_i)} c_{u_k} \right) \tag{8}$$

Where $S(u_i) = F_2(u_i)$ is the set of nearest and next nearest neighbors of user u_i, c_{u_k} denotes the local clustering coefficient of user u_k, and α is an additional parameter which ranges from 0 to 1.

4   Results and Discussion

The experimental result and analysis is based on social commerce platform Epinions which allocates users to post reviews on products to direct other users to make purchase decisions. The user on this website is also allowed to rate on other users' comments with a rating from 1 to 5 and mark other users as trust or distrust relationships. The trust

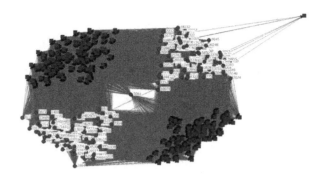

Fig. 2. Epinions dataset network.

and distrust mark is 1 and −1, respectively. Based on this, the platform takes the trust or distrust links into account in order to customize personalized recommendations. The dataset is contained of 32,016 users and 493,175 trust or distrust links, and the number of items is 246,968 with 893,154 ratings.

500 users are chosen from Epinions dataset to present their trust relationships with UCINET randomly. The example network diagram is drawn through visualization function.

Figure 2 shows the selected users are distributed into several communities and the subgroup division is obvious. The interactions are very close inside several communities. Some user nodes have more frequent communication with other nodes such as user ID = 5061, 10071 and so on.

The trust between users in this paper is influenced by four different attributes which are called familiarity trust, similarity trust, ability trust and prestige trust. The weight of each attribute is also different due to the importance degree when evaluating particular trust of different users. While entropy weight method will assign different weight values according to the contribution of each index to the whole. From this perspective, entropy weight method is taken to calculate the weight of each attribute. The trust value of the i-th user of j-th attribute is $t_{ij}(1 \leq i \leq m, 1 \leq j \leq n)$, then normalize t_{ij} to a certain value q_{ij} ranging from 0 to 1. Then the information entropy E_i of q_{ij} could be determined as follows:

$$E_i = -\frac{\sum\limits_{j=1}^{n} \ln p_{ij}}{\ln n} \tag{9}$$

If the information entropy of an indicator is smaller, it indicates that the greater the degree of variation of the indicator value, the more information it provides, the greater the role it can play in the comprehensive evaluation, and the greater its weight. Conversely, the larger the information entropy of an indicator, the smaller the role it can play in the overall evaluation, and the smaller its weight. The weight value w_i of trust attribute i is:

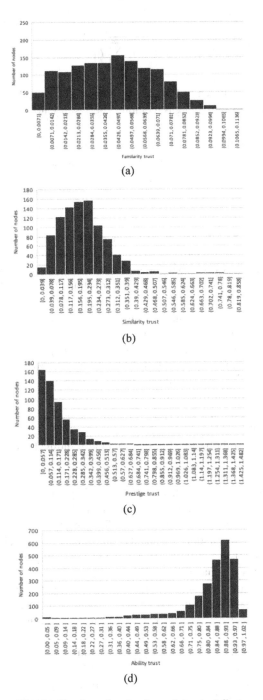

Fig. 3. Number of nodes in each trust attribute.

$$w_i = \frac{1 - E_i}{m - \sum\limits_{k=1}^{m} E_k} \tag{10}$$

Based on the results shown in Fig. 3, then the weight of each trust attribute could be calculated through entropy weight method. The result can be seen in Table 1.

Table 1. The weight value of each attribute.

Trust attribute	Familiarity trust	Similarity trust	Prestige trust	Ability trust
Weight value	0.1898	0.3392	0.3511	0.1197

The Fig. 3 shows the number of nodes in four trust attributes. It indicates that familiarity trust of users in Epinions is roughly ranging from 0 to 0.0781 as shown in Fig. 3(a), the interval with the largest number of user nodes is [0.0426, 0.0497]. The change of the range from [0, 0.0071] to [0.0426, 0.0497] is not obvious, while the amount of user nodes starts to reduce from the range [0.0426, 0.0497] drastically. The changing trend is more gradual, which means most of the relationships between users are strangers and they are relatively cautious about to establishing trust with other users. Figure 3(b) shows the user distribution in similarity trust, the trend is steeper compared with the changing trend in (a). It is shown that the weight value of similarity trust is 0.3392 while the value of familiarity trust is 0.1898 in Table 1. It can be inferred that the users in Epinions trust the users that have common preferences or interests, which also confirms from the fact that users in this social commerce platform are strangers on the whole.

The Fig. 3(c) and (d) shows the user distribution of indirect trust values. Compared with (a) and (b), the rate of change is more steeper and data range is more concentrated. From Fig. 3(c) we can conclude that fewer users have more prestige trust and most of users have very low prestige, but the prestige trust is pretty important to users when making purchase decisions or rating to some items. In Fig. 3(d), most users have high ability trust that almost ranges from 0.71 to 0.97, it means most users have common clear and consistent understanding of quality, appearance, practicality and durability that reflect the characteristics of products. So, when evaluating the weight of trust, the attribute of ability trust may take up a small space, i.e. 11.97%.

We calculate the total trust value of users which is the summary of direct trust and indirect trust based on four trust attributes and their particular weight values. Then three centrality measures consisted of Eigenvector Centrality, PageRank and Katz Centrality are used to detect the influential user nodes in network. The Fig. 4(a) shows that the correlation between total trust and Eigenvector Centrality is strong uphill, while in (b) and (c) the correlation is weak and moderate uphill, respectively. Overall, the more trust values the user node gets in the network, the more important it is. In other word, the user nodes having a high influence are positively trusted in the network.

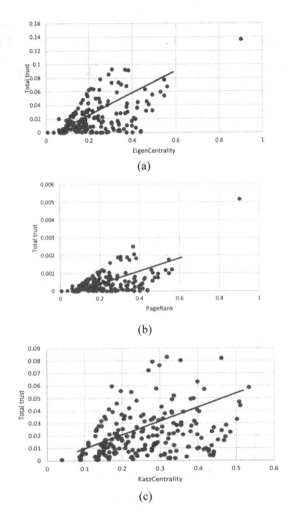

Fig. 4. Correlation between centrality and trust

5 Conclusion

This paper divides the trust between users into direct trust and indirect trust and presents in the form of four trust attributes: familiarity trust, similarity trust, prestige trust and ability trust. Then a trust model is proposed to calculate the trust values from users to users. Dataset named Epinions is set into the model to achieve the result, the dataset network diagram is drawn to demonstrate international connections between users in the dataset, besides. Entropy weight method is taken to evaluate the weight values of four trust attributes. The result shows that similarity and prestige trust is more important than both familiarity and ability trust relatively. Thus, users generally trust the users who have common interests or item appetite with them and users who have a higher reputation, i.e. opinion leaders. The correlation between user nodes♦trust and centrality is also calculated and drawn in the figure, it is shown that the users have higher trust values usually have a higher centrality value, i.e. more important in the network. In the future, we want to adapt this trust model into recommendation system and use it in a big data concept.

Acknowledgement. Supported by NSFC (No. 71671093), Natural Science Foundation of NJUPT (No. NY218024).

References

1. Yang, Y., Xie, G.: Efficient identification of node importance in social networks. Inf. Process. Manage. **52**, 911–922 (2016)
2. Deutsch, M.: Trust and suspicion. J. Confl. Resolut. **2**, 265–279 (1958)
3. Mayer, R.C., Davis, J.H., Schoorman, F.D.: An integrative model of organizational trust. Acad. Manage. Rev. **20**, 709–734 (1995)
4. Cho, J.-H., Chan, K., Adali, S.: A survey on trust modeling. ACM Comput. Surv. (CSUR) **48**, 1–40 (2015)
5. Daskapan, S., Van den Berg, J., Ali-Eldin, A.: Towards a trustworthy short-range mobile payment system. In: Proceedings of the IEEE International Conference on Systems, Man & Cybernetics, Washington. IEEE (2003)
6. Hajli, N., Sims, J., Zadeh, A.H., et al.: A social commerce investigation of the role of trust in a social networking site on purchase intentions. J. Bus. Res. **71**, 133–141 (2017)
7. Mao, C., Xu, C., He, Q.: A cost-effective algorithm for inferring the trust between two individuals in social networks. Knowl. Based Syst. **164**, 122–138 (2019)
8. Asim, Y., Malik, A.K., Raza, B., et al.: A trust model for analysis of trust, influence and their relationship in social network communities. Telematics Inform. **36**, 94–116 (2019)
9. Al Qundus, J., Paschke, A., Kumar, S., et al.: Calculating trust in domain analysis: theoretical trust model. Int. J. Inf. Manage. **48**, 1–11 (2019)
10. Amr Ali-Eldin, M.T.: Trsut prediction in online social rating networks. Ain Shams Eng. J. **9**, 3103–3112 (2019)
11. Yu, T., Guo, J.P., Li, W.H., et al.: Recommendation with diversity: an adaptive trust-aware model. Decis. Support Syst. **123**, 113073 (2019)

Digital Twins as Software and Service Development Ecosystems in Industry 4.0: Towards a Research Agenda

Yueqiang Xu[1]([⊠]), Tero Päivärinta[2], and Pasi Kuvaja[2]

[1] Martti Ahtisaari Institute, University of Oulu, Pentti Kaiteran katu 1,
90014 Oulu, Finland
yueqiang.xu@oulu.fi
[2] M3S Empirical Software Engineering on Software Systems, and Services,
Faculty of Information Technology and Electrical Engineering,
University of Oulu, Pentti Kaiteran katu 1, 90014 Oulu, Finland
{tero.paivarinta, pasi.kuvaja}@oulu.fi

Abstract. While research on digital twins of cyber-physical systems within industry 4.0 is emerging, the software development perspective on digital twins remains under-explored. Contemporary definitions and examples of digital twins have covered company- or product-specific solutions or discussed the use of digital twins in rather proprietary value chains. This paper addresses the importance of taking an ecosystem view on software development on digital twins for industry 4.0 and outlines a framework for building a research agenda for such ecosystems. The framework includes three dimensions: scope of the digital twin software platform (internal, value chain, ecosystem), life-cycle phases of the industry 4.0 system related with the digital twin (creation, production, operation & maintenance, disposal), and level of integration between the twin and the physical system (model, shadow, twin). As this research-in-progress addresses examples of research questions in light of the framework, further research to build a full-scale research agenda based on a systematic literature review is suggested.

Keywords: Digital twin · Software platform · Service ecosystem · Research agenda · Industry 4.0

1 Introduction

Industry 4.0 has attracted growing scholarly attention in recent years [1]. Progress in information technologies (IT), big data, and intelligent manufacturing have stimulated and enabled the global transformation in the manufacturing industry [2]. With the recent advances in the Internet of Things (IoT) in the modern industry, the conventional industrial production planning and management paradigm demands a shift or upgrade from purely providing surveillance-centric functions to building a comprehensive information framework of the industrial processes [3].

In this vein, an emerging concept of *digital twin* has gained momentum and much attention [4]. The term was coined by Michael Grieves in 2002 as a virtual, digital

© Springer Nature Singapore Pte Ltd. 2020
Y. Tian et al. (Eds.): ICBDS 2019, CCIS 1210, pp. 51–64, 2020.
https://doi.org/10.1007/978-981-15-7530-3_5

equivalent of a physical product [5] in the context of an executive course on Product Lifecycle Management (PLM) [6]. A digital twin is "a set of virtual information constructs that fully describes a potential or actual physical manufactured product" [6, p. 94]. Moreover, a digital twin can be defined at two levels: *digital twin prototype (DTP)*, which contains digital information "necessary to describe and produce a physical version that duplicates or twins the virtual version", and *digital twin instance (DTI)*, which "describes a specific corresponding physical product that an individual Digital Twin remains linked to throughout the life of that physical product" [6, p. 94].

From the viewpoint of cyber-physical systems (CPSs), a digital twin is defined as a specific applied technical framework as a realization of a CPS [7], while from the product life cycle perspective, a digital twin is a dynamic digital replica of physical assets, processes, and systems that comprehensively monitors the entire product lifecycle [3]. Grieves & Vickers propose also the concept of *Digital Twin Environment (DTE)* to cover an integrated multi-domain "application space for operating on Digital Twins for a variety of purposes" [6, p. 94]. Digital twin's backbone involves IoT technologies for real-time and multisource data acquisition. Additionally, artificial intelligence (AI) and software analysis are incorporated as part of the system to create digital simulation models that are dynamically updated and modified with their physical counterparts. The digital twin also advances the data visualization schemes, such as Virtual Reality (VR) and Augmented Reality (AR), so as to create more vivid, seamless, and user-friendly interfaces and user experience, for instance, for multimodal interactions with the physical system in question [8].

Overall, research (by Autumn 2019) on digital twins is emerging, diverse, scattered and weakly-linked. For example, there is a need for research in relation to the challenges of defining the unified framework for building the digital twin at the systemic level [9] while others call for the modular approach and continue to work on optimizing the synchronization framework between the cyber and physical worlds [10]. A majority of the literature has been primarily focused on the design schemes of the digital twin in narrow technical applications (e.g. surveillance signal processing [3], multi-modal user interface adaptation [11]), while [12] suggests that a (technological) system needs a coherent view at different levels or aspects such as core technology, platform, and application levels. Last but not least, the software development and implementation perspective on digital twin remains an under-explored territory in the existing studies. We argue that the development perspective on digital twins as software platforms within adjacent service development ecosystems is a crucial centerpiece to facilitate and enable the proliferation of digital twin applications in industry 4.0.

In the domain of Industry 4.0, asset administration related to an industrial plant and related CPSs requires multiple stakeholders throughout the plant life cycle, such as device manufacturers, system integrators, plant owners and Industry 4.0 architects (e.g., [13]). While architectural standards are still emerging, digital twins are expected to change current business models, development approaches, and technologies, while posing significant challenges to the architects and stakeholders in need to co-operate in this domain (e.g., [13, 14]). This trend highlights that development of innovative services and software applications on digital twins (such as those targeted to diagnostics, predictive maintenance, training, or virtual support for fieldwork on industrial artifacts) is increasingly taking place in platforms of actors in a value chain or even ecosystems of actors throughout the CPS life-cycle.

In an effort to understand the development of digital twins in industry 4.0, this paper outlines the challenges and proposes a framework for building a research agenda for the development of digital twins with related software and services at the platform and ecosystem levels. This paper sheds light on positioning digital twin research challenges related to the ecosystem and platform views on digital twins in the manufacturing industry.

The rest of this paper is organized as follows. Section 2 provides the review and discussion on the definition of the digital twin in the literature. Section 3 introduces the concepts of platform and ecosystem as an overarching framework to systematically identify the challenges and research agenda concerning the software development of a digital twin, especially in the ecosystem setting. Section 4 focuses on the presentation and proposition of the key research agenda for digital twins. Section 5 summarizes the contributions of our work and concludes the paper.

2 Analytical Dimensions of Digital Twins

2.1 High-Level Structure of Digital Twins

The fundamental idea of the digital twin includes the elements of the continuous real-time data exchange between the physical space, e.g. smart factory and the digital space, the data-driven training loop for continuous optimization and improvement of production as well as the integration of production and information elements [7]. A high-level illustration of the digital twin is presented in Fig. 1.

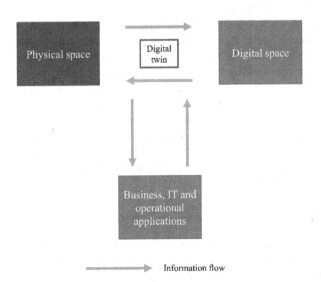

Fig. 1. A high-level illustration of digital twin (adapted from [15]).

Two key aspects of the digital twin system architecture are 1) a tight logical connection between the digital twins, the physical world counterparts and between different digital twins that are needed to realize a dedicated system functionality; 2) a changeable logical system architecture. Digital twin components may change properties like interfaces, connections to other components, behavior and simulation models, as well as communication protocols. Therefore, the initial logical architecture (of the DTP) may differ from the actual logical architecture (of a particular DTI) during runtime [14].

2.2   PLM Stages and Digital Twins

Based on the existing literature discussing digital twin in PLM [16], digital twin's integration into the PLM can include the following tasks and processes (at a coarse level): Creation, Production, Operations (and Maintenance), and Disposal [6].

In the Creation phase, a digital twin can be connected to design drawings, behavior prediction, design simulation, engineering data, manufacturing operations management key performance indicators (KPIs) and design tools. The digital twin can include order planning based on statistical assumptions, improved decision support by means of detailed diagnosis as well as automatic planning and execution from orders by the production units [17].

In the Production phase, the digital twin can focus on such issues as manufacturing instructions, virtual commissioning, and Hardware (HW)-in-the-loop tests [18].

In the Operations and Maintenance phase, digital twins can provide operation instructions, plant visualization, control performance, what-if studies, operational data, real-time movement, operational KPIs, and operational state display. The digital twin can be used to identify the impact of state changes on upstream and downstream processes of a production system [19, 20].

In maintenance actions, involved in the operations phase, digital twins are used to diagnose the system run-time, identification, and evaluation of anticipatory maintenance measures, the evaluation of machine conditions based on descriptive methods and machine learning algorithms [21]. As well, a digital twin can facilitate the integration, management, and analysis of machinery or process data during different stages of the machine life cycle to handle data/information more efficiently and further achieve better transparency of a machine's health condition [22].

The disposal phase has been so far less prominent in the mainstream discussion on digital twins. However, digital twin solutions within and after the disposal phase of the physical system life-cycle may appear important as well – for example, in the field of nuclear plants and spent nuclear fuel [6].

2.3   Three Levels of Digital Twin Integration

Digital twins were initially considered to be high fidelity mathematical models to reflect the behavior of the actual system as close as possible [18, 23]; this perception has evolved to include simulated and visible dynamic 3D models of real-world assets. The digital twin definition has been enriched over the time to be an evolving digital profile of the historical and current behavior and all properties of an asset, where an asset can be anything of value for an organization such as a physical device, a subsystem, a plant, or a software entity.

Based on the given definitions of a digital twin in any context, digital twins represent digital counterparts of physical objects. It is argued by [21] that three levels of how such counterparts interact are interchangeably used in the literature, namely, digital model, digital shadow and digital twin. Evidently, some digital representations are modeled manually and are not connected with any physical object in existence. At the same time, other digital twins are fully integrated with real-time data exchange. Thus, the definition of digital twins needs to be classified at different levels of how the digital counterparts interact with the physical objects to endorse a clear understanding of the existing and future research.

Based on the categorical classification of the digital twin [21], a digital model is a digital representation of an existing or planned physical object that involves no form of automated data exchange between the physical object and the digital object. Digital data of existing physical systems might still be in use for the development of such models, but all data exchange is done manually. A change in the state of the physical object has no direct effect on the digital object and vice versa as illustrated in Fig. 2.

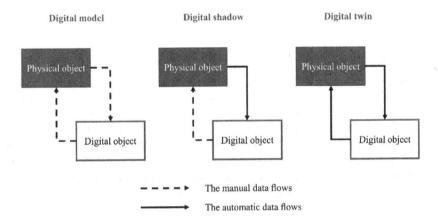

Fig. 2. Digital model, digital shadow, and digital twin [21].

The digital shadow utilizes automated one-way data flow between the state of an existing physical object and a digital object, becoming a virtual "shadow" of the physical object or system. A change in the state of the physical object or system changes the modeled state in the digital object [21]. In a full digital twin, the data flow between an existing physical object and a digital object is fully integrated to both directions. The digital object or system controls or affects a physical object. There might also be other physical or digital objects, which can make changes of state in the digital object. A change in the state of the physical object directly leads to a change in the state of the digital object, and this process goes in both directions as can be seen in Fig. 2.

3 Digital Twin Platforms and Ecosystems

3.1 Digital Platforms

When developing a variety of products that can meet the needs of a large number of customers, the manufacturers strive for commonalities and distinguishing features of the developed product variants. A common approach for this is the adoption of a platform approach [24], which is typically achieved by modularizing the product's architecture [25] or the production system [26]. The key to a platform approach is to achieve economies of scale in production [27] by using common components for a variety of product configurations [28].

In the literature, there are numerous platform types with different definitions and properties, e.g. the two-sided platform of [29]. To facilitate and navigate the literature of platform, the study of [30] divides the discussion of the digital platform into two perspectives: economics and engineering design. From an economic point of view, digital platforms are seen as markets where the platform facilitates exchanges between actors who otherwise would not be able to do business with each other. An example of this type of platform can be Airbnb, as the platform connects the business and leisure travelers with homeowners and enables the transaction between the buyers and sellers from different sides of the platform.

3.2 Digital Twin as Software Platform and Ecosystem

The technological perspective of the platform considers that a platform is a technological architecture that enables innovation [30, 31]. One of the basic ideas is that the platform inherently has the modularized features, functions, and components that can be used to decompose complex systems into manageable components connected by interfaces. Based on the level of authorization, the different modules are accessed and share data and information on the platform [28]. Furthermore, it is categorized by [30] the platforms into three organizational categories: the internal platform, the supply chain platform and the industry ecosystem platform (Table 1).

Table 1. Integrative classification of technological platforms (adapted from [30]).

	Internal platform	Supply-chain platform	Ecosystem platform
Unit of analysis	Company	Supply chain	Industry ecosystem
Degree of openness	Closed interfaces	Selectively open and closed interfaces	Open interfaces
The level of access	Company capabilities	Supply-chain capabilities	Unlimited number of external sources
Control/governance mechanisms	Managerial hierarchy	Contracts between supply chain companies	Ecosystem governance
Literature	[30, 32]	[30, 33, 34]	[30, 35, 36]

Digital Twin Platforms, Units of Analysis. Gawer [30] suggests the following units of analyses while looking at software and service platforms. An organization's *internal* platform often stands for the enterprise information system are sole available and accessible within a company or organization (e.g. an internal Enterprise resource planning (ERP) system of a factory), while the *supply chain* platform and *ecosystem* platform are outside a focal organization and exist in a broader network or ecosystem. As such, each platform type can be considered as a different unit of analysis. The internal platform only defines a single company/organization as the unit of analysis, while the boundary of an ecosystem platform covers multiple interconnected and interdependent actors with an ecosystem [30].

Digital Twin Platforms, Degree of Openness. The degree of openness is a defining characteristic of a platform. The traditional top-down enterprise management systems operate in a closed and hierarchical manner with higher-level controllers to plan, coordinate, and optimize production processes start to shift to changes that enable greater flexibility and adaptability to internal and external changes. In the world of networked production with multiple actors in complex manufacturing and production processes and ecosystems, the control process will inherently be a hybrid combination of hierarchical and heterarchical collaboration processes [15].

The equipment and technology vendors and software and system developers are all needed to become part of the ever-increasing complexity of larger and larger automated production networks [37], such as a digital twin network or ecosystem to support the production systems in industry 4.0 [15]. In this light, interconnectivity plays a crucial role not only within the boundaries of the manufacturing company in order to optimize production processes, but also beyond these limits. As a result, manufacturing is inherently a distributed control process [15].

A digital twin can improve the transparency of the production process beyond the organizational boundaries of the manufacturing company and data supports business applications on any device, anytime, anywhere [15]. The data-intensive nature of smart factory systems allows for timely, accurate, and detailed logging traces that enable real-time viewing of many systems and activities that were previously unavailable [15]. Evidently, today's production systems are no longer fully closed as [30]'s internal platforms.

Access to Capabilities and Resources. The platform's openness does not only affect actors' access to information, naturally, it also influences the platform's access to capabilities and resources as an increasing number of participators means a larger number of source pool and stronger capabilities, such as the open innovation capability in the literature [38, 39].

By incorporating the open innovation and ecosystem literature, we elaborate on [30]'s original proposition that focuses solely on the platform's innovation capabilities. We enrich this conceptualization and propose that platforms (especially in the ecosystem setting) can offer varying levels of access to resources and capabilities. Therefore, in contrast to a closed, internal platform focusing on internal development, a more open ecosystem platform supports also the external actors to access, exchange and share resources (e.g., software, information, and data) and capabilities (e.g., domain-based technical expertise) through the platform [30].

Platform Control and Governance. Orchestration and choreography [40] are two well-known composition strategies in the area of service-oriented architectures to create business processes from individual web services. According to [15], these concepts are partly related to the hierarchical and heterarchical functioning of manufacturing control systems. First, orchestration interacts with internal and external web services to take control from a stakeholder perspective. On the other hand, the choreography reflects a more collaborative interaction in which each involved stakeholder can describe his share of the interaction [15].

It is suggested by [41] that virtual factories that combine service-oriented computing and service-oriented workflows with the IoT. Similar to the typical roles of a service requester, a service provider, and a service register in a service-oriented architecture, they propose service providers, service consumers, and virtual factory brokers as essential roles of the virtual factory. The latter role is responsible for managing and controlling the virtual factory and uses services to model manufacturing processes and assemble products based on the results of factories of various business partners. The plug-and-play character of digital twin and virtual factories helps companies execute cross-organizational manufacturing processes as if they were running in a single company. Overall, as an emerging concept, the digital twin's technological development is at its nascent stage. Multiple aspects of the digital twin platform still require further development. This paper will focus more on software development with the platform and ecosystem perspective in the next section.

4   Framework for Building a Research Agenda

To outline existing (recognized) research issues and gaps, we constructed a three-dimensional framework based on the above-mentioned, three streams of literature related to the scope of the industrial organization and structure [30], the life-cycle perspective of the digital twin in industry 4.0 [6], and the levels of integration of digital twin [21].

First, **the scope dimension** consists of three organizational scopes: internal operations of a particular organization, the value chain of a group of suppliers, producers, and distributors, and the ecosystem that includes organizations beyond a particular value chain (see Fig. 3).

Second, we utilize the product **life-cycle perspective** on digital twins [6] as the second dimension. Essentially, the life-cycle dimension defines the four stages of the industrial 4.0 processes: creation and design of the products, the production process, operation and maintenance process, and the disposal of the wastes, defects, and decommissioned products (Fig. 3).

Third, we employ the categorization on the **levels of integration** between digital twins and the represented physical objects [21] as the third dimension of the framework (Fig. 3). The three levels of integration include the aforementioned concepts of the digital model, the digital shadow, and the digital twin. We use acronyms of DM (digital model), DS (digital shadow), and DT (digital twin), respectively, in Fig. 4. The level of integration dimension can be observed in each cell of the framework to assist the classification of the research issues and gaps concerning the digital twin studies.

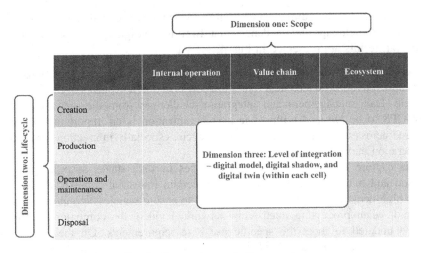

Fig. 3. Research agenda framework.

Dimension three: Level of integration (DM, DS, DT)	Dimension one: Scope		
	Internal operation	**Value chain**	**Ecosystem**
Creation	• Data management and integration (DS, DT)	• Data governance (DM, DS, DT)	• Ecosystem orchestration and governance (DM, DS, DT) • The degree of openness (DM, DS, DT) • Data provisioning and access (DM, DS, DT)
Production	• Data capture from IoT (DS, DT) • Data management and integration (DS, DT)	• Data interoperability (DM, DS, DT) • Data governance (DM, DS, DT) • Integration of intelligence (DS, DT)	• Ecosystem orchestration and governance (DM, DS, DT) • The degree of openness (DM, DS, DT) • Data provisioning and access (DM, DS, DT)
Operation and maintenance	• Understanding needs and opportunities for data utilization (DS, DT) • Data management and integration (DS, DT) • Understanding needs and opportunities for data utilization (DM, DS, DT)	• Data interoperability (DM, DS, DT) • Data governance (DM, DS, DT) • Integration of intelligence (DS, DT)	• Ecosystem orchestration and governance (DM, DS, DT) • The degree of openness (DM, DS, DT) • Data provisioning and access (DM, DS, DT)
Disposal	• Understanding needs and opportunities for data utilization (DM, DS, DT)	• Data governance (DM, DS, DT)	• Ecosystem orchestration and governance (DM, DS, DT)

Fig. 4. Examples of identified research issues in light of the framework.

By utilizing the three-dimensional framework as the conceptual lens, we mapped a number of research gaps and challenges that dwell in the digital twin research domain. The overall results are presented in Fig. 4.

Internal Digital Twin. Digital twin research focusing on internal operations of an organization has specific technical issues to address in different stages of the production life-cycle. Data management and integration challenges from the viewpoint of the whole CPS to be twinned within one host organization is an important issue to be addressed across the internal production life-cycle, especially in creation, production, and operation and maintenance stages.

Data capture from IoT represents challenges in such stages as production and operation and maintenance. For example, in certain industrial contexts, digital twin utilizes high-density intensive network cameras to ensure seamless monitoring. On the one hand, when processing intensively networked video, the computer architecture must be updated to meet the specific use case requirements. On the other hand, enabling a resource-constrained IoT device with modern analysis techniques, e.g., deep learning, can help relieve the pressure of cloud infrastructure and save the network bandwidth [3]. Another challenge lies within the internal organization is in regard to understanding needs and opportunities for data utilization in the later phases of the CPS life-cycle of a complex CPS, for instance, how predictive diagnosis can be utilized in operation and maintenance stage and even disposal stage. In general, the extant research in digital twin has made the process from the conventional digital model to the digital shadow and digital twin. However, the study identifies the fully digital twin development remains a gap to be addressed by the research community.

Value Chain-Focused Digital Twin. When we expand the digital twin scope from internal organization to the level of a value chain, new challenges regarding data interoperability and data governance emerge.

First, data interoperability challenges are related to enhancing data capture by component providers, for instance, how to standardize data acquisition and exchange within a value chain. Second, data governance challenges arise as the organizational boundary of digital twin shifts from internal operations to a value chain. As an example, the intellectual property rights (IPRs) within the value chain with regard to data analytics and processing is an important issue. Third, the integration of intelligence (e.g. AI and machine learning) in the value chain is a potential area for software or web applications to explore further. Supporting the integration of the AI and machine learning capabilities can resolve the resource constraints that exist in contemporary digital twin systems. Complexity increases when digital twins exit in the much wider application scope. Large technology companies like Google have been focusing on tackling the challenges and issues of data analytics integration. For example, Google has enabled TensorFlow (Google's machine learning and deep learning software library) to be able to be implemented in the mobile device through JavaScript, which solves the resource constrains for AI and machine learning integration in different systems and devices. In the context of the value chain, all three levels of integration (digital model, digital shadow, and digital twin) demand further research efforts.

Ecosystem-Focused Digital Twin. Currently, the digital twin ecosystem is primarily defined as a technical architecture that integrates the modeling and simulation while taking advantage of the industrial Internet of Things for data acquisition and information processing with cloud computing [42]. The technical ecosystem-focused digital twin system is visible and expected to be integrated into all phases of the PLM. The key challenges can be found in the areas of ecosystem governance mechanisms, degree of openness, and data sharing and access. The overall concept of suggesting digital twins as a basis for software and service development ecosystems represents a new contextual scope and view on related research. Such a view contributes to the existing digital twin research that mainly targets internal operations or value chain. Such a view will need to cover all the four stages of the CPS/product life-cycles.

5   Conclusion and Future Work

Digital platforms are transforming nearly every industry today [36] revolutionizing future value creation in the manufacturing industry as they enable companies to become more digitalized [46]. The advent of industry 4.0 fosters digital platforms and the concept of a digital twin to attract scholarly attention and interest as the industries start to realize and understand related technological and business opportunities [47].

Digital twin as an emerging concept represents new research issues crossing the disciplines of industrial engineering, software engineering, cyber-physical systems, AI and machine learning, and ecosystem and platforms. Digital twins need to be investigated holistically throughout three organizational scopes (internal operations, value chain, and ecosystem) while the challenges of interoperability through the combination of completely different models, systems and tools for digital twin become paramount. From the product and CPS life-cycle perspective [6], the digital twin must be seamlessly integrated with the existing systems, processes, and models [9] in different life-cycle stages to realize its true potential in industry 4.0. Additionally, this study incorporates the levels of integration for digital twin [21] to decrease the conceptual ambiguity in the existing digital twin research. New challenges and research issues are expected to emerge as novel applications on digital twins are required for system life-cycle phases of operations, maintenance, and disposal; built upon expanding software platforms opened for expanding digital service ecosystems, and involving increasingly integrated full-fledged twins instead of mere models or shadows of the physical systems. The key contributions of this study are constructing a three-dimensional framework to explore and analyze the research challenges and gaps in a structured manner and investigating the ecosystem context for digital twin that is rarely addressed in the digital twin studies Further studies can utilize the framework to systematically study the digital twin research in both theoretical and empirical contexts, in order to spot knowledge gaps and new research issues for the future research agenda.

Acknowledgement. This research has been partially funded by the ITEA3 project OXILATE (https://itea3.org/project/oxilate.html).

References

1. Uhlemann, T.H.J., Lehmann, C., Steinhilper, R.: The digital twin: realizing the cyber-physical production system for industry 4.0. Procedia CIRP 335–340 (2017)
2. Qi, Q., Tao, F.: Digital twin and big data towards smart manufacturing and industry 4.0: 360 degree comparison. IEEE Access **6**, 3585–3593 (2018)
3. He, Y., Guo, J., Zheng, X.: From surveillance to digital twin: challenges and recent advances of signal processing for industrial internet of things. IEEE Sig. Process. Mag. **35**, 120–129 (2018)
4. Enders, M.R., Hoßbach, N.: Dimensions of digital twin applications-a literature review. In: Twenty-fifth Americas Conference on Information Systems 2019. Association for Information Systems, Cancun (2019)
5. Grieves, M.W.: Virtually indistinguishable. In: IFIP International Conference on Product Lifecycle Management, Seville, Spain, pp. 226–242 (2012)
6. Grieves, M., Vickers, J.: Digital twin: mitigating unpredictable, undesirable emergent behavior in complex systems. Transdiscipl. Perspect. complex Syst. 85–113 (2017)
7. Min, Q., Lu, Y., Liu, Z., Su, C., Wang, B.: Machine learning-based digital twin framework for production optimization in petrochemical industry. Int. J. Inf. Manag. 1–18 (2019)
8. Saddik, A.E., Badawi, H., Alejandro, R., Velazquez, M., Laamarti, F.: Dtwins: a digital twins ecosystem for health and well-being. IEEE COMSOC MMTC Commun. - Front. **14** (2019)
9. Koulamas, C., Kalogeras, A.: Cyber-physical systems and Digital Twins in the industrial Internet of Things [cyber-physical systems]. Computer (Long. Beach. Calif.) 95–98 (2018)
10. Kuts, V., Otto, T., Tähemaa, T., Bondarenko, Y.: Digital twin-based synchronised control and simulation of the industrial robotic cell using Virtual Reality. J. Mach. Eng. **19** (2019)
11. Josifovska, K., Yigitbas, E., Engels, G.: Human-computer interaction. Des. Practice Contemp. Soc. **11568**, 398–409 (2019)
12. Quan, X.I., Sanderson, J.: Understanding the artificial intelligence business ecosystem. IEEE Eng. Manag. Rev. **46**, 22–25 (2018)
13. Wagner, C., et al.: The role of the Industry 4.0 asset administration shell and the digital twin during the life cycle of a plant. In: 2017 22nd IEEE International Conference on Emerging Technologies and Factory Automation (ETFA), pp. 1–8 (2017)
14. Bauer, T., Antonino, P.O., Kuhn, T.: Towards architecting digital twin-pervaded systems. In: Proceedings of the 7th International Workshop on Software Engineering for Systems-of-Systems and 13th Workshop on Distributed Software Development, Software Ecosystems and Systems-of-Systems, pp. 66–69. IEEE Press, Piscataway (2019)
15. Preuveneers, D., Ilie-zudor, E.: Robust digital twin compositions for industry 4.0 smart manufacturing systems. In: 2018 IEEE 22nd International Enterprise Distributed Object Computing Workshop (EDOCW), pp. 69–78. IEEE (2018)
16. Arianfar, S., Kallenbach, J., Mitts, H., Mäkinen, O.: Back to the Future – Prediction of Incremental and Disruptive Innovations (2012)
17. Boschert, S., Rosen, R.: Digital twin—the simulation aspect. In: Hehenberger, P., Bradley, D. (eds.) Mechatronic Futures: Challenges and Solutions for Mechatronic Systems and their Designers, pp. 59–74. Springer, Cham (2016). https://doi.org/10.1007/978-3-319-32156-1_5
18. Malakuti, S., Schlake, J., Ganz, C., Harper, K.E., Petersen, H.: Digital Twin: An Enabler for New Business Models. https://www.researchgate.net/profile/Somayeh_Malakuti/publication/334884420_Digital_Twin_An_Enabler_for_New_Business_Models/links/5d4413c44585153e59355a16/Digital-Twin-An-Enabler-for-New-Business-Models.pdf

19. D'Addona, D.M., Ullah, A.M.M.S., Matarazzo, D.: Tool-wear prediction and pattern-recognition using artificial neural network and DNA-based computing. J. Intell. Manuf. **28** (6), 1285–1301 (2015). https://doi.org/10.1007/s10845-015-1155-0
20. Susto, G.A., Schirru, A., Pampuri, S., McLoone, S., Beghi, A.: Machine learning for predictive maintenance: a multiple classifier approach. IEEE Trans. Ind. Inform. **11**, 812–820 (2014)
21. Kritzinger, W., Karner, M., Traar, G., Henjes, J., Sihn, W.: Digital Twin in manufacturing: a categorical literature review and classification. IFAC-PapersOnLine **51**, 1016–1022 (2018)
22. Lee, J., Lapira, E., Bagheri, B., Kao, H.: Recent advances and trends in predictive manufacturing systems in big data environment. Manuf. Lett. **1**, 38–41 (2013)
23. Bratthall, L.G., et al.: Integrating hundred's of products through one architecture-the industrial IT architecture. In: Proceedings-International Conference on Software Engineering, pp. 604–614 (2002)
24. Meyer, M.H., Lehnerd, A.P.: The Power of Product Platforms. Free Press, New York (1997)
25. Erixona, G., Anders, Y., Arnström, A.: Modularity – the basis for product and factory reengineering. CIRP Ann. - Manuf. Technol. **45**, 1–6 (1996)
26. Rogers, G.G., Bottaci, L.: Modular production systems: a new manufacturing paradigm. J. Intell. Manuf. **8**, 147–156 (1997)
27. Meyer, M.H., Osiyevskyy, O., Libaers, D., van Hugten, M.: Does product platforming pay off? J. Prod. Innov. Manag. **35**, 66–87 (2018)
28. Andersson, E., Eckerwall, K.: Enabling Successful Collaboration on Digital Platforms in the Manufacturing Industry A Study of Digital Twins (2019). http://www.diva-portal.org/smash/get/diva2:1324680/FULLTEXT02
29. Rochet, J.C., Tirole, J.: Two-sided markets: a progress report. RAND J. Econ. **37**, 645–667 (2006)
30. Gawer, A.: Bridging differing perspectives on technological platforms: toward an integrative framework. Res. Policy **43**, 1239–1249 (2014)
31. Henfridsson, O., Bygstad, B.: The generative mechanisms of digital infrastructure evolution. MIS Q. Manag. Inf. Syst. **37**, 907–931 (2013)
32. Mocanu, E., Nguyen, P.H., Gibescu, M., Kling, W.L.: Deep learning for estimating building energy consumption. Sustain. Energy Grids Netw. **6**, 91–99 (2016)
33. Yun, S., Park, J.H., Kim, W.T.: Data-centric middleware based digital twin platform for dependable cyber-physical systems. In: International Conference on Ubiquitous and Future Networks, pp. 922–926 (2017)
34. Evans, P.C., Gawer, A.: The Rise of the Platform Enterprise A Global Survey. New York (2016)
35. Gawer, A., Cusumano, M.A.: Industry platforms and ecosystem innovation. J. Prod. Innov. Manag. **31**, 417–433 (2014)
36. De Reuver, M., Sørensen, C., Basole, R.C.: The digital platform: a research agenda. J. Inf. Technol. **33**, 124–135 (2018)
37. Rajratnakharat, B.V., Jadhao, S., Marode, R.: Digital twin: manufacturing excellence through virtual factory replication. In: Nc-Race 18, pp. 6–15 (2014)
38. Chesbrough, H., Vanhaverbeke, W.: Open innovation: a new paradigm for understanding industrial innovation. Open Innov. **4**, 1–27 (2005)
39. Chesbrough, H., Vanhaverbeke, W., West, J.: New Frontiers in Open Innovation. Oxford University Press, Oxford (2014)
40. Peltz, C.: Web Services Orchestration and Choreography. Computer (Long. Beach. Calif.) (10) (2003)
41. Schulte, S., Schuller, D., Steinmetz, R., Abels, S.: Plug-and-play virtual factories. IEEE Internet Comput. **16**, 78–82 (2012)

42. Liu, Z., Meyendorf, N., Mrad, N.: The role of data fusion in predictive maintenance using digital twin. In: AIP Conference Proceedings (2018)
43. Borodulin, K.: Towards digital twins cloud platform: microservices and computational workflows to rule a smart factory. In: Proceedings of the 10th International Conference on Utility and Cloud Computing, pp. 209–210. ACM (2014)
44. Tao, F., Zhang, H., Liu, A., Nee, A.Y.C.: Digital twin in industry: state-of-the-art. IEEE Trans. Ind. Inform. **15**, 2405–2415 (2019)
45. Mourtzis, D., Doukas, M., Bernidaki, D.: Simulation in manufacturing: review and challenges. Procedia CIRP **25**, 213–229 (2014)
46. Müller, J.M.: Antecedents to digital platform usage in Industry 4.0 by established manufacturers. Sustainability **11**, 1121 (2019)
47. Landolfi, G., Barni, A., Menato, S., Cavadini, F.A., Rovere, D., Dal Maso, G.: Design of a multi-sided platform supporting CPS deployment in the automation market. In: 2018 IEEE Industrial Cyber-Physical Systems (ICPS), pp. 684–689 (2018)

A Click Fraud Detection Scheme Based on Cost-Sensitive CNN and Feature Matrix

Xinyu Liu[1(✉)], Xin Zhang[2], and Qianyun Miao[2]

[1] Nanjing Foreign Language School, Nanjing 210008, China
3060381407@qq.com
[2] School of Computer Science and Technology, Nanjing Tech University,
Nanjing 211816, China

Abstract. Around 30% revenue has been wasted due to different types of advertising fraud. In view of the continuous emergence of fraud and the improvement of fraudulent means, a click fraud detection of cost-sensitive convolutional neural network (CSCNN) based on feature matrix is proposed. In order to capture the pattern of click fraud, priori probability is introduced and a new feature set is derived from the knowledge of entropy. Then, using cost-based sampling method and threshold-moving cost sensitive learning algorithm to solve unbalanced data training problems. Features are transformed into feature matrix by different time windows to fit the input of a convolutional neural network. Finally, considering the convolution kernel size, the number of convolution kernels and the pooling size of different network structures in this work, effective CSCNN structure was chosen. Experiments on real-word data show that this method can complete click fraud detection effectively, and can complete multi classification without increasing the complexity of the model. A new effective method was provided on click fraud detection in mobile advertisement.

Keywords: Click fraud · Feature matrix · Cost-sensitive · Convolutional neural network · Imbalanced datasets

1 Introduction

Cost Per Click (CPC) is the main billing mode of mobile advertising. Almost 30% of mobile advertising revenue was consumed by different types of advertising fraud [1]. Click fraud has caused a serious loss of advertising budgets. Effective click fraud detection and prevention are key problems in the Internet advertising. Neural network algorithm performs well in large-scale calculation and nonlinear mapping. It is also very suitable for fraud detection scenarios [2]. In the field of natural language processing, word vectors were represented as matrices for input of CNN to complete the classification of sentences [3]. Inspired by this and based on the existing research, Convolutional neural network is used to classify in this paper to avoid feature redundancy and model over-fitting. It can further extract manual features and finally capture the intrinsic property of fraudulent behavior based on labeled sample data.

The performance of fraud detection technology much depends on feature selection, so it is necessary trying a lot of technical analysis on data to find effective features. In

© Springer Nature Singapore Pte Ltd. 2020
Y. Tian et al. (Eds.): ICBDS 2019, CCIS 1210, pp. 65–79, 2020.
https://doi.org/10.1007/978-981-15-7530-3_6

order to better show the characteristics of fraudulent clicks, this paper refers to the characteristics used in the existing advertisement click fraud detection, analyzes many click data, and re-examines the feature extracting to derive some aggregate attributes. Apart from statistical features such as difference and average, the prior probability is used to calculate the possibility of fraud by different publishers. Moreover, the knowledge of entropy is introduced to calculate multiple click entropies from different features. The spatial structure and spatial correlation of the image are very different from the features in this paper. Therefore, the structure of the input features needs to be considered. In this paper, the feature transformation is performed from a plurality of different time granularity windows, and the click feature is represented by a feature matrix which looks like a two-dimensional image. Then, a convolutional neural network is applied to identify each publisher sample category.

The extreme imbalance of click fraud data is another difficulty in anomaly detection. Nowadays, sampling methods are more commonly used, and cost-sensitive learning is also an effective solution to overcome class imbalance. Considering the existing of the data imbalance and different misclassification costs, this paper introduces cost-sensitive mechanism in both sample construction and training stage, and trains cost-sensitive convolutional neural network, which shows good performance finally.

2 Related Works

In order to obtain higher profits, click fraud methods come out one after the other. Online advertising system needs more accurate and effective click fraud detection methods. Researchers at home and abroad seek ways to identify and prevent click fraud in advertising, such as knowledge discovery and expert systems. But more methods based on user click behavior use massive data from the Internet to identify fraud. Based on the traditional characteristics of advertisement clicks, Perera et al. [4] derived a new feature set and used the decision tree to improve the efficiency of fraud detection. Kitts et al. [5] designed a data mining system to detect large-scale click fraud attacks. Crussel et al. [6] focused on mobile advertising fraud and developed MAdFraud, which aims to automatically detect fraud by performing a black box test on the application without having to manually reverse engineer the application. Oentaryo et al. [7] used a variety of machine learning methods for mobile advertising to perform click fraud detection, but the detection results were worse.

Click fraud has complex patterns and fraudulent clicks are similar to normal clicks, which leads to the characteristics of fraudulent clicks having a certain weak randomness, and it is difficult to find out. The integration method can improve the generalization ability of the algorithm. King MA [8] tests four integrated learning methods (Voting, bootstrap aggregation, Stacked Generalization, MetaCost) performed on four basic classification models (Naive Bayes, Logistic Regression, Decision Tree, SVM) to improve the performance of the classifier. In the latest research, He et al. [3] proposed an integration-based approach to detect fraudulent behavior in mobile advertising for mobile advertising data. In the previous research, we proposed a Boosting-SVM integrated detection method, which processed imbalanced dataset to obtain multiple balanced datasets. Using Boosting algorithm to train the SVM to generate multiple strong classifiers. The model finally integrates multiple strong classifiers to achieve effective detection of click fraud [9].

Ensemble methods are becoming more common in the field of detection, but integration methods can make the model too complex and cause model overfitting. In recent years, the rapid development of neural network pattern recognition methods has gradually replaced traditional machine learning methods, and has been widely applied to image recognition, natural language processing, and industrial fault detection. Among them, CNN, as the core technology of computer vision, has achieved good results in image classification. At present, CNN has also been well applied in the field of natural language processing. Kim et al. [10] proposed a sentence classification method based on single hidden layer CNN. He et al. [3] used word vectors to represent sentences as matrices as inputs, then comparing the similarities of sentences. Inspired by those, this paper uses the convolutional neural network as a classifier.

3   CSCNN Click Fraud Detection Model

This section mainly describes the construction of CSCNN advertising click fraud detection model based on feature matrix, the click fraud detection framework we use is shown in Fig. 1. It includes the training learning and classification prediction phases. The training learning phase is mainly carried out in four steps. Firstly, in order to capture the potential attribute characteristics of the click fraud publisher to better construct the classifier model, this paper analyzes the original data and refers to the existing click advertising fraud characteristics, using various statistical methods to extract the features of advertisement publishers from multiple angles. Secondly, since the fraud detection data sets are extremely unbalanced, this paper uses the cost-based sampling method and the threshold moving cost-sensitive learning algorithm. Finally, the cost-sensitive convolutional neural network is applied to the click fraud detection scenario to complete the classification of normal clicks and fraudulent clicks. In order to be more suitable for the CNN model, the feature needs to be transformed, and the feature matrix is constructed from multiple time granularities using time windows, similar to the input of a two-dimensional image. The specific structure of the convolutional neural network used here is given at the end of this section.

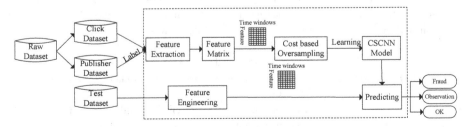

Fig. 1. The overall framework of the proposed CSCNN click fraud detection system

3.1   Feature Extraction

Real world click fraud data from a global mobile advertising company-BuzzCity provided the following information: *publiserid* (publisher's identifier), *bankaccount*, *adders*, *status* (Fraud, Observation, OK), *id* (unique identifier for each click), *numericip* (clicker's public IP address), *deviceua* (mobile device used), *campaignid* (the unique identifier of the published ad), *usercountry, clicktime, referredurl* (the URL where the ad was clicked), *channel* (the publisher's ad type, including Community, Entertainment and Lifestyle, Information, etc.).

The original data do not reflect the global behavior of the click, and cannot be directly used for the construction of the model. After the data is collated, some aggregate properties must be derived from the dataset for the classification of the training and test set of the classifier.

In order to construct new features, this paper refers to the features of Oentaryo [7] and Perera [4]. Consider the effects of the *deviceua, numericip, campaignid, usercountry, clicktime*, and *referredurl* attributes to discover the scope and usefulness of constructing new features to capture the spatial and temporal behavior patterns of each publisher. First, use the *clicktime* attribute to divide multiple fine-grained time window lengths T to better capture the time dynamic distribution of click fraud behavior. T is set to two different types of time granularity T_1, T_2. T_1 setting value is: *per min, per 5min, per 15min, per hour, per 3hours, per 6hours, per day*. T_2 setting value is: *first_15min (0-14), second_15min(15-29), third_15min(30-44), last_15min(45-59), night(0:00-5:59), morning(6:00-11:59), afternoon(12-17:59), evening (18:00-23:59), 3days*. A plurality of features are generated using these time windows T. Basic statistics are performed on the click volume of each publisher to construct feature: *Total_amount_clicks_T_2, Avg_amount _clicks_T, Std_amount_clicks_T, Clicks_percent _T_2, Max_amout_clicks_T, Min_amout_clicks _T* (attributes with T indicate that eigenvalues are calculated separately under the T_1 and T_2 windows). Next, we construct some *deviceua*-based derived features. The attribute *deviceua* is the device model and operating system platform used by the clicker, such as *Samsung_s5233, Nokia_3110c*, and so on. The feature shown in Table 1 is constructed based on the *deviceua* attribute.

Table 1. Description of Deviceua-based derived feature

Feature	Description
Distinct_deviceua_T_2	Number of different devices associated with the publisher
Avg_distinct_deviceua_T	Average number of different devices for publishers
Std_distinct_deviceua_T	Standard deviation of the number of different devices corresponding to the publisher
deviceua_click_ratio_T_2	Ratio of different devices to clicks
Std_samedeviceua_clicks_T_2	Standard deviation of the number of clicks for different devices
Max_samedeviceua_clicks_T	The maximum number of clicks for different devices
Entropy_deviceua_T_2	The number of clicks entropy corresponding to different devices

CPC is actually a more complicated mode. In order to better carry out training and learning, in addition to the basic statistical methods, the average value, and the standard deviation, the fraudster will continuously change the IP address and repeat clicks when the device is unchanged. This makes the distribution of random events of clicks change, so this paper introduces knowledge of entropy. The total number of clicks by the same publisher in the past T_2 is $Total\_amount\_clicks\_T_2$, which involves a different device. The total amount of clicks of the j-th device type is $amount\_clicks\_deviceua_j\_T_2$ $(j = 1, 2, \ldots, l)$, and the click ratio of the j-th device type is p_j:

$$p_j = \frac{amount\_clicks\_deviceua_j\_T_2}{Total\_amount\_Clicks\_T_2} \tag{1}$$

Click Entropy of l different devices are defined as $Entropy\_deviceua\_T_2$:

$$Entropy\_deviceua\_T_2 = -\sum_{j=1}^{l} p_j log p_j \tag{2}$$

When the probability of the sample is equal, that is, the sample distribution is uniform, the entropy value is the largest, and the fraudulent click will cause a certain amount of clicks corresponding to a certain device, so that the sample distribution has large unevenness and the entropy value is small.

The features based on the *numericip*, *campaignid*, *usercountry*, and *referredurl* attributes are defined in the same way. A public IP address may have different users, and a device may use multiple different IP addresses. Therefore, in addition to considering a single attribute, we also combine *numericip* with *deviceua* to calculate the combination of *numericip* + *deviceua*. Similar to the features of Table 1, 48 features were constructed under different time windows. The CNN model used in this paper can use the convolution layer for feature extraction and the pooling layer for feature mapping, effectively avoiding over-fitting of the model [11].

3.2 CSCNN Detection Model

CNN combines the feature extraction and classification process to train the neural network. The convolution layer is used for feature extraction, the pooling layer completes the feature selection to reduce the dimension, and the full connection layer is responsible for classification [12]. This paper uses CNN to complete the classification work of click data. After constructing the feature matrix for the input layer by using time window T, the cost-based oversampling method is used to deal with the unbalanced data set, and at the same time, the purpose of data expansion is achieved. Finally, the threshold is moved at the output layer to get the softmax classifier with the lowest expected cost. The CSCNN detection model is determined from the number and size of the convolutional layer filter, the pooling layer strategy, the deactivation rate of the dropout, the excitation function, and the fully connected layer.

Feature Matrix
In this paper, multiple one-dimensional features are constructed under multiple time granularities. Therefore, a method of constructing feature matrices by using multiple

time windows T for feature transformation is proposed. Similar to a two-dimensional image, the final input of the CNN is a 48×16 feature matrix. The specific method is showed in Fig. 2, and the feature attributes with different behaviors in the feature matrix are listed as time windows T of multiple time granularities. When the time window is T_2, such as *Total_amount_clicks_T_2*, only the value under the time window T_2 is calculated, and the value under the time window *T1* is set to 0. By analyzing the feature correlations in the matrix, it can be found that the same features in different time windows have a strong relationship and are placed in a closer position. Based on local correlation in the feature matrix, the CNN model can reduce the complex time complexity of data processing while retaining useful information.

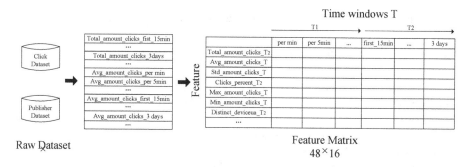

Fig. 2. Construction process of the feature matrix

Cost Sensitive Learning

Cost-sensitive learning method is a method proposed for different classification errors of imbalanced classification problems [13]. Cost-sensitive learning is usually divided into two classes: 1) Cost-sensitive meta-learning: reconstructing training samples, transforming any non-cost sensitive and classification algorithms into cost-sensitive learning algorithms, such as cost-sensitive BP neural networks; 2) Direct method: Without changing the samples' distribution, a cost-sensitive mechanism is introduced to the classification algorithm to redesign the cost-sensitive classification algorithm [14]. Most of the researches perform data reconstruction or pure cost-sensitive learning simply. Considering the dataset imbalance and different misclassification costs, this paper combines these two types of cost-sensitive learning, and introduces a cost-sensitive mechanism in both sample construction and training. First, the cost-based oversampling method is used to balance the data samples, and at the same time, the purpose of expanding the data set is achieved. Then, by considering the cost matrix, the threshold of the output of the mobile neural network is reached until the optimal value is reached. This paper proposes a CSCNN model structure based on cost sampling for the purpose of minimum classification cost.

Suppose a class C sample, the kth class contains N_k training samples, the cost matrix Cost[k, m](k, m $\in \{1, \ldots, C\}$) represents the loss of class k samples into m classes, and *Cost[k, k]* = 0, indicating correct classification. The cost of class k is:

$$Cost[k] = \sum_{m=1}^{C} Cost[k, m] \tag{3}$$

(1) Cost-based oversampling method

The cost-based oversampling method changes the distribution of training data by increasing the number of samples in the higher cost category, and directly reflects the cost into the sample data. After the sampling magnification is set, the number of samples of the k-th sample after sampling is N_k^*. The h class is a class that does not require sample copying. The specific calculation formula is as shown in Eq. (4). In this paper, the h class is a normal click.

$$N_k^* = \frac{Cost[k]}{Cost[h]} N_h \tag{4}$$

Samples defined as fraudulent clicks near the classification decision boundary have a higher probability of generating more artificial fraud samples, which be replicated by the higher cost fraud training samples, so that the sampled sample satisfies the formula (4). Firstly, calculating the cost of each fraud sample, and define the cost of the i-th fraudulent click publisher sample as $Cost_i$, as shown in (5), where d_{ij} is the distance between the i-th fraud publisher sample and the j-th publisher sample. The i-th fraudulent publisher neighborhood is defined by the function $g(x) = \begin{cases} 1, x < 0 \\ 0, x \geq 0 \end{cases}$ and the interrupt value C.

$$Cost_i = \frac{\sum_{j \in OK} g(d_{ij} - C) + \sum_{j \in Observation} g(d_{ij} - C)}{\sum_{r \in Fraud} g(d_{ir} - C)} \tag{5}$$

We use the SMOTE method to generate new samples, first using the k-means algorithm to divide the fraudulent publisher into several clusters. The fraud samples pub1 and pub2 in one of the clusters are selected as seed samples according to different costs, and a new artificial sample is constructed according to formula (6). The sample to be observed is then copied in the same way.

$$Pub_{new} = Pub_2 + rand(0, 1) \times (Pub_1 - Pub_2) \tag{6}$$

(2) Cost sensitive optimization layer

This paper uses the CNN structure and finally classifies it through the Softmax classifier. The formula of the Softmax function is:

$$a_j = p\left(y^{(i)} = j|x^{(i)}; \theta\right) = \frac{e^{\theta_j^T x^{(i)}}}{\sum_{l=1}^{C} e^{\theta_l^T x^{(i)}}} \tag{7}$$

Where C is the number of categories, $\sum_{j=1}^{C} a_j = 1$.

In the prediction phase, cost-sensitive mechanism is introduced, and the threshold-moving is used to offset the decision boundary of the non-cost sensitive neural network to the boundary of the lower cost class, so that the reduces of the risk of a higher-cost sample being misclassified. After introducing the cost sensitive mechanism, the probability that the sample x is classified as j is:

$$a_j^* = \eta \sum_{c=1}^{C} p(j|x)Cost[j,c] = \eta \sum_{c=1}^{C} a_j Cost[j,c] \tag{8}$$

Where η is the normalization term, $\sum_{j=1}^{C} a_j^* = 1$.

When performing backpropagation, the cross-entropy loss function is used to calculate the error, which ultimately enables the model to learn effectively from unbalanced data.

CSCNN Model Structure

The structure of CNN generally includes input layer, convolution layer, pooling layer, repeated convolution layer, pooling layer, fully connected layer, and final output result. The convolutional layer is calculated by different convolution checksums. The general process is shown in (9):

$$F_j^l = f\left(\sum_i F_i^{l-1} \otimes f_{ij}^{l-1} + b_j^l\right) \tag{9}$$

Where $\otimes$ is the convolution operator, F_j^l and F_i^{l-1} are the j-th feature map of the l layer and the i-th feature map of the l-1th layer, f_{ij}^{l-1} is the convolution kernel of F_i^{l-1} to F_i^l, and b_j^l is the offset term. $f()$ is a nonlinear excitation function. The activation function of all hidden layers in this paper uses ReLU. Compared with other functions, it can effectively avoid the problem of slow convergence and local maximum value caused by gradient missing. Each convolution layer has multiple filters. Each filter is the same size and convolved with the corresponding data to obtain multiple feature maps. The depth of the feature map is consistent with the number of convolution layer filters. Suppose the data input to each convolutional layer is of size $H_1 \times W_1 \times D_1$. Each convolution requires the following hyperparameters: filter size $f_1 \times f_2$, filter quantity d, step s, zero padding number p, the data size after convolution is $H_2 \times W_2 \times D_2$, Calculation formula such as (10):

$$H_2 = \frac{H_1 - f_1 + 2p}{s} + 1 \quad W_2 = \frac{W_1 - f_1 + 2p}{s} + 1 \quad D_2 = d \tag{10}$$

Each filter introduces $f_1 \times f_2 \times D_1$ weights, which requires a total of $f_1 \times f_2 \times D_1 \times d$ weights and d offset term parameters. According to formula (10), it can be found that the size of the region obtained by using the smaller convolution layer of the multi-layer filter is the same as the convolution layer with a larger filter. If two 3×3 convolutional layers are connected, they can be regarded as a 5×5 filter, and the three connected together can be regarded as a 7×7 filter. However, using a smaller filter can perform more nonlinear mapping to obtain more abstract features, so that the extracted feature expression performance is better. On the other hand, the introduction of parameters can be reduced, so this paper uses a plurality of filter smaller convolution layer stacks to be pooled again. At the same time, in order to maintain the boundary information, the dimensions are kept consistent before and after the convolution, and Zero Padding is performed before each convolution.

The pooling layer performs the down-sampling, and the depth of the feature map is unchanged every time. The dimension reduction is achieved by removing the unimportant features in each feature map. The general expression of the pooling layer is:

$$Z_j^l = down\left(F_j^l\right) \tag{11}$$

Where F_j^l and Z_j^l are the input and output of the pooling layer, and $down()$ is the pooling function. At present, the maximum pooling and the average pooling are the most commonly used methods. The pooling layer of this paper uses the maximum pooling to fully extract the significant features of different convolution mapping attributes.

The fully connected layer maps the operational maps of the convolutional layer, the pooling layer, the excitation function layer and the like into fixed-length feature vectors, wherein the output of each neural node is expressed as:

$$h\left(Z^D\right) = f\left(W^T Z^D + b\right) \tag{12}$$

Where $h()$ is the fully connected output, $f()$ is the excitation function, Z^D is the output of the previous layer of the full connection, D is the feature map depth, W is the full connection weight, and b is the offset term. In addition, in order to improve the generalization ability of the model and reduce the model overfitting, the dropout layer is added after the fully connected layer.

In this paper, we test different convolution layer levels, convolution kernel size, etc., and finally determine the CNN structure shown in Fig. 3 as the final classifier. The structure is similar to the typical VGG structure. The specific hyperparameters are given in the experimental part. The input is 48×16 feature matrix F, the first 10 layers are two convolutional layers, and the pooling layer is repeated twice, and then three convolutional layer stacks are added to the pooling layer. The last three layers are fully connected layers. In practical applications, full connections can be implemented by convolution operations. A fully connected layer that is fully connected to the front layer can be converted into a convolution kernel of 1×1 convolution. A global convolution of $h \times w$ (the height and width of the previous convolution result respectively) is used for the fully connected layer in which the front layer is a convolutional layer or a pooled layer. This article uses a global convolution kernel at the first fully connected layer. Finally, it is sent to Softmax to complete the classification, and the cost-sensitive optimized output layer calculates the distribution optimization loss and backpropagation for the predicted output and the expected output.

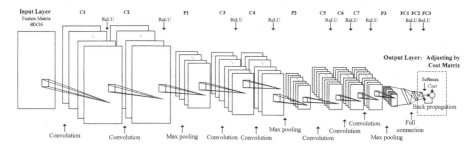

Fig. 3. CSCNN structure used in this paper

4   Experiments and Analysis

4.1   Experimental Dataset

The mobile advertising dataset in this paper is a real mobile advertising click dataset provided by BuzzCity for the FDMA2012 competition [7]. Table 2 shows the statistical data used in the experiment. It consists of the Click data and the publisher data. The dataset's format is CSV files containing three types of publisher samples (Fraud, Observation, ok), each sample belonging to only one class. The two datasets are linked by the *publisherid* property. The dataset in the experiment has two parts. Each part contains 3 days of click data: a training set of 6,145 publishers with a total of 5,862,839 clicks of the ad data stream and test set of 3,000 publishers with a total of 2,598,815 clicks ad data stream. This data has a strong non-imbalanced statistical distribution characteristic.

Before the experiment, the data needs to be preprocessed: 1) Setting the missing data in the original data to 0; 2) Extracting the click data designed by each publisher corresponding to the publisher data; 3) Normalizing the input features.

Table 2. Statistics of datasets used in this study

Dataset	Clicks	Publishers			
		OK	Observation	Fraud	Total
Training	5,862,839	5,824	164	157	6,145
Testing	2,598,815	2,847	71	82	3,000

4.2   Experimental Environment and Specific Parameter Setting

Data collation, feature extraction, data balance processing, and CNN model training test are all implemented by Python. The specific hardware environment is: i7-6800k,

16G DDR4, single channel 1080ti; software environment: Ubuntu 16.04LTS, Tensorflow-gpu1.5.0, Cuda9.0, Cudnn7.0.

To complete the feature extraction, we mainly use the Python scientific operation library numpy, Pandas, and spicy. There are a variety of open-source learning frameworks, and the training process of convolutional neural networks is also being simplified. This paper uses a convolutional neural network based on Tensorflow. The data balancing process uses the algorithm in imbalance-learn library. At the same time, in order to achieve comparison with the existing click fraud detection methods (such as SVM, decision tree J48, random forest and integration methods, etc.), the algorithm in the machine learning library sklearn is also used.

To determine the CNN structure, experiments were performed on different convolution layer levels, convolution kernel sizes, etc., and trained multiple hyperparameters W of CNN. The pre-training model is used to initialize the network parameters, and the parameters of the pre-training model are initialized as parameters of the model on new tasks. Table 3 shows the specific parameters of the CNN detection model that have been finalized after many experiments. Where f is the convolution kernel/filter size, s is the step size, and d is the number of convolution kernels in the layer (the number of channels is also called Feature map number), p is the padding parameter for zero Padding, δ is the deactivation rate of Dropout, C is the number of classification task categories, and the activation function of all hidden layers is ReLU. After completing the convolutionalization, the convolution kernel is firstly used to achieve the full connection of the front layer by using a 6×2 global convolution. Then, the mapping of the full connection layer is completed by a convolution kernel of 1×1. Finally, the softmax classifier with cost-sensitive is used to multi-classify.

Table 3. CNN network architecture and specific parameters

	Specific parameters	Input data	Output data
C1	$f = 3 \times 3; p = 1; s = 1; d = 32$	$48 \times 16 \times 1$	$48 \times 16 \times 32$
C2	$f = 3 \times 3; p = 1; s = 1; d = 32$	$48 \times 16 \times 32$	$48 \times 16 \times 32$
P1	$f = 2 \times 2; s = 2$	$48 \times 16 \times 32$	$24 \times 8\ 8 \times 32$
C3	$f = 3 \times 3; p = 1; s = 1; d = 64$	$24 \times 8 \times 32$	$24 \times 8 \times 64$
C4	$f = 3 \times 3; p = 1; s = 1; d = 64$	$24 \times 8 \times 64$	$24 \times 8 \times 64$
P2	$f = 2 \times 2; s = 2$	$24 \times 8 \times 64$	$12 \times 4 \times 64$
C5	$f = 3 \times 3; p = 1; s = 1; d = 128$	$12 \times 4 \times 64$	$12 \times 4 \times 128$
C6	$f = 3 \times 3; p = 1; s = 1; d = 128$	$12 \times 4 \times 128$	$12 \times 4 \times 128$
C7	$f = 3 \times 3; p = 1; s = 1; d = 128$	$12 \times 4 \times 128$	$12 \times 4 \times 128$
P3	$f = 2 \times 2; s = 2$	$12 \times 4 \times 128$	$6 \times 2 \times 128$
FC1	$f = 6 \times 2; s = 1; d = 512$	$6 \times 2 \times 128$	$1 \times 1 \times 512$
Dropout	$\delta = 0.5$	$1 \times 1 \times 512$	$1 \times 1 \times 512$
FC2	$f = 1 \times 1; s = 1; d = 128$	$1 \times 1 \times 512$	$1 \times 1 \times 128$
Dropout	$\delta = 0.5$	$1 \times 1 \times 128$	$1 \times 1 \times 128$
FC3	$f = 1 \times 1; s = 1; d = 128$	$1 \times 1 \times 128$	$1 \times 1 \times C$
Softmax	–	$1 \times 1 \times C$	–

4.3   Analysis of Experimental Results

Precision and Effectiveness Analysis
This paper proposes a cost-sensitive convolutional neural network structure to detect ad click fraud. The data is extremely imbalanced in this kind of detection, so an effective method is needed to achieve balanced processing of the data. It is more important to correctly classify fraud detection in fraud detection, Therefore, this paper introduces a cost-sensitive mechanism. The cost of the *OK* class's error is the smallest, so the cost factor of *OK* class is set to 1 firstly. The two stages of oversampling and threshold shifting are experimented with different cost factors. The cost factor of the oversampling stage is equivalent to the sampling rate. In this paper, the *Fraud* and *observation* samples are oversampled by 8 times, 12 times, 16 times and 20 times respectively. When the threshold is moving, the moving refer to the reference information and the need to use a variety of different cost factor matrices for experiments. This paper finally selects three different cost matrices in Table 4. In order to better prove that the cost sampling-threshold moving method of this paper is more effective in dealing with imbalanced data, it is also compared with the method of performing cost oversampling and threshold shifting only, and the cost factors of the two methods are based on the imbalance level.

Table 4. Different types of cost matrices

Cost $[i, j]$	Type(a)	Type(b)	Type(c)
Fraud	0 1 2	0 1 5	0 2 3
Observation	1 0 1	1 0 1	1 0 2
Ok	1 1 0	1 1 0	1 1 0

Using the precision rate, recall rate and F1-score to evaluate the classification performance, 10 experiments were performed in each group, and the best results were obtained. The method of combining cost oversampling with threshold shifting deals with imbalanced data, and classification performance is better than using only sampling or pure cost-sensitive learning. When the cost matrix is Type(c), the classification result is better than others. When a small number of samples in the training sample are sampled 12 times and the threshold value is moved using the Type(c) cost matrix, the classification perform best. The recall rate and the overall prediction accuracy are also improved. When the sampling magnification and the cost factor are getting larger, the classification performed worse. It is because when the sample is oversampled at a certain rate of cost, sample changes from the original extreme imbalance to relative balance. At this time, the cost and the sampling magnification are relatively high. It is possible to cause the model over-fitting, which leads to the classification performance worse., This paper selects 8 times sampling for oversampling after the experiments in this part, and uses the Type(c) cost matrix to perform threshold movement. Therefore, the precision and recall rate of the fraud samples are higher. It can also show that the algorithm proposed in this paper has a good generalization ability.

In order to prove the validity of multiple click entropy features constructed by the knowledge of entropy after determining the sampling rate and the cost matrix. The PR (precision-recall) curve is used to analyze the performance of the model with or without click entropy. shown Fig. 4 shows the result. The more the PR curve is to the upper right corner (1, 0), the better performance of the classifier. The BEP with the click entropy feature is larger than the BEP without the click entropy feature obviously The curve of the click entropy is introduced and the other one is completely covered. It indicates that the addition of multiple click entropy features further improves the classification accuracy.

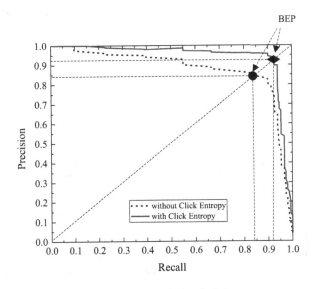

Fig. 4. Effectiveness analysis of click entropy

The Comparison of Different Methods

In order to show the superiority of detection model proposed in this paper is better, we select some representative models like J48 (C4.5), Random Forest (RF), SVM and advanced ensemble methods (Bagging with J48, Boosting with J48, Bagging with RF, Boosting with RF, Bagging with SVM, Boosting with SVM) as contrast test. In previous researches, data is usually binary classified. Therefore, we need to adjust tripartite results outputted from CSCNN further so that it can be compared with existed references better. The rules of judgement as follows: if result is fraud, this case is still fraud sample. If result is *observation* or *OK*, this case is normal sample. Meanwhile, fraud samples are positive class and normal samples are negative class. In this paper, the classification performance of multiple methods is measured by Precision, Recall, f1-score, g-mean and AUC indexes. Before model construction, the unbalanced data is processed by approach based on cost sampling and threshold moving sensitivity algorithm to select optimal sampling multiplier and cost matrix. Besides, in order to eliminate the influence of random factors, the performance of these classifiers is verified by means of $10\times$ cross validation. The result is shown as Fig. 5. By comparing with different analysis methods, it is found that the integration method improves the performance of classifiers to some extent but increases the complexity of model. However, in this paper, a CNN alternative integration method with a simpler structure is adopted, which does not increase the model complexity. While ensuring the classification accuracy, the recall rate has reached over 93%, and other indicators have been greatly improved, indicating that the classification performance has been improved and multi-classification can be conducted. Though the integration method can also conduct multiple classifications, the complexity of the model is further improved. This result shows that cost sensitive convolutional neural network detection model based on feature matrix proposed in this paper is simpler than the integration method, which can effectively adapt to the imbalance of data and detect fraudulent publishers in mobile ads better.

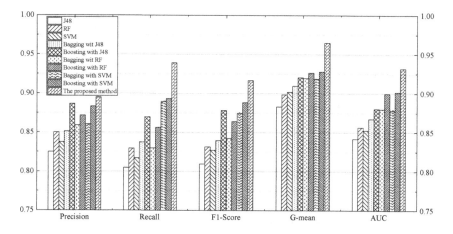

Fig. 5. The comparison of different methods

5   Conclusion

This paper proposes a cost-sensitive CNN mobile advertising click fraud detection model based on click feature matrix to explore the potential mode of advertisement publishers' click behavior. In addition to constructing features using simple statistical methods, prior probability is also introduced. The knowledge of entropy is applied to feature extraction to derive new feature sets. In order to solve the data imbalance, a cost mechanism is introduced. The reconstructed data sample method based on cost and the threshold moving cost sensitive algorithm considering the cost matrix are combined to obtain better results. Finally, the one-dimensional feature is transformed into the feature matrix by using multiple granular time windows to complete the construction of the CNN classification model, which effectively detects the click fraud publishers.

This paper applies CNN to the click fraud detection scenario of mobile advertising, and achieves good results. Currently, the dataset focuses on the detection of the behavior of publishers with some click data, which requires the construction of manual features first. In the following work, we will collect other mobile ad click datasets and use the deep neural network to extract features directly to achieve the detection of a single click data flow.

References

1. Haider, C.M.R., Iqbal, A., Rahman, A.H., et al.: An ensemble learning based approach for impression fraud detection in mobile advertising. J. Netw. Comput. Appl. **112**, 126–141 (2018)
2. Yang, Y.-H., Huang, H.-H., Shen, Q.-N., et al.: Research on intrusion detection based on incremental GHSOM. Chin. J. Comput. **5**, 1216–1224 (2014). (in Chinese)
3. He, H., Gimpel, K., Lin, J.: Multi-perspective sentence similarity modeling with convolutional neural networks. In: Proceedings of the 2015 Conference on Empirical Methods in Natural Language Processing (EMNLP2015), Lisbon, Portugal, pp. 1576–1586 (2015)
4. Perera, K.S., Neupane, B., Faisal, M.A., Aung, Z., Woon, W.L.: A novel ensemble learning-based approach for click fraud detection in mobile advertising. In: Prasath, R., Kathirvalavakumar, T. (eds.) MIKE 2013. LNCS (LNAI), vol. 8284, pp. 370–382. Springer, Cham (2013). https://doi.org/10.1007/978-3-319-03844-5_38
5. Kitts, B., et al.: Click fraud detection: adversarial pattern recognition over 5 years at microsoft. In: Abou-Nasr, M., Lessmann, S., Stahlbock, R., Weiss, G.M. (eds.) Real World Data Mining Applications. AIS, vol. 17, pp. 181–201. Springer, Cham (2015). https://doi.org/10.1007/978-3-319-07812-0_10
6. Crussell, J., Stevens, R., Chen, H.: Madfraud: investigating ad fraud in android applications. In: Proceedings of the 12th Annual International Conference on Mobile Systems, Applications, and Services, MobiSys 2014, Bretton Woods, NH, USA, pp. 123–134 (2014)
7. Oentaryo, R., Lim, E.P., Finegold, M., et al.: Detecting click fraud in online advertising: a data mining approach. J. Mach. Learn. Res. **15**(1), 99–140 (2014)
8. King, M.A., Abrahams, A.S., Ragsdale, C.T.: Ensemble learning methods for pay-per-click campaign management. Expert Syst. Appl. **42**(10), 4818–4829 (2015)
9. Zhang, X., Liu, X.-J., Li, B., et al.: Application of SVM ensemble method to click fraud detection. J. Chin. Comput. Syst. **39**(5), 951–956 (2018). (in Chinese)
10. Kim, Y.: Convolutional Neural Networks for sentence classification. In: Proceedings of the 2014 Conference on Empirical Methods in Natural Language Processing (EMNLP 2014), Doha, Qatar, pp. 1474–1480 (2014)
11. Wang, H.-Y., Dong, M.-W.: Latent group recommendation based on dynamic probabilistic matrix factorization model integrated with CNN. J. Comput. Res. Dev. **54**(8), 1853–1863 (2017). (in Chinese)
12. Jiao, L., Yang, S.-Y., Liu, F., et al.: Seventy years beyond neural networks: retrospect and prospect. Chin. J. Comput. **39**(8), 1697–1716 (2016). (in Chinese)
13. Li, H., Zhang, L., Zhou, X., et al.: Cost-sensitive sequential three-way decision modeling using a deep neural network. Int. J. Approx. Reason. **85**(C), 68–78 (2017)
14. Arar, F.M., Ayan, K.: Software defect prediction using cost-sensitive neural network. Appl. Soft Comput. **33**, 263–277 (2015)

Research on Table Overflow Ldos Attack Detection and Defense Method in Software Defined Networks

Shengxu Xie, Changyou Xing$^{(\boxtimes)}$, Guomin Zhang$^{(\boxtimes)}$, and Jinlong Zhao

Command and Control Engineering College,
Army Engineering University of PLA, Nanjing, China
changyouxing@126.com, zhang_gmwn@163.com

Abstract. As the key and precious resource of the SDN switch, the TCAM flow table is one of the core targets of network attackers. Among various attack methods, Low-rate dos (Ldos) attacks can exhaust the target switch's flow table resource with a very low attack rate, which degrades the network performance seriously. In order to detect the flow table overflow Ldos attacks in the SDN environment, we analyzed the two typical flow table overflow Ldos attack traffic models, and proposed a defense mechanism named SAIA (Small-flow Analysis and Inport-flow Analysis), which can detect the attack flows based on the flow size and position analysis method. Besides, we also implemented the traffic characteristics data acquisition and flow table overflow prediction algorithm. The experimental results show that SAIA can effectively detect the table overflow low-rate dos attacks and mitigate their impact on network performance.

Keywords: Software Defined Networking · Low-rate denial of service attack · Table overflow

1 Introduction

The data plane and control plane separation feature of SDN (Software Defined Networking) architecture makes network management and data collection more convenient and effective. However, the new architecture also introduces many security problems [1], of which the data plane security is a prominent problem [2]. On the one hand, most of the traditional network attacks can be applied to the SDN data plane, such as Ddos attacks [3], etc., on the other hand, due to the change of architecture, some new attacks against the data plane become possible, and one of the most typical attack is the SDN switch flow table overflow attack [4].

The flow table of SDN switches is usually implemented using TCAM (Ternary Content Addressable Memory) to meet the requirement of fast flow entry lookup and match. However, due to the limitation of TCAM implementation technology, the number of flow entries stored in the switch is very small, and can only be supported to several thousand at most [5]. It can be seen from the evolution process of the Openflow

© Springer Nature Singapore Pte Ltd. 2020
Y. Tian et al. (Eds.): ICBDS 2019, CCIS 1210, pp. 80–97, 2020.
https://doi.org/10.1007/978-981-15-7530-3_7

protocol v1.0 to the v1.5 version specification that the matching domain is getting more and more various, which is very important for fine-grained network management and control [6]. On the other hand, the finer the flow table matching granularity, the more the number of flow entries that need to be delivered, and the more likely the switch flow table space is saturated. When the flow table space of the switch is saturated, if a new flow arrives, the controller has three processing methods: (1) directly drop the new flow; (2) forward new flows through packet_out message; (3) select a flow entry from the switch to delete, and then install the corresponding flow entry for the new flow. The first method will cause a lot of packet loss in the network, resulting in a sharp decline in network performance. The second method will cause a large number of flows to be forwarded through the controller, causing a serious burden on the controller, and the network delay will also increase significantly. The third method will cause the original flow entry to be deleted, and the average latency of the flow increases due to frequent updates of the flow entries. Therefore, how to effectively deal with the switch flow table overflow is crucial to ensure the normal operation of SDN network, and targeted attack behavior is an important factor leading to this problem, which has been widely concerned by researchers in recent years [7, 8].

Ldos (Low-rate Denial of Service) attack can reduce the network's normal service capability by using well designed low rate attack traffic according to the characteristics of network protocol. Compared with traditional dos attacks, Ldos is more concealment [9]. According to the working mechanism of the OpenFlow protocol, after receiving the data of a flow, the switch first searches for the matching of the flow entry. If no match is found in the flow table space, the switch needs to send the request to the controller for corresponding processing rules. Therefore, Ldos attackers can send multiple small flows to the network to occupy the limited flow table space of the switch, so that the flow table space is in a saturated state for a long time, which leads to the flow entry of the normal flow in the network can't be correctly installed, thus reducing the network performance.

To solve the above problems, this paper studies two typical flow table overflow Ldos attack traffic models, and evaluates their impact on the performance of SDN network through experiment. According to the features of these two different Ldos attack traffic models, this paper proposes SAIA, a small-flow and inport-flow statistics analysis based defense mechanism. Based on the prediction of the flow table overflow situations, SAIA can alleviate the impact of network overflow attacks by detecting and deleting the flow entries of suspected attack flows.

2   Related Work

At present, most researches on the flow table overflow of OpenFlow switch focus on how to solve the flow table overflow problem caused by large traffic flows in a normal network environment. For example, setting an appropriate timeout value of flow entries to reduce the total number of flow entries in the flow table space [10]; balancing the utilization of flow table space by redirecting flows from switches with high flow table space utilization to switches with sufficient free flow table space [11]; aggregating flow entries [12]; finding out the most suitable flow entry to delete when the flow table space is in its saturation status [13, 14].

In essence, the above research is a mitigation mechanism for the table overflow under the normal network environment. On the other hand, under the attack of OpenFlow switch, the table overflow will be more serious, and how to deal with it is still a problem to be solved. Zhou et al. proposed a strategy to build a new flow aggregation algorithm and a multi-level flow table architecture to defense against the overflow attack launched by the attacker [4]. Cao studied the effects of the LOFT (Low-Rate Flow Table) overflow attacks on the SDN network, proposed a method for attackers to detect the SDN network configuration and build low-rate attack traffic, and gave two simple methods to prevent the network configuration detection [15]. However, there is no effective scheme to detect and mitigate the attack flow. Xu et al. studied the potential targets of table overflow attack, and used 3 metrics to detect the attack flows: GFFC (Growth of Foreign Flow Consumption), DFA (Deviation of Amount) and CFE (Commonness of Flow Entry) [16]. This work is mainly aimed at the defense of attacks that send a large number of flows in a short time. The corresponding mitigation mechanism is to limit the speed of installing flow entries from the controller by token bucket, so as to avoid exhausting the flow table space.

To sum up, there is still no systematic study on detection and defense of table overflow Ldos attacks. The main reason lies in that Ldos attack is relatively difficult to detect and defend due to their strong concealment feature. However, on the other hand, the flow table overflow Ldos attack has an important impact on the performance of SDN network. Thus, in this paper, we mainly focus on the detection and defense mechanism of Ldos attack against the flow table overflow.

3   Analysis of the Flow Table Overflow Ldos Attack

3.1   Controller Strategy Model

According to the OpenFlow protocol specification, the controller can use a combination of *hard_timeout* and *idle_timeout* to maintain the flow entries. In the hard timeout mechanism, when the existence period of a flow entry reaches the *hard_timeout* threshold, it will be deleted regardless of whether it is still in use, while in the soft timeout mechanism, the OpenFlow switch records the usage of each flow entry. once a flow table item is not used within the *idle_timeout* time, it will be deleted by the switch. In order to avoid the increase of network delay caused by the deletion of flow entries, and to ensure that the switch can actively delete obsolete flow entries, the controller generally adopts the timeout strategy of flow entries as shown in Eq. (1), where t is a non-zero normal number. Table 1 lists the configuration of default flow entry timeout times in the typical controller.

$$\begin{cases} hard\_timeout = 0 \\ idle\_timeout = t \end{cases} \tag{1}$$

Table 1. Timeout configuration in the typical controller.

Controller	Default timeout		Sample projects timeout		
	Hard	Idle	Project name	Hard	Idle
POX	0 s	0 s	l3_learning	0 s	10 s
RYU	0 s	0 s	rest_router	0 s	1800 s
ONOS	0 s	10 s	fwd	0 s	10 s
OpenDaylight	600 s	300 s	L2switch	3600 s	1800 s
Floodlight	0 s	5 s	learning_switch	0 s	5 s

Based on this strategy, the flow entry in the switch will remain in the flow table space after it is installed, and will be deleted due to timeout if it does not match the packet within the time of t.

3.2   Ldos Attack Model

According to the flow table space Ldos attack model proposed by [15], an attacker can send a lot of flows whose packet interval is less than the timeout of flow entries to the network. These attack flows are aggregated on the target switch in the network, which makes the target switch's flow table space always be saturated, thus causing the effect of denial of service to the new normal flow. Moreover, according to the differences in the distribution patterns of attack traffics, Ldos attacker has following two ways to occupy the flow table space:

Type-I Attack Flow: Uses a large flow to occupy the switch's one flow entry space. In this scenario, an attacker sends a small data packet to the network, and then sends the flow to the network again before the corresponding flow entry timeouts, so as to keep the flow entry alive in the switch due to the continuous matching of the flow. Its form is shown in Fig. 1(a).

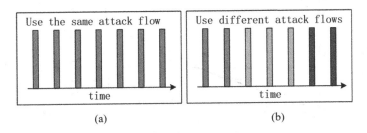

(a)   (b)

Fig. 1. Different attack flow patterns.

Type-II Attack Flow: Use multiple small flows to occupy the switch's one flow entry space. In this scenario, the attacker uses a small flow similar to the Type-I attack flow to occupy the flow table space of the switch. However, the difference is that each flow has a very short duration, and the newly generated flow is constantly replaced with a new flow, that is, the space vacated by the deleted flow entry due to the unmatched flow is occupied again by the arrival of the new attack flow. Compared with Type-I attack flow, Type-II attack flow is more difficult to detect due to its changing flow characteristics, as shown in Fig. 1(b).

3.3   Analysis of the Table Overflow Ldos Attack

Compared with traditional attack methods, the table overflow Ldos attack has the following detection and defense difficulties:

(1)   The low rate feature of the attack traffic makes it difficult to detect.

Compared with traditional dos attacks, the Ldos attack has the characteristics of small traffic and low rate, which can be well hidden in the normal flow and thus form the strong concealment feature. As shown in Fig. 2, we analyzed the network traffic in the univ dataset with about 17 million packets [17], and the results shows that more than 90% of the flows existed for less than 1 s. These flows accounted for about 30% of the data packets, while the average data packet size was 124 bytes (including the packet header). In addition, as can be seen from Fig. 3, about 64% of the flows have only one packet. Further analysis shows that most of these flows are the domain name request and reply packets. Therefore, attackers can take advantage of this characteristic of network traffic to simulate a large number of small flows by sending a small number of packets, thus causing the flow table overflow. At the same time, due to the packet size of each flow is small, the possibility of being discovered by the network manager is also low.

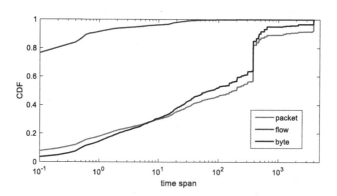

Fig. 2. Different time lengths correspond to the number of flows, packets, and bytes.

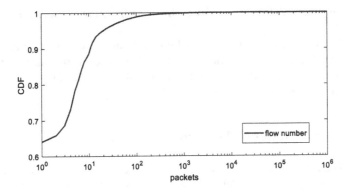

Fig. 3. The number of flows corresponding to the number of packets.

(2) The information that can be used for analysis is limited.

Without changing the architecture of the SDN switch and adding its extra functions, the controller can only collect very limited information. The network traffic is forwarded through the match of the flow table, and the statistics fields in the flow entries only have the packets number, bytes number, and the duration time of the flow entry, etc. It is difficult to extract useful information from these data for detecting the attack flow.

(3) It is necessary to comprehensively consider the mitigation of table overflow in a normal network state.

In the normal network state, there is also the table overflow problem caused by excessive traffics. Therefore, the defense mechanism of table overflow Ldos attack needs to be able to handle flow table overflow under the normal network state.

For problem (1) and (2), when launching an Ldos attack, the attacker needs to aggregate the low-rate attack traffic at the target switch, thus we can consider analyzing the flow information at the target switch, so as to find the attack flow. As can be seen from Fig. 2, there is an obvious heavy-tailed distribution of the normal flow in the real network. According to the discussion in Sect. 3.2, if an attacker uses Type-I attack flow, the switch will maintain the entry of the flow for a long time, but the number of packets and bytes matched by the flow entry are very small, which will be significantly different from the normal flow in the network. If attackers attack with Type-II flow, its feature is similar with a large number of small flows in the network. To detect such attack flows, we propose an inport flow statistics-based method, which uses the entire network information maintained by the controller to find out the source of the low-rate flow to the suspected attacked switch, and then establishes the <switch, inport> pair to analyze the low rate flow information. On this basis, the trend of flow quantity in the time domain is formed, so as to distinguish the attack flows from the normal flows. It can be seen from the above analysis that the information needed for the whole detection process can be obtained from the existing SDN architecture without any additional modification.

For problem (3), we can combine the flow table overflow detection and defense scheme under the Ldos attack condition with the flow table overflow mitigation scheme in the normal network together, so as to further alleviate the flow table overflow problem caused by normal flow in the network.

4   Detection and Defense Mechanism Design

In order to effectively detect and defend the table overflow Ldos attacks, we propose the corresponding detection and defense mechanism SAIA. As shown in Fig. 4, SAIA includes 4 main modules: Data Collection Module (DCM), Overflow Prediction Module (OPM), Attack Detection Module (ADM) and Overflow Mitigation Module (OMM). In our implementation, these modules are all running in the controller as components of the controller.

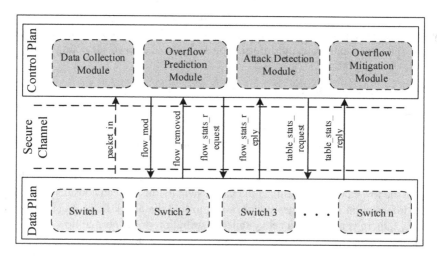

Fig. 4. Table overflow attack detection and defense mechanism logic architecture.

In order to accurately describe the working mechanism of SAIA, we first give the following symbol definition (Table 2):

Table 2. Symbol definitions.

Symbol	Definition
S_i	SDN switch i
C_i	The flow table capacity of the switch i
T	Sampling period
$A_i(t)$	The number of active flow entries in the switch i at the t th sampling
$p_i(t)$	The number of new flows arrived at the switch i during the t th sampling time
$F_{ij}(t)$	Flow entry j in the switch i at the t th sampling
$P_{ij}(t)$	The number of matched packets for the entry j in the switch i at the t th sampling
$B_{ij}(t)$	The number of matched bytes of entry j in the switch i at the t th sampling
$D_{ij}(t)$	Duration time of entry j of in the switch i at the t th sampling
$S_{i\_inport_k}$	Network access port k of the switch i (switch is edge switch)
$A_{i,jk}(t)$	The number of flow entries installed on switch i corresponding to the flow from the inport k of switch j
$P_{i,jk}(t)$	The number of new flows from the inport k of switch j to the switch i during the t th sampling time

4.1 Data Collection Module

The data collection module is mainly responsible for acquiring the data required by Ldos detection. The collection process includes two ways: 1) actively send requests to SDN switch to obtain the relevant data, such as obtaining counter fields of flow entries through *flow-stats-request* request; 2) record relevant messages reported by the switch to controller message, such as the arrival of new flows corresponding to *packet_in* events. Specifically, the messages between the controller and the switch used by the data collection module and the data analyzed are shown in Table 3.

Table 3. Message type description.

Message type	Message	Function	Analyzed data
Controller-to-switch	*flow-mod*	Install the flow entries to the switch	–
	flow-stats-request	Request the switch for flow entry statistics field information	–
	table-stats-request	Request the switch for flow table space usage	–
Asynchronous	*state-change*	Send switch connection and disconnect events to the controller	Update the number of SDN switches
	packet-in	Forward packets to the controller	The arrival rate of new flow
	flow-stats-reply	Reply flow entry statistics field information to the controller	Flow entries matched packet, bytes, and duration
	table-stats-reply	Reply flow table usage to the controller	Number of active flow entries
	flow-removed	Reports to the controller that the switch deletes the flow entry	Delete the corresponding flow entry data in the record

To determine whether a flow is a large flow or a small flow, we need to know the packets rate (packets/s) and the bytes rate (bytes/s) of the flow arriving at the switch. In addition, to distinguish an attack flow from the normal flows, we need to further construct the flow number variation trend over the time domain. Therefore, we design a periodic sampling-based data collection algorithm, and record the sampling data of each statistical metric within a period of time (20 sampling periods were used in our experiment). The data collected at each time are sent to the OPM for further analysis in the form of events, and $S_{i\_}inport_k$, $A_{i,jk}(t)$, $P_{i,jk}(t)$ and other data are sent to the ADM to detect whether there is an access port of Type-II attack flow.

Algorithm 1: Data Collection

---

1    $Topo = Controller.topo$

2    $C_i = Topo(i).capacity$

3   **while** (time elapse T)

4   **for** S_i in $Topo$

5   send $table\_stats\_request$ message to S_i

6   A_i = length($table\_stats\_reply.active\_count$)

7   send $flow\_stats\_request$ message to S_i

8   **for** $F_{ij}(t)$ in $flow\_stats\_reply$

9          $D_{ij}(t) = F_{ij}(t).duration$

10         $P_{ij}(t) = F_{ij}(t).packet$

11         $B_{ij}(t) = F_{ij}(t).byte$

12   **if** $timeSpan == ilde\_timeout/2$ **and** $F_{ij}(t)$ is $A_{i,jk}(t)$

13           $A_{i,ik}(t) = A_{i,jk}(t) + 1$

14    $p_i(t)$, $P_{i,jk}(t)$ //count the number of packet_in in this period

---

4.2   Overflow Prediction Module

OPM needs to be able to predict the occurrence time of the table overflow, so as to help the controller selectively delete a certain number of flow entries before such an event happens, and effectively mitigate the network performance degradation caused by the table overflow event.

In order to predict the switch flow table overflow event effectively, we propose an algorithm to predict the usage of flow table based on the analysis of switch flow table information. The algorithm predicts whether the flow table will overflow at the next time by combining the predicted number of new flows arriving at the switch in the next sampling period and the current usage of the flow table space of the switch. The specific algorithm description is shown in Algorithm 2.

Algorithm 2: Table Overflow Prediction

---

input: p_i, A_i, T

output: $pre(t_{n+1})$ // predicted value of A_i at the next sampling time t_{n+1}

1   $k_1 = (p_i(t_n) - p_i(tn-1))/T$

2   $k_2 = (p_i(t_{n-1}) - p_i(t_{n-2}))/T$

3   **if** $k_1 > k_2$

4      $k_0 = k_1 + \log_{10}(k_1 - k_2)$

5   **else**

6      $k_0 = k_1$

7   **end**

8   $p_i(t_{n+1}) = k_0 * T + p_i(t_n)$

9   $pre(t_{n+1}) = A_i(t_n) + p_i(t_{n+1})$

As shown in lines 3–7 of Algorithm 2, the prediction of the number of new flow arrivals is mainly based on the changing trend (slope) of new flow arrivals. When the slope k_1 between two points of $p_i(t_n)$ and $pi(t_{n-1})$ is greater than the slope k_2 between two points of $p_i(t_{n-1})$ and $p_i(t_{n-2})$, the predicted slope k_0 between two points of $p_i(t_{n+1})$ and $p_i(t_n)$ is equal to k_1 plus the logarithm of the increase of the slope, otherwise k_0 is equal to k_1. This algorithm not only effectively predict the number of new flows arriving at the switch, but also enlarge the predicted value according to the change of the number of new flows arriving. Figure 5 is a schematic diagram of new flow arrival quantity prediction. The circle point in the figure is the sampling value of the sampling point, and the triangle point is the predicted value of the sampling point. As can be seen from the part of region 1 in the figure, when the number of new flows reaches a sudden increase, the algorithm also has a good prediction effect. Meanwhile, combined with the flow table overflow mitigation mechanism, when the number of new flows reaches a high level, it is necessary to enlarge the predicted value appropriately, as shown in the part of regions 2 and 3 of the figure. This can effectively avoid the flow table overflow caused by the failure of accurately predicting a large number of new flows.

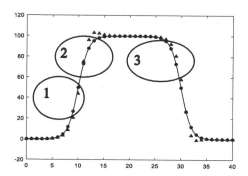

Fig. 5. New flow arrival quantity prediction algorithm.

When the predicted number $pre(t_{n+1})$ of flow entries in switch i is greater than the flow table space size C_i of the switch, some flow entries need to be deleted in advance to make room for the new arrival flows. Therefore, it is necessary to send the collected data of switch i to the ADM for detection, and find out the suspected attack flow for deletion.

4.3   Attack Detection Module

The main work of this module is divided into two parts: 1) when the OPM predicts there will be table overflow in switch S_i, it will analyze the flows that pass through switch S_i based on the obtained data information, so as to detect the Type-I attack flow; 2) periodically analyze the data such as $S_{i\_inport_k}$, $A_{i,\ jk}(t)$, $P_{i,jk}(t)$ collected by data collection module every half idle_timeout, so as to detect the network inport of Type-II attack flow.

For Type-I attack flow, in order to effectively distinguish from normal data flows in the network, the low-rate attack flow detection module evaluates the possibility of being attack flow from factors such as average packet interval, average packet size, and flow duration. The specific evaluation strategy is shown in formula (2), where the purpose of introducing parameter α is to optimize the impact of average packet interval on the evaluation results, whose value can be appropriately adjusted for different network scenarios. The constant $avgb$ is the average packet size (number of bytes) in the network.

$$f^1_{attack}(t) = \alpha \cdot \frac{D_{ij}(t) - idleTime}{P_{ij}(t)} + (1 - \alpha) \cdot \frac{P_{ij}(t)}{B_{ij}(t)} \cdot avgb \tag{2}$$

Since all packets for each flow are counted, for a normal flow, even with a heavy-tailed distribution, the average time interval of all packets is significantly smaller than the attack flow, and the average size of the packets is significantly larger than the attack flow. Therefore, the attack flow can be discriminated by defining a threshold $sh1$ according to different network scenarios. When $f^1_{attack} < sh1$, the flow is considered as an attack flow; when $f^1_{attack} > = sh1$, the flow is considered as a normal flow. When the module detects the Type-I attack flow, the attack flow information is sent to the OMM for precisely deleting the corresponding flow entries of the attack flow.

For Type-II attack flow, since each attack flow has a short time, it is difficult to evaluate them effectively through the above equation. Thus, we designed the identification pair <switch S, inport P>, which depicts the case that the traffic of a switch S comes from network access port P. As shown in Fig. 6, it is necessary to establish the identical pairs between 8 network access ports and 5 network switches, such as <S_1, $S_2\_inport_1$>, etc. The miscalculation caused by actions such as network source address spoofing can be effectively overcame in this method. According to the analysis in 3.3.1, a large number of small flows with only a single packet exist in the network. In order to effectively distinguish them from Type-II attack flow, we sue formula (3) to evaluate the flows with switch i and network access port as the port k of switch j. Due to Type-II attack flow sends new flows continuously, the switch generates new flow entries to replace the old ones that are about to expire, which makes the difference value of $A_{i,jk}$ between the two consecutive counts small while $P_{i,jk}$ is larger. Owing to the statistical period is half of $idle\_timeout$, for normal network access ports, even if there are a great deal of small flows of single data group, the difference value of $A_{i,jk}$ between two consecutive statistics is very large.

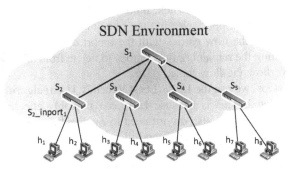

Fig. 6. Network topology.

$$f^2_{attack}(t) = \frac{\sum\limits_{n=0}^{3} P_{i,jk}(t_n)}{1 + \sum\limits_{n=0}^{4} \left(|A_{i,jk}(t_{n+1}) - A_{i,jk}(t_n)|\right)} \qquad (3)$$

Similarly, $sh2$ is defined according to different network scenarios. When $f^2_{attack} > sh2$, $S_j\_inport_k$ is considered to be the attack node of Type-II attack flow; when $f^2_{attack} <= sh2$, the inport is considered to be a normal network entry port. When the network inport of Type-II attack flow is detected, the <switch, inport> identification pair is sent to the OMM immediately, so that the OMM can delete the flow entries of flows that come from the specific network inport when the switch flow table overflows.

4.4 Overflow Mitigation Module

The OMM has two main functions: (1) maintaining the network access port of Type-II attack flows detected by the attack detection module; (2) selecting the appropriate flow entries to delete.

For the attack network access port maintenance function, when detected for the first time, the network access port is recorded in the form of <switch, inport> pair, and deleted after a certain time (the experimental setting is 5 times idle_timeout). The purpose of the deletion here is to remove the attack port mark timely and effectively after the attacked port becomes normal.

For the second function of the module, when the switch's flow table is about to overflow, in order to avoid the network performance degradation, we delete a certain number of n ($n = pre(t_{n+1}) - 0.9 * C_i$) flow entries proactively, by selecting the most suitable flow entries. Here, combining the ADM to detect the results of the two types of attack flows, it is divided into three steps to select the flow entries to be deleted:

First, when the attack detection module detects a Type-I attack flow, it directly deletes n flow entries according to the descending order of the f_{attack}^1 values.

Second, if no Type-I attack flow is detected, or if the number of detected attack flows is less than n, checking the <switch, inport> table maintained by the mitigation module. If there is an attack port, selecting the remaining number of flow entries that need to be deleted from the flow entries with the inport constraint.

Otherwise, selecting the remaining flow entries to delete from all flow entries in the switch that will overflow the flow table.

In the last two steps, we use the LRU (Least Recently Used) algorithm to select the flow entry to be deleted. This is because LRU can not only effectively reduce the overflow rate of flow table, but also do not need to modify the switch, so it is easy to implement [18]. Therefore, we designed the following formula:

$$f_{LRU} = \frac{\beta \cdot idleTime}{(1 - \beta) \cdot \left(P_{ij}(t_n) - P_{ij}(t_0) \right)} \tag{4}$$

IdleTime is the time interval between the last match of the flow entry and the current moment, and $P_{ij}(t_n) - P_{ij}(t_0)$ is the number of packets that the flow entry matched in the last n samples. From the formula, it can be seen that the higher the value of f_{LRU} is, the smaller the number of packets that the flow entry matched, and the flow entry is not matched for a long time. To a certain extent, the corresponding entries of the flow with certain attack flow characteristics can be selected with a high probability.

5 Implementation and Evaluation

By building a simulation environment of ryu+mininet, we verified the proposed attack detection and defense system through experiments. The experimental network topology is shown in Fig. 6. The controller processes *table_miss* by installing flow entries of four different matching fields of ARP, ICMP, TCP and UDP, where the matching field of

ARP is {eth_dst, eth_src, eth_type}, the matching field of ICMP is {eth_dst, eth_src, eth_type, ip_proto}, and the matching field of TCP (UDP) is {eth_dst, eth_src, eth_type, ip_src, ip_dst, ip_proto, TCP(UDP)_src, TCP(UDP)_dst}, and the *idle_timeout* of flow entry is set to 20 s.

5.1 Evaluation of the Ldos Attack Impact

To verify the impact of the Ldos attack, we tested the network performance under the circumstance that the controller did not actively handle the attack. That is, when the switch flow table space is full, the controller directly forwards the newly arrived flows without issuing flow entries. Figure 7 illustrates the comparison of the network transmission delay under Type-I attack flow and Type-II attack flow in normal condition, respectively.

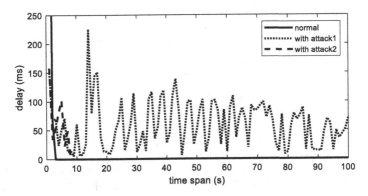

Fig. 7. The impact of two types of attacks on normal flow.

As can be seen from Fig. 7, when the table is not overflowed (solid line), for a flow, the delay of subsequent packets is almost 0, except that the first packet has a large delay. This is because the controller has to install the corresponding flow entry for the first packet. When the table overflow due to Type-I attack flow (dotted line), it can be clearly seen that the delay of all packets is around 50 ms. This is because the table is overflowed and each packet is treated as a new flow. However, when there is a Type-II attack flow that makes the table overflow (dashed line), the first few packets all have a large time delay. This is because the Type-II attack flow may have a few empty flow table space for a short time during the conversion process, which results in the installation of flow entries of normal packets. As the Type-II attack flow density increases, the probability that a normal packet will experience a higher delay will increase.

5.2   Evaluation of the Flow Table Usage Prediction

In order to further evaluate the effectiveness of the prediction algorithm, we generate traffic between 8 hosts in the topology shown in Fig. 6. The controller uses the DCM and the OPM to predict the flow table space changes of switch S1. The experimental results are shown in Fig. 8.

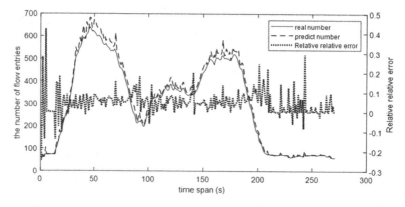

Fig. 8. Prediction effect.

As can be seen from Fig. 8, the prediction algorithm can make a relatively accurate prediction of the usage of the flow table space, and the predicted value is slightly higher than the actual value in most cases, which is beneficial to avoid the overflow of the flow table caused by burst flood flows. In addition, when the number of entries in the flow table is large, the relative error of prediction is less than 10%, and almost all of them are higher than the actual value, indicating that the flow table prediction algorithm can be well applied to the detection and defense system, and can effectively deal with the burst flood flows.

5.3   Evaluation of the Detection and Defense System

In order to further verify the effectiveness of the detection and defense system, we first carried out the experimental evaluation of the active deletion function of the flow table on the basis of Sect. 4.2. As shown in Fig. 9, the controller sets the flow table space size of S1 to 500 flow entries, while the actual flow table space size of the switch is not limited, and the solid line is the change curve of the number of flow entries in S1 over time. As can be seen from the figure, the number of real-time flow entries in the switch is always below 500, and in the case of heavy network load, the number of flow entries is close to 500. Therefore, it can be concluded that the active flow table deletion mechanism can delete a certain number of flow entries effectively when the flow table is about to overflow, so as to avoid the table overflow.

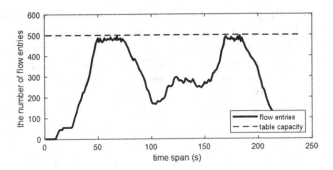

Fig. 9. Active deletion of flow table items.

Meanwhile, we further analyze the detection and defense capability of the system to table overflow Ldos attack. In the environment of Fig. 6, the hosts h2, h4, h6, and h8 are defined as normal users, and they generate normal flows with different distributions to each other through the D-ITG tool. Hosts h1, h3, h5, and h7 are controlled by the attacker and use hping3 tool to generate attack flows, among which h1 and h3 generate Type-I attack flows and h5 and h7 generate Type-II attack flows. Four groups of experiments were conducted for the ratios of different flows. The ratios of normal user flow, Type-I attack flow and Type-II attack flow were [1, 0, 0], [0.5, 0.5, 0], [0.5, 0, 0.5], [0.4, 0.3, 0.3], respectively. When the flow table overflow is predicted, the deleted flow entries in each group are shown in Fig. 10. Benign, attack1 and attack2 represent normal user flow, Type-I attack flow, and Type-II attack flow respectively. The x-axis represents the order in which flow table deletion events occur, and the y-axis represents the number of deleted flow entries.

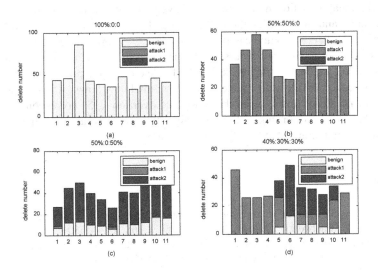

Fig. 10. Flow entries deletion.

From Fig. 10 (a) and (b), it can be seen that when there are only normal flows, entries deleted due to the table overflow events are all normal flow entries, and when the normal flow and Type-I attack flow each account for 50%, flow entries deleted due to the table overflow events contains only the Type-I attack flow entries. This shows that the system can effectively identify and eliminate the impact of Type-I attack flow on the network. In Fig. 10(c), when the normal flow and Type-II attack flow each account for 50%, the deleted entries of real attack flows accounts for 70%. Part of the reason for misjudgment is that the determination of Type-II attack flow needs to be based on the traffic information of the network port, that is, identifying the network port rather than the specific attack flow, which leads to some misjudgments. And the recognition rate of 70% also means that most of the attack flow entries can be detected and deleted. In addition, further analysis of the switch's feedback information shows that the Type-I attack flow in the first and sixth deletion processes is a misjudgment of the ARP data flow. Since ARP only needs one interaction in the end-to-end communication of the actual network, and deleting the corresponding flow entry will not affect the normal network communication. In Fig. 10(d), when the three types of flows account for 40%, 30%, and 30% respectively, it can be seen that the Type-I attack flow is deleted first, while the Type-II attack flow is deleted after a large number of Type-I attack flow are deleted. In conclusion, it can be found that the method proposed in this paper can effectively detect and defend the table overflow Ldos attack.

6 Conclusion

While enhancing the network control ability, SDN's new architecture also brings some new security threats. Among them, the table overflow Ldos attack is a destructive attack mode. In this paper, we study two typical table overflow Ldos attack traffic models, and propose the SAIA detection and defense mechanism accordingly. In SAIA, the data collection module can effectively collect the relevant data such as flow, flow table, and flow entries through active and passive means in real-time. The table overflow prediction module can predict the table overflow with a relative error of 10%, and can adapt to the traffic burst in the network. Attack detection module and mitigation module can detect the attack flow and delete the corresponding flow entries effectively, so as to provide a flow table space for normal new flows. At the same time, in the case of no attack flows, when the flow table overflows, the corresponding flow entries can be deleted according to the LRU algorithm, so as to alleviate the network performance degradation caused by the table overflow.

References

1. Yoon, C., Lee, S., Kang, H., et al.: Flow wars: systemizing the attack surface and defenses in software-defined networks. IEEE/ACM Trans. Netw. **25**(6), 3514–3530 (2017)
2. Dargahi, T., Caponi, A., Ambrosin, M., et al.: A survey on the security of stateful SDN data planes. IEEE Commun. Surv. Tutor. **19**(3), 1701–1725 (2017)

3. Kalkan, K., Gur, G., Alagoz, F.: Defense mechanisms against DDos attacks in SDN environment. IEEE Commun. Mag. **55**(9), 175–179 (2017)

4. Zhou, Y., Chen, K., Zhang, J., et al.: Exploiting the vulnerability of flow table overflow in software-defined network: attack model, evaluation, and defense. Secur. Commun. Netw. **2018**, 1–15 (2018)

5. Kreutz, D., Ramos, F.M.V., Veríssimo, P., et al.: Software-defined networking: a comprehensive survey. Proc. IEEE **103**(1), 14–76 (2015)

6. NOF: Openflow specifications [EB/OL], 19 May 2019. https://www.opennetworking.org/

7. Khan, M.K.A., Sah, V.K., Mudgal, P., et al.: Minimizing latency due to flow table overflow by early eviction of flow entries in SDN. In: 2018 9th International Conference on Computing, Communication and Networking Technologies (ICCCNT), pp. 1–4. IEEE (2018)

8. Zhang, M., Bi, J., Bai, J., et al.: FTGuard: a priority-aware strategy against the flow table overflow attack in SDN. In: The SIGCOMM Posters and Demos (2017)

9. Rabie, R., Drissi, M.: Applying sigmoid filter for detecting the low-rate denial of service attacks. In: 2018 IEEE 8th Annual Computing and Communication Workshop and Conference (CCWC), pp. 450–456. IEEE (2018)

10. Li, Q., Huang, N., Wang, D., et al.: HQTimer: a hybrid Q-learning-based timeout mechanism in software-defined networks. IEEE Trans. Netw. Serv. Manage. **16**(1), 153–166 (2019)

11. Qiao, S., Hu, C., Guan, X., et al.: Taming the flow table overflow in openflow switch. In: Proceedings of the 2016 ACM SIGCOMM Conference, pp. 591–592. ACM (2016)

12. Wang, C., Youn, H.Y.: Entry aggregation and early match using Hidden Markov Model of flow table in SDN. Sensors **19**(10), 2341 (2019)

13. Yang, H., Riley, G.F.: Machine learning based flow entry eviction for OpenFlow switches. In: 2018 27th International Conference on Computer Communication and Networks (ICCCN), pp. 1–8. IEEE (2018)

14. Xu, J., Wang, L., Song, C., et al.: Proactive mitigation to table-overflow in software-defined networking. In: 2018 IEEE Symposium on Computers and Communications (ISCC). IEEE (2018)

15. Cao, J., Xu, M., Li, Q., Sun, K., Yang, Y., Zheng, J.: Disrupting SDN via the data plane: a low-rate flow table overflow attack. In: Lin, X., Ghorbani, A., Ren, K., Zhu, S., Zhang, A. (eds.) SecureComm 2017. LNICST, vol. 238, pp. 356–376. Springer, Cham (2018). https://doi.org/10.1007/978-3-319-78813-5_18

16. Xu, T., Gao, D., Dong, P., et al.: Mitigating the table-overflow attack in software-defined networking. IEEE Trans. Netw. Serv. Manage. **14**(4), 1086–1097 (2017)

17. Data Set for IMC 2010 Data Center Measurement [EB/OL], 20 October 2019. http://pages.cs.wisc.edu/~tbenson/IMC10_Data.html

18. Nguyen, X.N., Saucez, D., Barakat, C., et al.: Rules placement problem in OpenFlow networks: a survey. IEEE Commun. Surv. Tutor. **18**(2), 1273–1286 (2016)

Human Factors Affecting XBRL Adoption Success in Lebanese Small to Medium-Sized Enterprises

A. Ayoub[1], Vidyasagar Potdar[1(✉)], A. Rudra[1], and H. Luong[2]

[1] School of Management, Faculty of Business and Law, Curtin University,
Perth, WA, Australia
a.ayoub2@postgrad.curtin.edu.au, {vidyasagar.potdar,
amit.rudra}@cbs.curtin.edu.au
[2] Otago Business School, Department of Accountancy and Finance,
Otago, New Zealand
hoa.luong@otago.ac.nz

Abstract. Firms use Extensible Business Reporting Language (XBRL), as a component of accounting information systems, to define and facilitate the exchange of sensitive and confidential big financial data, namely, financial reports of use to shareholders, stakeholders, competitors and public users. However, still, many companies have not, yet, successfully adopted XBRL despite its foreseen competitive advantages. Different factors affect the successful adoption of XBRL. The human factor, as a component of organizational culture, is deemed to impact the successful adoption of XBRL. Based on an in-depth literature review, and analysis of surveys collected from 78 small to medium-sized firms in Lebanon, using variance-based structural equation model analysis, the impact of human factors on XBRL successful adoption is defined. Results identified the impact of human factors impact on the successful adoption of XBRL by firms seeking to adopt the lateral mandatory financial reporting standards.

Keywords: Extensible Business Reporting Language (XBRL) · XBRL adoption success factors · Human factors · Organizational culture · XBRL adoption, big data, privacy

1 Introduction

XBRL adoption requires measures to manage big data, and this implies that the security of such data should not be compromised. Wahab (2019) advocates the importance placed on integrating blockchain in addressing the security concerns of the adoption of this system. With the enthusiasm surrounding the blockchain adoption, emphasis should be placed on the authentication of the system and the privacy required. For the XBRL system, concerns have been placed on the non-reliance of a single party when dealing with big data. As such, Wahab (2019) outlines the importance of using the peer-to-peer interlocking system as this will facilitate the involvement of more than two parties when accessing the system. The other factor that can compromise the security

© Springer Nature Singapore Pte Ltd. 2020
Y. Tian et al. (Eds.): ICBDS 2019, CCIS 1210, pp. 98–115, 2020.
https://doi.org/10.1007/978-981-15-7530-3_8

and privacy issues of XBRL adoption in the era of big data is the speed of processing information as the automation of the data provided in the organization can have an implication on the security breach (Wahab 2019).

According to Nair et al. (2018), segregation of the data presented in the XBRL adoption process should be based on a blockchain network, and most preferred being a private blockchain that is governed by a given selected individual serving the purpose of securing the system. Based on the private blockchain strategy, the level of control on such a network will be improved, and it will be the responsibility of a single individual where the organization reports privacy and security concerns (Nair et al. 2018). Also, Nair et al. (2018) study claims that the transparency of the information presented should be observed, but this should not be to the extent of revealing the pseudo-anonymity and privacy of the information (Nair et al. 2018). XBRL adoption should focus on employing harder security measures when using big data and this will prevent malicious accessibility of such data. Further, the big data infrastructure system needs to consider the integrity of the data, trust policies, and data quality (Nair et al. 2018).

In this context, one reason that led to the use of eXtensible Business Reporting Language (XBRL) in financial reporting is the elimination of time-consuming, labor-intensive and error-prone practices that are currently used by organizations to generate and exchange financial reports (Castro et al. 2015). Moreover, XBRL facilitates analysis and continuous auditing in different organizations, thereby increasing the transparency in the various activities that deal with financial information. XBRL serves as a derivative of Extensible Markup Language (XML) and takes advantage of the tag notion that involves contextual information with data points in financial statements (Castro et al. 2015). The tags are based on the standards of accounting used by different organizations and regulatory reporting regimes (Castro et al. 2015). XBRL taxonomies used in countries define the regimes and standards. In its role of providing digital financial reporting, XBRL relies on various organizational factors. It relies on both internal and external factors such as personnel issues (i.e., human resource policy and practice, unions, deployment, organizational structure, professional conduct) and operational issues (internal processes and external relations) (Castro et al. 2015). This study addresses the impact of human factors on the adoption success of XBRL through a review of relevant literature and a survey based study conducted on small to medium-sized firms in Lebanon.

2 Literature Review

Traditionally, organizations prepared financial data using non-interchangeable formats like PDF, HTML and Microsoft Excel. These methods face difficulties in the attempt of analyzing information that would lead annual reports. Idealists and financial specialists in the digital world are likely to use data developed by new technologies that will enhance efficiency in data storage and management. XBRL serves as an essential method of reporting financial information adopted in the digital age. Different authors found that the adoption of XBRL dramatically relies on human factors existing within or outside an organization.

In this regards, Malihe and Mahmoud (2015) established that the speed of the preparation, distribution, and comparability of financial information is an essential aspect of an organization that requires adequate utilization of available human resources to facilitate its success (Malihe et al. 2015). According to Malihe and Mahmoud (2015), any organization is defined by three types of factors that influence its operations. These factors are technological, organizational factors, and environmental factors. Human factors are mainly the resources available within an organization whose primary purpose is to facilitate the involvement of other entities to achieve a specific goal (Malihe et al. 2015). Researchers highlighted that human factors are like any other factor in the operation of an organization that affects the implementation of XBRL (Malihe et al. 2015). They added that human beings are entitled to the provision of knowledge about measurement indices used in financial instruments and make decisions used during the process of adopting an XBRL (Malihe et al. 2015).

Similarly, Doolin and Troshani highlighted that XBRL adoption success depends on the amount of support given by individuals participating in the entire exercise or taking the initiative. According to Doolin and Troshani (2007), XBRL adoption process requires interaction between various individuals with the intention of making trading partnership inform of institutions. Their argument shows that individuals or managers of different companies must develop an interest in making a business partnership to induce the desire of developing a language like XBRL that will facilitate financial communication and reporting. Doolin and Troshani (2007) also found that human factors affect the availability of information needed in the implementation of XBRL. For example, XBRL implementation in Australia required the government (through citizens) to run seminars, workshops and electronic newsgroups as well as the composition of articles to provide information on XBRL. Considering Australia as an organization, it took the responsibility of supplying the required personnel for passing information to different parts of the country to facilitate the implementation of XBRL. Doolin and Troshani (2007) added that the adoption of XBRL depends on the production and availability of appropriate taxonomies that are based on financial standards and reporting requirements. Human beings can provide the right taxonomies and set accounting standards that support the implementation of an effective XBRL (Doolin and Troshani 2007).

In another article, Malihe and Mahmoud (2015) identified XBRL as a tool for financial reporting whose outcome depends on the responsibility of stakeholders facilitating the activity. Malihe and Mahmoud (2015) found that success of XBRL adoption depends on factors that can be grouped into technological, organizational and environmental conditions. The authors placed human factors under the umbrella of organizational factors connected to the entire exercise of adopting XBRL (Malihe et al. 2015). According to Malihe and Mahmoud (2015), organizations that seek to adopt XBRL should get in touch with features such as availability of human resources, financial resources, and management structure of the entire organization. Malihe and Mahmoud (2015) also added that human beings are the champions within a business that influence the adoption decision and participate in displaying leadership within an organization to initiate behavioural change towards the adoption of new technology such as XBRL. Malihe and Mahmoud (2015) reinforced the idea about the influence of human factors on XBRL implementation, claiming that the adoption of this technology requires both in-depth technical and accounting knowledge. Therefore, humans or employees working in a company have the responsibility to supply the necessary technical and financial knowledge that does not facilitate the implementation of the technology but also enhance performance through the implemented technology (Malihe and Mahmoud 2015)

On the other hand, Henderson et al. (2012) explained that adoption of XBRL places organizations in need of appropriate tagging expertise and appropriate knowledge to integrate the XBRL-enabled system into the financial reporting supply chain. Henderson et al. (2012) believed that appropriate knowledge on the adoption of an XBRL lies with the personnel tasked with the duty of carrying financial reporting (Henderson et al. 2012). Therefore, organizations should encourage the use of new mechanisms that help in lowering knowledge barriers over time as a way of reducing challenges that may hinder the success of XBRL adoption (Henderson et al. 2012). Therefore, individuals working in an organization should take the responsibility of supplying the required level of knowledge expertise to eliminate barriers that may affect the implementation of new technology (Henderson et al. 2012). Moreover, human resources existing in an organization determines the extent that an organization learns about external sources and hence, a positive influence on private XBRL adoption. Henderson et al. (2012) highlighted that organizations do not only compete for legitimacy but also engage in innovative activities that lead to shared notions of appropriate behaviours. The authors added that human personnel sets the norms that may guide to concerns about the organization's legitimacy and adversely affect its capacity to obtain the required resources for new changes such as XBRL adoption (Henderson et al. 2012).

Rawashdeh and Selamat (2013), in the same context, examined the success factors that influence the adoption of XBRL adoption in Saudi Arabia. The authors found that human resources available in an organization determine conditions of adopting XBRL. Rawashdeh and Selamat (2013) identified that human resources determine the compatibility in an organization seeking to take XBRL technology. Compatibility is the state at which two things can exist or occur together without causing problems or conflicts. Rawashdeh and Selamat (2013) believed that human resources improve the rate of adopting XBRL by eliminating probable problems or coping with challenges that may hinder the adoption of new technology. Rawashdeh and Selamat (2013) also added that the adoption of XBRL requires one to deal with the complexity of an innovation that may lead the adoption to a negative direction (Rawashdeh and Selamat 2013) Their research confirmed that all organizations are faced with complexity existing among human beings assigned with various duties to adopt XBRL (Shubham 2015). Therefore, the adoption of similar technologies should commence with the inclusion of new ways of dealing with complexity to prevent the adoption process from moving in the negative direction. Finally, Rawashdeh and Selamat (2013) identified that individuals participating in the adoption of XBRL should undergo training that involves the acquisition of internet skills that necessitates internet communication (Rawashdeh and Selamat 2013).

Batcha et al. (2017) identified organization culture as one of the human factors that pose a significant impact on the adoption of XBRL. Batcha et al. (2017) defined organizational culture as the collective behaviour of people that serve as part of the organization formed by organization norms, working language, systems, symbols, visions, and values. Organizational culture determines the behaviour and norms governing the operations taking place within an organization (Batcha et al. 2017). It affects the way people and groups of participants interact with each other, clients and stakeholders of a company. In other words, organizational culture influences the performance of all the individuals interacting in different parts of the organization. Organizational culture can promote the performance of employees if it remains linked with superior properties of performance and create environmental conditions that allow changes (Batcha et al. 2017). Considering the adoption of XBRL technology, organizational culture instigates the willingness of employees to contribute towards the implementation of new technology as well as making the employees feel secure with new changes brought by the technology (Batcha et al. 2017). It makes employees working in an organization to explore comfortably with the activities taking place in the company and take the obligation to give their best in adopting XBRL (Batcha et al. 2017). Moreover, (Suwardi and Tohang 2017) also found a relationship between XBRL adoption and the systemic risk of financial institutions. The authors established that XBRL adoption is an essential tool for financial institutions to channel capital across the economy and achieve economic growth of a country. Suwardi and Tohang (2017) highlighted that corporate governance triggers financial development in financial institutions. It serves as the primary human factor discussed by these authors that influences the adoption of XBRL. Suwardi and Tohang (2017) established that proper use of corporate governance paves the way for many benefits for firms and helps in mitigating agency problems. Corporate governance plays a similar role during the adoption of XBRL technology and influences the willingness of employees to take part in the development of the highlighted technology (Suwardi and Tohang (2017).

Moreover, Rinku et al. (2015) found that financial institutions are increasingly exposed to risk behaviours whenever they attempt to make changes in their system of operation. Adoption of XBRL exists as one of the changes adopted in financial institutions that may suffer from risky behaviours. Therefore, corporate governance serves as a solution to risky behaviours that may hinder the adoption of XBRL. It involves the use of specific procedures to implement changes and adopt mechanisms that positively contribute to the development of a financial institution (Rinku et al. 2015). Ilias (2014) carried research on awareness of XBRL in Malaysia. Her research relied on the notion that users and preparers of XBRL encounter challenges in understanding the implementation and implication of XBRL adoption. Ilias (2014) highlighted that the problems affect the engagement of human resources in the process of adopting XBRL technology (Ilias 2014). Therefore, there is a need for a full understanding of concepts that help in improving the level of awareness of the parties participating in the adoption of XBRL or any digital reports. Individuals responsible for the adoption of XBRL need to know the importance and probable challenges they may face through digital financial reporting (Ilias 2014). According to Ilias (2014), the government should participate in educating stakeholders and organizations from different countries although under different jurisdictions, regulations and accounting standards to counter the challenges that may be experienced in an attempt to adopt a new technology that facilitates digital financial reporting (Ilias 2014). In a nutshell, both profit and non-profit organizations seeking to make financial reporting using digital resources such as XBRL ought to create awareness to the system developers and implementers (Ilias 2014). The awareness should inform the benefits and requirements of a successful XBRL system as well as strategies to solve problems affecting XBRL adoption (Ilias 2014).

Antônio et al. (2016) found that human factors, as part of the primary issues that influence the adoption and success of XBRL. The authors discussed this factor using the concept of electronic governance as a strategy used by different people to facilitate XBRL adoption. Antônio et al. (2016) defined electronic governing as the application and use of technologies by governments to promote control of economic agents and supervise their operations. This method of governing organization influences the adoption of XBRL because the government offers to the different actors of civil society using electronic means and encourages civil society to implement electronic materials to facilitate financial reporting (Antônio et al. 2016). Antônio et al. (2016) used an organizational context to examine the extent that electronic governance may influence the success of XBRL adoption (Antônio et al. 2016). They highlighted that companies usually have a higher propensity to innovate and become eager to rely on the advantage of gains from every initiative they undertake (Antônio et al. 2016). Antônio et al. (2016) added that companies might face significant challenges in innovating and making decisions on implementing new projects, especially situations with complex ideas. These conditions demand high levels of collaboration and coordination than taking projects in small firms. Therefore, electronic governing serves a vital role in implementing similar projects in complex organizations (Antônio et al. 2016).

In the same context, Jasmine (2016) also found that organizations may be influenced by many factors not to adopt XBRL for use in business reporting. Human factors are among the primary issues associated with an organization that influences the implementation or adoption of XBRL. Jasmine (2016) approached this factor using XBRL stakeholders as individuals or a group of people who may be affected by XBRL. XBRL stakeholders may be secondary or primary. Primary stakeholders that affect the success of XBRL adoption are the employees, shareholders, customers, suppliers, government, and communities surrounding an organization. Secondary stakeholders are the recipients or consumers of the services given by the company through XBRL technology. They involve environmentalists that are not attached to the organizations but make a critical impact on the survival of an organization (Jasmine 2016). Henderson et al. (2011) stressed on primary stakeholders that are potentially involved in the decisions that lead to the adoption of XBRL and determines its success in an organization. The author found that primary stakeholders are the governments, professional bodies, accounting firms, business organizations and other employees that determine the decision-making process during XBRL adoption. Henderson et al. (2011) deduced that all primary stakeholders should develop a positive attitude towards the development of new technology like XBRL adoption (Jasmine 2016).

Troshani (2005) also examined human factors that inhibit and drive the adoption of new technology. Troshani (2005) found employee education and availability of resources as primary human-related factors that determine the success of XBRL adoption. Employees that rely on XBRL functionality and enjoy its benefits need to understand XBRL's functionality as well as its benefits to the transfer of financial information. The understanding enables employees to be fluent with the applications are driven by XBRL to avoid the use of the applications to perform purposes that may not be successful (Troshani 2005). For example, XBRL adoption involves technical tasks like taxonomy development and maintenance. It is difficult for uneducated employees to accomplish functional tasks related to XBRL-enabled applications (Troshani 2005). Troshani added that the success of XBRL adoption is adversely affected by limited resources (Troshani 2005). Adoption of XBRL requires adequate resources like time, expertise and funding from an organization (Troshani 2005). Availability of resources also involves the formulation of national adoption strategy, development of taxonomy, software support, marketing and awareness campaigns as well as training of individuals participating in the entire exercise of XBRL adoption. Troshani (2005) also emphasized that the adoption success of XBRL is subject to agreement among the software vendors as well as triggering widespread adoption through the production of XBRL-enabled extension. It will allow adopters to do various experiments during the implementation/adoption period (Troshani 2005). As Troshani (2005) focused on stakeholders of an organization that influence the success of XBRL adoption, Bergeron (2003) pointed infrastructure as part of human factors aiding the adoption of new technology in an organization. According to Bergeron (2003), infrastructure offers a solution to business challenges by creating room for affordability, availability, and appropriateness of current technology. The author highlighted that any organization should acquire the appropriate infrastructure before any other intervention that may lead to the implementation of a technology-based solution such as XBRL adoption. For example, an organization should obtain a mobile phone or wireless personal digital assistant (PDA) solution to achieve communication-based solutions (Bergeron 2003). Bergeron (2003) suggested that organizations should consider information technology infrastructures like personal computers, a telephone network, internet and reliable employees that do not only participate in the adoption of XBRL but also facilitate the use of XBRL technology (Bergeron 2003). Bergeron (2003) added that information technology infrastructure helps in bringing lifeless XBRL statements to the real situation. Information technology does not only affect the organization towards the implementation of XBRL technology but also facilitate the inclusion of the business community in the world of using new technology for business purposes (Bergeron 2003). Therefore, organizations should acquire adequate and reliable infrastructure to facilitate XBRL adoption (Bergeron 2003). On the other hand, Rawashdeh et al. (2011) evaluated the characteristics of consumers that affect the adoption of XBRL adoption. Their research was founded on the fact that the adoption of XBRL technology relies on demographic factors such as gender, age, education, type of industry and experience. According to Rawashdeh et al. (2011), the adoption of XBRL and its success is associated with individual innovativeness that depends on their age, education, and occupation. Regarding age factor that affects the XBRL adoption success, Rawashdeh et al. (2011) established that the age groups that participate in the adoption of XBRL and use of computers in developed countries range between twenty-six to thirty-five years. However, youth and middle age groups are believed to be associated with XBRL adoption as opposed to old age group. Gender plays a vital role in the success of XBRL adoption. It is related to the hierarchical differences existing between men and women. Rawashdeh et al. (2011) found that males are primary users of computers in an organization as opposed to the female gender that are assigned other duties within an organization. Besides, Rawashdeh et al. (2011) found that education is not only an influence to the adoption of XBRL but also affects human capital by determining the competence to use and adopt XBRL within a firm. The source highlighted that education makes employees of an organization stay dedicated to technical tasks like taxonomy expansion, maintenance, configuration, growth and set-up of XBRL-enabled applications (Rawashdeh et al. 2011). Experience is the extent that consumers show their skills to use new technology. Rawashdeh et al. (2011) highlighted that internet financial reporting experience is the knowledge with consumers that enable them to interact with internet presentation format. It shows that employees should possess enough experience to enable them to communicate with internet presentation needed to prevail XBRL adoption success (Rawashdeh et al. 2011).

Enachi and Andone (2015) also examined human factors that influence the progress of XBRL in Europe. The authors established that development of XBRL language in Europe commenced with the appreciation of the language by the Europeans and their willingness to participate in actions aiming at the implementation and promotion of the modern standard (Martins and Oliveira 2011). The adoption success of XBRL did not only involve consumers but also relied on the engagement of regulatory bodies that chose to form jurisdictions for members of XBRL. Enachi and Andone (2015) added that Europe has the required human resources to facilitate efficient extraction, trans-mission, and processing of data needed to promote the development of XBRL tech-nology. The progress of XBRL adoption in Europe is also prevailed by the interest shown by software providers in Europe that participate in designing products and other operations needed in XBRL development. They facilitate the modification, mapping, validation and visualization and analysis of the data necessary to foresee the future of XBRL adoption in an organization (Enachi et al. 2015). In this respect, Ogundeji et al. (2014) investigated factors that influence the implementation of XBRL technology in Nigeria. Their investigation found that the adoption of XBRL technology in organi-zations in developing countries like Nigeria should start with technology acceptance made by employees working in different levels of a company. According to Ogundeji et al. (2014), employees should exhibit a high level of understanding among employees to provide positive support in various levels of XBRL adoption. Ogundeji et al. (2014) added that technology acceptance has much to do with job relevance, results demon-stration, output quality, subjective norm and the perceived ease of employees to use new technology (Ogundeji et al. 2014). Organizations that exhibit a high level of technology acceptance is said to have employees that understand the usefulness and show accountability in the financial statements that will lead to the success of XBRL adoption (Ogundeji et al. 2014).

Alturaigi and Altameem (2015) examined factors surrounding the adoption of XBRL in Saudi Arabia. The research addressed companies with high rate of XBRL adoption. The research suggested five success factors that are responsible for driving a high penetration rate of XBRL in companies within Saudi Arabia. Among the primary factors found relevant to the adoption success of XBRL system in Saudi Arabia, the authors highlighted that user's attitudes contribute to XBRL adoption or acceptance. Different magnitudes of attitudinal belief towards the use of personal computer among the XBRL adopters can be examined using perceived usefulness, compatibility and perceived ease of use. Alturaigi and Altameem (2015) deduced that companies that successfully achieved the adoption of XBRL could cope with attitudinal factors existing among the employees (Alturaigi and Altameem 2015). Furthermore, according to Utama and Ediraras (2004), the implementation of projects such as XBRL is determined by human factors that are technical and social. The authors explained that the technicalities and social nature of projects tend to influence the attractiveness to organizations and lead to the desire of organizations to undertake the project (Utama and Ediraras 2004). Utama and Ediraras (2004) reinforced their arguments by considering independent variables that led to the adoption of XBRL in companies within Indonesia. Their investigation found that implementation of projects like XBRL in Indonesia relied on independent factors like skills and knowledge. The factors exist within the human resources or personnel mandated with the task of implementing new technology. Individuals have the responsibility to provide the required skills and knowledge in various departments of an organization to integrate the existing applications as well as the implementation of the entire system (Utama and Ediraras 2004).

Doolin and Troshani (2007) through their study, identified issues and factors on organizational adoption that were consistent with the "Technology-Organization-Environment model". Through using exploratory research in a qualitative design methodology, they confirmed the suitability of this model. Doolin and Troshani (2007) found out that XBRL was a beneficial technology for software vendors and other auditing or professional accounting organizations. Secondly, Doolin and Troshani (2007) established that complexity was a significant factor because specialized tasks and knowledge were fundamental in ensuring that particular taxonomies and tagging of financial data are achieved. Doolin and Troshani (2007) revealed that trialability is an important factor in ensuring that it reduces the level of uncertainty when adopting new technology. Potential adopters try the new technology through observations and experience and this influences adoption. Observation offers a basis through which potential adopters will demonstrate an interest in XBRL applications to understand the suitability of the new technology in solving the problems of the current situation in the market (Doolin and Troshani 2007). Doolin and Troshani (2007) focused on stability as key in influencing the level of adoption. This is evaluated based on changes in the specifications and functionality. Relating to organization basis, Doolin and Troshani (2007) found out that innovations and organizational readiness were vital in influencing the level of adoption. On the environment, Doolin and Troshani (2007) postulated that market size is a key factor that influences adoption. Doolin and Troshani (2007) found out that trading partners were phenomenal in influencing adoption. Also, Doolin and Troshani (2007) underscored the importance of the availability of information about XBRL, especially concerning its benefits as integral in promoting the level of awareness for new reporting technology for potential adopters. Doolin and Troshani (2007) explained that active communication is important in ensuring that potential adopters are attracted towards incorporating XBRL technology ion their business. In particular, Doolin and Troshani (2007) found a low adoption of XBRL technology in Australia because of insufficient critical mass in the XBRL applications, software tools and its potential users. The study of Doolin and Troshani (2007) showed that software vendors were not ready to invest their time and resources to XBRL technology until a demand necessitated its incorporation. Also, Doolin and Troshani (2007) stated that the availability of support, especially for developing taxonomies and understanding accounting standards that are required for the innovations Doolin and Troshani (2007). In the same context, Pinsker and Li (2008) advanced the research based on an initial theoretical development in the earlier study. He intended to provide a better and clear understanding of XBRL adoption perspectives within middle-level managers for firms operating in the US business market. Pinsker and Li (2008) relied on respondents who were managers but with very little information and knowledge about XBRL with the bulk being MBA students specializing in accounting. Pinsker and Li (2008) found out that "Technology Acceptance Model" and Absorptive Capacity were important theories that could be utilized in analyzing the adoption of XBRL technology. Pinsker and Li (2008) established that XBRL innovative technology was perceived by a majority to be very useful. On the other hand, Pinsker and Li (2008) study noted that the attitudes of decision-makers failed to demonstrate a positive influence on XBRL technology. Concerning the absorptive capacity, Pinsker and Li (2008) revealed that convenience to learn was consistent with the decision of adopting XBRL. Bonson et al. (2009) undertook research through the Delphi Technique as a basis for identifying the factors that affect the companies that were willing to submit financial information through the XBRL technology. Bonson, Cortijo and Escobar (2009) study identified three important factors in promoting the level of voluntary adoption. Bonson et al. (2009) stated the factors as sufficient knowledge of XBRL, achieving the status of a company being the pioneer in the technology adoption, and enhancing the reputation of the company within the capital market.

Literature illustrated certain factors that can influence the level of adoption of XBRL technology within an organization. However, literature is limited and the factors influencing XBRL adoption in organizations are not yet well deciphered. According to Liu (2013), there is a need to identify human factors that have a higher significance in influencing the adoption of technology.

3 Derived Conceptual Framework

Grounded on theories such as the technology acceptance model, Delone and Mclean, organizational culture profile, competing values framework, culture audit theory, the following conceptual framework is derived. It presents the relationship between the independent and the dependent variables. In Fig. 1 below, the relationship between the exogenous and indigenous variables is presented. Exogenous variables are represented by the human factors dimensions and endogenous variable are represented by XBRL adoption success dimensions. 8 hypotheses are formulated in order to support or reject the relationship among the variables of the study.

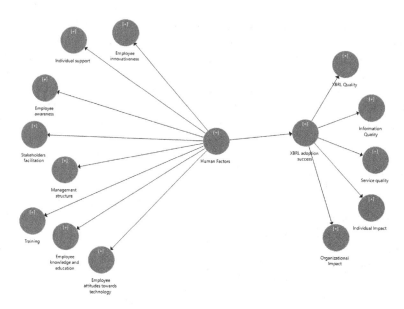

Fig. 1. The study conceptual framework

4 Methods

The study is conducted based on a survey distributed in the city of Beirut, Lebanon. Out of 120 surveys distributed to local small and medium-sized organizations across different industries, only 78 surveys were returned as useful. The analysis of the data was conducted based on a partial least square structural equation model. It is a hierarchical component model composed of two layers of constructs, lower and higher order constructs. Human factors and XBRL adoption success represent the higher order constructs while the dimensions of these constructs represent the first order variables.

This method verified the study hypotheses. The model is formulated using reflective measurements by testing first and second-order confirmations. The assessment of the reflection measurement model shows convergent and discriminant validities, indicator reliability, and internal consistency reliability. The structural model assessment is based on addressing multi-collinearity issues, path-coefficients, R^2, effect size F^2 and predictive relevant, Q^2.

The hypotheses of the study are presented as follows (Table 1):

Table 1. Study hypotheses

H	Constructs relationships
H1	Employee attitudes towards technology impacts XBRL adoption success in small to medium-sized organizations in Lebanon
H2	Employee awareness impacts XBRL adoption success in small to medium-sized organizations in Lebanon
H3	Employee motivation impacts XBRL adoption success in small to medium-sized organizations in Lebanon
H4	Employee knowledge and education impacts XBRL adoption success in small to medium-sized organizations in Lebanon
H5	Individual support impacts XBRL adoption success in small to medium-sized organizations in Lebanon
H6	Stakeholders facilitation impacts XBRL adoption success in small to medium-sized organizations in Lebanon
H7	Training impacts XBRL adoption success in small to medium-sized organizations in Lebanon
H8	Main Hypothesis: Human factors impact XBRL adoption success in small to medium-sized organizations in Lebanon

5 Results and Analysis

The assessment of the developed partial least square structural equation model follows two steps. In the first step, the assessment of the measurement model takes place focusing on the indicator reliability, Cronbach's alpha, indicator's validity and internal consistency. The indicator reliability is maintained as factor reliability values are higher than the minimum acceptance level of 0.7 (Chin 1998). Cronbach's alpha is higher than 0.7, and this indicates as well a high indicator's validity. AVE is higher than 0.5, and this indicates acceptable convergent reliability. Internal consistency is indicated by a CR that falls at an acceptable level which is higher than 0.7. The following table presents the results of the measurement model assessments pertaining loadings, CA, rho_A, CR and AVE (Table 2).

a. All item loadings >0.5 indicate indicator reliability (Hulland 1999, p. 198)
b. All of Cronbach's alpha >0.7 indicates indicator reliability (Nunnally 1978)
c. All composite reliability (CR) >0.7 indicates internal consistency (Gefen et al. 2000)
d. All Average Variance Extracted (AVE) >0.5 indicates convergent reliability (Bagozzi and Yi 1988)

The following table presents the reliability and validity results for the study main second order construct (Table 3).

This study adopted the Nunnally (1978) guidelines of 0.7. Therefore, all items with loadings lower than 0.7 are dropped as presented in the following table (Table 4).

The results of the analysis conducted show that there is convergent validity and reliable internal consistency in the measurement model. The acceptable cut-off point of

Table 2. Measurement model

Construct	Items	Loading	Cronbach's Alpha	rho_A	Composite reliability	Average Variance Extracted (AVE)
XBRL Quality	Q1-1	0.949	0.975	0.977	0.983	0.952
	Q1-2	0.984				
	Q1-3	0.963				
Inform. Quality	Q2-1	0.818	0.943	0.945	0.960	0.857
	Q2-2	0.985				
	Q2-3	0.931				
	Q2-4	0.960				
Service Quality	Q3-1	0.916	0.922	0.942	0.945	0.811
	Q3-2	0.946				
	Q3-3	0.934				
	Q3-4	0.798				
Indiv. Impact	Q4-1	0.939	0.951	0.953	0.965	0.873
	Q4-2	0.932				
	Q4-3	0.965				
	Q4-4	0.899				
Org. Impact	Q5-1	0.940	0.889	0.900	0.932	0.822
	Q5-2	0.986				
	Q5-4	0.818				
Emp Innovat.	Q6-1	0.932	0.907	0.930	0.937	0.790
	Q6-2	0.715				
	Q6-3	0.912				
	Q6-4	0.973				
Ind. Support	Q7-1	0.920	0.829	0.868	0.897	0.743
	Q7-2	0.807				
	Q7-3	0.856				
Emp. Awareness	Q8-1	0.889	0.903	0.913	0.932	0.775
	Q8-2	0.835				
	Q8-3	0.920				
	Q8-4	0.875				
Sharehold. Faci	Q9-1	0.831	0.907	0.933	0.934	0.780
	Q9-2	0.976				
	Q9-3	0.979				
	Q9-4	0.830				
Mang. Support	Q10-1	0.797	0.907	0.933	0.934	0.780
	Q10-2	0.826				
	Q10-3	0.832				
	Q10-4	0.850				
Training	Q11-1	0.943	0.954	0.963	0.967	0.880
	Q11-2	0.957				
	Q11-3	0.985				
	Q11-4	0.863				

(continued)

Table 2. (*continued*)

Construct	Items	Loading	Cronbach's Alpha	rho_A	Composite reliability	Average Variance Extracted (AVE)
Emp. Kno and Education	Q12-1	0.918	0.928	0.958	0.954	0.872
	Q12-2	0.959				
	Q12-3	0.923				
Emp. Attitudes	Q13-1	0.935	0.908	0.915	0.936	0.786
	Q13-2	0.898				
	Q13-3	0.905				
	Q13-4	0.802				

Table 3. Reliability and validity assessment of the measurement model (2nd order constructs)

Construct	Items	Loading	Cronbach's Alpha	rho_A	Composite reliability	Average Variance Extracted (AVE)
XBRL adoption success			0.975	0.984	0.979	0.708

Table 4. Measurement model dropped items

Respective construct	Dropped item/s
XBRL Quality	Q1-4
Organizational Impact	Q5-3
Employee knowledge and education	Q12-4

the composite reliability is 0.7. AVE is greater than 0.5. Cronbach's Alpha and rho_A minimum accepted point is 0.7 (Fornell and Larcker 1981; Nunally 1978). The analysis demonstrate that the values of the measurement model meet the minimum cut-off points for all constructs and thus, suggest good internal consistency and reliability (Fornell and Larcker 1981; Nunally 1978).

Pertaining discriminant validity analysis, the following Table 5 shows a high discriminant validity as the diagonals present the square root of the AVE of the latent variables. Thus, they represent the highest loading factors using Fornell-Larcker criterion.

The assessment of the measurement model showed satisfactory quality of internal consistency reliability, composite, convergent, and discriminant reliability and validity. Assessing the structural model of the study, results indicated that collinearity is not a critical issue. The path-coefficients results among the variables studied fall at

Table 5. Fornell-Larcker Criterion results

	Emp. Att.	Emp. Aw	Emp. Inn	Emp. K & Ed.	Indivi. Imp	Individ. Sup	Info. Qual.	Manag. Sup	Org. Imp.	Service Qua.	Stake. Facil.	XBRL Qual.
Emp. Att	0.922											
Emp. Aw	0.648	0.880										
Emp. Inn	0.881	0.799	0.899									
Emp. K & Ed.	0.822	0.640	0.725	0.934								
Indivi. Imp	0.649	0.802	0.799	0.790	0.934							
Individ. Sup	0.752	0.612	0.794	0.724	0.822	0.862						
Info. Qual.	0.545	0.705	0.762	0.549	0.641	0.748	0.926					
Manag. Sup	0.632	0.504	0.690	0.720	0.568	0.714	0.436	0.883				
Org. Imp.	0.775	0.844	0.785	0.549	0.701	0.822	0.709	0.661	0.907			
Service Qua.	0.411	0.675	0.622	0.835	0.707	0.709	0.720	0.428	0.725	0.900		
Stake. Facil.	0.633	0.399	0.582	0.876	0.535	0.702	0.333	0.709	0.728	0.262	0.938	
Training	0.663	0.665	0.799	0.635	0.721	0.765	0.693	0.455	0.909	0.525	0.592	0.976
XBRL Qual.	0.498	0.455	0.723	0.775	0.763	0.609	0.914	0.531	0.752	0.774	0.741	0.800

acceptable level. As a result, the analysis of the results support the study hypotheses as presented in the following table (Table 6).

R^2 value falls at a level of 0.508 which is considered significant. The effect size F2 follows Cohen (1998) guidelines which are 0.02, 0.15 and 0.35 indicate small, medium and large effect size respectively for exogenous constructs in the structural model. The results indicate large effects of the exogenous constructs in the study model as indicated by (Cohen 1988). For Q2, values of 0.02, 0.15 and 0.35 indicate small, medium and large predictive relevance respectively for exogenous constructs in the model (Hair et al. 2014; Fornell and Cha 1994). The results indicated a large effect size. The structural model supports the hypotheses of the study establishing that human factors have an impact on XBRL adoption success in small and medium-sized firms in Lebanon.

Table 6. Hypothesis testing results

Hypothesis	Constructs relationship	St. Beta	St. Error	t-value	p-value	Decision
H1	Human Factors -> Employee attitudes towards tech.	0.894	0.018	50.02	0.00	Supported
H2	Human Factors -> Employee awareness	0.904	0.012	73.557	0.00	Supported
H3	Human Factors -> Employee motivation	0.987	0.002	29.99	0.00	Supported
H4	Human Factors -> Employee know. & Educ.	0.89	0.015	57.651	0.00	Supported
H5	Human Factors -> Individual support	0.865	0.031	28.211	0.00	Supported
H6	Human Factors -> Stakeholders facilitation	0.883	0.014	62.437	0.00	Supported
H7	Human Factors -> Training	0.934	0.011	87.078	0.00	Supported
H8	Human Factors -> XBRL adoption success	0.713	0.066	346.737	0.00	Supported

6 Conclusion

The study concludes that human factors impact the successful adoption of XBRL in small and medium sized organizations in Lebanon. These factors include but are not limited to employee attitudes, employee awareness, employee motivation, employee knowledge and education, individual support, management support, stakeholder's facilitation and training. Human factors have a significant influence on the adoption success of XBRL because all the attempts to put in place the language requires human intervention or involvement. Therefore, human factors play a significant role in establishing XBRL as the study showed. The study faced some limitations, specifically, the size of the sample and the limited geography. Furthermore, human factors may be numerous and the study addressed only 8 human factors. However, this study established foundations for future research orientations addressing the relationship between the organizational human elements and the adoption success of XBRL.

References

Alturaigi, N.S., Altameem, A.A.: Critical success factors for m-commerce in Saudi Arabia's private sector: a multiple case study analysis. Int. J. Inf. Tech. Converg. Serv. **5**(6), 01–10 (2015)

Antônio, G., Luciano, N., Marco, B., Claudio, P.: Factors that influence the adoption and implementation of public digital accounting according 195 to the evaluation by managers of Brazilian companies. J. Inf. Syst. Technol. Manag. (2016)

Bagozzi, R.P., Yi, Y.: On the evaluation of structural equation models. J. Acad. Mark. Sci. **16**(1), 74–94 (1988). https://doi.org/10.1007/BF02723327

Batcha, M., Akbar, J., Subramani, A.K., Julie L.: Exploring the impact of organization culture on employees' work performance using structural equation modeling (SEM) approach. Int. J. Appl. Bus. Econ. Res. (2017)

Doolin, B., Troshani, I.: Organizational adoption of XBRL. Electron. Mark. **17**(3), 199 (2007)

Bonson, E., Cortijo, V., Escobar, T.: A Delphi investigation to explain the voluntary adoption of XBRL. Int. J. Digit. Account. Res. **9**(1), 193–205 (2009)

Castro, E., Santos, I., Velasco, M.: XBRL formula specification in the multidimensional data model. Inf. Syst. **57**, 20–37 (2015)

Cohen, J.: Statistical Power Analysis for the Behavioral Sciences. Lawrence Erlbaum Associates Inc, Hillsdale (1988)

Enachi, M., Andone, I.I.: The progress of XBRL in Europe – projects, users and prospects. Procedia Econo. Finance **20**, 185–192 (2015)

Fornell, C., Larcker, D.F.: Evaluating structural equation models with unobservable variables and measurement error. J. Mark. Res. **18**(1), 39–50 (1981)

Gefen, D., Straub, D.: The relative importance of perceived ease-of use in is adoption: a study of e-commerce adoption. JAIS (2000, forthcoming)

Henderson, D.L., Sheetz, S.D., Trinkle, B.S.: Understanding the intention to adopt XBRL: an environmental perspective. J. Emerg. Technol. Acc. **8**, 7–30 (2011)

Henderson, D., Sheetz, S.D., Trinkle, B.S.: The determinants of inter-organizational and internal in-house adoption of XBRL: a structural equation model. Int. J. Acc. Inf. Syst. **13**(2), 109–140 (2012)

Hulland, J.: Use of partial least squares (PLS) in strategic management research: a review of four recent studies. Strateg. Manag. J. **20**(2), 195–204 (1999)

Liu, C.: XBRL: a new global paradigm for business financial reporting. J. Global Inf. Manag. **21**(3), 1–26 (2013)

Liu, C., Wang, T., Yao, L.J.: XBRL's impact on analyst forecast behaviour: an empirical study. J. Account. Public Policy **1**(1), 10–104 (2013). https://doi.org/10.1016/j.jaccpubpol.2013.10.004

Martins, M.F., Oliveira, T.: Literature review of information technology adoption models at firm level. Electron. J. Inf. Syst. Eval. **14**(1), 110–121 (2011)

Nair, H., Wong, D., Fouladynezhad, N., Yusof, N.: Big data: ethical, social and political issues in the telecommunication industry. Open Int. J. Inf. **6**(1), 18–27 (2018)

Nunnally, J.C.: Psychometric Theory, 2nd edn. McGraw-Hill, New York (1978)

Ogundeji, G.M., Oluwakayode, E., Tijan, O.M.: Critical factors of XBRL adoption in nigeria: a case for semantic model-based digital financial reporting. Comput. Sci. Inf. Technol. **2**, 45–54 (2014)

Pinsker, R., Li, S.: Costs and benefits of XBRL adoption: early evidence. Commun. ACM **51**(3), 47–50 (2008)

Pinsker, R.: XBRL awareness in auditing: a sleeping giant? Manag. Audit. J. **18**(9), 732–736 (2003)

Rinku, D., Jyoti, M., Dr. Puri, M.M.: Exploring technology acceptance theories and models - a comparative analysis. In: International Conference (Special Issue) (2015)

Suwardi, A., Tohang, V.: An analysis of XBRL adoption towards systemic risk of financial institutions listed in NYSE. Aust. Acc. Bus. Finance J. **11**(4), 23–37 (2017)

Troshani, I., Doolin, B.: Drivers and inhibitors impacting technology adoption: a qualitative investigation into the Australian experience with XBRL. In: 18th Bled e Conference e Integration in Action Bled, Slovenia, 6–8 June, pp. 1–16 (2005)

Troshani, I., Rao, S.: Drivers and inhibitors to XBRL adoption: a qualitative approach to build a theory in under-researched areas. Int. J. E-Bus. Res. **3**(4), 98–111 (2007)

Troshani, I.: Drivers and inhibitors impacting technology adoption: a qualitative investigation into the Australian experience with XBRL. Int. J. E-Bus. Res. **3**(4), 98–111 (2005)

Utama, A.H., Ediraras, D.T.: Acceptance and implementation of extensible business reporting language in Indonesian companies: an empirical review. Gunadarma University (2004)

Wahab, Z.A.: Integrating XBRL and BlockChain to improve corporate transparency integrity and availability in Malaysia. Int. J. Acad. Res. Bus. Soc. Sci. **9**(6), 1194–1201 (2019)

Impact of Nepotism on the Human Resources Component of ERP Systems Implementation in Lebanon

A. Ayoub[1], Vidyasagar Potdar[1(✉)], A. Rudra[1], and H. Luong[2]

[1] School of Management, Faculty of Business and Law, Curtin University,
Perth, WA, Australia
a.ayoub2@postgrad.curtin.edu.au,
{vidyasagar.potdar,amit.rudra}@cbs.curtin.edu.au
[2] Otago Business School, Department of Accountancy and Finance,
Otago, New Zealand
hoa.luong@otago.ac.nz

Abstract. The adoption of enterprise resource planning (ERP) system is fundamental for organizational success as a tool to accumulate, store, and protect organizational critical and big data. However, very often, these systems fail for various reasons, and there are many high profile examples of ERP systems implementation. This study gathers evidence on the influence on nepotism, as a component of organizational culture, on the human element of ERP systems implementation success. We conducted our study by surveying 69 small to medium firms in Lebanon. Data was collected using questionnaires. Data analysis adopted variance-based structural equation modelling technique. The results of the study indicate that nepotism significantly impacts the human resources component of ERP systems implementation success. Such systems can be more effectively implemented in firms with an organizational culture that does not nurture nepotism.

Keywords: ERP systems · Nepotism · Human resources · ERP failure · ERP success · Organizational culture · Big data · Individual privacy

1 Introduction

Moghadam and Colomo-Palacios (2018) noted that big data is emerging to be an integral component in managing datasets that exceeds the capacity of the software tools used in an organization to capture and analyze the data. Enterprise resource planning system (ERP) deals with big data. Human resource components can be compromised in the development of ERP system due to the availability of big data. As such, Moghadam and Colomo-Palacios (2018) stated that secure applications should be developed in addressing the security issues faced in the ERP implementation process. The mechanism of adopting security systems is utilized by large companies such as Google, Yahoo, Facebook, and LinkedIn in processing data. For instance, Hadoop security has been successful in enhancing the privacy and security of the data as it utilizes the

© Springer Nature Singapore Pte Ltd. 2020
Y. Tian et al. (Eds.): ICBDS 2019, CCIS 1210, pp. 116–134, 2020.
https://doi.org/10.1007/978-981-15-7530-3_9

MapReduce model in processing the large datasets presented in ERP's (Moghadam and Colomo-Palacios 2018)

Aman and Mohamed (2017) study notes that human resources components can be easily compromised where the privacy of the data is not assured. As ERP systems rely on cloud storage, encryption of the data is vital in ensuring that the integrity and confidentiality of the sensitive data are realized (Aman and Mohamed (2017). For big data, it is important to consider the 'encrypt all or nothing' model as the ERP system can easily cause a collapse of the organization when the data is accessed by unauthorized people (Aman and Mohamed (2017). However, for the encryption of ERP system interactions, the involved parties should consider utilizing trust model which indicates that as long as the trusted parties in the system are exchanging keys and encrypted data; operation in the organization is secure (Aman and Mohamed 2017). Where the parties involved do not exchange trust, then data encryption will offer no protection on the data (Aman and Mohamed 2017). As such, human resource components that are denoted in the implementation of ERP systems should consider selecting trusted parties to encrypt the data (Aman and Mohamed 2017).

It is perplexing how the information system succeeds in one organization and fails in another. While technical causes may exist, other reasons cannot be ignored. Many researchers have detected an interplay between organizational culture and the success of ERP systems implementation (Pelit et al. 2015; Elbaz et al. 2018, Arshad et al. 2012; Kragh 2012). Across the world, companies are striving to stay competitive while meeting the demands of the global economy. The companies can achieve the objective of being competitive due to operational effectiveness and strategic positioning (Firfiray et al. 2018). Concerning the operational effectiveness, an enterprise resource planning (ERP) system plays a fundamental role. Enterprise resource planning implementation is an activity within an organization that entails the integration of systems that serve different functions within organizations (Firfiray et al. 2018). Implementation of successful ERP systems offers an integrated real-time view of core business processes (Firfiray et al. 2018). They help organizations to track primary business resources like production capacities, raw materials, cash as well as the overall status of the business (Firfiray et al. 2018). Such systems facilitate the flow of information from one business functions to another as well as bridging gaps that exist between managers and external stakeholders (Firfiray et al. 2018). The failure or success of most of ERP implementations has been associated with various factors like substantial cost overruns, time delays, data integration challenges, management complexity, disruptions during operation and socially and culturally related factors like nepotism (Arshad et al. 2012). According to Jaskiewicz et al. (2013), nepotism is the practice of hiring one's relatives as opposed to people that one is not related to. In the Middle Eastern and Asian organizations, this is a common practice, especially in family-controlled businesses (Jaskiewicz et al. 2013). Nepotism occurs at various levels of an organization and affects companies in different forms (Mustafa 2011). Its impact on ERP systems implementation exists as one of the primary issues affecting the development of various organizations operating in different environments (Mustafa 2011).

In Lebanon, a developing country in the middle east, suffers from corruption, nepotism and favoritism across its public as well as private sectors (Saffiedine 2019). Nepotism is blamed to have a negative impact on the Lebanese small and medium-sized organizations (Saffiedine 2019). This impact is posited to influence negatively the implementation success of ERP systems in such organizations. A limited number of previous research has addressed the impact of organizational culture on the implementation success of ERP systems. However, rare are the studies that have addressed the impact of nepotism on the human element of ERP systems implementation success. This research is particular to relationship between nepotism as a dimension of organizational culture and the human element as a fundamental component of ERP systems.

2 Literature Review

Different scholars have given different perceptions about the various ways that nepotism affects the implementation success of ERP systems. Elbaz et al. (2018) provided a theoretical perspective on the way nepotism affects the implementation of an ERP system. According to Elbaz et al. (2018), the performance of an organization lies in employee competencies. Researchers conducted a study based on the Egyptian tourism context that examined the relationship between organizational performance and employees' competencies. Elbaz et al. (2018) explained that intense competition and rapid technological advancement requires qualified employees chosen based on their competences. An organization made up of competent employees has all that is needed to compete with others and enjoy similar necessities of existing in the global economy (Elbaz et al. 2018). ERP system implementation is subject to the level of employee competencies existing within an organization. Building capable employees' competencies and competitive capabilities are one of the critical elements of building an active organization that is capable of achieving success in every initiative undertaken (Elbaz et al. 2018).

ERP system implementation is an initiative that mainly relies on two types of competencies in an organization (Elbaz et al. 2018). It relies on personal and organizational competencies (Elbaz et al. 2018). The implementation process requires both individuals and the entire organization to stay focused on accomplishing various duties that see the success of ERP system implementation (Elbaz et al. 2018). It relies on the knowledge, skills, and abilities that enable individuals to exhibit higher levels of personal strengths and weaknesses in the implementation of a system (Elbaz et al. 2018). However, Elbaz et al. (2018) mentioned nepotism as one of the primary factors that affect the implementation of various organizational systems like ERP. Elbaz et al. (2018) referred to nepotism as one of the poor employment practices existing within organizations that undermine the effectiveness of accomplishing most of the activities taking place within an organization. Elbaz et al. (2018) identify nepotism as a condition that enables one to enjoy privilege because of some irrelevant qualifications that do not relate to his/her profession. This type of privilege affects the implementation of an ERP system in several ways. It is associated with negative consequences like the loss of capabilities, dismissal of competent employees, indifferences within an organization, employee frustrations, and sense of social alienation among the employee and lack of teamwork (Elbaz et al. 2018). Elbaz et al. (2018) added that nepotism creates weaknesses of creativity, weak competition among employees, ineffective solutions for human resources planning and poor decision making by the employees.

In the same context, research has shown that there is a universal tendency of people to help those that are socially close to them; however, this tendency is not evenly distributed (Kragh 2012). In developing countries, especially developing countries, this is prevalent and is associated with particularistic social morality that has its root in the pre-industrial period of such countries. As such, in the African, Asian contexts and other countries like in the Middle East region, for instance, nepotism plays a vital role in the expression of social distance and reciprocity (Kragh 2012). Such concepts are central to the idea of nepotism and tribalism in the early stages of modernization (Kragh 2012). Research has shown that in places like Africa and Middle East countries, nepotism is rooted in the core of these organizations and has been accepted as normality (Kragh 2012). The culture of nepotism and favouritism in organizations in these countries, as well as the public sector, has been practiced at length, and it does not seem to end (Kragh 2012). Proponents of this practice have argued that nepotism is useful, especially for family businesses, while others have argued that nepotism is an outdated culture and everyone should have equal chances (Biermeier-Hanson 2015). In modern organizations, nepotism is perceived as the protection of relatives and friends, which is not invested or geared towards productivity but by a small cluster of family connections (Biermeier-Hanson 2015). This scenario has been seen to degrade the quality of human resource activities and in particular organizational performance. This is because the nepotism affects the objectivity of activities. Instead, subjectivity creeps in due to the existence of family interpersonal relationships. Although researchers have tried to separate nepotism from favouritism and protectionism, these themes are inseparable in modern organizations whose common denominator is one cluster (Calvard and Rajpaul-Baptiste, n.d; Urbanová and Dundelová, n.d 2015).

It has been argued and rightly so that for management of organizations in both private and public domains to be improved, ethical evaluation of nepotism should be done by refining organizational values and disintegrating the culture of nepotism and unfair decisions (Kragh 2012). According to Kragh (2012), nepotism, favouritism and protectionism exist side by side. Thus, for an organization to succeed, it must deal with the three of them. As such, nepotism has been viewed as a form of unwanted organizational culture, and their connection is prevalent in the developing world. In other researches, nepotism has been presented as being a dual organizational-management anomaly which affects organizational culture whose outcome is a sick organizational culture (Kragh 2012).

Other researchers have tried to connect organizational culture and nepotism by defining corporate culture as a set of beliefs and values that contribute to organizational behavior (Urbanová and Dundelová, n.d, P.59). In a study done by Hanson (2015), nepotism has been shown to accelerate the attraction-selection-attrition process in an organization. The argument in this regard is that individuals who are socially connected become more attracted to an organization because of human capital advantage (Hanson 2015). Further, the author argued that hiring family members to a family business has an advantage because they have been exposed to the business from a young age. Additionally, family members share a cultural connection and that their integration into the organization culture is more comfortable compared to people of different cultures. In an argument made by Hanson (2015), modern organizations tend to hire family members due to fear of turnover as a result of a cultural misfit. However, nepotism should not be viewed from one lens, but from different perspectives and objectively (Urbanová and Dundelová, n.d 2015).

According to organizational justice theory, organizational fairness is central to the success of any firm (Muhammad 2011). Research has shown that organizations that have embraced the culture of nepotism lack fairness and justice in the treatment of its employees (Muhammad 2011). As such, when employees view a firm as lacking justice and fairness in the way it handles issues regarding its workers, the morale of workers declines and intentions to leave the organization increases (Muhammad 2011).

Further, it has been shown that such organizations, there are higher chances of employees taking legal action against the organization, and it is less likely for an employee to help a co-worker. In other researches, it has been established that during the selection process, the justice perception greatly influences job acceptance by an applicant, re-application intentions, motivation to take tasks, and employee intention to recommend an applicant to the organization (Muhammad 2011). In addition, it has been shown that organizational justice affects employees, customers, and applicants from the point of interacting with the organization to the stage where they leave the organization. Thus, this phenomenon is the mediating variable between the unfair treatment and the reactions of employees and workers in regard to this construct (Muhammad 2011).

It has been established that organizations that practice nepotism as a part of their culture have little regard for organizational social justice. Due to the existing family and friendship ties that exist between employees and senior management, it has been shown that the employees are not equally treated. In research done by Muhammad (2011), it was established, for instance, that in Kenyan and Ghanaian organizational context, nepotism and tribalism are the core constructs that are rotting both public and private organizations (Muhammad 2011). In their study, it was shown that employees related to management were favored regarding promotions, task distribution, and allowances (Muhammad 2011). As such, the effect of this organizational behavior is low motivation for other employees and high turnover rate in such organizations. Further, the employees feel that justice cannot be served in case of an issue within the organization. It was shown that in case of disciplinary action, employees that were not related to senior management were likely to receive harsh disciplinary actions or even being terminated as compared to those that were related to the management (Muhammad 2011).

A keen look at such an organizational culture means that the family ties within the organization sway even decisions that regard crucial issues in the organizations (Muhammad 2011). It has been shown that corporate culture has a lot bearing in the adoption of information systems in any organization (Muhammad 2011). In this regard, organizations that practice nepotism and in extension organizational injustice will find it challenging to adopt information systems like AIS since the change will be rejected due to organizational politics of "Us vs. Them." (Muhammad 2011).

Although some proponents of nepotism have tried to argue for the benefits of this construct, when viewed from a postmodern social perspective, it is detrimental (Pelit et al. 2015). It reduces the contributions of employees who are not relatives or acquaintances of senior management (Pelit et al. 2015). According to contemporary management practices, humans are not machines (Pelit et al. 2015). Thus, they bring to work their emotions, which affect the way they work (Pelit et al. 2015). This conflicts with the free-speech and opinion paradigm that has been advocated for in the modern organizations (Pelit et al. 2015; Finelli 2011). Due to the presence of relatives and friends of senior leaders in the organization, the minority employees who are not related to these leaders have always been compelled to silence and alienation, which also results to a low commitment to the organization. The concept of organizational silence as a result of nepotism is a source of organizational problems and an obstacle to changes and progress in an organizational setting (Pelit et al. 2015).

The concept of organizational silence as a result of nepotism has been used to describe the attitudes of employees that are generated due to their inability to share their thoughts, feelings, concerns, and recommendations. According to Pelit et al. 2015, organizational silence can be viewed as an organizational problem and a phenomenon that is characterized by employees keeping silent about their knowledge, concerns, and views about work-related issues as opposed to sharing them with other organization members and management. It is essential, however, to note that organizational silence does not always mean opposition to changes, but can emanate from lack of opportunities to air views and opinions, or lack of information (Briggs and Wated 2012). This situation could be explained by the theory of planned behavior whereby if a worker anticipates that a particular behavior will result in a specific outcome. That individual will develop a particular behavior that suits the situation (Briggs and Wated 2012). In this regard, when individuals in an organization perceive their opinions and views as being dangerous and can lead to victimization, such employees will develop the behaviour of silence (Briggs and Wated 2012).

Concerning the adoption and successful implementation of an information system, organizational silence as a result of nepotism is detrimental. A research done by Briggs and Wated (2012) has established that for successful adoption and implementation of technologies like AIS to take place, it must be accepted by the majority of the users. When nepotism plays a central role in the hiring process, the employees that are not related to the management practice the act of silence to avoid being victimized (Briggs and Wated 2012). However, it has been shown that silence does not mean agreement. Thus, such employees might be opposed silently to the idea of AIS implementation. The result of such a scenario, especially in cases where such employees work directly with such a system is sabotage and sheer lack of commitment to the successful implementation (Briggs and Wated 2012).

Furthermore, research has shown that the commitment shown by employees towards an organization is a significant construct of organizational culture that affects organizational performance. Organizational commitment has been defined as the level of conviction and acceptance of organizational goals, values and the desire to remain at the organization to achieve these goals (Pelit et al. 2015). It has been shown that employees can either be committed to an organization due to the affection they feel towards the organization, when they feel they will be affected negatively by leaving and when employees are ethically bound to the organization (Pelit et al. 2015). In this context, organizational administration is concerned with the level of commitment shown by employees towards the organization because this translates to the execution of duties (Sarpong and Maclean 2015). It is argued that committed employees, in most cases, translate to the success of the organization (Sarpong and Maclean 2015).

Although other variables like job satisfaction and motivation have been seen to have a direct impact on employee commitment, nepotism is one variable that has been seen to predict organizational commitment (Sarpong and Maclean, 2015). It has been shown that especially in family-owned businesses, nepotism has been used to promote organizational commitment. Top leaders of such businesses hire and promote their relatives to key positions because they already understand the business having interacted with it from a young age. In the Arab region, nepotism has been practised for quite some time. It has become part of cultural normality in both private and public sectors (Kragh 2012). Other researchers have argued that there is a negative correlation between organizational commitment and nepotism. It has been established that once employees perceive organizational activities like recruitment and selection, promotions, and job lay-offs to be influenced by relationships rather than organizational policies. Such employees are demotivated and show less commitment to the organization (Sarpong and Maclean 2015).

Regarding commitment, nepotism has been seen to help in introducing changes to the organization as well as acting as a roadblock (Sarpong and Maclean 2015). A study conducted by Kragh (2012), revealed that when organizations have committed members, the introduction of technologies like AIS is often smooth and successful because everyone will agree on the need for such a change (Kragh 2012). As such, management of organizations appoint relatives in crucial decision-making positions so that the introduction of such technologies will be accepted readily (Kragh 2012). Other studies have shown that due to the discrimination shown in appointments and hiring process, some members who are not part of family cronies feel alienated and thus show less commitment towards the organization (Kragh 2012). This results in a sheer lack of interest and sometimes sabotage of any changes being implemented in the organization (Kragh 2012).

In the same context, according to Pelit et al. (2015), nepotism has a negative effect on the morale of employees who are forced to work with the relatives and friends of high ranking organizational officials especially those that have been promoted or hired with little regard to merits. In return, this has been found to harm the organizational relationships, cause inefficiency in the general working, weaken bonds between workers and reduce a sense of security (Pelit et al. 2015). In this regard, such organizations bring about the concept of alienation, which can be viewed as the state of exclusion from organizational processes (Pelit et al. 2015). When employee disassociates himself/herself from the organization, the morale and the feeling of belonging and part of the organization is affected massively (Pelit et al. 2015). Further, research shows that when an employee feels that selection and recruitment, promotion, work division, information flow, the delegation of authority and employee relations is based on nepotism, such an employee will feel alienated from the organization. Although little research has been done on this constraint as organizational culture, the little research that exists shows that in many organizations, the effect of nepotism has led to organizational alienation. Research has shown that organizational alienation can be explained in terms of employee powerlessness, employee meaninglessness, and self-estrangement (Pelit et al. 2015). It has been established that when family members are appointed to positions that they do not merit, the result is blind loyalty and powerlessness both to them and those that are not relatives (Pelit et al. 2015). In some organizations, such situations have led to organizational confusion and flawed decision-making processes. In such organizations, a minority of workers who are not relatives of the top leaders are bypassed in regards to promotions, salary increment, and employment. This makes them feel powerless and not part of the organization (Pelit et al. 2015). Often time, such employees feel a sense of meaninglessness and self-estrangement towards the organization (Pelit et al. 2015). When employees feel alienated from the organization, accepting change in the organization becomes very hard. Alienation, in most cases, is a form of rebellion from workers who feel discriminated and not part of the organization. Adoption of technologies and in particular, AIS requires the support of all employees. However, when some employees are kept away from organizational decisions, they can sabotage the adoption and successful implementation of such systems (Pelit et al. 2015).

Therefore, nepotism is unethical behaviour that leads to poor performance in every activity that an organization may try to implement (Elbaz et al. 2018). Elbaz et al. (2018) highlight that employees hired through nepotism create unproductive working environment that makes it challenging to implement an effective ERP system. The reason behind the highlighted effect of nepotism in the implementation of an ERP system lies in the fact that employees appointed by nepotism may misbehave during the implementation process under the umbrella offered by their sponsors (Elbaz et al. 2018). Besides, nepotism leads to inefficiency, lack of transparency and harmful behaviour during the implementation of an ERP system. It paves the way for negative motivation and lack of job satisfaction among employees assigned to various tasks within an organization (Elbaz et al. 2018). Implementation of a successful ERP system is an activity that requires a high level of job satisfaction among the employees (Elbaz et al. 2018). Nepotism has a negative relationship with job satisfaction and performance of employees (Elbaz et al. 2018).

In a similar context, Mustafa (2011) claimed that organizations suffering from nepotism do not make appointments based on competence and knowledge accumulation. Mustafa (2011) also explained that individuals applying for jobs with people enjoying privileges other than their competencies have low chances of getting employed by such organizations. Therefore, organizations end up working with incompetent employees that are subject to distressing situations experienced in a company (Mustafa 2011). In the same context, Wassenaar et al. 2002, described the ERP system implementation as a process that involves significant organizational changes that affect both human and non-human resources existing in an organization. Therefore, any change in the behaviour of human resources is expected to pose significant effects on ERP system implementation. Nepotism happens to be one of the primary factors within the human resources that affect the implementation of an ERP system. Wassenaar et al. (2002) identified that ERP system implementation might be affected during the four stages of implementation. These stages entail strategic visioning and contracting stage, project planning stage, adaptation stage, and institutionalization stage.

Mustafa (2011) also believed the nepotism affects organizational commitment that acts as one of the primary factors determining the success of an ERP implementation. It affects the way employees show their commitment and their level of engagement in the process of implementing an ERP system. Employees recruited through nepotism may demonstrate negative behaviours when interacting with other employees allocated with similar tasks of implementing an ERP system. The employees may think that the company should give more compensations than their workmates that lack blood relationship with their employers (Mustafa 2011). Regarding the effect of nepotism posed on the implementation of an ERP system, Firfiray et al. (2017) highlight that nepotism affects the entire process of decision making that exists as the primary task of family owners. In most of the family-owned organizations, owners find it challenging to make decisions on family member's performance and qualifications during recruitment. Therefore, firm owners may end up choosing the wrong employees to take different tasks like any task during the ERP system implementation (Firfiray et al. 2018).

AL-shawawreh (2015) did not keep off from examining the extent that nepotism affects employment processes taking place in different organizations. The effect of nepotism on the employment process among organizations undermines the accomplishment of various tasks like ERP system implementation. According to AL-shawawreh (2015), nepotism is the reason behind the increased rate of corruption among government institutions in Iraq. The author has identified that government institutions suffer from political, juridical and financial corruption that undermines the implementation of various activities within the institutions. The associated types of corruption existing in such institutions occur because individuals mandated with the duty of hiring new employees prioritize on family members thought to provide services to the organizations (AL-shawawreh 2015). Taking an example of a situation whereby an institution allocates an employee with a duty of implementing an ERP system, the subject may choose not to show full commitment in completing the assignment because of the favour is given by the employer who is a family member (AL-shawawreh 2015).

AL-shawawreh (2015) also found that employees working in nepotism oriented businesses may show unethical behaviours whenever they are assigned with duties of implementing ERP systems. Nepotism affects the sense of fairness existing among workers and damages the team spirit existing among employees that are expected to facilitate the success of the implementation process. The effect is prevalent in organizations whose employers use both nepotism and fairness when hiring their employees (AL-shawawreh 2015). Employees hired on the basis of their competence and skills may lack a sense of belonging when employers make decisions in favour of the family-related employees (AL-shawawreh 2015) Such employees may fail to show their highest levels of commitment during the implementation of an ERP system because of the increased rate of nepotism existing within the company (AL-shawawreh 2015). Moreover, managers in nepotism oriented businesses may invest their money and time in strengthening their social relations instead of completing tasks that see the success of the company (AL-shawawreh 2015). The impact entails giving rewards to workers without considering their competencies and achievements in the assigned duties. As a result, ERP system implementation may drag behind because of capital shortage and failure to allocate enough resources to the chosen team. The process may take more time than the expected duration because employers do not pressurize employees that share a family relationship (AL-shawawreh 2015). They allow the employees to spend the time allocated for ERP system implementation for other functions other than doing assignments that may influence the results of the system.

Firfiray et al. (2018), found that nepotism poses a significant threat to the management of human resources. Similarly, AL-shawawreh (2015) highlights that nepotism undermines the choices made by business managers on the resources owned by the companies as well as the distribution of the resources towards the accomplishment of various tasks in the company. AL-shawawreh (2015) claims that employees are expected to exhibit high levels of competency to utilize the allocated resources in pursuing duties given by managers of an organization. Nepotism tends to inflict organizations with employees that lack skills relevant to the implementation of an ERP system. Therefore, an organization may possess and allocate enough resources for the exercise. However, the employees fail to use the resources in accomplishing the proposed task (AL-shawawreh 2015). In the same context, Aldraehim et al. (2012) mentioned three adverse effects of nepotism that may affect the implementation of an ERP system. Aldraehim et al. (2012) explained that hiring employees based on their kinship expose organizations to problems of sibling rivalry over the managerial succession, family conflicts and difficulties in the decision-making process. Relating this effect with the implementation of an ERP system, team members selected by an organization to participate in the implementation of the system may encounter difficulties with corporate decision-making processes (Aldraehim et al. 2012). The team may comprise of family members that increase chances of family conflicts that hinder the completion of any process of implementing an ERP system (Aldraehim et al. 2012).

Aldraehim et al. (2012) also mentioned that allowing nepotism in a company reduces the morale of people that supervise employees known to share family relationships with high-level executives. Such workers may feel to be more close to the high-level executives than their supervisors despite being positioned in the lower class of jobs. Therefore, the supervisors may find it difficult to give instructions to such employees (Aldraehim et al. 2012). ERP implementation is a process that requires one to provide full supervision and ensure that the implementation team has a leader that presides over the activities taking place in that department. Nepotism tends to diminish the authorities of team leaders because they may find it difficult to create regulations that limit an employer who believes to be more superior to him/her. As a result, the supervisor may end up giving up with the instructions needed to follow during ERP implementation or give much freedom to ERP implementation team. Aldraehim et al. (2012) added that nepotism is characterized by incredible and unfair pressure on the employees. Putting irrelevant pressure on employees may hinder provision organizational rewards that increase the efficiency of employees in completing their duties (Aldraehim et al. 2012).

From another perspective, Aldraehim et al. (2012) brought some benefits of enrolling workers based on their kinship. The researcher proved that nepotism creates a family-oriented environment whereby relatives assist each other in building their morale and job satisfaction. The employees can interact within the same business environment and help one to improve his/her strengths of implementing duties while solving problems that may affect their efficiencies in the company (Aldraehim et al. 2012). Aldraehim et al. (2012) highlighted that nepotism within an organization encourages recognition of all employees that may play vital roles during ERP system implementation or any other task that may demand extraordinary skills. It ensures that organizations hire every member of the family that is believed to possess knowledge and skills that might be effective towards the organization rather than ignoring such employees because of their kinship. As a result, the recruitment and retention of competent employees are possible through nepotism. These employees can facilitate changes in an organization and ease the whole process of implementing new systems in a company. Therefore, Aldraehim et al. (2012) encourage the organization to consider hiring employees that offer benefits to the company instead of neglecting a person because of his/her blood relations with other employees.

Arshad et al. (2012) also used the idea of job satisfaction to determine the extent that nepotism affects the implementation of different organizational systems as well as the introduction of changes in companies. Arshad et al. (2012) defined nepotism as a situation whereby employees are chosen based on family relations regardless of their skills, educations or the capacity to accomplish various tasks existing in an organization. This method of recruiting workers exists in most of the family businesses because the owners of the business assume that they understand the business well than any other person from outside the family. The effect of nepotism on job satisfaction and its relationship with ERP implementation is pinpointed here because an organization can only implement a successful ERP system if it uses employees with high levels of job satisfaction (Arshad et al. 2012). Job satisfaction involves the creation of an environment whereby the employees develop a positive reaction towards pay, working atmosphere, supervision and the job they are pursuing (Arshad et al. 2012). Similarly, ERP implementation is a process that requires an organization to use employees with a positive reaction towards pay, working atmosphere, supervision and their engagement in implementing the system. Arshad et al. (2012) believe that employees with a positive reaction towards the activities taking place within a company are appropriate choices for implementing new changes. However, organizations whose employees are chosen based on their kinship are victims of poor job satisfaction (Arshad et al. 2012). This shows that employees working in these organizations have a negative attitude towards supervision, working atmosphere, and payments for the work they do (Arshad et al. 2012). Arshad et al. (2012) reinforced his deductions with a claim that nepotism affects the intrinsic job satisfaction that may enable employees to play their roles in a company with passion and devotion. Implementation of an ERP system requires employees that are intrinsically motivated by an organization (Arshad et al. 2012). This means that the drive towards the achievement of a set goal or objective comes from within the company (Arshad et al. 2012). Nepotism oriented business lacks any sort of intrinsic motivation or factors from within an organization that may boost the morale of workers towards the development of the company (Arshad et al. 2012). Therefore, employers should support any activity that improves the morale of employees and creates positive reactions towards activities the development of respective organizations (Arshad et al. 2012).

In a similar context, Al-Turki (2011) conducted a study that discusses some of the challenges faced during ERP implementation in Saudi Arabia. His study focused on factors that occur as threats to the success of an ERP system implementation. Al-Turki (2011) highlighted that ERP system implementation involves a set of activities that help in streamlining business processes and promote the integration of ideas from different sources to promote organizational development. According to Al-Turki (2011), ERP implementation may experience total success, partial success or total failure (Al-Turki 2011). The causes of the variations in the process of implementing an ERP system vary from one country to another. Considering the case of Saudi Arabia, most of the small enterprises existing in this country may suffer from knowledge constraints whose sources lie within the companies (Al-Turki 2011). In a nutshell, small enterprises in Saudi Arabia have high chances of recruiting employees from within the country. These employees may suffer from knowledge deficits when it comes to implementing tasks that demand a high level of experience (Al-Turki 2011). This problem affects Saudi Arabia because the recruitment process in this country is profoundly affected by nepotism (Al-Turki 2011). The companies prefer hiring workers from Saudi Arabia and pay little compensation for the work done by the employees. As earlier indicated, little compensation to the employees for a successful work kills the morale of employees towards the production of a successful ERP implementation (Al-Turki 2011). Similarly, medium-sized companies suffer this challenge connected to the behavior shown during employee recruitment. They prefer hiring employees from within the company but suffer from the same challenge of knowledge constraints (Al-Turki 2011).

Literature has established that a connection exists between nepotism and ERP implementation success, specifically, the human resource component. It has been shown that in the developing nations, it is not possible to separate organizational culture from nepotism. In such regions, it is normal for managers to hire their family members with disregard to merits. Although little studies have explored the extent of nepotism in organizations, it has been established that this construct of organizational culture is practised even by modern organizations. The effects of this practice are broad and vast concerning organizational performance. It has been shown in organizations that have embraced nepotism as a part of their organizational culture, there is a decline in organizational justice, commitment and has often led to organizational silence and alienation, which in return affect employee motivation and performance.

3 Derived Conceptual Framework

Nepotism becomes a part of the organizational culture with direct influence on ERP implementation success (Chan et al. 2017). The human resource component is manifested by seven first order constructs that are employee commitment, employee diversity, employee morale and fairness, frustration and social alienation, procedures, teamwork and employee competence. The human component of ERP is a second-order construct. It is the main dependent variable influenced by nepotism that is the main independent variable (Fig. 1).

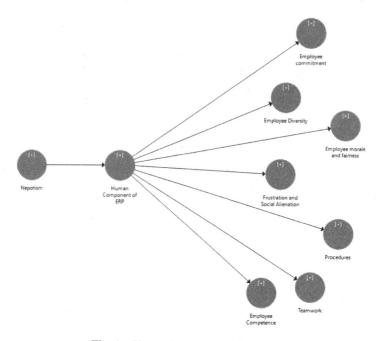

Fig. 1. The study conceptual framework

Study Hypotheses

The main study hypothesis is that nepotism has an impact on the human resources components of ERP systems in small and medium-sized organizations in Lebanon. This hypothesis is reflected by the following:

H1: Nepotism impacts employee competence in Lebanese small and medium-sized organizations

H2: Nepotism impacts employee diversity in Lebanese small and medium-sized organizations

H3: Nepotism impacts employee commitment in Lebanese small and medium-sized organizations

H4: Nepotism has an influence on the morale and fairness of employees in Lebanese small and medium-sized organizations

H5: Nepotism impact employee frustration and social alienation level in Lebanese small and medium-sized organizations

H6: Nepotism impacts procedures in Lebanese small and medium-sized organizations

H7: Nepotism impacts teamwork in Lebanese small and medium-sized organizations

Research Method Used

The study followed the exploratory research design attempting to explore the impact of nepotism on the HR component of ERP system implementation success. One hundred twenty-five companies are chosen in the City of Beirut, Lebanon. Only 69 surveys were returned. The survey questionnaire has two primary constructs. Table 1 lists the two

Table 1. Questionnaire primary constructs and its dimensions

S. No	Main constructs	Dimensions	No. of items
1	Nepotism	0	12
2	HR component of ERP implementation success	-Teamwork -Employee competence -Diversity -Moral and Fairness -Frustration and Social Alienation - Employee commitment - Procedures	42

primary constructs, dimensions and the number of items in measuring each dimension/construct in the questionnaire.

The collected data was coded and edited using Qualtrics Platform. The analysis technique used in this study variance-based SmartPLS structural equation modeling or partial least squares regression. This methodology verified the study hypotheses. The model is formulated using reflective measurements by testing first and second-order confirmations. The assessment of the reflection measurement model addresses convergent and discriminant validities, indicator reliability, and internal consistency reliability. The structural model assessment addresses multi-collinearity issues, path-coefficients, R^2, effect size F^2 and predictive relevant, Q^2.

4   Results and Discussions

Assessing the measurement model, the results of the model testing for the indicator reliability show that each indicator has a factor reliability value higher than the minimum acceptance of 0.7 (Chin 1998). Loadings on all items for latent construct are higher than 0.5, and this shows high indicator reliability. Cronbach's alpha is higher than 0.7, and this indicates as well a high indicator's validity. AVE is higher than 0.5, and this indicates acceptable convergent reliability. Internal consistency is indicated by a CR that is higher than 0.7 (Table 2).

Therefore, the test results for convergent validity were obtained using the average variance extracted. The results were above the minimum level, which means that every indicator that measures the construct meets the criteria of convergent validity. The test results show that nepotism impacts the human resource component of ERP systems implementations negatively. The test results indicated that successful ERP implementation could take place, considering other factors as stable, in a Lebanese small to medium organization that does not nourish nepotism. The latter is a significant factor that impacts the success of ERP implementation in contemporary organizations.

Table 2. Measurement model

	Items	Loadings[a]	Cronbach's Alpha[b]	rho_A	CR	AVE
Nepotism	Q9-1	0.965	0.966	0.971	0.971	0.771
	Q9-2	0.978				
	Q9-3	0.766				
	Q9-4	0.815				
	Q9-5	0.903				
	Q9-6	0.986				
	Q9-7	0.851				
	Q9-8	0.826				
Employee competence	Q2-1	0.882	0.938	0.964	0.955	0.842
	Q2-2	0.899				
	Q2-3	0.971				
	Q2-4	0.916				
Employee commitment	Q3-1	0.957	0.953	0.980	0.965	0.874
	Q3-2	0.904				
	Q3-3	0.929				
	Q3-4	0.948				
Employee diversity	Q4-1	0.844	0.936	0.976	0.953	0.835
	Q4-2	0.906				
	Q4-3	0.952				
	Q4-4	0.949				
Employee morale and fairness	Q5-1	0.972	0.951	0.956	0.965	0.872
	Q5-2	0.959				
	Q5-3	0.898				
	Q5-4	0.904				
Frustration and social alienation	Q6-1	0.955	0.866	0.931	0.922	0.752
	Q6-2	0.930				
	Q6-3	0.897				
	Q6-4	0.653				
Procedures	Q7-1	0.901	0.938	0.945	0.954	0.805
	Q7-2	0.932				
	Q7-3	0.944				
	Q7-4	0.777				
	Q7-5	0.922				
Teamwork	Q8-1	0.831	0.878	0.909	0.910	0.674
	Q8-2	0.875				
	Q8-3	0.839				
	Q8-4	0.609				
	Q8-5	0.917				

a. All item loadings > 0.5 indicate indicator reliability (Hulland 1999, p. 198)
b. All of Cronbach's alpha > 0.7 indicates indicator reliability (Nunally 1978)
c. All composite reliability (CR) > 0.7 indicates internal consistency (Gefen et al. 2000)
d. All Average Variance Extracted (AVE) > 0.5 indicates convergent reliability (Bagozzi and Yi 1988)

The following Table 3 shows a high discriminant validity as the diagonals present the square root of the AVE of the latent variables. Thus, they represent the highest loading factors.

Table 3. Discriminant validity: Fornell and Larcker criterion

	Emp Comp	Emp Divers	Emp Comm	Emp Moral	Frust and Al	H Comp.	Nepotism	Proce	Teamwk
Employee competence	**0.918**								
Employee diversity	0.118	**0.914**							
Employee commitment	−0.818	−0.263	**0.935**						
Emp. Morale	0.569	0.77	−0.742	**0.934**					
Frust and Al.	0.518	0.748	−0.701	0.952	**0.867**				
Human Comp.	0.557	0.814	−0.728	0.981	0.970	**0.814**			
Nepotism	0.525	0.78	−0.702	0.934	0.972	0.978	**0.878**		
Procedures	0.555	0.776	−0.702	0.966	0.979	0.989	0.978	**0.897**	
Teamwork	−0.586	−0.776	0.736	−0.916	−0.881	−0.96	−0.934	0.935	**0.828**

The diagonals are the square root of the AVE of the latent variables and indicate the highest in any column or row

Furthermore, assessing the structural model, The VIF values of the inner model are all below the threshold of 5. As a result, it is concluded that collinearity is not a critical issue. Multi-collinearity exists when two or more constructs are inter-correlated (Garson 2016).

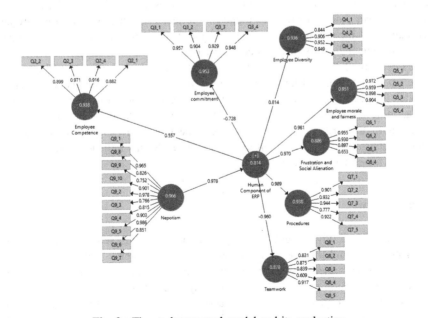

Fig. 2. The study structual model and its evaluation

The following Fig. 2 depicts the study structural model. The table following provides a comprehensive testing for the study hypotheses. The analysis of the results supports the 7 study hypotheses at high significance levels.

The following Table 4 presents the results of testing the study hypothesis. The analysis of the results supports the 7 study hypothesis at significant levels.

Table 4. Hypothesis testing

HP	Constructs Relationship	St. Beta	St. Error	t-value	p-value	Decision
H1	Nepotism -> Employee competence	0.545	0.117	4.664	0.00	Supported
H2	Nepotism -> Employee diversity	0.796	0.022	35.673	0.00	Supported
H3	Nepotism -> Employee commitment	0.712	0.047	15.264	0.00	Supported
H4	Nepotism -> Employee morale and fairness	0.96	0.007	145.718	0.00	Supported
H5	Nepotism -> Frustration and social alienation	0.949	0.007	140.739	0.00	Supported
H6	Nepotism -> Procedures	0.967	0.006	156.648	0.00	Supported
H7	Nepotism -> Teamwork	0.939	0.008	124.339	0.00	Supported

R^2 value falls at a level of 0.814 which is considered significant. The nature of hierarchical component model applied in this study does not require considering the R^2 value of the lower order constructs as it does not reflect any meaning since, they are just manifestations of the second order constructs and their measuring indicators are a part of the measuring indicators of the second order construct.

The effect size F2 follows Cohen (1988) guidelines which are 0.02, 0.15 and 0.35 indicate small, medium and large effect size respectively for exogenous constructs in the model. The results indicate large effects of the exogenous constructs in the study model as indicated by (Cohen 1988). For Q2, values of 0.02, 0.15 and 0.35 indicate small, medium and large predictive relevance respectively for exogenous constructs in the model (Hair et al., 2014, Fornell and Cha 1994). Results indicate large effect size respectively for exogenous construct in the model.

5   Conclusion

The outcome of the study presents a clear indication of a robust relationship that exists between nepotism and the HR component of the ERP system. Nepotism creates an unwelcoming environment for ERP systems. It impacts the human element of ERP systems implementation negatively. Therefore, system developers, industry specialists and top managers in organizations need to address and understand the negative impact of nepotism on the human resource factors in the ERP implementation process in order to increase the success of ERP systems implementations. The change will not happen overnight. It is a time-consuming process that will have a positive impact progressively. Despite the limitation of the study that was based on a limited sample of 68 collected surveys, it establishes a foundation for further, more in-depth, research orientations. Additional dimensions of research on the human component of ERP systems should be included. Other factors that could impact the successful implementation of ERP systems should be identified. Future research orientations may consider nepotism as a facet of organizational culture as literature presents limited studies in this context.

References

Aman, A., Mohamed, N.: The implementation of cloud accounting in the public sector. Asian J. Account. Gov. **8**(3), 1–6 (2017)

Aldraehim, M., Edwards, S.L., Watson, J., Chan, T.: Cultural impact on e-service use in Saudi Arabia: the role of Nepotism. Int. J. Infonomics **5**(3/4), 655–662 (2012)

Al-Salem, A.A.: A Case Study of the Organizational Culture of the Makkah Municipality in the Context of the Saudi Society (Unpublished doctoral dissertation). Temple University (1996)

AL-shawawreh, T.B.: Economic effects of using nepotism and cronyism in the employment process in the public sector institutions. Res. Appl. Econ. **8**(1), 58 (2016)

Al-Turki, U.M.: An exploratory study of ERP implementation in Saudi Arabia. Prod. Plan. Control **22**(4), 403–413 (2011)

Arshad, M., Hafiz Muhammad, Z., Yousuf, M., Muhammad, R.: Impact of Favoritism, Nepotism and Cronyism on Job Satisfaction a Study from the Public Sector of Pakistan. Institute of Interdisciplinary Business Research (2012)

Bagozzi, R.P., Yi, Y.: On the evaluation of structural equation models. J. Acad. Market. Sci. **16**(1), 74–94 (1988)

Biermeier-Hanson, B.: What about the rest of us? The importance of organizational culture in nepotistic environments. Ind. Organ. Psychol. **8**(1), 27–31 (2015). https://doi.org/10.1017/iop.2014.7

Briggs, E., Wated, G.: Proceedings of the National Conference on Undergraduate Research. In: Who's your Daddy? Addressing Nepotism from a Cultural Perspective, pp. 266–271. Utah, Weber State University (2012)

Chin, W.W.: The partial least squares approach for structural equation modeling. In: Marcoulides, G.A. (ed.) Modern Methods for Business Research. Methodology for Business and Management, pp. 295–336. Lawrence Erlbaum Associates Publishers, New Jersey (1998)

Cohen, J.: Statistical Power Analysis for the Behavioral Sciences. Lawrence Erlbaum Associates Inc., Hillsdale (1988)

Elbaz, A.M., Haddoud, M.Y., Shehawy, Y.M.: Nepotism, employees' competencies and firm performance in the tourism sector: a dual multivariate and qualitative comparative analysis approach. Tourism Manag. **67**, 3–16 (2018)

Finelli, G.M.: From The Dinner Table to the Boardroom: The Effect of Nepotism on Family Business (Unpublished doctoral dissertation). American University, Washington (2011)

Firfiray, S., Cruz, C., Neacsu, I., Gomez-Mejia, L.R.: Is nepotism so bad for family firms? A socioemotional wealth approach. Hum. Resource Manag. Rev. **28**(1), 83–97 (2018)

Fornell, C., Larcker, D.F.: Evaluating structural equation models with unobservable variables and measurement error. J. Market. Res. **18**(1), 39–50 (1981)

Garson, G.D.: Partial least squares regression & structural model statistical associates blue book series (2016)

Gefen, D., Straub, D.: The Relative Importance of Perceived Ease-ofUse in IS Adoption: A Study of e-Commerce Adoption. JAIS (forthcoming) (2000)

Hulland, J.: Use of partial least squares (PLS) in strategic management research: a review of four recent studies. Strategic Manag. J. **20**(2), 195–204 (1999)

Jaskiewicz, P., Uhlenbruck, K., Balkin, D.B., Reay, T.: Is nepotism good or bad? Types of nepotism and implications for knowledge management. Family Bus. Rev. **26**(2), 121–139 (2013). https://doi.org/10.1177/0894486512470841

Kragh, S.U.: The anthropology of nepotism: social distance and reciprocity in organizations in developing countries. Dev. Learn. Organ. Int. J. **27**(1) (2012). https://doi.org/10.1108/dlo.2013.08127aaa.006

Moghadam, R., Colomo-Palacios, R.: Information security governance in big data environments: a systematic mapping. Procedia Comput. Sci. **138**(7), 401–408 (2018)

Muhammad, R.S.: Bringing Along The Family: Nepotism In The Workplace (Unpublished master's thesis). University of Maryland, College Park (2011)

Mustafa, B.: The effects of nepotism and favoritism on employee behaviors and human resources practices: a research on Turkish public banks. Rev. Public Adm. (2011)

Nunnally, J.C.: Psychometric Theory, 2nd edn. McGraw-Hill, New York (1978)

Pelit, E., Dinçer, Fİ., Kılıç, İ.: The effect of nepotism on organizational silence, alienation and commitment: a study on hotel employees in Turkey. J. Manag. Res. **7**(4), 82 (2015). https://doi.org/10.5296/jmr.v7i4.7806

Saffiedine, K.: Lebanon's budget: Between fraudulent expenses and nepotism (2019). http://beirut-today.com/2018/02/01/lebanons-budget-fraudulent-expenses-nepotism/. Accessed 28 Oct 2019

Sarpong, D., Maclean, M.: Service nepotism in the multi-ethnic marketplace: mentalities and motivations. Int. Market. Rev. **32**(2), 160–180 (2015). https://doi.org/10.1108/imr-01-2014-0030

Urbanová, M., Dundelová, J.: Selected manifestations of social deviance in organizational culture. Romanian Sociol. **13**(2), 55–66 (2015)

Wassenaar, A., Shirley, G., Dirk, S.: ERP Implementation Management in Different Organizational and Cultural Settings (2002). https://www.researchgate.net/publication/228584084. Accessed 20 Nov 2019

Vveinhardt, J., Petrauskaitė, L.: Intensity of nepotism expression in organizations of Lithuania. Manag. Organ.: Syst. Res. **66**(66), 129–144 (2013a). https://doi.org/10.7220/mosr.1392.1142.2013.66.9

Vveinhardt, J., Petrauskaitė, L.: Nepotism as a cause and consequence of unhealthy organizational culture. Pridneprovsky Res. J. **7**(143), 90–95 (2013b)

Computationally Efficient Fine-Grain Cube CP-ABE Scheme with Partially Hidden Access Structure

Miada Murad, Yuan Tian, and Mznah A. Rodhaan[✉]

King Saud University, Riyadh, Saudi Arabia
rodhaan@KSU.EDU.SA

Abstract. In ciphertext policy attribute based encryption (CP-ABE), the private key is associated with the number of attributes and the data is encrypted with access policy. Most existing CP-ABE schemes suffer from the issue of having long ciphertext size. The ciphertext depends on the number of attributes in the access policy. Also, Most CP-ABE does not consider the recipients' anonymity, the encryptor-specified access structure is not hidden in the ciphertexts. Zhou et al. [1] proposed a construction of privacy preserving CP-ABE with constant ciphertext. However, [1] does not consider the importance of the attributes. On the other hand, existing weighted CP-ABE [2] consider the importance of the attributes but does not protect the recipients' anonymity and the efficiency, it requires increasing the ciphertext size with increasing number of attributes.

In this paper, we provide an affirmative answer to the above issue; we proposed a new construction of CP-ABE named as Computationally efficient Fine-Grain Cube CP-ABE with Partially Hidden Access Structure(denoted as Cube CP-ABE). CUBE CP-ABE reduces the ciphertext to constant size irrespective of the number of attribute in the access policy. Second, it protects the recipients" privacy. Third, it applies the idea of the weighted value. Forth, it is more granular than [2]. As far as we know, CUBE CP-ABE is the first construction with such properties. Our scheme is CPA-secure under Bilinear Diffie Hellman Exponent Assumption.

Keywords: CP-ABE · Efficiently · Hidden access-policy · Weighted attribute

1 Introduction

In fact, the data confidentiality and the data access control become one of the most important topics in cloud computing and in healthcare system, Nowadays nearly all patient information is transferred from old paper-based medical record to electronic medical record [3]. With the help of access control, the security of healthcare system is enhanced through different practices and policies, and only the authorized users can get access to resources [3–5].

The public key encryption is a tool to store the data in an encrypted format. In public key encryption, only the decryptor, who has the private key associated with public key which is one-to-one encryption, can decrypt. Recently, the Attribute-based encryption (ABE) is proposed, as it achieves one-to-many encryption. It is the solution

© Springer Nature Singapore Pte Ltd. 2020
Y. Tian et al. (Eds.): ICBDS 2019, CCIS 1210, pp. 135–156, 2020.
https://doi.org/10.1007/978-981-15-7530-3_10

to have secure fine-grain access control [6]. Fine-grain access control is the reliable solution to access the shared data on untrusted server, where the data is stored in an encrypted format, and only authorized users have the decryption key. Unauthorized user and the cloud server cannot collude to get the decryption key [7].

The attribute based encryption (ABE) can be divided into Key Policy ABE (KP-ABE) and Ciphertext-Policy ABE (CP-ABE). In KP-ABE [8], each private key is associated with an access structure P and each ciphertext is associated with a set of attributes S. In contrast, the situation in CP-ABE [2, 9, 10, 11, 12] is reversed, each private key is associated with a set of attributes S and each ciphertext is associated with an access structure P. A user can decrypt the ciphertext if S in the private key or the ciphertext satisfies an access structure P in the private key or the ciphertext. In both concepts, the collusion resistance property is an important property. Collusion resistance property means multiple users, whose private keys do not satisfy the ciphertext, cannot collude to decrypt that ciphertext.

ABE is either coarse-grain access control or fine-grain access control. In coarse-grain access control, a user with a set of attributes S is able to decrypt a ciphertext with a set of attributes S^* if $S^* \cap S = T$. This (S, T) threshold provides error tolerance, which is important especially for biometric applications. For Fine-grain access control like key-policy or ciphertext-policy, where a user with a set of attributes S is able to decrypt a ciphertext with a set of attributes S^* if $S^* \subseteq S$. The disadvantage of key-policy is that the encryptor encrypts with a set of descriptive attributes, thus the encryptor cannot decide who can decrypt the encrypted data. In addition, the encryptor should trust the key issuer that stores all access structure. However, in ciphertext-policy, the encryptor encrypt with a an access structure and can decide who can decrypt the encrypted data [13].

There are two approaches to hide access policy. It is partially hidden access structure and fully hidden access structure. Figure 1 shows an example of partially hidden access structure, the medical data is encrypted with access policy such that decryptor should be either (having id 13467 and patient) or (a doctor in a hospital in psychological department). In traditional CP-ABE everyone has the ciphertext can obtain the information in the access policy and know that there is a patient with id 13467 haveing psychological problem. In partially hidden CP-ABE, the attributed values are hidden and sent along with the encrypted data.

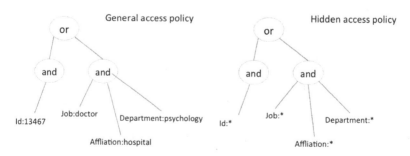

Fig. 1. General and hidden access policy.

There are several of ABE, where the ciphertext size, the private key size, and the decryption cost depend on the number of attributes in the access policy [2, 8, 14]. Actually, this is not suitable to send, store and share confidential data for resource-constraint applications.

Our contribution in this paper we present a computationally efficient fine-grain CUBE CP-ABE with partially hidden access structure denoted as (CUBE CP-ABE). First, Our scheme is efficient since it achieves constant ciphertext regardless of the number of attributes in CUBE access structure, while the previous scheme the ciphertext is increasing with the number of attributes. Second, CUBE CP-ABE scheme is more granular than previous scheme [2]; we can increase the number of weight value without decreasing the performance. Third, it is privacy preserving by having partially hidden CUBE access structure. Fourth, we propose CUBE Access System Model in which the attribute has weights according to its importance, and this structure is suitable for efficient CP-ABE. Fifth, we design a system to assign the attribute value and weights to users. Sixth, the CUBE CP-ABE scheme is CPA-secure under the Decisional Bilinear Diffie Hellman Exponent (ℓ-$BDFE$) Assumption.

In Sect. 2, we focus on the preliminaries that are used in our construction. In Sect. 3, the Proposed CUBE Access Control Model (CACM) is presented. Section 4 focuses on the Construction of Computationally Efficient Fine-Grain CUBE CP-ABE with Partially Hidden Access Structure Scheme. Section 5 explain the performance comparison respectively. Finally, in Sect. 6, we conclude the paper and propose some future work.

Related Work: The data is stored in encrypted format. The system access control needs to be designed so that users only access according to their permissions. And The system access control prevents an attacker from compromising authorized data. It requires authorization, authentication, safety and security. Previously, the data encrypted using users public key, and only users that have associate private key are able to decrypt. The traditional public key is coarse-grain access control and one-to-one encryption, where the data is encrypted for each specific user known in advance. Since there is a need to have fine-grained access control, there is also a need to have anonymous access control, and since the relation between users and resources is dynamic, the ABE is introduced, where a user's private keys and ciphertexts are associated with access policy. The access policy is defined by set attributes; the decryption is possible only if there is a match between the attributes of the ciphertext and the user's private keys. These attributes could include age, location, etc. Instead of specific identity in Identity Based Encryption (IBE) [15, 16].

The first attribute based encryption (ABE) was introduced [17] as fuzzy identity based encryption IBE. In this scheme, each biometric measurements of the identity is expressed as a set of attributes. It allows user *U1* with specific private key *PK1*, that reflect *U1* attribute list *L1*, to decrypt cipher text specified for user *U2* with private key *PK2* that reflect *U2* attribute list *L2*, if the lists *L1* and *L2* are close to each other and only subset of *PK1* are needed to decrypt. In fuzzy IBE, there are many decryptors for an encryptor. Each decryptor is associated with one attribute.

Many CP-ABE schemes with constant-size ciphertext and constant computation costs were proposed for a non-monotone AND gate access policy, [18, 19] and for threshold predicates in [20]. Both schemes are secure and have been proved using the decision Bilinear Diffie-Hellman Exponent assumption. In [21], CP-ABE with constant length was proposed..Irrespective of the increase in the number of attributes, the ciphertext and the secret key are constant in length, in addition, the decryption algorithm needs fewer and fixed numbers of pairings.

In [20, 21] the authors propose an attribute based encryption (ABE), where recipient-anonymous is preserved. The encryptor encrypts the ciphertext with hidden access structure, and the decryptor does not need to know(access) the access structure. If the set of attributes in the decryptors' private key satisfy the hidden access policy, the ciphertexts can be decrypted successfully. Else, the decryptors cannot decrypt the ciphertext or guess the hidden access structure.

The first privacy preserving ciphertext policy attribute-based encryption (ABE) construction was proposed [23]. It hides the encryptor-specific access structure, as it might reveal a clue of the encrypted data. In the hidden access structure, sets of the possible values of attributes are known in advance, the encryptors hide the values for successful encryption. For example, suppose a medical center encrypts medical files for patients with the access policy to allow psychologist and neurologist to decrypt the files. The access policy might give clues to the content; such as, encrypted files contain information about patients who have neurological diseases and psychological diseases.

One of the approaches to hide access policy is partially hidden access policy [23]. Each attribute includes two parts: attribute name and attribute value. The partially hidden access policy only hides attribute value. Also, in partially hidden access policy, the access policy has known format and known set of values that can be used to encrypt the ciphertext. In [23], two CP-ABE schemes are proposed with partially hidden ciphertext policies, where the encryptor hides subset of the possible value of each attribute to have successful decryption. In [24], the authors propose a policy anonymity ABE where a huge number of possible policies appeared but without specifying which exact policy is used to encrypt the ciphertext.

The other approach to hide access policy is Predicate Encryption (PE), which can be seen as a generalization of ABE with hidden policies. In predicate encryption schemes, the ciphertext is encrypted using Public Key PK. The ciphertext $CT(m, x)$ is a message M and access control policy x. The master key MK is used to generate the secret key $SK(y)$ for another secret policy y. The ciphertext $CT(m, x)$ is decrypted successfully using $SK(y)$ if $P(x, y) = 1$, if a set of ciphertext attributes and user attributes match. P is a predicate function defined as $P : X \times Y \Rightarrow \{0, 1\}$. The predicate function hides the information about the encrypted message as well as x, and it provides a good solution for privacy preserving ABE scheme.

Predicate encryption is an advanced class of encryption and it covers wide subclasses Anonymous IBE, hidden vector encryption (HVE) and inner-product encryption (IPE). Anonymous IBE is the simplest subclass and it includes a simple equality test. HVE subclass provides a conjunctive equality test. Finally, inner-product encryption (IPE) provides conjunctive or disjunction and equality test. To use inner-product encryption (IPE), the formula must be written in conjunction normal form (CNF) or disjunction normal form (DNF) that can cause super polynomial blowup in size. Unfortunately, while some PE constructions are very expressive, they are still quite limited. IPE implies HVE and HVE implies IBE [24, 25].

In [26–28] Anonymous IBE is proposed, where the message is encrypted for specific identity, the adversary can't guess which the identity that is allowed to have a successful decryption. In [28], Blind anonymous IBE is proposed, where the blind means that the user can request the decryption key for an identity, without revealing the identity for the key generation entity. In [27, 28, 31], a HVE is introduced. In a HVE, two attribute vectors are associated with a private key and a ciphertext. Similar to ABE schemes, HVE is classified into CP-HVE and KP-HVE, it depends if the wildcards {*} appear on encryption attribute vector on the ciphertext or the private key. In [27, 28], KP-HVE is presented, where the wildcards appear in the private key. The ciphertext attributes are vectors $\vec{x} = \{x_1, \ldots, x_\ell\}$ over alphabet $\sum$, the keys are associated with vectors $\vec{k} = \{k_1, \ldots, k_\ell\}$ over alphabet $\Sigma \cup \{*\}$. The predicate $match\left(\vec{x}, \vec{k}\right)$ is true, if for all $k_i \neq *$ implies $k_i = x_i$. In [31], two constant-size CP-HVE is introduced, where the wildcards appear in the ciphertext.

In [2, 8], the authors propose two weighted attribute based encryption schemes (WABE). In [2], they propose a cipher-text policy attribute based encryption (CP-ABE) scheme, which is proven to be secure under decision l-Expanded bilinear Diffie-Hellman exponent (l-Expanded BDHE) assumption. In [8], (KP-ABE) is proposed, it is proven to be secure under l-th Bilinear Diffie-Hellman Inversion Assumption. In WABE, a set of attributes is treated on a different level according to their importance in real life. The private key or the ciphertext is associated with weighted attributes or weighted access tree. A user can decrypt the ciphertext, if a set of weighted attributes in the private key or the ciphertext satisfies a weighted access tree in the private key or the ciphertext. However, in WABE construction, the length of ciphertext increases linearly with the number of attributes. When the number of attributes involved in the system is very large, it can greatly increase the storage space and the transmission cost.

2 Preliminaries

2.1 Bilinear Map

Let G and G_T be two multiplicative cyclic group of prime order p. Let g be a generator of G and e be a bilinear map, $e : G \times G \to G_T$. The bilinear map e has the following properties:

    I. Bilinearity: for all $u, v \in G$ and $a, b \in Z_p$, we have $e\left(u^a, v^b\right) = e(u, v)^{ab}$.
    II. Non-degeneracy: $e(g, g) \neq 1$.
    III. Computability: it is efficient to compute $e(u, v)$ for all $u, v \in G$

We say that G is a bilinear group if the group operation in G and the bilinear map $e : G \times G \to G_T$ are both efficiently computable. The map e is symmetric since $e\left(g^a, g^b\right) = e(g, g)^{ab} = e\left(g^b, g^a\right)$.

2.2   Complexities Assumption

The security of our system is based on a complexity assumption, which is Bilinear Diffie-Hellman Exponent assumption (ℓ-BDFE). Let G be a bilinear group of order q, g and h are random elements of G and α is a random element of Z_p. ℓ-BDFE is as follow:

For any polynomial time algorithm A, the probability shown in the Eq. 1 is negligible.

$$\left| \begin{array}{l} \Pr\left[A\left(g, h, g^{\alpha^1}, \ldots, g^{\alpha^\ell}, g^{\alpha^{\ell+2}}, \ldots, g^{\alpha^{2\ell}}, e(g,h)^{\alpha^{\ell+1}} = 1 \right) \right] - \\ \Pr\left[A\left(g, h, g^{\alpha^1}, \ldots, g^{\alpha^\ell}, g^{\alpha^{\ell+2}}, \ldots, g^{\alpha^{2\ell}}, Z = 1 \right) \right] \end{array} \right| \tag{1}$$

Definition 1: Decisional ℓ-BDFE is held in G if there is no efficient algorithm can solve ℓ-BDFE with non-negligible advantages.

2.3   CP-ABE Algorithms: Setup, Key Generation, Encryption and Decryption

The CP-ABE consists of four fundamentals algorithms: setup, key generation, encryption and decryption.

Setup: the setup algorithm takes an implicit security parameter. It outputs the public parameter PK and the secret key SK.

Key generation (PK, MK, S): The key generation takes public parameter, master key and a set of attributes S that describe the key and outputs the Private key SK.

Encryption (PK, W, M): The Encryption Algorithm takes the public Key PK, the Access structure W and the message M. It encrypts the message M and produces the ciphertext. Such that, only the user that has a set of attributes S, that satisfy the access structure W, will be able to decrypt the message.

Decryption (PK, SK, CT): The decryption algorithm takes as input the public key, the private key (for a set of attributes S), and the ciphertext that contains the access structure W. The algorithm will decrypt the ciphertext if S satisfies W.

2.4   Security Model for CP-ABE

Init: the Adversary $\mathcal{A}$ chooses the Access Structure W that he wishes to be challenged.

Setup: The challenger $\mathcal{B}$ runs the setup algorithm (CP-ABE) and gives the public parameter to the $\mathcal{A}$.

Phase 1: $\mathcal{A}$ is allowed to issue queries for a private key (for a set of attributes L) where $L| \neq W$. These queries can be repeated adaptively.

Challenge: $\mathcal{B}$ runs the encryption with W to obtain $\{ <c_0, c_1>, key\}$ and flips a random coin b. Then, he sets $key_0 = key$ and picks a random key_1. Finally, he sends $\{ <c_0, c_1>, key_b\}$ to $\mathcal{A}$.

Phase 2: as phase 1, $\mathcal{A}$ issues queries for private key, for a set of attribute L, where $L| \neq W$. These queries can be repeated adaptively.

Guess: the adversary output the guess b' of b where $b' \in \{0, 1\}$.

The advantage of $\mathcal{A}$ in this game is defined as $Adv(\mathcal{A}) := |Pr(b' = b) - \frac{1}{2}|$.

Definition 2: A CP-ABE is secure in selective-set model of security if no polynomial time adversary $\mathcal{A}$ has non-negligible advantages in the selective set game.

3   Proposed Cube Access Control Model (CACM)

Before introducing Cube CP-ABE, we first give the proposed a system model. The proposed system model is Cube Access Control Model. Figure 2 shows how to use attribute to form data access policy.

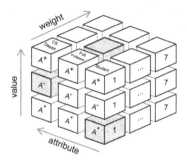

Fig. 2. The proposed CUBE access structure.

3.1   Cube Access Control Model (CACM)

In this paper, we propose 3D Access Structure instead of 2D Access Structure introduced in [2, 8, 16]. The proposed access structure has the same access structure denote as $AND^*_{-,+}$ gate proposed in [32]. Each attribute has three values positive value, negative value, and wildcards. The Cube access structure is like [2, 8] since each attribute is described by its weight. The attribute value has different weights according to its importance in the access control system, as in tree access structure in [2, 8]. Cube access structure is proposed to have an efficient weighted CP-ABE.

Cube Access structure: let $U = \{A_1, A_2, A_3, \ldots, A_k\}$, a set of attributes in the system and $|A| = k$. Each A_i, where $1 \leq i \leq k$, can receive one of three values $\{V_i^+, V_i^-, V_i^*\}$ where $|V_i| = 3$. Each attributes could take any weight value ranging from 1 to 7. Let's suppose the range of weight value for A_i and V_j is $W_{i,j} = \{W_{i,j,1}, W_{i,j,2}, \ldots, W_{i,j,7}\}$, where $|W_{i,j}| = 7$.

Definition 3: A user's attribute list is defined as $L = \{L[i] | i \in [1, 2k]\}$, where $L[i] \in \{A_i^+, A_i^-, A_i^*\}$ for $i \in [1, k]$, $S = S^+ \cup S^-$ Where $S^+ = \{A^+ | i \in [1, k]\}$ and $S^- = \{A^- | i \in [1, k]\}$, and $S^+ \cup S^- = \phi$. A_i^* denotes to a wildcard value, which means do not care of the value A_i. $L[i] \in \{1, 2, 3, \ldots, 7\}$. For $i \in [1+k, 2k]$.

Definition 4: The user list, $S = \{A_1, A_2, A_3, \ldots, A_{2k}\}$, satisfies the Cube access policy, $W = \{W_1, W_2, W_3, \ldots, W_{2k}\}$, denoted as $S| = W$ if $A_i = W_i$ for $i \in [1, 2k]$.

For example, Eq. 2 defined the list of user attributes, can be presented in Fig. 2.

$$L[u] = \left\{ \begin{array}{c} (cs\ Depart,\ A^-, 1), \\ (Full\ Professor, A^+, 2), \\ (Student, A^*, 1) \end{array} \right\} \tag{2}$$

3.2 Anonymized Cube Access Control Model

In order to define an anonymized CUBE Access Policy, we remove all identifying attribute values $\{A^+, A^-\}$ where ⌘ represent "do not care". Also, we remove all the weighted values. Let $W = \{W[i]\}, i \in [1, 2k]$ where $W[i]$ is the value of the attribute for $i \in [1, k]$ and $W[i]$ is the value of the weights of the attribute respectively for i $\in [k + 1\ to\ 2k]$. Figure 3 and Fig. 4 show an example of anonymized CUBE access policy.

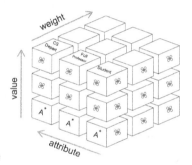

Fig. 3. The proposed anonymized CUBE access structure

Figure 3 shows an example of an anonymized CUBE access structure, where the values of the attributes are hidden except for the wildcard values A^*.

Figure 4 shows an example of a user anonymized Cube access structure. It shows three sub-cubes from the Cube access policy in the left and three sub-cubes from the anonymized Cube access policy on the right. Each sub-cubes represents specific attribute value and weight. For example, the sub-cube CS department has value A^- and weight 1. The three sub cube on the right shows that the values of CS department and full professor are hidden, but the attribute student is not.

3.3 The Weighted Value

In a real scenario, different attributes have different importance. We will give an example to explain why different attributes have different importance in practical scenario. For instance; the doctor wants both the general nurse and the nurse manager to decrypt a patient's medical record. We assign the nurse manager with attribute value nurse as weight 2, also, we assign the general nurse with attribute value nurse as weight 1.

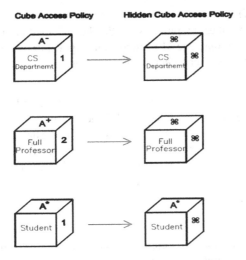

Fig. 4. Sub-cubes of the proposed anonymized cube access structure.

The general nurse does not have the right to read patients medical records encrypted for the nurse manager.

We may choose to give a third nurse the right to read specific patients medical records because of emergency. We give him/her the right by assigning the nurse with attribute value nurse as weight 3.

We encrypt the patients' medical records, so nurse with the highest weight (3) can decrypt it.

4   Construction of Computationally Efficient Fine-Grain Cube CP-ABE with Partially Hidden Access Structure Scheme

The Cube CP-ABE schemes consist of four algorithms based on the general CP-ABE algorithms defined in Sect. 2.3:

Setup (1λ, k)
The Setup algorithm takes the security parameter 1λ, the number of weights k, and the number of attributes in the system k as input. It returns public key PK and master key MK. The public key is used for encryption while central authority holds the master key for private key generation.

KeyGen (PK, MK, L)
The KeyGen algorithm takes the public key PK, the master key MK and the user's weighted attribute list L as input. It outputs the private key SK associated with user's weighted attribute list L.

Encrypt (PK, W, M)

The Encrypt algorithm takes the public key PK, the specified partially Hidden CUBE access policy W, and the message M as input. The algorithm outputs ciphertext CT, if the user with L satisfying W can decrypt the message $(L| = W)$.

Decrypt (PK, SK, CT)

It takes the public key PK, the private key SK of the user and the ciphertext CT as input. CT includes the partially hidden CUBE access policy W. It returns a valid plaintext M if $L| = W$, where L is the user's weighted attribute list and W is the weighted access policy hidden from the ciphertext. The Decrypt algorithm decrypts the ciphertext when the user's weighted attribute list satisfies the partially hidden CUBE access policy.

4.1 Computationally Efficient Fine-Grain CUBE CP-ABE with Partially Hidden Access Structure Scheme

We present a Computationally efficient Fine-Grain Cube CP-ABE with Partially Hidden Access Structure Scheme denoted as (Cube CP-ABE) and provide security under bilinear diffie Hellman Exponent Assumption (ℓ-BDHE). In our CP-ABE, we use the proposed CUBE Access Control Model (CACM). In CACM, we have a set of attributes. Each attribute has three values positive value, negative value, and wildcards. This is similar to access structure in [32]. Our access structure includes a weighted value as in [2, 8] for each attribute with specific value. The Cube access control model is proposed to have efficient weighted CP-ABE. In Cube CP-ABE, The size of the ciphertext is not related with the number of attributes. To the best of our knowledge, no scheme has advantages of our proposed scheme Cube CP-ABE, because Cube CP-ABE enables a constant ciphertext length, it has Partially hidden Cube Access Structure, and its attributes have weights. Finally, in Cube CP-ABE, increasing the granularity does not affect the performance in the same time. The concrete construction of Cube CP-ABE is as follows:

Setup. Assuming we have k attribute value and k Weights $\{A_1, \ldots, A_k, W_1, .., W_k\}$ in the system. We have $\ell = 10 \times k$. Each attribute A_i has 3 values $\{A_i^+, A_i^-, A_i^*\}$ and each attribute value $W_{i,j}$ has 7 values $\{W_{i,1}, \ldots, W_{i,7}\}$. We map the weight value and the attribute value to integer as shown in Table 1.

Increasing the number of weights ω, increases the granularity and does not decrease the performance. The chosen value ω depends on the tradeoff between the granularity and preprocessing regarding to the calculating the table in the setup process. In our construction, the value ω is chosen randomly from a finite set of rational number $\omega \in Z_p$. In this paper, we set ω to 7.

The trusted authority uses symmetric pairing and chooses two bilinear group $e : G_0 \times G_0 = G_1$ of prime order p. Then it picks a random generator $g \in G_0$ and $\alpha \in Z_P$. It computes g_i as shown in Eq. 3. Then, it takes random $\gamma \in Z_P$ and set v as shown in Eq. 4. The public key and the master key are shown in Eq. 5 and Eq. 6 respectively.

Table 1. Mapping weight and attribute values to integer.

Attribute & value	A1	A2	A3	...	Ak
W1	1	2	3	...	K
W2	k + 1	k + 2	k + 3	...	2k
W3	2k + 1	2k + 2	2k + 3	...	3k
W4	3k + 1	3k + 2	3k + 3	...	4k
W5	4k + 1	4k + 2	4k + 3	...	5k
W6	5k + 1	5k + 2	5k + 3	...	6k
W7	6k + 1	6k + 2	6k + 3	...	7k
A+	7k + 1	7k + 2	7k + 3	...	8k
A−	8k + 1	8k + 2	8k + 3	...	9k
A*	9k + 1	9k + 2	9k + 3	...	10k

$$g_i = g^{\alpha^i}$$
$$For\ i = 1, 2, 3, \ldots, \ell, \ell+1, \ell+2, \ldots, 2\ell. \tag{3}$$
$$Where\ \ell = 10 \times k$$

$$v = g^{\gamma} \in G_0 \tag{4}$$

$$PK = \{g, g1, g2, \ldots, g\ell, g\ell+2, \ldots, g2\ell, v\} \in G_0^{2\ell+1} \tag{5}$$

$$MS = \{\gamma, \alpha\} \tag{6}$$

Key Generation. Each user u is tagged with a weighted attribute list. The list contains k attributes and k weights value as shown in Eq. 7.

$$L_u = \left\{ L_u[i]_{i \in [1,2k]} \right\}$$
$$L_u = \{V_1, \ldots, V_k, W_1, \ldots, W_k\}$$
$$where\ 8k \geq L_u \geq 9k\ For\ i \in [1, k] \tag{7}$$
$$and\ 1 \geq L_u \geq 7k\ For\ i \in [1+k, 2k]$$

Then, it Compute D, D_i, F_i and SK_u _for the user u as shown in the Eq. 8 to Eq. 12 respectively. The trusted authority selects random number $\{r_i\}$ for attribute vector for $i \in [1, k]$ and for weighted vector for $i \in [1+k, 2k]$ where $r_i \in Z_p$:

$$r = \sum_{i=1}^{i=2k} r_i \tag{8}$$

$$D = g^{\gamma \cdot r} = v^r \tag{9}$$

$$D_i = g^{\gamma \left(\alpha^{L_u[i]} + r_i \right)}$$
$$D_i = g^{\gamma}_{L_u[i]} \cdot g^{\gamma \cdot r_i} \tag{10}$$
$$\forall i \in [1, 2k]$$

$$F_i = g^{\gamma \left(\alpha^{9k+i} + r_i \right)}$$
$$F_i = g^{\gamma}_{9k+i} \cdot g^{\gamma \cdot r_i} \tag{11}$$
$$\forall i \in [1, k]$$

$$SK_u = \left\{ \begin{array}{c} \{D\} \\ \{D_i\}_{i \in [1,2k]} \\ \{F_i\}_{i \in [1,k]} \end{array} \right\} \tag{12}$$

Encryption. We suppose the Cube Access Structure is W with key attributes and corresponding weights. The value of weights is from 1 to 7 where 1 means no weight is given and 7 is the highest weight. The values of attributes from 8k to 10k are positive, negative or wildcard. The Encryptor picks a random t in Z_p and uses one time symmetric encryption as shown in the Eq. 13 and Eq. 14. The encryptor first encrypts the message 9 using symmetric key and set c_0 and c_1 as shown in Eq. 15 and Eq. 16.

$$key = (g\ell, g1)^{2kt} \tag{13}$$

$$\{M\}_{key} \tag{14}$$

$$C_0 = g^t \tag{15}$$

$$C_1 = \left(v \prod_{j \in W} g\ell + 1 - j \right)^t \tag{16}$$

The encryptor anonymizes the access policy. The anonymized Cube access policy is shown in Eq. 17. The encryptor hides the attribute value and the weights value except do not care value A^*. Assume the Cube access policy is W.

$$\bar{W} = \left(W \cap A_i^* \right) \forall i \in [1, 2k] \tag{17}$$

We adopt an anonymized Cube access policy construction. So that, each decryptor needs to decrypt once on each ciphertext header. The ciphertext is shown in Eq. 18.

$$CT = \left(\bar{W}, \{M\}_{key}, g^t, \left(v \prod_{j \in W} g\ell + 1 - j \right)^t \right)$$

$$CT = \left(\bar{W}, \{M\}_{key}, Hdr \right) \tag{18}$$

Where the ciphertext header $Hdr = \{C_0, C_1\}$

The user u has little information about the anonymized access policy. If $L_u| = \bar{W}$, then u can recover the plaintext and the access policy. If $L_u|| = \bar{W}$, then u cannot recover the plaintext neither the access policy. u should not try a large number of access policies when performing decryption.

Decryption. The user u constructs a local guess of the Cube access policy, the anonymized Cube access policy denoted as $\bar{W}$. The algorithm works by only one guess for $\bar{W}[i]$ for $i = 1$ to $2k$ as shown in Fig. 5. The algorithm is proposed in [1]. It will replace hidden value in the $\bar{W}$ with corresponding value of the u. If the guess is identical to actual Cube access policy, the decryption succeeds otherwise it fail.

Initialize $\hat{W} = \bar{W}$

   For $i = 1$ *to* $2k$

If $\bar{W}[i] == ⌘$ then

        $\hat{W}[i] = L[i]$

    End if

  EndFor

Return $\hat{W}$

Fig. 5. Algorithm to construct a local guess.

Then, u calculates T_0 and T_1 $\forall i \in [1, 2k]$, as shown in Eq. 19, Eq. 20 and Eq. 21. For $i \in [1, 2k]$, u calculates T_0 as shown in Eq. 19. For $i \in [1, k]$, u computes T_1 as shown in Eq. 20 if $\hat{W}[i] \in L_u$ or as in Eq. 21 if $\hat{W}[i] \in A^*$. For $i \in [1 + k, 2k]$ which is the weighted vector. u computes T_1 as in Eq. 19.

$$T_0 = e\left(g_{\widehat{W}[i]}, C_1\right)$$

$$T_0 = e\left(g^{\alpha^{\widehat{W}[i]}}, g^{t\left(\gamma + \sum_{j\in W}\alpha^{\ell+1-j}\right)}\right) \tag{19}$$

$$T_0 = e(g,g)^{t\gamma\alpha^{\widehat{W}[i]}} + t\sum_{j\in\widehat{W}}\alpha^{\ell+1-j+\widehat{W}[i]}$$

$$T_1 = e\left(D[i]. \sum_{j\in\widehat{W}, j\neq\widehat{W}[i]} g_{\ell+1-j+\widehat{W}[i]}, C_0\right)$$

$$T_1 = e\left(g^t g^{\gamma\left(\alpha^{\widehat{W}[i]} + r_i\right)} + \sum_{j\in\widehat{W}, j\neq\widehat{W}[i]}\alpha^{\ell+1-j+\widehat{W}[i]}\right) \tag{20}$$

$$T_1 = e(g,g)^{t\gamma\left(\alpha^{\widehat{W}[i]} + r_i\right)} + \sum_{j\in\widehat{W}, j\neq\widehat{W}[i]}\alpha^{\ell+1-j+\widehat{W}[i]}$$

$$T_1 = e\left(F[i]. \sum_{j\in\widehat{W}, j\neq\widehat{W}[i]} g_{\ell+1-j+\widehat{W}[i]}, C_0\right)$$

$$T_1 = e\left(g^t g^{\gamma\left(\alpha^{\widehat{W}[i]} + r_i\right)} + \sum_{j\in\widehat{W}, j\neq\widehat{W}[i]}\alpha^{\ell+1-j+\widehat{W}[i]}\right) \tag{21}$$

$$T_1 = e(g,g)^{t\gamma\left(\alpha^{\widehat{W}[i]} + r_i\right)} + \sum_{j\in\widehat{W}, j\neq\widehat{W}[i]}\alpha^{\ell+1-j+\widehat{W}[i]}$$

After that, u calculates $\frac{T_0}{T_1}$ for $i \in [1, 2k]$ as shown in Eq. 22. It calculates the production of all the quotient value for all k values in attribute vector and k values in weighted vector as shown in Eq. 23. Then, u calculates $e(D, C_0)$ as shown in Eq. 24. Then, it multiplies the result with Eq. 23 and Eq. 24. We get the symmetric key as in Eq. 25. The symmetric key will be used to decrypt the message. The symmetric $key = e(g,g)^{2kt\alpha^{\ell+1}} = e(g\ell, g1)^{2kt}$ if the guessed access policy is equal to encrypted access policy $\widehat{W} = W$.

$$\frac{T_0}{T_1} = e(g,g)^{-t\gamma r_i + t\alpha^{\ell+1}}$$

$$\text{(22)}$$

$$For \; i \in [1, 2k]$$

$$e(g,g)^{-t\gamma(r_1 + r_2 + r_3 + \dots + r_{2k}) + 2kt\alpha^{(\ell+1)}}$$
$$= e(g,g)^{-t\gamma r + 2kt\alpha^{\ell+1}}$$

$$\text{(23)}$$

$$e(D_c, D_0) = e(g,g)^{t\gamma r}$$

$$\text{(24)}$$

$$e(g,g)^{-t\gamma r + 2tk\alpha^{\ell+1}} \times e(g,g)^{t\gamma r}$$
$$= e(g,g)^{2tk\alpha^{\ell+1}} = e(g\ell, g1)^{2tk}$$

$$\text{(25)}$$

5 Performance Comparison

We will compare the efficiency, privacy, and expressiveness with applied weighted value among different available ABE schemes. Table 2 and Table 3 show the performance comparison between our construction and the previous CP-ABE constructions. We compare our scheme with **CZF-1** and **CZF-2** by C. Chen [19], **ZH** scheme by Z. Zhou [9], **ZHW** scheme by Z. Zhou [1] and **LMXM** scheme by X. Liu [2]. Our construction has partially hidden access policy and constant ciphertext size like **ZHW** scheme and applies the weighted value like **LMXM** scheme.

Table 2. Comparisons with other attribute based encryption.

Scheme	Enc	Dec	SK	Ciphertext	Weighted value
[19] CZF-1	3e	2p	$\ell\mathbb{G}$	$\|\mathbb{G}_T\| + 2\|\mathbb{G}\|$	No
[19] CZF-2	6e	6p + 2e	$\ell\mathbb{G}$	$\|\mathbb{G}_T\| + 3\|\mathbb{G}\| + \mathbb{Z}_p$	No
[9] ZH	2e	(2 t +1) p	$(2\ell+1)\mathbb{G}$	$\|\mathbb{G}_T\| + 2\|\mathbb{G}\|$	No
[1] ZHW	2e	(2 t +1) p	$(2\ell+1)\mathbb{G}$	$\|\mathbb{G}_T\| + 2\|\mathbb{G}\|$	No
[2] LMXM	E	((m.w) + m +1)p	$4\|X\|\|\mathbb{G}\| + 4\|X\|\|\omega\|\|\mathbb{G}\|$	$\|\mathbb{G}_T\| + 2\|Y\|\|\mathbb{G}\|$	Yes
Ours	2e	(2 t +1) p	$(2\ell+1)\mathbb{G}$	$\|\mathbb{G}_T\| + 2\|\mathbb{G}\|$	Yes

Let us discuss about the memory requirement of our construction based on secret key size $|SK|$ and ciphertext size $|CT|$. We compare with other construction in term of first, G and G_T, the size of element of bilinear group. Second, ℓ the number of attributes used in attribute university $\mathbb{U}$ in AND gate access structure. Third $|X|$ the size of the attributes set in tree based access structure. Forth, $|Y|$ the number of the leaf node in the

Table 3. Comparisons with other attribute based encryption.

Scheme	Expressiveness	Hidden policy
[19] CZF-1	AND-Gate	No
[19] CZF-2	AND-Gate	No
[9] ZH	AND-Gate	No
[1] ZHW	AND-Gate	Yes
[2] LMXM	Weighted tree structure	No
Ours	Weighted cube structure	Yes

tree Access structure. Finally, $|\omega|$ the size of weighted set. In case of $|CT|$, Table 2 and Fig. 6 show that our scheme has constant size like CZF-1, CZF-2 and ZH, but in LMXM scheme $|CT|$ increased linearly with $|Y|$ and $|\omega|$.

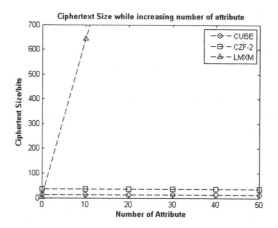

Fig. 6. Ciphertext size comparison with other CP-ABE.

For $|SK|$, Table 3 shows that for our scheme, the $|SK|$ is increasing linearly with ℓ like all other system CZF, ZH and ZHW. In LMXM the $|SK|$ increased linearly with $|X|$ and $|\omega|$. The performance of our scheme is better than LMXM as shown in the Fig. 7.

Let us compare the computation time for encryption Enc and the computation time for decryption Dec between our scheme and other schemes. Since all CP-ABE schemes shown in Table 2 are pairing-based encryption scheme, we assume the highest computation cost for decryption and encryption are pairing computation p and exponential computation e. The *Enc* is constant in all CP-ABE Schemes as all have constant number of e. The number of pairing in the decryption is constant in CZF-1 and CZF-2, increasing linearly with t in ZH and ZHW, where t is the number of attributes the user has to hold in order to satisfy the access policy. While d increases linearly with m in LMXM, where m is the minimal size of the leaf node that satisfy the access structure. In

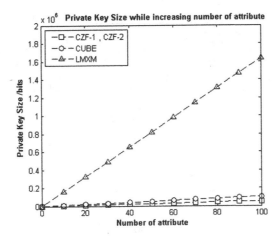

Fig. 7. Secret key size comparing with others CP-ABE.

our Cube CP-ABE, the decryption cost increase linearly with t but the performance is better than LMXM as shown in Fig. 8.

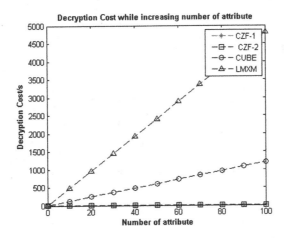

Fig. 8. Decryption cost comparison with other CP-ABE.

Figure 9 shows the tradeoff between granularity and efficiency when choosing the number of weights value w. In Fig. 10, we set w to 2,7 and 20. For LMXM, Fig. 9 shows that the increase of w, will increase the granularity but at the same time increase $|SK|$. The increase of the $|SK|$ decrease the efficiency. For Cube, Fig. 9 shows that the increase of w do not affect the $|SK|$ or the performance. Figure 10 shows the tradeoff between granularity and efficiency when choosing the number of weights value w. In Fig. 10, we set w to 2, 7 and 20. For LMXM, Fig. 10 shows that the increase of w this

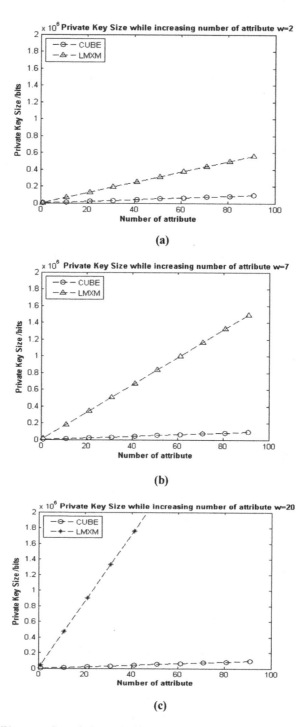

Fig. 9. Tradeoff between Granularity and Efficiency regarding to the private key (a) when w = 2 (b) when w = 7 (c) when w = 20.

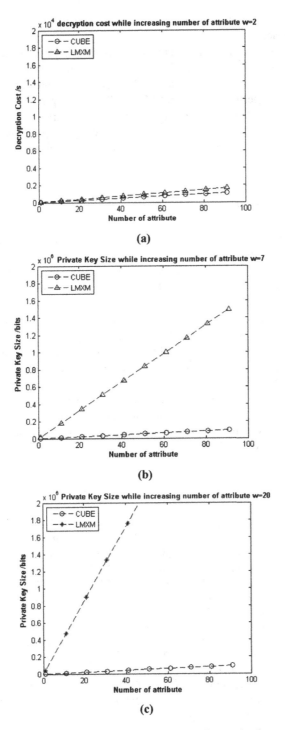

Fig. 10. Tradeoff Between Granularity and Efficiency regarding to the decryption cost (a) when w = 2 (b) when w = 7 (c) when w = 20.

will increase the granularity but at the same time increase d. The increase of the d decreases the efficiency.

In general, our scheme has advantages over LMXM since it uses the proposed Cube access structure to apply the idea of weighted value and make the ciphertext size constant instead of increase linearly like LMXM. Second, in our scheme, the $|SK|$ size and d cost has better performance than LMXM. Third, it is privacy preserving since it applies the idea of hidden access structure as in ZHW. Fourth, in our scheme we can increase the granularity by increasing w without affecting the performance in term of d and $|SK|$. In LMXM, the computation of d and $|SK|$ decrease when increasing the value of w.

6 Conclusion and Future Work

In this paper, we have presented a Cube CP-ABE scheme. In Cube CP-ABE, the attributes have different weight values according to their importance in the system as in [2, 8]. CUBE CP-ABE is efficient by having constant size ciphertext. The decryption cost and the secret key size in CUBE CP-ABE increases linearly while increasing the number of attribute. It has a better performance than the previous Ciphertext-Policy Weighted Attribute Based Encryption (CP-WABE) scheme [2]. In CUBE CP-ABE we increase the granularity by increasing the number of weighted value. This increase does not affect the performance of the secret key size and the decryption cost, while for [2] the increase of weighted value will decrease the performance of secret key size and decryption cost. Our Scheme is privacy preserving by using partially hidden Access structure. The future research of our scheme can be easily extended to be more efficient with constant private key size and constant number of pairing, and constant decryption cost irrespective of the number of attribute. Also, Our work could be extended to have Fully Hidden Cube Access Structure.

References

1. Zhou, Z., Huang, D., Wang, Z.: Efficient privacy-preserving ciphertext-policy attribute based encryption and broadcast encryption. IEEE Trans. Comput. **PP**(99), 1 (2013)
2. Liu, X., Ma, J., Xiong, J., Li, Q., Ma, J.: Ciphertext-policy weighted attribute based encryption for fine-grained access control. In: 2013 5th International Conference on Intelligent Networking and Collaborative Systems (INCoS), pp. 51–57 (2013)
3. Røstad, L.: Access control in healthcare information systems. Norwegian University of Science and Technology (2008)
4. Aydogan, Y., Stunkel, C.B., Aykanat, C., Abali, B.: Adaptive source routing in multistage interconnection networks. In: Parallel Processing Symposium 1996, Proceedings of IPPS 1996, The 10th International, pp. 258–267 (1996)
5. Gunti, N., Sun, W., Xu, M., Liu, Z., Niamat, M., Alam, M.: A healthcare information system with augmented access controls. In: Sheng, Q.Z., Wang, G., Jensen, Christian S., Xu, G. (eds.) APWeb 2012. LNCS, vol. 7235, pp. 792–795. Springer, Heidelberg (2012). https://doi.org/10.1007/978-3-642-29253-8_80

6. Balu, A., Kuppusamy, K.: Privacy preserving ciphertext policy attribute based encryption. In: Meghanathan, N., Boumerdassi, S., Chaki, N., Nagamalai, D. (eds.) CNSA 2010. CCIS, vol. 89, pp. 402–409. Springer, Heidelberg (2010). https://doi.org/10.1007/978-3-642-14478-3_40

7. Yuan, Q., Ma, C., Lin, J.: Fine-grained access control for big data based on CP-ABE in cloud computing. In: Wang, H., Qi, H., Che, W., Qiu, Z., Kong, L., Han, Z., Lin, J., Lu, Z. (eds.) ICYCSEE 2015. CCIS, vol. 503, pp. 344–352. Springer, Heidelberg (2015). https://doi.org/10.1007/978-3-662-46248-5_42

8. Liu, X., Zhu, H., Ma, J., Ma, J., Ma, S.: Key-policy weighted attribute based encryption for fine-grained access control. In: 2014 IEEE International Conference on Communications Workshops (ICC), pp. 694–699 (2014)

9. Zhou, Z., Huang, D.: On efficient ciphertext-policy attribute based encryption and broadcast encryption: extended abstract. In: Proceedings of the 17th ACM Conference on Computer and Communications Security, New York, NY, USA, pp. 753–755 (2010)

10. Pérez, S., Rotondi, D., Pedone, D., Straniero, L., Núñez, M.J., Gigante, F.: Towards the CP-ABE application for privacy-preserving secure data sharing in IoT contexts. In: Barolli, L., Enokido, T. (eds.) IMIS 2017. AISC, vol. 612, pp. 917–926. Springer, Cham (2018). https://doi.org/10.1007/978-3-319-61542-4_93

11. Sandhia, G.K., Kasmir Raja, S.V., Jansi, K.R.: Multi-authority-based file hierarchy hidden CP-ABE scheme for cloud security. Serv. Oriented Comput. Appl. **12**(3), 295–303 (2018)

12. Zhang, L., Cui, Y., Mu, Y.: Improving privacy-preserving CP-ABE with hidden access policy. In: Sun, X., Pan, Z., Bertino, E. (eds.) ICCCS 2018. LNCS, vol. 11065, pp. 596–605. Springer, Cham (2018). https://doi.org/10.1007/978-3-030-00012-7_54

13. Qiao, Z., Liang, S., Davis, S., Jiang, H.: Survey of attribute based encryption. In: 2014 15th IEEE/ACIS International Conference on Software Engineering, Artificial Intelligence, Networking and Parallel/Distributed Computing (SNPD), pp. 1–6 (2014)

14. Bethencourt, J., Sahai, A., Waters, B.: Ciphertext-policy attribute-based encryption. In: Proceedings of the 2007 IEEE Symposium on Security and Privacy, Washington, DC, USA, pp. 321–334 (2007)

15. Masood, R., Shibli, M.A., Ghazi, Y., Kanwal, A., Ali, A.: Cloud authorization: exploring techniques and approach towards effective access control framework. Front. Comput. Sci. **9** (2), 297–321 (2014). https://doi.org/10.1007/s11704-014-3160-4

16. Samarati, P., de Vimercati, S.C.: Access control: policies, models, and mechanisms. In: Focardi, R., Gorrieri, R. (eds.) FOSAD 2000. LNCS, vol. 2171, pp. 137–196. Springer, Heidelberg (2001). https://doi.org/10.1007/3-540-45608-2_3

17. Sahai, A., Waters, B.: Fuzzy identity-based encryption. In: Cramer, R. (ed.) EUROCRYPT 2005. LNCS, vol. 3494, pp. 457–473. Springer, Heidelberg (2005). https://doi.org/10.1007/11426639_27

18. Tran, P. V. X., Dinh, T. N., Miyaji, A.: Efficient ciphertext-policy ABE with constant ciphertext length. In: 2012 7th International Conference on Computing and Convergence Technology (ICCCT), Seoul, pp. 543–549 (2012)

19. Chen, C., Zhang, Z., Feng, D.: Efficient ciphertext policy attribute-based encryption with constant-size ciphertext and constant computation-cost. In: Boyen, X., Chen, X. (eds.) ProvSec 2011. LNCS, vol. 6980, pp. 84–101. Springer, Heidelberg (2011). https://doi.org/10.1007/978-3-642-24316-5_8

20. Ge, A., Zhang, R., Chen, C., Ma, C., Zhang, Z.: Threshold ciphertext policy attribute-based encryption with constant size ciphertexts. In: Susilo, W., Mu, Y., Seberry, J. (eds.) ACISP 2012. LNCS, vol. 7372, pp. 336–349. Springer, Heidelberg (2012). https://doi.org/10.1007/978-3-642-31448-3_25

21. Doshi, N., Jinwala, D.: Hidden access structure ciphertext policy attribute based encryption with constant length ciphertext. In: Thilagam, P.S., Pais, A., Chandrasekaran, K., Balakrishnan, N. (eds.) ADCONS 2011. LNCS, vol. 7135, pp. 515–523. Springer, Heidelberg (2012). https://doi.org/10.1007/978-3-642-29280-4_60

22. Li, J., Ren, K., Zhu, B., Wan, Z.: Privacy-aware attribute-based encryption with user accountability. In: Samarati, P., Yung, M., Martinelli, F., Ardagna, C.A. (eds.) ISC 2009. LNCS, vol. 5735, pp. 347–362. Springer, Heidelberg (2009). https://doi.org/10.1007/978-3-642-04474-8_28

23. Nishide, T., Yoneyama, K., Ohta, K.: Attribute-based encryption with partially hidden encryptor-specified access structures. In: Bellovin, S.M., Gennaro, R., Keromytis, A., Yung, M. (eds.) ACNS 2008. LNCS, vol. 5037, pp. 111–129. Springer, Heidelberg (2008). https://doi.org/10.1007/978-3-540-68914-0_7

24. Müller, S., Katzenbeisser, S.: Hiding the policy in cryptographic access control. In: Meadows, C., Fernandez-Gago, C. (eds.) STM 2011. LNCS, vol. 7170, pp. 90–105. Springer, Heidelberg (2012). https://doi.org/10.1007/978-3-642-29963-6_8

25. Park, J.H., Lee, K., Susilo, W., Lee, D.H.: Fully secure hidden vector encryption under standard assumptions. Inf. Sci. **232**, 188–207 (2013)

26. Izabachène, M., Pointcheval, D.: New anonymity notions for identity-based encryption. In: Cortier, V., Kirchner, C., Okada, M., Sakurada, H. (eds.) Formal to Practical Security. LNCS, vol. 5458, pp. 138–157. Springer, Heidelberg (2009). https://doi.org/10.1007/978-3-642-02002-5_8

27. Boyen, X., Waters, B.: Anonymous hierarchical identity-based encryption (without random oracles). In: Dwork, C. (ed.) CRYPTO 2006. LNCS, vol. 4117, pp. 290–307. Springer, Heidelberg (2006). https://doi.org/10.1007/11818175_17

28. Camenisch, J., Kohlweiss, M., Rial, A., Sheedy, C.: Blind and anonymous identity-based encryption and authorised private searches on public key encrypted data. In: Jarecki, S., Tsudik, G. (eds.) PKC 2009. LNCS, vol. 5443, pp. 196–214. Springer, Heidelberg (2009). https://doi.org/10.1007/978-3-642-00468-1_12

29. Angelo De Caro, V.I.: Hidden Vector Encryption Fully Secure Against Unrestricted Queries. IACR Cryptol. EPrint Arch., vol. 2011, p. 546 (2011)

30. Blundo, C., Iovino, V., Persiano, G.: Private-key hidden vector encryption with key confidentiality. In: Garay, J.A., Miyaji, A., Otsuka, A. (eds.) CANS 2009. LNCS, vol. 5888, pp. 259–277. Springer, Heidelberg (2009). https://doi.org/10.1007/978-3-642-10433-6_17

31. Phuong, T.V.X., Yang, G., Susilo, W.: Efficient hidden vector encryption with constant-size ciphertext. In: Kutyłowski, M., Vaidya, J. (eds.) ESORICS 2014. LNCS, vol. 8712, pp. 472–487. Springer, Cham (2014). https://doi.org/10.1007/978-3-319-11203-9_27

32. Zhang, Y., Zheng, D., Chen, X., Li, J., Li, H.: Computationally Efficient Ciphertext-Policy Attribute-Based Encryption with Constant-Size Ciphertexts. In: Chow, S.S.M., Liu, J.K., Hui, L.C.K., Yiu, S.M. (eds.) ProvSec 2014. LNCS, vol. 8782, pp. 259–273. Springer, Cham (2014). https://doi.org/10.1007/978-3-319-12475-9_18

The Impact of Organizational Culture on the Internal Controls Components of Accounting Information Systems in the City of Beirut, Lebanon

A. Ayoub[1]([✉]), Vidyasagar Potdar[1], A. Rudra[1], and H. Luong[2]

[1] School of Management, Faculty of Business and Law, Curtin University, Perth, WA, Australia

`a.ayoub2@postgrad.curtin.edu.au`, {`vidyasagar.potdar`, `amit.rudra`}`@cbs.curtin.edu.au`

[2] Otago Business School, Department of Accountancy and Finance, Otago, New Zealand

`hoa.luong@otago.ac.nz`

Abstract. The adoption of accounting information systems (AIS) is fundamental for organizational success as it improves accumulation, management, and control of big organizational data. However, such systems often fail, causing significant operational problems and financial losses. This study gathers evidence on the impact of organizational culture on the internal controls components of accounting information systems (AIS). We conducted this study by surveying 72 small to medium enterprises in the city of Beirut, Lebanon. Data analysis adopted a partial least squares regression. The results of the study indicate that organizational cultural traits significantly influence the internal controls components of accounting information systems, and thus, such systems can be more successful in firms with supporting organizational cultural traits.

Keywords: Organizational culture · AIS · Accounting information systems · Internal controls · Big data · Individual privacy · Security

1 Introduction

Internal controls play a critical role in enhancing the privacy and security of data. Kumar and Shafi (2019) advocates for the internal control to implement cloud computing strategy in which the complexity of the specifications when implementing AIS can improve the security of the data. The service-based systems that are developed will focus on codifying the AIS security system, and this can be integral in overcoming the security configurations that are utilized when designing such a system. Most of the internal controls are developed to address the departmental data, but with the proliferation of technology and innovation, big data has been integrated into the AIS implementation process. Also, Kumar and Shafi (2019) claims that the implementation of AIS should align the architect solutions to the service-oriented approach where the service delivery should meet the desired privacy and security measures for cloud

© Springer Nature Singapore Pte Ltd. 2020
Y. Tian et al. (Eds.): ICBDS 2019, CCIS 1210, pp. 157–177, 2020.
https://doi.org/10.1007/978-981-15-7530-3_11

computing. Yayla and Sarkar (2018) appreciates the dynamics in security adoption when dealing with big data in AIS implementation. Internal control measures should foster the need to secure storage data and this done in three distinct levels – network level, authentication level, and data level. In the case of the network level, there is a need to articulate to the security and protocol issues and this includes focusing on data distributed notes and communications' internode. The network communication is always encrypted using secure sockets layer (SSL), and internal control should articulate to this security measure. For the authentication level, administrative permissions, logging, and applying authentication techniques for encryption should be prioritized in the internal control mechanism for the AIS implementation (Yayla and Sarkar 2018). Finally, data-level security and privacy are based on securing distributed data by assuring the users on data integrity and availability. It is important to always have backup servers for the AIS implementation for ease of data retrieval in case of technical problems and/or natural disasters.

The advent of the 21st century has seen many organizations embrace technology as a way of making management easier. Consequently, many organizations have embraced particularly the use of accounting information systems (AIS) to maximize their qualitative characteristics and boost their internal controls (Ahmad 2017; Zare and Mohammad (2016). As such, when AIS is used in an organization, there is an assurance in regard to financial information processes as well as improved performance. Various studies have shown that AIS when used well, it improves internal control, which encompasses the reliability of financial reporting and adherence to the laws and guidelines. According to Domnisoru et al. (2017), the organizational level of internal control relates to how reliable is the financial reporting, how timely is the feedback, and whether there is adherence to laws and policies. On the other hand, transactional level internal control relates to actions that are taken to achieve a specific goal. Therefore, internal control mechanisms reduce variations in processes and as such, ensure a more predictable outcome (Ali et al. 2016; Budi and Nusa 2015).

As emphasized by various authors such as Ju (2014), Nakiyaga et al. (2017) and Weixing (2003), AIS has been used by many organizations to make sure that the internal control procedures are adhered to. As a consequence, these procedures are set to ensure that reliable accounting and financial reports are produced, assets are protected, and efficiency is promoted whilst encouraging adherence to laws and policies of the organization (Mahadeen et al. 2016; Zare and Khan 2016). The internal control procedures have also been seen to be important in the achievement of objectives such as conducting accounting transactions, preventing and detecting errors as well as safeguarding company assets. However, it is important to understand that every organization has a culture. Culture has been defined as a set of shared values, rules and assumptions within a group of people (Ahmad 2017; Ju 2014). In the organizational context, these may include procedures, customs, unwritten rules, and practices that bind the organization personnel together (Ahmad 2017; Ju 2014). As such, organizational culture can be defined as a system of shared values, customs, guidelines, actions and beliefs that directs and guides the behaviour of all members of the organization. Therefore, all the traditions, principles and values that influence the way of doing things in an organization and can distinguish one organization from the rest, constitute an organizational culture (Mahadeen et al. 2016). Owing to this definition, organizational culture consists of many aspects that include human factors, customs, and values (Mahadeen et al. 2016). Human factors may include any action by human beings to influence the way things are done or do things in a certain way (Aldegis 2018). In essence, the human side of organizational culture could be explained in various dimensions that include innovation and risk-taking, attention to detail, a people orientation, team orientation, stability, and aggressiveness. According to Zare and Khan 2016), these dimensions have been seen to affect the adoption and utilization of AIS as a system that would foster internal control. Organizational culture, specifically, the human factors affect significantly the implementation of AIS and its ability to enhance internal controls (Zare and Khan 2016). As such, this review focuses on assessing the impact of organizational culture on AIS and its ability to enhance internal control and specifically focusing on human factors.

2 Literature Review

2.1 Organizational Culture and Accounting Information Systems (AIS)

The corporate culture is widely speculated as to the way a business aligns operations and resources based on experience from the market participation, hence creating value and the underlying belief that the corporate image is built on (Tian and He 2016). Based on the fundamental lessons from the market anticipation, it is expected that the management formulates assumptions on these issues and forms response processes such as adaptation and learned organizational transformation towards delivering solutions concerning areas of the business activities. Here, Tian and He (2016) shows that as many researchers have identified the direct connection between corporate culture and respective staff behaviour, where the respective articulation of business expectations and employee performance is highly dependent on the organization's current environment. As a result, the corporate culture is transferred through communication, management, and worker to worker interaction and behaviour, and the existence of clear communication and transparency between workers and management as well as the other shareholders.

According to Mahadeen et al. (2016), culture can be considered a key platform for communication and attainment of the business objectives, where the subsequent business operations and soundness of internal standards is a mere reflection of the quality of established standards and business culture. As a result, the mere establishment of business standards and the image is not enough towards establishing a competitive advantage, instead, creating a clear understanding of the market operations and cultural expectations would allow the management to tailor operations towards the targeted audience market (Mahadeen et al. 2016). Expectedly, the only way businesses can achieve efficient operations is through a highly trained workforce that emulates the business culture as well as the industrial norms and operational standards. According to Hamdan (2012), AIS could be viewed as a unified system that employs physical resources and aspects to turn economic data into useful accounting information to be utilized by both internal and external users. Further, the researcher argues that for any AIS to be useful, it must be able to transform financial data into information that would be used to make informed decisions. In their argument, the researchers also posited that AIS depends on resources such as specialists, hardware, software, data and networks to be successful. In another study, Budi and Nusa (2015), argued that the success of any AIS is based on the user satisfaction in the way the system is utilized daily to digest, analyze and produce accounting reports. It is in regard to these definitions that other researchers identified five variables that could be used to measure the success of accounting systems, which include user satisfaction, high level of use, the attitude of the user, achieved objectives and financial payoff. Further, other researchers identified six dimensions of AIS that define the success of the system that include information quality, system quality, user satisfaction, use of the system, impact to both individuals and organizations (Handoko et al. 2017; Vlasta et al. n.d.). Whether one looks at the variables or dimensions, it is clear to note that human cultural factors are at the centre of AIS implementation at any organization. For example, user satisfaction and the impact of the system on the organization are aspects that management could look at before the implementation of AIS. A study conducted by Medina et al. (2014) defined leadership as the capability to influence a group of people in achieving organizational goals and objectives. In this regard, therefore, one can explain leadership as a strategy that fosters progress in an organization by influencing the subjects and making crucial decisions on behalf of the organization. As such, planning and implementing AIS in an organization needs a robust leadership that will support and lead the members in the process of successful implementation. Regarding this, many studies have linked technology adoption in an organization with its leadership style (B. M. B. Ahmad 2017; Handoko et al. 2017; Zare and Khan 2016). The studies have shown that the attitudes, behaviours, and vision portrayed by the management are central to the perceptions of employees in regard to technology adoption and use. A leadership that is flexible and can communicate the vision of the organization to the employees is more likely to influence them (Nakiyaga et al. 2017; Newswire 2018). Therefore, organizational leadership must exhibit a culture of flexibility whereby they are ready to accept change (Nakiyaga et al. 2017; Newswire 2018). In many occasions, organizations have not been able to successfully implement new technologies due to poor leadership or lack of management support (Nakiyaga et al. 2017; Newswire 2018). Managers and organizational leaders ought to realize the benefits of implementing systems like AIS in the realization of organizational goals and objectives. It is in light of this that instead of looking at AIS as a threat, they should look at the benefit that the organization would realize in the process. Such benefits include the generation of accounting reports and using these reports to make informed decisions (Nakiyaga et al. 2017; Newswire 2018). AIS plays a critical role in the success of any business organization due to their nature of providing information that is correct and reliable for making managerial decisions (Agung 2015; Wisna 2015). As such, when AIS is used to generate correct accounting reports, internal control is improved in the process as variations and errors are avoided or detected and corrected early enough (Agung 2015; Wisna 2015). More so, AIS produces reports that serve as the basis for strategic decisions and exercise of control over organizational activities and assets. In this regard, it means that the culture of leadership in an organization has a lot of bearing in the adoption and implementation of AIS. Flexibility and open-mindedness are the key aspects that are required in such leadership if AIS is to be adopted in order to enhance internal control through generation of reports that are free of errors (Qamruzzaman 2014; Stefanou 2002).

2.2 Internal Control Context

Research has defined internal control as systems and procedures that are put in place to safeguard assets, promote compliance to laws and policies as well as enable reliable financial reporting in an organization (Mahadeen et al. 2016). From another perspective, it was reported that these systems are broad and do not just regard accounting only, but also relate to both internal and external communication procedures, management of staff and handling of errors (Newswire 2018). As such, internal controls include everything pertaining handling of funds received and spent by a firm, preparation of financial reports for board members and management, auditing financial statements, evaluation of staff and organizational programs, evaluation of the performance of the organization, keeping organizational records and implementing policies (Budi and Nusa 2015; Domnisoru et al. 2017).

However, internal controls must be effective and sound so as to ensure that an organization meets its objectives whilst utilizing its resources effectively and minimizing the risk of fraudulent activities within the organization (Domnisoru et al. 2017). Additionally, a sound control system should be able to detect and minimize errors by continuous monitoring and evaluation (Domnisoru et al. 2017). It is in this regard that a sound internal control system has been seen to help in aligning the organizational performance with the overall objectives by continually monitoring the activities and performance parameters of the organization (Domnisoru et al. 2017). Additionally, a sound internal control system has encouraged good management practices by allowing the management of organizations to make informed decisions because managers receive comprehensive, timely and accurate financial reports (Mahadeen et al. 2016). Also, the internal control system ensures proper financial reporting through maintaining correct and complete reports. These reports are most often required by authorities and management and are used to minimize errors and to help in proper allocation of resources (Mahadeen et al. 2016). In regard to safeguarding assets, internal control systems ensure that organization's properties, both physical, intellectual and monetary assets are protected from fraud, errors, and theft (Mahadeen et al. 2016). As well, internal control is put in place to help detect and deter errors and also reduce exposure to risk. According to Susanto (2016), effective internal controls need to be planned well and assessed by the organization from the beginning, especially in cases where personnel and financial power are limited. As such, internal controls must be established within the confines of the organization in terms of available resources and personnel (Suzanto 2016).

Literature has also noted that for internal control to be put in place effectively, there must be an environment to hold it (Tate and Calvert 2017). This environment is basically the organizational culture of the firm in context (Tate and Calvert 2017). An enabling environment in this context is one that each person in the organization understands his/her responsibilities, and limits to his/her authority and knowledgeability. As well, everyone must exhibit a commitment to do the right thing and doing it the right manner (Mahadeen et al. 2016). This aspect is what brings organizational culture and especially the human factors into focus. For internal controls to be successful, everyone must be committed to the organizational culture and therefore, adhere to policies and guidelines that anchor the organizational culture (Mahadeen et al. 2016). This means that a controlled environment is created by setting policies and procedures that are in line with the organizational objectives and goals. Therefore, the underlying organizational culture and in specific human factors is paramount to the adoption and implementation of AIS in an organization that wants to have a sound internal control system. Research has shown that whilst many organizations have tried to adopt and utilize AIS, very few have succeeded owing to the culture of organizations that does not embrace technology (Ali et al. 2016; Nakiyaga et al. 2017). Although adoption of technology and explicitly accounting information systems (AIS) is still increasing especially in developing economies, the importance of AIS in improving internal control systems in an organization cannot be underrated (Ali et al. 2016; Nakiyaga et al. 2017). It is through AIS that accurate financial reports will be generated and will allow for informed decision making by management. Therefore, organizational culture must be discussed in line with the adoption of AIS as a way of improving internal control mechanism in an organization (Domnisoru et al. 2017; Handoko et al. 2017).

In other studies, it has been argued that internal controls ensure that reliability and integrity of financial information is maintained (Nakiyaga et al. 2017; Stefanou 2002). As such, management has access to accurate, timely and correct information that can be used for the better decision-making process. Moreover, internal controls ensure that employees and management are able to maximize the efficiency brought about by internal control systems (Nakiyaga et al. 2017; Stefanou 2002). Owing to these aspects, it is clear that the internal control mechanism helps management to monitor and make sure that operational goals and objectives are maintained (Mahadeen et al. 2016). It is in light of this that the AIS becomes the central foundation under which accurate and timely accounting information is produced and therefore establishing a sound internal control system in the organization (Mahadeen et al. 2016).

Pfister and Hartmann (2011) cite that internal control comes from the connotation of the internal business environment where the management alongside staff put efforts towards attainment or coordination of activities within the business which results in better alignment in the industry and creation of competitive advantage. The aspect of increasing corporation of the internal operations specifically targets attaining speculated high operational and organization standards, which are in line with industrial compliance and operating expectations while working towards achieving competency (Wright 2009). As a result, one can simply put that internal controls include deliberate acts by management, staff, and the business at large in efforts not only to achieve effectiveness but also transform the norm of expected business performance through innovation and alignment of respective business operations to ensure that the set expectations are followed at every stage of business acts and representation. Wright (2009) identifies that the staff is at the centre of implementing these expectations, who work closely with the management to enhance the business alignment to operational procedures and corporate policies. Ideally, this case builds on the assumption that internal control systems are not only business procedures but also platforms that represent opportunities for engaging respective shareholders in the decision-making model, where sound internal control operations facilitate clear communication and interaction, and systems through which the respective people and standards collaborate to achieve a common objective. According to Alina et al. (2013), this is achieved through engaging management that selects other dedicated teams towards attaining operational effectiveness, with clear communication that the intent of business operations, lie solely on satisfactory output, and the extent to which such an objective is to be achieved depends on each and every member of the staff. The final aspect of these internal operations is adherence to the set industrial standards and expected operations where the law provides for minimum operating efficiency and assurance that the business activities and financial statement are in line with the expected business operations and performance guideline (Fitrios 2016). Admittedly, achieving the law as well as the business expectations should be considered an essential step towards the attainment of a sustainable relationship between the management and shareholders as well as industrial expectations and performance threshold, all of which emanate from the sound internal control operations (Fitrios 2016).

2.3 Employee Involvement

Research has shown that for any organization to make progress, employee involvement should be at the core of the organization (Ali et al. 2016). Many organizations have failed and rightly so, because of the lack of involvement of employees in the implementation of serious changes within an organization. Employee involvement could be viewed as making sure that all employees are aware and asked about their opinions when an organization needs to make some changes (Wisna 2015). Research has further noted that even to improve the overall performance of an organization, the adoption of an information system is inevitable. Accounting department being a sensitive department, adoption of AIS is important so as to produce credible and accurate accounting reports (Wisna 2015).

However, even with this type of knowledge, the adoption rate of information systems has been minimal, and companies that tried to implement have significantly failed. In the 1980s, it was reported that the failure of information systems and in particular AIS, was as high as 80%, which prompted researchers to conduct researches on the possible factors leading to this type of failure (Ali et al. 2016). Among the many researches that were conducted in various parts of the world, it was shown that lack of employee involvement was the primary cause of systems failure at the implementation phase (Wisna 2015). The researchers showed that due to lack of employee engagement employees tended to resist the implementation of AIS in their companies. This is because employees need to know the importance of these systems and how they fit in into the new technology. The fear of losing jobs and being deemed redundant has been seen to lead to employee resistance to new technologies due to changes in power and content caused by new technologies (Agung 2015; Ahmad 2012; Ekaterina Rosenkrans 2015). For example, one would wonder whether the adoption of AIS by an organization would make his/her role redundant. In such cases, an employee is likely to resist the adoption of AIS for fear of losing a job. However, if this employee was engaged and assured of job security and a more natural way of doing things, he/she will likely support the new technology. As such, an organization that has a culture of involving its employees in the running of the organization is likely to succeed especially when it comes to adopting new technologies, as compared to organizations that have a culture of not involving employees (Soudani 2012; Stefanou 2002).

Employee resistance to new technology could be based on various theories, including status quo bias theory, people-oriented theory and systems interaction theory (Weixing 2003). Whatever theory one bases his/her perspective on, the focus remains on the people resisting the technology, the reason for resisting, the behaviour and effect of resistance (Agung 2015). All the theories mentioned show that if an employee foresees that a system like AIS could reduce their interests or when the benefits of the system are inferior, or maybe the income of an employee is not equal to the endeavour, the majority of the employees will resist the new technology (Agung 2015). However, the central aspect of the resistance of new technology is always engagement or lack of it. When employees in an organization are engaged or involved in the whole process of adoption and implementation of any new technology, resistance could be very minimal (Ahmad 2012; Fanxiu n.d.; Wanyama and Zheng 2010). Management ought to understand that employees and every stakeholder in the organization need to understand the benefits of adopting new technology and how everyone will fit in for it to be implemented successfully without resistance (Ahmad 2012; Fanxiu, n.d.; Wanyama and Zheng 2010).

Considering other studies, when employees view AIS as a problem to their way of doing things, they are likely to resist it, and most likely the actions will be violent at the beginning (Fanxiu, n.d.; Wanyama and Zheng 2010). However, the resistance of new systems in an organization could be divided into various levels that include passive, active and attack and each level of resistance cause different damage. As such, this level of understanding the resistance places employees involvement at the centre of information system adoption in an organization (Fanxiu n.d.; Wanyama and Zheng 2010). Bearing in mind that AIS is a very sensitive system because of the nature of data it is required to analyze, employees and other stakeholders must be involved in its adoption and implementation process (Xiao and Dasgupta 2005). Thus, when the implementation of AIS is problematic, it means even the internal control system will be compromised (Xiao and Dasgupta 2005). AIS is in many occasions at the centre of improving and making sure the internal control mechanism is sound and could be used to avert errors and ensure laws and procedures are followed (Xiao and Dasgupta 2005). Various studies have shown that any information system that lacks the backing of all stakeholders is deemed to fail (Xiao and Dasgupta 2005). As such, if employees feel threatened by the implementation of AIS, the system will fail, and that means that accounting department will face serious problems (Ali et al. 2016; Xiao and Dasgupta 2005). Finances and physical assets could be lost, and many errors could be committed that could cost the organization a fortune. As such, when the accounting department is not able to produce accurate and reliable financial reports either because AIS has not been adopted or employees have compromised the system, the internal control mechanism will face significant challenges (Soudani 2012).

2.4 Communication

According to Mahadeen et al. (2016), communication is the process of transmitting information and understanding from one person to another in an organizational set-up. From this definition, it is clear that unless a common understanding is derived from the exchange of the information, communication has not taken place. Therefore, communication channels must be developed in an organization that will be used to pass correct information among the stakeholders in a timely manner. Being part of the internal control, communication is vital in ensuring that a sound control system is in place. Any information system used in an organization is geared towards making communication easier by enabling the generation of required reports. In the case of AIS, the financial reports generated must be accurate and timely and should be relayed to management for decision making. When the reports generated from the AIS are not well interpreted and communicated, then wrong decisions can be made and thus compromising internal control system of an organization (Agung 2015; Mahadeen et al. 2016).

Further, Mahadeen et al. (2016) assert that effective communication must include both formal and informal aspects, as both have been seen to have a correlation with internal control mechanisms. Particularly, organizations dealing with consumers or clients must think about communication processes (Ahmad 2012; Karagiorgos et al. 2008). Most of the times, when systems like AIS are used to generate reports, mathematical and accounting knowledge is required to interpret the information. As such, the employees generating such reports must be aware that not all stakeholders understand the accounting language. Therefore, the way they communicate the information to the stakeholders matters a lot (Ahmad 2012; Karagiorgos et al. 2008). This is because studies have shown that communication issues affect all the aspects of an organization's operations and assist in supporting its internal control system. Therefore, when both management and employees establish a good communication network, it helps to foster a sound internal control mechanism. This is due to the fact that through communication, feedback received can help the management evaluate the effectiveness of their control mechanism and whether the improvement is required (Ahmad 2012; Karagiorgos et al. 2008).

According to a study conducted by Nakiyaga and Anh (2017), Luhmann's Social System theory could be utilized to establish the relationship between organizational culture and internal control. The researchers argued that the communication process used in an organization is important in relating organizational culture to internal controls since both the internal control mechanisms and the system theory underline the need for effective communication (Nakiyaga et al. 2017). The theory looks at an organization as a system composed of various components that need to communicate regularly in order to function well. Therefore, all departments are dependent on each other and communication from the accounting department to other departments is vital (Nakiyaga et al. 2017).

According to Budi and Nusa (2015), the implementation of AIS is overly dependent on organizational culture and especially human factors like communication. Therefore, AIS cannot be run effectively if it is not supported by the organization culture and trained human experts. Further, the study argued that culture is characterized by trust, open communication, supportive leadership, and information sharing. Other studies (Ahmad 2012; Budi and Nusa 2015; Wisna 2015) elaborated this statement by explaining that a culture of open communication within an organization is central to adoption and implementation of AIS. For example, the operators of AIS should be very quick in detecting an accounting error, report the error and fix the error. Failure to act on the error and communicate the error to the relevant stakeholders compromises the internal control system that should otherwise be advanced by the adoption of AIS (Ahmad 2012; Budi and Nusa 2015; Wisna 2015).

2.5 Compliance with Procedures

Research has proved that an internal control system in an organization is the foundation under which laws and procedures are complied with (Domnisoru et al. 2017; Mahadeen et al. 2016). It is important to note that no business organization operates in a vacuum. All firms operate in an environment that is guided by-laws, procedures, and procedures. These may be state laws, federal laws, and regulations or even local regulations that guide how accounting should be carried out in an organization (Domnisoru et al. 2017; Mahadeen et al. 2016). Therefore, organizations must adhere to these laws and procedures to make sure they do not get into legal and regulatory issues. For example, some financial reporting in the world is governed by the International Financial Reporting Standards (IFRS). As such, an organization ought to make sure that they report according to IFRS. To standardize the reporting procedures and enhance internal control mechanism that will ensure that accounting information is correct and accurate, AIS ought to be adopted and implemented. Through AIS, accounting information is generated accurately and in a timely manner (Agung 2015; Ahmad 2012).

2.6 Organizational Learning

According to a research carried out by Tate and Calvert (2017), organizational learning can broadly be defined as a learning practice within an organization that brings together the interaction between individuals and collective group levels of analysis geared towards achieving common organizational goals. They further argued that organizational learning is the main aspect that controls the organizational capability to accumulate knowledge (Michael 2016; Tate and Calvert 2017). It is important to note that learning capability is composed of pre-conditions such as management commitment, openness, knowledge transfer, and integration, among others. In regard to managerial commitment, it refers to the role of management to support and create a culture of learning (Ju 2014; Tate and Calvert 2017). The management should view learning as being central to the performance of the organization. An organization that uses systems such as AIS need a management team that will create an environment that is conducive for users to learn and understand the system. As such, managers should participate and encourage employees to learn (Michael 2016; Tate and Calvert 2017). In a study conducted by Michael (2016), it was shown that organizational learning is aligned to the creation of a shared vision as well as mental models in an organization. As such, openness and experimentation are two aspects of learning that are associated with welcoming new ideas and learning, which is particularly important for an organizational change. Therefore, the integration and knowledge transferability are a pure representation of the extent to which an organization is able to pass knowledge to its members. If a firm can develop a culture of learning, especially in this era of technology, then it is likely to succeed in the adoption of new technology. Technologies like AIS are important because of the type of information that they handle, and therefore, employees must learn to use them and interpret information generated by AIS. It is through this learning therefore that AIS will be seen to improve the internal control of an organization and thus prevent fraud cases and assets theft (Edmonson and Moingeon 1998; Michael 2016; Tate and Calvert 2017).

2.7   Organizational Culture: The Denison Model

Denison and his colleagues developed and supported a theory of organizational culture (Denison 1990; Denison and Mishra 1995; Fey and Denison 2003; Denison et al. 2004). This theory builds on four cultural traits that reflect on organizational performance. These traits are involvement, consistency, adaptability and mission. The involvement trait addresses the competence of employees as well as their level of engagement and responsibility. This cultural trait is developed to detect the contributions of organizational members to the well-being and the overall goals and performance of the organization. The second cultural trait addressed by Denison theoretical model is consistency which builds on the overall coordination and consistency level of the organization. It reflects on the internal cultural traits that are identified as core values, agreement, coordination and integration. Adaptability reflects how quickly and successfully can an organization adapt to changes in the external environment and how well these changes can be absorbed inside the organization. The mission is one cultural trait that refers to the share function and goals and behaviours of organizational members. It identifies the path of organizational performance towards the achievements of strategies goals and objectives (Denison 1990; Denison and Mishra 1995; Fey and Denison 2003; Denison et al. 2004). Denison and Mishara (1995), considering 764 top organizational executives, identified that the four cultural traits are correlated with a variety of measures of effectiveness inside an organization. One measure that we consider for the purpose of this study is the efficiency of internal controls inside an organization. Therefore, this study aims to investigate the impact of organizational culture on the internal controls components of Accounting Information Systems. Denison's model suggested that organizations that are characterized by a higher combined measure of the four considered traits of organizational culture show a better level of efficiency and performance and thus, our hypothesis for this study are as follows:

- H1: Organizational culture has a positive relationship or correlation with the effectiveness of the internal controls of Accounting Information Systems
- H2: The cultural traits of involvement, consistency, adaptability and mission in an organization have a positive influence on the effectiveness of the internal controls of Accounting Information Systems

The review has shown that at the organizational level, internal control is paramount and could be affected by many factors. AIS, which is an accounting tool, is central to making sure that internal control in an organization is improved through reliable financial reporting, timely and correct feedback and compliance with set laws and procedures. Using systems like AIS ensures that these aspects of internal control are taken care of, and thus internal control is maintained. However, for AIS to be adopted and implemented successfully, the culture of the organization should be favorable. Cultural factors and especially human factors such as management and leadership style, communication, organizational learning and compliance with laws are some of the human cultural factors that can jeopardize the adoption of AIS and thus putting internal control into a disaster. Thus, the culture of leadership must be one that accepts change and leads the organization into making changes that help the organization to achieve its objectives. If the leadership does not support the adoption of AIS, then the internal control systems will be a problem. Further, communication is paramount in the process of reporting on financial matters, which helps the management in the decision-making process. Moreover, the AIS ensures that local, international and national policies are adhered to while preparing financial reports, and thus errors and variations are avoided.

3   Conceptual Framework

Adapting the Denison Model of organizational culture, the following figure one depicts the impact of organizational culture traits on the success of internal controls components of AIS (Fig.1).

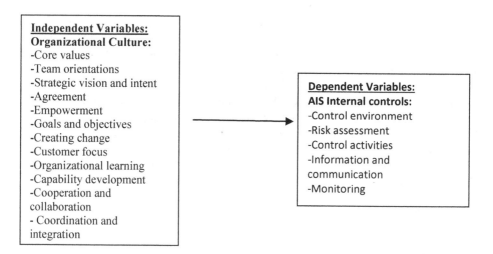

Fig. 1. The study conceptual model

4   Methodology

The study has adopted a survey research to conduct an investigation to determine if organizational culture impacts the internal controls component of Accounting Information Systems. The study was conducted by collecting primary data with the help of adopted questionnaire items disseminated to employees of 95 organizations in the city of Beirut, Lebanon. Only 72 usable responses were received. Sampling was conducted based on the assumption that the opportunities provided by the population are similar to those pursued by the sample. For the purpose of this study, items were drawn from the Denison organizational culture survey measuring organizational culture that used 60 items on a five-point Likert scale. 42 Items measuring the dimensions of the internal control of accounting information systems were adopted from a survey that uses 73 items. The items measured the general control environment, risk assessment, control activities, information and communication, and monitoring. The analysis technique that was used in this study is variance based on structural equation modelling. This method addresses the formulated problem and verifies the developed hypotheses. The model is constructed using higher-order components, formative elements. The assessment of formative measurement model includes indicator reliability, internal consistency reliability, convergent validity and discriminant validity.

5   Results and Discussion

The results of the first test for the indicator reliability shows that each indicator has a factor reliability value that is higher than the minimum limit acceptance of 0.7 (Chin 1998). The composite reliability indicator follows the internal consistency reliability (Bagozzi and Yi 1988; Hair et al. 2012). The composite reliability indicator for each construct are higher than the minimum limit of 0.7 according to the results, and this provides a clear indication that each indicator is consistently measuring the first as well as the second-order constructs. The average variance extracted (AVE) provides a clear indication about the convergent validity of the constructs. The value of each construct is higher than the minimum limit of 0.5, and this indicates that the first, as well as the second-order constructs, meet the criteria of convergent validity. Discriminant validity testing was conducted using the Hetrotrait Monotrait ratio of correlations (HTMT). The criteria are applied to compare HTMT inference with the lower and upper limits at 90% confident interval. The results showed that the HTMT inference value for each of the constructs meeting the criteria of discriminant validity. The results of the study showed clearly that organizational culture impacts the internal controls components of accounting information systems (AIS). The results of the measurement model are presented in the following Table 1.

The test results indicated that organizational culture has a direct influence on the internal controls components of accounting information systems (AIS). The findings are consistent with the assumption that several organizational dimensions impact the accounting information systems internal controls. In this context, the literature has supported that the effectiveness of the internal controls structure is linked to the environment that holds it (Tate and Calvert 2017). Commitment to organizational core

Table 1. Measurement model

Construct	Items	Loadings[a]	Cronbach's alpha[b]	Rho_A[c]	Composite reliability	AVE[e]
Empowerment	Item 1	0.823	0.957	0.964	0.967	0.855
	Item 2	0.940				
	Item 3	0.981				
	Item 4	0.942				
	Item 5	0.929				
Cooperation and Collaboration	Item 1	0.875	0.956	0.957	0.967	0.853
	Item 2	0.912				
	Item 3	0.962				
	Item 4	0.969				
	Item 5	0.896				
Capability development	Item 1	0.919	0.953	0.964	0.963	0.812
	Item 2	0.941				
	Item 3	0.77				
	Item 4	0.891				
	Item 5	0.926				
	Item 6	0.946				
Coordination and integration	Item 1	0.869	0.912	0.924	0.934	0.739
	Item 2	0.861				
	Item 3	0.884				
	Item 4	0.899				
	Item 5	0.781				
Agreement	Item 1	0.967	0.981	0.982	0.985	0.93
	Item 2	0.955				
	Item 3	0.967				
	Item 4	0.949				
	Item 5	0.982				
Core values	Item 1	0.971	0.978	0.979	0.982	0.918
	Item 2	0.956				
	Item 3	0.975				
	Item 4	0.913				
	Item 5	0.975				
Creating change	Item 1	0.945	0.979	0.98	0.984	0.924
	Item 2	0.941				
	Item 3	0.983				
	Item 4	0.981				
	Item 5	0.954				

(*continued*)

Table 1. (*continued*)

Construct	Items	Loadings[a]	Cronbach's alpha[b]	Rho_A[c]	Composite reliability	AVE[e]
Customer focus	Item 1	0.921	0.965	0.966	0.973	0.877
	Item 2	0.916				
	Item 3	0.973				
	Item 4	0.959				
	Item 5	0.912				
Organizational learning	Item 1	0.895	0.962	0.966	0.971	0.87
	Item 2	0.934				
	Item 3	0.964				
	Item 4	0.961				
	Item 5	0.906				
Strategic direction and intent	Item 1	0.933	0.976	0.978	0.981	0.911
	Item 2	0.968				
	Item 3	0.973				
	Item 4	0.916				
	Item 5	0.982				
Vision	Item 1	0.946	0.964	0.969	0.972	0.876
	Item 2	0.882				
	Item 3	0.974				
	Item 4	0.965				
	Item 5	0.909				
Goals and objectives	Item 1	0.971	0.991	0.991	0.993	0.964
	Item 2	0.984				
	Item 3	0.988				
	Item 4	0.983				
	Item 5	0.983				
General control environment	Item 1	0.95	0.979	0.983	0.982	0.856
	Item 2	0.933				
	Item 3	0.863				
	Item 4	0.909				
	Item 5	0.945				
	Item 6	0.927				
	Item 7	0.966				
	Item 8	0.96				
	Item 9	0.869				
Risk assessment	Item 1	0.841	0.927	0.943	0.944	0.742
	Item 2	0.605				
	Item 3	0.913				
	Item 4	0.909				
	Item 5	0.932				
	Item 6	0.924				

(*continued*)

Table 1. (*continued*)

Construct	Items	Loadings[a]	Cronbach's alpha[b]	Rho_A[c]	Composite reliability	AVE[e]
Control activities	Item 1	0.912	0.975	0.975	0.979	0.869
	Item 2	0.888				
	Item 3	0.919				
	Item 4	0.952				
	Item 5	0.946				
	Item 6	0.946				
	Item 7	0.96				
Information and Communication	Item 1	0.846	0.96	0.961	0.965	0.737
	Item 2	0.788				
	Item 3	0.88				
	Item 4	0.889				
	Item 5	0.942				
	Item 6	0.879				
	Item 7	0.825				
	Item 8	0.866				
	Item 9	0.824				
	Item 10	0.832				
Monitoring	Item 1	0.905	0.974	0.976	0.978	0.829
	Item 2	0.940				
	Item 3	0.963				
	Item 4	0.912				
	Item 5	0.875				
	Item 6	0.936				
	Item 7	0.934				
	Item 8	0.879				
	Item 9	0.824				

a. All item loadings > 0.5 indicate indicator reliability (Holland 1999, p. 198)

b. All of Cronbach's alpha > 0.7 indicates indicator reliability (Nunally 1978)

c. All Rho_A > 0.7 indicates the reliability indices for each construct (Dijkstra and Henseler 2015)

d. All composite reliability (CR) > 0.7 indicates internal consistency (Gefen et al. 2000)

e. All Average Variance Extracted (AVE) > 0.5 indicates convergent reliability (Bagozzi and Yi 1988) values, strategic directions and visions, guidelines and policies are essential for the success of internal controls (Mahadeen et al. 2016) (Table 2).

Table 2. Path Coefficient, T Statistics, P Values for hypotheses testing

	Path coefficient	T Statistics (O/STDEV)	P values
Internal controls -> Control Activities	0.957	190.432	0.000
Internal controls -> General control environment	0.890	33.799	0.000
Internal controls -> Information and communication	0.970	111.563	0.000
Internal controls -> Monitoring	0.976	187.984	0.000
Internal controls -> Risk assessment	0.959	105.125	0.000
Organizational culture -> Agreement	0.981	316.207	0.000
Organizational culture -> Capability development	0.951	166.862	0.000
Organizational culture -> Cooperation and collaboration	0.959	127.193	0.000
Organizational culture -> Coordination and Integration	0.931	111.409	0.000
Organizational culture -> Core values	0.973	288.593	0.000
Organizational culture -> Creating change	0.942	92.111	0.000
Organizational culture -> Customer focus	0.957	71.654	0.000
Organizational culture -> Empowerment	0.966	275.527	0.000
Organizational culture -> Goals and objectives	0.966	183.926	0.000
Organizational culture -> Internal controls	0.936	82.829	0.000
Organizational culture -> organizational learning	0.961	112.615	0.000
Organizational culture -> strategic direction and intent	0.940	97.998	0.000
Organizational culture -> Vision	0.944	135.366	0.000

The test results indicate that the success of internal controls can be achieved in an environment of organizational culture that supports agreement, capability development, cooperation, collaboration, adaptability to change, customer focus, empowerment, organizational learning and strategic visions and directions. Therefore, the findings are consistent with the assumption that several organizational culture traits affect the internal controls component of accounting information systems (AIS) (Fig. 2).

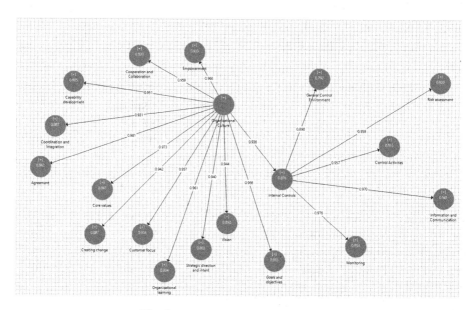

Fig. 2. Study structural equation model

6   Conclusion

The research aimed mainly on investigating the impact of organizational culture on the internal controls component of accounting information systems (AIS). There is a strong view in the literature that organizational culture has a direct impact on the internal controls components of Accounting Information Systems (AIS). The study concludes that organizational culture affects the internal controls components of Accounting Information Systems (AIS). Companies ought to consider the impact of organizational culture and thus, maintain an organizational culture with strong core values and vision, higher level of agreement, coordination, cooperation, integration, collaboration, empowerment, learning, capability development, strategic direction, change adaptability, and customer focus in order to maintain robust accounting information systems internal controls structure. Subsequent research on the same variables involving organizations in the city of Beirut, Lebanon as well as other cities across the globe should be conducted to provide a more profound understanding of the organizational culture impact on the internal controls components of accounting information systems (AIS). Additional dimensions of research on organizational culture as well as the internal controls components of accounting information systems, should be considered. Despite the limitations of the study that are represented by a small sample size of organizations operating in the city of Beirut, Lebanon, and across a limited variety of business sectors, it establishes a foundation for relevant future research orientations.

References

Alina, C.M., Cerasela, S.E., Andreea, T.R.: Internal audit, internal control and organizational culture active ingredients in conquering the crisis. Ovidius Univ. Ann. Ser. Econ. Sci. **13**(2), 553–557 (2013)

Ahmad, B.M.B.: Organizational culture is crucial to the company's risk management system, but how can it be measured ? pp. 1–5 (2017)

Ahmad, M.A.: Problems and internal control issues in AIS from the view point of Jordanian certified public accountants. J. Emerg. Trends Comput. Inf. Sci. **3**(12), 1622–1625 (2012)

Agung, M.: Internal control part of fraud prevention in accounting information system. Int. J. Econ. Commer. Manag. **III**(12), 724–737 (2015). http://ijecm.co.uk/wp-content/uploads/2015/12/31249.pdf

Aldegis, A.M.: Impact of accounting information systems' quality on the relationship between organizational culture and accounting information in Jordanian industrial public shareholding companies. Int. J. Acad. Res. Account. Finan. Manag. Sci. **8**(1), 70–80 (2018). https://doi.org/10.6007/IJARAFMS/v8-i1/3829

Ali, B.J.A., Ahmad, W., Omar, W., Bakar, R.: Accounting information system (AIS) and organizational performance: moderating effect of organizational culture. Int. J. Econ. Commer. Manag. U.K. **IV**(4), 138–158 (2016). http://ijecm.co.uk/

Budi, I., Nusa, S.: Influence of organizational culture and structure on the quality of the accounting information system. Int. J. Sci. Technol. Res. **4**(05), 257–267 (2015)

Chien, M.-H.: A study of the factors affecting organizational effectiveness

Denison, D.R.: Corporate Culture and Organizational Effectiveness. Wiley, New York (1990)

Denison, D.R., Mishra, A.K.: Toward a theory of organizational culture and effectiveness. Organ. Sci. **6**, 204–222 (1995)

Denison, D.R.: Organizational culture: can it be a key lever for driving organizational change (2000)

Denison, D.R., Haaland, S., Goelzer, P.: Corporate culture and organizational effectiveness: is Asia different from the rest of the world?" Organ. Dyn. **33**, 98–109 [7] (2004)

Dijkstra, T.K., Henseler, J.: Consistent partial least squares path modeling. MIS Q. **39**(X), 297–316 (2015)

Domnisoru, S., Ogarca, R., Dragomir, I.: Organizational culture and internal control. Audit Financ. **15**(148), 628 (2017). https://doi.org/10.20869/AUDITF/2017/148/628

Edmonson, A., Moingeon, B.: From organizational learning to the learning organization. Manag. Learn. **29**(1), 5–20 (1998). https://doi.org/10.1177/1350507698291001

Rosenkrans, E.: The interrelationship between different components of internal control, pp. 1–42 (2015)

Fanxiu, G.A.O.: A study of the internal controls of accounting information systems in the network environment, pp. 9–13 (n.d.). https://doi.org/10.5013/IJSSST.a.17.18.09

Fitrios, R.: Factors that influence accounting information system implementation and accounting information quality. Int. J. Sci. Technol. Res. **5**(4), 193 (2016)

Hamdan, M.W.: The impact of accounting information systems (AIS) development life cycle on its effectiveness and critical success factors. Eur. Sci. J. ESJ **8**(6), 19–32 (2012). http://eujournal.org/index.php/esj/article/view/98

Handoko, B.L., Sabrina, S., Hendra, E.: The influence of leadership styles on accounting information systems quality and its impact on information quality survey on state-owned enterprises, vol. 6, no. 11, pp. 1989–1993 (2017)

Hegtvedt, K.A., Turner, J.H.: A Theory of Social Interaction. Social Forces, vol. 68 (1989). https://doi.org/10.2307/2579266

Ju, C.: Management & engineering research on the internal control of small and medium-sized enterprise. Manag. Eng. **16**, 33–37 (2014). https://doi.org/10.5503/J.ME.2014.16.007

Karagiorgos, T., Chatzispirou, I., Drogalas, G.: Internal control system and management information systems. S. Eur. Rev. Bus. Finan. Account. **6**(1), 91–111 (2008). http://www.drogalas.gr/uploads/publications/INTERNAL_CONTROL_SYSTEM_AND_MANAGEMENT_INFORMATION_SYSTEMS.pdf

Kumar, Y., Shafi, M.: A model-driven platform for service security and framework for data security and privacy using key management in cloud computing. Int. Res. J. Eng. Technol. **10**(6), 1464–1471 (2019)

Mahadeen, B., Al-Dmour, R.H., Obeidat, B.Y., Tarhini, A.: Examining the effect of the organization's internal control system on organizational effectiveness: a Jordanian empirical study. Int. J. Bus. Adm. **7**(6), 22–41 (2016). https://doi.org/10.5430/ijba.v7n6p22

Qamruzzaman, Md.: Accounting information system (AIS) enhance efficiency level of the organization: evidence from the insurance industry in Bangladesh. Bangladesh Res. Publ. J. **9**(4), 297–304 (2014)

Medina, J., Victoria, C., Jiménez, D.K., Mora, A., Victoria, C., Ábrego, M.S.D., Victoria, C.: Training in accounting information systems for users' satisfaction and decision making. Int. J. Bus. Soc. Sci. **5**(7), 134–145 (2014)

Michael, G.: Theories of Organizational Learning as resources of Organizational Education (2016) (1990). https://doi.org/10.1007/978-3-658-10086-5

Nakiyaga, B., Thi, D., Anh, L.: How organizational culture affects internal control effectiveness: the role played by top case study, Uganda Revenue Authority (2017)

Newswire: Fraud prevention & detection : the impact of corporate Governance, internal controls, and culture, pp. 1–2 (2018)

Pfister, J., Hartmann, F.: Managing organizational culture for effective internal control: from practice to theory. Account. Rev. **86**(2), 738–741 (2011)

Salih, W.K., Hla, D.T.: Impact of organizational culture to improve audit quality assurance in the public sector (n.d)

Soudani, S.N.: The usefulness of an accounting information system for effective organizational performance. Int. J. Econ. Finan. **4**(5), 136–145 (2012). https://doi.org/10.5539/ijef.v4n5p136

Stefanou, C.J.: Accounting information systems (AIS) development/acquisition approaches by greek SME AIS flexibility and development/acquisition approaches - research. In: European Accounting Information Systems Conference, pp. 23–24 (2002)

Susanto, A.: The effect of internal control on accounting information system. Int. Bus. Manag. **10**(23), 5523–5529 (2016). https://doi.org/10.3923/ibm.2016.5523.5529

Tate, M., Calvert, P.: Intellectual capital, organizational learning capability, and ERP implementation for strategic benefit. In: Twenty-Fifth European Conference on Information Systems (ECIS), pp. 1–16 (2017)

Teru, S.P., Hla, D.T.: Internal control frameworks. Int. J. Sci. Res. Publ. **5**(9), 1–3 (2015)

Tian, J., He, S.: Study of factors for internal control effectiveness of listed companies (2016)

Vlasta, R., Jasenka, B.: Accounting information systems from management decisions: empirical research in Croatia (n.d.)

Wanyama, I., Zheng, Q.: Organizational culture and information systems implementation: a structuration theory perspective. In: 2010 2nd IEEE International Conference on Information and Financial Engineering, pp. 507–511 (2010). https://doi.org/10.1109/ICIFE.2010.5609410

Weixing, W.: The establishment of an internal control system. J. Bus. Manag. **5**(5), 104–113 (2003)

Wright, R.M.: Internal audit, internal control and organizational culture, Doctoral dissertation, Victoria University (2009)

Wisna, N.: Organizational culture and its impact on the quality of accounting information systems. J. Theor. Appl. Inf. Technol. **82**(2), 266–272 (2015)

Xiao, L., Dasgupta, S.: The impact of organizational culture on information technology practices and performance. In: 11th Americas Conference on Information Systems, AMCIS 2005: A Conference on a Human Scale, vol. 7, Association for Information Systems (2005)

Yayla, A., Sarkar, S.: The dynamics of information security policy adoption. In: Proceedings of the 13th Pre-ICIS Workshop on Information Security and Privacy, San Francisco, 13 December 2018 (2018)

Zare, M.M., Khan, M.H.: Effect of culture on quality of internal controls in companies listed on tehran stock exchange. Int. J. Hum. Cult. Stud. 2108–2115 (2016). ISSN 2356-5926

A Security Vehicle Network Organization Method for Railway Freight Train Based on Lightweight Authentication and Property Verification

Congdong Lv[1,2(✉)] and Yucai Li[3]

[1] School of Information Engineering,
Nanjing Audit University, Nanjing 211815, China
lvcongdonglv@163.com
[2] School of Computer and Information Technology, Beijing Jiaotong University,
Beijing 100044, China
[3] Information Technology Centre of Ministry of Railways,
Beijing 100055, China

Abstract. With the development of railway transportation, it has put forward higher requirements for the safety of freight train. The present ground vehicle safety monitoring system, due to technical limitations, can't meet the security requirement for real time information report of the train. Vehicular sensor can collect real-time vehicle information, to guarantee the safety of the train. Vehicle network is the basic of the communications between vehicular sensors. Because of the particularity of the freight train, a security vehicle network organization algorithm is proposed for the railway freight train based on lightweight authentication and property verification. Distance measured by distance sensor is the trigger event of the algorithm. The lightweight authentication makes the node trusted. Authenticating with speed and direction make the nodes belong to the same train. And ultimately vehicle network is established. Through the vehicle network, vehicle sensors collect data in real time and transmit to the ground processing system. Finally, ensure the safety of railway freight train.

Keywords: Lightweight authentication · Vehicle network · Wireless sensor · Security organization algorithm · Noninterference · Formal analysis

1 Introduction

The maintenance system of China's railroad trucks is repaired on a regular basis. At present, it is obviously unreasonable for regular-cycle vehicles to run regardless of the number of tonne-kilometres they operate, how the vehicle is operating, and how bearing technology is used, and vehicles that are scheduled to be on a regular basis will be regularly repaired [1]. Due to the lack of precise control over the use of vehicles and conditions, the optimal use of the vehicle in a safe and safe manner cannot be achieved. This will not only reduce the repair expenses, but also affect the vehicle usage rate [2].

© Springer Nature Singapore Pte Ltd. 2020
Y. Tian et al. (Eds.): ICBDS 2019, CCIS 1210, pp. 178–189, 2020.
https://doi.org/10.1007/978-981-15-7530-3_12

The vehicle-mounted IoT system aims at the intelligentization of freight vehicles and realizes the on-board detection of the vehicle [3]. Through the onboard sensors, it collects the shaft temperature, sound, weight, and eccentric load, and wheels in real time during the loading and running of the truck. Information such as size and treading, plus ambient temperature, speed, etc., data transmitted through the on-board network and the establishment of terrestrial big data systems, and the sensing system collects sufficient data to create a database of freight vehicle operating status, which is a potential safety hazard for vehicles [4]. Comprehensive analysis of data and operational status data to improve the accuracy of the monitoring system. The ground big data system can record data on the use of vehicles and their major components. These data will provide support for the status quo of freight vehicles and can effectively save vehicles. Maintenance costs [5]. The on-board network can provide accurate information for tracking the entire process of rail freight transportation, improving the service quality and utilization of vehicles [6]. At present, the on-vehicle train safety detection system is mainly for passenger cars, and the communication between the systems mainly depends on the cable, and the system hardware has sufficient power protection [7]. This on-board safety inspection system is not suitable for freight trains [8]. Unlike passenger trains, freight trains are frequently organized and require the use of sensors to form self-organizing networks [9] and collect relevant information [10].

The freight train vehicle network has the following characteristics:

(1) Different trigger conditions. According to different networking algorithms, when the network nodes are in communication range, they authenticate each other, and the vehicle-mounted network nodes must be based on distance attributes. When the cars are connected, two network nodes will authenticate the two nodes [11].

(2) The node authentication conditions are different. The usual authentication is to ensure that the network node is a trusted node, and the nodes in the vehicle network need not only to be trusted but also to be in the same group [12].

In view of the above characteristics of the freight train network of freight trains, this paper proposes an onboard network method for railway freight trains based on lightweight identity authentication and attribute authentication. The distance attribute between cars is the condition that triggers the network node networking, and lightweight identity authentication. Ensure that all network nodes are trusted nodes, and the network nodes of the vehicle speed attribute and direction attribute authentication and guarantee networking are in the same group.

2 Freight Train Vehicle Network Security Networking Method

Each car of the train corresponds to a network node in the network. After the formation of trains, the network composed of train cars is fixed and it is a linear topology. To compose these nodes into a network, we need to overcome three difficulties: (1) Whether the network nodes need to form a network (that is, whether the two cars are connected); (2) How network nodes judge whether they belong to the same network (that is, two sections) Whether the cars are actually grouped into a train or not;

(3) Whether the network node is trusted (i.e. whether there is a malicious network node). In this article, we use distance sensors to solve the problem of whether network nodes need to form a network; use direction and speed attributes to solve whether network nodes belong to the same network problem; and use lightweight authentication protocols to solve network nodes for credible problems.

2.1   Train Network Topology

The topological structure of the freight train network is linear, and the network nodes where the two connected cars are located are also adjacent in the network. Because there may be non-adjacent situations in the network (that is, two cars are connected, but the car's network node equipment is damaged or no equipment is installed), a train can be divided into multiple networks. If all train vehicles are equipped with network nodes, the train is a network.

The state of the node is divided into 3 different states: 1) The election state, which is the initial state of the node. Among them, the head node defaults to the master node, and other nodes default to slave nodes. 2) The master node, which is in the position of the linear network head, is responsible for the management of the network; 3) The slave node belongs to the management of the master node. All the information collected from the nodes is summarized to the master node. The master node can be divided into two types: the front car master node and the car master node. The car head master node may not become a slave node, and the car master node may become a slave node.

Each node is given a unique identifier called the node identification number (English abbreviation: UUID, available car number here), each node has a status value, the node can only be in one of the above three states. The attribute of the node indicates which network the node belongs to, and the identifier of the network is expressed using the identification number of the master node. If the node number and the attribute value of the node are the same, the node is the master node. If the node is not the same, the node belongs to a network. The master node is generally generated by the election of the nodes on both sides of the linear structure network.

2.2   Lightweight Authentication Protocol

Before the network node is installed, a digital certificate (Digital ID/Certificate) has been issued by the Certificate Authority (CA).

When network node A and network node B are connected for the first time, the identity authentication between A and B uses a third-party authentication method, such as PKI. The CA verifies the identity certificate and private key signature of network node A and network node B, confirms the identity of the node, and returns the verification result of both. After identity authentication is completed, A and B perform key agreement. The key that is negotiated can be used as the communication session key or identity authentication key of both parties.

The lightweight authentication protocol is based on the success of the first round of authentication. When A and B are connected again, a lightweight authentication protocol is used to complete two-way authentication without CA participation. The implementation of this agreement requires the following:

1) The protocol uses the shared key K_{AB} generated by key agreement as the identity authentication key. A and B store K_{AB} in a key database with protection measures, indexed by UUID.
2) After the first authentication succeeds, both parties save the other party's digital certificates ID_A and ID_B.
3) The mutual sharing K_{AB} must be updated after the first authentication is completed. After a specified valid period of the authentication key or exchange of a certain amount of data, authentication keys can be re-negotiated between A and B (Fig. 1).

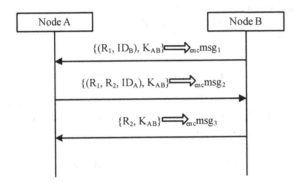

Fig. 1. Lightweight authentication protocol.

The specific description is as follows:

1) B → A: $\{(R_1, ID_B), K_{AB}\} \Rightarrow_{enc} msg_1$.

When B and A initiate a connection, B generates an authentication challenge random number R_1, and encrypts the message msg_1 using B and A's shared authentication key K_{AB}, and then sends the message msg_1 to A as an identity authentication request.

2) After A receives the message msg_1 sent by B, it first decrypts msg_1, $\{msg_1, K_{AB}\} \Rightarrow_{dec} \{R_1, ID_B\}$, first verifies the certificate ID_B, verifies the certificate, and generates a reply message msg_2, that is, $\{(R_1, R_2, ID_A), K_{AB} \Rightarrow_{enc} msg_2$. If the certificate is incorrectly verified or cannot be decrypted, skip to step 7).
3) A → B: $\{(R_1, R_2, ID_A, ID_B), K_{AB}\} \Rightarrow enc\ msg_2$.

A sends an identity authentication message msg_2 to B, including the random number R_1 sent by B, the authentication challenge random number R_2 generated by A, the identity certificate ID_A of A, and is encrypted using the shared authentication key K_AB of A and B to obtain the message msg_2. Send message msg_2 to B as a response authentication request and authentication.

4) After B receives the message msg_2 sent by A, it first decrypts msg_2, $\{msg_2, K_{AB}\}$ $_{dec}$ $\{R_1, R_2, ID_A\}$, first verifies the certificate ID_A and the previously sent authentication challenge random number R_1, certificate and random The number is verified correctly, and a reply message msg_3 is generated, namely $\{R_2, K_{AB}\} \Rightarrow_{enc} msg_3$. If

the certificate or random verification is incorrect or cannot be decrypted, skip to step 7).

5) B → A: $\{R_2, K_{AB}\} \Rightarrow_{enc} msg_3$.

B sends msg_3 to A, which contains the authentication challenge random number R_2 sent by A.

6) After A receives the message msg_3 sent by B, it first decrypts msg_3, $\{msg_3, K_{AB}\} \Rightarrow_{dec} \{R_2\}$, and verifies the random number R_2. The random number is verified correctly and the connection is successful. If the random number is incorrectly verified or cannot be decrypted, skip to step 7).

7) When the shared key of the two is not stored in the library, remote CA authentication is started.

2.3   Network Node Networking and Network Fusion Algorithm

The algorithm in this section describes that any node can establish a network. When the networks established by different nodes meet the conditions, they can be integrated into one network. When the distance between two network nodes is less than the threshold, and the speed attribute and direction attribute, when the speed is within the error and the direction is consistent, follow the following fusion rules:

(1) When a head node exists in a network, the head node is the converged network master node;

(2) When there are no front nodes in the two networks, the main nodes of the merged network are selected by the network nodes on both sides of the linear network.

Specific steps are as follows:

Assuming network nodes A and B, B and A use a lightweight authentication protocol for identity authentication. The authentication passes and B establishes a connection with A.

1) When A is the front node, A is the main node,

1.1) When B is in the election state, modify the B attribute to the identification number of A;

1.2) When B is the master node or the slave node, the attributes of all the network nodes in the network B or the network where B is located are changed to the identification number of A;

2) When B is the front node, B is the main node.

2.1) When A is in the election state, modify the A attribute to the identification number of B;

2.2) When A is the master node or the slave node, the attribute of all network nodes in the network A or the network where A is located is modified as the identification number of B;

3) When A and B are not front nodes,

3.1) When A is in a state of election,

3.1.1) When B is in a state of election, both A and B generate a random number in the interval [1–100], and a node with a larger random number becomes a master node, and another node is a slave node, if a random number Equal, the random number comparison is regenerated until the size is divided. The node attribute is modified to the identification number of the primary node.

3.1.2) When B is a slave node,

    3.1.2.1) When the main node of the network where B is the head node, the A attribute is modified to the primary node's identification number;

    3.1.2.2) When the main node of the network where B is located is not the head node, both A and B's network master node generate a random number in the interval [1–100], and the node with the larger random number becomes the master node. A node is a slave node. If the random numbers are equal, the random number comparison is repeated until the size is divided. The node attribute is changed from the node attribute to the primary node identifier.

3.1.3) When B is the primary node, both A and B end nodes of the network generate a random number in the interval [1–100]. The node with the larger random number becomes the master node, and the other node is the slave node. If the random numbers are equal, the random number comparison is regenerated until the size is divided. The node attribute is modified as the identification number of the primary node.

3.2) When A is the main node,

3.2.1) When B is in the election state, the tail nodes of the B and A networks both generate a random number in the interval [1–100]. The node with a larger random number becomes the master node, and the other nodes are slave nodes. If the random numbers are equal, the random number comparison is regenerated until the size is divided. The node attribute is modified as the identification number of the primary node.

3.2.2) When B is a slave,

    3.2.2.1) When the host node of the network where B is located is the head node, the attributes of all nodes of the A network are modified to the identification number of the primary node of the network where B is located;

    3.2.2.2) When the main node of the network where B is located is not the head node, both the master node of the B network and the tail node of the A network generate a random number in the interval [1–100], and the node generating the larger random number becomes The master node and all other nodes are slave nodes. If the random numbers are equal, the random number comparison is regenerated until the size is divided. The slave node attribute is modified as the identification number of the master node.

3.2.3) When B is the master node, both the tail node of the A network and the tail node of the B network generate a random number in the interval [1–100], and a node with a large random number becomes a master node, and other nodes All are slave nodes. If the random numbers are equal, the random number comparison is repeated until the size is divided. The node attribute is modified as the identification number of the primary node.

3.3) When A is a slave node,

    3.3.1) When B is in a state of election,

        3.3.1.1) When A is the master node of the network, modify the B attribute to be the identification number of the master node;

        3.3.1.2) When the main node of the network where A is located is not the head node, the main nodes of the B and A networks both generate a random number in the interval [1–100], and the node with the larger random number becomes the master node. The nodes are all slave nodes. If the random numbers are equal, the random number comparison is repeated until the size is divided. The node attribute is modified as the identification number of the master node.

    3.3.2) When B is a slave,

        3.3.2.1) When A is the master node of the network, modify the attributes of all the nodes in the network where B resides as the identification number of the master node of the A network;

        3.3.2.2) When B is the master node of the network where the host is located, the attributes of all the nodes on the network where A is located are modified to be the identification number of the primary node on the B network;

        3.3.2.3) In other cases, both the master node of the B network and the master node of the A network generate a random number in the interval [1–100], and a node with a large random number becomes a master node, and other nodes are slave nodes. If the random numbers are equal, the random number comparison is regenerated until the size is divided. The node attribute is modified as the identification number of the primary node.

    3.3.3) When B is the primary node,

        3.3.3.1) When the network node where A resides is the head node, the attributes of all the nodes in the network where B resides are modified as the identification number of the primary node of the A network;

        3.3.3.2) In other cases, the tail node of the network where B resides and the master node of network A both generate a random number in the interval [1–100]. The node with the larger random number becomes the master node, and the other nodes are slaves. Nodes, if the random numbers are equal, regenerate the random number comparison until the size is divided, and the node attribute will be modified as the identification number of the primary node.

2.4   Vehicle Network Separation Algorithm

When the distance measured by the distance sensor is greater than the separation threshold, it indicates that the physical connection between the two nodes is removed and the network needs to be removed. The specific steps are as follows:

When the distance between network node A and network node B is greater than the threshold, A and B are disconnected.

1) If A is the master node and B is the slave node,

  1.1) If there is more than one network node in the part where B is located, and B and the other node on the network where B is located, generate a random number in the interval [1–100], and generate a node with a larger random number to become the master node, and all other nodes For the slave node, if the random numbers are equal and the random number comparison is regenerated until the size is divided, the node attribute will be modified as the identification number of the master node.

  1.2) If B is only part of the B network node, leave the Node B attribute blank, and the B status is changed to the election status.

2) If A is a slave node,

  2.1) If there is only one A network node in the part where A is located, the A node attribute is set to blank, and the A status is changed to the election status.

  2.2) If there is more than one network node in part A,

    2.2.1) If there is a master node in the part where A is located, the network is not changed.

    2.2.2) If A does not exist in the part where the master node exists, A and the other node both generate a random number in the interval [1–100], and the node with the larger random number becomes the master node, and the other nodes are slaves. Nodes, if the random numbers are equal, regenerate the random number comparison until the size is divided, and the node attribute will be modified as the identification number of the primary node.

  2.3) If B is only part of the network node B and the head node of the B site, the B node attribute is set to blank, and the B status is changed to the election state.

3 Security and Performance Analysis

3.1 Lightweight Protocol Security Formal Verification

According to the description of the identity authentication protocol in Chapter 2, establish an idealized model of the protocol:

1) $B \rightarrow A$: $\{R_1, B\}(K_{AB})$;
2) $A \rightarrow B$: $\{R_1, R_2, A\}(K_{AB})$;
3) $B \rightarrow A$: $\{R_2\}(K_{AB})$.

Let's consider whether this protocol can perform secure two-way authentication. If whenever the responder gets the evidence that the initiator knows the shared key K_{AB} (B receives R_1), the initiator must also get the evidence that the responder knows the shared key K_{AB} (A receives R_2), then we say that the protocol implementation t he sponsor and responder's two-way identity authentication.

The CryptoSPA description of the lightweight authentication protocol is shown in Table 1:

Table 1. CryptoSPA description of light weight authentication protocol.

$$B(R_1, K_{AB}) \overset{\text{def}}{=} \bar{c}_1 msg_1 \cdot c_2(v) \cdot check_{msg_2}(v) \cdot \bar{c}_1 msg_3 \overline{done}$$

$$A(R_2, K_{AB}) \overset{\text{def}}{=} c_1(q) \cdot check_{msg_1}(q) \cdot \bar{c}_2 msg_2 \cdot c_1(u) \cdot check_{msg_3}(u) \cdot \overline{done}$$

$$P(n, m) \overset{\text{def}}{=} B(n, K_{AB}) || A(m, K_{AB})$$

其中: $\bar{c}_1 msg_1 = [< (R_1, B), K_{AB} >_{\Rightarrow enc} p] \bar{c} p$

$check_{msg_1}(q) = [< q, K_{AB}^{-1} >_{\Rightarrow dec} i][i \Rightarrow_{fst} s][i \Rightarrow_{snd} r][r = B]$

$\bar{c}_2 msg_2 = [(s, R_2, A), K_{AB} >_{\Rightarrow enc} t] \bar{c} t$

$check_{msg_2}(v) = [< v, K_{AB}^{-1} >$

$\Rightarrow_{dec} i][i \Rightarrow_{fst} s][i \Rightarrow_{snd} d][s \Rightarrow_{fst} z][s \Rightarrow_{snd} x][z = R_1][d = A]$

$\bar{c}_1 msg_3 = [x, K_{AB} >_{\Rightarrow enc} y] \bar{c} y$

$check_{msg_3}(u) = [< u, K_{AB}^{-1} >_{\Rightarrow dec} o][o = R_2]$

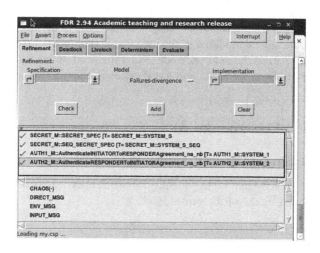

Fig. 2. Result of verification by FDR.

Among them, c1, c2 $\in$ puAct, done $\in$ prAct. Use Casper and FDR to verify the security of this protocol. The verification result is as follows:

The adversary satisfies the Dolev-Yao model. There are four verifications in Fig. 2, and no attacks were found. In the authentication process, the random messages R_1, R_2 are secure and no cryptographic information is disclosed; B vs. A, A vs. B Implemented bidirectional authentication.

The lightweight authentication protocol guarantees the legitimacy, direction attributes, and speed attributes of participating entities to ensure the correctness of participating entities.

3.2 Safety Performance Analysis

In the lightweight authentication protocol,

1) B and A have the shared authentication key KAB after the first round of authentication. In the authentication process, the authentication message $V_1 = \{R_1, ID_B\}$ (K_{AB}) is generated using the shared key K_{AB}, the random numbers R1, R2 generated by the two authentication parties, and the platform certificate ID_A of the both parties, $V_2 = \{R_1, R_2, ID_A\}(K_{AB})$, $V_3 = \{R_2\}(K_{AB})$. The authentication message V_1, V_2, V_3 is used as the signature of the two parties to verify and provide identity authentication evidence for dual-issue.

2) The freshness of the authentication messages V_1, V_2, V_3 of both parties can be verified by the random numbers R1, R2 to ensure that the authentication value of this message has no relation with the previous authentication value and can effectively resist replay attacks.

To effectively illustrate the performance advantages of the lightweight authentication protocol, the original TCA authentication used for the first access is compared with the lightweight authentication protocol, as shown in Table 2. The TCA first authentication protocol only analyzes the identity authentication protocol itself and does not include the key negotiation part. Send or receive 1 message for 1 exchange. Compared with the original protocol, the lightweight authentication protocol has obvious advantages in communication and computing efficiency under the premise of accomplishing the same task.

Table 2. Comparison between authentication protocols.

Protocol	Number of data exchange	Computation		
		A	B	PM
TCA protocol	5	1S+1V	1S+1V	1S+1V
Lightweight authentication protocol	3	1E+1D	1E+1D	0

Among them, A and B are two parties that participate in identity authentication, and PM is a strategy manager in TCA. S is an RSA-1024 bit signature operation; V is an RSA-1024 bit verification signature operation; E is a 128-bit block encryption operation; and D is a 128-bit block decryption operation.

1) Communication load

The lightweight authentication protocol data exchange has been reduced to 3 times 5 times, and the two-way identity authentication between A and B can be fully realized while reducing the number of interaction steps. The reduction of the number of data exchanges directly leads to the improvement of the performance of the authentication protocol; and a large number of public and private key operations are changed to encryption and decryption operations, occupying less network communication bandwidth during protocol execution, and improving the usability of the protocol.

2) Calculation load

Compared with the original TCA authentication protocol, the lightweight authentication protocol is less computationally intensive. The one-signature operation and one-time verification signature operation of B and A are reduced to one symmetric cryptographic operation and one symmetric decryption operation. Reducing the participation of trusted third parties has obvious performance advantages.

4   Conclusion

Aiming at the identity authentication of network nodes, this paper proposes a lightweight authentication protocol. After a remote CA authentication, the re-authentication between network nodes can be completed through a shared key, without the need for remote CA participation. Based on the lightweight authentication protocol and the distance attribute between freight train compartments, vehicle speed attributes, and direction attributes, a safe networking method is proposed. The distance attribute between cars triggers a networking algorithm, and the networking algorithm uses a lightweight authentication protocol pair. The network node performs identity authentication and verifies the network node's speed attributes and direction attributes to form a secure railway freight train on-board network.

References

1. Sarkar, R., Pathak, S., Kela, D.H.: Root cause analysis of low impact toughness of cast steel yokes used in railway freight cars. J. Fail. Anal. Prev. 19(1), 76–84 (2019)
2. Abuobidalla, O., Chen, M., Chauhan, S.: A matheuristic method for planning railway freight transportation with hazardous materials. J. Rail Transp. Plan. Manag. 10, 46–61 (2019)
3. Ludicke, D., Lehner, A.: Train communication networks and prospects. IEEE Commun. Mag. 57(9), 39–43 (2019)
4. Ma, X.D., Li, H., Ma, J.F., et al.: Lightweight position awareness recommendation system privacy protection framework. Chin. J. Comput. 40(5), 1017–1030 (2017)
5. Xin, Y., Feng, X., Li, T.T.: Position-dependent lightweight Sybil attack detection method in VANET. J. Commun. 38(4), 110–119 (2017)
6. Wei, G.J., Qin, Y.L., Zhang, H.G.: ECC-based lightweight radio frequency identification security authentication protocol. J. Huazhong Univ. Sci. Technol. (Nat. Sci. Ed.) (1), 49–52 (2018)
7. Gope, P., Hwang, T.: A realistic lightweight authentication protocol preserving strong anonymity for securing RFID system. Comput. Secur. 55, 271–280 (2015)
8. Abdallah, A., Shen, X.S.: Lightweight authentication and privacy-preserving scheme for V2G connections. IEEE Trans. Veh. Technol. 66(3), 2615–2629 (2017)

9. Abbasinezhad-Mood, D., Nikooghadam, M.: Design and hardware implementation of a security-enhanced elliptic curve cryptography based lightweight authentication scheme for smart grid communications. Future Gener. Comput. Syst. **84**, 47–57 (2018)

10. Arafin, M.T., Gao, M., Qu, G.: VOLtA: voltage over-scaling based lightweight authentication for IoT applications. In: 2017 22nd Asia and South Pacific Design Automation Conference (ASP-DAC), pp. 336–341. IEEE (2017)

11. Lai, C., Lu, R., Zheng, D., et al.: GLARM: group-based lightweight authentication scheme for resource-constrained machine to machine communications. Comput. Netw. **99**, 66–81 (2016)

12. Reddy, A.G., Yoon, E.J., Das, A.K., et al.: Lightweight authentication with key-agreement protocol for mobile network environment using smart cards. IET Inf. Secur. **10**(5), 272–282 (2016)

Lightweight Identity Authentication Scheme Based on IBC Identity Cryptograph

Yongbing Lian$^{(\boxtimes)}$ and Xiaogang Wei

Nari Group Corporation/State Grid Electric Power Research Institute,
Nanjing 21003, Jiangsu, China
lianyongbing@sgepri.sgcc.com.cn

Abstract. With the widespread use of Public Key Infrastructure (PKI), some defects in PKI management have also been exposed, such as occupying a lot of valuable network resources, needing large storage resources and computing resources. Based on IBC identification cryptograph, this paper proposes a lightweight identity authentication scheme which uses SAKI private key distribution protocol and SM9 national secret algorithm. The scheme mainly includes three parts: online secure distribution of private key, identity authentication, key agreement. And the protocol interaction among Key Generation Center (KGC), Edge Computing Agent and Internet of Things terminal is introduced. Compared with common PKI verification, the lightweight authentication scheme proposed in this paper greatly saves network resources, and has higher security performance, shorter length key and more convenient key management. It can be combined with device identification in the Internet of Things to solve key security problems such as identity authentication, link encryption and data protection in the Internet of Things.

Keywords: IBC · SAKI · SM9 · Lightweight

1 Introduction

As the key information infrastructure supporting the operation of power grid, the safe operation of power information network is related to national security and social stability. In recent years, with the continuous evolution of network security policies in various countries, network space has become the focus of competition in various countries, and the security threats to power grid information network are increasing day by day.

With the development of the Internet of Things (IOT), the network boundary becomes more complex and vague, and network security protection is facing many new problems. Firstly, the lack of authenticating capability of trusted identity for the IOT terminal results in the risk of being counterfeited and sensitive data leaking. Massive and heterogeneous terminals lack trusted identity identification and authentication mechanism, which makes it difficult to achieve trusted network access and data encryption transmission. Secondly, the extension of open and shared network endings leads to the blurring of the boundary of the material federation. The construction of ubiquitous power Internet of things breaks through the original security protection

© Springer Nature Singapore Pte Ltd. 2020
Y. Tian et al. (Eds.): ICBDS 2019, CCIS 1210, pp. 190–198, 2020.
https://doi.org/10.1007/978-981-15-7530-3_13

system based on network isolation. The network security exposure is increasing, and the border security protection is becoming more and more difficult.

Based on this, we need to study a lightweight identity authentication system suitable for the current ubiquitous power Internet of Things, to achieve reliable access to Internet of Things equipment and secure data transmission, and to strengthen the security protection capabilities of IOT.

2 Research Status

PKI is a universal technical specification and standard that uses the principle and technology of asymmetric encryption algorithm to realize and provide security services. It is a system that manages the key and confirmation information of asymmetric encryption algorithm, integrates digital certificate, public key encryption technology and CA. PKI system is the most widely used and most mature cryptographic security system in the world. However, the PKI system needs to manage a huge certificate group, which requires a high cost of construction and maintenance. Ubiquitous terminals of IOT have a large base, and most of them have low cost. Depending on the PKI system, the security of the terminals of IOT will lead to high construction costs and greatly increase the management costs [1].

IBC (identity-based Cryptograph) is an encryption method that uses a user's unique identity as a public key. It enables any pair of users to communicate securely and verify everyone's signature without exchanging private and public keys, and does not need to save key directories and third-party services. Compared with the PKI system, the IBC system has the characteristics of low construction cost, low operation cost, flexible and convenient use by users. At present, it has been applied in the mail system and financial system.

3 Basic Knowledge

3.1 SAKI Private Key Distribution Process [2]

Step 1:   Users with ID are randomly selected $r \in Z_q^*$ as blind factors to calculate $Q = H(ID)$, $Q' = rQ$, $T = H(\text{pwd})$, $T' = r^{-1}T$. Send (Q', T') as the user's private key application message to KGC.

Step 2:   After KGC receives (Q', T'), the following calculations are made:

- Verify that $e(Q', T') = e(Q, T)$ is valid. If it is not valid, return fails, otherwise enter next step.
- Computation $S' = sQ' = srQ$, which S' will be sent to the user.

Step 3:   After the user receives S', the following calculations are made:

- Verify that $e(S', P) = e(Q', P_{pub})$ is valid.
- Get rid of blindness: $S = r^{-1}S' = sQ$ to get the real private key.

3.2   Elliptic Curve Encryption

Here's the formula $K = kG$, the points K, G is on the elliptic curve $Ep(a, b)$, n is the order of $G(nG = O_\infty)$, and k is an integer which is less than n. Given k and G, it is easy to calculate K according to the rule of addition, but conversely, given K and G, it is very difficult to find k. Because the ECC in practice set n to very big, it is impossible to get all points. This is the mathematical basis of elliptic curve encryption algorithm [3].

- G is base point
- $k(k < n)$ is private key
- K is public key

The process of elliptic curve encrypted communication [4]:

Step 1:   User A chooses an elliptic curve $Ep(a, b)$ and takes a point on the elliptic curve as the base point G;

Step 2:   User A selects a private key k and generates a public key $K = kG$;

Step 3:   User A send $Ep(a, b)$ and K, G to User B;

Step 4:   When user B receives the information, the plaintext to be transmitted is coded to the previous point M and a random number $r(r < n)$ is generated;

Step 5:   User B calculates $C_1 = M + rK$ and $C_2 = rG$;

Step 6:   User B sends C_1, C_2 to User A;

Step 7:   When user A receives the information, calculate $C_1 = kC_2$, and the result is point M;

Step 8: $C_1 - kC_2 = M + rK - k(rG) = M + rkG - krG = M$, Decode M to get plaintext.

3.3   Ubiquitous Power Internet of Things

The overall architecture of IOT for power transmission is divided into four layers: perception layer, network layer, platform layer and application layer [5] (Fig. 1).

The perception layer is composed of various field acquisition components, intelligent service terminals, local communication networks and edge computing agent. It is divided into sensor layer and data aggregation layer. Field acquisition components must be accessed to the platform layer through edge computing agent. Intelligent service terminals can not directly access the platform layer through edge computing agent, and must be encrypted.

Lightweight authentication system is needed to ensure reliable access and secure communication between field acquisition components, intelligent service terminals and edge computing agent (Fig. 2).

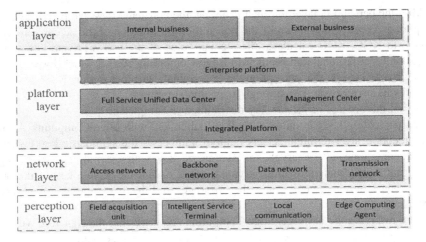

Fig. 1. Architecture of IOT [6].

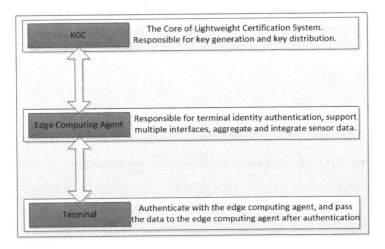

Fig. 2. Architecture of lightweight.

4 Scheme Description

Edge Computing Agent is the "gateway" for the data of the perception layer terminal to enter the upper layer. This scheme solves the problem of trusted access and secure communication between the perception layer terminal and Edge Computing Agent.

Key Generation Center (KGC) is generally deployed on the platform layer. After Edge Computing Agent is online, it establishes a trusted channel with KGC (optical fiber private network, wireless APN, etc.). Edge Computing Agent registers with KGC through the trusted channel. KGC generates the IBC private key of Edge Computing Agent and sends it down to KGC through the trusted channel.

After the perception layer terminal is online, the registered message is sent to Edge Computing Agent, which forwards the registration information of the perception layer terminal to KGC. KGC calculates the median value of the user's private key of the perception layer terminal and sends it to Edge Computing Agent, which forwards the user's private key of the perception layer terminal. The perception layer terminal calculates its own private key through a specific algorithm.

So far, the process of private key distribution is completed.

The perception layer terminal exchanges public key with Edge Computing Agent. The perception layer terminal selects random number as the symmetric key for subsequent communication, encrypts the symmetric key with the public key of Edge Computing Agent, and signs the encrypted message with the private key of the perception layer terminal, and sends the message to Edge Computing Agent after completion.

After receiving the message, Edge Computing Agent verifies the signature with the public key of the perceptual terminal, and decrypts the message with its own private key to obtain the symmetric key.

So far, the process of identity authentication and key agreement is completed.

Finally, Edge Computing Agent and the perceptual terminal use the negotiated symmetric key and the symmetric encryption algorithm to encrypt the data communication.

4.1   Key Distribution

All terminal devices need to preset the public key (ID) of KGC (Fig. 3).

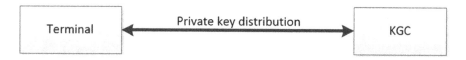

Fig. 3. Terminal and KGC.

Step 1:   The terminal device selects the registration password, encrypts the password with the public key of KGC, and sends the encrypted registration password and the plaintext device ID to KGC.

Step 2:   After KGC receives it, it decrypts the device ID and the registration password with its own private key.

Step 3:   The terminal device combines device ID+application time+validity period into terminal public key, chooses random number r, calculates the private key application message (Q', T') with terminal public key, random r and registration password according to SAKI protocol, and the private key application message has two signature private key application messages and encrypted private key application messages. The key plaintext is sent to KGC

Step 4:   KGC obtains the application time and validity period from the public key plaintext, verifies the validity of the application time and validity period according to the preset information of the database, calculates the private key distribution information S' after that, S' divides the signature private key distribution information and the encryption private key distribution information into two parts, and sends them to the terminal.

Step 5:   The terminal calculates the user's signature private key and user's encryption private key with r and S' in step 3.

4.2   Identity Authentication and Key Agreement

According to the security requirements, identity authentication can be divided into two types: one-way authentication from the terminal to Edge Computing Agent and two-way authentication between the terminal and the edge agent (Fig. 4).

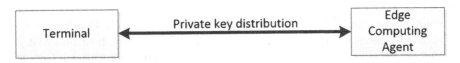

Fig. 4.   Terminal and edge computing agent.

The terminal and Edge Computing Agent exchange the public key first.

One-way Verification Scheme:

Step 1:   The terminal selects the random number R as the symmetric encryption key, encrypts the R with the public key of Edge Computing Agent, and signs the encrypted message with the terminal signature private key, and sends the encrypted random number and signature message to Edge Computing Agent.

Step 2:   Edge Computing Agent receives and verifies the signature with the terminal public key first, and then decrypts the signature with the private key of Edge Computing Agent to obtain the symmetric key R.

Two-way Verification Scheme:

Step 1:   The terminal chooses the random number R1, encrypts R1 with the public key of Edge Computing Agent, and signs the encrypted message with the terminal signature private key. The encrypted random number R1 and signature message are sent to Edge Computing Agent.

Step 2:   Edge Computing Agent receives and verifies the signature with the terminal public key first, then decrypts the signature with the private key of Edge Computing Agent, and obtains R1. The edge couplet agent selects the random number R2, encrypts R2 with the terminal public key, and signs the encrypted message with Edge Computing Agent, and sends the encrypted random number R2 and signature message to the terminal;

Step 3:   The terminal receives and verifies the signature with the public key of Edge Computing Agent, decrypts the signature with the private key of the terminal, and obtains R2. It does XOR operation on R1 and R2, and sends them to Edge Computing Agent after hashing.

Step 4:   Edge Computing Agent confirms with the local result after receiving, and the confirmation will be used as the symmetric key.

5   Scheme Analysis

5.1   Safety

Point 1: The system private key is generated by KGC, and the system security depends entirely on the trusted key generation center, so the protection of KGC is particularly important.

Point 2: Private key distribution is based on SAKI Private Key Distribution Protocol. SAKI constructs a blind signature to protect the private key. It enables KGC to transmit the generated blind private key to the user in a non-secure channel. Only the user with blind factor can recover the real private key.

5.2   Advantage

Point 1: It supports key distribution online and is easy to implement. The PKI system supports certificate online application, but the construction cost of PKI is high and the maintenance cost is high. It is not suitable for the scenario of millions of terminals. Other lightweight authentication systems, such as CPK combined public key [7], do not support key online distribution.

Point 2: Network overhead is low. PKI system needs to transmit certificate + certificate chain + encrypted symmetric key + signature to complete certificate verification. In this scheme, lightweight authentication system needs to transmit "device identification + application time + validity period + encrypted symmetric key + signature". The certificate generated by OpenSSL has more than 300 bytes, and the certificate chain has at least 300 bytes. Symmetric key +signature" does not exceed 200 bytes, and PKI completes one-way authentication with a minimum transmission of 800 bytes; device identification + application time + validity period has a total of dozens of bytes, and lightweight completes one-way authentication with a maximum transmission of 300 bytes.

Point 3: The calculation efficiency is high and the calculation process is simple. In this scheme, the lightweight authentication system needs "validity period of validation + one verification + one decryption" and the validity period of validation is negligible compared with 1-N certificate validation. The lightweight authentication system is better than the PKI.

5.3 Inferiority

SM9 has Pair Operations, and has certain requirements for computing power of equipment.

5.4 Design and Analysis of Network Overhead Testing Scheme

Design of Test Scheme. Develop the lightweight key system terminal and Edge Computing Agent DEMO proposed in this scheme. Use the third-party package grabbing tool tcpdump to grab packets, count the number of message interaction bytes in the process of identity authentication and key agreement, and compare with the results of packet grabbing in PKI system.

The PKI scheme is implemented based on OpenSSL library [8]. RSA algorithm is adopted and the key length is 2048 bits. Openssl is a widely used software library, and the implementation of PKI scheme with OpenSSL is representative. PKI certificate is a self-verifying certificate generated by openssl, and the certificate chain is a first-level certificate chain.

Lightweight authentication scheme is implemented based on sm9. The identification length is 6 bytes and the key strength is equivalent to 3072 bits RSA [9].

The longer the key length, the larger the certificate generated, the more bandwidth resources needed [10]. 2048-bit RSA has consumed much more network resources than the lightweight key system based on sm9, so 3072-bit RSA has not been selected for testing.

Analysis of Test Results. OpenSSL synthesizes multiple processes into a single message, resulting in four interactions (Table 1).

Table 1. Openssl statistics.

Process	Bytes
Client Hello	373
Server Hello\Certificate\ Certificate Request\Server Hello Done	2003
Certificate\Client Key Exchange Certificate Verify\Change Cipher Spec\ Encrypted Handshake Message	2476
New Session Ticket\Change Cipher Spec\ Encrypted Handshake Message	1156
Total	6008

There are five lightweight interactions, which complete the process of identity access and key agreement (Table 2).

It can be seen from the table that 6008 bytes of interaction are needed for PKI to complete authentication and password negotiation. The lightweight authentication and password negotiation proposed in this scheme only need 806 bytes. Compared with PKI, lightweight greatly saves network overhead.

Table 2. Lightweight statistics.

Process	Bytes
Public key application	84
Public key reply	84
Application for identity authentication	292
Identity authentication response	292
Identity authentication	108
Total	806

6   Conclusion

This paper proposes a lightweight authentication scheme based on SM9, which solves the complicated certificate management problem of traditional PKI, and solves the online distribution problem of private key in other lightweight authentication systems by referring to SAKI private key distribution protocol. It realizes the trusted access and secure communication of the terminals in the power Internet of Things.

Acknowledgments. This work is supported by the science and technology project of State Grid Corporation of China: "Research on Fundamental Protection Architecture and Terminal Layer Security Monitoring and Protection Technology of SG-eIoT" (Grand No. SGGR0000XTJS 1900274).

References

1. Zhang, J., Wu, J.C., Dan, C.: Application of identity-based cryptosystem in intelligent substation. Zhejiang Electr. Power. **10**, 7–11 (2013)
2. Yang, B., Xiong, X.D., Su, K.J.: Improved saki private key distribution protocol. Comput. Eng. Appl. 102–104 (2009)
3. Zhou, L.S., Qing, Y., Tan, P.Z., Yang, J., Pang, F.: Implementation of an improved identification-based authentication system. Inf. Secur. Commun. Encryption 61–63 (2002)
4. Freebuf. https://www.freebuf.com/articles/database/155912.html. Accessed 11 Dec 2017
5. Xu, S.W., Li, X.Y., Wang, R.R.: A new solution to IBC key escrow problem. Comput. Appl. Softw. 308–310 (2018)
6. Baidu. https://baijiahao.baidu.com/s?id=1627795739580530244&wfr=spider&for=pc. Accessed 12 Mar 2019
7. Nan, X.H., Chen, Z.: Summary of Network Security Technology. National Defense Industry Press (2003)
8. Guan, H.M.: Performance analysis of CPK and PKI. Comput. Secur. (030), 17–18 (2003)
9. Huang, H.B., Zhang, M.: Application of IBC in LTE authentication and key agreement. Beijing University of Posts and Telecommunications (2012)
10. Zhou, C.Y., Wang, J.W., Li, M.: Research on identity password application in Internet of Things. Res. Inf. Secur. **3**(11) (2017)

Security Analysis and Improvement on Kerberos Authentication Protocol

Guangyao Yuan, Lihong Guo$^{(\boxtimes)}$, and Gang Wang

School of Information and Communications Engineering,
Nanjing Institute of Technology, Nanjing 211167, China
yuanguangyao0403@163.com

Abstract. Kerberos is a third-party network authentication protocol based on symmetric key technology which is widely used in major operating systems and Hadoop ecosystems. However, the original Kerberos's fragility is gradually emerging and no longer suitable for current requirements with the changes of the times. We need to improve it based on previous versions. In this paper, we propose an improved the process of Kerberos authentication and its vulnerabilities and deficiencies which solve the limitation of Kerberos symmetric key by using two-factor authentication. Besides, we uses zero-knowledge proof to eliminate the hidden trouble caused by using plaintext when Kerberos-clients first interact with AS. Then we apply Kerberos in the SSL handshake protocol in order to test the performance of improved Kerberos. The experimental results show that the scheme effectively improves the authentication performance of Kerberos.

Keywords: Kerberos · Two-factor authentication · Zero-Knowledge proof · SSL

1 Introduction

With the rapid development of communication infrastructure construction and the improvement of Internet technology, all industries of life have entered a new era of information reform. However, it is the rapid development of information technology that makes information security become a new hot topic. How to ensure the convenient and safe access of resources by legitimate users and how to ensure the safe operation of the system, reducing the impact on work efficiency has become an urgent problem to be solved.

Currently, Kerberos is generally used as safe authentication protocol in the network. Kerberos developed by the Massachusetts Institute of Technology is a third-party network authentication protocol based on symmetric key technology. However, while people's requirements for network security performance gradually increase and many security protocols are gradually emerging, the shortcomings of Kerberos are gradually exposed. So, it is significant security risks that Kerberos-based applications, which are still in use now [1].

© Springer Nature Singapore Pte Ltd. 2020
Y. Tian et al. (Eds.): ICBDS 2019, CCIS 1210, pp. 199–210, 2020.
https://doi.org/10.1007/978-981-15-7530-3_14

If we try to revise some parts of Kerberos, without prejudice to the compatibility of original Kerberos-based applications, we will solve the existing problems on its original protocol to optimize the security benefits of the entire system.

2 Related Work

2.1 The Process of Kerberos Authentication

The Description of Parameters. In Table 1, there are some symbols and parameters needed brief explanations. They are ID, Times, Nonces, Ticket, Message, Authentication et al. The explanations of these parameters are shown in the following table.

Table 1. Some symbols and parameters.

Symbols	Meaning
ID_A	ID of A
Times	Timestamp
Nonces	Random value
$Ticket_A$	Permit to visit A
$Message_A$	Certification Information from A
Authentication	Authentication code

The Detailed Kerberos Authentication Procedure [2, 3]

(1) C - > AS certification process

$$\lceil ID_C \mid ID_{tgs} \mid Times \mid Nonces \rfloor \tag{1}$$

First, the client sends a request to the authentication server AS in simple text for gaining permission to access an application server v.

(2) AS - > C certification process

$$\lceil ID_C \mid Ticket_{tgs} \mid Message_{as} \rfloor$$

$$Message_{as} = EK_{c,a}\{K_{c,tgs} \mid Times \mid Nonces \mid ID_{tgs}\}$$
$$Ticket_{tgs} = EK_{c,tgs}\{K_{c,tgs} \mid ID_{mathsfc} \mid AD_c \mid Times\} \tag{2}$$

If AS verifies that C is a valid user, AS will send a ticket that is encrypted by a symmetric key for interaction between C and TGS and a message-packet used to inspect C own message. This whole packet is encrypted by a symmetric key between C and AS.

C needs to encrypt the message-packet using the symmetric key between C and AS after receiving the reply message from AS. Then, C needs to ensure that the difference value between the accepted parameter 'Times' and the parameter 'Times' sent to the AS is within an acceptable range. Then, C checks whether the parameter 'Nonces' has changed and checks for repetition to prevent replay attacks.

(3) C - > TGS certification process

$$\lceil ID_v \mid Times \mid Nonces \mid Ticekt_{tgs} \mid Authentication \rfloor$$
$$Message_{tgs} = EK_{c,tgs}\{K_{c,v} \mid Times \mid Nonces \mid ID_v\}$$
(3)

C sends the ticket received from AS, Times, Nonces to TGS. Besides, There is also a parameter 'Authentication' in this packet which is roughly composed of ID_c and timestamp so that TGS can query the permissions possessed by C.

(4) TGS - > C certification process

$$\lceil ID_c \mid Ticket_v \mid Message_{tgs} \rfloor$$
$$Ticket_v = EK_{c,v}\{K_{c,v} \mid ID_c \mid AD_c \mid Times\}$$
$$Message_{tgs} = EK_{c,tgs}\{K_{c,v} \mid Times \mid Nonces \mid ID_v\}$$
(4)

When C has the right to access the server V after the authentication, the TGS sends a ticket and a key that interacts between C and V to C so that the client C can access server V by the access ticket symbolized by $Ticket_v$. This whole process is encrypted using a symmetric key between C and TGS.

(5) C - > V certification process

$$\lceil Ticket_v \mid Authentication \rfloor$$
$$Authentication = Ek_{c,v}\{ID_c \mid TimeSample \mid Subkey\}$$
(5)

C sends the ticket received from TGS, Times, Nonces to V. Besides, There is also a parameter 'Authentication' in this packet which is roughly composed of ID_c, Subkey and TimeStamp so that V can query the permissions possessed by C.

(6) V - > C certification process

$$\lceil EK_{c,v}\{TimeSample \mid subkey\} \rfloor$$
(6)

Through the above authentication process, the identity of both parties between the C and V has been trusted. During the validity period of $Ticket_v$, C can use $Ticket_v$ to apply for services from V and the message communicated between the two is encrypted by the Subkey. After C successfully sends a message to V, V will add a small increment to the obtained TimeSample that received from C. This increment is usually 5 ms.

2.2   Problems Existing in Kerberos Authentication Protocol

Vulnerable to Password Guessing Attacks. In the Kerberos protocol, a one-way hash function is used to convert the user's password into the key Kc. When performing the hash operation, the user's name and the name of the user's region are added to perform the operation. The specific algorithm adds a password to the Kerberos region's name and the customer's name to generate a string, and padding ASCII null ensure an 8-byte boundary. The string is XORed by itself to form an 8-byte DES key. The parity bit of the key is corrected and the parity bit is used to generate the DES-CBC checksum of the initial string (with region and name) and the next parity check CBC checksum. If the result matches the "fragile" or "semi-fragile" key described in the DES specification, it will be XORed with the constant 000000000000000FO. The final result is used as the key.

According to the generation algorithm of the user key, the user key Kc is obtained by encrypting the user password by a public cryptographic algorithm. Because the attacker can request a large number of accesses to the TGS from the AS, the attacker can collect a large number of TGTs. When the number of TGTs is enough, the attacker can perform password guessing by calculating and analyzing the key Kc. In a word, The attacker can gain passwords just by guessing attacks, if the password selected by the user is not strong enough [4].

Vulnerable to Clock Synchronization Attacks. In Kerberos, in order to avoid replay attacks leading the system that is damaged, timestamps are added to both the ticket and the authenticator. In this way, the receiver can judge whether the data has been replayed based on whether difference value of timestamps is within an acceptable range, but the method needs to ensure that the clocks of the communication parties maintain the synchronous clock authentication protocol. Although there are many excellent clock authentication protocols, some people still use the unauthenticated clock authentication protocol, which is very vulnerable to clock synchronization attacks [5].

Difficult to Manage Symmetric Keys. Kerberos uses common symmetric keys for encryption to ensure the confidentiality of communication. However, when users increase in a large amount, the key to be used will also increase in a corresponding trend. Assuming the number of users is n, and then the number of required keys is

$$\frac{n \cdot (n - 1)}{2} \tag{7}$$

This will impose a heavy burden on the server so that the efficiency of the program is reduced greatly reduced and a lot of memory space on the server is wasted greatly. Also, the cost of the entire system is much higher.

3 Improvement for Kerberos Authentication Protocol

3.1 Two-Factor Kerberos Authentication

Concept and Characteristics of the Two-Factor Kerberos Protocol. Two-factor authentication is a form of multi-factor authentication that can combination with passwords and physical conditions (such as credit cards, SMS phones, tokens, or fingerprints). Two-factor authentication adds an extra layer of security to the authentication process by increasing the difficulty of a functional attacker accessing the user's online account. Two-factor authentication has long been used to control access to sensitive systems and data, and online service providers are increasingly using two-factor authentication to protect their users' data to prevent hackers from stealing password databases or user password [6].

The Kerberos system itself is a very complex system involving many aspects of security considerations. Excessive changes to the Kerberos protocol can easily lead to problems in system implementation. The two-factor Kerberos protocol not only improves the security of the Kerberos protocol, but also avoids excessive modification of the Kerberos protocol, making the system simple and easy to implement.

The USB card needs to be inserted into the computer, and then the password is entered when the system logs in during the user's using. The operation of the two-factor Kerberos is transparent to the legitimate user.

The original Kerberos system uses encrypted passwords as the only authentication method for legitimate users resulting in the attacker can obtain it by password guessing. However, Combining of the password and the symmetric key and separating storage can increase security in the two-factor Kerberos system. If the stealer obtains an USB card but does not know user account or password, it still cannot be used; if the user account and password are obtained but no USB card, it also cannot be used.

In the two-factor Kerberos system, the symmetric key of the user is no longer calculated based on the user's password and the password is not transmitted in the network thereby avoiding the eavesdropping of the encryption key when C and AS interact for the first time.

The Principle of Two-Factor Kerberos Protocol. When the encryption algorithm is known by everyone, it is very vulnerable to be attacked by password guessing since Kerberos uses the symmetric key system for identity authentication. Therefore, how to enable the user to securely verify their identity while keeping the Kerberos symmetric key system intact is an issue that must be addressed.

From the perspective of two-factor authentication mechanism, it is not difficult to find that Kerberos's inherent user identity authentication is a cognitive factor. We can combine it with other factors to improve the security performance of the user identity. Such as, the unique sequence in the user's USB authentication can be combined with the user's password.

Safety Performance of Two-Factor Kerberos Protocol. While two-factor authentication does improve the security performance because access no longer depends solely on the strength of the password. The two-factor authentication scheme is only as secure as the weakest component. Although the SMS-based two-factor Kerberos protocol is easy to implement and inexpensive, it is also vulnerable to a large number of attacks. For example, NIST mentioned in its publications against the use of SMS in two-factor Kerberos protocol services. NIST believes that the one-time password sent via SMS is too fragile due to the portability of the mobile phone number.

Improvement of Two-Factor Kerberos Protocol. Since the two-factor Kerberos protocol only changes the way the user key is generated, there is no major change in the workflow of the protocol itself, so that the security vulnerability caused by the revision is hardly brought to the Kerberos protocol.

$$\lceil IDc \mid ID_{tgs} \mid Times \mid Nonces \rfloor \tag{8}$$

Here, $K_{c,as}$ is a user key obtained by hashing and XORing the password of the client C with the key in the USB card owned by the user. After receiving the client request message, the AS generates a random session key $K_{c,tgs}$ and a TGS ticket, which is encrypted by the client's key $K_{c,as}$ a response message. The session key $K_{c,tgs}$ is used for encrypted communication between the client C and the TGS. The contents of the Ticket include:

$$Tickettgs = EKc, tgs[Kc, tgs \mid IDc \mid ADc \mid Times] \tag{9}$$

The data is encrypted using the TGS key K_{tgs} to ensure that only the ticket can be decrypted. The AS sends a response to the client C, and the response content is encrypted with the client's key $K_{c,as}$ so that only the client C can decrypt the contents of the message. If the customer cannot answer the response message, the customer's identity is a fake customer. After receiving the response message returned by the AS, client C decrypts with its own key $K_{c,as}$, and obtains the ticket of the TGS. The client can send the ticket to the TGS in the next step to prove that he has the legal identity to access the TGS. The client C also obtains the session key $K_{c,tgs}$ from the packet which comes from AS, and uses the key to perform encrypted communication with the TGS.

3.2   Zero-Knowledge Proof Kerberos

Concepts and Characteristics of Zero-Knowledge Kerberos Protocol. The notion of a Zero-Knowledge Proof System was first introduced for a particular communication model between the prover and the verifier in the 1980s. Zero-knowledge proof is a cryptographic protocol. One side of the protocol is called a prover, and the other side of the agreement is a verifier. Zero-knowledge proof means that the prover proves to the verifier that a statement is correct, but does not provide any relevant information to the verifier or that the verifier cannot obtain any relevant information from the prover's argument.

Principle of Zero-Knowledge Kerberos Protocol. We all know that in the first information exchange process of Kerberos, client C sends the verification information to AS in clear text to prove that C is a valid user. This way will inevitably lead to information leakage. Therefore, how to solve the problem that Kerberos can securely authenticate C under the condition of clear text transmission is a problem to be solved. The homomorphic-hidden proof is used to ensure the security of the first interaction in plaintext transmission. Since only the way how the user key is generated is changed, there is no major change in the working process of the protocol itself, so that there is almost no security trouble caused by the revision of the Kerberos protocol. If C wants to pass the AS certification, he only needs to prove to the AS that he has the correct password and doesn't need to transmit the password.

Mathematical Realization of Zero-Knowledge Kerberos Protocol. Pcan be any integer, but in order to obtain some special properties, P generally takes a prime number, such as 7. The so-called modulo P addition is to modulate P after adding (divide by P to take the remainder). The example showed in Table 2.

Table 2. Addition mode p.

Variable	Value						
x	0	1	2	3	4	5	6
(x + 1) mod	1	2	3	4	5	6	0

Putting the collection

$$\{0, 1, \ldots, p - 1\}\{0, 1, \ldots, p - 1\}\{0, 1, \ldots, p - 1\} \tag{10}$$

Together with the modulo P addition, it is called a finite group. The number of elements in the set is called the order of the finite group, so the above is a 7-order finite group. Similar to the modulo P addition, the modulo P multiplication is multiplied and then modulo P. The example displayed in Table 3.

Table 3. Multiplication mode p.

Variable	Value						
x	0	1	2	3	4	5	6
(x * 2) mod 7	1	2	3	4	5	6	0

If you let each element in the collection

$$\{0, 1, \ldots, p - 1\}\{0, 1, \ldots, p - 1\}\{0, 1, \ldots, p - 1\} \tag{11}$$

Continually do modulo p multiplication on itself, as shown in Table 4.

It is not difficult to find that the calculated results of 3^x mod 7, 5^x mod 7 are generators, the other calculated results are cyclic groups. All the finite groups of prime orders are cyclic groups. If taking the above example as an example, the generator element is

Table 4. Square mode p.

Variable	Value					
x	0	1	2	3	4	5
1^x mod 7	1	1	1	1	1	1
2^x mod 7	1	2	4	1	2	4
3^x mod 7	1	3	2	6	4	5
4^x mod 7	1	4	2	1	4	2
5^x mod 7	1	5	4	6	2	3
6^x mod 7	1	6	1	6	1	6

$$g \in \{3,5\} \tag{12}$$

Assuming that the generator is 3, define a homomorphic hidden function is in Eq. (13).

$$E(x) = g^x \bmod p = 3^x \bmod 7 \tag{13}$$

E(x + y) can be calculated from E(x) and E(y), but the range of values of x and y. is {0, p − 2}, here the addition is the modulo p-1 operation and the formula can be obtained in Eq. (14).

$$E(x+y) = g^{(x+y)} \bmod (p-1) = (g^x \cdot g^y) \bmod (p-1) = E(x) \cdot E(y) \tag{14}$$

Improving Ideas and Processes of the Zero-Knowledge Kerberos Protocol. First, C and AS need to reach a large prime p consensus, which does not need to be kept secret and can be made public. Divide password into two paragraphs pw1,pw2. Divide times into two paragraphs t1,t2, a large prime The p and pw1|t1 and pw2|t2 modulo operations yield E(a) and E(b), respectively.

$$\lceil \text{IDc} \mid \text{IDtgs} \mid E(a) \mid E(b) \mid \text{Nonces} \rfloor$$

$$\begin{aligned} E(a) &= (\text{pw1}|\text{t1}) \bmod p \\ E(b) &= (\text{pw2}|\text{t2}) \bmod p \end{aligned} \tag{15}$$

After the AS receives the authentication information from the client C, it only needs to authenticate it. The equation is shown in (16).

$$(E(a) + E(b)) \bmod p = E(password + times) \bmod p \tag{16}$$

If the condition is met, the identity of C is valid. If the condition is not met, the identity of C is invalid. The randomness of each data transmission is guaranteed, and the malicious party replay attack is prevented effectively.

4   Application for Improved Kerberos Protocol in SSL

4.1   The Design of Security Policy

Through the analysis of the characteristics of some current communication protocols and their applicable environments, the system uses the SSL protocol as the communication protocol used by the two parties. By analyzing the research results of the SSL protocol by domestic and foreign security experts and technicians, the authentication mechanism of the SSL protocol has some security risks. By analyzing the authentication mechanism of the SSL, the SSL handshake protocol can be improved by using Kerberos identity authentication. So, security policy of Kerberos-SSL can be used as security policy of the system [7].

4.2   Analysis of SSL Security

Analysis from Encryption Method of the Public Key. When using the Kerberos identity authentication mode, the client obtains the ticket authorized to access the server and the session key for the session with the server through the ticket authorization center TGS. The client generates a message, including the entity information of the client and the pre-master key required to generate the master key. Then, the client encrypts the session key with the client and the server, and sends the message together with the ticket to the server. The application server decrypts the ticket with its own secret key to obtain a session key with the client, and decrypts the first message with the session key to obtain the pre-master key and the client entity information. The customer entity information in the ticket compared with the customer entity information therein, and if it is consistent, the verification passed. At this point, the client and server authentication ends, and the pre-master key required to generate the master key is obtained. Kerberos identity authentication has been added to the SSL communication protocol.

Analysis from the Current Certificate. It is possible for an attacker to exploit an attack during the time when one of the parties' communications has been logged out but the new certificate list has not been updated. If the certificate is logged out due to the leakage of the certificate private key, the attacker can use the leaked private key to attack when the new certificate is not used, so that obtain the sensitive information content of the interaction between the two parties. Through the above analysis, the use of certificates has certain security risks. Kerberos is a network security authentication system based on symmetric encryption of shared keys, which avoids the authentication information of the two parties communicating on the Internet in clear text. It uses the password of both parties as the symmetric encryption key, verifies the identity of the user by correct decryption, and generates a shared key to protect the interaction information of the two parties. It is effective to avoid the hidden dangers of using certificate authentication. Therefore, this paper proposes to enhance the security of the SSL handshake protocol by adding a Kerberos authentication method to the SSL protocol.

4.3   Implement of Kerberos Authentication Method

The SSL protocol supports the scalable add-in service model, which allows the addition of a new authentication scheme and the design and implementation of a secure Kerberos-SSL-based data transport system. Therefore, it is feasible to add the Kerberos authentication method to the SSL protocol.

Password Group that Supports the Kerberos Authentication Option. In the initial stage of the SSL protocol handshake, the client and the server can flexibly negotiate the cipher suite used in the communication through the interaction of the Hello message. The specific step is that the client encapsulates the cipher suite that it supports in the Client-Hello message and sends it to the server. The server selects the cipher suite it supports from the server and sends it to the client in the Server-Hello message. The cipher suite for both parties' communication is determined. If the negotiated cipher suite includes the Kerberos authentication option, the Kerberos authentication mode can be selected when the client and the SSL server perform key negotiation. According to RFC 2246, each encryption component contains a key exchange algorithm, a symmetric encryption algorithm (including key length), and a MAC algorithm. According to the RFC 2246 specification, a cipher suite set containing Kerberos authentication options is defined.

Because the Kerberos authentication process does not require the use of a certificate, the client obtains the services provided by the server by having access to the server's tickets. When using the Kerberos authentication option, the certificate request packet, the client certificate packet, and the client key exchange packet in the SSL handshake protocol are affected.

Certificate Request Packet. In the SSL handshake protocol, the server may choose to accept the certificate request from the client. If the server accepts the certificate request, it needs to return a corresponding type of certificate request packet to the client. The content of the packet mainly includes list of a certificate type and list of authorities.

When using the RSA asymmetric encryption algorithm, the relevant content of the certificate is defined by the X.509 certificate system. When using Kerberos authentication, the certificate content should be able to represent Kerberos related information.

Certificate Request Packet. If the client uses Kerberos for authentication, the client needs to provide the server with the certificate containing the client information when it receives the certificate request information sent by the server. The client sends its own ticket information to the server through the Kerberos type message in the certificate. After receiving the certificate information of the client, the server verifies the client through the content in the AP-REQ packet. The client can choose the type of ticket to be sent to the server through the key management center..

Client Key Exchange Packet. When using the Kerberos identity authentication mode, the client obtains the ticket authorized to access the server and the session key for the session with the server through the ticket authorization center TGS. The client generates a message, including the entity information of the client and the pre-master key required to generate the master key. Then, the client encrypts the session key with the client and the server, and sends the message together with the ticket to the server. The application server decrypts the ticket with its own secret key to obtain a session key with the client, and decrypts the first message with the session key to obtain the premaster key and the client entity information. The customer entity information in the ticket compared with the customer entity information therein, and if it is consistent, the verification passed. At this point, the client and server authentication ends, and the premaster key required to generate the master key is obtained. Kerberos identity authentication has been added to the SSL communication protocol [8, 9].

5   Conclusions

In this paper, based on Kerberos's authentication process and the characteristics analysis of Kerberos protocol, we propose an improvement Kerberos authentication scheme.

According to Kerberos's vulnerabilities and deficiencies, in the improvement scheme, we use two-factor authentication method to solve the limitation of Kerberos symmetric key, at the same time, zero-knowledge proof is proposed to eliminate the hidden trouble caused by using plaintext when Kerberos first interacted with AS. In order to test the performance of improved Kerberos, we apply it the SSL, the experiment results show that the scheme effectively improves the authentication performance of Kerberos. In the future, the research on Kerberos authentication scheme is continuing, so it has better application prospects in many aspects [10, 11].

Acknowledgements. This work was supported by Innovation and Entrepreneurship Training Program for College Students in Jiangsu Province (No. 201911276128H), and the Innovation Funding of Nanjing Institute of Technology (No. CKJB201704).

References

1. Gao, X.H.: Design and implementation of quantum trusted authentication system based on Kerberos. Beijing University of Posts and Telecommunications (2019)
2. Qi, Z.X.: Design and implementation of authentication system for web application system based on Kerberos. Beijing Industry University (2014)
3. Cheng, C.: Design and implementation of email service authentication based on Kerberos protocol and DES encryption algorithm. University of Electronic Science and Technology (2013)
4. Yang, P.: Research and improvement of Kerberos security analysis and its authentication mode. Tianjin University of Technology (2015)
5. Yang, P., Ning, H.Y.: Security analysis and countermeasure research of Kerberos protocol. Comput. Eng. **41**(451), 150–154 (2015)
6. Qiong, S.C., Hao, H.Z.: RFID two-way authentication protocol based on Kerberos. Comput. Eng. **39**(425), 133–137 (2013)
7. Wang, Y.: Design and implementation of enterprise data security transmission system based on Kerberos + SSL. Dalian University of Technology (2013)
8. Sun, C.Y.: Design and implementation of Kerberos unified authentication and authorization system based on PKI. Beijing University of Posts and Telecommunications (2012)

9. Xu, B.: Research on improvement of Kerberos protocol. China Shipbuilding Engineering Society (2017)
10. Huang, L.: Research and implementation of campus network unified identity authentication system. Tianjin University (2013)
11. Mo, Y.: Attack on Kerberos protocol and countermeasures. In: National Computer Network and Information Security Management Center, China Communications Society Communication Security Technical Committee, China Communications Society (2004)
12. Sun, J.B., Gao, Z.: Improved mobile application security mechanism based on Kerberos. In: Proceedings of 2019 4th International Workshop on Materials Engineering and Computer Sciences 2019, pp. 108–112. Francis Academic Press, UK (2019)
13. Shen, P., Ding, X.M., Ren W.J.: Research on Kerberos technology based on hadoop cluster security. In: Proceedings of the 2018 2nd International Conference on Advances in Energy, Environment and Chemical Science 2018. Advances in Engineering Research, vol. 155, pp. 238–243. Atlantis Press (2018)

Distributed Differential Privacy Protection System for Personalized Recommendation

Zongsheng Lv[1], Kaiwen Huang[1], Yuanzhi Wang[2], Ruikang Tao[1], Guanghan Wu[1], Jiande Zhang[2], and Yuan Tian[2(✉)]

[1] School of International Education,
Nanjing Institute of Technology, Nanjing, China
[2] School of Computer Engineering, Nanjing Institute of Technology,
Nanjing, China
1547393771@qq.com

Abstract. Personalized recommendation systems become increasingly popular and have been widely applied in various fields nowadays. The release of users' private data is required in order to provide users recommendations with high accuracy, yet this has put the users in danger. Unfortunately, existing privacy preserving methods are either developed under trusted server settings with impractical private recommendation systems or lack of strong privacy guarantees.

In this paper, we propose a new scheme that can achieve a better balance between security and usability, effectively solving the above problem. The innovation lies in improving the method of adding noise to the Laplace mechanism in local differential privacy. It adopts a univariate noise increase method, combined with wavelet clustering and multiple cluster identification methods to ensure the lowest data distortion rate. At the same time, it is safe to ensure the data.

Keywords: Local differential privacy · Wavelet transform · Significant grid identification · Cluster identification

1 Introduction

With the rapid development of information technology, especially network technology, data storage technology and high-performance processor technology, the collection management and analysis of massive data becomes more and more convenient. Knowledge discovery and data mining are in some deep level applications [1]. Played a positive role. However, at the same time, it also brings many problems in terms of privacy protection. For example, illegal records in the public security system, transaction behavior of bank card customers, personal information of telecommunications users, and the relationship between purchases and other information are of great importance to government and corporate decision-making, at the same time they are highly valued by citizens. personal privacy. More and more organizations share resources by exchanging or publishing unorganized information about individuals. At the same time, data and privacy leaks have become more frequent [2].

© Springer Nature Singapore Pte Ltd. 2020
Y. Tian et al. (Eds.): ICBDS 2019, CCIS 1210, pp. 211–222, 2020.
https://doi.org/10.1007/978-981-15-7530-3_15

1.1 Research Status and Current Problem

About privacy protection technology, 2006, Dwork et al. A new definition of privacy protection model is proposed, which is strict and independent of background knowledge-differential privacy [1]. Berlioz et al. In 2015, the privacy protection of collaborative filtering algorithms based on matrix decomposition was studied. For the first time, differential privacy protection techniques are applied to the potential factors of matrix decomposition no mathematical proof of related algorithms is given [2]. Therefore, improving the accuracy of the recommendation system is as important as providing privacy assurance to users. Differential privacy protection technology has rigorous mathematical proof and has the advantage of ensuring that its processing results are credible. Privacy-protected collaborative filtering algorithm based on differential privacy protection technology effectively improves data loss due to excessive noise by improving the differential privacy method and reducing the number of Laplacian noise increases. Compared with the collaborative filtering algorithm under typical differential privacy protection, we divide the differential privacy processing into two steps, which reduces the data processing pressure of the client and avoids the risk of the third-party server leaking data.

1.2 Improved System and Optimized Solutions

In order to improve the above problems, we have improved the traditional data processing method. First, we divided the process of differential privacy into two parts to further ensure the security of the data. Compared with similar improvement studies, we use wavelet transform, effective mesh recognition and other methods to greatly improve the accuracy of the recommendations. At the same time, it can make good use of the research results in the traditional recommendation field. In the follow-up study, the relationship between the degree of data customization and the privacy protection budgets and the accuracy of algorithm recommendation will be studied to further improve the accuracy of the algorithm. Privacy protection is a great challenging problem in the recommendation system: on the one hand, in order to provide a better user experience, it is necessary to continuously improve the accuracy of the recommendation; on the other hand, accurate recommendations will reveal the user's private information, which will Causes the user to lose trust in the recommendation system.

This paper combines differential privacy with local differential privacy and divides the whole part into two steps. First, it performs preliminary data scrambling on the local end, then sends the processed data to the aggregator for single-parameter differential privacy processing. The process of conversion and important grid identification sends the most accurate and secure data to the shopping company's servers, feeds back accurate data to the customer.

This article is divided into five parts, namely introduction, related work, P2R-εDP Approach, Experimental Results & Analysis and Conclusion and Future Work. Through this arrangement, we can clearly analyze the current problem and solve the problem and give accurate and intuitive data information.

2   Related Work

We have combined the local differential privacy with wavelet transform to improve the Laplace mechanism and control the number of noise increases. At the same time, the Fourier transform is also improved, which solves the problem of instability in Fourier transform, and demonstrates wavelet transform, which combines with cluster recognition and important grid recognition to ensure the accuracy of the data.

2.1   Collaborative Filtering in Recommendation System

Collaborative Filtering as a classic recommendation algorithm and the best machine learning algorithm for recommending systems. Collaborative filtering algorithms can be mainly divided into two categories [3]: *userCF* and *ItemCF*. For e-commerce, the number of users generally exceeds the number of products. At this time, the computational complexity of *ItemCF* is low. In non-social networking sites, intrinsic links to content are important recommendation principles that are more effective than recommendations based on similar users. The importance of this recommendation goes beyond the comprehensive recommendation of the user on the homepage of the website. In this case, the recommendation of *ItemCF* becomes an important means of guiding users to browse. It uses all users' preferences for an item as a vector to calculate the similarity between items. After obtaining similar items of the item, it predicts the items that the user has not expressed preference based on the preferences of the user history, and calculates a sorted item.

As shown in Fig. 1 McSherry et al. used differential privacy in the collaborative filtering recommendation system [4, 5] to perform differential privacy processing on the Item-to-Item covariance matrix, and divided the recommendation system into a learning phase and a prediction phase (i.e., recommendation), which stated that there is no seriousness. It is feasible to implement differential privacy protection in the case of loss recommendation accuracy does not consider the latent factor model [6].

2.2   Wavelet Transform and Significant Grid Identification

Wavelet transform is a new transform analysis method. It inherits and develops the idea of localization of short-time Fourier transform. At the same time, it overcomes the shortcomings of window size and frequency variation, and can provide a "time-frequency" window with frequency change. It is an ideal tool for signal time-frequency analysis and processing. Its main feature is that it can fully highlight some aspects of the problem through transformation, can localize the analysis of time (*space*) frequency, and gradually multi-scale the signal (*function*) through the telescopic translation operation, and finally reach the high frequency [7]. Time subdivision, frequency subdivision at low frequency, can automatically adapt to the requirements of time-frequency signal analysis, so that it can focus on any detail of the signal, solve the difficult problem of Fourier transform, and become a major breakthrough in scientific methods since the Fourier transform.

In wavelet variation, we quantify a specific space into a grid of sizes and create a count matrix. Wave clusters decompose the matrix into average subbands. Important

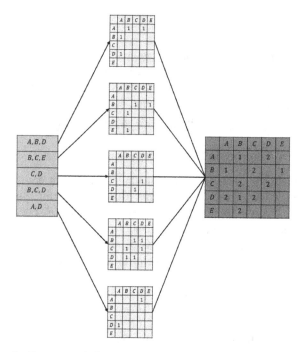

Fig. 1. Recommendation matrix generated by collaborative filtering

grid recognition will identify valid grids from the average subbands, and Wave Cluster constructs an ordered sequence list for the positive wavelet transform values obtained from the wavelet transform value matrix [8]. The user sends information to the aggregator in the form of a user identity, indicating the user's new information coordinates. When the aggregator receives the information sent by the user, the current grid is [11].

2.3 Differential Privacy and Local Differential Privacy

The core idea of the differential privacy protection model has two main points [9]. It can ensure that the operation of inserting or deleting a record in the input data set does not affect the output of any calculation (such as counting query). The model does not care about the attacker. With the background knowledge, even if the attacker has mastered sensitive information of all records except one record, the sensitive information of the record cannot be disclosed [10].

In local differential privacy method, the differentially private mechanism is applied to the real data on local device instead of sending them to the third-party aggregator. The aggregator receives the data that is already anonymized, and the aggregator will not have any access to real data [11, 12]. Local differential privacy method offers a great advantage that the third-party aggregator does not have to be fully trusted. The user's private date is safe even if the aggregator is malicious, which make the local differential privacy model well-suited to wider conditions where the third party is barely trusted

3 P²R-εDP Approach

At present, differential privacy has become a new and generally considered strict and robust privacy protection model. By randomly adding noise to the data set of the user's local information to protect privacy, usually only a small amount of noise is added to protect a large amount Data sets, meanwhile, this method can take into account both the level of privacy protection and data availability. Compared with the traditional method, this method has the advantage that it can rigorously and quantitatively analyze the risk of privacy leakage and does not rely on the background knowledge of the attacker [13, 14]. At present, the research on differential privacy recommendation systems is popular. These studies also consider the trade-off between privacy security and recommendation accuracy.

In order to maximize the balance between security and accuracy, we proposed a new system model, *HPIDP*. In this model, we improved the traditional differential privacy method, and made a lot of recommendations on the recommendation system. The system, while greatly improving the accuracy of the recommendation, also fits the system more perfectly, making the entire mechanism efficient and stable.

3.1 Overview

The *HPIDP* model includes a client (*local device*), a base station, a wireless network, an information aggregation server, and a personalized recommendation system server. Each information aggregation server can connect multiple base stations, mainly to record information updates of users in the cell. The structure of the system is shown in Fig. 2. The user inputs personal information into the client. The information aggregator transforms the user's real data into anonymized data and performs mesh segmentation according to the degree of confidentiality of the information [15, 16]. The aggregator is a trusted third party, the aggregator sends the anonymous data to the personalized recommendation system server, and the service provider sends the searched candidate (*cs*) set to the aggregator for refinement, i.e., important mesh identification, and finally through the aggregator. Send results that meet user needs to the user.

3.2 Distributed ε-Differential Privacy Method

The basic idea of differential privacy is to convert the original data or add noise to the statistical results to achieve the effect of privacy protection [17], that is, to ensure that the overall or fuzzy information is given the individual information is not revealed. Queries in the recommendation system tend to have higher sensitivity. Therefore, the application of differential privacy technology can introduce a lot of noise, resulting in poor data availability.

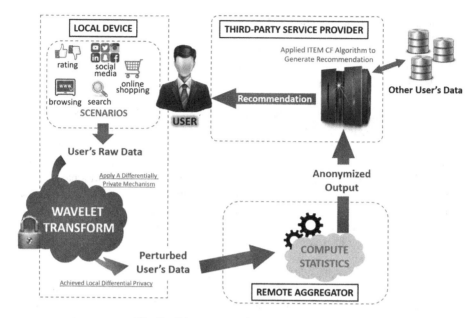

Fig. 2. Privacy protection structure system

3.2.1 Single Parameter Local Differential Privacy

To protect privacy, each user first uses a random perturbation function f to perturb their tuples and then sends the perturbed data $f(t)$ instead of the original real data t to the aggregator or service provider. The perturbation function determines the trade-off between privacy security levels and service recommendation accuracy. If $f(t) = t$ is directly used, in this case, the user sends the real data directly to the aggregator, and the aggregator performs modeling calculation based on the real similar data, which will reach the extreme of the recommended service precision, and at the same time. This is also the fact that the aggregator completely receives the user's private data and will have no user privacy. If you let f output a tuple unrelated to t, the aggregator will not perform computational modeling based on any valid user data, which also achieves an extreme user privacy the recommended service accuracy will be reduced to zero.

Definition 1 ($\in$-Local Differential Privacy)
The random function f satisfies $\in -local$ differential privacy if and only if any two input tuples $t, t' \in Dom(f)$. At this point for any possible output $(t) = t^*$, we have:

$$Pr[f(t) = t^*] \leq e^{\in} \times Pr[f(t') = t^*] \tag{1}$$

LDP is a special case of *DP* because random perturbation in *LDP* are performed by the user rather than by the aggregator [18], which means that the aggregator does not have the user's real private data.

According to the definition above, it can be ensured that the aggregator accepting the disturbed data tuple t^* cannot distinguish whether the true tuple is t or another tuple t' (controlled by the privacy parameter $\in$). This also provides users with certain denial. At the same time, in the $\in - local$ differential privacy, since the random disturbance is performed by the user himself, depending on the different privacy requirements of the users, different users further achieve the privacy protection by giving different values of the privacy parameter $\in$.

3.2.2 Data Processing Method on the Aggregator Side (Combination of Wavelet Transform and Important Grid Recognition)

Wavelet transform is a new transform analysis method. It inherits and develops the idea of localization of short-time Fourier transform. At the same time, it overcomes the shortcomings of window size and frequency variation and can provide a "time-frequency" window with frequency change. It is an ideal tool for signal time-frequency analysis and processing. Its main feature is that it can fully highlight some aspects of the problem through transformation, can localize the analysis of time (*space*) frequency, and gradually multi-scale the signal (*function*) through the telescopic translation operation, and finally reach the high frequency. Time subdivision, frequency subdivision at low frequency, can automatically adapt to the requirements of time-frequency signal analysis, so that it can focus on any detail of the signal, solve the difficult problem of Fourier transform, and become a major breakthrough in scientific methods since the Fourier transform.

The basic idea is to first calculate the number of iterations of the two algorithms based on the degree of anonymity k that the user wants to achieve, then calculate the number of grids included in the final results of the two algorithms, compare the grid numbers of the two algorithms, and finally select the algorithm that generates the least number of grids. This selection mechanism can reduce the anonymous processing of unnecessary grids, reduce data distortion, and improve the privacy protection against data.

Assume that the amount of user data onto each $N \times M$ cell is evenly distributed (ideally), the number n, k is the degree of anonymity indicating user data. Assuming that the number of columns and rows in the final anonymous area is increased or decreased, then $\mu = \sqrt{\frac{k}{n}}$.

μ^2 indicates the number of cells required, and the number of cells in the ideal state formed is μ row and μ column. Assume that the maximum anonymous area calculated according to the maximum spatial resolution is a row and b column, and the value of sum can be estimated according to the maximum resolution (d_x, d_y) and the grid parameter (N, M), as follows:

$$a = 2 \times \left(\frac{d_y}{M}\right) + 1 \quad B = 2 \times \left(\frac{d_x}{N}\right) + 1 \tag{2}$$

For the *Bottom − Upgrid* algorithm to dynamically expand from a cell containing the user, the number of cells after the final anonymous region is expanded is $a \times b$, that is, the $a - 1$ row $b - 1$ column needs to be added. Ideally, you need to add $\mu - 1$ rows and $\mu - 1$ columns. For the *Top - Downgrid* algorithm, the anonymous area that satisfies the condition is a row and b column, and the $a - (\mu - 1)$ row and $b - (\mu - 1)$ column will be removed on average. Therefore, the number of iterations required by the *Bottom - Upgrid* algorithm is represented by x, and the value is estimated as follows:

$$x = 2 \times \left(\sqrt{\frac{k}{n}} - 1 \right) \tag{3}$$

The number of iterations required by the *Top - Downgrid* algorithm is represented by y, and the value is estimated as follows:

$$y = a - \left(\sqrt{\frac{k}{n}} - 1 \right) + b - \left(\sqrt{\frac{k}{n}} - 1 \right) \tag{4}$$

3.3   Recommended Information Protection Based on LDP

Although the traditional recommendation system model can also provide some user privacy protection, with the increasing enhancement of hacker technology, the user's recommendation information may not be so highly protective. Hackers can still steal user data through offline description files stored on the client.

Therefore, we propose a local differential privacy strategy to solve this problem, namely LDP. The basic idea of differential privacy is to transform the original data or add noise to the statistical results to achieve the effect of privacy protection, that is, to ensure that overall or vague information is given not to disclose individual information. Through LDP technology, we encrypt user data at the local client, then upload it to the server for processing of the recommendation algorithm, which greatly reduces the possibility of user data being plagiarized.

Queries in recommendation systems often have a high sensitivity. Therefore, the application of differential privacy technology will cause a lot of noise, resulting in poor data availability. Fortunately, we thought of a solution. Project-first send the data to an aggregator, use wavelet transformation in the aggregator, then re-acquire the original discrete data by the important grid recognition technology. After such an operation, it is sent to our server for recommendation processing.

On the server side, we use distributed servers, that is, multiple servers accept user data and integrate information through aggregation algorithms. Under this decentralized mechanism, unless you have a service provider specific aggregation algorithm, it is difficult for a hacker to steal the information he wants from the server.

So far, we have proposed a highly protective recommendation system model that does not lose recommendation quality while improving the security of user data.

4 Experimental Results and Analysis

This paper uses the standard dataset *MovieLens* dataset for verification. The *MovieLens* dataset contains 100,000 real ratings from 1682 movies by anonymous users, with ratings ranging from 1–5. In order to make the verification more accurate, records with scores less than 3 are deleted, some documents are called coarse-grained processes.

Accuracy and recall are two measures widely used in the fields of information retrieval and statistical classification to evaluate the quality of results. Among them, accuracy is the ratio of the number of retrieved related documents to the total number of retrieved documents, which measures the accuracy rate of the retrieval system; the recall rate refers to the ratio of the number of retrieved related documents to the total number of relevant documents in the document library. It is the recall of the retrieval system. The value of the two is between 0 and 1. The closer the value is to 1, the higher the precision or recall.

In a real system, the recommendation algorithm usually only returns a recommendation list of length L to the user. The products in the list are the top L products with the highest prediction score. In this way, the user is concerned about how many products the user really likes in the recommendation list of length L. For this reason, the accuracy rate and recall rate are often used as two commonly used indicators to measure the effectiveness of the recommendation. Accuracy is defined as the proportion of users who like a product in a recommendation list of length L.

Formula 1:

$$P(L)_i = \frac{N_i}{L} \tag{5}$$

Among them, N_i represents the number of products the user likes in the recommendation list of length L. By averaging the accuracy rates of all users in the system, the accuracy rate $P(L)$ of the system is obtained.

Recall indicates the proportion of products that the user likes appearing in the recommendation list.

Formula 2:

$$R(L)_i = \frac{N_i}{B_i} \tag{6}$$

Among them, N_i represents the number of products that the user likes in the recommendation list of length L; B_i represents the total number of products that the user likes. By averaging the recall rate of all users in the system, the system recall rate $R(L)$ is obtained. Both the accuracy rate and the recall rate need to calculate the number of products that the user likes to appear in the recommendation list of length L. The difference is the denominator. The denominator for calculating the accuracy is a fixed value L. The experiment usually sets $L = 50$.

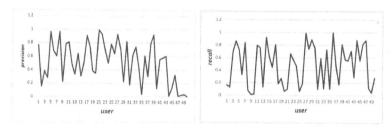

Fig. 3. The precision rate and recall rate of the system

The higher the precision and recall of the search results, the better the presentation effect. In fact, the two are contradictory in some cases. For example, in extreme cases, we only search for one result and it is accurate, then Precision is 100%. Recall is low; and if we return all results, for example, Recall is 100%, Significantly reduced accuracy. Therefore, in different occasions, you need to judge for yourself whether you want a higher Precision or a higher Recall. Figures 1 and 2 are the user's Precision and Recall. By averaging the accuracy rates of all users in the system, the system's accuracy rate $P(L)$ is obtained. By averaging the recall rates of all users in the system, the system's Recall rate $R(L)$. In the recommendation system using *HPIDP*, the Enhancement of $P(50)$ is 0.69%, and the Enhancement of $R(50)$ is 2.16%. The experimental results show that the recommendation method in *HPIDP* improves the recommendation effect.

In order to check the recommendation effect using *HPIDP*, the data set is divided into two parts: the training set and the test set, and the ratio of the training set to the test set is 9 : 1. The data in the training set is known information, while the information in the test set is not allowed to be used for prediction. Then, compare the ratings and predictions to determine whether the protected data will affect the accuracy of the recommendation. As shown in Fig. 4:

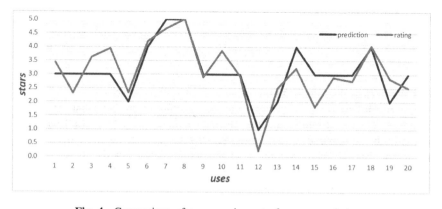

Fig. 4. Comparison of accuracy impact of recommendations

In the case of the same data set, there is a slight difference between the prediction result of the recommendation system and the user's own choice. After calculating the data for each star rating, the accuracy of the prediction and the recommendation without *HPIDP* the method is almost the same.

5 Conclusion and Future Work

Most of the personalized recommendation systems in life focus on how to improve the accuracy of recommendations, while ignoring the importance of their privacy. This article aims to improve the privacy of personalized recommendation systems, while also applying differential privacy. Based on the privacy protection algorithm of the protection technology, by improving the differential privacy method and reducing the number of Laplacian noise increases, the data loss caused by the excessive number of noises is effectively controlled, so that the recommendation accuracy does not meet the requirements. Compared with the collaborative filtering algorithm under typical differential privacy protection, we divide the process of differential privacy into two steps, which alleviates the ergonomic pressure of the user and solves the risk of data leakage of the third-party server. However, there are still some limitations in the proposed *HPIDP* mechanism. Though the user's private data can have a strong protection through the differentially private method in local device, and wavelet transform and so on from remote aggregator, and meanwhile have an acceptable accuracy. The accuracy of recommendation service still has a big improving room for current system, which is also our focusing point in the future work.

References

1. Friedman, A., Schuster, A.: Data mining with differential privacy. In: Proceedings of the 16th ACM SIGKDD International Conference on Knowledge Discovery and Data Mining, Washington, DC, USA (2010)
2. Polat, H., Du, W.: Achieving private recommendations using randomized response techniques. In: Ng, W.-K., Kitsuregawa, M., Li, J., Chang, K. (eds.) PAKDD 2006. LNCS (LNAI), vol. 3918, pp. 637–646. Springer, Heidelberg (2006). https://doi.org/10.1007/11731139_73
3. Ning, X., Desrosiers, C., Karypis, G.: A comprehensive survey of neighborhood-based recommendation methods. Comput. Sci. Eng. 37–76 (2015)
4. Dwork, C., McSherry, F., Nissim, K., Smith, A.: Calibrating noise to sensitivity in private data analysis. In: Halevi, S., Rabin, T. (eds.) TCC 2006. LNCS, vol. 3876, pp. 265–284. Springer, Heidelberg (2006). https://doi.org/10.1007/11681878_14
5. Wanyu, D., Qinghua, Z., Lin, C.: Study on the rapid learning method of neural network. Chinese J. Comput. 33(2), 279–287 (2010)
6. Chaudhuri, K., Monteleoni, C., Sarwate, A.D.: Differentially private empirical risk minimization. J. Mach. Learn. Res. 12, 1069–1109 (2009)
7. Chen, L., Yu, T., Chirkova, R.: WaveCluster with differential privacy. In: International Conference on Information and Knowledge Management, Proceedings, Melbourne, Australia (2015)

8. Berlioz, A., Friedman, A., Kaafar, M.A., Boreli, R., Berkovsky, S.: Applying differential privacy to matrix factorization. In: Proceedings of the 9th ACM Conference on Recommender Systems, Vienna, Austria (2015)

9. Dwork, C.: Differential privacy. In: Bugliesi, M., Preneel, B., Sassone, V., Wegener, I. (eds.) ICALP 2006. LNCS, vol. 4052, pp. 1–12. Springer, Heidelberg (2006). https://doi.org/10.1007/11787006_1

10. Zhao, R., Mao, E.: Semi-random projection for dimensionality reduction and extreme learning machine in high-dimensional space. IEEE Comput. Intell. Mag. **10**, 30–41 (2015)

11. Bassily, R., Smith, A.: Local, private, efficient protocols for succinct histograms. In: STOC (2015)

12. Duchi, J.C., Jordan, M., Wainwright, M.J.: Privacy aware learning. J. ACM **61**(6), 38:1–38:57 (2014)

13. Erlingsson, Ú., Korolova, A., Pihur, V.: RAPPOR: randomized aggregatable privacy-preserving ordinal response. In: CCS, pp. 1054–1067 (2014)

14. Fanti, G., Pihur, V., Erlingsson, Ú.: Building a RAPPOR with the unknown: privacy-preserving learning of associations and data dictionaries. In: Proceedings of Privacy Enhancing Technology, pp. 41–61 (2016)

15. Nguyên, T.T., Xiao, X., Yang, Y., Hui, S.C.: Collecting and Analyzing Data from Smart Device Users with Local Differential Privacy (2016). https://arxiv.org/abs/1606.05053

16. Liu, B., Xia, S.-X., Meng, F.-R., Zhou, Y.: Manifold regularized extreme learning machine. Neural Comput. Appl. **27**(2), 255–269 (2015). https://doi.org/10.1007/s00521-014-1777-8

17. Li, C., Sánchez, R.V., Zurita, G.V., Cerrada, M.: Multimodal deep support vector classification with homologous features and its application to gearbox fault diagnosis. Neurocomputing 168 (2015)

18. Dwork, C., Nissim, K.: Privacy-preserving datamining on vertically partitioned databases. In: Franklin, M. (ed.) CRYPTO 2004. LNCS, vol. 3152, pp. 528–544. Springer, Heidelberg (2004). https://doi.org/10.1007/978-3-540-28628-8_32

An Improved Dynamic Certificateless Authenticated Asymmetric Group Key Agreement Protocol with Trusted KGC

Haiyan Sun[✉], Lingling Li, Jianwei Zhang, and Wanwei Huang

Software College, Zhengzhou University of Light Industry,
Zhengzhou 450002, China
18703618726@126.com

Abstract. Asymmetric group key agreement allows a group of users to negotiate a common public encryption key, and each user only holds his own secret encryption key. Authenticated asymmetric group key agreement (AAGKA) protocol is a kind of AGKA protocols which can be secure against active attacks. Dynamic asymmetric group key agreement allows any member to join and leave at any point. This paper studies dynamic AAGKA in certificateless cryptography. We first pointed that Wei et al.'s dynamic certificateless AAGKA protocol suffers from a key compromise impersonation attack, and cannot provide secrecy or forward secrecy. We then proposed an improved dynamic certificateless AAGKA protocol. Security proofs show that our protocol can provide security attributes including secrecy, known-key security, key compromise impersonation resistance, forward security, non-repudiation, and privacy. Furthermore, the proposed protocol is still efficient.

Keywords: Asymmetric group key agreement · Certificateless key cryptography · Provable security · Dynamic groups

1 Introduction

Group key agreement (GKA) protocol allows a group of users to negotiate a common secret key over an open network, which can be used to establish a confidential communication channel among these users via symmetric encryption. Hence, GKA protocols are proverbially exploited in numerous present collaborative and distributed application systems, for instance, multicast communications, audio-video meetings and chat systems. Since this primitive was proposed, many GKA protocols (e.g., [1–4]) have been built. However, GKA protocol is subject to a problem, i.e., every user external the group cannot send messages to the members in the group (group members), on account of the public secret key is the uniquely known mid the group members. In addition, many now available GKA protocols (e.g., [1–4]) need two or more rounds to set up a secret session key. It would be more interesting they can be done by one-round communication. A two round GKA protocol requires all participants to be online concurrently, which is in fact difficult for them to be online at the same time.

© Springer Nature Singapore Pte Ltd. 2020
Y. Tian et al. (Eds.): ICBDS 2019, CCIS 1210, pp. 223–237, 2020.
https://doi.org/10.1007/978-981-15-7530-3_16

In 2009, Wu et al. [5] proposed the asymmetric key agreement (AGKA), which allows a group of users to negotiate a common encryption key, and each group member holds his own decryption key. In this way, anyone who knows the negotiated public key can send messages to group members. The protocol in [5] is a one-round AGKA protocol. However, this only secure prevents passive opponents from eavesdropping on the message. In the real world, attackers are usually active and control the communication channel to modify, replay, insert or delete messages. It is promotes the need for authenticated asymmetric group key agreement (AAGKA) protocols.

Authenticated key agreement protocols guarantee that only their expected peers can know the secret session keys. Dynamic asymmetric group key agreement protocols allow member joining or leaving at any point. Dynamic asymmetric group key agreement protocols can be implemented in different public-key cryptosystems, including the traditional public-key infrastructure (PKI), identity-based cryptography [6] or certificateless cryptography [7]. In 2010, Zhang et al. [8, 9] extended their PKI-based AAGKA protocol to a broadcast encryption, which can be viewed as a dynamic PKI-based AAGKA protocol. However, Wu et al. [10] pointed out that their protocol requires a trusted third party to maintain an electronic billboard, which seems hard to realize in the ad hoc networks. They also proposed a dynamic asymmetric group key agreement protocol without a trusted third party. Zhao et al. [11] also proposed a dynamic asymmetric group key agreement. Different from other AGKA protocols, in their protocol every participant holds the same decryption key and their protocol is a three-round protocol while other AGKA protocols are one-round protocols. Lv et al. [12] presented a generic construction of asymmetric GKA protocol based on Chinese Remainder Theorem and public-key cryptosystems with key homomorphism. However, protocols in [10, 12] are unauthenticated protocols while protocols [8, 9, 11] are PKI-based protocols, which have a heavy certificate management burden. To avoid these problems, several dynamic identity-based AAGKA protocols [13, 14] were proposed. However, dynamic identity-based AAGKA protocols are subject to the inherent key escrow problem. To avoid the problem, Wei et al. [15] proposed a certificateless AAGKA protocol for dynamic groups, called WYS protocol.

In this paper, we noticed that the WYS protocol cannot satisfy key compromise impersonation resistance, secrecy or forward secrecy. Furthermore, we found that the WYS protocol cannot provide secrecy or forward secrecy. To improve security, we proposed an improved protocol, which can catch security properties including secrecy, known-key security, key compromise impersonation resistance, forward security, non-repudiation, and privacy.

2   Preliminaries

2.1   Bilinear Maps

Let g be the generator of an additive group $\mathbb{G}$ of prime order q and $\mathbb{G}_T$ be a multiplicative group of q, and. A map $\hat{e} : \mathbb{G} \times \mathbb{G} \to \mathbb{G}_T$ is said to be a bilinear map if it meets the following requirements [9]:

(1) Bilinearity: $\hat{e}(g^a, g^b) = \hat{e}(g,g)^{ab}$ for any $a, b \in \mathbb{Z}_q^*, Q \in \mathbb{G}$.

(2) Non-degeneracy: $\hat{e}(g,g) \neq 1_{\mathbb{G}_T}$.

(3) Computability: e is efficiently computable.

2.2 Complexity Assumption

ℓ-**Bilinear Diffie-Hellman Exponent (ℓ-BDHE) Problem** [8]: Given g, g_1 and $t_i = g^{\alpha^i}$ in $\mathbb{G}$ for $i = 1, 2, \cdots, \ell, \ell+2, \cdots, 2\ell$, compute $\hat{e}(g, g_1)^{\alpha^{\ell+1}}$.

ℓ-BDHE assumption means that for any polynomial-time algorithm $\mathcal{CH}$, $\text{Adv}(\mathcal{CH}) = Pr[\mathcal{CH}(g, g_1, t_1, \cdots, t_\ell, t_{\ell+2}, \cdots, t_{2\ell}) = \hat{e}(g, g_1)^{\alpha^{\ell+1}}]$ is negligible.

2.3 Security Properties

According to [13], the famous security properties for AAGKA protocols are as follows:

- **Secrecy:** Only the **group** members can read the messages encrypted by the negotiated public key.
- **Known-key security:** If an adversary learns the group encryption/decryption keys of other sessions, he cannot compute subsequent group decryption keys.
- **Key compromise impersonation resistance:** The compromise of user A's long-term private key will allow an adversary to impersonate A, but it should not make the adversary be able to impersonate other users to A.
- **Forward secrecy:** The disclosure of long-term private keys of group members must not compromise the secrecy of the previously established group decryption keys.
- **Non-repudiation (sender):** A sender cannot deny his/her transmission of a message.
- **Privacy (sender):** An **attacker** cannot identify the identity of the sender.

3 Weaknesses of the WYS Protocol

In this section, we point out the weaknesses of the WYS protocol. Here, we do not review the WYS protocol, one can refer to [15] for details.

3.1 Key Compromise Impersonation Attack

Suppose that U_i's private key $sk_i = (D_i, v_i)$ has been compromised. In the following we will show that an adversary $\mathcal{A}$ can impersonate $U_j (j \neq i)$ with U_i's private key to communicate with U_i and other users.

Assume $\mathcal{A}$ can obtain U_j's previously generated message $\{ID_j, \sigma_{j,1}, \cdots, \sigma_{j,j-1},$ $null, \sigma_{j,j+1}, \cdots, \sigma_{j,N}, (x_j, A_j)\}$, which is actually open and everyone can obtain it. When $\mathcal{A}$ joins the system, $\mathcal{A}$ sends $\{ID_j, \sigma_{j,1}, \cdots, \sigma_{j,j-1}, null, \sigma_{j,j+1}, \cdots, \sigma_{j,N}, (x_j, A_j)\}$ to the billboard maintainer. Since this message only depends on the sender's private keys rather than random numbers, the message from the same user in each session is same.

Since it can be verified valid by the billboard maintainer, $\mathcal{A}$ joins the systems successfully.

$\mathcal{A}$ then computes the group private key gsk_i of U_i as the group private key and decrypts received ciphertexts. Since $\mathcal{A}$ knows U_i's private key $sk_i = (D_i, v_i)$, he can compute $\sigma_{i,i} = D_i g_i^{v_i}$ and gsk_i. Thus the WYS protocol cannot resist key compromise impersonation attack.

3.2 Lack of Secrecy

In the WYS protocol, if the billboard part II is not full, then the billboard maintainer always has the ability to decrypt the group messages. Since the billboard maintainer is an extraordinary user of the system, then the secrecy of the WYS protocol is not satisfied.

3.3 Lack of Forward Secrecy

Suppose that U_i's private key $sk_i = (D_i, v_i)$ has been compromised. With the knowledge of $sk_i = (D_i, v_i)$, $\mathcal{A}$ can compute $\sigma_{i,i} = D_i g_i^{v_i}$, from which $\mathcal{A}$ can compute the previously established group decryption keys. Thus the WYS protocol cannot provide forward secrecy.

4 Our Improved Protocol

In this section, we propose our dynamic certificateless AAGKA from bilinear pairings.

4.1 Protocol Description

- **System-Setup (SS):** Taking a security parameter k as input, KGC does the following:

  (1). Choose two multiplicative groups $\mathbb{G}$ and $\mathbb{G}_T$ with prime order q. such that a bilinear pairing $\hat{e} : \mathbb{G} \times \mathbb{G} \to \mathbb{G}_T$ can be constructed and pick an arbitrary generator g of $\mathbb{G}$.

  (2). Choose a random number $s \in \mathbb{Z}_q^*$ as the master key and set the master public key $mpk = g^s$.

  (3). Choose six cryptographic hash functions $H_1 : \{0,1\}^{\lambda_0 + \lambda_1} \to \mathbb{G}$, $H_2 : \{0,1\}^{\lambda_0 + 2\lambda_1} \to \mathbb{Z}_q^*$, $H_3 : \{0,1\}^* \to \mathbb{G}$, $H_4 : \{0,1\}^* \to \mathbb{G}$, $H_5 : \mathbb{G}_T \to \{0,1\}^{\lambda_0 + \lambda_2 + \lambda_1}$ and $H_6 : \{0,1\}^{\lambda_0 + \lambda_1 + \lambda_2 + \lambda_1} \to \mathbb{Z}_q^*$, in which λ_0, λ_1, and λ_2 are the binary lengths of an identity, an element in $\mathbb{G}$, and a plaintext, receptively.

  (4). Publish the system parameters $params = (\mathbb{G}, \mathbb{G}_T, \hat{e}, g, mpk, H_1, \cdots, H_6)$ while keeping the master key s secret.

- **Set-Secret-Value (SSV)**: This algorithm takes *params* and U_i's identity ID_i as inputs. The user randomly selects $v_{i,0}, v_{i,1} \in \mathbb{Z}_q^*$, and sets $v_i = (v_{i,0}, v_{i,1})$ as his secret value.
- **Set-Public-Key (SPK)**: Inputting *params*, and U_i's identity ID_i and secret value $(v_{i,0}, v_{i,1})$, it computes $pk_{i,0} = g^{v_{i,0}}, pk_{i,1} = g^{v_{i,1}}$, and constructs U_i's public key as $pk_i = (pk_{i,0}, pk_{i,1})$.
- **Partial-Private-Key-Extract (PPKE)**: On input *params*, s and U_i's identity ID_i and public key $pk_i = (pk_{i,0}, pk_{i,1})$, KGC computes $Q_{i,0} = H_1(ID_i, pk_{i,0}), Q_{i,1} = H_1(ID_i, pk_{i,1})$, $D_{i,0} = Q_{i,0}^s$, $D_{i,1} = Q_{i,1}^s$ and outputs the partial private key $D_i = (D_{i,0}, D_{i,1})$ for U_i. U_i can check the correctness of $D_{i,0}$ and $D_{i,1}$ by verifying $\hat{e}(D_{i,0}, g) = \hat{e}(Q_{i,0}, P_{pub})$ and $\hat{e}(D_{i,1}, g) = \hat{e}(Q_{i,1}, P_{pub})$, respectively.
- **Set-Secret-Key (SSK)**: Inputting *params*, and U_i's partial private key $(D_{i,0}, D_{i,1})$ and secret value $(v_{i,0}, v_{i,1})$, U_i constructs his private key as $sk_i = (D_{i,0}, D_{i,1}, v_{i,0}, v_{i,1})$.
- **Billboard-Initialization (BI)**: Assume that the group size is n and the group manager (i.e., the billboard maintainer) U_t, which holds identity ID_t, private key $sk_t = (D_{t,0}, D_{t,1}, v_{t,0}, v_{t,1})$ and public key $pk_t = (pk_{t,0}, pk_{t,1})$, is the 1-th participant in the group. U_t initializes the billboard part I (as shown in Table 1) as follows:

Table 1. Billboard part I

Column	1	2	3	$\cdots$	n	n + 1
	Null	$\sigma_{1,2}^0$	$\sigma_{1,3}^0$	$\cdots$	$\sigma_{1,n}^0$	$(ID_t, R_1^0, pk_{t,0})$
$\mathbb{L}_2$		Null	$\sigma_{2,3}^0$	$\cdots$		
$\mathbb{L}_3$		$\sigma_{3,2}^0$	Null	$\cdots$	$\sigma_{3,n}^0$	
$\vdots$	$\vdots$	$\vdots$	$\vdots$	$\ddots$	$\vdots$	
$\mathbb{L}_n$		$\sigma_{n,2}^0$	$\sigma_{n,3}^0$	$\cdots$	Null	

(1). For $1 \leq i \leq n$, pick $r_i^0 \in \mathbb{Z}_q^*$ at random and calculate $R_i^0 = g^{r_i^0}, h_i^0 = H_2(ID_t, R_i^0, pk_{t,0})$ and $Z = H_3(params)$.

(2). For $1 \leq i, j \leq n$, compute $\sigma_{i,j}^0 = D_{t,0} Z^{h_i^0 v_{t,0}} H_4(j)^{r_i^0}$.

(3). Publish $\mathbb{L}_i = \{\sigma_{i,1}^0, \cdots, \sigma_{i,i-1}^0, null, \sigma_{i,i+1}^0, \cdots, \sigma_{i,n}^0, (ID_t, R_i^0, pk_{t,0})\}$.

For the billboard part II, as shown in Table 2, U_t sets the first row to be $\mathbb{L}'_1 = \{null, \sigma_{1,2}^0, \cdots, \sigma_{1,n}^0, (ID_t, R_1^0, pk_{t,0})\}$, and the rest rows to be

$$\mathbb{L}'_i = \{\overbrace{null, null, \cdots, null}^{n+1}\}, 2 \leq i \leq n.$$

- **Join**: When a user $\mathcal{U}_i$ with a private/public key pair $(sk_i, pk_i) = ((D_{i,0}, D_{i,1}, v_{i,0}, v_{i,1}), (pk_{i,0}, pk_{i,1}))$ wants to join the group, he first checks whether there is a row with all null elements on billboard part II. If there is no such row, it

Table 2. Billboard part II

Column	1	2	3	$\cdots$	n	n + 1
	Null	$\sigma_{1,2}^0$	$\sigma_{1,3}^0$	$\cdots$	$\sigma_{1,n}^0$	$(ID_t, R_1^0, pk_{t,0})$
$\mathbb{L}'_2$	Null	Null	Null	$\cdots$	Null	Null
$\mathbb{L}'_3$	Null	Null	Null	$\cdots$	Null	Null
$\vdots$	$\vdots$	$\vdots$	$\vdots$	$\ddots$	$\vdots$	$\vdots$
$\mathbb{L}'_n$	Null	Null	Null	$\cdots$	Null	Null

means the group is full. Otherwise, assuming that he/she would be the i-th group participant for simplicity (i.e., the i-th row on billboard part II), $\mathcal{U}_i$ does the following:

(1). Choose a random number $r_i \in \mathbb{Z}_q^*$ and compute $R_i = g^{r_i}$, $h_i = H_2(ID_i, R_i, pk_{i,0})$ and $Z = H_3(params)$.

(2). For $1 \leq j \leq n$, compute $\sigma_{i,j} = D_{i,0} Z^{h_i v_{i,0}} H_4(j)^{r_i}$.

(3). Publish $\{\sigma_{i,1}, \cdots, \sigma_{i,i-1}, null, \sigma_{i,i+1}, \cdots, \sigma_{i,n}, (ID_i, R_i, pk_{i,0})\}$ to the group manager.

When the group manager receives this message, he/she sets the elements in i-th row on billboard part II to be $\mathbb{L}'_i = \{\sigma_{i,1}, \cdots, \sigma_{i,i-1}, null, \sigma_{i,i+1}, \cdots, \sigma_{i,n}, (ID_i, R_i, pk_{i,0})\}$.

- **Leave: Suppose** that the i-th group participant (the i-th row on billboard part II) is leaving the group and the group manager is the 1-th group participant.

(1). If $i \neq 1$, the group manager sets $\mathbb{L}'_i = \overbrace{(null, null, \cdots, null)}^{n+1}$.

(2). Else, a new group manager $\mathcal{U}_{t'}$ is elected. Both tables maintained by $\mathcal{U}_t$ are passed to $\mathcal{U}_{t'}$. The new group manager $\mathcal{U}_{t'}$ needs to update messages in Table 1 and the first row in Table 2 in the same way described in the BI algorithm.

- **Group-Public-Key-Derivation (GPKD):** Let $\mathbb{S}$ be the set of indexes such that $\mathbb{L}'_i = \overbrace{(null, null, \cdots, null)}^{n+1}$ and $\bar{\mathbb{S}}$ be the set of indexes such that $\mathbb{L}'_i \neq \overbrace{(null, null, \cdots, null)}^{n+1}$ on the billboard part II, respectively. To derive the group private key, a user first computes $Z = H_3(params)$, $Q_{t,0} = H_1(ID_t, pk_{t,0})$, for $i \in \mathbb{S}$ computes $h_i^0 = H_2(ID_t, R_i^0, pk_{t,0})$, for $i \in \bar{\mathbb{S}} \setminus \{1\}$ computes $h_i = H_2(ID_i, R_i, pk_{i,0})$ and $Q_{i,0} = H_1(ID_i, pk_{i,0})$

Any user first verifies the correctness of elements on the billboard part I and the billboard part II by verifying the following two equations.

$$\hat{e}(\sigma_{1,2}^0, g) = \hat{e}(Q_{t,0}, mpk)\hat{e}(Z, pk_{t,0}^{h_i^0})\hat{e}(H_4(2), R_1^0) \tag{1}$$

$$\hat{e}(\prod_{i\in S} \sigma_{i,1}^0 \prod_{i\in \bar{S}\setminus\{1\}} \sigma_{i,1}, g) \overset{?}{=} \hat{e}(\prod_{i\in S} Q_{t,0} \prod_{i\in \bar{S}\setminus\{1\}} Q_{i,0}, mpk)\hat{e}(H_4(1), \prod_{i\in S} R_i^0 \prod_{i\in \bar{S}\setminus\{1\}} R_i)$$
$$\times \hat{e}(Z, \prod_{i\in S} pk_{t,0}^{h_i^0} \prod_{i\in \bar{S}\setminus\{1\}} pk_{i,0}^{h_i})$$
$$\tag{2}$$

If Eqs. (1) and (2) hold, he/she computes the group public key $gpk = (x, A)$, where
$x = \prod_{i\in S} R_i^0 \prod_{i\in \bar{S}} R_i$, $A = \hat{e}(\prod_{i\in S} Q_{t,0} \prod_{i\in \bar{S}} Q_{i,0}, mpk)\hat{e}(Z, \prod_{i\in S} pk_{t,0}^{h_i^0} \prod_{i\in \bar{S}} pk_{i,0}^{h_i})$.

- **Group-Secret-Key-Derivation (GSKD)**: In order to compute the group private key gsk_j, each participant U_j calculates $gsk_j = \prod_{i\in S} \sigma_{i,j}^0 \prod_{i\in \bar{S}} \sigma_{i,j}$ and validates the equality of $\hat{e}(gsk_j, g) = A\hat{e}(H_4(j), x)$, where x and A are computed according to the GPKD algorithm. If it holds, user U_j accepts gsk_j as the group decryption key.
- **Encryption (Enc)**: Assume **that** the sender holds identity ID_s, private key $sk_s = (D_{s,0}, D_{s,1}, v_{s,0}, v_{s,1})$ and public key $pk_s = (pk_{s,0}, pk_{s,1})$. With the knowledge of the system parameters $params$ and the group public key $gpk = (x, A)$, the sender can sign and encrypt any plaintext m from the message space as follows:

  (1). Select a random $t \in \mathbb{Z}_q^*$ and calculate $c_1 = g^t$, $h = H_6(ID_s, c_1, m, pk_{s,1})$, $W = H_3(params)$ and $S = D_{s,1}mpk^{hv_{s,1}}W^t$.
  (2). Calculate $c_2 = x^t$, $c_3 = H_5(A^t) \oplus (ID_s, m, S)$, and output the ciphertext $c = (c_1, c_2, c_3)$.

- **Decryption (Dec)**: To decrypt the ciphertext $c = (c_1, c_2, c_3)$, user U_j which holds the group decryption key gsk_j does the following:

  (1). Calculate $(ID_s, m, S) = c_3 \oplus H_5(e(gsk_j, c_1)e(H_4(j)^{-1}, c_2))$.
  (2). Calculate $W = H_3(params)$, $Q_{s,1} = H_1(ID_s, pk_{s,1})$ and $h = H_6(ID_s, c_1, m, pk_{s,1})$, and verifies whether the equality $\hat{e}(S, g) = \hat{e}(Q_{s,1}pk_{s,1}^h, mpk)\hat{e}(W, c_1)$ holds. If it holds, user U_j accepts m.

4.2 Protocol Correctness

We can easily verify the correctness via the following equations.

$$\hat{e}(gsk_j, g)$$

$$= \hat{e}(\prod_{i \in \S} \sigma_{i,j}^0 \prod_{i \in \bar{\S}} \sigma_{i,j}, g)$$

$$= \hat{e}(\prod_{i \in \S} D_{t,0} Z^{h_i^0 v_{i,0}} H_4(j)^{r_i^0} \prod_{i \in \bar{\S}} D_{i,0} Z^{h_i v_{i,0}} H_4(j)^{r_i}, g)$$

$$= \hat{e}(\prod_{i \in \S} D_{t,0} \prod_{i \in \bar{\S}} D_{i,0}, g) \hat{e}(\prod_{i \in \S} Z^{h_i^0 v_{t,0}} \prod_{i \in \bar{\S}} Z^{h_i v_{i,0}}, g) \hat{e}(\prod_{i \in \S} H_4(j)^{r_i^0} \prod_{i \in \bar{\S}} H_4(j)^{r_i}, g)$$

$$= \hat{e}(\prod_{i \in \S} Q_{t,0}^s \prod_{i \in \bar{\S}} Q_{i,0}^s, g) \hat{e}(\prod_{i \in \S} Z^{h_i^0 v_{t,0}} \prod_{i \in \bar{\S}} Z^{h_i v_{i,0}}, g) \hat{e}(\prod_{i \in \S} H_4(j)^{r_i^0} \prod_{i \in \bar{\S}} H_4(j)^{r_i}, g)$$

$$= \hat{e}(\prod_{i \in \S} Q_{t,0} \prod_{i \in \bar{\S}} Q_{i,0}, g^s) \hat{e}(Z, \prod_{i \in \S} g^{h_i^0 v_{t,0}} \prod_{i \in \bar{\S}} g^{h_i v_{i,0}}) \hat{e}(H_4(j), \prod_{i \in \S} g^{r_i^0} \prod_{i \in \bar{\S}} g^{r_i})$$

$$= \hat{e}(\prod_{i \in \S} Q_{t,0} \prod_{i \in \bar{\S}} Q_{i,0}, mpk) \hat{e}(Z, \prod_{i \in \S} pk_{t,0}^{h_i^0} \prod_{i \in \bar{\S}} pk_{i,0}^{h_i}) \hat{e}(H_4(j), \prod_{i \in \S} R_i^0 \prod_{i \in \bar{\S}} R_i)$$

$$= A \hat{e}(H_4(j), x),$$

$$c_3 \oplus H_5(\hat{e}(gsk_j, c_1) \hat{e}(H_4(j)^{-1}, c_2))$$

$$= (ID_s, m, S, pk_{s,1}) \oplus H_5(A') \oplus H_5(\hat{e}(gsk_j, g^t) \hat{e}(H_4(j)^{-1}, x'))$$

$$= (ID_s, m, S, pk_{s,1}) \oplus H_5(A') \oplus H_5(A^t \hat{e}(H_4(j), x)^t \hat{e}(H_4(j)^{-1}, x'))$$

$$= (ID_s, m, S, pk_{s,1}) \oplus H_5(A') \oplus H_5(A') = (ID_s, m, S, pk_{s,1}).$$

5 Security Proof

In this section, the security proof of our proposed protocol is given.

5.1 Known-Key Security

Theorem 1. The proposed protocol can provide known-key security under the randomness of ri and the collision resistance of H_2.

Proof. The group private key(s) is computed from $\sigma_{i,j} = D_{i,0} Z^{H_2(ID_i, g^{r_i}, pk_{i,0}) v_{i,0}} H_4(j)^{r_i}$, where it is different, uniformly and independently for different sessions since r_i is randomly selected and H_2 is collision-resistant. Therefore, the group private key(s) is also different, uniformly and independently for different sessions, which makes it is impossible for an adversary to compute the group private key(s) of any other session by the group private key(s) of one session.

5.2 Key Compromise Impersonation Resistance

Theorem 2. The proposed protocol can provide key compromise impersonation resistance under the CDH assumption.

Proof. Given a CDH instance $(X = g^x, Y = g^y)$, we next show that if an adversary $\mathcal{A}$ can successfully forgery a message $\{\sigma_{j,j}, (ID_j, R_j, pk_{j,0})\}$, then the challenger $\mathcal{CH}$ can compute $CDH(X, Y) = g^{xy}$.

(1). The challenger $\mathcal{CH}$ first produces $params = (\mathbb{G}, \mathbb{G}_T, \hat{e}, g, mpk = X = g^x, H_1, \cdots, H_6)$.

(2). $\mathcal{CH}$ sets the private key of U_i and $U_j (j \neq i)$ as $sk_i = (X^{k_{i,0}}, X^{k_{i,1}}, v_{i,0}, v_{i,1})$ and $sk_j = (\perp, X^{k_{j,1}}, v_{j,0}, v_{j,1})$, respectively, where $Q_{j,0} = Y = g^y$.

(3). $\mathcal{A}$ creates a forgery $\{\sigma_{j,j}, (ID_j, R_j, pk_{j,0})\}$ on $(ID_j, j, pk_{j,0})$.

(4). If $\{\sigma_{j,j}, (ID_j, R_j, pk_{j,0})\}$ is correct, $\mathcal{A}$ must query $H_4(j)$ and $H_2(ID_j, R_j, pk_{j,0})$. And then $\mathcal{CH}$ returns g^{z_j} and t as answers to $H_4(j)$ and $H_2(ID_j, R_j, pk_{j,0})$ respectively.

(5). At last, $\mathcal{CH}$ computes $\text{CDH}(X, Y) = \sigma_{j,j} pk_{j,0}^{-t} R_j^{-z_j}$ as the answer.

5.3   Forward Secrecy

Theorem 3. The proposed protocol can provide forward secrecy under the DLC assumption in the random model.

Proof. Given a CDH instance $(X = g^x, Y = g^y)$, we next show that if an adversary $\mathcal{A}$ can successfully forgery a message $\{\sigma_{i,i}, (ID_i, X, pk_{i,0})\}$, then the challenger $\mathcal{CH}$ can compute $\text{CDH}(X, Y) = g^{xy}$.

(1). The challenger $\mathcal{CH}$ first gives the master key $s \in \mathbb{Z}_q^*$ and the system parameters $params = (\mathbb{G}, \mathbb{G}_T, \hat{e}, g, mpk = g^s, H_1, \cdots, H_6)$.

(2). $\mathcal{CH}$ sets the private key of U_i as $sk_i = (D_{i,0}, D_{i,1}, v_{i,0}, v_{i,1})$.

(3). $\mathcal{CH}$ sets the messages of U_i as $(\sigma_{i,j} = D_{i,0} Z^{h_i v_{i,0}} X^{z_j}, (ID_i, X, pk_{i,0}))$, where $1 \leq j \leq n, j \neq i$, and publishes $\{\sigma_{i,1}, \cdots, \sigma_{i,i-1}, null, \sigma_{i,i+1}, \cdots, \sigma_{i,n}, (ID_i, X, pk_{i,0})\}$.

(4). At a moment, $\mathcal{A}$ obtained $sk_i = (D_{i,0}, D_{i,1}, v_{i,0}, v_{i,1})$ from $\mathcal{CH}$.

(5). If $\mathcal{A}$ can compute the session key of U_i, he must know $\sigma_{i,i}$, which is not open. Next, $\mathcal{A}$ creates a forgery $\sigma_{i,i}$.

(6). If $\sigma_{i,i}$ is correct, $\mathcal{A}$ must query $H_4(i)$ and $H_2(ID_j, R_j, pk_{j,0})$. And then $\mathcal{CH}$ returns Y and t as answers to $H_4(i)$ and $H_2(ID_i, R_i, pk_{i,0})$ respectively.

(7). At last, $\mathcal{CH}$ computes $\text{CDH}(X, Y) = \sigma_{i,i} D_{i,0}^{-1} Z^{-t v_{i,0}}$ as the answer.

5.4   Non-repudiation (Sender)

Theorem 4. The proposed protocol can provide non-repudiation (sender) under the CDH assumption.

Proof. Given a CDH instance $(X = g^x, Y = g^y)$, we next show that if an adversary $\mathcal{A}$ can successfully forgery a message $c^* = (c_1^*, c_2^*, c_3^*)$, then the challenger $\mathcal{CH}$ can compute $\text{CDH}(X, Y) = g^{xy}$.

(1). The challenger $\mathcal{CH}$ first produces $params = (\mathbb{G}, \mathbb{G}_T, \hat{e}, g, mpk = X = g^x, H_1, \cdots, H_6)$.

(2). $\mathcal{CH}$ sets the private key of U_i as $sk_i = (\perp, \perp, v_{i,0}, v_{i,1})$, where $Q_{i,1} = Y = g^y$.

(3). $\mathcal{A}$ creates a forgery $c^* = (c_1^*, c_2^*, c_3^*)$

(4). $\mathcal{CH}$ calculates $(ID_s, m, S) = c_3^* \oplus H_5(e(gsk_j, c_1^*)e(H_4(j)^{-1}, c_2^*))$, calculates $W = H_3(params) = g^z$, $Q_{s,1} = H_1(ID_s, pk_{s,1})$ and $h = H_6(ID_s, c_1^*, m, pk_{s,1})$, and verifies whether the equality $\hat{e}(S, g) = \hat{e}(Q_{s,1}pk_{s,1}^h, mpk)\hat{e}(W, c_1^*)$ holds. If it holds, $\mathcal{CH}$ accepts m.

(5). If $c^* = (c_1^*, c_2^*, c_3^*)$ is correct, the above equality must hold, i.e., (c_1^*, S) is valid.

(6). At last, $\mathcal{CH}$ computes $\text{CDH}(X, Y) = S(mpk)^{-hv_{s,1}}(c_1^*)^{-z}$ as the answer.

5.5 Privacy (Sender)

Theorem 5. The proposed protocol can provide privacy (sender) under the ℓ-BDHE assumption.

Proof. Given a ℓ-BDHE instance $(g, g_1, t_1, \cdots, t_\ell, t_{\ell+2}, \cdots, t_{2\ell})$, we next show that if an adversary $\mathcal{A}$ can successfully guess $c^* = (c_1^*, c_2^*, c_3^*)$ is the message from $ID_{s,0}$ or $ID_{s,1}$, then the challenger $\mathcal{CH}$ can compute $\hat{e}(g, g_1)^{\alpha^{\ell+1}}$.

(1). The challenger $\mathcal{CH}$ first produces $params = (\mathbb{G}, \mathbb{G}_T, \hat{e}, g, mpk = t_1 = g^\alpha, H_1, \cdots, H_6)$.

(2). $\mathcal{CH}$ sets $H_1(ID_i, pk_{i,0}) = g^{\mu_i}$ if $1 \leq i \neq I \leq n$, and $H_1(ID_i, pk_{i,0}) = g^{\mu_i}t_\ell$ if $i = I$, where $\mu_i \in \mathbb{Z}_q^*$.

(3). $\mathcal{CH}$ sets $H_2(ID_i, R_i, pk_{i,0}) = h_i, H_3(params) = g^\beta$, $H_5(\chi_i) = \omega_i$, $H_6(ID_i, c_1, m, pk_{i,1}) = h_i^6$, where $h_i, \beta, \omega_i, h_i^6 \in \mathbb{Z}_q^*$.

(4). $\mathcal{CH}$ sets $H_4(j) = g^{c_j}t_j$ if $j \leq \ell$, and $H_4(j) = g^{c_j}$ if $j > \ell$, where $c_j \in \mathbb{Z}_q^*$.

(5). If $i \neq I$, $\mathcal{CH}$ computes $R_i = g^{r_i}t_{\ell-i+1}, h_i = H_2(ID_i, R_i, pk_{i,0})$, and $\sigma_{i,j} = t_1^{\mu_i}pk_{i,0}^{\beta h_i}R_i^{c_j}t_j^{r_i}t_{\ell+j-i+1}$ for $1 \leq j \leq n, i \neq j$; otherwise, $\mathcal{CH}$ computes $R_i = g^{r_i}\prod_{k=1}^{n,k \neq i}(t_{\ell-k+1})^{-1}, h_i = H_2(ID_i, R_i, pk_{i,0})$, and $\sigma_{i,j} = t_1^{\mu_i}pk_{i,0}^{\beta h_i}R_i^{c_j}t_j^{r_i}\prod_{k=1}^{n,k \neq i, k \neq j}(t_{\ell+j-k+1})^{-1}$ for $1 \leq j \leq n, i \neq j$.

(6). $\mathcal{CH}$ sets $c_1 = g_1, c_2 = \prod_{k=1}^{n}g_1^{r_k^*}$, picks $b \in \{0, 1\}$ and $\rho_i \in \mathbb{Z}_q^*$, calculates $h = H_6(ID_{s,b}, c_1, m, pk_{s,b,1})$ and $S = t_1^{\rho_i + hv_{s,b,1} + \beta}$, picks $\theta \in \{0, 1\}^{\lambda_0 + \lambda_2 + \lambda_1}$, and calculates $c_3 = \theta \oplus (ID_{s,b}, m, S)$.

(7). If $\mathcal{A}$ can successfully guess $c^* = (c_1^*, c_2^*, c_3^*)$ is the message from $ID_{s,0}$ or $ID_{s,1}$, $\mathcal{A}$ has made a H_5 query on $\hat{e}(g_1^{\sum_{k=1}^{n}\mu_i}, g^{\alpha^{\ell+1}})\hat{e}(g_1^\beta, \prod_{k=1}^{n}pk_{i,0}^{h_i})$. Then, $\mathcal{CH}$ computes $\hat{e}(g, g_1)^{\alpha^{\ell+1}} = \chi_i^{-\sum_{k=1}^{n}\mu_i}\hat{e}(g_1^{-\beta}, \prod_{k=1}^{n}pk_{i,0}^{h_i})$ as the solution, where (χ_i, ω_i) is the tuple $\mathcal{CH}$ has set in steps (3).

5.6   Secrecy

Theorem 6. The proposed protocol can provide secrecy under the ℓ-BDHE assumption.

Proof. Given a ℓ-BDHE instance $(g, g_1, t_1, \cdots, t_\ell, t_{\ell+2}, \cdots, t_{2\ell})$, we next show that if an adversary $\mathcal{A}$ can successfully guess $c^* = (c_1^*, c_2^*, c_3^*)$ is the message under m_0 or m_1 for ID_s, then the challenger $\mathcal{CH}$ can compute $\hat{e}(g, g_1)^{\alpha^{\ell+1}}$.
This proof is almost the same as that of Theorem 5 except steps (6) and (7). Steps (6) and (7) are modified as follows:

(6) $\mathcal{CH}$ sets $c_1 = g_1, c_2 = \prod_{k=1}^{n} g_1^{r_k^*}$, picks $b \in \{0,1\}$ and $\rho_i \in \mathbb{Z}_q^*$, calculates $h = H_6(ID_s, c_1, m_b, pk_{s,1})$ and $S = t_1^{\rho_i + hv_{s,1} + \beta}$, picks $\theta \in \{0,1\}^{\lambda_0 + \lambda_2 + \lambda_1}$, and calculates $c_3 = \theta \oplus (ID_s, m_b, S)$.

(7)   If $\mathcal{A}$ can successfully guess $c^* = (c_1^*, c_2^*, c_3^*)$ is the message under m_0 or m_1, $\mathcal{A}$ has made a H_5 query on $\hat{e}(g_1^{\sum_{k=1}^{n} \mu_i}, g^{\alpha^{\ell+1}}) \hat{e}(g_1^\beta, \prod_{k=1}^{n} pk_{i,0}^{h_i})$. Then, $\mathcal{CH}$ computes $\hat{e}(g, g_1)^{\alpha^{\ell+1}} = \chi_i^{-\sum_{k=1}^{n} \mu_i} \hat{e}(g_1^{-\beta}, \prod_{k=1}^{n} pk_{i,0}^{h_i})$ as the solution.

6   Protocol Comparison

In this section, we compare our protocol with several dynamic AAGKA protocols [9, 11, 13–15] in terms of functionality and efficiency.

6.1   Functionality Comparison

Table 3 lists the functionality comparison results. As shown in Table 3, our design achieves more security requirements compared to previous protocols. Note that, KCIR is not analyzed for the protocol in [11] since their security model cannot capture KCIR.

Table 3. Functionality comparison

Protocols	Secrecy	KCIR	FS	PS	NRS	Privacy	NCM	NKE:	TL
[9]	No	Yes	Yes	No	No	No	No	Yes	III
[11]	Yes	–	Yes	Yes	No	No	Yes	No	I
[13]	Yes	Yes	Yes	Yes	Yes	Yes	Yes	No	I
[14]	Yes	Yes	Yes	Yes	No	No	Yes	No	I
[15]	No	No	No	No	No	No	Yes	Yes	II
Ours	Yes	Yes	Yes	Yes	Yes	Yes	Yes	Yes	III

FS: forward secrecy; PS: Provably security; NRS: Non-repudiation (sender); Privacy: Privacy (sender); NCM: No certification management; NKE: No key escrow; TL: Trust level; –: no analysis

6.2   Computation Performance Comparison

To estimate the computational performance, Table 4 lists the expensive cryptographic operations used in our comparison. We use the experiment results in [16], i.e., the time consuming of T_P, T_h, and T_E, are $87T_m$, $29T_m$, and $21T_m$, respectively.

Table 4. Cryptographic operations used in the comparison of protocols

Notation	Explanation (The execution time of)
T_P	A pairing $e : \mathbb{G} \times \mathbb{G} \rightarrow \mathbb{G}_T$
T_E	A modular exponentiation in $\mathbb{G}$
T_h	A hash-to-point in $\mathbb{G}$
T_m	A multiplication in $\mathbb{G}$
T_S	A signature generation
T_V	A signature verification
T_{VC}	A certificate verification

Next, we calculate the computation cost at agreement and key generation of our protocols and the competitive protocols and compare them. The comparison result is shown in Table 5 and Fig. 1.

Table 5. Computation efficiency comparison

Protocols	Agreement and key generation
[9]	$1T_P + (5n + 4)\ T_E \approx (105n + 171)\ T_m$
[11]	$2(n + 1)\ T_P + (n + 3)\ T_h + 6T_E \approx (203n + 387)\ T_m$
[13]	$10T_P + 3(n + 1)\ T_h + 2\ (n + 2)\ T_E \approx (129n + 1041)\ T_m$
[14]	$10T_P + 3(n + 1)\ T_h + 2\ (n + 2)\ T_E \approx (129n + 1041)\ T_m$
[15]	$2\ (n - 1)\ T_P + n\ T_E \approx (195n - 174)\ T_m$
Ours	$10T_P + 2(n + 2)\ T_h + 2\ (n + 1)\ T_E \approx (100n + 1028)\ T_m$

For our protocol, computation cost at key agreement is $(n + 1)\ T_h + (n + 2)\ T_E$, computation cost at group public key derivation is $8T_P + (n + 1)\ T_h + nT_E$, computation cost at group private key derivation is $2T_P$, and therefore computation cost at key agreement and key generation is $10T_P + 2\ (n + 2)\ T_h + 2\ (n + 1)\ T_E$. For [9], computation cost at key agreement and key generation is $1T_P + 1T_S + nT_V + (n + 1)\ T_E + (n + 1)\ T_{VC}$. If Schnorr signature scheme [17] is selected to secure the protocol in [9], then we can obtain that $1\ T_V = 1\ T_{VC.} = 2\ T_E$, $1\ T_S = 1\ T_E$ and computation cost at cost at key agreement and key generation for [9] is $1\ T_P + (5n + 4)\ T_E$.

The results show that our protocol almost have the lowest computation cost at agreement and key generation. According to Fig. 1, our protocol will be more and more efficient than other protocols [11, 13–15] with the growth of the group size.

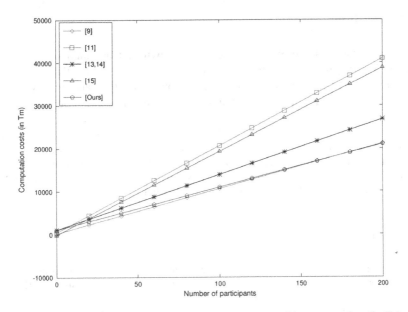

Fig. 1. Comparisons of computation cost at agreement and key generation (in T_m).

6.3 Communication Performance Comparison

Let λ_0, λ_1, λ_2, λ_3, λ_S, λ_{CV}, λ_q and λ_T be the binary lengths of an identity, an element in $\mathbb{G}$, a plaintext, an element in $\mathbb{G}_T$, a signature based on PKI, a PKI certificate, an element in $\mathbb{G}_T$, and a timestamp, receptively. Table 6 gives our protocol with other protocols in terms of communication efficiency.

Table 6. Communication efficiency comparison

Protocols	Agreement/Join	Ciphertext	Round
[9]	$n\lambda_1 + \lambda_3 + \lambda_S + \lambda_{CV}$	$2\lambda_1 + \lambda_3$	1
[11]	$3\lambda_1 + 2\lambda_0 + 3\lambda_q + 2\lambda_T$	$2\lambda_1 + \lambda_0$	3
[13]	$(n+1)\lambda_1 + \lambda_0$	$\lambda_0 + \lambda_2 + 3\lambda_1$	1
[14]	$(n+1)\lambda_1 + \lambda_0$	$\lambda_0 + \lambda_2 + 3\lambda_1$	1
[15]	$n\lambda_1 + \lambda_3$	$2\lambda_1 + \lambda_3$	1
Ours	$(n+1)\lambda_1 + \lambda_0$	$\lambda_0 + \lambda_2 + 3\lambda_1$	1

From Table 6, we can see that only the protocol [11] has the constant communication cost at agreement/join phase, however the protocol in [11] is a three-round protocol while protocols [9, 13–15] and our protocol are one-round protocols. Although the communication cost of our protocol is a litter higher than that of protocol [15], only our protocol achieves the most security properties.

7   Conclusions

The security flaws of the WYS protocol are shown and an improved protocol is proposed. Security proofs show that the improved protocol can avoid the security flaws and can hold other security properties including non-repudiation, and privacy. Protocol comparison shows that our protocol is more suitable for dynamic groups.

Funding. This work is supported by National Natural Science Foundation of China (No. 61502436, 61672471), Science and Technology Program of Henan Province (No. 172102210060), Plan for Scientific Innovation Talent of Henan Province (No. 184200510010), Program for Innovative Research Team in Science and Technology in University of Henan Province (No. 18IRTSTHN012) and Doctor Fund Project of Zhengzhou University of Light Industry (No. 2014BSJJ081).

References

1. Burmester, M., Desmedt, Y.: A secure and efficient conference key distribution system. In: De Santis, A. (ed.) EUROCRYPT 1994. LNCS, vol. 950, pp. 275–286. Springer, Heidelberg (1995). https://doi.org/10.1007/BFb0053443
2. Bresson, E., Chevassut, O., Pointcheval, D., Quisquater, J.J.: Provably authenticated group Diffie-Hellman key exchange. In: Proceedings of the 8th ACM Conference on Computer and Communications Security, Philadelphia, USA, pp. 255–264 (2001)
3. Choi, K.Y., Hwang, J.Y., Lee, D.H.: Efficient ID-based group key agreement with bilinear maps. In: Bao, F., Deng, R., Zhou, J. (eds.) PKC 2004. LNCS, vol. 2947, pp. 130–144. Springer, Heidelberg (2004). https://doi.org/10.1007/978-3-540-24632-9_10
4. Anitha Kumari, K., Sudha Sadasivam, G.: Two-server 3D ElGamal Diffie-Hellman password authenticated and key exchange protocol using geometrical properties. Mob. Netw. Appl. **24**(3), 1104–1119 (2019)
5. Wu, Q., Mu, Y., Susilo, W., Qin, B., Domingo-Ferrer, J.: Asymmetric group key agreement. In: Joux, A. (ed.) EUROCRYPT 2009. LNCS, vol. 5479, pp. 153–170. Springer, Heidelberg (2009). https://doi.org/10.1007/978-3-642-01001-9_9
6. Shamir, A.: Identity-based cryptosystems and signature schemes. In: Blakley, G.R., Chaum, D. (eds.) CRYPTO 1984. LNCS, vol. 196, pp. 47–53. Springer, Heidelberg (1985). https://doi.org/10.1007/3-540-39568-7_5
7. Al-Riyami, S.S., Paterson, K.G.: Certificateless public key cryptography. In: Laih, C.-S. (ed.) ASIACRYPT 2003. LNCS, vol. 2894, pp. 452–473. Springer, Heidelberg (2003). https://doi.org/10.1007/978-3-540-40061-5_29
8. Zhang, L., Wu, Q. H., Qin, B.: Authenticated asymmetric group key agreement protocol and its application. In: Proceedings of the International Communications Conference, Cape Town, South Africa, pp. 1–5 (2010)
9. Zhang, L., Wu, Q.H., Qin, B., Domingo-Ferrer, J.: Asymmetric group key agreement protocol for open networks and its application to broadcast encryption. Comput. Netw. **55**(15), 3246–3255 (2011)
10. Wu, Q.H., Zhang, X.Y., Tang, M., Yin, P., Qiu, Z.: Extended asymmetric group key agreement for dynamic groups and its applications. China Commun. **8**(04), 32–40 (2011)
11. Zhao, X., Zhang, F., Tian, H.: Dynamic asymmetric group key agreement for ad hoc networks. Ad Hoc Netw. **9**(5), 928–939 (2010)
12. Lv, X.X., Li, H., Wang, B.C.: Group key agreement for secure group communication in dynamic peer systems. J. Parallel Distrib. Comput. **72**(10), 1195–1200 (2012)

13. Li, J.T., Zhang, L.: Sender dynamic, non-repudiable, privacy-preserving and strong secure group communication protocol. Inf. Sci. **414**, 187–202 (2017)
14. Zhang, L., Wu, Q.H., Domingo-Ferrer, J., Qin, B., Dong, Z.M.: Round-efficient and sender-unrestricted dynamic group key agreement protocol for secure group communications. IEEE Trans. Inf. Forensics Secur. **10**(1), 2352–2364 (2015)
15. Wei, G.Y., Yang, X.B., Shao, J.: Efficient certificateless authenticated asymmetric group key agreement protocol. KSII Trans. Internet Inf. Syst. **6**(12), 3352–3365 (2012)
16. Karati, A., Islam, S.H., Biswas, G.P.: A pairing-free and provably secure certificateless signature scheme. Inf. Sci. **450**, 378–391 (2018)
17. Schnorr, C.P.: Efficient identification and signatures for smart cards. J. Cryptol. **4**, 161–174 (1991)

Research on Medical Image Encryption Method Based on Chaotic Scrambling and Compressed Sensing

Yubin Liu[1] and Ming Pang[2(✉)]

[1] State Key Laboratory of Robotics and System, Harbin Institute of Technology, Harbin, China
[2] College of Automation, Harbin Engineering University, Harbin, China
pangm@hrbeu.edu.cn

Abstract. In order to improve the security of medical images, a new image encryption method is proposed in this paper. In this method, the chaos theory is used to set the initial state and key, and then the measurement equation constructed by compressed sensing is used to complete the fusion encryption. The fusion of the two theories achieves the effect of chaotic uniform scrambling on the one hand, and on the other hand, the encrypted image can still accurately recover the real image when it is compressed to a fairly small size. Experiments are carried out on three groups of medical images. The experimental results show that the proposed encryption method achieves an ideal encryption effect for medical images. Under the condition that the encrypted image is compressed to 1/4 of the original image, the decryption can still be completed effectively.

Keywords: Medical image · Initial state · Measurement matrix · Image encrytion

1 Introduction

With the rapid development of Internet technology, various types of data information have become indispensable and important resources in people's daily life and production activities. Among these data information, image information has become the most commonly used one. Among them, medical image reading is of great significance for both patients and doctors to assist in diagnosis [1].

Medical image information is not only informative, but also visually intuitive. It is convenient for users to grasp the essence of information at the first time. However, the breadth and depth of the Internet have also brought various hidden dangers to information security to a considerable extent. The security protection of medical image information has become an important issue to be solved urgently [2].

In order to realize the security of medical image information, the most common methods are watermarking embedding and image encryption [3]. Among them, medical image encryption has become the focus of research in the field of Information Science in recent years. The security of medical image information encryption includes two meanings: first, in the process of image information transmission and storage, the

© Springer Nature Singapore Pte Ltd. 2020
Y. Tian et al. (Eds.): ICBDS 2019, CCIS 1210, pp. 238–246, 2020.
https://doi.org/10.1007/978-981-15-7530-3_17

encrypted image information can not be cracked by those who have no authority to interpret [4]; second, for those who have authority to interpret, they should be able to recover the true and complete original image information. Therefore, how to construct an excellent image encryption method from these two aspects is of great significance for image information security [5].

The essence of medical image encryption is the transformation and scrambling of image pixels in the same or different space. Through this transformation and scrambling, the original visual effect of the image is hidden and new visual effect is formed.

In the early stage of medical image encryption research, many methods have been proposed from the perspective of image transformation, such as image encryption based on matrix transformation and image encryption based on transform domain [6]. In the matrix transformation encryption method, Baker matrix and magic cube matrix are widely used [7]. However, due to the reversibility and repeatability of matrix transformation, this method makes image decryption relatively easy, and encrypted images are often attacked [8]. Transform-domain encryption methods are commonly used to transform images from geometric space to frequency space, from position expression to phase expression, and so on. But this kind of method and matrix encryption face similar problems. Once the encryption mode is realized, it is easy to find the decryption method.

Since the 21st century, with the further development of chaos theory, the sensitivity of chaotic system to initial values and the uniform scrambling performance of pixel positions have made it widely used in the field of medical image encryption [9]. Encryption methods based on different chaotic systems and high-dimensional chaotic systems are constantly emerging. This kind of method has very ideal encryption security, even if it is known that it is encrypted in chaotic mode, it is difficult to crack it effectively. Encrypted medical images are faced with the requirement of transmission and storage energy, so it is a new requirement to express the encrypted images with fewer pixels and restore the original image information completely in the decryptor [10]. In this respect, compressed sensing can express the image through sparse feature matrix, so that the encrypted image can be transformed into a smaller format for easy transmission, and then the image decryption can be completed without distortion in the decryptor.

Based on the above analysis, this paper hopes to give full play to the advantages of chaos theory and compressed sensing theory and construct an ideal medical image encryption method.

2 Image Encryption Based on Chaos and Compressed Sensing

Compressed sensing can achieve sparse representation of image information, compression measurement of image information and reconstruction of image information. Therefore, it has good adaptability to image encryption and decryption. Chaos theory has random and irregular motions and is sensitive to the initial state. These performances are especially suitable for image encryption. For this reason, this paper constructs an image encryption method based on chaos and compressed sensing.

2.1   Chaotic System and Initial Value Setting

In order to form a reliable mapping of image encryption process, a new type of nonlinear chaotic system is selected here. The advantage of this chaotic system is that it has good memory performance and strong randomness of signal appearing. It is suitable for image encryption and decryption. The mathematical model of this new chaotic system is as follows:

$$\begin{cases} \dot{x} = -ax + by + yz \\ \dot{y} = -xz + cx - dxW(\varphi) \\ \dot{z} = xy - rz \\ \dot{w} = gx \end{cases} \tag{1}$$

In order to get the initial state of the chaotic system, a key of 256 bits is set, which can form 32 decimal numbers according to a group of 8 bits.

These decimal numbers are expressed in this way such as Z_1, Z_2, ..., and Z_{32}. Thus, four median values can be calculated as follows:

$$\begin{cases} g_1 = \frac{1}{256}(Z_1 \oplus Z_2 \oplus \cdots \oplus Z_8) + k_1 \\ g_2 = \frac{1}{256}(Z_9 \oplus Z_{10} \oplus \cdots \oplus Z_{16}) \times k_2 \\ g_3 = \frac{1}{256}(Z_{17} \oplus Z_{18} \oplus \cdots \oplus Z_{24}) \\ g_4 = \frac{sum(Z_{25}, Z_{26}, \cdots Z_{32})}{\max(Z_{25}, Z_{26}, \cdots Z_{32})} \times k_3 \end{cases} \tag{2}$$

where, k_1, k_2, and k_3 is part of the whole key, and their range is positive numbers greater than 0. According to the four parameters calculated above, the initial state of the chaotic system can be further formed according to the following rules:

$$\begin{cases} x_0 = (g_1 + g_2) \times 10^{10} \bmod N \\ y_0 = (g_3 \times k_4 + g_4) \times 10^{10} \bmod N \\ z_0 = \bmod(g_3 + g_4, 1) \\ w_0 = \bmod\left(\frac{g_4}{7}, 1\right) \end{cases} \tag{3}$$

where, k_4 is part of the whole key, and its range is positive numbers greater than 0. N represents the total number of image pixels to be processed.

2.2   Chaotic Encryption Processing of Image

Firstly, the Hash value of 256 bits length is calculated for the image to be encrypted. From these 256 Hash values, the 0-chaotic sequence and 1-chaotic sequence with length N are selected and marked as R and C respectively, which represent row coordinates and column coordinates.

The next step is to clarify how to screen R and C.

Choose R from the 256-bit Hash value of the image to be encrypted. Consider three situations:

Firstly, if N is in the interval of [1, 256], the sequence of 0 or 1 with length of N is screened in reverse order from back to front. Secondly, if N is between [256, 512], 0 or

1 sequence strings with length N/2 are screened in reverse order from back to front, and 0 or 1 sequence strings with residual length N/2 are selected in positive order. Thirdly, if N is greater than 512, we select enough 512-bit 0 or 1 sequence strings according to the second step method. If N is more than 512, we still filter repeatedly according to such rules.

Choose C from the 256-bit Hash value of the image to be encrypted. Consider three situations:

Firstly, if N is in the interval of [1,256], the sequence of 0 or 1 with length of N is screened in positive order from front to back. Secondly, if N is between [256, 512], 0 or 1 sequence strings with length of N/2 are screened in positive order from front to back, and 0 or 1 sequence strings with residual length of N/2 are selected in reverse order. Thirdly, if N is greater than 512, we select enough 512-bit 0 or 1 sequence strings according to the second step method. If N is more than 512, we still filter repeatedly according to such rules.

2.3 Design of Compressed Sensing Measurement Matrix

In order to facilitate the use of compressed sensing theory in encryption process, a measurement matrix is constructed here. Here, the compressed sensing measurement matrix is set in the form of a circular matrix, in which each row of matrix elements can be obtained by shifting the previous row of matrix elements.

Firstly, the initial state x_0, y_0, z_0, and w_0 of chaotic sequence calculated in Sect. 2.1 is used as input to set up a new chaotic system. Among the possible numerical values in chaotic systems, the first 1000 are discarded. After 1000, four sequences of length and size N are obtained, which are set as follows:

$$\begin{cases} X = [x_1, x_2, \cdots, x_N] \\ Y = [y_1, y_2, \cdots, y_N] \\ Z = [z_1, z_2, \cdots, z_N] \\ W = [w_1, w_2, \cdots, w_N] \end{cases} \tag{4}$$

Three new sequences are further designed and calculated as follows:

$$\begin{cases} \phi_1(i) = [X(i) + Y(i) - Z(i)] \\ \phi_2(i) = [X(i) + Z(i) - Y(i)] \\ \phi_3(i) = [X(i) + Y(i) - X(i)] \end{cases} \tag{5}$$

According to the variance of the distribution of the pixel value of the image to be encrypted, $\phi_1(i)$, $\phi_2(i)$, and $\phi_3(i)$ are selected separately as the measurement matrices of compressed sensing.

2.4 Design of Encryption Algorithms

After the preparation of the first three steps, the image encryption method based on chaos and compressed sensing is designed in detail. The specific flow is as follows:

In the first step, the encrypted image is decomposed by discrete wavelet transform, and the sparse matrix of image based on wavelet sparse is obtained.

In the second step, according to the method and process shown in Sect. 2.1, the initial state four initial values of the new chaotic system are obtained.

In the third step, R and C are selected according to the method shown in Sect. 2.2 to form the initial configuration of the image to be encrypted.

In the fourth step, the sparse coefficient matrix obtained in the first step is mapped in one dimension to satisfy the subsequent processing requirements.

The fifth step is to scramble the encrypted image according to the initial state of the chaotic system and form a new image with irregular pixel position.

In the sixth step, combined with the sparse coefficient matrix obtained in the fourth step and the measurement matrix constructed in Sect. 2.3, the encrypted image is sampled and stored by compressed sensing, and the final encryption process is completed.

3   Experimental Results and Analysis

In order to validate the effectiveness of the proposed image encryption method based on chaos and compressed sensing, some experiments on image encryption and decryption are carried out in the following work.

3.1   Selection of Experimental Images and Configuration of Relevant Parameters

In the verifiable encryption experiment, three medical images were selected, one vertebral image, two vertebral images and cranial cavity images. The resolution of these three images is 256 * 256 pixels.

In order to control the encryption method effectively, the key parameters are given, as shown in Table 1.

Table 1. Key parameter configurations in this paper's algorithm

Para	a	b	c	d	k_1	k_2	k_3	k_4
Value	10	10	20	8	21.5731	4.0589	2.5632	3.2771

3.2   Analysis of the Effect of Image Encryption and Decryption

In the case of the above parameter configuration, the experiment of image encryption and decryption effect is carried out first, and the experimental results are shown in Fig. 1.

In Figs. 1 a), 1 b), and 1 c) are the original images of vertebral 1 image, vertebral 2 image and cranial image respectively; d), e), and f) are the encrypted result images of vertebral 1 image, vertebral 2 image and cranial image respectively; g), h), and i) are

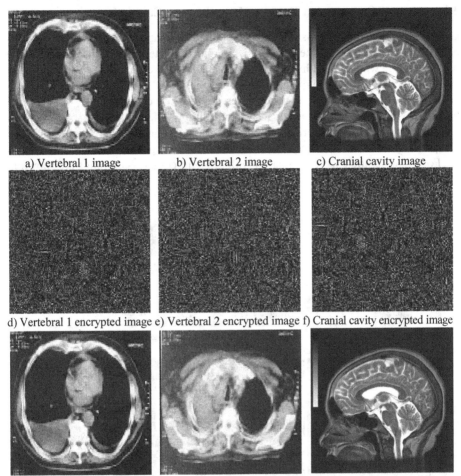

a) Vertebral 1 image   b) Vertebral 2 image   c) Cranial cavity image

d) Vertebral 1 encrypted image e) Vertebral 2 encrypted image f) Cranial cavity encrypted image

g) Vertebral 1 dencrypted image h) Vertebral 2 dencrypted image i) Cranial cavity dencrypted image

Fig. 1. Encryption and decryption of 3 sets of medical images

the decrypted images of vertebral image, vertebral image and cranial image respectively.

As can be seen from Fig. 1, after the proposed encryption method based on chaos and compressed sensing, the three images of vertebral 1 image, vertebral 2 image and cranial cavity image are evenly scrambled, which has formed a good encryption effect. According to the inverse process of encryption method, the original image can be restored accurately. This fully proves the effectiveness of the proposed method in the process of image encryption and decryption.

3.3   Effect of Compression Rate on Medical Image Encryption

Compressive sensing theory is fully integrated into the image encryption method in this paper. Compressive sensing technology is used to generate image sparse matrix in the first step of the whole algorithm, and to complete the final compression and encryption in the sixth step of the whole algorithm.

By adjusting and controlling the compression ratio, we can further adjust the size of the encrypted image, which has greater adaptability to different storage space. For this reason, in the following experimental process, we investigate the influence of different compression ratios on the encrypted image and the encrypted effect.

For example, the encrypted images with different compression ratios are shown in Fig. 2.

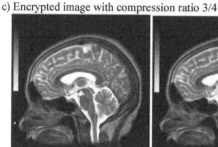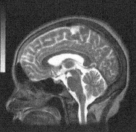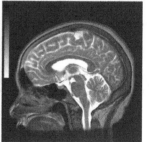

a) Encrypted image with compression ratio 1/4 b) Encrypted image with compression ratio 1/2
c) Encrypted image with compression ratio 3/4

d) Dencrypted image with compression ratio 1/4 e) Dencrypted image with compression ratio 1/2 f) Dencrypted image with compression ratio 3/4

Fig. 2. Encrypted and decrypted images with different compression ratios

As can be seen from Fig. 2, the size of the encrypted image will change significantly under different compression ratios, so that it can be adapted to the needs of different storage space sizes. However, from the perspective of decrypted images, because of the successful application of compressed sensing method, no matter how large the compression ratio is, ideal decryption results are still achieved and the original image is restored vividly.

Next, we need to consider whether the reconstructed image after decryption will be affected under different compression ratios in Fig. 2. Still take the three images in Fig. 1 as an example, after encrypting and decrypting under three compression ratios, the effect of decrypting the image is almost the same. The MSSIM values of the reconstruction effect of the decrypted image under three compression ratios are further compared, as shown in Table 2.

Table 2. MSSIM value comparison of decrypted image reconstruction under three compression ratios

	Vertebral 1 image	Vertebral 2 image	Cranial cavity image
Compression ratio 1/4	0.9669	0.9744	0.9523
Compression ratio 1/2	0.9712	0.9754	0.9581
Compression ratio 3/4	0.9755	0.9801	0.9603

From Table 2, we can see that the MSSIM values of decoding and reconstructing vertebral image, vertebral image and cranial image are all over 0.95 under three compression ratios, which fully proves that the quality of image reconstruction is very ideal. This further shows that the method has achieved good results even in the case of large-scale compression encryption and decryption.

4   Conclusion

Compressive sensing theory can realize image restoration with sparse features. Chaos theory is sensitive to the initial state and uniform scrambling of the pixel space. It has a very prominent applicability for image encryption and decryption. In the implementation of medical image method, a new non-linear chaotic system is used to set the initial state, and then the initial configuration of image encryption is completed. The measurement matrix is constructed based on compressed sensing theory. Finally, a six-step encryption process is designed. In the course of the experiment, vertebral image, vertebral image and cranial image were selected as experimental objects. The experimental results show that the encryption method constructed in this paper can treat the encrypted image with uniform scrambling and ideal encryption effect. Further experiments and analysis of the effect of compression ratio show that the proposed method can achieve ideal decryption and reconstruction results under different compression ratios. Even if the compression ratio reaches 1/4, the MSSIM values of vertebral image, vertebral image and cranial image reconstruction are all over 0.95, which shows that the decryption reconstruction effect is good.

Acknowledgement. This work is supported by National Key R&D Program of China (N0. 2017YFB1303600).

References

1. Pisarchik, A.N., Zanin, M., Nonlinear, P.: Image encryption with chaotically coupled chaotic maps. Physica D **237**(20), 2638–2648 (2008)
2. Chang, H.T., Hwang, H.E., Lee, C.L., et al.: Wavelength multiplexing multiple-image encryption using cascaded phase-only masks in the Fresnel transform domain. Appl. Opt. **50** (5), 710–716 (2011)
3. Liu, Z., Guo, Q., Xu, L., et al.: Double image encryption by using iterative random binary encoding in gyrator domains. Opt. Express **18**(11), 12033–12043 (2010)
4. Khan, M.A., Ahmad, J., Javaid, Q., et al.: An efficient and secure partial image encryption for wireless multimedia sensor networks using discrete wavelet transform, chaotic maps and substitution box. Optica Acta Int. J. Opt. **64**(5), 531–540 (2017)
5. Kwok, H.S., Tang, W.K.S.: A fast image encryption system based on chaotic maps with finite precision representation. Chaos, Solitons Fractals **32**(4), 1518–1529 (2007)
6. Mirzaei, O., Yaghoobi, M., Irani, H.: A new image encryption method: parallel sub-image encryption with hyper chaos. Nonlinear Dyn. **67**(1), 557–566 (2012)
7. Parvaz, R., Zarebnia, M.: A combination chaotic system and application in color image encryption. Opt. Laser Technol. **101**, 30–41 (2017)
8. Patidar, V., Pareek, N.K., Purohit, G., et al.: A robust and secure chaotic standard map based pseudorandom permutation-substitution scheme for image encryption. Opt. Commun. **284** (19), 4331–4339 (2011)
9. Volos, C.K., Kyprianidis, I.M., Stouboulos, I.N.: Image encryption process based on chaotic synchronization phenomena. Sig. Process. **93**(5), 1328–1340 (2013)
10. Wei, D., Wang, X., Hou, J., et al.: Hybrid projective synchronization of complex Duffing-Holmes oscillators with application to image encryption. Math. Methods Appl. Sci. **40**(12), 112–119 (2017)
11. Mozaffari, S.: Parallel image encryption with bitplane decomposition and genetic algorithm. Multimedia Tools Appl. **77**(19), 25799–25819 (2018)
12. Xiong, Y., He, A., Quan, C.: Security analysis of a double-image encryption technique based on an asymmetric algorithm. J. Opt. Soc. Am. A Opt. Image Sci. Vis. **35**(2), 320–326 (2018)
13. Özkaynak, F.: Brief review on application of nonlinear dynamics in image encryption. Nonlinear Dyn. **92**(2), 305–313 (2018)
14. Parvaz, R., Zarebnia, M.: A combination chaotic system and application in color image encryption. Opt. Laser Technol. **101**, 30–41 (2018)
15. Liu, L., Miao, S., Hu, H., et al.: N-phase logistic chaotic sequence and its application for image encryption. Iet Sig. Process. **10**(9), 1096–1104 (2017)
16. Muhammad, K., Hamza, R., Ahmad, J., et al.: Secure surveillance framework for IoT systems using probabilistic image encryption. IEEE Trans. Ind. Inform. 1–11 (2018)
17. Chuman, T., Kiya, H.: Security evaluation for block scrambling-based image encryption including JPEG distortion against jigsaw puzzle solver attacks. IEICE Trans. Fundam. Electron. Commun. Comput. Sci. **12**, 2405–2408 (2018)
18. Praveenkumar, P., Amirtharajan, R., Thenmozhi, K., et al.: Fusion of confusion and diffusion: a novel image encryption approach. Telecommun. Syst. **65**(1), 65–78 (2017)
19. Ismail, S.M., Said, L.A., Radwan, A.G., et al.: Generalized double-humped logistic map-based medical image encryption: J. Adv. Res. **10**, 85–98 (2018)
20. Li, J., Xiong, J., Zhang, Q., et al.: A one-time pad encryption method combining fully phase image encryption and hiding. J. Opt. **19**(8), 85–91 (2017)

Design and Optimization of Evaluation Metrics in Object Detection and Tracking for Low-Altitude Aerial Video

Li Wang[1], Xin Shu[1], Wei Zhang[1,2], and Yunfang Chen[1(✉)]

[1] Nanjing University of Posts and Telecommunications,
Nanjing 210023, Jiangsu, China
chenyf@njupt.edu.cn
[2] Jiangsu Key Laboratory of Big Data Security and Intelligent Processing,
Nanjing University of Posts and Telecommunications,
Nanjing 210023, Jiangsu, China

Abstract. The combination of Unmanned Aerial Vehicle (UAV) technology and computer vision has become popular in a wide range of applications, such as surveillance and reconnaissance, while popular evaluation measures are sometimes not applicable for specific tasks. In order to evaluate visual object detection and tracking algorithms of low-altitude aerial video properly, we first summarize the evaluation basis of computer vision tasks, including ground truth, prediction-to-ground truth assignment strategy and distance measures between prediction and ground truth. Then, we analyze the advantages and disadvantages of visual object detection and tracking performance measures, including average precision (AP), F-measure, and accuracy. Finally, for the low-altitude (nearly 100 m) surveillance mission of small unmanned aerial vehicles, we discuss the threshold optimization method of popular measures and the design strategy of application measures. Our work provides a reference in the aspect of performance measures design for researchers of UAV vision.

Keywords: Performance metrics · Object detection · Visual object tracking · Unmanned Aerial Vehicle (UAV) · Low-altitude aerial video

1 Introduction

UAV has become an essential part of surveillance and reconnaissance in recent years. Beside their widespread usage in the entertainment and media production industries, UAV is used for many military and civil applications. These applications include search and rescue, traffic control, border patrol and security. In order to more efficiently and accurately process the videos or images captured by UAV in these applications, the combination of computer vision and UAV becomes very important. Object detection and tracking are key steps in these applications and have been extensively studied in recent years. There have been many algorithms for UAV vision, and how to choose appropriate performance measures to evaluate these algorithms becomes very important.

© Springer Nature Singapore Pte Ltd. 2020
Y. Tian et al. (Eds.): ICBDS 2019, CCIS 1210, pp. 247–262, 2020.
https://doi.org/10.1007/978-981-15-7530-3_18

Since UAV vision is an extension of computer vision, it is necessary to study the performance measures of computer visual object detection and tracking firstly. However, the performance measures are even different in different periods or datasets. Leonardis et al. [1] homogenize the tracking performance measures and increase the interpretability of results, which is very important for the understanding of performance measures in the object tracking field. Pascal VOC [2] first considered multi-classification problems in object detection field, and proposed mAP measure, which gradually became the most recognized performance measure in the field of object detection. At present, many literatures contain the research of performance measures on computer vision: For common field, there are object detection benchmark e.g. [2, 3] and single object tracking benchmark e.g. [4, 5]; in application field, there are face detection [6] and pedestrian detection [7, 8], etc.

Further, we research the application scenarios of UAV visual object detection and tracking. For security purpose, the UAV is required to perform aerial surveillance missions. In order to ensure a wider view and to avoid interference with the masses, the flying height of the UAV should be nearly 100 m [9], which belong to low-altitude range. The view of low-altitude UAV dataset is more like a "bird" perspective which is essentially different from the traditional "human" perspective dataset. And the UAV aerial videos are featured with a top-down view and small object scale, etc. Although there have been some studies on the UAV vision in recent years, these studies mainly propose related datasets or algorithm improvements, such as [10–13], which are not specific studies to performance measures. However, the DAC competition designs the evaluation methodology for the lower power object detection challenge (LPODC). Intuitively, the UAV detection or tracking performance measures should be different from the common measures, and more scientific and reasonable measures should be designed to guide the research of specific scenarios projects. It should be noted that in this article, the object tracking we refer to is single-object tracking. The contribution of our paper can be summarized as the following three aspects:

(1) We extract the basis of evaluation metrics in object detection and single object tracking fields, including the definition of the annotation (i.e. ground truth) in datasets, the measures of prediction-to-target assignment, and the assignment strategy;
(2) We summarize the popular performance measures in the current object detection and single object tracking fields, and analyze the advantages and disadvantages of different metrics;
(3) We discuss the threshold optimization of common metrics for low-altitude (nearly 100 m) UAV surveillance task, and analyze other application metrics to measure speed and energy consumption.

2 Basis of Evaluation

At present, the popular object detection and tracking algorithms are based on ground truth annotation to verify the accuracy. In most cases, the verification dataset annotates the ground truth of each target object. Therefore, the performance of the task is evaluated at the object level based on the alignment accuracy of the system output results relative to ground truth. In this section, we first introduce the ground truth, then introduce the assignment method of the prediction detection and annotation bounding boxes.

2.1 Ground Truth Annotation

In machine learning, the term "ground truth" refers to the accuracy of the training set's classification for supervised learning techniques. This is used in statistical models to prove or disprove research hypotheses. For object detection problems, the ground truth includes the image, the classes of the objects in it and the ground truth bounding boxes of each of the objects in that image [14]. Figure 1 is an image (i.e., a frame of a video) with ground truth annotations. These annotations are in a single file as text or other formats, which can be superimposed and visualized on the image by some simple programming. In most detection or tracking datasets, axially aligned rectangular boxes are used to describe the regions where the objects are located. In Table 1, each record represents the ground truth of an object in Fig. 1. "X" and "Y" represent the coordinates of the upper left corner of the bounding box. "Box Width" and "Box Height" represent the width and height of the rectangle box. In addition, more complex shapes are used in some datasets, such as the rotating rectangle used in the 2016 VOT challenge.

Fig. 1. Human visualisation of the ground truth [14].

For single-object tracking, the ability to track a specific object is examined. Generally, there is no need to care about the class of an object. Therefore, "Class" is not required when designing ground truth in single-object tracking dataset. In the multi-object tracking task, there is a judgment on the object identity (ID), so the ground truth should include the IDs of the objects in addition to the class.

Table 1. The ground truth annotations of objects in Fig. 1 [14].

Class	X	Y	Box width	Box height
Dog	100	600	150	100
Horse	700	300	200	250
Person	400	400	100	500

2.2   Prediction-to-Target Assignment Strategy

The same object may be predicted by multiple predictions in object detection. The constraint that must be considered is that an actual object should correspond to at most one prediction result, and one prediction cannot match with more than one target.

The accuracy measures for object detection and tracking are designed to compare the assignment degree between prediction and ground truth bounding boxes. At present, there are two popular matching strategies: One is the greedy algorithm, which traverses the detection images in descending order of the confidence scores and searches for the prediction boxes that satisfy the certain threshold (ImageNet and Pascal VOC use this strategy). Another is the Hungarian algorithm, which models the prediction-to-target assignment as an overall allocation optimization problem, maximizing the total intersection over union (IoU, in Sect. 2.3). The evaluation strategy is used in the FDDB face detection dataset, and the MOT (Multiple object tracking) challenge.

There is at most one prediction in one frame of single target tracking. If the prediction assigns with the ground truth correctly, it is the true positive (TP), otherwise is false positive (FP). If there is a target in a certain image and is erroneously determined to be non-existent, it is false negative (FN). For multi-object tracking and detection, the relationship between output results and ground truth annotations of each image is a many-to-many. If there is prediction describes a certain annotation object correctly, it is called true positive (TP), otherwise it is false alarm (or false positive, FP). While an object is not matched to any prediction, the object is called false negative (FN). This decision is typically made by thresholding based on a defined distance (or dissimilarity) measure (see Sect. 2.3). A good result is expected to have as few FPs and FNs as possible.

2.3   Assignment Distance Measure

Distance measure between the prediction bounding box and the ground truth bounding box earliest take the central error metric in the single-object tracking field. We first establish a general definition of an object state description in a sequence with length N as [1]:

$$\Lambda = \{(R_t, x_t)\}_{t=1}^{N} \qquad (1)$$

Where $x_t \in \mathcal{R}^2$ denotes a center of the object and R_t denotes the region of the object at time t. In some cases, the annotated center can be automatically derived from the region, but for some articulated objects, the centroid of region R_t does not correspond to x_t, therefore it is best to separately annotate x_t [1].

Central Error: It has its roots in aeronautics [1] and is still a popular object tracking measure which measures the difference between the target's prediction center and the ground truth center. We use δ_t to indicate the center distance of the prediction bounding box to the ground truth bounding box in the t-th frame (time t), then:

$$\delta_t = \| x_t^G - x_t^P \| \tag{2}$$

The results are usually shown in a plot, or summarized as average center location error or root-mean-square error [1]. It is relatively straightforward to use the central error calculation to predict the deviation from the real object, but the central error ignores the scale of the object, so the metric based on region overlap is paid more attention to in the subsequent object tracking.

Region overlap: The overlap-based measures [15–17] take the problem of the object scale into account, which apply the Jaccard index. Jaccard index [18] can measure the similarity between two sets. Given the set A and B, their Jaccard index is the intersection size of the two divided by the union size of the two. The formula is as follows:

$$J(A, B) = \frac{|A \cap B|}{|A \cup B|} \tag{3}$$

Considering the pixel region within the bounding box as a collection of pixels. Thus, the Jaccard index of the pixel collection of the two bounding boxes is used to measure the similarity of the two bounding boxes, where the Jaccard index is usually called intersection over union (IoU). An appealing property of region overlap measures is that it accounts for both position and size of the prediction and ground truth bounding boxes simultaneously, and do not result in arbitrary large errors at tracking failures, as is the case on center-based error measures [1]. Because of this feature, all performance measures used to evaluate object detection [2] and tracking [19, 20] depend on IoU.

3 Common Evaluation Metrics

3.1 Object Detection Metrics

Metrics. Because the object classification is implicit in the object detection task, the object detection draws on some measures in the classification task, such as precision, recall, which can be defined as follow:

$$Precision = \frac{TP}{TP + FP} \tag{4}$$

$$\text{Recall} = \frac{TP}{TP + FN} \tag{5}$$

TP represents the number of true positives, FP represents the number of false positives, and FN represents the number of false negatives. The best case is that the precision and recall are both 1. But in reality, this situation cannot be achieved. Although the above metrics are relatively intuitive, they are one-sided and cannot fairly rank the detection algorithms. The object detection community introduces AP and F-score metrics from the field of information retrieval field. Both of the two metrics are based on precision and recall. And AP is determined by PR curve.

PR curve: Precision and recall metrics are affected by IoU and confidence. Fixed IoU threshold, different P-R pairs are obtained by changing the confidence threshold of the prediction result, and they compose the P-R curve. Apart from PR curve, the "miss rate vs. false positives per-image (FPPI)" curve was also used as a measure in single-class detection task, which generally report the miss rate (1-recall) value under a certain FPPI as an evaluation metric.

mAP: Mean average precision (mAP) is the sum of all classes' APs divided by the number of classes. The calculation of the AP value for each class is equivalent to the area under the interpolated PR curve, in which the precision at each recall level r is interpolated by taking the maximum precision measured for a method for which the corresponding recall exceeds r. In actual calculations, mAP does not take all the test results into account. On the contrary, it considers the top 100 results of each image. If it is a dataset of dense scenes, this number should be improved.

For different types of objects, APs may be very different. When analyzing the performance of the model, it is helpful to observe the AP of each class separately, which can be used as an indicator to add more training samples. For example, by analyzing the AP of popular algorithms on the COCO dataset, Kisantal et al. [25] draw the conclusion that the detection effect on the small object in the COCO were poor, and they amplify the small object in the dataset to improve the overall performance of the object detection algorithm on the COCO.

AR: Average recall (AR) is a measure of recall. It cannot only report recall at particular IoU thresholds, but also report the average recall (AR) between IoU 0.5 to 1. In COCO dataset evaluation, AR is the maximum recall given a fixed number of detections per image, averaged over classes and IoUs (between IoU 0.5 to 1). If considering all the prediction bounding box, we can always reach recall = 100%. Therefore, in the COCO evaluation system, 1, 10 and 100 results with max predicted score are generally considered, namely $AR^{max=1}, AR^{max=10}$ and $AR^{max=100}$.

F-score: F-measure can be defined as the harmonic mean of the recall and precision under non-negative weight β. Calculated as follows:

$$F = \frac{(1 + \beta^2) Recall \times Precision}{\beta^2 Precision + Recall} \tag{6}$$

Where, $\beta > 1$ means that precision is more important, and $\beta < 1$ means that recall is more important. When $\beta = 1$, F-measure becomes F1-measure. The F-measure captures the combined performance of detectors based on recall and precision better.

Development of Metrics. This question how to evaluate object detection algorithms may even have different answers at different time [21]. In the early time's detection community, there is no widely accepted evaluation measures on detection performance. For example, in the early research of pedestrian detection [22], the "miss rate vs. false positives per-window (FPPW)" was usually used as a metric. However, Wojek et al. [23] proved that the higher detection precision of a single window does not mean the higher detection precision of the image. In 2009, the Caltech pedestrian detection benchmark was created [23] and since then, the evaluation metric has changed from per-window (FPPW) to false positives per-image (FPPI).

The currently popular object detection definition of mAP was first formalized in the PASCAL Visual Objects Classes (VOC) challenge in 2007. The intention in interpolating the precision-recall (PR) curve was to reduce the impact of the 'wiggles' in the PR curve, caused by small variations in the ranking of examples. However, the downside of this interpolation was that the evaluation was too crude to discriminate between the methods at low AP [24]. Therefore, starting in 2010 the method of computing AP changed to use all data points. The object localization precision is measured by the IoU, usually taking a threshold of 0.5.

After 2014, due to the popularity of MS-COCO datasets, researchers started to pay more attention to the accuracy of the bounding box location [21]. Instead of using a fixed IoU threshold, AP is averaged over multiple IoU thresholds between 0.5 (coarse localization) and 0.95 (perfect localization). This change of the metric has encouraged more accurate object localization and may be of great importance for some real-world applications.

3.2 Object Tracking Evaluation Metrics

The mainstream evaluation metrics in the single-object tracking come from two benchmarks: VOT (Visual Object Tracking Challenge) and OTB (Object Tracking Benchmark). OTB contain two datasets: OTB50 and OTB100. The evaluation metrics are the precision score and the success score. The VOT benchmark comes from the VOT challenge that began in 2013, which is designed to evaluate the performance of single-object short-time tracking in complex scenarios. The VOT dataset and the evaluation metrics are adjusted yearly, but accuracy and robustness are the most basic evaluation metrics, because [26] points out that the two metrics are weakest correlation. Besides, EAO is the main evaluation metrics which was proposed in 2015. Before it, the main evaluation metric in VOT challenge was AR-rank. In 2018, VOT add LTB35 dataset, which is for long-term tracking. It exists object reappears, which requires the participating algorithm to re-detect the object. So, in this task, the VOT challenge evaluation metrics are precision, recall and F1-score. The follow of this section, we introduce the two evaluation systems and analyze their differences and connections.

OTB Evaluation Methodology. Precision score: This performance measure is calculated based on center error. OTB evaluation system estimates the number of frames within a given threshold distance of the ground truth position, i.e., precision score. The precision plot shows the percentage of frames whose location is within the given threshold distance (typically 0 to 50 pixels) of the ground truth. As the representative precision score for each tracker, OTB evaluation use the score for the threshold = 20 pixels.

Success score: The calculation of the measure is based on region overlap. When the overlap rate (i.e., IoU) in one frame is greater than a given threshold, the frame is regarded as successful tracking. Success score is equal to the number of successful frames divided by the total number of frames in the sequence. The method of overlapping threshold evaluation comes from the target detection community, and the threshold is generally set to 0.5. The same threshold is also used as a performance assessment for target tracking, as in [15] and [16], however this threshold is too high for the evaluation of normal target tracking, and only a visually well-overlapped rectangle can reach this threshold, so using a success score at a specific threshold (e.g. threshold = 0.5) for tracker evaluation may not be fair. In contrast, OTB2013 benchmark [27] ranks the tracking algorithms using the area under the curve (AUC) of success plot.

A popular way to evaluate trackers is to run them throughout a test sequence with initialization from the ground truth position in the first frame and report the precision plot or success plot. This is one-pass evaluation (OPE), which has two main drawbacks: First, the tracking algorithm may be sensitive to the initialization of the first frame. Second, for the algorithms without reinitialization, the tracking result after tracking failure cannot provide meaningful information [26]. Therefore, in [26], different frames are used as starting frames to report success plot and precision plot, which are called time robustness evaluation (TRE). OTB2013 [27] evaluation system uses different scales of ground truth bounding box, which named spatial robustness evaluation (SRE). And the scale ratio varies from 80 to 120% of the ground truth at the increment of 10%.

VOT Evaluation Methodology. The VOT benchmark evaluation system uses a reinitialization mechanism, and the system reinitializes the trace after fails. However, the reinitialization of trackers might introduce a bias into the performance measures. If a tracker fails at a particular frame, e.g., due to occlusion, it will likely fail again immediately after re-initialization. To reduce this bias, the tracker is re-initialized $N_{skip} = 5$ frames after the failure [26]. In addition, in the calculation of accuracy, it is considered that the overlaps in the frames after initialization is biased toward a higher value, and a burn-in period of several frames is required to reduce the bias. The period depends on the frame rate and the speed at which the object moves. [29] experimentally determined that the aging period on the VOT dataset is $N_{burnin} = 10\,frame$.

Accuracy: A tracker is run on each sequence N_{rep} times which allows dealing with the potential variance of its performance. The overlap rate (i.e., IoU) of each frame of the video has been defined in Sect. 2.3. Here, the overlap rate of the t-th frame in the k-th repetition is defined as $\phi(t, k)$. According to [29], the average precision of the t-th frame is:

$$\phi(t) = \frac{1}{N_{rep}} \sum_{k=1}^{N_{rep}} \phi(t, k) \tag{7}$$

Furthermore, the average accuracy of the tracker is defined as:

$$\rho_A = \frac{1}{N_{valid}} \sum_{t=1}^{N_{valid}} \phi(t) \tag{8}$$

Robustness: In the VOT, robustness is an independent metric to evaluate the stability of the tracker, and the larger the value, the worse the stability. Define F(k) as the number of times the tracker failed to track (IoU dropped to 0) in the k-th repetition. According to [29], F(k) is defined as follows:

$$\rho_R = \frac{1}{N_{rep}} \sum_{k=1}^{N_{rep}} F(k) \tag{9}$$

AR-rank: In [26], the tracker's accuracy and robustness are ranked separately for each attribute (e.g. occlusion, scale variation) sequence. Then get an accuracy or robustness rank by averaging each tracker's ranks on different attributes. Finally, average the two ranks (accuracy rank and robustness rank) to get the AR-rank. However, the statistical significance of performance differences does not directly imply actual differences. To solve this problem, the AR-rank has been improved [30], in which the practical difference measure is added to evaluate equivalence.

EAO: While ranking does convert the accuracy and robustness to equal scales, the averaged rank cannot be interpreted in terms of a concrete tracking application result. A tracker is initialized at the beginning of the sequence and left to track until the end. If a tracker drifts off the target, it remains off until the end of the sequence. The tracker performance can be summarized in such a scenario by computing the average of per-frame overlaps, Φ_i, including the zero overlaps after the failure [29], i.e.

$$\Phi_{N_s} = \frac{1}{N_s} \sum_{i=1}^{N_s} \Phi_i \tag{10}$$

While $N_s = N$, where N is the length of the sequence, we can get the average overlap (AO). By averaging the average overlaps on a very large set of N_s frames long sequences, we can obtain the expected average overlap $\hat{\Phi}_{N_s} = \Phi_{N_s}$. Evaluating this measure for a range of sequence lengths (i.e., $N_s = 1 : N_{max}$) results in the expected average overlap curve.

$$\Phi_{N_s} = \frac{1}{N_{max}} \sum_{i=1}^{N_{max}} \Phi_i \tag{11}$$

Actually, calculating the ideal EAO is a cumbersome task, because you need to find a lot of videos that are long enough to ensure the comprehensive evaluation of the tracker, and then measure the average overlap in a range. In the VOT, trace will be reinitialized after the drift, so that a video can be divided into several segments according to the failure point, which expanding the number of videos and saving the calculation amount. The number of frames of the video is counted as a statistic distribution map. Since the distribution is discrete, the KDE method is used to interpolate into continuous, and then the highest point is found. The boundary is satisfied $P(N_{low}) = P(N_{high})$ and $\int_{N_{low}}^{N_{high}} P(N_s)dN_s = 0.5$. Finally, for each of the divided N videos, the average overlap is calculated for each $N_s = N_{low} : N_{high}$.

EFO: In order to reduce the difference of speed generated by different computer hardware, EFO was proposed in VOT2014. Before using the vot-toolkit to evaluate the tracker, people first measure the time of filtering with a 30 * 30 maximum filter on a 600 * 600 gray image to obtain a base unit, and then use this basic unit to measure the speed of the tracker.

$EAO_{realtime}$: Since the EFO is still heavily affected by the performance of the hardware platform, in order to further solve the impact of the hardware platform, the VOT2017 Challenge introduces $EAO_{realtime}$. The specific calculation method is to limit the response time of the tracker while using VOT evaluation system. If the tracker fails to feedback the tracking result in real time (i.e., 25 fps, 40 ms per frame), the toolkit will no longer wait and use the tracking result of the previous frame.

The Difference Between the Two Evaluation Methodologies. The OTB evaluate methodology' robustness by changing the initialization on temporal and spatial. However, the non-detection tracking algorithms may fail at the beginning because same factors, e.g. due to occlusion, and cannot re-track, so the final evaluation system may only use a small part of the sequence, resulting in waste. VOT proposes that the evaluation system should detect the tracking failure and reinitialize the tracker after few frames of the failure, so that the dataset can be fully utilized.

In 2015, OTB [31] borrowed the VOT restart mechanism and proposed spatial robustness evaluation with restart (SRER) and one-pass evaluation with restart (OPER). If the tracker fails to track on a frame, the tracker is restarted for the rest of the sequence. In VOT2016, the metric AO (learning from the success score in OTB) is introduced, which is equivalent to EAO without restart mechanism.

The VOT benchmark evaluation is constantly updated and is more challenging, which gradually becomes mainstream. While the dataset of the OTB2013 benchmark is invisible to the previous algorithm, so the evaluation result is relatively accurate, and the link [28] contains the comparison results of single object tracking on the OTB benchmark evaluation system, and has been updating and maintaining, so in the single-object tracking field, researchers generally use both OTB and VOT evaluation systems to evaluate their algorithms.

4   UAV Visual Metrics

4.1   The Metrics of UAV Challenge

Benefiting from flourishing global drone industry, drones, or general UAVs, equipped with cameras have been fast deployed to a wide range of applications, such as security and surveillance, search and rescue, and sports analysis. Different from traditional video dataset, UAV aerial video has the inherent advantages of large view scope, and uniform scale. Meanwhile, it also brings new challenges to existing detection and tracking technologies, such as:

(1)   Small object. Objects are usually small or tiny due to high altitude of UAV views, resulting in difficulties to detect and track them.
(2)   Bird's-eye view. The object of the video is a bird's-eye view, which has fewer visual features than a normal surveillance video or video of an unmanned vehicle view.
(3)   Real-time. For most visual inspection and tracking applications, such as military reconnaissance or intelligent monitoring, the real-time image processing should be considered.
(4)   Low power consumption. The algorithms should maintain comparable accuracy on embedded devices of UAV for practical application, which requires the algorithms with relatively small network size.

The UAV vision challenges mainly including two types: Object detection and object tracking. There are two general types of hardware, namely embedded devices and high-performance GPUs. Embedded devices can be installed on UAV, making it easy for UAV to process video directly under various conditions, but limited by hardware conditions. On the contrary, high-performance GPUs can run more complex and efficient algorithms, but need to consumes a lot of power. So, it cannot be installed on small UAV, and can only handle video returned by UAV.

Visdrone challenge, the UAV visual object detection and recognition competition held by ICCV, divides the UAV visual challenge into four parts: object detection in image, object detection in video, single object tracking and multi-object tracking. In the object detection (in both images and videos) task, there are AP and AR metrics, which are same as COCO [3] (Sect. 3.1). In the single object tracking, the metrics are success score and precision score from OTB evaluation system. The 55th Design Automation Conference (DAC) held its first System Design Contest (SDC) in 2018 which features a lower power object detection challenge (LPODC) on designing and implementing novel algorithms based on object detection in images taken from unmanned aerial vehicles (UAV) [32]. The images of the dataset are the real image captured by the DJI drone [32], but the competition only involves video single-target detection. And metrics of this challenge include IoU, energy and speed. The evaluation metrics of the two challenges follow the traditional metrics, and pay more attention to real-time performance evaluation.

However, these common competitions are different from the scenarios we discussed (nearly 100 m' low-altitude surveillance). The UAV of these competitions are not fixed in height, and the minimum height is only a few meters. For the scenario we proposed, we can select the proper threshold for the general metrics to better adapt to the small object. And for this scenario, the measurement of inference speed and energy consumption is very important, which we discussed in Sect. 4.3.

Table 2. Evaluation metrics in target detection and tracking challenges of UAV.

Challenge	Metrics	Description
2019 Visdrone-DET&VID challenge [33]	AP	AP at IoU = 0.5:0.05:0.95
	$AP^{IoU=0.5}$	AP at IoU = 0.5
	$AP^{IoU=0.75}$	AP at IoU = 0.75
	$AR^{max=1}$	AR given 1 detection per image
	$AR^{max=10}$	AR given 10 detection per image
	$AR^{max=100}$	AR given 100 detection per image
2019 Visdrone SOT challenge [33]	Success score	The percentage of correct frames (with AUC)
	Precision score	The percentage of correct frames (with 20 pixels)
	mAP	mAP with thresholds 0.25, 0.50, 0.75
DAC-SDC LPODC Challenge [32]	IoU	The average IoU of an object detector
	Energy	Consumption for processing all the images
	FPS	Frame Per Second

4.2   Threshold Selection of Common Metrics

Choosing an appropriate value for the threshold may affect the order and can also be potentially misused to influence the results of a comparison. It is sometimes better to avoid the use of a single specific threshold altogether, especially when the evaluation goal is general and a specific threshold is not a part of the target task. However, in the specific UAV project for small target detection and tracking, the threshold can be adjusted in order to get a more realistic algorithm.

Threshold Selection of mAP. As shown in Table 2, the metric AP of the object detection of the UAV is calculated based on the IoU threshold. While different sizes of objects are sensitive to IoU. For example, an 18 * 35 pixels prediction box matches a 10 * 20 pixels ground truth bounding box, as shown in Fig. 2, the error of the prediction box is within the acceptance range of people, but the IoU is only 0.32. Since the objects of the UAV vision are small objects, IoU = 0.5 is unfairly to evaluate the algorithm for this application. ImageNet's evaluation system also takes into account the size of the object. When evaluating smaller objects, the threshold of the IoU is reduced. The formula is as follows:

$$\text{thr(B)} = \min\left(0.5, \frac{w * h}{(w + 10) * (h + 10)}\right) \qquad (12)$$

Where, w is the width and h is the height of the ground truth bounding box.

Fig. 2. The image is derived from the dataset of visdrone challenge, in which all non-pedestrians are defined as the category "person". The image on the left is the original image, and the four images on the right are enlarged views of the "person". The green box is the ground truth bounding box; the red box is prediction bounding box. (Color figure online)

Threshold Selection of Precision Score. The precision score is a popular evaluation metric in the single-object tracking competition of the UAV, which is based on the central error. The precision score in the common single-object tracking is defined as the percentage of bounding boxes within a distance threshold of 20 pixels, which because this threshold roughly corresponds to at least 50% overlap between the tracker bounding box and the ground truth [34]. However, in the actual application scenario assumed in this paper, the small unmanned aerial vehicle performs the surveillance mission, which the flying height is about 100 m, so that the object is small. So, the central error threshold can be defined smaller. However, sometimes in order to avoid selecting a specific threshold, the result can also be reported as a plot whose threshold from 0 to 50 pixel.

4.3 Application Metrics Design

Most of the current models with good detection and tracking effects are based on convolutional neural networks. However, real-time scene parsing through object detection running on a UAV platform is very challenging, due to limited memory and computing power of embedded devices. Inferring speed and energy consumption are major concern for current deep learning models, especially in practical applications.

The Measure of Inferring Speed. There are two quantitative measures of detection and tracking speed: One is the number of images processed per second, i.e., frame per second (f/s or FPS); the other is the time t for processing each image, i.e., inference speed t = 1/N, where N is the number of processing images per second. The frame rate of video capture is generally 24 FPS, and the algorithm could be considered as real-time detection if it achieves or exceeds 24 FPS. Otherwise, only the FPSs obtained on the same computing device are comparable. In order to reduce the influence of external factors such as hardware platform and programming language on the tracking speed, the EFO metric is introduced in the VOT evaluation system (Sect. 3.2).

The Measures of Energy Consumption. Energy consumption is also an important metric. Considering that in some practical applications, it may be necessary to process images on embedded devices of small UAV. For example, [32] DAC-SDC LPODC Challenge, officially provided Nvidia TX2 GPU and Xilinx Ultra96 FPGA as the platform. Only the algorithms running on the same device and on the same dataset have comparable power consumption. Considering a more intuitive comparison of power consumption on different devices, the space and time complexity of the model itself can measure the energy consumption of the algorithm to some extent. If the model has more parameters, more memory will be applied, which results in more energy consumption. Spatial complexity is measured by parameter size, and parameter is the weight that a model has to learn, or the required variables to define the model. The time complexity is measured by floating point operations (FLOPs). In the appendix of [35], the calculation method of the FLOPs metric is mentioned, whose main idea is to ignore the overhead of nonlinear calculation and compare the FLOPs of the convolution kernel and the fully connected layer.

5 Conclusion

In this paper, we study the design and optimization of evaluation metrics in object detection and tracking for low-altitude aerial video. As far as we know, our paper is the first work to study this issue, and is a reference for the performance evaluation of detection and tracking algorithms in domain-specific research. Comprehensive consideration of metrics will be our future research direction.

References

1. Cehovin, L., Leonardis, A., Kristan, M.: Visual object tracking performance measures revisited. IEEE Trans. Image Process. **25**(3), 1261–1274 (2016)
2. Everingham, M., Gool, L.V., Williams, C.K.I., et al.: The PASCAL visual object classes (VOC) challenge. Int. J. Comput. Vis. **88**(2), 303–338 (2010)
3. Lin, T.Y., Maire, M., Belongie, S., et al.: Microsoft COCO: common objects in context. In: Fleet, D., Pajdla, T., Schiele B., Tuytelaars, T. (eds.) Computer Vision–ECCV 2014, LNCS, vol. 8693, pp. 740–755. Springer, Cham (2014). https://doi.org/10.1007/978-3-319-10602-1_48

4. Kristan, M., et al.: The sixth visual object tracking VOT2018 challenge results. In: Leal-Taixé, L., Roth, S. (eds.) Computer Vision–ECCV 2018 Workshops, LNCS, vol. 11129, pp. 3–53. Springer, Cham (2019). https://doi.org/10.1007/978-3-030-11009-3_1

5. Wu, Y., Lim, J., Yang, M.H.: Object tracking benchmark. IEEE Trans. Pattern Anal. Mach. Intell. **37**(9), 1834–1848 (2015)

6. Vidit, J., Erik, L.M.: FDDB: a benchmark for face detection in unconstrained settings. Technical Report UM-CS-2010-009, Department of Computer Science, University of Massachusetts, Amherst (2010)

7. Wojek, C., Dollar, P., Schiele, B., et al.: Pedestrian detection: an evaluation of the state of the art. IEEE Trans. Pattern Anal. Mach. Intell. **34**(4), 743–761 (2012)

8. Geiger, A., Lenz, P., Urtasun, R.: Are we ready for autonomous driving? The KITTI vision benchmark suite. In: Proceedings of the 2012 IEEE Conference on Computer Vision and Pattern Recognition, pp. 3354–3361. IEEE, Providence (2012)

9. Baykara, H.C., Bıyık, E., Gül, G., et al.: Real-time detection, tracking and classification of multiple moving objects in UAV videos. In: 29th International Conference on Tools with Artificial Intelligence (ICTAI), pp. 945–950. IEEE, Boston (2017)

10. Du, D.W., Qi, Y.K., Yu, H.Y., et al.: The unmanned aerial vehicle benchmark: object detection and tracking. In: Ferrari, V., Hebert, M., Sminchisescu, C., Weiss, Y. (eds.) Computer Vision–ECCV 2018. LNCS, vol. 11214, pp. 375–391. Springer, Cham (2018)

11. Mueller, M., Smith, N., Ghanem, B.: A benchmark and simulator for UAV tracking. In: Leibe, B., Matas, J., Sebe, N., Welling, M. (eds.) Computer Vision–ECCV 2016. LNCS, vol. 9905, pp. 445–461. Springer, Cham (2016). https://doi.org/10.1007/978-3-319-46448-0_27

12. Zhang, P.Y., Zhong, Y.X., Li, X.Q.: SlimYOLOv3: Narrower, Faster and Better for Real-Time UAV Applications. CoRR abs/1907.11093 (2019)

13. Zhu, P.F., Wen, L.Y., Du, D.W., et al.: VisDrone-VDT2018: the vision meets drone video detection and tracking challenge results. In: Leal-Taixé, L., Roth, S. (eds.) Computer Vision–ECCV 2018 Workshops. LNCS, vol. 11133, pp. 496–518. Springer, Cham (2018). https://doi.org/10.1007/978-3-030-11021-5_29

14. Measuring Object Detection models-mAP-What is Mean Average Precision? https://towardsdatascience.com/what-is-map-understanding-the-statistic-of-choice-for-comparing-object-detection-models-1ea4f67a9dbd. Accessed 07 Oct 2019

15. Smeulders, A.W.M., Chu, D.M., Cucchiara, R., et al.: Visual tracking: an experimental survey. IEEE Trans. Pattern Anal. Mach. Intell. **36**(7), 1442–1468 (2014)

16. Zhang, K.H., Zhang, L., Yang, M.H.: Real-time compressive tracking. In: Fitzgibbon, A., Lazebnik, S., Perona, P., Sato, Y., Schmid, C. (eds.) Computer Vision–ECCV 2012. LNCS, vol. 7574, pp. 864–877. Springer, Heidelberg (2012). https://doi.org/10.1007/978-3-642-33712-3_62

17. Godec, M., Roth, P.M., Bischof, H.: Hough-based tracking of non-rigid objects. Comput. Vis. Image Underst. **117**(10), 1245–1256 (2013)

18. Kosub, S.: A note on the triangle inequality for the Jaccard distance. Pattern Recogn. Lett. **120**, 36–38 (2019)

19. Leal-Taixé, L., Milan, A., Reid, I.D., et al.: MOTChallenge 2015: Towards a Benchmark for Multi-Target Tracking. CoRR, abs/1504.01942 (2015)

20. Kristan, M., et al.: The visual object tracking VOT2016 challenge results. In: Hua, G., Jegou, H. (eds.) Computer Vision – ECCV 2016 Workshops, LNCS, vol. 9914, pp. 777–823. Springer, Cham (2016). https://doi.org/10.1007/978-3-319-48881-3_54

21. Zou, Z.X., Shi, Z.W., Guo, Y.H., et al.: Object Detection in 20 Years: A Survey. CoRR abs/1905.05055 (2019)

22. Dalal, N., Triggs, B.: Histograms of oriented gradients for human detection. In: 2005 IEEE Computer Society Conference on Computer Vision and Pattern Recognition, vol. 1, pp. 886–893. IEEE, San Diego (2005)

23. Dollar, P., Wojek, C., Schiele, B., et al.: Pedestrian detection: a benchmark. In: 2009 IEEE Conference on Computer Vision and Pattern Recognition, pp. 304–311. IEEE, Miami (2009)

24. Everingham, M., Eslami, S.M.A., Gool, L.V., et al.: The Pascal visual object classes challenge: a retrospective. Int. J. Comput. Vis. **111**(1), 98–136 (2015)

25. Kisantal, M., Wojna, Z., Murawski, J., et al.: Augmentation for small object detection. CoRR abs/1902.07296 (2019)

26. Kristan, M., Pflugfelder R., Leonardis A., et al.: The visual object tracking VOT2013 challenge results. In: 2013 IEEE International Conference on Computer Vision Workshops, pp. 98–111. IEEE, Sydney (2013)

27. Wu, Y., Lim J., Yang, M.H.: Online object tracking: a benchmark. In: 2013 IEEE Conference on Computer Vision and Pattern Recognition, pp. 2411–2418. IEEE, Portland (2013)

28. Foolwood Homepage. https://github.com/foolwood/benchmark_results. Accessed 07 Oct 2019

29. Kristan, M., Matas, J., Leonardis, A., et al.: A novel performance evaluation methodology for single-target trackers. IEEE Trans. Pattern Anal. Mach. Intell. **38**(11), 2137–2155 (2016)

30. Kristan, M., Pflugfelder, R., Leonardis, A., et al.: The visual object tracking VOT2014 challenge results. In: Agapito, L., Bronstein, M., Rother, C. (eds.) Computer Vision - ECCV 2014 Workshops. LNCS, vol. 8926, pp. 191–217. Springer, Cham (2014). https://doi.org/10.1007/978-3-319-16181-5_14

31. Kristan, M., Pflugfelder, R., Matas, J., et al.: The visual object tracking VOT2015 challenge results. In: 2015 IEEE International Conference on Computer Vision Workshop, pp. 564–586. IEEE, Santiago (2016)

32. Xu, X.W., Zhang, X.Y., Yu, B., et al.: DAC-SDC Low Power Object Detection Challenge for UAV Applications. CoRR abs/1809.00110 (2018)

33. Zhu, P.F., Wen, L.Y., Bian, X., et al.: Vision Meets Drones: A Challenge. CoRR abs/1804.07437 (2018)

34. Babenko, B., Yang, M.H., Belongie, S.J.: Robust object tracking with online multiple instance learning. IEEE Trans. Pattern Anal. Mach. Intell. **33**(8), 1619–1632 (2011)

35. Molchanov, P., Tyree, S., Karras, T., et al.: Pruning convolutional neural networks for resource efficient inference. arXiv preprint arXiv:1611.06440 (2016)

People Flow Analysis Based on Anonymous OD Trip Data

Tianxu Sun[1], Yunlong Zhao[1,2(✉)], and Zuowei Lian[1]

[1] Nanjing University of Aeronautics and Astronautics, Nanjing, China
zhaoyunlong@nuaa.edu.cn
[2] Collaborative Innovation Center of Novel Software Technology
and Industrialization, Nanjing, China

Abstract. With the development of cities, analyzing people flow in city become more and more important. Meanwhile, with the development of intelligence sensing technology especially mobile crowd-sensing, the concept of smart city was proposed by many scholars, and sensing data in smart cities provides the possibility for analysis of people flow. Based on the idea of protecting users, this paper analyzing people flow from OD trip data that not including user information with a simple structure by an improved density-based clustering algorithm named ST-DBSCAN based on the thinking of clustering; then introduce some improvements of the clustering algorithm to adapt to the urban environment, Including the use of spherical distance formulas, adding iterative steps and defining cluster centers; finally experiment on a real dataset of Nanjing, China, analyze the results and interpret some insights of the results.

Keywords: People flow · Smart city · Clustering algorithm · OD trip

1 Introduction

With the rapid development of the city, the growing population has brought tremendous pressure on the city's public resources such as transportation by the urbanization. Due to the uncertainty of people flow, it is also prone to serious incidents such as traffic accidents and trampling, affecting the safety and quality of life of urban residents. Therefore, People Flow Analysis is an important part of urban development. With the development of intelligence sensing technology, especially crowd-sensing, the concept of smart city has been proposed by many scholars. Data collected by various sensing devices in the city is used more for urban people flow analysis, such as mobile phone cellular data, monitoring video, GPS data, WiFi, intelligent traffic IC card data, etc. [1, 2]. Different from general text or image data, data collected in city has spatial features and temporal features. Spatial features include attributes such as distance and geographic level. Time features include time series, trend and periodicity. These characteristics usually contain personal information, such as travel habits, etc. How to analyze people flow from anonymous data is a problem in smart city system. In this paper, we:

1. Propose an analyze method based on clustering thought. We first transforming the analyze problem into a clustering problem of three-dimension data, then propose a

Y. Tian et al. (Eds.): ICBDS 2019, CCIS 1210, pp. 263–273, 2020.
https://doi.org/10.1007/978-981-15-7530-3_19

clustering algorithm improved by DBSCAN (Density-Based Spatial Clustering of Applications with Noise) named ST-DBSCAN (Spatio-Temporal DBSCAN) to solve the clustering problem.

2. In order to adapt our clustering method to urban environments, we used the spherical distance formula in ST-DBSCAN, then add iterative steps to limit the coverage of the cluster to make the clustering method suitable for transportation applications. Finally, define the center of the cluster to represent the spatiotemporal characteristics of cluster.

3. Apply algorithm proposed in this paper to a real data set, and the results are analyzed and evaluated based on the actual geographic information. We can find that the obtained results are consistent with the people flow in city, which proves the effectiveness of our method.

The rest of this paper is organized as follows. Section 2 introduce related work in recent years. Section 3 introduce our clustering algorithm named ST-DBSCAN to solve the problem, Sect. 4 introduce some improvements of the clustering algorithm to adapt to the urban environment. Section 5 presents evaluation results. Finally, we conclude this paper in Sect. 6.

2   Related Work

In terms of the source of spatiotemporal data, the large amount of data generated by modern communication technologies such as Bluetooth, radio frequency technology, 4G LTE, etc. plays an increasingly important role in the study of spatio-temporal distribution of people flow [4]. For example, mobile phone signaling data owned by operators is one of the innovative tools for analyzing the spatial and temporal distribution and mobility patterns of human flow [5]. Many scholars have combined multi-source data to carry out research work. For example, Masahiko I combined IC card data with social media data to explore changes in passenger behavior and abnormalities in subway traffic from multiple perspectives. Scenario [1], the social media data combined in this study can better reflect the individual behavioral characteristics of travel passengers. At the same time, many scholars have carried out different research on different spatial and temporal data of different granularity. For example, Merkebe G et al. applied signaling data to model the overall traffic distribution pattern of Senegal countries [6], and in another study, Traffic demand was estimated by him [7], which proposed traffic planning for the less developed Senegal. In a more granular scenario, Fei X et al. clustered the operational information of bus lines [8], and divided The state of operation of several bus lines is used to estimate the traffic conditions of the city based on the state of the vehicle. In terms of the analysis of the flow pattern of people flow, the Zheng Y system expounds the main research methods and techniques for the flow pattern of the trajectory data mining [9]; Liu Z et al. based on the travel chain of urban residents [10], by exploring the home address and The daily movement behavior is used to construct the flow pattern of people flow; similarly, Takihiro Y et al. combined the travel chain and disaster data [11] to analyze the impact of different disaster modes on the movement pattern of people. Do C et al. used the starting-destination matrix [12] to process the mobile phone data using the decision tree classification algorithm to explore the travel mode. In higher-level applications, Lyu Y et al. proposed a customized bus route planning method using the flow pattern of people flow [3], which improved the revenue of the bus system.

3 ST-DBSCAN

DBSCAN (Density-Based Spatial Clustering of Applications with Noise) proposed by Ester in 1996 is a typical density clustering algorithm. Compared with clusters only applicable to convex sample sets such as K-Means, DBSCAN Can be applied to convex sample sets or non-convex sample sets. Given a set of points in a space, DBSCAN can cluster nearby points and mark outliers in low-density areas.

Considering the various features of people flow in time and space dimensions, traditional DBSCAN is not enough to cluster Spatio-temporal Data, so we propose ST-DBSCAN to solve this problem. When defining a neighborhood, our algorithm enters a set of spatio-temporal neighborhood radii (c_s, c_t), so the neighborhood can be divided in terms of time and space. The relevant definitions of the algorithm are as follows:

Definition 1 (Spatio-Temporal Neighborhood). There is a sample set $D = (x_1, x_2, ..., x_m)$, for any $x \in D$, its spatio-temporal neighborhood is a sample set containing the time-space distance of x in the sample set D and not greater than the neighborhood radius threshold, which is:

$$N_{c_s, c_t}(x_i) = \{x_j | spatiodist(x_i, x_j) < c_s, temporaldist(x_i, x_j) < c_t\} \tag{1}$$

Definition 2 (Core Point). There is a sample set $D = (x_1, x_2, ..., x_m)$, for any $x \in D$, if its spatio-temporal neighborhood $N_{cs,\ ct}(x_i)$ contains at least *MinPts* samples, then x is called the core point. which is:

$$\left| N_{cs,ct}(x_i) \right| > MinPts \tag{2}$$

Definition 3 (Spatio-Temporal Distance). There is a sample set $D = (x_1, x_2, ..., x_m)$, for any $x = (o_{i,x}, o_{i,y}, d_{i,x}, d_{i,y}, t_i, t_{i,off})$, The spatio-temporal distance between any two points is:

$$spatiodist(x_i, x_j) = \sqrt{||o_i - o_j||_2^2 + ||d_i - d_j||_2^2} \tag{3}$$

$$temporaldist(x_i, x_j) = |t_{i,o} - t_{j,o}| + |t_{i,d} - t_{j,d}| \tag{4}$$

Algorithm 1. ST-DBSCAN

Input: $D = (x_1, x_2, ..., x_m), (c_s, c_t, MinPts)$

Output: $Labels = (l_1, l_2, ..., l_m)$

1: $cores = \emptyset, seeds = \emptyset$;

2: $k = 0$

3: **for** each element E in sample set D

4:     **if** E is a core point

5:         add E to core set $cores$

6:     **end if**

7: **end for**

8: **for** each core point C in core set $cores$

9:     mark C with label k

10:     $seeds = get\_seedset(C)$

11:     **while** seeds not empty

12:         $seed = seeds.pop()$

13:         mark $seed$ with label k

14:         seed_neighbour = get_neighbour($seed$)

15:         **if** seed is core point:

16:             add point in seed_neighbour to $seeds$

17:         **end if**

18:     $k = k+1$

19: **end for**

$$\left\| o_i - o_j \right\|_2 = \sqrt{\left(o_{i,x} - o_{j,x} \right)^2 + \left(d_{i,x} - d_{j,x} \right)^2} \tag{5}$$

According to the above three definitions, our algorithm are shown in Algorithm 1.

4 People Flow Clustering

In order to discover the characteristics of human flow, we define human flow extraction issue as a clustering problem for 3D data, including the location of the origin and destination, and the start time of each trip. When dealing with GPS data containing longitude and latitude information, we need to use the spherical distance formula to calculate the distance between the two points, to reduce errors due to uneven distribution of longitude and latitude in two-dimensional space. The spherical distance formula as follows

$$S = \Delta\sigma \times R \tag{6}$$

$$\Delta\sigma = 2\arcsin\left(\sqrt{sin^2(\Delta\varphi/2) + cos\varphi_A cos\varphi_B sin^2(\Delta\gamma/2)} \right) \tag{7}$$

where S means actual spherical distance between two points, R represents the average radius of the earth; $\Delta\sigma$ which is calculated in formula (6) represents the central angel of two lines which link two points with the center of sphere respectively; φ and γ are radians of each points latitude and longitude $\Delta\varphi$ and $\Delta\gamma$ denote the difference values between two radian corresponding to the longitude and latitude, respectively

Based on this distance formula and the ST-DBSCAN algorithm, we can solve this 3D clustering problem. However, in some smart transportation applications, we usually do not want the coverage area of the origin or destination to be too large, such as bus-stop locations determining for customized bus systems [t2cbs]. To prevent the area of a single cluster from being too large, we added an iterative step after getting the results of ST-DBSCAN. We check the coverage area of each cluster first, If the area S_i of the i-th cluster is greater than a given preset threshold S_0, the space radius c_s in our algorithm is halved, and then a clustering step is performed until the coverage area of all clusters meets the constraints. Similarly, in the time dimension, we set a threshold T_0 so that the length of the period covered by each cluster is less than T_0. If the result of the clustering algorithm does not satisfy the constraint, an iterative step will be performed and the time radius c_t will be halved.

Also we need to define a cluster center to describe a people flow, including the location of its origin and destination and the time of movement in all the flow. We utilize formulas (8), (9) and (10) to define cluster centers [13]

$$lat_{center} = \sum_{i=1}^{n} lat_i \Big/ n \tag{8}$$

$$lon_{center} = \sum_{i=1}^{n} lon_i \Big/ n \tag{9}$$

$$time_{center} = \sum\nolimits_{i=1}^{n} time_i \Big/ n \qquad (10)$$

where n is the number of elements in the cluster; lat_i and lon_i mean the latitude and longitude of *i-th* point in cluster, $time_i$ mean the time of movement of *i-th* trip in cluster, lat_{center}, lon_{center} and $time_{center}$ represent the latitude, longitude and time of the cluster center, respectively.

5   Evaluation

This chapter first introduces the real taxi dataset of a Chinese city, then apply ST-DBSCAN algorithm proposed in this paper to the dataset and evaluates the results.

5.1   Settings

The taxi GPS data used in this paper collected by 100 taxis in Nanjing, China during the period from October 1, 2018 to October 26, 2018. Table 1 shows one sample data of the data set. In the data pre-processing, taxis whose trip records were less than 10 in a whole day have been omitted. Table 1 shows a sample of the data set, including the ID of the sample, the sampling time stamp *UTC*, the geographical location latitude *Lat* and longitude *Lng*, and the occupation state *State*.

Table 1. Sample of the data set

ID	UTC	Lat	Lng	State
38801	1539409634	32.003	118.725	0

Table 2. Sample of OD trip data

Lat-O	Lng-O	Lat-D	Lng-D	UTC
32.003	118.725	32.003	118.725	1539409634

In order to keep the anonymity of the data, we only consider the location of origin and destination of each taxi trip, without the travel trajectory and user information. After the data processing process, we converted taxi location records into OD trips data by checking the change of *state*. Table 2 shows a sample of OD trip data, including the travel time stamp *UTC*, the geographical location of both origin and destination.

5.2   Result Analysis

– Time distribution and hotspot area in city

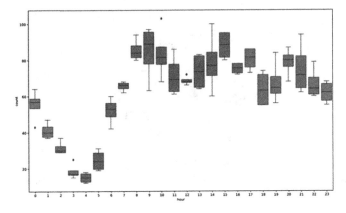

Fig. 1. Trip distribution during the working day

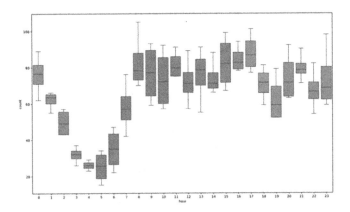

Fig. 2. Trip distribution during the rest day

We first select the daily flow data for the two weeks from October 8 to October 21, 2018 and count them by the working day and the rest day in the time dimension. The results are shown in Figs. 1 and 2; the heat map is drawn in the space dimension. The result is shown in Fig. 3.

In Figs. 1 and 2, we can find the people flow has certain characteristics in the time distribution of one day. During the working day, the movement of crowd is concentrated in the morning and evening commuting peaks, and the activity is the least at noon. During the rest day, there is no time pressure on commuting, so the overall distribution is more uniform, and the number of nighttime activity is obviously higher than the working day. In Fig. 3, we can find there are several obvious hotspots in city. We combine real geographic information and these areas, that we can find these hotspots are in line with the facts.

– Case Study: People Flow in Nanjing South Railway Station

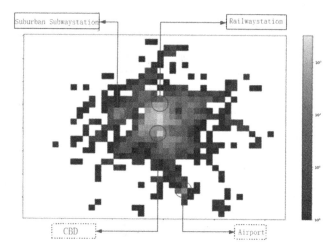

Fig. 3. Hotspot area in city

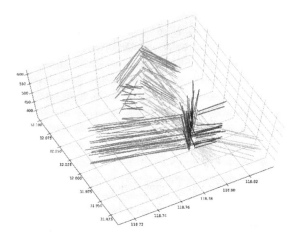

Fig. 4. Overview of clustering results

After the clustering process, we can get the results as shown in Fig. 4, where each line represents a set of travel behavior. We can find that the travel behavior of people flow is unevenly distributed on the spatial and temporal scales. This is because the OD trip data used in this paper is converted from taxi data. These data represent the travel demands and behaviors of a part of passengers in city for example commuting travel. It is very meaningful to find these pattern for urban planning and other smart city applications.

In this article, we will give an example to analyze the flow of people at the Nanjing South Railway Station to give some results. Nanjing South Railway Station is an important transportation hub in Nanjing, and it is located far away from the city center.

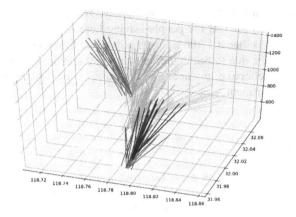

Fig. 5. People flow of Nanjing South Railway Station

Fig. 6. Main location in Nanjing of people flow

So there are so many taxi trips around the train station. When we focus on the people flow of Nanjing South Railway Station, we can get the results as shown in Fig. 5. The x-axis and the y-axis represent longitude and latitude, respectively, and z represents time. When we combine the map and draw the center of the cluster, we can get Fig. 6.

In the spatial dimension, the centers of several clusters are mainly concentrated on 4 points, they are basically located on the subway network. In the time dimension, the clusters at each point are quite different. We can find but not limited to the following phenomena.

- Between 22:30 and 7:00 the next day, the people flow at the station mainly consists of two-way movement between the station and Xinjiekou and Yuantong. This phenomenon is mainly due to the operation time of the subway. During the daytime, the station's people flow is mainly from the station travel to the city center.
- Although most people follow a two-way pattern, people flow near YunjinRoad locate at different positions in different directions, this is mainly because Yuantong

is a transportation hub in the suburbs of the city. We can find from the character-istics of the people flow that the people leaving here is greater than arriving.

- Another exception is that at 17:00 a cluster will travel from the station to Guanghua Road, which may be due to traffic pressure during commuting time. Such a people flow can provide effective guidance for the transportation planning of the city's transportation department.

6 Conclusion

In the context of smart city, this paper proposes a method of analyzing people flow based on simple and anonymous OD trip data. Firstly, we design an improved density-based clustering algorithm. Extend the input parameters of DBSCAN and re-define the neighborhood in Spatio-temporal dimension. Then introduce some improvements of the clustering algorithm to adapt to the urban environment. Finally analyze our results and interpret some insights. We have discovered some phenomena from the distribu-tion of people low which can provide guidance for the development of the city. This proves the effectiveness of the analyzing method. In the next research work, we hope to focus on particular people flow for specific city optimize application, this will play a big role in the city development.

Acknowledgement. This research was supported by Defense Industrial Technology Develop-ment Program under Grant No. JCKY2016605B006, Six talent peaks project in Jiangsu Province under Grant No. XYDXXJS-031.

References

1. Itoh, M., Yokoyama, D., Toyoda, M., et al.: Visual exploration of changes in passenger flows and tweets on mega-city metro network. IEEE Trans. Big Data 2(1), 85–99 (2016)
2. Alessandrini, A., Gioia, C., Sermi, F. et al.: WiFi positioning and Big Data to monitor flows of people on a wide scale. In: 2017 European Navigation Conference (ENC). IEEE (2017)
3. Lyu, Y., Chow, C.Y., Lee, V.C.S., et al.: T2CBS: mining taxi trajectories for customized bus systems. In: Computer Communications Workshops. IEEE (2016)
4. Hashem, I.A.T., Chang, V., Anuar, N.B., Adewole, K., Yaqoob, I., et al.: The role of big data in smart city. Int. J. Inf. Manag. 36(5), 748–758 (2016)
5. Steenbruggen, J., Tranos, E., Nijkamp, P.: Data from Mobile Phone Operators, vol. 39, no. 3, pp. 335–346. Pergamon Press, Oxford (2015)
6. Demissie, M.G., Phithakkitnukoon, S., Kattan, L.: Trip distribution modeling using mobile phone data: emphasis on Intra-Zonal trips. IEEE Trans. Intell. Transp. Syst. 20(7), 2605–2617 (2019)
7. Demissie, M.G., Phithakkitnukoon, S., Kattan, L., Sukhvibul, T., Antunes, F., et al.: Inferring passenger travel demand to improve urban mobility in developing countries using cell phone data: a case study of Senegal. IEEE Trans. Intell. Transp. Syst. 17(9), 2466–2478 (2016)
8. Fei, X.Q., Gkountouna, O.: Spatiotemporal clustering in urban transportation: a bus route case study in Washington DC. SIGSPATIAL Spec. 10(2), 26–33 (2018)

9. Zheng, Y.: Trajectory data mining: an overview. ACM Trans. Intell. Syst. Technol. **6**(3), 29 (2015)

10. Liu, Z., Yu, J., Xiong, W., et al.: Using mobile phone data to explore spatial-temporal evolution of home-based daily mobility patterns in Shanghai. In: International Conference on Behavioral, Economic and Socio-Cultural Computing, pp. 1–6. IEEE (2017)

11. Yabe, T., Tsubouchi, K., Sekimoto, Y.: CityFlowFragility: measuring the fragility of people flow in cities to disasters using GPS data collected from smartphones. Proc. ACM Interact. Mob. Wearable Ubiquitous Technol. **1**(3), 117 (2017)

12. Do, C.X., Tsukai, M.: Exploring potential use of mobile phone data resource to analyze inter-regional travel patterns in Japan. Data Mining Big Data 314–325 (2017)

13. Wang, W., Tao, L., Gao, C., Wang, B., Yang, H., Zhang, Z.: A C-DBSCAN algorithm for determining bus-stop locations based on taxi GPS data. In: Luo, X., Yu, J.X., Li, Z. (eds.) ADMA 2014. LNCS (LNAI), vol. 8933, pp. 293–304. Springer, Cham (2014). https://doi.org/10.1007/978-3-319-14717-8_23

Agile Methods and Cyber-Physical Systems Development—A Review with Preliminary Analysis

Muhammad Ovais Ahmad[✉]

Department of Mathematics and Computer Science, Karlstad University,
Karlstad, Sweden
Ovais.ahmad@kau.se

Abstract. The software companies are using Agile methods and practices to tackle challenges in the rapidly changing environments and increasingly complex software systems. However, companies developing cyber physical systems (CPS) are still infancy in the use of Agile methods and hesitate to adopt. This systematic literature review was conducted in order to analyze the current trends of Agile methods use for CPS development. The search strategy resulted in 101 papers, of which 15 were identified as primary studies relevant to our research. The results show growing trend of Agile processes and Scrum is widely used reported for CPS development. The primary studies also exhibits a growing interest in teaching Agile in embedded systems, CPS and other engineering degree programs. The reported challenges included synchronization of software and hardware development, software and hardware developers use different vocabulary, lack of visibility and track of software releases and project progress. Additionally, lesson learned were extracted from the primary studies for guiding the practitioners interested in adopting Agile for CPS development.

Keywords: Agile · Scrum · Cyber physical systems · Software development

1 Introduction

In 2011, at Hannover fair, the term Industry 4.0 presented as fourth industrial revolution driven by the Internet [1]. The background on the term industry 4.0 came from the German government initiative to promote manufacturing industry using latest information and communication technologies. In general, there are forces which brings industrial revolution such as constant pressure to improve software, product and service quality, stay competitive in the market, enhance safety, sustainability and more important to remain profitable etc. To cope with these forces and become more agile the companies in every sector paying more attention to take advantages of technology and digitalization. The industry 4.0 focuses on interconnectivity, automation, machine learning, smart digital technology and real-time data. According to Hermann et al. [2] there are four key component of Industry 4.0: Cyber-physical systems (CPS), Internet of things (IoT), Internet of services (IoS), Smart factory. This digital transformation bring the traditional engineering closer to software engineering and create new interesting technical challenges and opportunities.

© Springer Nature Singapore Pte Ltd. 2020
Y. Tian et al. (Eds.): ICBDS 2019, CCIS 1210, pp. 274–285, 2020.
https://doi.org/10.1007/978-981-15-7530-3_20

CPS is one of the important and fastest growing area in today ICT development paradigm. *"Cyber-physical systems (CPS) are physical and engineered systems whose operations are monitored, coordinated, controlled and integrated by a computing and communication core"* [8]. According to Leitao et al. [10] CPS extends the concept of embedded systems: *"in embedded systems the focus is on computational elements hosted in stand-alone devices, while CPS is designed as a network of interacting computational and physical devices"* [10]. Developing such complex systems are extremely challenging to complexity and strict regulated standards and guidelines. One example could be complexity comes when everything getting smart, e.g., phones, houses, cars, aircrafts, factories, cities etc. On the other, hand complexity in our systems are not visible to user and package as making life easier feature. In case of a smart car, the complexities such senor inter-communications, with operating system and internet connection is hidden from a driver.

CPS constitute of the physical part (hardware and its integration) and software with capability exposure as services *(services on-device, i.e. running within the CPS, and in network, i.e. other services running outside the CPS such as the cloud or even in other CPS* [10]. It is evident that binding force of today's CPS components is software. It is the core for development and maintaining smart environment where systems are interconnect intelligently. Agile approaches are widely used in classical software and systems development due to various benefits such as reduce time to market, better meet customer requirements, improve software quality, deliver value added feature to customer and many more [11, 12]. However, directly adopting Agile methods to CPS development is not explored and Lee [13] propose a research direction to *"Rethink the hardware and software split"* and its development. This leads to a question, what are the techniques are there to develop and maintain software for CPS. There are attempts to use Agile methods in the development of various CPS. Cawley et al. [14] investigated lean and agile methods in regulated, safety-critical systems; Huang et al. [15] reported positive experiences of Agile use in systems engineering for satellite development. Despite these attempts on Agile use in CPS, existing scientific literature seems to disperse and fragmented. This become the motivation for study to investigate the status of Agile methods in cyber physical systems development in existing literature. The goal of this systematic literature review is to identify the methods and practices used in the development of cyber physical systems, and faced challenges while using Agile in CPS as well as lessons learned along with future research direction.

The article is organized as follows: Sect. 2, Introduces the systematic review protocol in detail; Sect. 3, Reports the results of the review; Sect. 4, Discuss the validity threat; Sect. 5 conclude the paper with future research direction.

2 Research Method

In this section, we discuss our literature review protocol based on Kitchenham guidelines [6]. The review protocol has the following key elements: motivation and identification of research questions, Search Strategy, inclusion and exclusion criteria, quality assessment and data extraction.

2.1   Motivation and Research Question

The motivation and formulation comes under the umbrella of planning literature review phase. According to Kitchenham et al. (2011), *"classification and thematic analysis of literature on a software engineering topic"*. Our motivation for this study is to provide a state-of-the-art of Agile methods use in the context of cyber physical systems between 2010 and 2018. The main objective is to identify and categorize Agile methods use in CPS development, distil the reported challenges of Agile methods in CPS, lessons learned and future research direction in the topic area. These broad objectives can be achieve with the following research questions.

- RQ 1. What is the status of applying agile methods use in context of CPS development?
- RQ 2. What are the challenges involved in Agile use for CPS development?
- RQ 3. What are the lessons learned from existing literature for the industry and the research community?

2.2   Search Strategy and Selection

The search string for this study was based Kitchenham et al. [6] guidelines-define 'population' and 'intervention'. *Population* refers to the application area, which is software, and *intervention* is Agile. Software is the expected search that will include all documents with the word "software" in title, abstract or keyword [3]. The search string was "(software AND (Agile OR Scrum) AND "cyber physical systems")". The rationale for using the term "software" is that, this study will cover studies that discuss software, software development, or software intensive products, services, and systems including cyber physical systems.

We chose four major databases in the field to search for relevant literature: Scopus, IEEE Xplorer, Web of Science, ACM digital Library. The retrieved papers from these databases are listed in the following Table 1.

The mentioned databases resulted into 101 papers. In step 1, was to sort the paper in one excel sheet and remove the duplicates. In total 32 duplicate papers were removed. The second step was to examine papers based on titles. Paper is exclude, if it clearly showing that they were outside the focus of this study. However, excluding decisions were not in all cases based only on titles, as some of the titles did not reveal the contents of the papers clearly enough. In such cases the papers were included for review in the next step.

In third step, each paper abstract, keywords are examine against the inclusion and exclusion criteria; which resulting into 38 papers exclusion. The remaining 31 papers were left for full reading. This fourth step yielded into 15 primary studies.

2.3   Inclusion and Exclusion Criteria

Studies were eligible for inclusion in this review if they are: written in English, published between 2010–2018, reported on applying the agile method or practices to CPS software development; argue for or against using any agile method or practices when developing CPS. The paper were excluded if their focus was not specifically Agile

Table 1. Selected databases and retrieved papers.

Databases	Full Query with filter	No. of retrieved papers
Scopus	TITLE-ABS-KEY (software AND (agile) AND "cyber physical systems") AND (EXCLUDE (PUBYEAR, 2019)) AND (LIMIT-TO (LANGUAGE, "English")) AND (EXCLUDE (DOCTYPE, "ch")) AND (EXCLUDE (SRCTYPE, "k"))	35
Web of Science	(software AND (Agile) AND "cyber physical systems") Refined by: LANGUAGES: (ENGLISH) AND [excluding] PUBLICATION YEARS: (2019) Timespan: All years. Indexes: SCI-EXPANDED, SSCI, A&HCI, CPCI-S, CPCI-SSH, ESCI.	20
IEEE Xplorer	software AND (Agile) AND "cyber physical systems" Filters Applied: Conferences, Journals	26
ACM Digital Library	Searched for software AND (Agile OR Scrum) AND "cyber physical systems" Published since: 2010 Published before: 2018	20
Total		101

methods in the context of CPS, short articles, duplicate papers, simulation studies, not peer reviewed papers.

3   Results

We identified 14 primary studies on Agile methods use in cyber physical systems domain (see Appendix A). From the year 2010 to 2013, no studies were identified which is dealing specifically with Agile in cyber physical systems development. Although the search process bring some papers published in that timeframe about Agility, however, they were related to systems technical agility and responses or algorithmic agility. The following Table 2 highlighted the increase in number of papers on Agile use in CPS development.

Table 2. Primary papers published annually

Years	2010–13	2014	2015	2016	2017	2018
Papers	–	1	3	3	7	1
Percentage	–	6.66%	20%	20%	46.66%	6.66%

Almost half of primary studies (46.66%) were published in year 2017, which can be considered as indicator of growing interest in using Agile method in cyber physical systems development and reporting about it. Furthermore, the primary studies mostly published in conferences, most of which are experienced based and qualitative studies (See Table 3).

Table 3. Paper distribution according to publication channel and occurrence

Source	Type	No. of papers
International Workshop on Rapid Continuous Software Engineering	Conference	2
International Conference on Computer Science and Software Engineering	Conference	1
International Conference on Parallel and Distributed Systems	Conference	1
Proceedings of the IEEE	Conference	1
Annual Conference of the IEEE Industrial Electronics Society	Conference	1
International Conference on Software Engineering: Software Engineering Education and Training Track	Conference	1
International Conference on Cyber-Physical Systems, Networks, and Applications	Conference	1
Cluster Computing	Journal	1
Americas Conference on Information Systems	Conference	1
CEUR Workshop Proceedings	Conference	1
Proceedings of NordDesign	Conference	1
International Conference on ICT Management for Global Competitiveness and Economic Growth in Emerging Economies	Conference	1
Ambient Intelligence - Lecture Notes in Computer Science	Conference	1
Annual Conference of the IEEE Industrial Electronics Society	Conference	1
Total		15

The primary studies didn't explicitly shows which Agile methods are dominantly used for CPS development. However, our analysis exhibits that Scrum practices dominantly reported. The primary studies are further categories based on themes as shown in the following Table 4. At higher level, two categories were identified. The categories are based on the number of primary studies discuss a specific theme.

Table 4. Primary studies categorization

#	Agile use theme wise in CPS	Primary studies
1	Development	P1, P2, P5, P8, P9, P11, P14, P12
	Requirements and Testing	P4, P6
	Continuous Deployment	P3
2	Teaching Agile in CPS engineering curriculum	P7, P10, P13, P15

Agile methods are well known and widely used in the software industry; while companies developing software cyber-physical systems hesitant to adopt such processes [P1, P2]. Wagner [P1] highlighted that in software development the final design is product, however, in hardware and mechanics it is the starting point of production. There are several proposed ways to implement Agile in CPS development. For example Wagner [P1] propose Scrum extension Scrum CPS. The extension helps to handle concurrent hardware and software development (See Fig. 1, Adopted from [P1]).

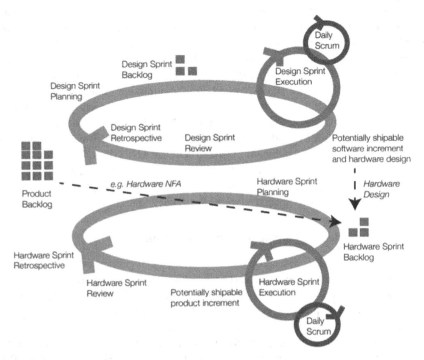

Fig. 1. Wagner propose Scrum CPS process [P1]

The central idea is to bring harmony between software and hardware development. In this regard, starting sprint could be the architecture of CPS and build operational software. The hardware design is a central part of software development backlog. The developed software going to be tested together with hardware simulations from design models, which build in parallel [P1]. One proposal is to adapt the idea of Agile Release Train from Leffingwell model [4], to ensure sprints synchronization and produce coherent CPS. It is important to bring closer and empower the development and hardware teams to collaborate with customer openly.

A single contact from the CPS team to customer can bring hurdle to process of development that is why to split product owner responsibilities to a number of persons [P2, P8]. For iterative development, Buchmann and Karagiannis [P9] experiment Agile modelling. Further, Pfeiffer et al. [P5] propose to create ad hoc personas to obtained global view of users. These personas should be iterative in nature in order to refine it based on data gathered from user research and make it more real. The proposed persona approach was adopted from Pruitt and Adlin [5].

Testing CPSs makes are extremely prone to human error due to complex modelling [P4]. Spichkova et al. [P4] propose a human-centered agile modelling and testing approach (HCATD) for CPSs. HCATD helps to increase efficiency of testing of CPSs and reduce the testing cost and time. The basic behind HCATD is combinatorial test design-test-planning technique. Further, functional requirements for reconfigurable cyber-physical system is challenging task. Boschi et al. [P6] described a methodology based on the requirement engineering concepts. It helps to in identification and deployment of general business and strategic requirements needed to implement new plug-and-produce paradigms into traditional production systems.

Continuous deployment in mission-critical CPS should be reliable and failure tolerant, where failure recovery is timely and predictable, and minimizes the negative impact on quality of service [P3]. A number of continuous deployment techniques exists for the CPSs, such as Locality-Enhanced Deployment and Configuration Engine (LE-DAnCE), Lightweight CORBA Component Model, a Methodology for Architecture and Deployment of Cloud Application Topologies based on iterative refinement (MADCAT), Dynamic IoT Application Deployment (DIANE) [P3]. To handle the CPS complexity, synchronization, failure detection, and state preservation, a solution could be microservices architecture [P3]. Microservices architecture helps to independently deployment of service on its own resources, scalability that are manage at runtime.

3.1 Teaching Agile in CPS Engineering Curriculum

Preparing student for the fast growing ICT industry is important. The engineers requires multi-disciplinary technical and soft skills. It is essential for software engineering and other ICT students to know about Agile development, model-driven engineering, and cyber physical systems [P7, P10]. Various universities included the Agile software development in their engineering education programmes. However, the primary studies highlighted that directly using Agile methods in other engineering domains are challenging and it need to be adapted [P7, P10, P13]. Marusik et al. [P10] proposed a task-centric holistic agile teaching approach. This approach utilized the problem/project based teaching and encourage students to do research in order to understand and adapt specific techniques in given situation. Furthermore, Mäkiö et al. [P15] stress more to include social and other software skills development in the education, which will result in well-prepared engineers for future jobs. This approach is similar to the software factory projects and courses in the field of software engineering [7, 8].

3.2 Challenges in CPS Development

The following challenges are reported in the primary studies while using Agile methods and practices in CPS development:

- CPS are complex systems, and to handle the complexities of highly networked and real-time components is difficult [P1, P11].

- The CPS is a combination of software and hardware development and synchronization of both is bigger challenge [P1, P11, P14].
- Insufficient visibility and control to efficiently manage and track software releases and project progress [P2].
- The software and hardware developers use different vocabulary, which makes it difficult to understand the cross-functional design issues [P11].
- CPS dependability is a major concern. It is measures in term of availability, reliability, durability, safety and security of a system. For example, automotive standard ISO26262, impose a rigorous process on development team, which bring difficult to implement Agile methods [P11].
- Critical system has a long lifespan and their maintenance are in form of patches, updates and repairs will form a major expenditure and requires more well advanced planning [P2]. Additionally, non-portability and lack of robustness will become easily suicidal for the system [P2].
- Need for complete deployment notations to allow stakeholders specifying and visualizing large-scale deployments from different perspectives and levels of abstraction [P3].
- A need for notation and tool support for linking design and runtime deployment concept [P3].
- Tool support for the evolution of deployment specifications and configuration management at runtime [P3].
- During the designing of CPS, developers do not take in consideration time to market [P11].
- Mismatches in the abstraction levels of the different components [P2, P11].

3.3   Lessons Learned

During the implementation of Agile methods and practices for CPS development, the following lessons learned are reported in the primary studies:

- Adapt agile software development principles and practices into real, every-day used, well and thoroughly understood and accepted ways of working, is hard work [P2, P14].
- Establish a dual-track requirement handling process to handle false assumptions about a feature [P2].
- Split the product owner responsibilities to a number of persons in team, which will help to have effective, communicate with both the customer and the teams [P2].
- The teams should have direct access to a real customer (or at least a legitimate customer proxy). Customer should proactively help the team to pick value added items for backlog [P2].
- Organization should aims to enable the mechanisms for the continuous improvement [P2].
- CPS emphasize the connectedness of many quite different components. To some degree, the availability of models for simulations and in-the-loop tests helps to test these aspects. In addition, the Agile Release Train ensures compatible interfaces between components connected via networks [P1].

- Agile modelling satisfy requirements from the client IoT application [P9].
- Show working system to customer at regular intervals - early system-level evaluation; which will help to avoid wrong design and development assumptions [P11, P14].
- Optimize the processes to enable shorter time-to-market, for example performing independent tasks concurrently [P11, P14].

4   Threats to Validity and Reliability

In this study, Wohlin et al. [16] guidelines were followed, to evaluate validity threats (i.e. construct validity, external validity, external validity, and conclusion validity). Firstly, construct validity meaning obtaining the right measures for the concept being studied. This threat was reduced with the help of data collection process presented by Pilar et al. [3] and apply clearly sorted out the inclusion and exclusion criteria's. Secondly, external validity which is related to generalizability of study results. To enhance the generalizability to this study results, data collection procedures were carefully executed and context of each primary study was examined. Thirdly, Internal validity examine the causal relationships of investigated factors. This literature review doesn't aim to examine or establish statistical causal relationship of the topic; hence this threat is not considered in this study. Fourthly, conclusion validity, meaning researcher biasness during interpretation of data. This is tricky and cannot be fully eliminated. However, measure were taken to reduce the researcher biasness by keeping full trail of data collection till obtaining 15 primary studies. Furthermore, the publications were obtained only from four databases Scopus, IEEE Xplorer, Web of Science, ACM digital Library. It is claimed that these databases has most of the relevant scientific article and used in similar literature review studies, such as Pilar et al. [3].

5   Conclusion

This literature review was aiming to analyze the current usage of Agile methods in cyber physical systems development, along with its challenges and lesson learned. The review exhibit that currently there is a lack of rigor in scientific literature on Agile methods use for cyber physical systems development. However, this study analysis provide valuable information for further investigations.

The results show that agile methods and practices are used at abstract level for CPSs development. Not a single industrial study clearly demonstrated that how Agile methods can be implemented. Only the Wagner [P1] proposed Scrum CPS process provide a bigger picture, but with limited implementation. However, the publication trend of primary studies shows that there is a growing interest in the use of Agile methods for CPSs development. The main reason is the iterative development and active customer role to reach the market on time. It also helps to build crossover team to design and build the systems collaboratively.

A number of challenges were highlighted in primary studies, such as; combining the software and hardware developers is difficult to the use of different vocabulary. The highly regulated CPSs requires following a variety of international standards that slow down the use of Agile implementation. Organizations needs to understand that being Agile is a continuous journey, which requires commitment and active role of all stakeholders. There is no silver bullet and CPS development teams requires optimizing processes based on their needs and project requirement.

To prepare graduate for fasted growing ICT domain, the educational institutes need to offer multi-disciplinary courses. The current hardware and software developers find it challenge to communicate efficiently due lack of common vocabulary. Additionally, soft skills including teamwork and collaboration need to be integrated to such engineering teaching programs.

The current literature does not provide reliable and depth of Agile use for CPSs development, however, it shows a positive tendency toward using the Agile methods. The future research direction could be replicate the some of primary studies as well as this literature review adding forward and backward snowballing.

Appendix A – Primary Studies

P1. Wagner, S.: Scrum for cyber-physical systems: a process proposal. In Proceedings of the 1st International Workshop on Rapid Continuous Software Engineering, pp. 51-56. ACM. (2014).

P2. Koski, A., Mikkonen, T.: Rolling out a mission critical system in an agilish way. reflections on building a large-scale dependable information system for public sector. In 2015 IEEE/ACM 2nd International Workshop on Rapid Continuous Software Engineering, pp. 41-44. IEEE. (2015).

P3. Jiménez, M., Villegas, N. M., Tamura, G., Müller, H. A.: Deployment Specification challenges in the context of large-scale systems. In Proceedings of the 27th Annual International Conference on Computer Science and Software Engineering, pp. 220-226. IBM Corp. (2017).

P4. Spichkova, M., Zamansky, A., Farchi, E.: Towards a human-centred approach in modelling and testing of cyber-physical systems. In 2015 IEEE 21st International Conference on Parallel and Distributed Systems (ICPADS), pp. 847-851. IEEE. (2015).

P5. Pfeiffer, T., Hellmers, J., Schön, E. M., Thomaschewski, J. Empowering user interfaces for Industrie 4.0. Proceedings of the IEEE 104(5), 986-996 (2016).

P6. Boschi, F., Zanetti, C., Tavola, G., Taisch, M.: Functional requirements for reconfigurable and flexible cyber-physical system. In IECON 2016-42nd Annual Conference of the IEEE Industrial Electronics Society, pp. 5717-5722. IEEE. (2016).

P7. Ringert, J. O., Rumpe, B., Schulze, C., Wortmann, A. Teaching agile model-driven engineering for cyber-physical systems. In Proceedings of the 39th International Conference on Software Engineering: Software Engineering and Education Track, pp. 127-136. IEEE Press. (2017).

P8. Scheuermann, C., Verclas, S., Bruegge, B.: Agile factory-an example of an industry 4.0 manufacturing process. In 2015 IEEE 3rd International Conference on Cyber-Physical Systems, Networks, and Applications, pp. 43-47. IEEE. (2015).
P9. Buchmann, R. A., Karagiannis, D.: Domain-specific diagrammatic modelling: a source of machine-readable semantics for the Internet of Things. Cluster Computing 20(1), 895-908 (2017).
P10. Mäkiö-Marusik, E., Mäkiö, J., Kowal, J.: Implementation of task-centric holistic agile approach on teaching cyber physical systems engineering. Twenty-third Americas Conference on Information Systems, Boston (2017).
P11. Denil, J., Salay, R., Paredis, C., Vangheluwe, H.: Towards agile model-based systems engineering. In CEUR workshop proceedings, pp. 424-429. (2017).
P12. Luedeke, T. F., Köhler, C., Conrad, J., Grashiller, M., Sailer, A., Vielhaber, M.: CPM/PDD in the context of design thinking and agile development of cyber-physical systems. DS 91: Proceedings of NordDesign 2018, Linköping, Sweden, 14th-17th August 2018. (2018).
P13. Mäkiö-Marusik, E., Mäkiö, J.: Implementation of task-centric holistic agile approach on teaching cyber physical systems engineering and distributed software development. ICTM 115. (2016).
P14. Wessling, F., Gries, S., Ollesch, J., Hesenius, M., Gruhn, V.: Engineering a cyber-physical intersection management–an experience report. In European Conference on Ambient Intelligence, pp. 17-32. Springer, Cham. (2017).
P15. Mäkiö, J., Mäkiö-Marusik, E., Yablochnikov, E., Arckhipov, V., Kipriianov, K.: Teaching cyber physical systems engineering. In IECON 2017-43rd Annual Conference of the IEEE Industrial Electronics Society, pp. 3530-3535. IEEE. (2017).

References

1. Jasperneite, J.: Was hinter begriffen wie industrie 4.0 steckt. Comput. Autom. (2012). www.computer-automation.de/steuerungsebene/steuern-regeln/artikel/93559/0/
2. Hermann, M., Pentek, T., Otto, B.: Design principles for industrie 4.0 scenarios. In: 2016 49th Hawaii International Conference on System Sciences (HICSS), pp. 3928–3937. IEEE (2016)
3. Rodríguez, P., Haghighatkhah, A., Lwakatare, L.E., Teppola, S., Suomalainen, T., Eskeli, J., Oivo, M.: Continuous deployment of software intensive products and services: a systematic mapping study. J. Syst. Softw. **123**, 263–291 (2017)
4. Leffingwell, D.: Agile Software Requirements. Lean Requirements Practices for teams. Programs, and the Enterprise. Addison-Wessley, Boston (2011)
5. Pruitt, J., Adlin, T.: The persona lifecycle: keeping people in mind throughout product design. Elsevier (2010)
6. Kitchenham, B.: Guidelines for performing systematic literature reviews in software engineering, version 2.3, EBSE technical report EBSE-2007-01, Keele University and University of Durham (2007)
7. Ahmad, M.O., Liukkunen, K., Markkula, J.: Student perceptions and attitudes towards the software factory as a learning environment. In: 2014 IEEE Global Engineering Education Conference (EDUCON), pp. 422–428. IEEE (2014)

8. Taibi, D., et al.: "Free" innovation environments: lessons learned from the software factory initiatives. In: IARIA (2015)
9. Rajkumar, R., Lee, I., Sha, L., Stankovic, J.: Cyber-physical systems: the next computing revolution. In: Design Automation Conference, pp. 731–736. IEEE (2010)
10. Leitão, P., Colombo, A.W., Karnouskos, S.: Industrial automation based on cyber-physical systems technologies: Prototype implementations and challenges. Comput. Ind. **81**, 11–25 (2016)
11. Dybå, T., Dingsøyr, T.: Empirical studies of agile software development: a systematic review. Inf. Softw. Technol. **50**(9–10), 833–859 (2008)
12. Rodríguez, P., Markkula, J., Oivo, M., Turula, K.: Survey on agile and lean usage in Finnish software industry. In: Proceedings of the 2012 ACM-IEEE International Symposium on Empirical Software Engineering and Measurement, pp. 139–148. IEEE (2012)
13. Lee, E.A.: Cyber-physical systems-are computing foundations adequate. In: Position Paper for NSF Workshop on Cyber-Physical Systems: Research Motivation, Techniques and Roadmap, vol. 2, pp. 1–9. Citeseer (2006)
14. Cawley, O., Wang, X., Richardson, I.: Lean/agile software development methodologies in regulated environments – state of the art. In: Abrahamsson, P., Oza, N. (eds.) LESS 2010. LNBIP, vol. 65, pp. 31–36. Springer, Heidelberg (2010). https://doi.org/10.1007/978-3-642-16416-3_4
15. Huang, P.M., Darrin, A.G., Knuth, A.A.: Agile hardware and software system engineering for innovation. In: 2012 IEEE Aerospace Conference, pp. 1–10. IEEE (2012)
16. Wohlin, C., Runeson, P., Höst, M., Ohlsson, M.C., Regnell, B., Wesslén, A.: Experimentation in Software Engineering. Springer, Heidelberg (2012). https://doi.org/10.1007/978-3-642-29044-2

Optimizing the Reservoir Connection Structure Using Binary Symbiotic Organisms Search Algorithm: A Case Study on Electric Load Forecasting

Lina Pan$^{(\boxtimes)}$ and Bo Zhang

School of Computer Engineering, Jinling Institute of Technology, Nanjing, China
{panln19,zhangb}@jit.edu.cn

Abstract. ESN (Echo state network) is a novel recurrent neural network and it is also acknowledged as a powerful temporal processing method, especially in real-valued, time-series forecasting fields. The current research results believe that the connection structure of the reservoir has significant effect for ESN's forecasting performance. However, the randomly generated reservoir is hard to establish a optimal reservoir structure for a given task. Optimizing the connection structure of reservoir can be considered as a feature selection issue and this issue can be solved by binary optimization algorithm. SOS (Symbiotic organisms search) is a recently proposed heuristic algorithm and its superior performance is confirmed via many mathematical benchmark functions and engineering design problems. It's worth noting that the original SOS is only suitable for continuous numerical optimization problems. In this paper, a binary SOS, called BSOS, is employed to optimize the connection structure of reservoir of the standard ESN. To verify the effectiveness of the proposed model, a real electric load series derived from New South Wales in Australia is adopted as benchmark dataset. The experimental results demonstrate that the proposed model can significantly improve the forecasting accuracy and it is a hopeful forecasting model.

Keywords: Echo state network · Binary symbiotic organisms search algorithm · Reservoir connection structure · Electric load forecasting

1 Introduction

It is vital issue to accurately forecast the electric load, because electricity is an energy source that cannot be stored, but it plays a critical role in the economic and secure operation of power systems. However, the forecasting precision frequently could not be desired due to the influence of the uncontrollable and uncertain factors [10].

Reservoir computing (RC) is a hot approach to design and train recurrent neural networks. As one of the most promising RC approaches, ESN takes advantages over classic recurrent neural networks [5]. The reservoir contains mass

© Springer Nature Singapore Pte Ltd. 2020
Y. Tian et al. (Eds.): ICBDS 2019, CCIS 1210, pp. 286–297, 2020.
https://doi.org/10.1007/978-981-15-7530-3_21

randomly and sparsely connected neurons. The sole trainable component is the readout weights, which can be calculated through any simple linear regression. The relatively simple architecture and design makes it successfully applied to various time-series prediction tasks, for instance, short-term electric load and temperature forecasting [3].

It has been demonstrated that connection structure of the reservoir has significant effect on ESN's prediction performance [8], however, the reservoir generated randomly is an issue to establish optimal reservoir for a given task [7]. The structure optimization of ESN can be treated as a feature selection problem and need use feature selection methods to solve it. Recently, some conventional feature selection methods such as random deletion, and novel heuristic algorithms such as binary particle swarm optimization (BPSO) have been employed to optimize the ESN by excluding irrelevant output connection [4,9]. Symbiotic organisms search (SOS) algorithm is a novel powerful and robust metaheuristic algorithm imitating the symbiotic interaction strategies adopted by organisms to survive and propagate in the ecosystem [2]. However, the original version of this algorithm is only suitable for continuous problems, so it cannot be applied to feature selection problems directly. A binary version of SOS algorithm named BSOS is proposed simultaneously in that paper, which not only keeps the merits of the SOS algorithm but also can be applied to feature selection problems directly [1].

Inspired by above research achievement, a novel optimized ESN, based on binary symbiotic organisms search algorithm called BSOS-ESN, is proposed.

The rest of the paper is organized as follows: Sect. 2 provides a brief overview of ESN; Sect. 3 introduces the BSOS algorithm in detail; Sect. 3 detail the BSOS-ESN; The experimental results are demonstrated in Sect. 4; and Sect. 5 presents conclusions.

2   Echo State Network

Owing to ESN's important role in our study, it is described briefly in this section. The standard structure of ESN is shown in Fig. 1. As it can be seen, the structure of ESN mainly comprises input layer, internal layer and output layers. N internal neurons constitute a dynamic structure, named reservoir, via several sparse connections. K input neurons are connected to the reservoir and they can be also directly connected to the output neurons via full connections. L output neurons receive the network output from reservoir neurons and input neurons, depending on output connections. In addition, the output neurons can be connected to reservoir via the optional output feedback connections.

At the time step t, the state of the reservoir can be expressed by the states $\mathbf{x}(t)$ of neurons, the states of neurons of reservoir are determined by Eq. (1).

$$\mathbf{x}(t) = f(\mathbf{W}^{in}\mathbf{u}(t) + \mathbf{W}\mathbf{x}(t-1) + \mathbf{W}^{back}\mathbf{y}(t-1)) \qquad (1)$$

where bold font letters denote vectors. $f(\cdot)$ is a activation function, such as sigmoid function. In this study, tanh function is adopted as activation function. At

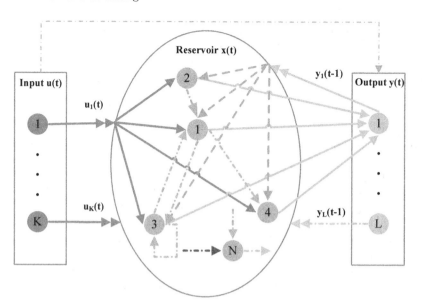

Fig. 1. The standard structure of ESN

the time step t, the input and output of the network are expressed by $\mathbf{u}(t)$ and $\mathbf{y}(t)$. The connection weights between the input neurons and reservoir neurons are collected in a $N \times K$ matrix, $\mathbf{W}^{in}$. The connection weights of reservoir neurons are collected in a $N \times N$ matrix, $\mathbf{W}$. In addition, the feedback connections from output neurons to the reservoir neurons are collected in a $N \times L$ weight matrix, $\mathbf{W}^{back}$. The weight matrixes mentioned above are randomly generated before training.

Similar to the other application scenarios, feedback connections are also omitted in this study. Thus, $\mathbf{W}^{back}$ is uninvolved in training, Eq. (1) can be rewritten as Eq. (2).

$$\mathbf{x}(t) = f(\mathbf{W}^{in}\mathbf{u}(t) + \mathbf{W}\mathbf{x}(t-1)) \tag{2}$$

The output neurons can be treated as a readout layer for the reservoir. The output of the network can be calculated by Eq. (3).

$$\mathbf{y}(t) = f^{out}(\mathbf{W}^{out}\mathbf{x}(t)) \tag{3}$$

where f^{out} is activation function. $L \times N$ weight matrix $\mathbf{W}^{out}$ collects the connections of neurons between reservoir and output layer.

3   Echo State Network Optimized by Binary Symbiotic Organisms Search Algorithm

3.1   Symbiotic Organisms Search Algorithm

SOS algorithm is a novel heuristic optimization algorithm, proposed by [2] in 2014. Inspired by symbiotic interaction strategies, organisms are use to survive in the ecosystem. Compared to other metaheuristic algorithms, an obvious advantage of SOS is that it require no specific parameters in whole calculation process.

In mutualism phase, the interaction benefits both organisms, which can be described by Eq. (4–6).

$$mutualVector = (x_j + x_i)/2 \tag{4}$$

$$x_i^{new} = x_i + rand(0, 1) * (bestOrg - mutualVector * BF_1) \tag{5}$$

$$x_j^{new} = x_j + rand(0, 1) * (bestOrg - mutualVector * BF_2) \tag{6}$$

where x_i and x_j are two organisms in the ecosystem. Both of them engage in a mutualistic relationship with the purpose of increasing mutual survival benefit in the ecosystem. This mutualistic relationship is described by $mutualVector$. BF_1 and BF_2 are two benefit factors which denote the benefit level, determined randomly as either 1 or 2.

In commensalism phase, the interaction benefit one side and do not impact the other side, which is described by Eq. (7).

$$x_i^{new} = x_i + rand(-1, 1) * (bestOrg - x_j) \tag{7}$$

In parasitism phase, the interaction benefit one side but injure the other side, expressed by artificial parasite called $parasiteVector$. The $parasiteVector$ is a duplicate of x_i by modifying the randomly selected dimension using a random number.

3.2   Binary Symbiotic Organisms Search Algorithm

BSOS is a binary version of SOS algorithm that not only reserves the merit of the SOS algorithm but also can be applied to feature selection problems directly. The V-shape transfer function used in SOS is described as Eq. (8) and is visualized in Fig. 2.

$$V(v(d)) = \frac{2}{\pi} arctan(\frac{\pi}{2} v(d)) \tag{8}$$

In mutualism phase, selected two organisms can be updated according to Eq. (9) to Eq. (12).

$$x_i^{new}(d) = \begin{cases} x_i^{new}(d)^{-1} & rand < V(v_i(d)) \\ x_i^{new}(d) & rand \geq V(v_i(d)) \end{cases} \tag{9}$$

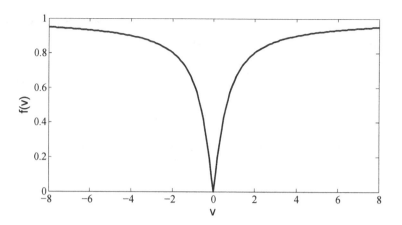

Fig. 2. The v-shaped transfer function

$$v_i(d) = rand(0, 1) * (bestOrg(d) - mutualVector(d) * BF_1) \qquad (10)$$

$$x_j^{new}(d) = \begin{cases} x_j^{new}(d)^{-1} & rand < V(v_j(d)) \\ x_j^{new}(d) & rand \geq V(v_j(d)) \end{cases} \qquad (11)$$

$$v_j(d) = rand(0, 1) * (bestOrg(d) - mutualVector(d) * BF_2) \qquad (12)$$

where v is the update velocity of corresponding organism x, d denotes the dth dimension. $x(d)^{-1}$ is the complement of $x(d)$.

In commensalism phase, the update of organisms is implemented relying on Eq. (9) and Eq. (13).

$$v_i(d) = rand(-1, 1) * (bestOrg(d) - x_j(d)) \qquad (13)$$

In parasitism phase, the *parasiteVector* is a duplicate of x_i by modifying the randomly selected dimensions using the complement of corresponding dimension. The pseudo code of BSOS algorithm is summarized in Algorithm 1.

3.3 Echo State Network Optimized by Binary Symbiotic Organisms Search Algorithm

The fundamental idea of BSOS-ESN can be described as follows and its flowchart is shown in Fig. 3.

Step 1. Dataset are divided into two parts, namely, training data and testing data.
Step 2. Initialize the untrained ESN according to appropriate reservoir size N and spectral radius γ and set the sparse connectivity l as 1. Randomly initialize the input weight matrix $\mathbf{W}^{in}$ obeying uniform distribution with an interval $[-1, 1]$ and generate weight matrix $\mathbf{W}$ of reservoir with the specified parameters N, γ and l.

Algorithm 1. BSOS Algorithm

Input: Ecosystem size $ecoSize$
Output: Best organism $bestOrg$
1: **function** SOS($ecoSize$)
2:    Define fitness function $f(x)$ and initialize ecosystem randomly
3:    $i = 1$
4:    **while** (Not up to the maximum iteration) **do**
5:        Identify $bestOrg$
6:        **while** $i <= ecoSize$ **do**
7:            Select an organism randomly as x_j and $x_j \neq x_i$
8:            $mutualVector = (x_j + x_i)/2$
9:            **for** $d = 1 : length(x_i)$ **do**
10:               Update $x_i(d)$ using Eq. (8) to Eq. (10) as $x_i^{new}(d)$
11:               Update $x_j(d)$ using Eq. (8) , Eq. (11) and Eq. (12) as $x_j^{new}(d)$
12:            **end for**
13:            **if** $f(x_i^{new}) > f(x_i)$ **then**
14:               Update x_i with x_i^{new} and its fitness with $f(x_i^{new})$
15:            **end if**
16:            **if** $f(x_j^{new}) > f(x_j)$ **then**
17:               Update x_j with x_j^{new} and its fitness with $f(x_j^{new})$
18:            **end if**
19:            Select an organism randomly as x_j and $x_j \neq x_i$
20:            **for** $d = 1 : length(x_i)$ **do**
21:               Update $x_i(d)$ using Eq. (8) , Eq. (9) and Eq. (13) as $x_i^{new}(d)$
22:            **end for**
23:            **if** $f(x_i^{new}) > f(x_i)$ **then**
24:               Update x_i with x_i^{new} and its fitness with $f(x_i^{new})$
25:            **end if**
26:            Select an organism randomly as x_j and $x_j \neq x_i$
27:            Create a parasite as $parasiteVector$ from x_i
28:            **if** $f(parasiteVector) > f(x_j)$ **then**
29:               Update x_j with $parasiteVector$ and   its   fitness   with
    $f(parasiteVector)$
30:            **end if**
31:        **end while**
32:        $i + +$
33:    **end while**
34:    **return** $bestOrg$
35: **end function**

Step 3. Specify the ecosystem size $ecoSize$, the maximum iterations of BSOS and the fitness function.

Step 4. Randomly initialize the organisms $\mathbf{x}_i, i = 1...ecoSize$, and the dimension of each organism is N.

Step 5. Reshape each $\mathbf{x}_i$ to a $N \times N$ matrix $\mathbf{X}_i$, then generate the similar ESNs. The method is to utilize each matrix to multiply the reservoir weight matrix $\mathbf{W}$ via Eq. (14). The fitness of each organism is defined as NMSE value

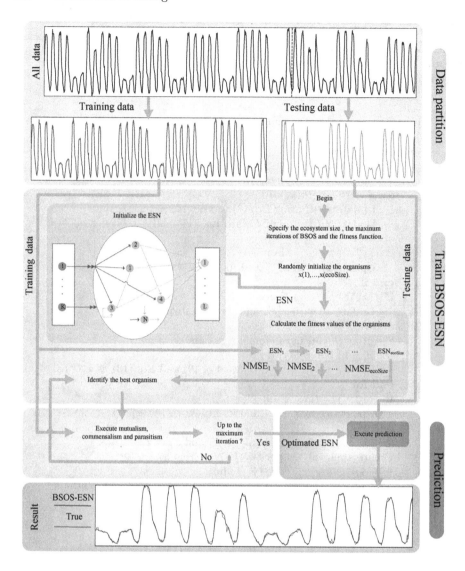

Fig. 3. The flowchart of BSOS-ESN

of corresponding ESN.

$$\mathbf{W}_i = \mathbf{X}_i . * \mathbf{W} \tag{14}$$

Step 6. Execute the mutualism, commensalism and parasitism phases of BSOS.
Step 7. Execute iteratively Step 5 and Step 6 until the maximum iteration is satisfied.
Step 8. Use the best organism to generate the corresponding reservoir, then use this optimized reservoir to train the ESN again.

Step 9. Finally, use the trained ESN to check out the forecasting capability of model, and obtain the final forecasting result.

4   Experiments and Discussion

4.1   Experiments

In this study, the proposed model is verified by a real time-series dataset. The data resource is half-hourly electrical power data of New South Wales in Australia, collected from July 9th to August 9th, 2013 (48 data points starting from 0:00 AM to 23:30 PM per day). The data set contains 1538 samples, shown in Fig. 4.

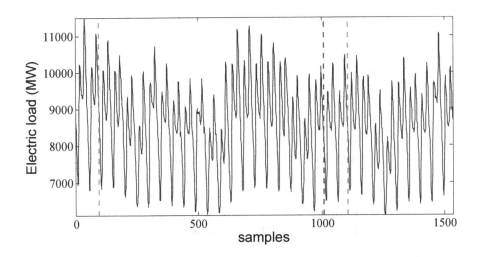

Fig. 4. The electric load time-series

For the sake of evaluating the forecasting capability of the proposed model, mean absolute percentage error (MAPE), normalized root mean square error (NRMSE), and index of agreement (IA) are adopted as evaluation criteria.

$$MAPE = \frac{1}{I} \sum_{i=1}^{I} |\frac{y_i - \hat{y}_i}{y_i}| \times 100\% \tag{15}$$

$$NRMSE = \sqrt{\frac{1}{I\sigma^2} \sum_{i=1}^{I} (y_i - \hat{y}_i)^2} \tag{16}$$

$$IA = 1 - \frac{\sum_{i=1}^{I} (y_i - \hat{y}_i)^2}{\sum_{i=1}^{I} (|y_i - y_{ave}| + |\hat{y}_i - y_{ave}|)^2} \tag{17}$$

where I is the data length, y_i and $\hat{y}_i$ represent ith observed value and ith forecasting value, σ^2 is the variance of the observed values, y_{ave} is the average of all observed values.

MAPE and NRMSE are the universal measure of evaluating the forecasting accuracy of model. The smaller MAPE and NRMSE, the better the forecasting capability. The IA is a dimensionless index within the range of $0-1$. The higher IA means more agreement between forecasting result and real result [6]. It should be pointed out that all forecasting results listed in Table 1 are the mean value of 50 time predictions in order to eliminating the influence of randomness.

Some intelligent models are used to baseline for comparison in this paper, they are standard ESN, the back propagation neural network (BPNN), support vector regression (SVR), Autoregressive Integrated Moving Average (ARIMA), optimized echo state network with binary particle swarm optimization(BPSO-ESN). The comparison of the BSOS-ESN and other models is displayed in Table 1.

Table 1. The evaluation criteria of BSOS-ESN and comparison models

Model	Electric load		
	MAPE(%)	NRMSE	IA
ESN	0.7982	0.0825	0.9982
BPNN	1.0772	0.1162	0.9963
SVR	1.0393	0.1141	0.9967
ARIMA	1.3100	0.1408	0.9952
BPSO-ESN	0.7844	0.0803	0.9983
BSOS-ESN	**0.7792**	**0.0794**	**0.9984**

4.2   Discussion

The experimental results indicate that BSOS-ESN can achieve the better prediction performance compared with the standard ESN and the other models. The Fig. 5 shows the fit results of standard ESN and BSOS-ESN. Table 1 lists the forecasting criteria of all models. We can draw a conclusion that all models are valid for the Electric load prediction tasks. Nevertheless, the values of MAPE and NRMSE of BSOS-ESN are less than that of the standard ESN, and the value of IA are greater than that of the standard ESN, which indicates that the prediction accuracy of the BSOS-ESN is definitely higher than standard ESN. Compared with the other models, such as BPNN, SVR, ARIMA, BPSO-ESN, the experimental results also demonstrate that BSOS-ESN has the higher prediction accuracy.

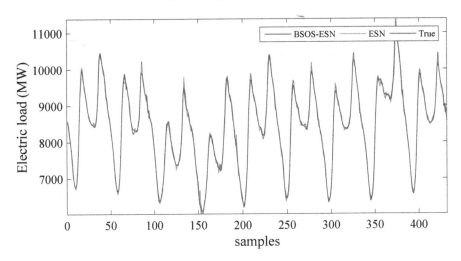

Fig. 5. Electric load forecasting curves

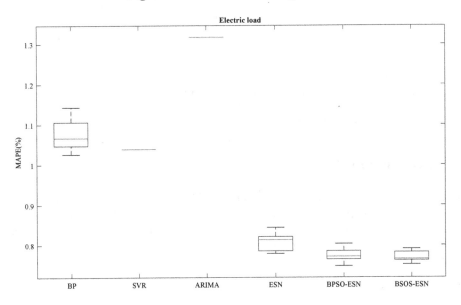

Fig. 6. Box plots of all models

Figure 6 displays the box plot of all models' prediction results, which suggests that the optimized ESN models could achieve higher accuracy than the other models for the optimization ability. The searching process of the optimized ESN models is shown in Fig. 7, and it suggests that BPSO and BSOS could find a subset of reservoir weight connections to improve the prediction performance of standard ESN. The search optimization result of BSOS is the best and the prediction accuracy of BSOS-ESN is higher than that of BPSO-ESN. To sum

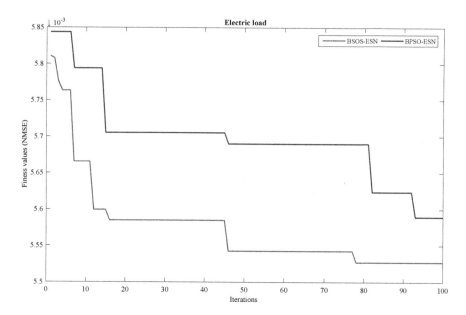

Fig. 7. Fitness curves of the optimazed ESNs

up, optimizing the reservoir connection structure with BSOS can improve the prediction accuracy of ESN and BSOS is an efficient search technique for feature selection than BPSO.

5   Conclusion

In this paper, a novel model called BSOS-ESN is employed in electric load series forecasting. The experiment results demonstrate that it is able to achieve better prediction results comparing with the standard ESN and other prediction models and it is a hopeful forecasting model.

References

1. Research and application of neural network and its combination model in time series forecasting. Ph.D. thesis, LanZhou University (2018)
2. Cheng, M.Y., Prayogo, D.: Symbiotic organisms search: a new metaheuristic optimization algorithm. Comput. Struct. **139**, 98–112 (2014)
3. Deihimi, A., Orang, O., Showkati, H.: Short-term electric load and temperature forecasting using wavelet echo state networks with neural reconstruction. Energy **57**, 382–401 (2013)
4. Dutoit, X., Schrauwen, B., Van Campenhout, J., Stroobandt, D., Van Brussel, H., Nuttin, M.: Pruning and regularization in reservoir computing. Neurocomputing **72**(7), 1534–1546 (2009)

5. Jaeger, H.: The "echo state" approach to analysing and training recurrent neural networks-with an erratum note. Bonn, Germany: German Natl. Res. Center Inf. Technol. GMD Tech. Rep. **148**, 34 (2001)

6. Nastos, P., Paliatsos, A., Koukouletsos, K., Larissi, I., Moustris, K.: Artificial neural networks modeling for forecasting the maximum daily total precipitation at Athens, Greece. Atmosph. Res. **144**, 141–150 (2014)

7. Ozturk, M.C., Xu, D., Príncipe, J.C.: Analysis and design of echo state networks. Neural Comput. **19**(1), 111–138 (2007)

8. Song, Q., Feng, Z.: Effects of connectivity structure of complex echo state network on its prediction performance for nonlinear time series. Neurocomputing **73**(10), 2177–2185 (2010)

9. Wang, H., Yan, X.: Optimizing the echo state network with a binary particle swarm optimization algorithm. Knowl.-Based Syst. **86**, 182–193 (2015)

10. Zhang, X., Wang, J., Zhang, K.: Short-term electric load forecasting based on singular spectrum analysis and support vector machine optimized by cuckoo search algorithm. Electric Power Syst. Res. **146**(2), 270–285 (2017)

On the Character Relations Between Nodes for Data Forwarding in Mobile Opportunistic Networks

Runtong Zou[1], Xuecheng Zhang[1], Wei Jiang[2], and Linfeng Liu[1(✉)]

[1] School of Computer Science and Technology, Nanjing University of Posts and Telecommunications, Nanjing 210023, China
liulf@njupt.edu.cn
[2] School of Telecommunications and Information Engineering, Nanjing University of Posts and Telecommunications, Nanjing 210023, China

Abstract. In this paper, a data forwarding algorithm based on character relations (DFCR) for mobile opportunistic networks (MONs) is proposed. DFCR first endows the nodes with some characters according to the coordinates of nodes and the corresponding time. Note that each character is determined by a unique binary combination which consists of time periods and regions, and thus each character can describe some moving habits of nodes. It is obvious that the nodes with the same character are prone to encounter with each other. However, the nodes not with the same character still can encounter with each other if their characters are closely related. To analyze the character relations, an index Characters-Relation (CR) comprised of time-relation and frequency-relation is proposed. The time-relation denotes the ratio of the encountering durations between the nodes with two different characters to the maximum encountering durations, and the frequency-relation denotes the ratio of the number of encounters between the nodes with two different characters to the number of total encounters. The time-relation and frequency-relation can reflect the character relations between nodes effectively. Finally, simulation results demonstrate the preferable performance of DFCR, i.e., DFCR performs well in terms of the delivery ratio, number of forwarded copies and propagation delay.

Keywords: Mobile opportunistic networks · Data transmission · Character relations

1 Introduction

With the development of mobile facilities and wireless communication technology, various mobile networks play an essential role in modern society, and many mobile applications have been served for human beings, such as Wireless Fidelity (Wi-Fi), mobile payments, mobile communications, Bluetooth communications and so on. Most of the mobile applications require the stable communication paths, however, in some severe environments such as earthquakes or snowstorms, the communication infrastructures are probably destroyed, and hence the end-to-end transmission mechanisms are difficult to realize the communications between mobile devices. Thus, the

© Springer Nature Singapore Pte Ltd. 2020
Y. Tian et al. (Eds.): ICBDS 2019, CCIS 1210, pp. 298–308, 2020.
https://doi.org/10.1007/978-981-15-7530-3_22

opportunistic forwarding manner is introduced to transmit the data packets through several intermittent hops.

Mobile Opportunistic Networks (MONs) are greatly different from the traditional multi-hops networks: (*a*) The network size of MONs is not fixed, and the nodes in MONs typically move continuously; (*b*) the stable paths from the source nodes to the destination nodes would never emerge. And thus, the data transmissions from the source nodes to the destination nodes are always realized by utilizing the intermittent multi-hops. Although the opportunistic manner can maintain the communications in severe environments, it is still confronted with several challenges, such as the long propagation delay, large number of forwarded data copies and low delivery ratio. This paper investigates the character relations of nodes, which are then applied to improve the data forwarding process.

2 Related Works

The opportunistic forwarding manner has been employed into some types of networks, such as opportunistic mobile sensor networks (OMSNs) [1, 2], vehicular networks [3], ad hoc networks in disaster scenarios [4] and so on. Some research works based on encountering prediction, nodal activity or social relationship have been conducted on the data forwarding issue in MONs.

At present, some data forwarding algorithms based on the prediction of encounters between nodes have been proposed. For example, Zhou *et al.* propose an efficient temporal closeness and centrality-based data forwarding strategy (TCCB) [5] to predict nodes' social contact patterns from the temporal perspective and finally to improve the performance of data forwarding in OMNs. The basic idea of TCCB is to capture and utilize the temporal correlations to infer the future temporal social contact patterns. The node with a higher probability to meet the destination node is selected to serve as the relay node. This algorithm effectively reduces the storage occupancies of data packets, while it cannot achieve an ideal delivery ratio.

Some data forwarding algorithms focusing the nodal activities have attracted some attentions as well. Reference [6] proposes a Data Dissemination Algorithm based on Nodal Activities (DDANA). This algorithm calculates the nodal activities according to the number of encountered nodes during a specific period. Since a higher activity will be obtained when the node has encountered more other nodes, and the correlations between nodes and the destination is exploited for the data dissemination, DDANA improves the delivery ratio and shortens the delivery time.

The social relationship has been investigated and applied to forward the data packets, e.g., Tao *et al.* propose a Contacts-Aware Opportunistic Forwarding scheme (CAOF) [7], which includes an inter-community phase and an intra-community phase, to handle the data forwarding issue in heavy traffic scenarios. CAOF considers that the nodes have more opportunities to contact with each other if they stay in the same community for a longer period. The node with a higher global activeness and a larger source-to-destination probability in the intra-community phase is preferentially selected to be the relay node. Similarly, in [8] an Effective Transmission strategy based on Node Socialization (ETNS) is presented, and ETNS divides the network into several communities, and the data packets are forwarded to the nodes in the same community where the destination node stays. However, when the nodes move very fast, the aforementioned works cannot obtain a preferable delivery ratio.

The outstanding problem of data forwarding mechanisms is to enhance the delivery ratio and shorten the transmission delay while the storage occupancy is confined. Note that in social networks the nodes usually are with some characters, and the character relations between nodes can reflect the moving regularities of nodes, which has not been carefully investigated in previous works. To this end, we exploit the character relations to help forward the data packets, and a data forwarding algorithm based on character relations (DFCR) is then proposed. DFCR can guarantee a high delivery ratio, a short transmission delay and a confined storage occupancy.

3   Problem Modeling

Each node in MONs is assigned a unique ID. The deployment area of nodes is divided into y regions, and each region at each time slot is mapped into a unique character. Especially, each node at one time slot is only with one character. The number of time slots during which each data packet can be forwarded (the life cycle of each data packet) is set as *NTTL*. The length of each time slot is denoted by t_s.

The source node and the destination node are denoted by a_s and a_d, respectively. The relay node is denoted by f_a $(a = 1, 2, 3, \ldots)$. The character of a_e at the i-th time slot is denoted by $K(a_e, i)$. To confine the forwarded copies of each data packet, each data-holding node is allowed to transmit the data packet to at most n_f relay nodes at each time slot.

Suppose there are m nodes $\{a_1, a_2, a_3, \ldots, a_m\}$ in the j-th region at the i-th time slot with the character K_{ji}, and there are n nodes $\{a_{m+1}, a_{m+2}, a_{m+3}, \ldots, a_{m+n}\}$ in the k-th region at the i-th time slot with the character K_{ki} at the i-th time slot.

With regard to any two characters K_{ji} and K_{ki}, the character relation between K_{ji} and K_{ki} is denoted by $CR(K_{ji}, K_{ki})$.

Suppose a_b is with the character $K_{ji}(b = 1, 2, 3 \ldots m)$, the maximum communication duration of a_b and K_{ki} is expressed as:

$$TS(a_b, K_{ki}) = n \cdot t_s \tag{1}$$

which indicates that the value of $TS(a_b, K_{ki})$ is depends on the number of nodes which belong to K_{ki}.

Then, the maximum communication duration of K_{ji} and K_{ki} is given by:

$$TTS(K_{ji}, K_{ki}) = \sum_{b=1}^{b=m} TS(a_b, K_{ki}) \tag{2}$$

The real communication duration of a_b (with K_{ji}) and another node a_c (with K_{ki}, and $c = m+1, m+2, m+3, \ldots, m+n$) is marked as $TR(a_b, a_c, i)$, and thus the real communication duration of a_b and K_{ki} is written as:

$$TR(a_b, K_{ki}) = \sum_{c=m+1}^{c=m+n} TR(a_b, a_c, i) \tag{3}$$

By (3), the real communication duration of K_{ji} and K_{ki} is expressed as:

$$TTR(K_{ji}, K_{ki}) = \sum_{b=1}^{b=m} TR(a_b, K_{ki}) \tag{4}$$

Then, the time-relation and frequency-relation between K_{ji} and K_{ki} are calculated as following formulas:

$$TR(K_{ji}, K_{ki}) = \frac{TTR(K_{ji}, K_{ki})}{TTS(K_{ji}, K_{ki})} \tag{5}$$

$$FR(K_{ji}, K_{ki}) = \frac{\sum_{c=m+1}^{c=m+n} M(a_c, K_{ji})}{\sum_{p \neq j, p \leq y} \sum_{c=m+1}^{c=m+n} M(a_c, K_{pi})} \tag{6}$$

where $M(a_c, K_{pi})$ denotes the number of nodes (with the character K_{pi}) falling into the communication range of a_c at the i-th time slot.

Finally, the character relation between K_{ji} and K_{ki} is calculated as:

$$CR(K_{ji}, K_{ki}) = [TR(K_{ji}, K_{ki})]^\alpha \cdot [FR(K_{ji}, K_{ki})]^\beta \tag{7}$$

where α and β are preset parameters which can measure the importance of time-relation and frequency-relation, respectively.

4 DFCR Algorithm

In the data forwarding algorithm based on character relations (DFCR), at the beginning of each time slot the data-holding nodes broadcast the inquiry messages to inquire for neighboring nodes. If the destination node has falling to the communication range of any data-holding node, the data packet will be forwarded to the destination node immediately; otherwise, the neighboring nodes with the largest forwarding values will be selected as the relay nodes. This process is repeated until the data packet has been delivered to the destination node or the *TTL* of data packet has been reduced to 0. The detailed steps are given as follows:

4.1   Step 1

At each time slot, each node updates the current coordinate and the current time slot. Neighboring nodes exchange the information of their historical movements. The nodes reserve the character information of the latest N cycles. Note that nodes with the same character in the same cycle are considered to be in the communication range of each other. Besides, *TTL* is initialized as *NTTL*, and after each time slot, $TTL \leftarrow TTL - 1$.

4.2   Step 2

When a data-holding node a_b encounter an ordinary node a_c at the i-th time slot, a_b will calculate the forwarding value of a_c (denoted by $FV(a_c, a_d)$), which considers the character relation and character adscription.

Each node is with a single character at each time slot, and in the N historical cycles, each node is possible to be with different characters at different time slots. To measure the relation between a node a_c and a character K_{ji}, there are only two relation possibilities: a_c belongs to K_{ji} or not. And it can be expressed as:

$$R(a_c, K_{ji}, \tau) = \begin{cases} 0, & K(a_c, i) \neq K_{ji} \\ 1, & K(a_c, i) = K_{ji} \end{cases} \tag{8}$$

where τ denotes the last τ-th cycle. Then, the character adscription between a_c and K_{ji} is calculated as:

$$CA(a_c, K_{ji}) = \sum_{\tau=1}^{N} \frac{R(a_c, K_{ji}, \tau)}{2^{\tau}} \tag{9}$$

And the character of a_c is determined by:

$$K(a_c, i) = \max_{1 \leq j \leq y} CA(a_c, K_{ji}) \tag{10}$$

Besides, the forwarding value of a_c is expressed as:

$$FV(a_c, a_d) = \sum_{i=w+1}^{i=w+\frac{TTL}{t_s}} \left[CA(a_c, K(a_c, i)) \cdot CA(a_d, K(a_d, i)) \cdot CR(K(a_c, i), K(a_d, i)) \cdot \frac{t_s}{TTL} \right] \tag{11}$$

Where $\frac{t_s}{TTL}$ denotes the weight of $CA(a_c, K(a_c, i)) \cdot CA(a_d, K(a_d, i)) \cdot CR(K(a_c, i), K(a_d, i))$ at the future time slots.

At the end of this time slot, a_b will select n_f ordinary nodes with the highest forwarding values.

4.3 Step 3

Step 2 is repeated until the destination node has received the data packet or *TTL* is reduced to 0. Two cases are discussed as follows:

Case 1: At the last time slot of the life cycle of each data packet, the destination node is still out of the communication ranges of all data-holding nodes. Then, the further forwarding will be terminated.

Case 2: The destination node has received the data packet, and then it broadcasts a message-received (MR) packet to prevent the data-holding nodes from disseminating this data packet. Thus, the storage occupancy of nodes can be reduced for the forwarding of other data packets. When *TTL* is reduced to 0, the stored copies of this data packet on the data-holding nodes will be deleted.

5   Simulation Evaluation

DFCR is evaluated by observing the performance of different model paraments and by comparing with other algorithms. The simulation is realized in ONE (Opportunistic Networks Environment), which can generate the node mobilities using various movement models and transmit the data packet with different forwarding algorithms. The simulation results are averaged over 50,000 runs. The main parameter settings are given in Table 1.

Table 1. Simulation parameters

Parameters	Description	Value
NN	Number of total nodes	1000
S	Deployment space size	10,000 m^2
BR	Maximum communication range	15 m
MV	Maximum speed at each time slot	10 m per time slot
NC	Number of characters at each time slot	16
$NTTL$	Life cycle of each data packet	40 min
n_f	Number of forwarded copies at each time slot	2
t_s	Length of each time slot	10 min

5.1   Impacts of n_f and NN

NN denotes the number of total nodes in the simulation, and n_f denotes the number of forwarded copies at each time slot. Figure 1(a) illustrates that the deliver ratio decreases with the increase of NN. This is because when the number of nodes is reduced, the proportion of data-holding nodes is increased, i.e., the destination node has a higher probability to encounter the data-holding nodes. Figure 1(a) also suggests that with the increase of n_f, the delivery ratio increases rapidly. In Figs. 1(b) and 1(c), both the number of forwarded data copies and the propagation delay are almost invariable with the variation of *NN*. Besides, the number of forwarded data copies grows continuously with the increase of n_f, while the propagation delay increases slightly, which is attributed to the fact that the increase of n_f always leads to more data-holding nodes.

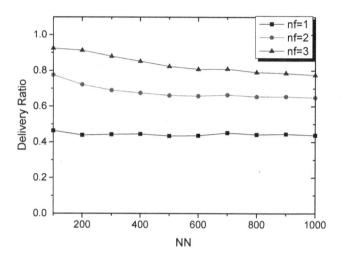

(*a*) Delivery ratio vs. *NN* and n_f

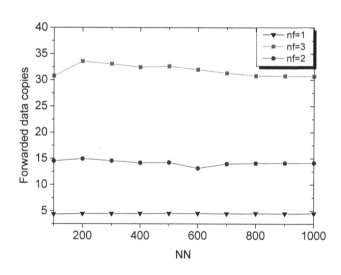

(*b*) Number of forwarded data copies vs. *NN* and n_f

Fig. 1. Impacts of *NN* and n_f.

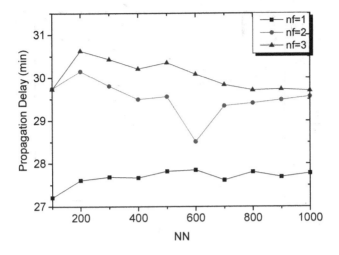

(c) Propagation delay vs. *NN* and n_f

Fig. 1. (*continued*)

5.2 Algorithm Comparisons

Figure 2 provides the results of the simulation comparisons among DFCR, EF (epidemic), DIR (direct transmission) and TCCB, in terms of the delivery ratio, number of forwarded data copies and propagation delay, respectively. In Fig. 2(a), the curves of delivery ratio indicate that DFCR performs much better than DIR and TCCB. Moreover, the delivery ratio of DFCR is very close to that of EF.

As shown in Fig. 2(b), the number of forwarded copies of EF is much larger than other because EF adopts a flooding manner. Besides, the number of forwarded copies of DFCR is slight larger than DIR and TCCB, while a much larger delivery ratio and a much shorter propagation delay will be achieved by DFCR, as shown in Figs. 2(a) and 2(c), respectively.

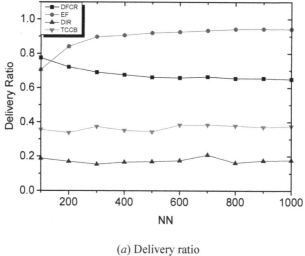

(*a*) Delivery ratio

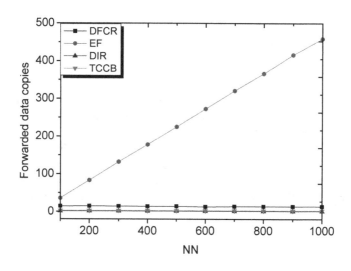

(*b*) The number of forwarded data copies

Fig. 2. Comparisons of DFCR, EF, DIR, TCCB.

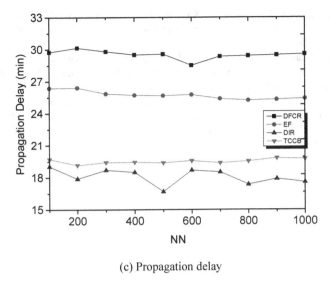

(c) Propagation delay

Fig. 2. (*continued*)

6 Conclusions

By exploiting the characters' relations between nodes (comprised of time-relation and frequency-relation), a data forwarding algorithm based on character relations (DFCR) for mobile opportunistic networks is proposed, and DFCR can achieve the preferable results in terms of the delivery ratio, number of forwarded copies and propagation delay.

Acknowledgement. This research is supported by National Natural Science Foundation of China under Grant Nos. 61872191, 61872193, 61972210; Six Talents Peak Project of Jiangsu Province under Grant No. 2019-XYDXX-247; Technology Innovation and Application Demonstration Major Program of Chongqing (cstc2018jszx-cyztzxX0015).

References

1. Francesco, M.D., Das, S.K.: Data collection in wireless sensor networks with mobile elements: a survey. ACM Trans. Sens. Netw. **8**(1) (2011)
2. He, L., Kong, L., Gu, Y., Pan, J., Zhu, T.: Evaluating the on-demand mobile charging in wireless sensor networks. IEEE Trans. Mob. Comput. (2015)
3. LeBurn, J., Chuah, C.N., Ghosal, D., Zhang, M.: Knowledge-based opportunistic forwarding in vehicular wireless ad hoc networks. In: Proceeding of IEEE 61st Vehicular Technology Conference, Stockholm, Sweden (2005)
4. Martín-Campillo, A., Crowcroft, J., Yoneki, E., Martí, R.: Evaluating opportunistic networks in disaster scenarios. J. Netw. Comput. Appl. **36**(2), 870–880 (2013)

5. Zhou, H., Leung, V.C.M., Zhu, C.S., Xu, S.Z., Fan, J.L.: Predicting temporal social contact patterns for data forwarding in opportunistic mobile networks. IEEE Trans. Veh. Technol. **66** (11), 10372–10383 (2017)
6. Zhong, K.X., Zhang, S.R., Zou, A., Liu, L.F., Tang, J.: A data forwarding algorithm based on nodal activities in opportunistic networks. In: Proceeding of the 18th International Conference on Communication Technology, Chongqing, China (2018)
7. Tao, J., Wu, H.T., Shi, S.J., Hu, J., Gao, Y.: Contacts-aware opportunistic forwarding in mobile social networks: a community perspective. In: Proceedings of 2018 IEEE Wireless Communications and Networking Conference, Barcelona, Spain (2018)
8. Yan, Y.Q., Chen, Z.G., Wu, J., Wang, L.L., Liu, K.H., et al.: Effective data transmission strategy based on node socialization in opportunistic social networks. IEEE Access **7**, 22144–22160 (2019)

Research on Interference of LTE Wireless Network in Electric Power System

Shanyu Bi[(✉)], Junyao Zhang, Weiwei Kong, Long Liu,
and Pengpeng Lv

NARI Group Corporation/State Grid Electric Power Research Institute,
Nanjing, China
bishanyu@sgepri.sgcc.com.cn

Abstract. In view of the problems of electric power wireless communication and to serve the power consumer better, On the basis of the basic principles of TD-LTE's network structure, interference in the wireless network optimization of power system are analyzed in detail, and put forward a method of interference remediation for power system. Based on the actual, cases, the feasibility of interference remediation is verified by means of data processing and comparative analysis. The interference analysis provides a technology support for electric power communication access network construction and late operation and lays the foundations for popularization and application of LTE power wireless private network, and the security of the power network is guaranteed.

Keywords: TD-LTE · Barrage jamming · Intermodulation interference · Network security · Spurious emission · Network optimization

1 Introduction

As one of the important technologies of power communication network, wireless communication has been widely used in national network marketing, transportation inspection and other systems [1, 2]. At present, many provincial and municipal districts have carried out pilot applications of power private networks based on different wireless communication technologies, including WiMAX, McWILL, 230 MHz LTE, and data transmission stations [3]. Business applications include distribution automation, power information collection, monitoring of transmission and transformation status and so on [4]. At the same time, some problems in power wireless network are gradually exposed. The interference problem will affect the performance of the network, therefore, it is urgent to study the interference analysis of wireless network optimization technology in power system. In this paper, the interference in the power system is introduced in detail, and different kinds of interference is analyzed in detail.

2   Process for Interference Analysis

For wireless communication networks, the premise of ensuring service quality is to use a clean spectrum, this band is not used or interfered by other systems [5]. Otherwise, the performance of the interference system and the terminal will be affected negatively [6].

The screening of interference cells is to screen out the high interference cells that need to be dealt with according to certain conditions [7]. Interference analysis is the

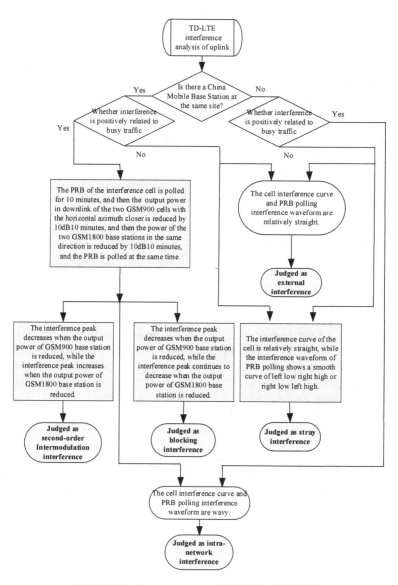

Fig. 1.   Interference process of uplink in TD-LTE.

third step in the overall process of interference trouble shooting, and is a very important step. Interference analysis determines the next working direction of site interference detection [8]. Correct interference analysis is helpful to improve the overall efficiency of interference checking. The flow chart of interference analysis is shown in Fig. 1.

3   Analysis and Treatment of Intermodulation Interference

3.1   Analysis of Intermodulation Interference

Intermodulation interference is generally caused by the fact that the Intermodulation signal transmitted by nearby radio equipment falls into the frequency band received by the TD-LTE base station [9]. At present, the Intermodulation interference is mainly the second-order Intermodulation interference produced by China Mobile GSM900 system, which interferes with the F-band of TD-LTE. In addition, in other places, because the frequency band used in GSM1800 system reaches 1870 MHz, the third or fifth order Intermodulation interference will also fall in the F band of TD-LTE. The characteristics of interference are as follows.

The average interference level of the cell is closely related to the traffic of 2G. The busier the traffic of 2G is, the greater the interference of TD-LTE is. The smaller the isolation between the antenna of 2G cell and the antenna of TD-LTE cell, the more serious the interference is.

The interference curve of a cell is shown in the following figure (Fig. 2).

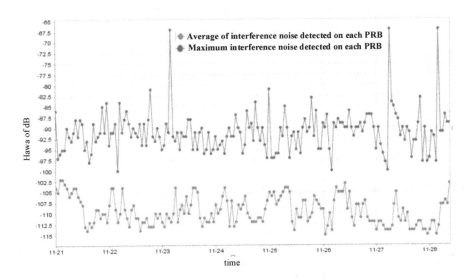

Fig. 2. Intermodulation interference curve.

The interference of PRB level is shown in the following figure (Fig. 3).

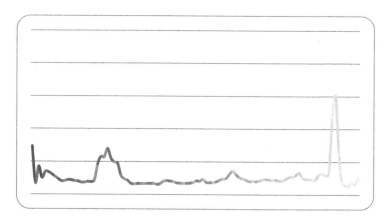

Fig. 3. Intermodulation interference in class PRB.

The characteristics of interference can be clearly seen from the interference of the cell. The interference in the early hours of the morning is the least, because traffic in the early hours of the morning is lower. According to the parameters of information, there are GSM900 base stations in the same sector of the site, and there are many frequency points. The frequency point of BCCH is 69, and the frequency point of TCH is 13/10. The calculated second order intermodulation and second harmonics are shown in the following table (Table 1).

Table 1. Two order intermodulation and two harmonic

Second order intermodulation & frequency point of second harmonic	Interference with the number of PRB in F band
Second-order Intermodulation generated by frequency points 69 and 10	PRB25 ～ 27
Second-order Intermodulation generated by frequency points 69 and 13	PRB28 ～ 31
Second harmonic produced by frequency point 69	PRB91 ～ 93

Therefore, it can be judged from the above table that the sector of TD-LTE is interfered by the second order Intermodulation of GSM900 cell.

Because the antenna is about the same height, the site can be initially determined to be subjected to blocking interference from the GSM900/1800 base station. And because of the frequent occurrence of BCCH frequency points, the second harmonic interference is the most obvious, which is of course related to the low traffic volume in the cell.

3.2   Treatment of Intermodulation Interference

There are two ways to regulate the interference of Intermodulation. First, the antenna of the interference source base station and the antenna of the interfered base station are transformed from horizontal isolation to vertical isolation, the isolation degree can generally be increased by more than 10 dB. Second, the horizontal distance between the antenna of interference source base station and the antenna of the interfered base station is more than 2 meters, or in the case of vertical isolation, the antenna of the interference source base station can be replaced with the antenna with higher second-order intermodulation suppression system. At present, the antenna with intermodulation index of 100 dBm and 43 dBm can be replaced.

4   Analysis and Treatment of Blocking Interference

4.1   Analysis of Blocking Interference

Blocking interference is generally caused by a strong signal transmitted by a nearby radio device received by the device of the TD-LTE. The blocking interference found at this stage is mainly caused by China Mobile GSM900 base station and closer base station. The characteristics of interference are as follows.

The average interference level of the cell is related to the traffic of the interference source, and the busier the traffic of the interference source is, the greater the interference is. The smaller the antenna isolation between the interference base station and the TD-LTE cell, the more serious the interference. Of course, it is impossible to know the isolation degree of the antenna between the systems only through the information of the working parameters, but the isolation degree of the antenna can be roughly understood

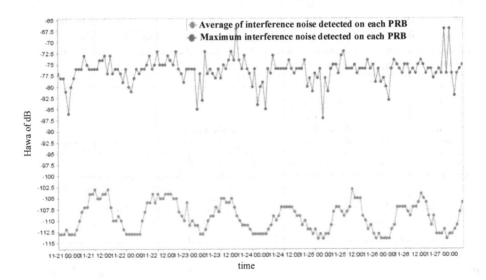

Fig. 4. Block interference curve.

from the antenna height and the horizontal azimuth angle of the antenna. The characteristic of PRB interference is that there is an obvious protruding before PRB10, and there is no obvious interference waveform behind the raised PRB (Fig. 4).

The interference of PRB level is shown in the following figure (Fig. 5).

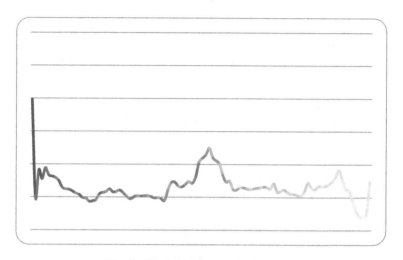

Fig. 5. Block interference in class PRB

The interference characteristics of the cell can be clearly seen from the interference of the cell. The interference in the early hours of the morning is the least, because traffic in the early hours of the morning is lower. From the interference of PRB, we can see that there is a large uplink interference in the cell around PRB1. According to the information of working parameters, there is a GSM900/1800 base station in the same sector, and the antenna of the base station is the same as that of the LTE base station. Therefore, the site can be initially determined to be subjected to blocking interference from the GSM900 base station.

4.2   Treatment of Blocking Interference

There are three ways to deal with blocking interference.

First, filters in the corresponding frequency band can be installed on interfered TD-LTE base stations. It should be noted that the filter installed in the RRU, common mode with the TD-SCDMA in the A band must be 2010–2025 MHz compatible.

Second, increase the isolation between the two systems, for example, raise the antenna height of the interference source base station or the interfered base station, change it from horizontal isolation to vertical isolation

Third, replace the interfered RRU with the RRU of more anti-blocking. For example, replace it with RRU produced after 2012, and its anti-blocking ability is developed and produced according to the latest 3GPP specification, compared with the previous RRU, the resistance to stopper is obviously enhanced, so the number of blocking interference sites is small.

5 Analysis and Treatment of Stray Interference

5.1 Analysis of Stray Interference

Stray interference is the interference caused by stray transmission outside the transmission band of one system falling into the receiving band of another system. Stray interference directly affects the receiving sensitivity of the system. If the stray falls into the receiving frequency band of the system, the receiver system of the interfered system can not filter out the stray signal, therefore, the filter must be added to the input port of the transmitter to control the stray interference.

In the process of actual investigation, it is found that the stray interference mainly comes from three aspects. One is the stray interference from China Mobile GSM1800MHz base station, second, the 1G FDD-LTE base station of China Telecom at present, third, the TD-LTE base station in E band is vulnerable to the stray interference of WLAN AP.

The diagram of interference curve is as follows (Fig. 6).

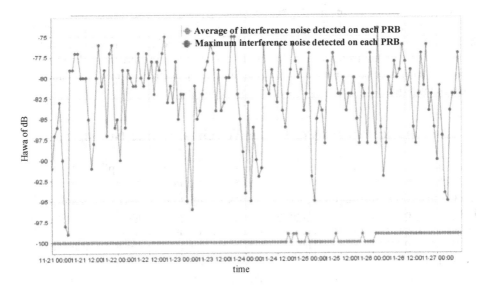

Fig. 6. Stray interference curve.

From the diagram, the interference curve of the cell affected by stray interference is relatively straight, and the fluctuation is generally about 1 dB.

The interference of PRB level is shown in the following figure.

From the interference curve, we can obviously see that the interference of the cell has obvious busy characteristics, and there are many interference peaks in the interference polling waveform of PRB (Fig. 7).

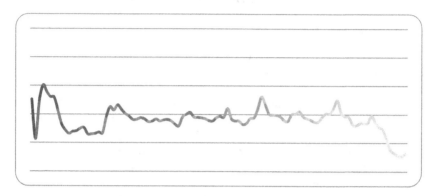

Fig. 7. Interference curve in class PRB

5.2   Treatment of Stray Interference

There are two kinds of treatment methods for stray interference.

First, by increasing the isolation between the antenna of the base station and the base station of the interference source, the purpose of reducing the interference can be achieved, horizontal isolation can generally be changed to vertical isolation. The second is to reduce stray interference by adding bandpass filter to the base station of interference source.

6   Interference Analysis of Power Wireless Private Network

There are two main ways to find interference. One is to statistics the uplink interference through the base station side, the other is to collect the downlink interference through the terminal side. Taking Y city as an example, the interference index in uplink of the last week is extracted, and the granularity is the one day. The uplink interference can only be extracted on the base station side, and the downlink interference can only be collected on the terminal side. Uplink interference is ideal when the low noise is below −120 dbm, and can be determined as interference when it is higher than −120 dbm. When the uplink interference is higher than-110dbm, it is considered that the interference begins to deteriorate, and when it is higher than-105 dbm, it is considered that the interference is more serious (Table 2 and Fig. 8).

Table 2. Uplink interference statistics

RSSI	Number of samples	Proportion
$[0 \sim -95)$	891	85.84%
$[-95 \sim -105)$	144	13.87%
$[-105 \sim -110)$	3	0.29%
$[-110 \sim -115]$	0	0.00%
$[-115 \sim -120]$	0	0.00%

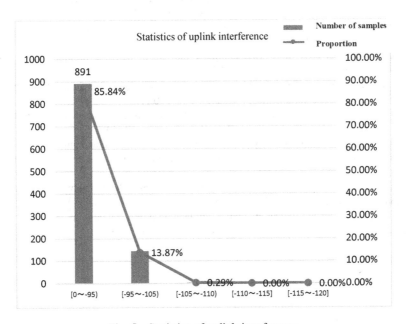

Fig. 8. Statistics of uplink interference.

From the above statistics, we can see that, the proportion of interference above −95 dbm is very high, reaching 85.84%, it shows that the interference in the frequency band is very serious and needs to be checked.

7   Conclusion

This paper is based on the basic principle of TD-LTE network structure, the frequency sweep test, interference analysis, alarm processing and coverage optimization in wireless network optimization of power system are analyzed in detail. In this paper, an optimization method in TD-LTE wireless private network is proposed. The network optimization scheme provides technical support for the construction of power network, and lays a solid foundation for the popularization and application of power wireless private network.

References

1. Qiu, J., Ding, G., Wu, Q., et al.: Hierarchical resource allocation framework for hyper-dense small cell networks. IEEE Access **4**(99), 8657–8669 (2017)
2. Chen, X., Jiang, Y.Z., Wang, X., et al.: Research on the development of energy internet from the perspective of internet. Autom. Electr. Power Syst. **41**(9), 2–11 (2017)
3. Gao, F., Zeng, R., Qu, L., et al.: Research on identification of concept and characteristics of energy internet. Electr. Power, 1–6 (2018)
4. Xu, X.L.: Time-sensitive network technology and its application in industrial network. Telecommun. Netw. Technol. **5**, 1–5 (2018)
5. Craciunas, S.S., Oliver, R.S.: Combined task and network-level scheduling for distributed time-triggered systems. Real-Time Syst. **52**(2), 161–200 (2016)
6. Sun, G.D.: Research and Simulation of clock synchronization and scheduling algorithm in time-sensitive networks. Beijing Univ. Posts Telecommun. (2018)
7. Bahnasse, A., Louhab, F.E., Oulahyane, H.A., et al.: Novel SDN architecture for smart MPLS traffic engineering-diff serv aware management. Future Gener. Comput. Syst. **11**(2), 212–219 (2018)
8. Li, B.L., Zhou, J., Ren, X.H.: Research on key issues of TD-LTE network optimization. Telecom Eng. Tech. Stand. **1**, 57–61 (2015)
9. Zheng, L., Tse, D.N.C.: Diversity and multiplexing: a fundamental tradeoff in multiple antenna channels. IEEE Trans. Inf. Theory **49**, 1073–1096 (2003)

Research on High Reliability Planning Method in Electric Wireless Network

Zewei Tang[1]([⊠]) and Chengzhi Jiang[2]

[1] School of Management and Engineering,
Nanjing University, Nanjing 210093, China
tzw@nju.edu.cn
[2] Nanjing Institute of Technology, Nanjing 211167, China

Abstract. Aimed at the problems existing in the planning of power wireless communication, in order to better serve smart grid and carry out the application of time-sharing long-term evolution technology in power communication, a highly reliable planning method for wireless private network is proposed. It improves the survival of the user's service by using overlapping coverage of base station signals, and the overlapping cells are merged to avoid the same frequency interference. By optimizing the deployment of the organization of the base station, in the case of the same number of base stations, the average inter station distance of overlapping coverage is increased, and the network reliability is improved on the premise of ensuring network performance. The planning scheme solves the problem of mutual interference caused by the same frequency overlapping coverage between base stations.

Keywords: TD-LTE · Network planning · High reliability · Interference · Electric wireless network

1 Introduction

To support the core tasks and objectives of the smart grid, the power system needs to build a terminal access network with wide access and flexibility [1]. Optical fiber access is the best access method for users, but there are some problems, such as difficult laying, long construction cycle, long fault recovery time, high investment cost and so on [2, 3]. The reliability and security of communication network are very important in power system. Power monitoring system should be isolated from data network and external information network of electric enterprises. Therefore, the wireless private network is the necessary path for the construction of the power system terminal access network [4, 5].

Wireless network planning is the foundation of wireless construction [6, 7]. The coverage of the power wireless private network shall meet the needs of automatic power distribution, power utilization information acquisition, power transmission and transformation status monitoring [8, 9], etc. In power application, if the base station fails due to sudden power outage, equipment failure and cable damage, shutdown maintenance must be arranged. And under normal circumstances, the traffic accessed by the base station will not be maintained, which will have a serious impact on the

© Springer Nature Singapore Pte Ltd. 2020
Y. Tian et al. (Eds.): ICBDS 2019, CCIS 1210, pp. 319–329, 2020.
https://doi.org/10.1007/978-981-15-7530-3_24

power system [10–13]. Therefore, the reliability of the service should be strengthened, and it must ensure that the key service is covered by two or more base stations [14]. One service is covered by multiple base stations, which leads to self-interference [15]. In the public network, interference avoidance is realized in the self-interference region through hetero-frequency network. However, due to the shortage of frequency resources in power system, hetero-frequency network may not be implemented, therefore, it is necessary to study the high reliability planning method under the same frequency.

2   Novel Networking Structure

Each base station in the power wireless private network includes a remote radio frequency unit (RRU), the baseband unit (BBU), connected to the optical fiber between the remote radio frequency unit and the baseband unit [16]. A baseband unit can usually support multiple remote radio frequency units. In this section, it first describes the structure of the traditional cellular network, and then introduces two improved structures with low self-interference and high reliability.

2.1   Traditional Cellular Networking

According to the general description of physical layer, the cell of the base station is recorded as $C_{N^{ID}}$, where N^{ID} is a physical cell identification, $N^{ID} = 3N^{ID(1)} + N^{ID(2)}$, Where $N^{ID(2)}$ is the primary synchronous sequence identifies (PSSI). ID represents the identification of the cell of a base station, and the regular value is $\{0,1,2\}$. The direction of the three cells of the base station refers to the direction angle of the three cells whose PSSI is 0, 1 and 2, the conventional cellular communication system is deployed as shown in Fig. 1.

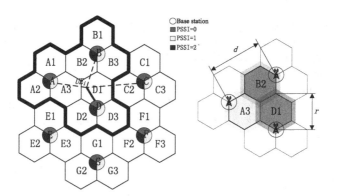

Fig. 1. Traditional cellular network structure.

The coverage radius of the base station is recorded as r, r is also the diameter of the cell. The distance between base stations is recorded as d, the area covered is recorded as

S, the number of base stations in the area is recorded as N, Cell A1 represents the first cell of base station A.

The user i in the base station D of cellular networking is recorded as UE_i. The received signal-to-noise ratio is

$$SINR_i = \frac{\rho(D,i)}{\sum_{\substack{k \in \Psi \\ k \neq D}} \rho(k,i) + P_N} \tag{1}$$

2.2 Network Structure 1

In LTE network, by increasing the density of base station, the same terminal can receive more than one signal from the base station to avoid service failure caused by the failure of base station. In a single coverage network, the overlap of coverage can be increased by adding the same configuration of the base station. The existing base station is called the backbone base station. The new base station is called disaster recovery base station, represented by set Φ, the signal-to-noise ratio (SNR) at UE_i after adding the station is as follows.

$$SINR_i = \frac{\rho(D,i)}{\sum_{\substack{k \in \Psi \\ k \neq D}} \rho(k,i) + \sum_{j \in \Phi} \rho(j,i) + P_N} \tag{2}$$

In that case of not changing the original site, the site selection method for doubling redundant coverage is shown in Fig. 2.

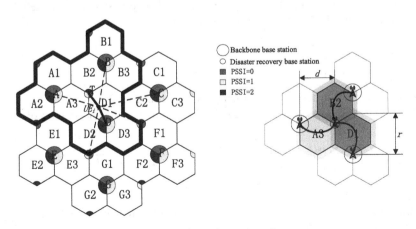

Fig. 2. Network structure 1.

Because the backbone base station D is merged with the adjacent disaster recovery base station T cell, the signal-to-noise ratio of UE_i is

$$SINR_i = \frac{\rho(D,i) + \rho(T,i)}{\sum_{\substack{k \in \Psi \\ k \neq D}} \rho(k,i) + \sum_{\substack{j \in \Phi \\ j \neq T}} \rho(j,i) + P_N} \tag{3}$$

Formula (3) is obviously larger than (2), so SINR is improved and the self-interference is reduced.

The calculation method of one station spacing in networking structure is shown as follows. The relationship of the distance between disaster recovery base station and backbone base station d_D and cell radius r is as follows.

$$d_D = \sqrt{3}r/2 \tag{4}$$

The number of network base stations is $N_D = 2N$, and the relationship between the coverage area S and the number of base stations N_D is.

$$S = 9\sqrt{3}N_D r^2/16 = 3\sqrt{3}N_D d_D^2/4 \tag{5}$$

The networking structure is obtained by adding N disaster recovery base stations in a cellular network composed of N backbone base stations,

The distance between stations in uniform distribution is shown in the following formula.

$$\bar{d} = 3r/2\sqrt{2} = \sqrt{3/2}d_D \tag{6}$$

Because the failure of base station is due to the power outage, the dug out optical cable is dug up and so on, increasing the distance between stations is beneficial to increase the independence between disaster tolerant base stations and backbone base stations.

2.3   Network Structure 2

The second method of networking structure is shown in Fig. 2.

For the user UE_i of the base station D in Fig. 3, the signal-to-noise ratio of UE_i is

$$SINR_i = \frac{\rho(D,i) + \rho(T,i)}{\sum_{\substack{k \in \Psi \\ k \neq D}} \rho(k,i) + \sum_{\substack{j \in \Phi \\ j \neq T}} \rho(j,i) + P_N} \tag{7}$$

Formula (7) it is obviously larger than (2), so the SINR is improved and the self-interference is reduced.

There are two station spacing d_1 and d_2 in the repeat area. Due to symmetry, the distance between the first backbone base station and the adjacent second disaster

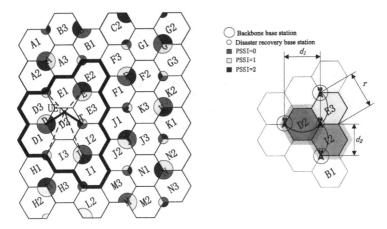

Fig. 3. Network structure 2.

recovery base station, as well as the distance between the second backbone base station and the adjacent first disaster recovery base station, are recorded as d_1, $d_1 = r$. The distance between the first backbone base station and the first disaster recovery base station, and the distance between the second backbone base station and the second disaster recovery base station are recorded as d_2, $d_2 = \sqrt{3}r/2$.

Since the number ratio of d_1 and d_2 is 1:2, the average station spacing is

$$
\begin{aligned}
d_{D'} &= \left(1 + \sqrt{3}\right)r/3 \\
&= \left(1 + \sqrt{3}\right)2d_D/3\sqrt{3} \\
&= \left(1 + \sqrt{3}\right)2\sqrt{2}\bar{d}/9
\end{aligned}
\tag{8}
$$

Under the condition that the coverage overlap and anti-interference ability are the same as the structure-1, the average distance between the base stations is increased by 5.2%, and the distance between the stations is increased by 85.9%, which increases the reliability of disaster recovery.

3 The Process of Network Planning

In the above two networking structures, the former's networking scheme is to add disaster recovery base station to the single coverage cellular network, which is suitable for the reinforcement of the built network. The latter is a kind of networking structure with larger station spacing, which provides better disaster recovery effect in different places and needs to change the traditional cellular network structure, so it can be used in the new network. Two kinds of networking structures and the particularity of power service are integrated into the process of wireless network planning, as shown in Fig. 4.

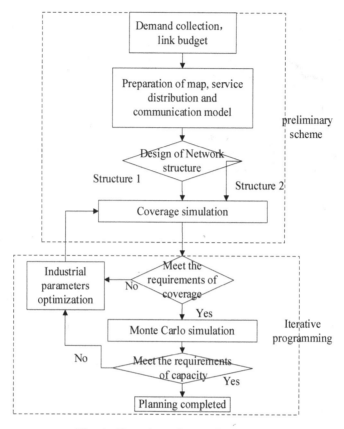

Fig. 4. Flow chart of network planning.

4 Simulation Analysis

The simulation adopts atoll, a professional planning simulation software for wireless communication. City Y is a small city, with an area of 132 km², the overall elevation is flat, the terrain of the city fluctuates within 3 m, and 2 base stations have been built. There is a need for full coverage of 58 km² of urban areas and to ensure the reliability of service in central and industrial areas. The installed terminal is a fixed CPE terminal with an edge rate of 256 kbps, the link budget results are as follows (Table 1):

Based on the results of the link budget, the cell radius of the service at the rate of 256 kbps is about 1.36 km, 5 new backbone base stations are built in the urban area, and 4 disaster recovery stations are deployed in the central urban and industrial areas. A total of 11 base stations were built. The base station distribution and coverage simulation during co-channel networking are shown in the following figure. The results of the simulation are shown in Table 2 (Fig. 5).

The proportion of RSRP >-115 dBm is 99.3% and that of SINR >-3 dB is 79.2%. From the simulation results, it can be seen that when the disaster recovery base station

Table 1. Link budget.

CPE-256kbps link budget table	
Antenna gain of base station (dBi)	17.0 dBi
Processing gain of base station (dB)	0.0 dB
Loss of feeders and joints (dB)	0.5 dB
Number of RB in uplink	12
Thermal noise power spectral density (dBm/Hz)	−173.98
Demodulation bandwidth thermal noise power (dBm)	−110.6 dBm
Noise coefficient of receiver (dB)	3.0 dB
Demodulation bandwidth receiver noise power (dB)	−107.6 dB
Demodulation threshold (dB)	−5.8 dB
Sensitivity of receiver (dBm)	−113.4 dBm
Interference margin (dB)	3.0 dB
Body loss (dB)	0.0 dB
he minimum received level of the demodulated bandwidth (dBm)	−110.4 dBm
Transmission power of terminal (dBm)	23.0 dBm
Antenna gain of terminal (dBi)	0.0 dBi
Feeder and joint loss of terminal (dB)	0.0 dB
Requirements for coverage probability	95.0%
Fading variance of shadow	10.0 dB
The margin of shadow fading (dB)	11.7 dB
Penetration loss (dB)	0.0 dB
Antenna height of terminal (m)	1.5 m
Antenna height of base station (m)	45.0 m
Center frequency (MHz)	1795 MHz
Maximum allowable path loss (dB)	138.2 dB
The radius of coverage in uplink	1.36 km

Table 2. Results of the coverage simulation.

RSRP (dBm)	Area of coverage (km^2)	Fraction of coverage (%)	SINR (dB)	Area of coverage (km^2)	Fraction of coverage (%)
≥ -75	10.3755	17.4	≥ 9	9.0549	15.2
≥ -95	50.9343	85.6	≥ 3	24.5682	41.3
≥ -115	59.0764	99.3	≥ -3	47.1537	79.2

and the backbone base station cover a terminal together, it will cause serious co-frequency self-interference.

The table shows the static simulation results of user UE$_i$, in which RSRP = −102.1, SINR = −5.47, indicates that the user in this location can not be connected to the network due to self-interference (Table 3).

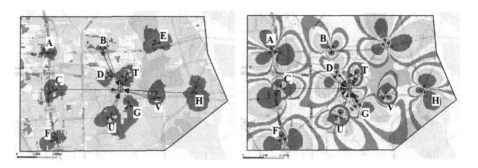

Fig. 5. Simulation (RSRP & SINR) of overlap coverage with co-channel interference.

Table 3. Results of the UE_i single point simulation.

The strongest cell	The distance of propagation (m)	Path loss (dB)	SINR (dB)	RSRP (dBm)
D	961	139.1	−5.47	−102.1
T	670	139.6	–	−102.6
G	847	151.2	–	−116.6
U	1459	157.6	–	−123.0

In Fig. 6, the coverage simulation after the scheme proposed in this paper is applied. The simulation results are shown in Table 4, in which the coverage area of RSRP >-115 dBm is 99.3%, and that of SINR >-3 dB is 93.1%.

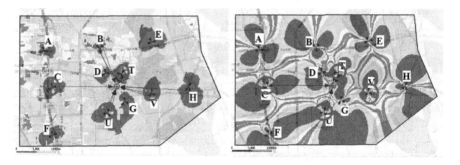

Fig. 6. Simulation (RSRP & SINR) of overlap coverage with SFN cell merging.

From the simulation results, it can be seen that due to the merger of interference cells, the problem of self-interference is significantly reduced, and the coverage of SINR is increased by 13.9%, which meets the coverage requirements of power wireless special network.

Table 4. Results of the coverage simulation

RSRP (dBm)	Area of coverage (km²)	Fraction of coverage (%)	SINR (dB)	Area of coverage (km²)	Fraction of coverage (%)
≥ −75	10.3635	17.4	≥ 9	26.7093	44.9
≥ −95	50.9598	85.6	≥ 3	40.4271	67.9
≥ −115	59.0841	99.3	≥ −3	55.4436	93.1

Table 5 shows the static simulation of user UE_i in the same location, where the RSRP = −101.4, SINR = 1.51, signal-to-noise ratio (SNR) is improved by about 7 dB.

Table 5. Results of the UE_i single point simulation

The strongest cell	The distance of propagation (m)	Path loss (dB)	SINR (dB)	RSRP (dBm)
D/T merged cell	961 (D) 6709 (T)	139.1	1.51	−101.4
U/G merged cell	847 (G) 1459 (U)	151.2	–	−114.4
V	1718	168.1	–	−130.6

Figure 7 shows the coverage simulation results of the proposed scheme in the event of base station failure in the key area. Suppose station D and G fail, and they are marked with ⊗ in the figure. Table 6 shows the result of simulation, in which the coverage area of RSRP >-115dbm is 98.9%, and that of SINR >-3 dB is 94.8%, the results are similar to those in Table 4 without failure. The results show that due to the existence of disaster tolerant base station, the field strength and signal quality in the coverage area do not change significantly, which meets the coverage requirements of the power network and achieves the purpose of disaster recovery.

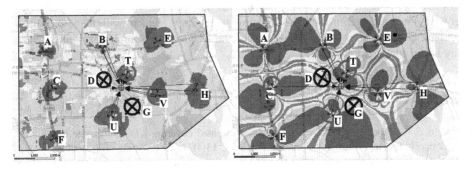

Fig. 7. Simulation (RSRP & SINR) of coverage with eNodeB failure.

Table 6. Results of the coverage simulation.

RSRP (dBm)	Area of coverage (km²)	Fraction of coverage (%)	SINR (dB)	Area of coverage (km²)	Fraction of coverage (%)
≥ -75	8.0613	13.5	≥ 9	23.3397	39.2
≥ -95	49.6422	83.4	≥ 3	42.2874	71
≥ -115	58.8942	98.9	≥ -3	56.4336	94.8

Table 7 shows the static simulation results of user UE_i in the same location, where RSRP = −101.99, SINR = 3.95, it shows that users can connect to the network.

Table 7. Results of the UEi single point simulation.

The strongest cell	The distance of propagation (m)	Path loss (dB)	SINR (dB)	RSRP (dBm)
D/T merged cell	670 (T)	139.5	3.95	−101.99
U/G merged cell	1459 (U)	158	–	−120.49
V	1718	169.8	–	−133.37

5 Conclusion

In this paper, a high reliability planning method for power wireless private networks with low self-interference is proposed based on SFN technology. It improves the survival of the user's service by using overlapping coverage of base station signals, and the overlapping cells are merged to avoid the same frequency interference. By optimizing the deployment of the organization of the base station, in the case of the same number of base stations, the average inter station distance of overlapping coverage is increased, and the network reliability is improved on the premise of ensuring network performance. The scheme solves the mutual interference of the same frequency between the base stations of the existing technology, which will lead to mutual interference, and it also solves problems of the frequency resource constraints which may be unable to implement.

References

1. Sun, S.W., Chen, Y.: Research on business-oriented covering LTE power wireless private network. Electr. Power Inf. Commun. Technol. **13**(4), 6–10 (2015)
2. Yao, J.M.: Random access technology of electric dedicated LTE network based on power priority. Autom. Electr. Power Syst. **40**(10), 127–131 (2016)

3. Cao, J.P., Liu, J.M., Li, X.Z.: A power wireless broadband technology scheme for smart power distribution and utilization network. Autom. Electr. Power Syst. **37**(11), 76–80 (2013)
4. Yu, J., Liu, J.S., Cai, S.L.: Performance simulation on TD-LTE electric power wireless private network. Guangdong Electr. Power **30**(1), 39–45 (2017)
5. Cao, J.P., Liu, J.M.: A two-stage double-threshold local spectrum sensing algorithm research for the power private communication network. In: Proceedings of the CSEE, vol. 35, no. 10, pp 2471–2479 (2015)
6. Yan, J.M., Xu, J.B., Ni, M., et al.: Impact of communication system interruption on power system wide area protection and control system. Autom. Electr. Power Syst. **40**(5), 17–24 (2016)
7. Sun, W., Lu, W., Li, Q.Y., et al.: Reliability confidence interval prediction for communication link of wireless sensor network in smart grid. Autom. Electr. Power Syst. **41**(4), 29–34 (2017)
8. Han, J.H., Duan, Z.L.: Optimal base station selection based on dynamic programming for reprogramming in mine wireless network. J. Commun. **38**(3), 7–15 (2017)
9. Hamza, A.S., Khalifa, S.S., Hamza, H.S., et al.: A survey on inter-cell interference coordination techniques in OFDMA based cellular networks. IEEE Commun. Surv. Tutor. **15**(4), 1642–1670 (2013)
10. Bjomson, E., Zakhour, R., et al.: Cooperative multicell precoding: rare region characterization and distributed strategies with instantaneous and statistical CSI. IEEE Trans. Sig. Process. **58**(8), 4298–4310 (2010)
11. Garcia, V., Zhou, Y., Shi, J.: Coordinated multipoint transmission in dense cellular networks with user-centric adaptive clustering. IEEE Trans. Wirel. Commun. **13**(8), 4297–4308 (2014)
12. Shi, Y., Zhang, J., Letaief, K.B., et al.: Large-scale convex optimization for ultra-dense Cloud-RAN. IEEE Wirel. Commun. **22**(3), 84–91 (2015)
13. George, K.: Green network planning of single frequency networks. IEEE Trans. Broadcast. **56**(4), 541–550 (2010)
14. Chen, H., Zhong, X., Wang, J.: Optimal deployment of assisting cells for multimedia push in single frequency network. J. Commun. Netw. **19**(2), 114–123 (2017)
15. GPP. TS 36.201 LTE physical layer: General description. 3GPP Technical Specification (2017)
16. Li, C., Wen, C., Bin, W., Xin, Z.: System-level simulation methodology and platform for mobile cellular systems. IEEE Commun. Mag. **49**(7), 148–155 (2011)

Research on Service Support Ability of Power Wireless Private Network

Yu Chen[(✉)], Kun Liu, and Ziqian Zhang

NARI Group Corporation/State Grid Electric Power Research Institute, Nanjing,
China
Chenyu1@sgepri.sgcc.com.cn

Abstract. In view of the problems of electric power wireless communication
and to serve the power consumer better, on the basis of the basic principles of
TD-LTE's network structure, traffic model of power service is analyzed in
detail, and in the actual case, through the data processing method and comparison analysis method, the technical parameters, theoretical analysis and field
test results of 1.8 G and 230 M LTE systems are compared, and the ability of
power wireless private network to support power service is verified. The analysis and testing provide a technology support for electric power communication
access network construction and lays the foundations for popularization and
application of LTE power wireless private network.

Keywords: TD-LTE · Wireless private network · Hybrid networking · Traffic
model · Bandwidth analysis

1 Introduction

With the development of the construction of smart grid, the types of power communication services are becoming more and more abundant, network coverage and construction scale are expanding year by year [1–3]. In order to support the core tasks and
objectives of smart grid construction, it is necessary to construct a terminal access
network that has a wide access and flexibility [4, 5].

Fiber access network has many advantages, such as high bandwidth, anti-
interference, anti-damage, security, reliability and so on. It is the best access method of
user experience [6]. However, there are many problems in fiber-optic access network,
such as the difficulty of laying, the long construction period, the long time of fault
recovery, the high cost of investment, and so on, which can not meet the needs of mass
access or mobile access [7]. Wireless technology system becomes a necessary sup-
plement to optical fiber access.

At present, we mainly use the way of public network leasing to realize [8, 9], this
approach has the following problems, one is that many intranet service applications can
not be extended to the wireless terminal of the outer network, the second is that
applications with high bandwidth requirements, such as pictures and videos, will
generate expensive traffic costs, the third is restricted by the national network information security factors, video surveillance and other services can not access the
intranet, there is a lot of inconvenience in the application of the business. In addition,

© Springer Nature Singapore Pte Ltd. 2020
Y. Tian et al. (Eds.): ICBDS 2019, CCIS 1210, pp. 330–339, 2020.
https://doi.org/10.1007/978-981-15-7530-3_25

with the development of clean energy substitution and electric energy substitution, distributed photovoltaic, electric vehicle charging piles and other business will be explosive growth [10, 11]. Power wireless private network is one of the most important technologies to realize access and acquisition of power network terminal services, therefore, more and more attention has been paid to the establishment of power wireless communication broadband private network based on special authorized frequency band [12, 13]. In order to ensure that the construction of power wireless private network can meet the current and even future needs of power business applications, in this paper, the traffic model of electric power business is obtained at the present stage and on this basis, the power service support capability of power wireless special network is analyzed and verified.

2   Architecture of Power Wireless Private Network

2.1   Base Station

The base station is generally located in the power supply building [14], including network management platform, monitoring center, data center, etc. The network management platform is mainly responsible for network state monitoring, fault diagnosis and alarm. At the same time, it can integrate the existing electric power information management, and form a unified dispatching command system on the basis of various multimedia means and GIS (Geographic Information System) technology, mainly including dispatching command center, field emergency command and dispatch system, videophone scheduling system and monitoring system.

2.2   Core Network

The core network is directly connected to the base station [15]. It mainly provides the connection for the user, manages the user and carries the service, including responsible for terminal authentication, terminal IP address management, mobility management, etc. The core network of the power wireless private network system can provide basic services including distribution automation, load management, power information collection, emergency repair and maintenance, dispatching command and visual management of mobile assets, etc.

2.3   Terminal

Terminal equipment module is the general name of remote terminal modules such as user data acquisition, power monitoring and dispatching, power video transmission, etc. It is the executive unit of information collection and monitoring and dispatching in Internet of things terminal, such as collector, concentrator, control switch and so on. The wireless terminal (also referred to as the UE) and the base station are air interfaces that provide communication between the terminal device and the base station.

3 Bandwidth Analysis

We use Okrmuram-Hata model to calculate the coverage ability of power wireless private network system. The model is established according to the measured data, which provides complete data and is widely used in 150–1920 MHz frequency band. The basic transmission loss formulas of Okumuram-Hata model in different propagation environments are as follows

$$
\begin{aligned}
\Delta = {} & 69.55 + 26.16 \times \log_{10}(f_c) - 13.82 \times \log_{10}(h_t) + \\
& (44.9 - 6.55 \times \log_{10}(h_t)) \times \log_{10}(d) - \\
& ((1.1 \times \log_{10}(f_c) - 0.7) \times h_r - 1.56 \times \log_{10}(f_c) + 0.8) + C
\end{aligned} \tag{1}
$$

where f_c is the working frequency, h_t is the effective antenna height transmitted by the base station, h_r is the effective antenna height received by the terminal, and d is the overlay distance, and C is the environmental compensation factor, the value is as follows

$$
\begin{cases}
city: & C = 0 \\
suburbs: & C = -2 \times \left(\log_{10}(f_c/28)\right)^2 - 5.4
\end{cases} \tag{2}
$$

When the path loss is achieved, the link budget is then analyzed. Assume that the transmission power of the signal is p (dBm), Then the sensitivity of the receiver is $p - \Delta$ (dBm). If the bandwidth of the signal is π (dB-Hz), the noise coefficient of the receiver is ζ (dB), and the corresponding noise power of the receiver is $\pi + N_0 + \zeta$ (dBm), where N_0 (dBm/Hz) denotes the noise power spectral density (-174 dBm/Hz). It is known that the minimum receiving SNR of the receiver is $\Gamma = (p - \Delta) - (\pi + N_0 + \zeta)$, which is also the minimum SNR that requires the receiving device to be able to work.

Since power infrastructure mainly depends on the uplink data transmission, the capacity of uplink is analyzed here. In the uplink, the uplink signal transmitted by the user device can take up all of its transmit power, $p = P_{UL}$. The corresponding receiving SNR on the receiving end is

$$
\Gamma = (P_{UL} - \Delta) - (\pi + N_0 + \zeta) \tag{3}
$$

And then use the modified Shannon formula

$$
r = \pi \cdot \log_2(1 + \beta \cdot \Gamma) \text{ (bit/s)} \tag{4}
$$

The calculation of the channel capacity is carried out, where β is the compensation parameter used to compensate for the theoretical formula and the actual situation.

To simplify the analysis, a cell is divided into three regions according to SNR, as shown in Fig. 1. The three regions are 20 dB regions with SNR above 20 dB, 10 dB region with SNR between 10 dB and 20 dB, and 0 dB region with SNR between 0 dB and 10 dB. In urban environment, the corresponding radius of the three regions are

0.75 km, 1.45 km and 2.8 km, respectively. In the suburban environment, the radius of the three regions are 1.65 km, 3.2 km and 6.1 km respectively. The area percentage and spectral efficiency of each region are given by simulation, as shown in Table 2.

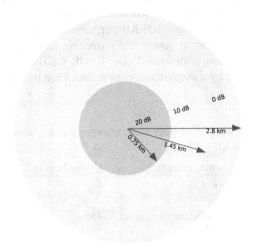

Fig. 1. Plot diagram of district division

The average transmission rate per RB can be expressed as

$$\bar{r} = \sum_{n=1}^{3} r_n b \alpha_n = r_1 b \alpha_1 + r_2 b \alpha_2 + r_3 b \alpha_3 \text{ (bits/RB)} \tag{5}$$

$b=144$ is the number of available resources per RB, r_i is the spectral efficiency of the region in Table 1, and α_i is the area percentage of the region in Table 1. Bring the data from Table 1 to get the average number of bits transmitted by a single RB $\bar{r} \approx 200$ bits/RB. It is worth noting that the average rate is basically the same because the percentage of area between the city and the suburb is similar. The transmission rates that each RB can support can be represented as

Table 1. Area percentage and spectral efficiency of each region within the cell

	Area percentage %		Spectral efficiency bits/s/Hz
20 dB	$\alpha_1 =$	$\begin{cases} 7.2, & urban \\ 7.3, & \text{suburban} \end{cases}$	$r_1 = 4.9$
10 dB	$\alpha_2 =$	$\begin{cases} 19.6, & urban \\ 20, & suburban \end{cases}$	$r_2 = 2.5$
0 dB	$\alpha_3 =$	$\begin{cases} 73.2, & city \\ 72.7, & suburban \end{cases}$	$r_3 = 0.82$

$$\bar{r} = 200 \times 0.6/0.001 = 120 \text{ kbps} \tag{6}$$

Table 2 shows the number of power terminals to be accommodated in each cell by 2020 and the requirements of different power infrastructure services for wireless communication transmission rates. For wireless meter reading, there are currently two solutions, one is that 1 poll per day, 300 KB per poll, including positive and negative active power, voltage and current power, daily freezing data, etc., and another is that 1 h 1 poll, 28 kB each time, additional 1 day 1 poll, 8 KB each time. For cities, an average of 92 m are hung by a single concentrator, and 53 m by a single concentrator in suburban areas.

Table 2. The demand of wireless communication rate for power basic service

Type of traffic	Single terminal transmission rate	Number of terminals in cell	Total rate demand (kbps)
92 m hanging under concentrator	300 KB/day	485	13.5
92 m hanging under concentrator	28 KB/hour + 8 KB/day	485	30.5
53 m hanging under concentrator	182 KB/day	763	12.85
53 m hanging under concentrator	20 KB/hour + 6 KB/day	763	34.33
Load control	6 MB/month	Urban: 365 Suburban: 277	Urban: 6.8 Suburban: 5.1
Distribution automation	800 MB/month	Urban: 83 Suburban: 84	Urban: 205 Suburban: 207
Distributed photovoltaic	100 MB/month	Urban: 10 Suburban: 250	Urban: 3.1 Suburban: 77.1
Charging pile	150 MB/month	Urban: 150 Suburban: 235	Urban: 69.5 Suburban: 108.8

According to Table 2, these four types of basic power services require approximately 315 kbps (cities) and 433 kbps (suburbs) for transmission rates, as a result, at least 3 RBs and 4 RBs need to be reserved for urban and suburban areas, respectively. Considering the overhead of uplink control channel, at least 1.4 MHz bandwidth is required for TD-LTE system, which is exactly the minimum bandwidth of existing LTE system.

It can be seen from Table 2 that power distribution automation requires the highest transmission rate in four types of services. But with the progress of science and technology, the collection of electricity information will become particularly important. In general, the minimum bandwidth requirement for a power wireless private network is 1.4 MHz if only basic power services are considered. When the user information acquisition interval is reduced to 5 min, the minimum bandwidth is 3 MHz. When it is necessary to transmit the data of distribution automation with high precision, the minimum bandwidth is 5 MHz. The minimum bandwidth required to support other extended services, such as video conferencing, emergency repair, etc., is 10 MHz.

4 Road Survey

4.1 Test Location Selection

The total area of the test area is 927.68 km^2. At present, the area has been fully covered by 230 M wireless private network, and 14 base stations have been set up. Through careful planning, and considering the system capacity, coverage and other problems, the average radius of the base station is set to 4.8 km.

The contrast test of LTE1.8 G and 230 M is within the 5 km coverage radius of a base station. A representative wireless communication scene is selected for field measurement, and the throughput, delay and diffraction capability are compared and tested. In the north, a variety of sheltered environments, such as visual field transmission, buildings, bridges and trees, were selected for community coverage testing.

4.2 Relationship Between Distance and Throughput

The uplink transmit rate can reach 10 Mbps in the 1.8 G wireless private network when the distance between the base station and test point is about 2 km, and the downlink transmit rate can reach 12.5 Mbps. It can support the application of video conference. The uplink transmit rate can reach 2 Mbps when the distance between the base station and test point is about 3.5 km, and the downlink transmit rate can reach 5 Mbps. It can support the application of power data monitoring. The uplink transmit rate can reach 0.5 Mbps when the distance between the base station and test point is about 5 km, and the downlink transmit rate can reach 0.8 Mbps. It can support the application of power data monitoring (Figs. 2 and 3).

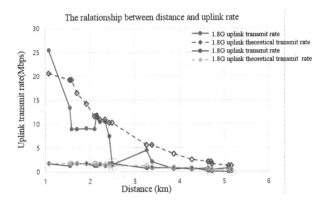

Fig. 2. Comparative diagram of the relationship between test distance and uplink rate

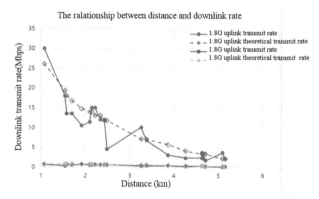

Fig. 3. Comparative diagram of the relationship between test distance and downlink rate

The uplink transmit rate can reach 1.5 Mbps in the 230 M wireless private network when the distance between the base station and test point is about 2 km, and the downlink transmit rate can reach 0.5 Mbps. The uplink transmit rate can reach 800 kbps when the distance between the base station and test point is about 3.5 km, and the downlink transmit rate can reach 300 kbps. It can support the application of power data monitoring.

4.3 Relationship Between Distance and Delay

The bidirectional average delay of 1.8 G is within 50 ms, and the packet loss rate is "0". one-way transmission delay of 230 M is about 140 ms (Fig. 4).

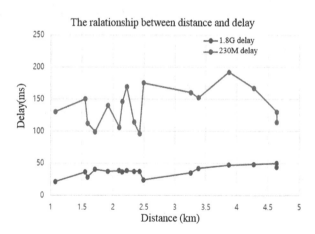

Fig. 4. Comparative diagram of the relationship between test distance and delay

4.4   Relationship Between Distance and Traffic Support Capability

By comparing the technical parameters of 1.8 G and 230 M, the theoretical analysis and field test results show that, in addition to being slightly superior to the former in terms of cell coverage radius, the 230 M system is much weaker than the 1.8 G system in terms of throughput, delay, service support capability, and the smoothness of subsequent technology evolution, and can only support static state. Small amount of basic power business. Therefore, 1.8 G is more suitable for urban area, and 230 M has a certain coverage advantage in suburbs and rural areas, which is about 1.6 times of 1.8 GHz, suitable for the construction of special network of small granular area with fewer service terminals (Figs. 5 and 6).

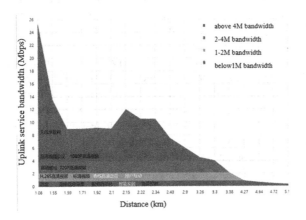

Fig. 5. Distance and traffic support capability diagram of 1.8 G

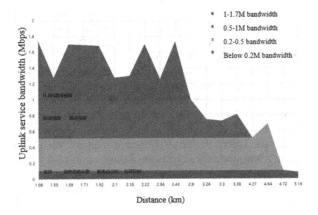

Fig. 6. Distance and business support capability diagram of 230 M

In addition, through theoretical simulation analysis, we can see that the minimum bandwidth of power wireless private network is 1.4 MHz under the condition of considering only the basic power services. When the information collection interval is reduced to 5 min, the minimum bandwidth is 3 MHz. The minimum bandwidth required is 5 MHz when high precision data transmission is required for distribution automation, and 10 MHz is the minimum bandwidth required to support other extended services, such as videoconferencing, emergency repair, etc.

5 Conclusion

On the basis of the basic principle of TD-LTE network structure, this paper analyzes the traffic model, and takes the actual case as the background, the technical parameters of 1.8 G and 230 M system are compared by data processing method and comparative analysis method. The theoretical analysis and test results verify the ability of power wireless private network to support power service. By comparing the technical parameters of 1.8 G and 230 M, the theoretical analysis and test results show that, in addition to being slightly superior to the former in terms of cell coverage radius, the 230 M system is much weaker than the 1.8 G system in terms of throughput, delay, service support capability and so on. The analysis and test provide technical support for the unified construction of power terminal communication access network and lay a solid foundation for the popularization and application of LTE power wireless private network.

References

1. Yao, J.M.: Random access technology of electric dedicated LTE network based on power priority. Autom. Electr. Power Syst. **40**(10), 127–131 (2016)
2. Cao, J.P., Liu, J.M., Li, X.Z.: A power wireless broadband technology scheme for smart power distribution and utilization network. Autom. Electr. Power Syst. **37**(11), 76–80 (2013)
3. Yu, J., Liu, J.S., Cai, S.L.: Performance simulation on TD-LTE electric power wireless private network. Guangdong Electr. Power **30**(1), 39–45 (2017)
4. Sun, S.W., Chen, Y.: Research on LTE power wireless private network for service coverage. Electr. Power Inf. Commun. Technol. **13**(4), 6–10 (2015)
5. Yu, J., Liu, J.S., Cai, S.L.: Research on LTE wireless network planning in electric power system. Electr. Power Inf. Commun. Technol. **10**(2), 7–11 (2016)
6. Gao, X., Zhu, J., Chen, Y.: Research on multi-services bearing solution of LTE power wireless private network. Electr. Power Inf. Commun. Technol. **12**(12), 26–29 (2014)
7. Liu, J.C., Quan, H.D.: RF interference cancellation based on multi-tap delay and orthogonal combination in multipath channel. J. Electron. Inf. Technol. **39**(3), 654–661 (2017)
8. Zhang, L.J., Liu, Z.H., Zhang, H.B.: Wireless secure enhancement with cooperative jamming. J. Commun. **38**(2), 183–195 (2017)
9. Wang, J., Zhao, H.Z., Tang, Y.X.: Quick adaptive self-interference cancellation at RF domain in full duplex systems. J. Univ. Electron. Sci. Technol. China **46**(4), 505–512 (2017)

10. Cao, J.P., Liu, J.M.: A two-stage double-threshold local spectrum sensing algorithm research for the power private communication network. In: Proceedings of the CSEE, vol. 35, no. 10, pp. 2471–2479 (2015)
11. Li, B.L., Zhou, J., Ren, X.H.: Research on key issues of TD-LTE network optimization. Telecom Eng. Tech. Stand. 1, 57–61 (2015)
12. Gesbert, D., Shafi, M., Smith, P., Shiu, D., Naguib, A.: From theory to practice: an overview of MIMO space-time coded wireless systems. IEEE J. Sel. Areas Commun. 21, 281–302 (2004). Special Issue on MIMO systems, guest edited by the authors
13. He, S., Huang, Y., Yang, L., et al.: Coordinated multiuser procoding for maximizing weighted sum energy efficiency. IEEE Trans. Sig. Process. 62(3), 741–751 (2014)
14. Wu, J., Zhang, Y., Zukerman, M., et al.: Energy-efficient base-stations sleep-mode techniques in green cellular networks: a survey. IEEE Commun. Surv. Tutor. 17(2), 803–826 (2015)
15. Garcia, V., Zhou, Y., Shi, J.: Coordinated multipoint transmission in dense cellular networks with user-centric adaptive clustering. IEEE Trans. Wirel. Commun. 13(8), 4297–4308 (2014)

A Method of UML Sequence Diagram Verification Based on a Graph Grammar

Zhan Shi[1], Chenrong Huang[1($\boxtimes$)], Xiaoqin Zeng[2], Jiande Zhang[1],
Lei Han[1], and Ying Qian[1]

[1] School of Computer Engineering, Nanjing Institute of Technology,
Nanjing, China
chenrong_h@qq.com
[2] Institute of Intelligence Science and Technology, Hohai University,
Nanjing 211100, China

Abstract. With the increasing scale and complexity of software, the description of software structure plays a more and more important role. In order to ensure the quality of the software and improve the reliability of the software, it is a feasible way to combine the relevant parts of the software structure with the formal methods. In this paper, based on an existing context-sensitive temporal graph grammar, the formal method for UML sequence diagrams is proposed. Then, new productions are presented, which could be used to verify and analyze the temporal semantics in UML sequence diagrams. Finally, a case study of ATM withdrawal operation is provided to show how the formal method works.

Keywords: UML · Sequence diagram · Graph grammar · TEGG

1 Introduction

The integration and complexity of computer software systems are continuously improving, and the concurrency and interactivity of these systems are also continuously enhanced, which makes software architecture plays an important role in describing software systems. Software architecture is often represented by means of multiple model views. Modelling is the core of any software architecture.

There are many architecture description languages (ADLs), such as Rapide [1], Wright [2], xADL3.0 [3], ACME [4], UniCon [5], ABC/ADL [6], and so on, to specify the software architecture. Nowadays, UML (Unified Modeling Language) is the most popular language for object-oriented paradigm which recognized by the Object Management Group to specity, visualize, construct, and model software applications [7, 8].

However, most of the proposed ADLs with a textual format and self-defined graphic notations (including UML) are based on informal diagrams, which lacks precise formal descriptions and semantic definitions. So, it is difficult to make models' consistency, and fail to verify the software architectures. Moreover, the difficulty and cost of later maintenance of the system is also increased because of the inability to detect potential problems early in the system design.

© Springer Nature Singapore Pte Ltd. 2020
Y. Tian et al. (Eds.): ICBDS 2019, CCIS 1210, pp. 340–351, 2020.
https://doi.org/10.1007/978-981-15-7530-3_26

As a strict mathematical description, the formal modelling method can not only precisely describe the requirements of the system, but also formally verify the system. This feature of the formal modelling method has made it widely used in all stages of system development.

At present, there is a lot of research work on the formal verification of UML diagrams. Schafer et al. [9] presented a prototype tool to support verification of the objects interactions in UML diagrams. In [10], the authors provided a transformation approach of UML Statechart and Communication diagrams to Colored Petri nets. A MCC+ tool was introduced in [11] and [12] to verify consistencies in UML models.

As a useful formalism tool, graph grammars provide a rigorous but intuitive way to specify visual languages. In 1997, Rekers and Schürr [13] proposed the Layered

Graph Grammar (LGG) for specifying visual languages. Its parsing algorithm is complicated, and the parsing algorithm has exponential time complexity. In order to solve the problems faced by LGG, Zhang et al. [14] proposed another contextsensitive grammar, Reserved Graph Grammar (RGG). In 2008, Zeng et al. [15] proposed another contextsensitive graph grammar formalism, called Edge-based

Graph Grammar (EGG). The main advantage of the EGG over the LGG is its simplified context expression by using an edge instead of a node, and that over the RGG is its simplified node structure with only one level instead of two levels. Based on EGG, a new attempt of transformation between BPMN and BPEL [16] was provided, which presented mapping steps and a parsing algorithm.

There are also many studies using the graph grammar for software design and development. In [17] and [18], authors proposes a formal definition for this previously proposed translation, using graph grammars.

However, most of existing graph grammars could be difficult to meet the time-related requirements. So, there is a new context-sensitive graph grammar formalism called the Temporal Edge-based Graph Grammar (TEGG) proposed in [19]. TEGG introduces some temporal mechanisms to grammatical specifications, productions, operations and so on in order to tackle time-related issues. In this paper, based on the TEGG, a formal method of UML sequence diagrams is proposed. Then, new productions are provided, which could be used to verify and analyze the temporal semantics in UML sequence diagrams.

The rest of the paper is organized as follows. Section 2 introduces some basic definitions of the TEGG as the preliminaries to Sect. 3, which presents a formal method based on the TEGG to verify and analyze the temporal semantics in UML sequence diagrams. Section 4 explains a case study on how to realize our purpose by using the formal method. Finally, Sect. 5 concludes the whole paper.

2 Preliminaries

The TEGG is based on the EGG, while the former includes a temporal mechanism to deal with time-related issues. In this way, the TEGG not only has certain features of the EGG, but also includes a set of temporal attributes for each node and edge in graphs, and some time-related productions, called T-productions, to operate on the attributes, and so on. So, the TEGG has the ability to tackle time-related requirements in real applications, and to check the structural correctness of this graph. Below are some formal definitions of the TEGG, which are fundamental to the discussion in the next section.

Definition 2.1. *A node n on a label set L_n is defined as a two-tuple, denoted as $n \equiv (lab, Natts)$, where*

- *L_n can be expressed as $L_n = T \cup \overline{T}$ which is a set of node labels, where T represents a label set of N_T, $\overline{T}$ represents a label set of N_N, N_T represents a set of terminal nodes and N_N represents a set of non-terminal nodes;*
- *$lab \in L_n$, representing the label of n;*
- *Natts is a set of temporal attributes owned by node n, while $Natts = Nka \cup \overline{Nka}$ with $Nka = \{statusflag\}$ being a set of key temporal attributes of n, and $\overline{Nka}$ a set of non-key temporal attributes of n.*

The above definition introduces the Natts for handling temporal semantics. Different applications should include the key temporal attribute of all nodes. For example, to deal with the UML sequence diagram, there is the statusflag attribute with the values WAITING, WORKING, or COMPLETED. According to these three values of statusflag, node n could have one of the following statuses:

$n.Natts.statusflag = WAITING$, that is to say, n is in the waiting status;
$n.Natts.statusflag = WORKING$, that is to say, n is in the working status;
$n.Natts.statusflag = COMPLETED$, that is to say, n is in the completed status.

To intuitively express the status of a node in a TEGG graph, the following graphical notations of a solid triangle or solid circle are used, which are shown in Fig. 1. The notations are placed in the upper right of a node.

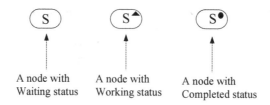

A node with   A node with   A node with
Waiting status   Working status   Completed status

Fig. 1. A Nodes with waiting, working, and completed statuses.

Of course, different applications may require time-related attributes in the $\overline{Nka}$ of the Natts. For example, the attributes starttime and durationtime need to be introduced into each node in Fig. 1, which represent the start and duration time of an activity respectively.

Definition 2.2. *An edge e on a label set L_e is defined as a four-tuple, denoted as $e \equiv (lab, n_s, n_t, Eatts)$, where*

- *L_e is a set of edge labels;*
- *$lab \in L_e$, representing the label of e;*

- n_s *is a node defined in Definition* 3.1, *representing the source node of e;*
- n_t *is a node defined in Definition* 3.1, *representing the target node of e;*
- *Eatts is a set of attributes owned by edge e, while Eatts* $= Eka \cup \overline{Eka}$ *with Eka* $=$ *{edgeflag} being a set of temporal attribute of an edge e, called key attributes of e, and* $\overline{Eka}$ *being a set of attributes which could have finite or infinite values, called non-key attributes of e.*

The Eatts is an attributes' set which can be divided into two sets, and the attributes in these two sets can be varied for different applications. In general, edges with different labels have different non-key attributes.

To intuitively express an edge with the temporal attribute edgeflag in a TEGG graph, the following lines with different colors are used, which are shown in Fig. 2.

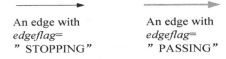

An edge with
edgeflag=
" STOPPING "

An edge with
edgeflag=
" PASSING "

Fig. 2. Edges with different values of the edgeflag. (Color figure online)

Definition 2.3. *A temporal graph TG on a label set L is defined as a six-tuple, denoted as* $TG \equiv (N, E, CurrentTime, l, p, q)$, *where*

- *N is a set of nodes defined in Definition* 2.1, *and* $N = N_T \cup N_N$;
- *E is a set of edges defined in Definition* 2.2;
- *CurrentTime is a self-increasing global variable and can be changed by some operations in the productions;*
- $l : N \cup E \rightarrow L$ *is a mapping from N and E to L, and L can be expressed as* $L = L_n \cup L_e$;
- $p : E \rightarrow N$ *is a mapping from E to N, indicating the source node of an edge;*
- $q : E \rightarrow N$ *is a mapping from E to N, indicating the target node of an edge.*

To show the CurrentTime in a temporal graph, a special node can be used, which is given in Fig. 3. The node is independently placed in a graph and CurrentTime is assigned to it as an attribute.

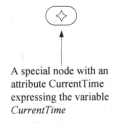

A special node with an
attribute CurrentTime
expressing the variable
CurrentTime

Fig. 3. A special node to express the variable current time.

Usually, there are two typical grammatical operations that have reverse functions. One is called L-application (deduction) and the other is called R-application (reduction). More detailed information about the content of the TEGG is available in the literature [19].

3   A Formal Method Based on the TEGG

The UML model abstractly defines the system according to the static properties and dynamic behavior of the system. Static properties describe the inherent information of objects contained in the UML models, as well as implicit or explicit relationships between different objects. Dynamic behavior describes the mechanisms for communicating and interacting between objects in order to complete system functions.

3.1   Formal Definitions of UML Sequence Diagrams

Sequence diagrams of UML are diagram that illustrate how objects in software architecture interact with each other. These diagrams are two-dimension, while the horizontal direction represents the transmission of information between objects, and the longitudinal direction describes the life time of the object.

In order to use the TEGG to analyze the UML diagrams, this section first introduces the formal definitions of elements in the UML sequence diagrams.

Definition 3.1. *A node n on a label set L_n is defined as a four-tuple, denoted as $n \equiv (id, lab, type, Natts)$, where*

- *L_n is the same as that defined in Definition 2.1;*
- *$id \in \{0, 1, 2, \ldots k\}$, representing the identifier of n, is used to distinguish other nodes;*
- *$lab \in L_n$, representing the label of n;*
- *type, representing which category of node this node belongs to, while type = $\{Object, Event, Frag\_Connection\}$, these values are corresponding to a object node, an event, and a fragment in UML sequence diagrams respectively;*
- *Natts is the same as that defined in Definition 2.1.*

As introduced in the second section, the Natts of a node n for handling temporal semantics. To deal with UML sequence diagrams, there is the statusflag attribute with the values WAITING, WORKING, or COMPLETED.

Of course, different applications may require other attributes in the $\overline{Nka}$ of the Natts. For a object node, an event, and a fragment in UML sequence diagrams, there are different attributes in the $\overline{Nka}$. First of all, for a object, there is $\overline{Nka} = \{starttime, durationtime\}$ of its corresponding node, which represent the start and duration time of this object respectively. The meaning of these two attributes is the same in the following. Second, for an event, there is $\overline{Nka} = \{serial\_no, is\_belong\_fregment, fregment\_id, starttime, durationtime\}$ of its corresponding node. Finally, for a fragment, there is $\overline{Nka} = \{serial\_no, starttime, durationtime\}$ of its corresponding node, while the attribute serial_no indicates the serial number of this node.

A unique identifier is given for each node with a id, as mentioned in Definition 3.1. Similar to the TEGG graph, if a node with an id is also expressed as n_i, the attribute att in the set Nka of the node can be denoted as $n_i.Nka.att$, or $n_i.Natts.att$, while the notation $n_i.lab$ represents the label.

Definition 3.2. *An edge e on a label set L_e is defined as a six-tuple, denoted as $e \equiv (id, lab, type, n_s, n_t, Eatts)$, where*

- *L_e is the same as that defined in Definition 2.1;*
- *$id \in \{0, 1, 2, \ldots k\}$, representing the identifier of e, is used to distinguish other edges;*
- *$lab \in L_e$, representing the label of e;*
- *type, representing which category of edges this edge belongs to, while $type = \{Controlflow, Messageflow\}$, these values are corresponding to a control edge, and a message in UML sequence diagrams respectively;*
- *n_s is a node defined in Definition 3.1, representing the source node of e;*
- *n_t is a node defined in Definition 3.1, representing the target node of e;*
- *Eatts is the same as that defined in Definition 2.2.*

Usually, the set type may include multiple elements and each element indicates each of edge types in a TEGG graph. This means edges have strong expressive power.

For the UML sequence diagrams involved in this paper, the non-key attribute "cond" is assigned to each edge, so $\overline{Eka} = \{cond\}$. This attribute represents the conditions of a control flow, or constraints of a message in UML sequence diagrams.

Definition 3.3. *A uml-sequence-attributed graph USAG on a label set L is defined as a five-tuple, denoted as $USAG \equiv (N, E, l, p, q)$, where*

- *N is a set of nodes defined in Definition 3.1, and $N = N_T \cup N_N$ like that in Definition 2.1;*
- *E is a set of edges defined in Definition 3.2;*
- *L, l, p, and q are the same as those defined in Definition 2.3.*

Definition 3.4. *A uml-sequence-attributed graph with dangling edges $\overline{USAG}$ on a label set L is defined as a seven-tuple, denoted as $\overline{USAG} \equiv (N, \hat{E}, M, l, \overline{p}, \overline{q}, m)$, where*

- *N, L, and l are the same as those defined in Definition 3.3;*
- *$\hat{E}$ is a set of edges, which can be expressed as $\hat{E} = E \cup \overline{E}$, where E is the same as that in Definition 3.2 and $\overline{E} = \overrightarrow{E} \cup \overleftarrow{E}$ is a set of dangling edges. $\overrightarrow{E}$ represents a set of edges which only have source nodes, while $\overleftarrow{E}$ represents a set of edges which only have target nodes;*
- *M is a unique marks' set of $\overline{E}$, also called marks;*

- $\bar{p} : (E \cup \overrightarrow{E}) \to N$ is a mapping for source nodes of an edge;
- $\bar{q} : (E \cup \overleftarrow{E}) \to N$ is a mapping for target nodes of an edge;
- $m : \overline{E} \to M$ is an injective mapping from $\overline{E}$ to M, indicating the mark of a dangling edge.

Definition 3.5. *Two uml-sequence-attributed graphs with dangling edges $\overline{USAG}_1$ and $\overline{USAG}_2$ are isomorphic, denoted as $\overline{USAG}_1 \approx \overline{USAG}_2$, if and only if there exist two bijective mappings $f_N : \overline{USAG}_1.N \leftrightarrow \overline{USAG}_2.N$ and $f_E : \overline{USAG}_1.\hat{E} \leftrightarrow \overline{USAG}_2.\hat{E}$, and the following conditions are satisfied:*

$$\forall n \forall att((n \in \overline{USAG}_1.N) \to (n.type = (f_N(n)).type \wedge \\ ((att \in n.Nka) \to (n.Nka.att = (f_N(n)).Nka.att)))$$;

$$\forall e \forall att((e \in \overline{USAG}_1.\hat{E}) \to (e.lab = (f_E(e)).type) \wedge \\ (\overline{USAG}_2.\bar{p}(f_E(e)) = f_N(\overline{USAG}_1.\bar{p}(e))) \wedge \\ (\overline{USAG}_2.\bar{q}(f_E(e)) = f_N(\overline{USAG}_1.\bar{q}(e))) \wedge \\ ((att \in e.Eka) \to (e.Eka.att = (f_E(e)).Eka.att)))$$.

Definition 3.6. *A uml-sequence graph USG on a label set L is defined as a six-tuple, denoted as $USG \equiv (N, E, CurrentTime, l, p, q)$, where*

- *N,E,L, l, p, and q are the same as those defined in Definition 3.3;*
- *CurrentTime is the same as the defined in Definition 2.3.*

3.2 Formal Definition of Productions

In order to check the structural correctness and analyze the temporal semantics of a graph, there are two types of productions in TEGG. One is called E-production, which is similar to productions in the EGG for dealing with the structural aspect. While the other is called T-production, which only deals with the temporal aspect.

To verify the UML sequence diagrams from the sequence aspect, T-productions in the TEGG are used in this section. According to the definition of T-productions, they consist of not only the left and right graphs, but also Con and Fun. In Fig. 4, it shows T-productions that deal with uml-sequence graphs.

The function Source Node (Edge e) can return all the source nodes of an edge e. There are some notations in T-productions that need to be further explained. A notation * is used to indicate an arbitrary natural number. So, an edge with * means no edge or several edges. In addition, a notation {} containing a set of marks is employed to indicate dangling edges' marks.

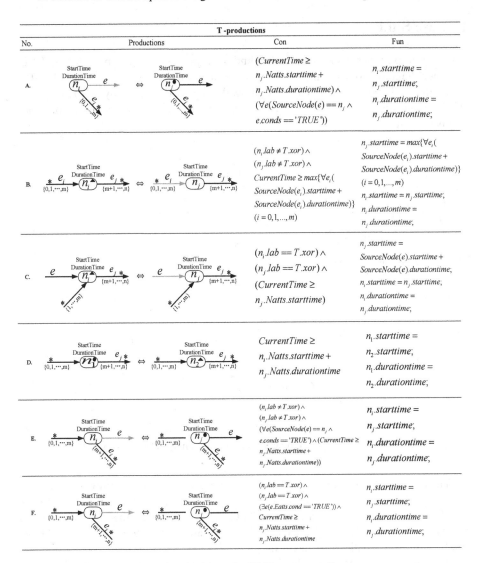

Fig. 4. T-productions of a UML sequence diagram.

4   Case Study

This section provides a case of a cash withdrawal process at ATM modeled by UML sequence diagrams to show how the sequence diagram can be verified using TEGGs.

Figure 5 shows a simple cash withdrawal process described by UML sequence diagrams. In this process, there are three object nodes, six messages and a combined fragment "Alt".

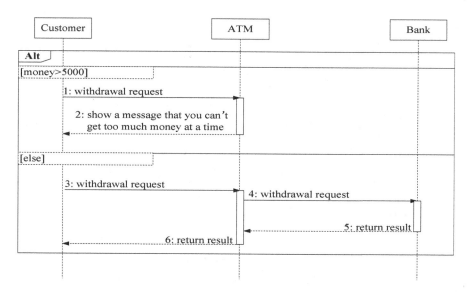

Fig. 5. A UML sequence diagram of a cash withdrawal process at ATM.

There are three steps to verify this UML sequence diagram as follows.

First, executing pretreatment and initialization. Through graph transformation from a UML sequence diagram to a graph of TEGGs, we can obtain the host graph of the TEGG in Fig. 6(a). Meanwhile, some of the nodes are added into the generated TEGG graph in order to facilitate the analysis.

Next, according to the T-productions, verifying the correctness of the host graph by means of R-application. After searching the host graph with the right graph of each T-production, there are redexes, which will be replaced by the left graph of this T-production. Therefore, there are intermediate graphs in Fig. 6(b)-(d) reflecting the situations after the redexes are replaced.

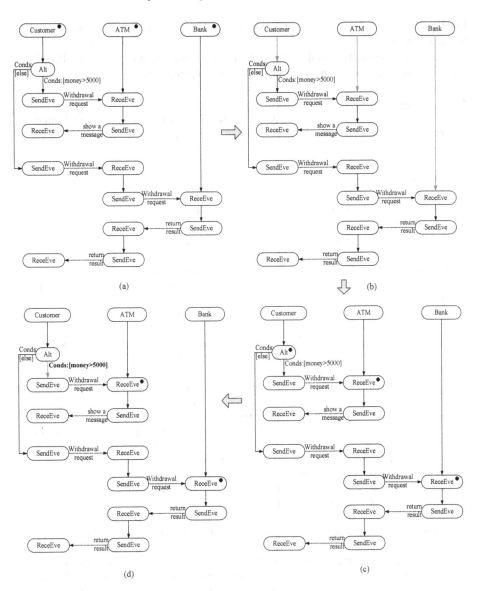

Fig. 6. Verifying a UML sequence diagram in Fig. 5 using TEGG.

5 Conclusion

Based on the existing graph grammar TEGG, this paper introduces a formal method for verifying UML sequence diagrams which include the attributes of each node and each edge in graphs, new productions, and so on. According to a set of properly designed productions, the proposed method is able to check the correctness of host graphs.

Finally, a case study is provided to illustrate how the sequence diagram can be verified using TEGGs.

Our future research includes the applications of the TEGG to more UML related problems and the development of more effective parsing algorithm.

Acknowledgments. This work is supported by the Natural Science Foundation of the Jiangsu Youth of China under grant BK20181019 and Science Foundation of Nanjing Institute of Technology under grant YKJ201723.

References

1. Luckham, D., Vera, J.: An event-based architecture definition language. IEEE Trans. Softw. Eng. **21**(9), 717–734 (1995)
2. Allen, R., Garlan, D.: A formal basis for architectural connection. ACM Trans. Softw. Eng. Methodol. (TOSEM) **6**(3), 213–249 (1997)
3. Dashofy, E., Van der Hoek, A., Taylor, R.: A highly-extensible, xml-based architecture description language. In: 2001 Proceedings, Working IEEE/IFIP Conference on Software Architecture, pp. 103–112. IEEE (2001)
4. Garlan, D., Monroe, R., Wile, D.: Acme: an architecture description interchange language. In: CASCON First Decade High Impact Papers, pp. 159–173. ACM (2010)
5. Shaw, M., DeLine, R., Klein, D., Ross, T., Young, D., Zelesnik, G.: Abstractions for software architecture a nd tools to support them. IEEE Trans. Softw. Eng. **21**(4), 314–335 (1995)
6. Mei, H., Chen, F., Wang, Q., Feng, Y.: ABC/ADL: an ADL supporting component composition. In: George, C., Miao, H. (eds.) ICFEM 2002. LNCS, vol. 2495, pp. 38–47. Springer, Heidelberg (2002). https://doi.org/10.1007/3-540-36103-0_6
7. Object Management Group (OM G): Unified modeling language specification (2004). http://www.uml.org
8. Object Management Group: UML 2.1.1 specification, (2008). http://www.omg.org/technology/documents/formal/uml.htm
9. Schafer, T., Knapp, A., Merz, S.: Model checking UML state machines and collaborations. Theoret. Comput. Sci. **47**(1), 1–13 (2001)
10. Kerkouche, E., Chaoui, A., Bourennane, E., Labbani, O.: A UML and colored Petri nets integrated modeling and analysis approach using graph transformation. J. Object Technol. **9**(4), 25–43 (2010)
11. Simmonds, J., Bastarrica, M.C., Hitschfeld-Kahler, N., Rivas, S.: A tool based on DL for UML model consistency checking. Int. J. Softw. Eng. Knowl. Eng. **18**(6), 713–735 (2008)
12. Simmonds, J., Bastarrica, C.: Description logics for consistency checking of architectural features in UML 2.0 models, Technical report, Department of Computer Science, University of Chile (2005)
13. Rekers, J., Schürr, A.: Defining and parsing visual languages with layered graph grammars. J. Vis. Lang. Comput. **8**(1), 27–55 (1997)
14. Zhang, D.Q., Zhang, K., Cao, J.N.: A context-sensitive graph grammar formalism for the specification of visual languages. Comput. J. **44**(3), 187–200 (2001)
15. Zeng, X.Q., Han, X.Q., Zou, Y.: An edge-based context-sensitive graph grammar formalism. J. Softw. **19**(8), 1893–1901 (2008). (in Chinese)
16. Shi, Z., Zeng, X.Q., et al.: Bidirectional transformation between BPMN and BPEL with graph grammar. Comput. Electr. Eng. **51**, 304–319 (2016)

17. Kong, J., Zhang, K., et al.: A graph grammar approach to software architecture verification and transformation. In: Proceeding of the 27th Annual International Computer Software and Applications Conference (2003)
18. Bisi, N.N., Pazzini, V., et al.: Using graph grammars to develop embedded systems based on UML models. In: 2011 Workshop-School on Theoretical Computer Science, pp. 81–87 (2011)
19. Shi, Z., Zeng, X.Q., et al.: A temporal graph grammar formalism. J. Vis. Lang. Comput. **47**, 62–76 (2018)

A Bus Passenger Flow Estimation Method Based on POI Data and AFC Data Fusion

Yuexiao Cai[1], Yunlong Zhao[1,2(✉)], Jinqian Yang[1],
and Changxin Wang[1]

[1] Nanjing University of Aeronautics and Astronautics, Nanjing, Jiangsu, China
{yuexiaocai,zhaoyunlong,jq.yang,cx.wang}@nuaa.edu.cn
[2] Collaborative Innovation Center of Novel Software Technology
and Industrialization, Nanjing, Jiangsu, China

Abstract. The unreasonable location of bus stations and scheduling has been a serious problem in public transportation for a long time. To provide a comfortable travel experience, effective bus scheduling and reasonable station location is essential. In order to estimate bus passenger flow at different location and time, this paper proposes a method using ridge regression and stepwise regression to estimate passenger flow with POI and AFC data fusion. The results show that all categories of POI have different capacity to influence passenger flow, and people can estimate number of passengers of arbitrary time and place based on the method, which will contribute to optimization of public transportation system.

Keywords: AFC data · POI data · Regression · Urban bus transit systems · Passenger flow

1 Introduction

As the most widely used public transportation in many cities, bus service still has a lot of room to improve in order to meet the demand of citizens. In the past, fare was collected manually. Therefore, people had to optimize the bus schedule and location of bus stations in an empirical method, which is inaccurate and costly. With the help of Automatic Fare Collection (AFC) and On-Board Unit (OBU), experts are able to look into statistics recorded by these devices and improve the quality of bus service more efficiently and effectively. However, statistics just imperfectly reflect the real demand for public transportation. People have to take the existing bus lines, although their real demand is slightly different from the existing one and they may sometimes need to transfer to another bus. They have to do so, but these records are used to prove 'they prefer to do so' in the perspective of statistics, which is nonconforming to the situation. So, it is urgent to study citizens' real demand for public transportation. The current method is to give out questionnaires, but which is costly and only applicable for small scale datasets. Also, due to concerns about privacy, it is difficult to get accurate demand information. Such a status quo is extremely unfavorable for bus companies and the general public. On the one hand, bus companies cannot accurately get passengers' demand, resulting in waste of human resources and vehicle resources, which involves

© Springer Nature Singapore Pte Ltd. 2020
Y. Tian et al. (Eds.): ICBDS 2019, CCIS 1210, pp. 352–367, 2020.
https://doi.org/10.1007/978-981-15-7530-3_27

schedules of buses and location of sites, affecting operating profits; On the other hand, passengers keep complaining about the situation that it takes forever to wait until the bus they want to come, and they always have to walk a long journey to take buses.

In this paper, we developed a method using ridge regression and stepwise regression to calculate the weight (influence coefficient) of each category of POI with multi-source data. And based on this method, the demand for the passenger carrying capacity of the bus at any point on the map can be roughly estimated, thereby optimizing the layout of the bus stop location. In addition, if the time interval is set as a particular one, POI weight at any time can be estimated as well, so do the demand for the bus carrying capacity at each moment. Optimized adjustments can be made to solve the problem of insufficient carrying capacity of buses during peak hours, which caused by unreasonable schedule.

Since the method of manual counting can only be applied to rather small scale, automated data-collection systems have been developing rapidly and show promising future. The AFC devices system can record payments of each passenger, including line ID, vehicle ID, card ID, boarding time, latitude and longitude. A kind of GPS embedded OBU that can record the position and speed information of the vehicle is also widely installed. With the help of the mentioned in-vehicle data collecting system, we finally have the opportunity to use the long-term unutilized information to optimize our urban Bus Transit System (BTS).

As is known to us, people always take public transport with a purpose or specific destination. Considering the good urban morphological representation ability, Point of Interest (POI), which have long been used for urban functional area division, can be a powerful tool for study passenger flow. POI data is relatively easy to get access to. It can be downloaded from the map provider. The POI data mainly covers the specific name, land type, latitude and longitude information of the objects in the selected area.

Although the analysis and prediction of traffic flow seems to be a job only involves statistics, there are still many difficulties to overcome. The main challenges are as follows:

- The passenger's demand for the bus is an amount that cannot be directly counted. The reason is that AFC records will only be generated in the place where the bus station is set up, but this does not mean that citizens have no demand for public transport in the 'no records' area. As a matter of fact, the records will never be generated without a bus stop.
- The bus station will also have a certain siphon effect on the surrounding area. It means people will gather there to take the bus rather than get on bus anywhere like taxis do. Therefore, bus travels in a certain area will be concentrated to the site, so the number of AFC records will be greater than the actual demand at this site. As the consequence, the statistical law based on past records cannot truly reflect the demand for public transportation at any location on the map, especially the area far from the bus line.
- Current on-board devices cannot automatically count the number of passengers getting on and off the bus. We still need to export data and perform manual processing.

- The POI update is slow, so the resulting model is insufficient to reflect real-time passenger flow variation due to traffic accidents and weather.

In summary, it is of great value to optimize bus stop locations and schedule, but to our best knowledge, there is no existing method for this problem in large scale. In this paper, by analyzing the relationship between AFC and POI data, we propose a method involving temporal POI-weight model, to predict demands for public transportation of any place at any time. To make this possible, we made the following contributions:

- First, we analyze the AFC data and calculate the number of people getting on at each station. We match AFC records to the nearest bus stop according to location and time information which generated respectively by OBU and AFC devices.
- Secondly, we obtain the POI information in a particular buffer zone around the site. Furthermore, we calculate the correlation coefficient between various POI types, and merge the highly correlated types in order to eliminate collinearity. Then, we input the number of AFC records and the number of different types of POIs as independent variables and dependent variable and apply the ridge regression/weight decay model to get the coefficients of each major class of POIs (the ability to attract passengers).
- Third, we reduce the granularity of AFC data to 1 h and apply the similar method, finding out the relationship between the ability of POIs to attract passenger flow and time ultimately.
- Finally, applying this model, we can estimate the demand for public transportation at any location.

We divided the Nanjing Public Transport AFC data into a training set and a test set and applied our model on the test set, which achieved very good results and consequently proved the validity of the model.

The rest of the paper is organized as follow: After a brief introduction of the related work in Sect. 2, we give an overview of the problem and our solution in Sect. 3. In Sect. 4, we focus on the whole procedure of estimation method and followed by Sect. 5, which revolves around applying our solution in the city of Nanjing and evaluate the performance. And we will end up the paper with conclusion In Sect. 6.

2 Related Work

The research on the temporal and spatial distribution of passenger flow in cities provides important support for urban functional area planning, customized bus route formulation, regional emergency warning and evacuation plan planning with the application of big data technique. [1] As an important part of trajectory data mining, research has attracted the attention of academic and industry circles at home and abroad [2].

Majority of the POI-related researches focus on POI selection in multi-scale map [3], extracting hierarchical landmarks [4], POI recommendation [5] and urban functional partitions [6]. However, becoming known of the impact POIs have on traffic situation, bus travel time prediction algorithm was proposed [7]. At the same time, researchers begin to study AFC data and try to help guide the operators to allocate and schedule the bus route and timetable dynamically [8].

Similar to topic of this paper, Jinbao Zhao et al. uses multiple ordinary least squares (OLS) regressions were run to evaluate the impacts of the population, employment and some other independent variables on Metro ridership [9]. Based on the study, Guoqiang Li et al. explored the influence factors of railway ridership, which came to a conclusion that the number of households, commercial facility, cultural facility and bus route have a remarkable effect on ridership [10]. Though Guoqiang Li et al. s' study is really thought-provoking, the method to calculate coefficients has no essential difference with ordinary multiple linear regression and results in collinearity, which led to negative coefficients. What's more, due to the special mechanism of subway, we can get the number of alighting passengers, which is hardly to achieve in bus issue. Fortunately, Jun Zhang et al. proposed some reliable models to estimate number of getting off passengers [7].

3   Problem Statement

In this section, we first illustrated motivation of building this AFC&POI-based model to solve the problem. Then we present the dataset and the rough work flow of the system.

3.1   Motivation

Based on the analysis of passenger flow of bus stations, it is found that the patterns of passenger flow at the bus station can be roughly classified into residential-intensive, employment-intensive, and transportation hub patterns according to their different land use types [10].

These patterns show totally different characteristics. The peak of residential-intensive stations' passenger flow occurs at 7:00–9:00, which happens to be the morning rush hour. The peak of employment-intensive stations' passenger flow appears at 17:00–19:00 and 21:00–22:00, sharing the time period with evening rush hour and the end of overtime. The traffic hub pattern combines characteristics of the first two, and there is always a delay of about 30 min comparing to the peak of patterns above, which is exactly the time people spend on travelling to traffic hubs from their living and working place.

There are also some special patterns, such as the sites around the health care facilities, whose passenger flow does not increase significantly during the morning and evening rush hours, but the peak appears at 10:00–11:00 and 15:00–16:00. The peak of passenger flow of stations set around restaurants appears after three meals, which is just the same as our common sense. However, except for sites with a single feature, the traffic characteristics of most stations are not that clear, but complicated. The reason is that, in fact, most of the land use types in the city are mixed, and there are various kinds of facilities around the site. Therefore, the characteristics of most stations cannot be classified into a single pattern, but the superposition of various passenger flow characteristics.

Therefore, we believe that the passenger flow of most sites should also be able to be split into different parts. Since POIs are often used in geographic information systems to represent all kinds of facilities, we have chosen POI as a tool to reflect the pattern of land used in the particular area. In a large number of literatures researching POIs and urban functional partitions, researchers assume that number of POI has linear relationship with passenger flow, which is correct in a large scale. However, in our research, we found that the number of POI points is not linearly related to passenger flow some single cases, shown as Fig. 1.

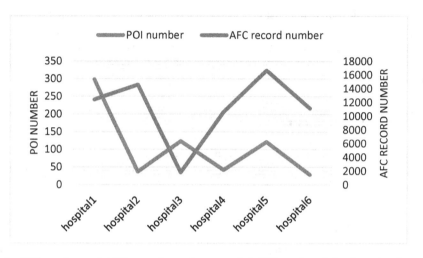

Fig. 1. POI number and AFC records number around 6 different hospitals show that in some cases POI number and AFC number are not linear related.

Namely, POI number may not be the only factor. In fact, in the POI data set, a newsstand and a hospital are just counted as a point without a difference, except for their classification. It is quite unreasonable to have no weight difference between the categories. We use ridge regression and stepwise regression to get the weights (influential coefficients) of various POIs. Once we get the weights of different kinds of POIs through machine learning models, after counting the number all kinds of POIs in the selected area respectively and multiplying the influence coefficients, the rough passenger flow of the region can be obtained.

In addition, based on the fact that regional traffic flows will exhibit significant time-related characteristics within areas of single land use, we believe that this feature still exists in the mixed land type region. That is to say, the weights (influence coefficients) of each type of POI in each time of the day are also significantly changed. If the time granularity of the ridge regression is reduced to 1 h or less, the POI weights (influence coefficients) in every hour can be obtained as well. With this result, it is also possible to obtain the passenger flow for each time period in a certain region.

3.2   The Architecture and Datasets

The architecture of the estimation and prediction system is shown as Fig. 2. Four datasets are involved in the process of estimation. The data dictionary is elaborated in Table 1, 2, 3, 4. The smartcard dataset records every single tapping event. The bus station dataset is static and provides with bus station information to figure out which station does the passenger get on the bus. Arrival/Departure dataset is an auxiliary one. It helps when the bus stations are too close to figure out which one is the station getting aboard by checking the time intervals. POI dataset records the information about POIs, which helps in machine learning. In this paper, we do not take mid category and sub category of POI into consideration, since it will bring about too many independent variables, which will take too much effort to merge.

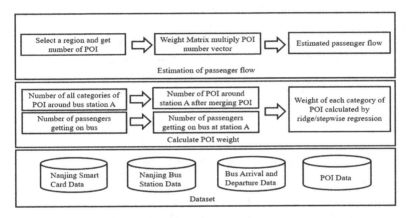

Fig. 2. Work flow of the system.

4   Estimate Bus Passenger Flow with POI-Weight Model

In this section, we will describe our approach to estimating passenger flow, to begin with, Part A will show how to formulate the problem as a model and prepare the normalized data, Part B will show the essential algorithm to calculate POI weight, Part C of it will be how to processed data to estimate the overall traffic flow.

4.1   Data Preparation and Formulation

Since the smart card (AFC) data is collected by OBU, it is under the WGS-84 coordinate system, which has an offset comparing to the GCJ-02 bus station coordinate and POI coordinate provided by Gaode Map API. In order to determine which bus station does passengers get onboard, we need a unified geographic coordinate system. Theoretically, we can choose any one of the two coordinate systems, and in this paper the standard will be GCJ-02 coordinate system. Therefore, the AFC data requires to be converted into GCJ-02 system [11].

Table 1. Smart card dataset.

Content	Remarks
Line ID	The line number of the bus
Vehicle ID	The registration ID of the vehicle
Card ID	The number of IC card
Onboard Time	The time of tapping card
Longitude	The longitude of tapping card
Latitude	The latitude of tapping card

Table 2. Bus station dataset.

Content	Remarks
Station ID	The number of the station
Station Name	The name of the station
Direction	The direction buses will go
Station Distance	The distance to next station
Longitude	The longitude of station
Latitude	The latitude of station

Table 3. Arrival/Departure dataset.

Content	Remarks
Line ID	The line number of the bus
Vehicle ID	The registration ID of the vehicle
Station Name	The name of the station
In/Out Sign	1 represent arrive, 2 represent depart
Arrive/Depart Time	The time bus arrive/depart from station
Longitude	The longitude of station
Latitude	The latitude of station

Table 4. Point of Interest dataset.

Content	Remarks
POI Name	The name of POI
Category	The category of POI
Mid Category	The mid category of POI
Sub Category	The sub category of POI
Longitude	The longitude of POI
Latitude	The latitude of POI

The location where the smart card data is generated is actually on the bus, so it possibly not completely coincides with the POI point on the map. Therefore, it is necessary to take the smart card records within a certain range around the station into account. Considering that most bus stations are set at an interval of 500 m–2 km, the buffer zone selected in this paper is a square with 100 m length of a side and its center is the bus station. However, due to the possible OBU error and uncertain locations of the station, such a radius may cause the smart card data to be mis-recorded in upstream stations, which should be recorded in downstream stations, since these two stations may set too close or just on the other side of the street. Therefore, it is necessary to detect the vehicle ID that the passenger boarded while clustering smart card data, and look up the vehicle ID in the arrival/departure data to determine the up or down direction of the vehicle, thereby determining whether the passenger boarding station is in the upstream direction or the downstream direction. Besides, we need to check whether the vehicle have entered the station at the moment when the smart card data is generated, and at the same moment, it has not departed the station. If there is data that is out of the interval, it will be discarded.

After finishing the above preprocess steps, the AFC and OBU data has been well and normalized prepared. Its normalized form should be as matrix N.

$$N = \begin{pmatrix} N_{\sum i,1,0} & N_{\sum i,1,1} & \cdots & \cdots & N_{\sum i,1,23} \\ N_{\sum i,2,0} & N_{\sum i,2,1} & \cdots & \cdots & N_{\sum i,2,23} \\ \vdots & \vdots & \ddots & \ddots & \vdots \\ N_{\sum i,j,0} & \vdots & N_{\sum i,j,t} & N_{\sum i,j,t+1} & \vdots \\ \vdots & \vdots & \vdots & \vdots & \vdots \end{pmatrix} \tag{1}$$

$N(i, j, t)$ denotes the number of passengers who get on Bus #i at Station #j at Time #t. $P(k, j)$ denotes the number of Class #k POIs in the range of a square whose edge is 500 m and center is Station #j. $\beta(k, t)$ denotes the weight(influence coefficient) of Class #k POI at the Time # t, and $I(j, t)$ denotes the number of passengers attracted to the Station #j at Time #t due to the siphon effect of the bus stop when the number of all classes of POI are zeros.

Next, the latitude and longitude of all the sites are input in order to get POI data, and the picking range is determined to be a square which length of a side is 500 m, all POI points in the area are acquired, and the number of different categories POIs can therefore be counted according to the data dictionary. The initial data has a total of 20 categories. We discard some non-entity categories of POI, such as the road name, holiday events and end up with 13 remaining categories:

(1) catering services
(2) shopping services
(3) life-related services
(4) sports and leisure services
(5) health care services
(6) accommodation services

(7) scenic spots
(8) residences
(9) government agencies
(10) education and cultural services
(11) transportation facilities
(12) financial insurance services
(13) corporate enterprises

How to choose the variables as the independent variables in regression model is a difficult problem. In paper [10], Guoqiang Li et al. select population live round the station, number of employments, whether in CBD or not etc. as the independent variables. However, that will result in some errors in linear regression model, and it did in the paper. Due to collinearity using the linear regression model directly will result in the weight of some categories (influence coefficient) being negative, which is impossible to explain its meaning. If we do not merge the correlated categories, POI weight getting from linear regression will be like results shown in Table 5.

Table 5. POI Weight without eliminating collinearity.

POI Category	Weight
Catering services	27.65563686
Shopping services	20.64133616
Life-related services	−29.91145993
Sports and leisure services	−323.97398154
Health care services	214.38562792
Accommodation services	102.37563036
Scenic spots	131.55610907
Residences	108.28456801
Government agencies	−74.87660339
Education services	−48.81027063
Transportation facilities	70.8657459
Financial services	187.08495514
Corporate enterprises	−5.08927465
I(j, t)/intercept	2569.4090543280445

In multiple linear regression analysis, when there are many independent variables, not all independent variables may have significant influences, and some may be related, and there is information overlap and collinearity. In general, it is more desirable to introduce statistically significant independent variables into the regression equation to make the equation simpler and easier to interpret. The reason why the model produces negative numbers is that there is a high degree of collinearity in the categories of catering services, shopping services, and life-related services, and the variance of parameter fluctuations is large. In order to eliminate the influence of collinearity, we first analyze the correlation coefficients of 13 categories of variables and combine the POI categories with highly correlated. The coefficient of correlation matrix is shown in Fig. 3.

	catering services	shopping services	life-related services	sports and leisure services	health care services	accommodation services	scenic spots	residences	government agencies	education services	transportation facilities	financial services	corporate enterprises
catering services	1	0.580877	0.692182	0.593331	0.486513	0.292574	0.002875	0.272449	0.07757	0.236064	0.320442	0.211263	0.24154
shopping services	0.580877	1	0.532762	0.536762	0.355837	0.133007	0.027573	0.237808	0.0327	0.245375	0.277848	0.173255	0.225785
life-related services	0.692182	0.532762	1	0.482134	0.439352	0.356094	0.005867	0.339481	0.10725	0.388881	0.304823	0.333391	0.416905
sports and leisure services	0.593331	0.536762	0.482134	1	0.369868	0.104074	0.046582	0.194819	0.033377	0.271336	0.289881	0.308063	0.305308
health care services	0.486513	0.355837	0.439352	0.369868	1	0.128726	0.089034	0.133358	0.110219	0.151871	0.275704	0.228361	0.279461
accommodation services	0.292574	0.133007	0.356094	0.104074	0.128726	1	0.026102	0.383765	0.128086	0.431248	0.360709	0.287941	0.196186
scenic spots	0.002875	0.027573	0.005867	0.046582	0.089034	0.026102	1	-0.014563	-0.011727	0.05256	0.05708	0.038139	0.035949
residences	0.272449	0.237808	0.339481	0.194819	0.133358	0.383765	-0.014563	1	0.268854	0.476624	0.495099	0.4631	0.389484
government agencies	0.07757	0.0327	0.10725	0.033377	0.110219	0.128086	-0.011727	0.268854	1	0.297565	0.24961	0.217352	0.179621
education services	0.236064	0.245375	0.388881	0.271336	0.151871	0.431248	0.05256	0.476624	0.297565	1	0.486714	0.636251	0.625403
transportation facilities	0.320442	0.277848	0.304823	0.289881	0.275704	0.360709	0.05708	0.495099	0.24961	0.486714	1	0.562153	0.436386
financial services	0.211263	0.173255	0.333391	0.308063	0.228361	0.287941	0.038139	0.4631	0.217352	0.636251	0.562153	1	0.709353
corporate enterprises	0.24154	0.225785	0.416905	0.305308	0.279461	0.196186	0.035949	0.389484	0.179621	0.625403	0.436386	0.709353	1

Fig. 3. Coefficient of correlation matrix

We find that catering services, shopping services, life-related services and sports and leisure services are highly related, so we merge them into catering services as the representative category. After that, using the same method, we finally merge them into 5 categories: catering services, health care services, scenic spots, residences, corporate enterprises.

After merging the highly correlated categories, the input data for ridge regression and stepwise regression are ready.

4.2   Calculate POI-Weight

After the data preparation is completed based on the above method, the collinear relationship between the classes and the classes is eliminated, but the implicit multicollinearity relationship which cannot be observed directly by coefficient matrix has not been solved yet, which will also result in the coefficients in some particular time periods being negative. Therefore, we still need to further optimize the model using ridge regression or stepwise regression. And we will make comparisons between these two methods in Sect. 5.

Tikhonov regularization, named for Andrey Tikhonov, is a method of regularization of ill-posed problems. Also known as ridge regression/weight decay. It is particularly useful to mitigate the problem of multicollinearity in linear regression, which commonly occurs in models with large numbers of parameters [12]. We apply this method to our work considering the multicollinearity between different categories of POI, which will definitely result in negative coefficients. We arrange the data like the matrix below, and input into SPSSAU to do ridge regression.

$$INPUT = \begin{pmatrix} P_{1,1} & P_{2,1} & \cdots & P_{5,1} & N_{\sum_{i,1},\sum_t} \\ P_{1,2} & P_{2,2} & \cdots & \cdots & N_{\sum_{i,2},\sum_t} \\ \vdots & \vdots & \ddots & \ddots & \vdots \\ P_{1j} & \vdots & P_{kj} & P_{5j} & \vdots \\ \vdots & \vdots & \vdots & \vdots & \vdots \end{pmatrix} \qquad (2)$$

We input matrix INPUT, which take $N(i, j, t)$ as the dependent variables and $P(k, j)$ as the independent variables. The ridge regression will give out POI coefficient vector β (k, t) denotes the weight (influence coefficient) of Class #k POI at the Time # t, and intercept $I(j, t)$ as is shown in Table 6.

Table 6. POI Weight after merging and ridge regression.

POI Category	Weight
Catering services	18.983
Health care services	188.639
Scenic spots	165.24
Residences	147.822
Corporate enterprises	115.78
I(j, t)/intercept	2702.608

If we take Time #t as x-axis, and β (k, t) as y-axis, then a weight-time graph can be observed clearly. The graph shows that weights (influence coefficients) of each type of POI in each time of the day are also significantly changed as our assumption in Fig. 4, 5, 6, 7, 8. For example, the ability of POIs to attract passengers in restaurant-intensive region is significantly higher during the morning, evening and evening meals than that of the normal time periods.

Different from the method above, we could also use stepwise regression directly. Stepwise regression is a method of fitting regression models in which the choice of predictive variables is carried out by an automatic procedure [14–16]. However, calls to stop using stepwise model building altogether have been rising, since it cannot reflect model uncertainty correctly [17–20].

4.3   Estimate Bus Passenger Flow

In this part we will predict the traffic flow based on the results obtained by the Ridge regression.

First, divide Nanjing into squares whose length of a side is 500 m, calculate the number of all categories of POIs in each square, and then multiply the coefficient matrix obtained in Sect. 4.2 and add to $I(j, t)$ to obtain Estimated passenger flow in each square in each time period. It should be noted that although the input training data of machine learning only uses data at bus stops, this method can theoretically be

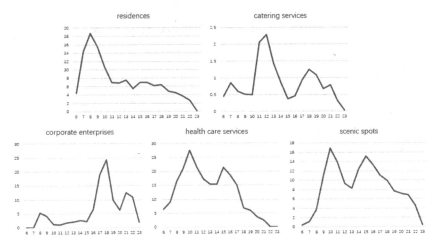

Fig. 4. Weights of 5 categories of POI vary over time.

Fig. 5. Heat map of predicted bus passenger flow (not actual flow but demand for bus).

applied not only to predict the passenger flow of a bus stop, but also to predict "if a bus stop is set up in a certain place, then the traffic here will be", as Fig. 5 shows. Such results are meaningful for the optimization of bus site location and scheduling optimization. In any other traditional method, as well as statistical methods, the conclusions can only predict the future passenger flow of a certain site, but cannot estimate the passenger flow generated by the area without a bus station.

According to the result above, based on the research of Jinbao Zhao et al. [9] and the data of NICTP in 2010, the proportion of passengers travelling by bus in all traffic is 17.63% - although the 2010 data is not accurate reference value for the current situation, but we are here only to verify the feasibility of the model - so that we can roughly infer the overall passenger flow in a certain area. However, such an estimate is

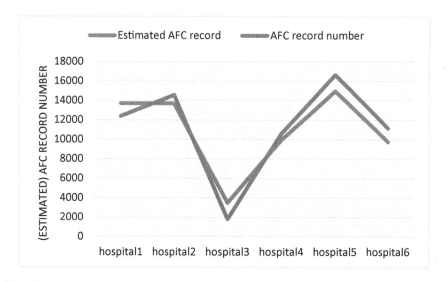

Fig. 6. Estimated passenger number and AFC records number around 6 different hospitals.

	Coefficient	Standard Coefficient	t	p	VIF
	B	Beta			
intercept	2702.608	-	11.815	0.000**	-
catering services	18.983	0.054	1.101	0.271	1.393
healthcare services	188.639	0.106	2.205	0.028*	1.358
residence	165.24	0.087	1.818	0.07	1.335
scenic spots	147.822	0.043	1.03	0.304	1.012
corporate enterprises	115.78	0.113	2.391	0.017*	1.322
		* p<0.05 ** p<0.01			

Fig. 7. Result of ridge regression.

	Coefficient	Standard Coefficient	t	p	VIF
	B	Beta			
intercept	2903.247	-	15.251	0.000**	-
healthcare services	225.058	0.126	3.001	0.003**	1.06
residence	100.251	0.158	3.681	0.000**	1.095
corporate enterprises	118.846	0.116	2.669	0.008**	1.137
		* p<0.05 ** p<0.01			

Fig. 8. Result of stepwise regression.

inaccurate because the NICTP data only provides a percentage of the total number of people using various vehicles, with a time granularity of one year and the entire region of Nanjing. Therefore, it cannot be guaranteed to maintain such a ratio in all of the area and at all of the time.

5   Evaluation and Experiment

Since we have no dataset to prove the accuracy that our model estimated in no-station area, we have to split our smart card dataset into training set and test set. To prove the effectiveness of the method, we did experiments as follow:

5.1   Evaluation the Accuracy of the Estimation

We split 6 months of AFC dataset which contains 13,000,000 smart card records in Nanjing into test set and training set. The test set accounts for 33 percent of the total dataset. Evaluation of passenger flow is carried out between the real number of smart card records in test set and predicted number of passengers using coefficient vector β (k, t) and intercept I (j, t). To evaluate the accuracy of result, we applied fit and predict function in scikit-learn (α in ridge regression is set to 0.5 manually). And the accuracy ranges from 76.62% to 83.14% according to different split of training and test dataset (this procedure is automatically done by scikit-learn).

Besides, we also do the evaluation manually and try to estimate passenger flow around hospital. The estimated number of passengers in Fig. 6 is relatively close to actual number comparing to Fig. 1.

5.2   Comparison Between Ridge Regression and Stepwise Regression

In the process of calculating POI weight in Sect. 5, we mentioned that Ridge Regression and Stepwise Regression are both used in our experiment. The result of Ridge regression SPSSAU give out is shown in Fig. 7. B denotes coefficient in regression. Beta denotes coefficient in regression when the intercept is 0. t is an intermediate variable to calculate p. p is used to measure the significance level of the independent variables. And independent variables are significant if p is less than 0.05. VIF is less than 5 means the variables are not collinear. Since we have already merged POI of highly collinearity, the VIF will not greater than 5. The result ensures that POI weights are positive numbers. However, some variables are not significant enough.

Comparing to Ridge Regression, Stepwise Regression is far more significant than it. However, we can hardly tell the meaning of categories in reality. If we use Stepwise Regression to estimate the passenger flow, whose result lies in Fig. 8, then the passenger flow can be expressed as:

Total number of passengers

$$= 2903.247 + 225.058 * healthcare\ services\ POI\ number \\ + 100.251 * residence\ POI\ number + 118.846 \\ * corporate\ enterprises\ POI\ number. \tag{3}$$

The result may be correct, but so many categories are merged that 'corporate enterprises POI number' may be actually the sum of POI number of many categories, which makes people confusing and sometimes contradict to common sense.

6 Conclusion

In this paper, we present a method to analyze and estimate demand for public transport and real-time passenger flow at any place, any time in the city with the help of AFC data, POI data and two kinds of regression model in machine learning.

We find that sometimes traffic flow is not in proportion to POI numbers. We come to a conclusion that every category of POI has its weight, which means they have different impact on traffic flow, and this weight also varies by time. We calculate the weight or influence coefficients of some categories of POI with ridge regression and stepwise regression, and finally find out a pattern how weight varies by time.

After proving the method is reliable, we compare the result caused by two different regression model. Bus companies can discard the old method of just doing counting, and combine POI and AFC data together to estimate the accurate passenger flow and demand for bus. Then they will be able to optimize time scheduling of buses and setting location of bus stations to meet the demand of citizens.

Acknowledgements. This research was supported by Defense Industrial Technology Development Program under Grant No. JCKY2016605B006, Six talent peaks project in Jiangsu Province under Grant No. XYDXXJS-031.

References

1. Nagy, A.M., Simon, V.: Survey on traffic prediction in smart cities. Pervasive Mob. Comput. **50**, 148–163 (2018)
2. Sun, T.X.: Mobility pattern mining from people flow based on spatio-temporal data
3. Shen, Y., Chen, J., Cao, X., et al.: POI selection with the reference of linear roads in multi-scale map. Surv. Mapp. Eng. **23**(7), 6–11 (2014)
4. Zhao, W., Li, Q., Li, B.: Extracting hierarchical landmarks from urban POI data. Yaogan Xuebao-J. Remote Sens. **15**(5), 973–988 (2011)
5. Ye, M., Yin, P., Lee, W.C., et al.: Exploiting geographical influence for collaborative point-of-interest recommendation. In: Proceedings of the 34th International ACM SIGIR Conference on Research and Development in Information Retrieval, pp. 325–334. ACM (2011)
6. Chi, J., Jiao, L., Dong, T., et al.: Quantitative identification and visualization of urban functional area based on poi data. J. Geomat. **41**(2), 68–73 (2016)

7. Ma, L.H., Chen, T.W., Hao, M., Zhang, L.: Us travel time prediction algorithm based on multi-line information fusion. Comput. Sci. http://kns.cnki.net/kcms/detail/50.1075.TP. 20190814.1443.048.html

8. Zhang, J., Shen, D., Tu, L., et al.: A real-time passenger flow estimation and prediction method for urban bus transit systems. IEEE Trans. Intell. Transp. Syst. **18**(11), 3168–3178 (2017)

9. Zhao, J., Deng, W., Song, Y., et al.: What influences Metro station ridership in China? Insights from Nanjing. Cities **35**, 114–124 (2013)

10. Li, G.Q., Yang, M., Wang, S.H.: Influence factors exploration of rail station-level ridership using AFC data and POI data. Urban Transp. **17**(01), 106–112+124

11. Kim, Y.I.: Method for converting coordinate values of map data: U.S. Patent 7,197,393, 27 March 2007

12. Kennedy, P.: A Guide to Econometrics, 5th edn., pp. 205–206. The MIT Press, Cambridge (2003). ISBN 0-262-61183-X

13. Efroymson, M.A.: Multiple regression analysis. In: Ralston, A., Wilf, H.S. (eds.) Mathematical Methods for Digital Computers. Wiley, New York (1960)

14. Hocking, R.R.: The analysis and selection of variables in linear regression. Biometrics **32**, 1–49 (1976)

15. Draper, N., Smith, H.: Applied Regression Analysis, 2nd edn. Wiley, New York (1981)

16. Flom, P.L., Cassell, D.L.: Stopping stepwise: why stepwise and similar selection methods are bad, and what you should use. In: NESUG 2007 (2007)

17. Harrell, F.E.: Regression Modeling Strategies: With Applications to Linear Models, Logistic Regression, and Survival Analysis. Springer, New York (2001). https://doi.org/10.1007/978-3-319-19425-7

18. Chatfield, C.: Model uncertainty, data mining and statistical inference. J. Roy Statist. Soc. A **158**(Part 3), 419–466 (1995)

19. Efron, B., Tibshirani, R.J.: An Introduction to the Bootstrap, Chapman & Hall/CRC, London (1998)

Big Data

Research Character Analyzation
of Urban Security Based on Urban Resilience
Using Big Data Method

Yi Chen[1(✉)], Zhuoran Yang[2], Zhicong Ye[1], and Hui Liu[1]

[1] School of Architecture and Urban Planning,
Nanjing Tech University, Nanjing 211800, China
njut_chenyi@126.com, 286493466@qq.com,
1663297128@qq.com
[2] State Grid Nanjing Power Supply Company, Nanjing 210019, China
2654068649@qq.com

Abstract. Contemporary urban development faces many uncertainties and complexities. Resilience research based on big data method provides new ideas for improving urban security. This paper analyzes the research on foreign urban security considering resilience from 1993 to 2018 with Citespace software. The big data algorithm provided by Citespace proves that the urban resilience research can be characterized by three aspects. Firstly, urban resilience and climate change adaptation are mostly at the national scale and regional scale, and there are few studies on community scale and family scale. In the future, the community scale should be emphasized to improve the research accuracy. Secondly, the urban resilience governance model and social dynamic mechanism should be based on the Chinese institutional background and localized and embodied and be socially fair. The combination of public participation, system resilience, economic resilience, and social resilience can still be further improved. Lastly, research can focus on interdisciplinary integration with geography, economics and sociology, considering big data and smart cities. The research scale should strengthen the comparative study of community scales.

Keywords: Urban resilience · Big data · Urban security · Knowledge map · Citespace analysis

1 Introduction

Extreme climate and rapid urbanization have brought many challenges to the city. Urban security problems such as smog, haze, hurricanes and epidemic diseases have emerged in cities. Columbia University's International Earth Science Information Network Center (CIESIN) shows that out of 450 cities in 633 large cities, about 900 million people are exposed to at least one disaster risk [1]. The urban system is a huge and complex system, and uncertainty and complexity are the main themes in urban development. In the past, the traditional methods have become difficult to deal with urban problems with increasingly diverse types, increasingly complex causes, and increasingly widespread influences [2]. How to improve the urban security has drawn

© Springer Nature Singapore Pte Ltd. 2020
Y. Tian et al. (Eds.): ICBDS 2019, CCIS 1210, pp. 371–381, 2020.
https://doi.org/10.1007/978-981-15-7530-3_28

the attention of researchers all over the world. In 1973, Holling first introduced the concept of resilience to ecosystem research, arguing that the toughness is the ability to return to a stable state after the ecosystem is disturbed. After 2000, resilience gradually expanded from social-ecological systems to socio-economic systems, and corresponding studies on economic resilience, disaster resilience, infrastructure resilience, and urban security resilience emerged. Gunderson and Holling proposed adaptive cycle theory to decompose socio-ecological system evolution into four stages of development, protection, release, and renewal. Resilience toughness should not be seen merely as a recovery of the initial state of the system, but as a capability of change, adaptation, and change that a complex social ecosystem motivates in response to stress and constraints [3, 4].

In recent years, resilient analyzation includes not only the redundancy of infrastructure, the reliability of environmental systems (low exposure, ecological barriers, etc.), but also the support for economic capabilities, social organization, and institutional conditions [2]. To improve the resilience research, it is necessary to provide an overall review of the progress of the urban resilience in last decades. This paper uses big data method provided by Citespace and the knowledge map to study the progress of resilience cities in urban planning in the past 25 years from the perspective of quantitative analysis of literature. Three aspects of previous research character are summarized in this paper. This can be a guide for the future city resilience research of Chinese cities.

2   Big Data Source and Analyzation Method

2.1   Data Source Selection

Based on CiteSpace's requirements for big data sources, this study selected Web of Science (WOS) as a document search engine. The Resilience Research Institute covers a wide range of fields. In order to limit the scope of research to the policy research of urban planning, the four most representative and authoritative urban planning magazines are selected as sources of literature based on research experience. They are LANDSCAPE AND URBAN PLANNING, URBAN STUDIES, CITIES, HABITAT INTERNATIONAL. Use "resilience" as the key word and "article", "proceeding paper" and "review" as the literature type. In order to cover all the research results, the research time ranges from 1900 to present. The Citespace parameter is set to 25 years, which is from 1993 to 2018. With one year as a time span, pathfinder is selected to streamline each year's network and merged network. The data acquisition time was July 10, 2018, and 178 articles were obtained in total. Among them, LANDSCAPE AND URBAN PLANNING includes 76 articles, URBAN STUDIES includes 27 articles, CITIES includes 48 articles, and Regional Studies includes 27 articles. It should be pointed out that there are many literatures on the study of resilience in urban studies, but such documents cannot be restricted by specific search conditions. Therefore, only representative urban planning type magazines can be selected for research.

2.2 Analyzation Methods

CiteSpace is used to analyze the keywords of the above-mentioned four magazines in the WOS from 1993 to 2018. A time slice is defined as one year and the top 20 keywords in each slice are selected to form a knowledge network. The Pathfinder is finally applied to form the knowledge map. The algorithm tailors the knowledge network of each time slice and the merged network of all slices to achieve the purpose of streamlining the network structure and highlighting important nodes and connections. It is shown that a total of 104 nodes (keywords) are obtained, and there are 305 links between each other.

As shown in Fig. 1, the keywords that have a co-citation relationship with resilience (the nodes that are connected to resilience) include: cities, climate change, climate change adaptation, social ecosystems, land use, sustainability, governance, vulnerability, risk and disaster. On this basis, it has led to research on multiple extension areas, including: community departments, sustainability theory, land use change, nature conservation, urban waterscape, geographic design, urbanization, etc.

Fig. 1. Key map of foreign tough cities in 1993–2018.

3   Results Analyzation and Discussion

3.1   Results Analyzation

Considering the basic knowledge map in last section, the time trend of hot keywords in resilience research has been shown since 1993 (see in Fig. 2). The larger the node range stands for the higher occurrence frequency. The nodes marked by red-brown outer ring are highly central and important in the knowledge map. Since 2009, climate change and social ecosystems have become the focus of resilience research. Since 2013, issues such as urbanization, ecosystem services, land use, urban resilience and vulnerability, and biodiversity have become hot topics of research. Of course, the hot topics in 2009 have not been left out in the new era, and the links between hot keywords are intensive.

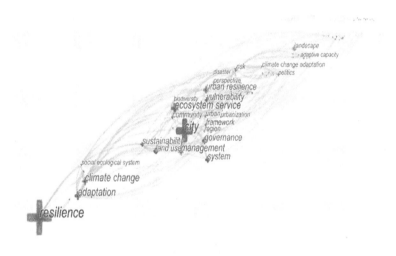

Fig. 2. Annual changes in keywords.

Cluster analysis of knowledge network based on keyword construction is also conducted and the result shows that the knowledge map can be classified into 7 clusters with the Modularity = 0.5018 and the Mean Sihouette = 0.6822. This result reflects a distinctive feature of resilience research: the research topics are broad and diverse, and the research perspectives within the same subject are diverse. Figure 3 shows the clusters with the strongest similarity (Sihouette > 0.7) and the largest number of keywords: community sector, promotion of urban sustainability theory, land use change, nature conservation, urban waterscape, Geographic design, urbanization.

As shown in the Fig. 4, the most active urban resilience research scholar since 1980. Early researchers included Folke C, Guy C, Tzoulas K, Grimm NB, and Farr D. Mid-term researchers include Barthel S, Mewman P, Ernstson H, and Bulkeley H. Recent researchers include Ahern J, Davoudi S, Colding J, Buhaug H, and Wolch Jr. Long-term active researchers include Ahern J, Xiang Wu, Barthel S, Colding J, and Folke C.

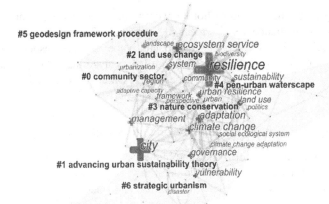

Fig. 3. Keyword construction knowledge network clustering analysis results.

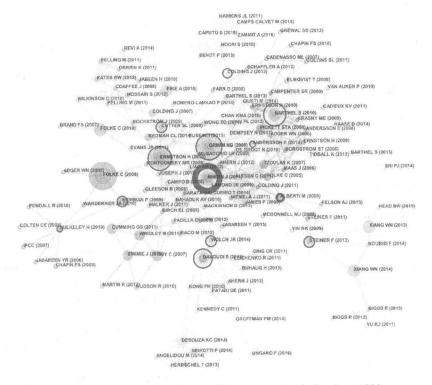

Fig. 4. The most active urban resilience research scholar since 1980.

3.2 Discussion

According to the time trend of hot keywords and the clusters in knowledge map, the characters of resilience research can be achieved. The clusters show that climate change, social dynamic mechanism and landscape are three aspects which are most frequently mentioned. It is necessary to further analyze the detail research program in these areas in order to reveal the necessary research needed to be conducted in the future.

3.3 Urban Resilience and Climate Change Adaptation

It is shown that the keywords with the highest collinear frequency are climate change, adaptation, risk perception, social vulnerability, flood-prone area, etc. Climate change and adaptability have drawn many attentions. The scale of research covers the nation, region, community and family. Issues related to climate change began to appear after 2008, and the research results in 2015–2018 showed a clear growth trend. The researches are relatively concentrated and most of them explore climate change and adaptability. Some studies explore from the perspective of tourism management, rural social vulnerability and wildfire management. According to Fig. 4, some typical research can be summarized [5–11]. Manoj Roy et al. [5] explored the mitigation of climate change and adaptation in Dhaka, Bangladesh. Chiang et al. [8] believed that community risk perception is an inherent part of the decision-making process and helps to strengthen the community. Chu et al. [11] assesses the social vulnerability of Indian cities to climate change and argues that social, economic and geographic differences lead to large differences in climate change.

Another important area concerns climate change and urban resilience is sustainable development. The trend of research based on Fig. 4 is shown. Ahern [12] explored new sustainability from a resilience perspective and argued that sustainable development should change from "fail prevention" to "can fail safely". Spaans [13] evaluates the state of Rotterdam's urban resilience, which is one of the 100 resilience cities.

It is also important to explore urban resilience from a design perspective, and to optimize and improve the harsh environment through urban design. The focus of research is the construction of flood-accessible areas, the construction of water-resistant buildings, and green buildings. Typical studies include: Samuelsson [14] combines accessibility analysis with public participation in GIS (PPGIS) to explore how environmental characteristics affect people's lives. Liao [15] took the flood of the Mekong Delta in Vietnam as an example and proposed a flood adaptation model that allows floods to enter the city.

Obviously, most researches are conducted on the national scale and regional scale. There are few studies on community scale and family scale. The research methods are influenced by the research scale. Usually, the study of national scales uses 100-year historical data while research on community and family-scale is based on survey data. There is a significant difference between two kinds of research in the field of urban resilience and sustainability research. On a global scale, urban resilience emphasizes more on self-protection and ecosystem restoration, while urban sustainability pays more attention to the use and protection of ecological resources. On a regional scale, urban sustainability emphasizes local economic self-sufficiency and economic activities while urban resilience pays more attention to the stability and diversification of urban economic structure. On the urban scale, urban resilience pays more attention to policy management, emphasizes institutional arrangements to strengthen urban structure while urban sustainability considers more about urban and land use. The research scale of urban resilience determines the accuracy of the research. Therefore, it is necessary to strengthen the research at the community level and improve the division of research units. The resilience evaluation method needs to be further improved and adjusted according to the needs.

3.4   Urban Resilience Governance Model and Social Dynamic Mechanism

Urban resilience governance model and selection research focuses on urban resilience governance principles, governance methods and power relations. Figure 4 shows the typical studies [9, 16–23]. Torabi, Elna [16] used two Australian cities as examples, to explore how key elements of urban resilience (subjects, institutions, and systems) interact and the impact of stakeholders on resilience. Meerow [20] used bibliometrics to determine the six characteristics of understanding resilience, and based on this, proposed a new definition of resilience. Chmutina [23] explores the different views and outcomes of the government on resilience by analyzing relevant UK policy documents.

In addition, the research on the social dynamic mechanism of urban resilience focuses on institutional resilience, economic resilience and social resilience. Among them, institutional resilience covers urban-rural dual system and cross-border cooperation; economic resilience covers industry and retail industry resilience; social resilience covers landless farmers and apartments. Typical studied are as follows [24–29]. Brendan Gleeson [24] reported the impact of climate change and energy insecurity on Australian cities, emphasizing that the main role of planning in addressing climate warming will be adaptation rather than mitigation. Castanho [27] discussed the key factors for the success of cross-border cooperative development projects. 14 key factors, including clear common goals and master plans, political transparency and support, connectivity and mobility between cities were identified.

It is clear that the model of resilience governance is greatly influenced by national conditions and policies. The resilience governance model based on national conditions is very necessary. However, the domestic research foundation of resilience governance model is weak. The model lacks the governance of urban resilience and institutional construction. Moreover, the lack of research on existing government documents, government workers, community volunteers, and institutional personnel makes it difficult to explore urban resilience from a governance perspective. The model of resilience governance should be based on the Chinese institutional background and localized and embodied. The model of resilience governance should also be combined with social equity and public participation. There is still room for further discussion on economic resilience. Social resilience research combined with urbanization and Chinese characteristics will be the future direction of development.

3.5   Relationship Between Urban Resilience and Landscape

The last important aspect drawn from the knowledge map is urban resilience and landscape ecology. The current research focuses on the relationship between urbanization and the environment, the assessment of resilience of specific landscapes, the contribution of agricultural landscapes to cities, residential gardens, biodiversity and floods. The resilience of landscape research is closely related to rainwater management. The literature review, case study, measurement model, GIS, data platform, etc. are used, and the research methods are more advanced and diversified. Analyzation in previous section shows the typical researches [30–40]. Michael Batty [30] puts emphasis on the resilience of urban systems from urban multi-core landscapes. Lezlie Morinière [34] explored the relationship between urbanization and the environment through literature review, and 93% of the literature described urbanization as the coercion of the environment, clarifying the relationship between the two is essential for promoting adaptation without compromising elasticity. Langemeyer [40] conducted field observations and remote sensing of 27 urban gardens in Barcelona to explore the actual feelings of parks and users, and proposed that urban green space planning could enhance the potential of urban garden management.

The research results of urban resilience and land use can also be obtained in knowledge map. The research involves housing, urban renewal, high-speed railway, etc. The research topics include land use and biodiversity, land use and landscape security pattern, land use and earthquake mitigation. From the perspective of research, land use is regarded as natural and ecological process, and social-ecological resilience is discussed. Important studies are as follows. Peng, Jian [41] used Shenzhen as a case to link the ecological degradation risk with the rapid urbanization landscape security pattern and distinguish the ecological protection boundary of Shenzhen. Su Jeong [43] used Geographic Information System (GIS), Multi-Criteria Decision Analysis (MCDA), and Fuzzy Evaluation (DEMATEL) to conduct research on the rural area of Alange, Spain, to explore the adaptive evaluation of rural housing construction in the reservoir area.

Ecological wisdom is an important research perspective that affects the principles of urban development and the interaction between cities and natural systems. Most of the existing researches are qualitative research [44–47]. Young, Robert F [45] used a multi-agent model to explore the influential framework for sustainable landscapes and urban planning from an ecological perspective. Patten [46] explored the role of management in sustainable, interdependent cities and natural systems from ecological wisdom.

It can be seen that the landscape ecology and urban resilience has a natural connection. The existing research focuses on the relationship between urbanization and environment, landscape resilience assessment, agricultural landscape, residential gardens and biodiversity. Most of these researches were conducted from the micro-level empirical research, qualitative research and survey data. Few of them introduced big data and other methods. The research content focuses on landscape ecology, land use, ecological wisdom and smart cities. Future research can focus on interdisciplinary integration with geography, economics and sociology, combined with big data, smart cities and land use analyzation. The research object can be further broadened, not limited to biodiversity and landscape.

4   Conclusions

Modern cities are facing more and more uncertainties, and urban resilience research as an effective tool to deal with urban uncertainty has developed rapidly in recent years. Theoretical innovation has begun to take shape, and the field has gradually broadened to form more abundant research results. This paper analyzes the research characters of urban resilience with big data method. The following conclusions can be obtain.

(1) The big data analyzation is effective in the study of research character analyzation of urban security based on urban resilience. The result can be presented in the form of visualization patterns.

(2) According to the knowledge map, the previous researches can be classified in to 7 clusters, including community sector, promotion of urban sustainability theory, land use change, nature conservation, urban waterscape, Geographic design, urbanization. These clusters can be further summarized as three characters, which are urban resilience and climate change adaptation, urban resilience governance model and social dynamic mechanism, and relationship between urban resilience and landscape.

(3) Based on the knowledge map, it is found that to strengthen the research at the community level and improve the division of research units is necessary in the area of climate change adaption. Social resilience research combined with urbanization and Chinese characteristics will be the future direction when it comes to governance model and social dynamic mechanism. In the field of landscape, future research can focus on interdisciplinary integration with geography, economics and sociology, combined with big data and smart cities.

Funding. This project is supported by the National Natural Science Foundation of China (41701186). Humanity and Social Science Youth Foundation of Ministry of Education (17YJCZH029).

References

1. Brecht, H., Deichmann, U., Wang, H.G.: A Global Urban Risk Index. The World Bank, Washington, D.C. (2013)
2. Xiu, C., Wei, Y., Wang, Q.: Evaluation of urban resilience of Dalian city based on the perspective of "Size-Density-Morphology". Acta Geogr. Sin. **73**(12), 2315–2328 (2018)
3. Walker, B., Holling, C.S., Carpenter, S., et al.: Resilience, adaptability and transformability in social–ecological systems. Ecol. Soc. **9**(2), 5 (2004)
4. Gunderson, L.H.: Panarchy: Understanding Transformations in Human and Natural Systems. Island Press, Washington, D.C. (2001)
5. Roy, M.: Planning for sustainable urbanisation in fast growing cities: mitigation and adaptation issues addressed in Dhaka, Bangladesh. Habitat Int. **33**(3), 276–286 (2009)
6. Alves, D., Barreira, A.P., Guimarães, M.H., et al.: Historical trajectories of currently shrinking Portuguese cities: a typology of urban shrinkage. Cities **52**, 20–29 (2016)
7. Muller, B.: Mending man's ways: wickedness, complexity and off-road travel. Landsc. Urban Plan. **154**, 93–101 (2016)

8. Chiang, Y.-C.: Exploring community risk perceptions of climate change - a case study of a flood-prone urban area of Taiwan. Cities **74**, 42–51 (2018)

9. Chu, E.K.: Urban climate adaptation and the reshaping of state–society relations: the politics of community knowledge and mobilisation in Indore, India. Urban Stud. **55**(8), 1766–1782 (2018)

10. Fang, Y., Zhao, C., Rasul, G., et al.: Rural household vulnerability and strategies for improvement: an empirical analysis based on time series. Habitat Int. **53**, 254–264 (2016)

11. Yenneti, K., Tripathi, S., Wei, Y.D., et al.: The truly disadvantaged? Assessing social vulnerability to climate change in urban India. Habitat Int. **56**, 124–135 (2016)

12. Ahern, J.: From fail-safe to safe-to-fail: sustainability and resilience in the new urban world. Landsc. Urban Plan. **100**(4), 341–343 (2011)

13. Spaans, M., Waterhout, B.: Building up resilience in cities worldwide–Rotterdam as participant in the 100 Resilient Cities Programme. Cities **61**, 109–116 (2017)

14. Samuelsson, K., Giusti, M., Peterson, G.D., et al.: Impact of environment on people's everyday experiences in Stockholm. Landsc. Urban Plan. **171**, 7–17 (2018)

15. Liao, K., Le, T.A., Van Nguyen, K.: Urban design principles for flood resilience: learning from the ecological wisdom of living with floods in the Vietnamese Mekong Delta. Landsc. Urban Plan. **155**, 69–78 (2016)

16. Torabi, E., Dedekorkut-Howes, A., Howes, M.: Adapting or maladapting: building resilience to climate-related disasters in coastal cities. Cities **72**, 295–309 (2018)

17. Poku-Boansi, M., Cobbinah, P.B.: Are we planning for resilient cities in Ghana? An analysis of policy and planners' perspectives. Cities **72**, 252–260 (2018)

18. Zhang, X., Li, H.: Urban resilience and urban sustainability: what we know and what we do not know? Cities **72**, 141–148 (2018)

19. Aoki, N.: Adaptive governance for resilience in the wake of the 2011 Great East Japan Earthquake and Tsunami. Habitat Int. **52**, 20–25 (2016)

20. Meerow, S., Newell, J.P., Stults, M.: Defining urban resilience: a review. Landsc. Urban Plan. **147**, 38–49 (2016)

21. Marks, D., Lebel, L.: Disaster governance and the scalar politics of incomplete decentralization: Fragmented and contested responses to the 2011 floods in Central Thailand. Habitat Int. **52**, 57–66 (2016)

22. Jones, G., Meegan, R., Kennett, P., et al.: The uneven impact of austerity on the voluntary and community sector: a tale of two cities. Urban Stud. **53**(10), 2064–2080 (2016)

23. Chmutina, K., Lizarralde, G., Dainty, A., et al.: Unpacking resilience policy discourse. Cities **58**, 70–79 (2016)

24. Gleeson, B.: Critical commentary. Waking from the dream: an Australian perspective on urban resilience. Urban Stud. **45**(13), 2653–2668 (2008)

25. Bouzarovski, S., Salukvadze, J., Gentile, M.: A socially resilient urban transition? The contested landscapes of apartment building extensions in two post-communist cities. Urban Stud. **48**(13), 2689–2714 (2011)

26. Cowell, M.M.: Bounce back or move on: regional resilience and economic development planning. Cities **30**, 212–222 (2013)

27. Castanho, R., Loures, L., Fernández, J., et al.: Identifying critical factors for success in Cross Border Cooperation (CBC) development projects. Habitat Int. **72**, 92–99 (2018)

28. Abramson, D.B.: Periurbanization and the politics of development-as-city-building in China. Cities **53**, 156–162 (2016)

29. Hudec, O., Reggiani, A., Šiserová, M.: Resilience capacity and vulnerability: a joint analysis with reference to Slovak urban districts. Cities **73**, 24–35 (2018)

30. Batty, M.: Polynucleated urban landscapes. Urban Stud. **38**(4), 635–655 (2001)

31. Stoms, D.M., Chomitz, K.M., Davis, F.W.: TAMARIN: a landscape framework for evaluating economic incentives for rainforest restoration. Landsc. Urban Plan. **68**(1), 95–108 (2004)
32. Ernstson, H.: The social production of ecosystem services: a framework for studying environmental justice and ecological complexity in urbanized landscapes. Landsc. Urban Plan. **109**(1), 7–17 (2013)
33. Pyke, C., Warren, M.P., Johnson, T., et al.: Assessment of low impact development for managing stormwater with changing precipitation due to climate change. Landsc. Urban Plan. **103**(2), 166–173 (2011)
34. Morinière, L.: Environmentally influenced urbanisation: footprints bound for town? Urban Stud. **49**(2), 435–450 (2012)
35. McClintock, N., Mahmoudi, D., Simpson, M., et al.: Socio-spatial differentiation in the Sustainable City: a mixed-methods assessment of residential gardens in metropolitan Portland, Oregon, USA. Landsc. Urban Plan. **148**, 1–16 (2016)
36. Coles, R., Costa, S.: Food growing in the city: exploring the productive urban landscape as a new paradigm for inclusive approaches to the design and planning of future urban open spaces, pp. 1–5 (2018)
37. Campellone, R.M., Chouinard, K.M., Fisichelli, N.A., et al.: The iCASS Platform: nine principles for landscape conservation design. Landsc. Urban Plan. **176**, 64–74 (2018)
38. Duckett, D., Feliciano, D., Martin-Ortega, J., et al.: Tackling wicked environmental problems: the discourse and its influence on praxis in Scotland. Landsc. Urban Plan. **154**, 44–56 (2016)
39. Karlo, T., Sajna, N.: Biodiversity related understorey stability of small peri-urban forest after a 100-year recurrent flood. Landsc. Urban Plan. **162**, 104–114 (2017)
40. Langemeyer, J., Camps-Calvet, M., Calvet-Mir, L., et al.: Stewardship of urban ecosystem services: understanding the value(s) of urban gardens in Barcelona. Landsc. Urban Plan. **170**, 79–89 (2018)
41. Peng, J., Pan, Y., Liu, Y., et al.: Linking ecological degradation risk to identify ecological security patterns in a rapidly urbanizing landscape. Habitat Int. **71**, 110–124 (2018)
42. Weil, K.K., Cronan, C.S., Meyer, S.R., et al.: Predicting stream vulnerability to urbanization stress with Bayesian network models. Landsc. Urban Plan. **170**, 138–149 (2018)
43. Jeong, J.S., García-Moruno, L., Hernandez-Blanco, J., et al.: Planning of rural housings in reservoir areas under (mass) tourism based on a fuzzy DEMATEL-GIS/MCDA hybrid and participatory method for Alange. Spain. Habitat Int. **57**, 143–153 (2016)
44. Wang, X., Palazzo, D., Carper, M.: Ecological wisdom as an emerging field of scholarly inquiry in urban planning and design. Landsc. Urban Plan. **155**, 100–107 (2016)
45. Young, R.F.: Modernity, postmodernity, and ecological wisdom: toward a new framework for landscape and urban planning. Landsc. Urban Plan. **155**, 91–99 (2016)
46. Patten, D.T.: The role of ecological wisdom in managing for sustainable interdependent urban and natural ecosystems. Landsc. Urban Plan. **155**, 3–10 (2016)
47. Marsal-Llacuna, M., Segal, M.E.: The Intelligenter Method (I) for making "smarter" city projects and plans. Cities **55**, 127–138 (2016)

Privacy Issues in Big Data from Collection to Use

Alaa A. Alwabel[(⊠)]

King Khaled University, Abha, Kingdom of Saudi Arabia
alwbel@kku.edu.sa

Abstract. Big data management and analysis has become an important matter in academic and industry research. In fact, big data can be very powerful and have significant positive impact on most organizations. However, a large portion of big data in service today is personal data. One of the methods currently in use to preserve privacy of personal data that are collected from big data, is to control the process of data collection according to corresponding privacy policies. In this paper we aim to highlight issues need to be resolved in order to achieve a sustainable balance of growth and protection in the use of big data. We have discussed three main issues including: the advanced definition of personal data, the concern of collecting big data: how and why big data collected and which challenges big data faced, the main privacy principles required in preserving privacy of collected big data, and finally we have proposed a case study to analyze the most famous online organization – Google- privacy policy in collecting big data and decide to which extent privacy is preserved.

Keywords: Big data · Knowledge management · Privacy policy

1 Introduction

Due to recent technological development, the amount of data produced by social networking sites, sensor networks, Internet, online games, online shopping, online education, healthcare applications, and many other companies, is significantly increasing day by day. All the big amount of data produced from various sources in several formats with very high speed is described as big data. Big data has become a very active research area for last couple of years [14]. In fact, big data can be very powerful and have significant positive impact on most organizations. Big data has become the power for better decision making, faster time to market; and enhanced customer service [1]. However, a large portion of big data in service today is personal data. The World Economic Forum describes the personal data gained from big data as—the new oil—a valuable resource of the 21st century, and the analytics of this data as—the new engine of economic and social value creation [2, 3]. Big data about individual including demographic information, social interaction, and internet activity are being collected by different service provider. Personal data is collected and used in order to add value to the business of the organization. The personal data of a person when collected with external large data sets leads to the implication of new facts and secret about that person. This could be done by making insight on people lives without

© Springer Nature Singapore Pte Ltd. 2020
Y. Tian et al. (Eds.): ICBDS 2019, CCIS 1210, pp. 382–391, 2020.
https://doi.org/10.1007/978-981-15-7530-3_29

their knowing while they might not want the data owner to know or any person to know about them [4]. The other hand, the data overflow presents privacy concerns that could lead to a regularity backlash, moving down the data economy and stifling innovation. Fail to protect data privacy is unethical and can cause harm to data subjects and the data provider. Big Data privacy is the most critical issue since the very early stage of data communication and management. To preserve the privacy of Personal data that are collected from big data, the most efficient way is to control the process of data collection according to corresponding privacy policies [5]. In this paper, we aim to highlight issues that need to be resolved in order to achieve a sustainable balance of growth and protection in the use of big data. We discuss few main questions as following: what is Personal data? Why do service provider collect big data? How do they collect big data? What are the challenges in collecting big data? What are main privacy principles in collecting big data? And finally, we will provide a case study of the most famous online organization -Google- to analyze its privacy policy in collecting big data and decide to which extent privacy is ensured.

2 Personal Data

The usefulness of processing big data is mainly unquestioned, however it arises high privacy risks when working on personal data. This is mostly due to two facts about big data. First, the bigger the amount of data the higher the possibility of re-identifying individuals even in datasets which seem like not to have personal connecting information. Second, it is able to extract from safe personal data new information that is much more important and was not expected to be discovered by the affected person [12]. Personal data meaning is evolving with the advanced technologies to include new dimensions. Traditionally, the definition was pre-determined and governed using personally identifiable information whereas the non-personally identifiable information was often uncontrolled [3]. However, the definition of personal data is changing with new personal preferences, new applications, context of uses, and changes in cultural and social norms. According Teresa Scassa [6], it recognized that personal data means a name, an address and other information that you might give to someone, but now personal data can be any information about our activities, about everything we do online, and even elsewhere [7, 8]. Personal data is a term that may be used in a slightly different manner by different people, but in this paper, we mean by personal data the following two dimensions [9].

2.1 Personally Identifiable Information

Any information that could be used to identify or locate an individual including individual name or characteristics that may be made part of the individual personal data such as age, gender, and relationship status, and it may refer to information that can be correlated with other information to identify an individual like credit card number, and postal code.

2.2   Non-personally Identifiable Information

Any information that could be considered as private and related to the individual life. It could be divided in three sub-dimensions as following.

Social Life. Any information could be used to identify the social life of the individual and considered sensitive such as religion race, health, union membership, personal financial information and job performance information, his interests in hobbies, his interests in entertainment as well as his interests in commercial products.

Cognitive/Expert Life. Any information could be used to identify the expert of the individual including his knowledge, his background and his skills, his professional interests. In addition, individual goal or intention could be also considered to be sensitive and that represent what individual wishes to achieve in a given context.

Digital Life. Any information could be used to identify the individual usage of the digital data, and his unique device identity. The repetitive behaviors of the individual that can be observed and stored in their profiles such as viewing habits for digital content, users' recently visited websites or product usage history, and the history of the individual actions considered under this type of data. Moreover, uniquely traceable to the individual device considered sensitive and may affect individual such as IP addresses, Radio Frequency Identity (RFID) tags, and unique hardware identities.

3   Big Data Collection Concern

Day by day individuals are transacting more and more data online and service provider have begun exploring what insights and lessons they can gather from users of data through collecting, storing, processing, and analysis of extremely large data sets [11]. Although, the collect of data creates influence with each additional use, it leads to the challenges of the complexity in controlling the way of collecting data. Different concerns regarding big data collection including how and why big data is collected, and which challenges does it face will be discussed in this part.

3.1   How Big Data Is Collected

Big Data is collected by billions of connected devices, people and sensors that trace trillions of transactions and behaviors each day. The unexpected amount of data being generated is created in multiple ways. Big Data is actively collected from individuals who provide it in traditional ways by filling out forms, surveys, registrations and so on. They are also passively collected as a by-product of other activities by web browsing, location information from phones and credit card purchases, social media, search engine, free applications and by many other services. The increasing use of machine-to-machine transactions, which do not involve human interaction, is generating more and more data about individuals. All this data is further analyzed and commingled to create inferred data [4].

3.2   Why Big Data Is Collected

According to a report of the standing committee on access to information and ethics (2012) personal data was collected to be used in transaction purpose whereas personal data is now itself the valued commodity [8]. In Professor Scassas view, the data is collected to profile us to define our consumption habits, to decide our fitness for products or services, or to apply price unfairness in the delivery of wares or services. We become data subjects in the fullest sense of the word [8]. Consequently, free online services are not free, but rather a means to commercialize access to users and their personal data. As noted by Jason Zushman of the Merchant Law Group, —the archiving and monitoring of information that's provided by users is what provides the monetary benefits to the companies [10].

3.3   Challenges in Collecting Big Data

World Economic Forum found that the Data-driven opportunities are not without risk and uncertainty. The issue is how to gain new insights and make better decisions, and to do so in a manner that recognizes and protects individual privacy. The profitable incentive in collecting data to share with secondary and tertiary parties is strong and deeply embedded in existing Internet business models. Although, more and more data are collected and combined, the insights, discoveries, value and possible risks increase; particularly, if this activity performed by parties not directly known by individual. With more than 6 billion people connected to mobile devices, more diversity of data is also becoming capable of being linked to individual identity. Smart phones are now able to capture and track an individual location patterns as well as facilitate create new levels of authentication. Moreover, individuals are no longer just the subjects of data they are also being recognized as producers of data. For example, digital personal-health devices measure daily physical activities. They present a new way of capturing a rich data set about an individual [4]. Collecting big data have raised questions regarding the appropriate balance of control between individuals and service provider, and how best to protect personal privacy interests. Researchers argue that individuals have a legitimate interest in the collection of data by third parties. Certainly, big data collection practices rather than bad uses or outcomes are enough to trigger an individual privacy interests. Nowadays, big data collection practices are for the most part unregulated [11]. The key challenge is to regulate the optimal balance between enhanced privacy protection and the helpfulness of the data for decision making. In one hand, the data must be used for extracting value, and, on the other hand, the re-identification of the data must be minimized [13]. Consequently, there is a great need to address the truly activation privacy principles required in collecting big data in order to balance between beneficial uses of big data and the protection of individual privacy.

4 Privacy Principles of Big Data Collection

Principles have been and need to be a core part of the future governance in collecting personal data. Principles can set the foundation for trustworthy collecting data and help empower users. Identifying the principles that reflect communal and cultural norms and ensuring ways to activate them will enable trustworthy data practices, persuading individuals to be more willing to share data about themselves. Existing principles associated with the collection, handling and use of personal data have formed the basis of most privacy and data-protection legislation around the world. Privacy policies must be made available to clients, and be understandable [4]. We briefly describe and discuss the nine privacy principles that should be considered in big data collection process [9, 12].

Notice, Openness and Transparency. This principle refers to that anyone who wants to collect user's information must inform them what and why they want to collect, how they want to use it, how long they will keep it, with whom they will share it, and any other uses they intend for the information. They must also notify users if they want to make any change in how the information is being used. If they want to pass the information to third parties, users must be notified too.

Choice, Consent and Control. This principle refers to that users must be given the choice of whether they want this information to be collected or not. Data subjects must give their approval to the collection, use and disclosure of their Personal identifiable information.

Scope/Minimization. This principle refers to that only information that is necessary to fulfill the stated purpose should be collected or shared. The collection of data should be minimized.

Access and Accuracy. This principle refers to that users must be able to get access to their personal data; to observe what is being collected about them, and to check its accuracy.

Security Safeguards. This principle refers to that safeguards must prevent unauthorized access, disclosure, copying, use or modification of Personal identifiable information.

Challenging/Compliance. This principle refers to that clients must be able to challenge an agency's privacy process. Transactions must be compliant to privacy legislation. One feature of this is respecting cross border transfer obligations.

Purpose. This principle refers to that data usage has to be limited to the purpose for which it was collected. There must be a clearly specified purpose for the collection and sharing of personal data. Data subjects should be informed why their data is being collected and shared at or before the time of collection.

Limiting Use-Disclosure and Retention. This principle refers to that data can only be used or disclosed for the purpose for which it was collected and should only be divulged to those parties authorized to receive it. Personal data should be aggregated or anonymized wherever possible to limit the possible for compute matching of records. Personal data should only be kept as long as is necessary.

Accountability. This principle refers to that an organization must appoint someone to ensure that privacy policies and practices are followed. Audit functions must be present to monitor all data accesses and modifications.

5 Case Study

In our study we are going to analyze the privacy policy of the most famous online organization – Google Company- to address the non-resolved areas in their privacy policy of collecting bid data through online tool that named as policy score. Privacy Score is a project of Privacy Choice, which was founded in 2009 by Jim Brock to make privacy easier for websites, apps and their users. Privacy Score analyses the privacy policies of companies along for clear criteria and assess the privacy risk of using a website. Privacy Score covers two kinds of data: it estimate privacy risk to personal data such as your name or email address based on the published policies of the website, and estimate privacy risk to anonymous data such as your interests and preferences based on the privacy qualifications of the other companies who collect this kind of data across websites [12]. However, Privacy Scores reflects nine factors based on the site's privacy policy and the privacy qualifications of the other companies collecting data there. Four site-policy factors cover how websites promise to collect and handle your personal data. Five tracking data factors cover the privacy policies and oversight of companies that collect anonymous profile data on the site and elsewhere for things like ad selection [12]. Based on these factors, a Privacy Score of 100 would indicate two points as mentioned in the following (Table 1).

Table 1. Privacy score factors.

Privacy Indicator			
How websites promise to handle user personal data		The privacy policies qualification site tracker that collect anonymous profile data	
Factor	Score	Factor	Score
Sharing	30	Anonymity	20
Deletion	10	Boundaries	5
Notice	5	Choice	5
Vendors	5	Retention	10
		Oversight	10
Total = 100			

The Privacy Scores first indicate the site's policies expressly limit the sharing and use of personally identifiable data in four different ways. First, personal data like name, phone number and email address should not be provided to marketers without permission and should be deleted on request. Second, a user's request to delete personal data should be honored. Third, notice should be provided in the case of disclosure of personal data pursuant to legal process or government requests, where legally allowed. Fourth, if service providers have access to personal data, their use of it should be restricted by contract. The other hand, the Privacy Scores indicate that all trackers seen on the site pledge to respect different five criteria. First, personal data should not be collected or use, or should be separated from behavioral data. Second, boundaries should be recognized in areas like health conditions and financial data. Third, choice should provide as to whether data will be collected or applied for the purpose of ad targeting. Fourth, Retention should provide whether data will be deleted data within one year or lose points ratably. Finally, Accountability should be provided through both regular compliance reviews of internal processes by industry organizations such as the Network Advertising Initiative or independent auditors, as well as ongoing external monitoring of practices by industry organizations.

5.1 Google Privacy Issues

Google has drawn considerable criticism for its privacy practices. It were reported that Google used user name and profile pictures in advertisement. In addition, it provides special government access without notifying their user as reported that they participate in PRISM program. In October 2011, it was reported by the United States Federal Trade Commission (FTC) that Google Company are sharing user information without their consent. In August 2012, it was fined $22.5 million by the United States Federal Trade Commission (FTC) for bypassing the privacy settings in Apple's Safari browser in order to track the browser's users and show them advertisements, thereby violating a prior agreement with the FTC.

5.2 Assurances Scale in Google Privacy Policy

Google earns 30 points out of 30 in sharing privacy policy based on the latest updated in their company privacy policy they don't share personal data, like your name, email or phone. Furthermore, they gain 10 out of 10 in their deletion privacy policy as they will delete data promptly when you terminate your account. While they gain zero out of 5 in their notice privacy policy as they don't notify users of government requests for personal data. And finally, they gain 5 out of 5 in their vendor's privacy policy as they require confidentiality from service providers with data access.

5.3 Privacy Qualifications Scale of Trackers on Google Site

Google gain 20 out of 20 in their anonymity privacy policy as they don't associate personal identification data with your profile. Moreover, they got 5 out of 5 in their Boundaries privacy policy as they keep out of sensitive areas like health history, financial records or religion. In addition, Google gained 5 out of 5 in their Choice privacy policy as they allow users to opt-out of behavioral ad targeting. Furthermore, they got 10 out of 10 in their Retention privacy policy as they delete data within one year or lose points ratably. And finally, they gained 10 out of 10 in their Oversight privacy policy as they are subject to oversight from industry organizations. We can summarize Google privacy policy level as following (Table 2).

Table 2. Google privacy policy assessment.

Privacy Indicator			
How websites promise to handle user personal data		The privacy policies qualification site tracker that collect anonymous profile data	
Factor	Score	Factor	Score
Sharing	30	Anonymity	20
Deletion	10	Boundaries	5
Notice	0	Choice	5
Vendors	5	Retention	10
		Oversight	10
Total = 95			

As a result, we can say that during the last two years Google has drawn considerable criticisms for its privacy practices. Although, Google privacy policy has updated to reach better lever and gained 95 scores in both assurance scale and privacy qualification scale for all trackers, Privacy Score has considered other privacy issues of Google Company that could badly affect their users. First, Users will have one profile across all Google services. This means user personal data, searches and behavior are available to all Google applications and advertising. User should log out and use private browsing for Google services that they do not want associated with their Google profile. Second, Concentration of data increases privacy risk. Google's privacy score does not reflect the additional risk posed by the breadth of Google's data collection. If users make extensive Google services–such as Google Search and Gmail - this increases the impact on their privacy if Google does not honor its privacy policies. Third, new privacy policy. This Privacy Score is based on Google's revised and unified privacy policy, which has effective from March 1, 2012.

6   Conclusion

This paper addressed the new perspectives of Personal Data that gained from Big Data and should be protected by service provider. In order to preserve privacy of Big Data, the most efficient way is to control the process of collecting data. Consequently, the paper introduced the way of collecting Big Data, reasons of collecting Big Data and the challenges facing Big Data. The paper also introduced the international privacy principles of Big Data Collection. In order to achieve a sustainable balance of growth and protection in the use of big data, the paper highlighted the no resolved areas in the most famous online organization–Google- privacy policy through analysis tool. Finally, we conclude that privacy principles are not enough and there is a need to translate principles into practice through a model that inform service provider how to manage the use of the personal data in trusted way with economic growth.

References

1. ISACA: Privacy and Big Data (2013). http://www.isaca.org
2. World Economic Forum: Personal Data: The Emergence of a New Asset Class (2011). www.weforum.org/reports/personal-dataemergence-new-asset-class
3. World Economic Forum: Unlocking the Value of Personal Data: From Collection to Usage (2013). www3.weforum.org/docs/WEF_IT_UnlockingValuePersonalData_Collection Usage_Report_2013.pdf
4. Katal, A., Wazid, M.: Big data: issues, challenges, tools and good practices. In: IEEE 6th International Conference on Contemporary Computing (IC3). Department of CSE, Graphic Era University, Dehradun, India (2013)
5. Ng, W.S., Wu, H., Wu, W., Xiang, S., Tan, K.L.: Privacy preservation in streaming data collection. In: IEEE 18th International Conference on Parallel and Distributed Systems. Institute for Infocomm Research, A*STAR, Singapore (2012)
6. Scassa, T.: Standing Committee on Access to Information, Privacy and Ethics. 1st Session, 41st Parliament, May 31, 2012. House of Common, Canada (2012)
7. Pierre-Luc, D.: Privacy and Social Media in the Age of Big Data. House of Commons, Canada (2012)
8. Hasan, O., Habegger, B., Brunie, L., Bennani, N., Damiani, E.: A discussion of privacy challenges in user profiling with big data techniques: the EEXCESS use case. In: 2013 IEEE International Congress on Big Data, Santa Clara, CA (2013)
9. Jason, Z.: Standing Committee on Access to Information, Privacy and Ethics. 1st Session, 41st Parliament, October 16, 2012, 1645 Merchant Law Group (2012)
10. Justin, B.: Why Collection Matters: Surveillance as a Defector Privacy (2012). http://www.futureofprivacy.org/wpcontent/uploads/Brookman-Why-CollectionMatters.pdf
11. Siani, P.: Taking Account of Privacy When Designing Cloud Computing Services. Hewlett-Packard Development Company, L.P. (2009)
12. Jim, B.: Privacy Score Project (2009). http://privacyscore.com
13. Gruschka, N., Mavroeidis, V., Vishi, K., Jensen, M.: Privacy issues and data protection in big data: a case study analysis under GDPR. In: 2018 IEEE International Conference on Big Data (Big Data), pp. 5027–5033. IEEE (2018)

14. Bachlechner, D., La Fors, K., Sears, A.M.: The role of privacy-preserving technologies in the age of big data. In: WISP 2018 Proceedings, vol. 28 (2018). https://aisel.aisnet.org/wisp2018/28
15. Abid, M., Iynkaran, N., Yong, X.: Protection of big data privacy. IEEE Access **4**, 1821–1834 (2016). https://doi.org/10.1109/ACCESS.2016.2558446

Trusted Query Method Based on Authorization Index and Triangular Matrix in Big Data

Lihong Guo[1,2(✉)], Haitao Wu[1], and Jie Yang[1]

[1] Department of Information and Communications Engineering,
Nanjing Institute of Technology, Nanjing 211167, China
`guolihongnj@163.com`
[2] College of Computer Science and Technology,
Nanjing University of Aeronautics and Astronautics, Nanjing 210016, China

Abstract. Owing to the increasing of XML data on the web, the security search for a shared XML document in the cloud becomes a central issue in the database and information retrieval. In this paper, a new authorization and trusted query method is proposed to finish the security search for big data, which uses index vector to represent the authorization of content and uses the triangular matrix to represent XML's structure. It not only provides the authorization of content but also considers the structure information. At the same time, query vector is created based on query keywords in order to improve the speed of search, and with the help of triangular matrix and authorization index, which also can efficiently speed up the process of search. Experiment shows that this method has good performance in security search for big data.

Keywords: Trusted query · Authorization index · Triangular matrix · Big data

1 Introduction

At present, with the development of information technology, it makes the information more and more abundant, and the data are growing rapidly on the Internet. Facing with more and more complex data, how to effectively organize, store and manage these data has become an important problem in the development of network and database now. Especially with the semi-structured XML appearing, its scalability and portability make a lot of organizations and agencies using XML as the information carrier. Therefore, XML plays an important role in the field of data storage and exchange. In the face of a large amount of XML data, developing high performance techniques for efficiently managing extremely large collections of XML data becomes essential in information retrieval fields. About XML, it relates to many techniques including data classification, clustering technology and privacy protection, security search, data similarity detection and so on [1–3]. In them, XML security search plays a very important role in the related research fields [4, 5].

In this paper, a trusted query scheme based on the authorization index and triangular matrix is proposed. For XML document we know that the main information is

© Springer Nature Singapore Pte Ltd. 2020
Y. Tian et al. (Eds.): ICBDS 2019, CCIS 1210, pp. 392–401, 2020.
https://doi.org/10.1007/978-981-15-7530-3_30

located at the leaf node, so the core of authorization is on the leaf node, and the structure also has a certain impact. In this paper, using triangular matrix to represent the structure and using index vector to indicate the authorization of leaf node. Combination of authorization index and triangular matrix, it can make legitimate users obtain effective queries.

In summary, the contributions of this paper are as follows:

(1) A new trusted query method is proposed for XML document, which uses the triangular matrix to represent the structure and uses index vector to indicate the authorization of content, so XML's trusted query is changed into the combined calculation between triangular matrix and index vector.
(2) Compare with whole XML document's authorization, the content's index authorization relieves the pressure on the server side.
(3) In order to test the effectiveness of the algorithm the simulation software is designed to verify the trusted query scheme. Experiment shows that this method has good performance in security search for big XML data.

The rest of this paper is organized as follows. We describe existing classical XML trusted query methods, and analyze their core ideas in Sect. 2. In Sect. 3, we present some preliminaries. In Sect. 4, we provide the trusted query method, which includes the extraction of main structure, the creation of structure matrix, and the authorization of leaf nodes. In Sect. 5, we show the simulation software and the experiment data, which verifies the performance of the scheme. Section 6 presents the conclusion and summaries about XML trusted query.

2 Related Work

There are a lot of studies on trusted query. The traditional trusted query method is to encrypt XML document, if the user wants to obtain some information, he must get the corresponding decryption key and then decrypt the document, which increases the burden on the user or server. These methods achieve confidentiality and credibility, but lose flexibility.

In recent years, a good trusted query way is to directly search information on the encrypted document. Searchable encryption becomes an active research area in the cloud model to improve the usage of outsourced encrypted data [6]. In 2018, MB Smithamol [7] proposed a novel privacy enhanced conjunctive search (PECS) over encrypted data in the cloud supporting parallel search and dynamic updating to achieve search efficiency. In 2019, Song [8] established a set of strict privacy requirements for full-text retrieval in cloud storage systems and designed a Bloom filter based tree index. In 2019, Li [9] proposed a secure and efficient client-side encrypted data deduplication scheme (CSED). In CSED, a dedicated key server is introduced in generating MLE keys to resist brute-force attacks. Nowadays, homomorphic encryption technology [10–12] has been proposed and provides the ability to perform calculations on encrypted data without decrypting them. For the search on the encrypted document, it is convenient to the user, but the process is too complex, and query efficiency also needs to be improved.

Access control is one of effective methods to implement trusted queries, which restricts the access through all kinds of authorization schemes. Many researches have been done to specify a fine-grained authorization on XML data [13–15]. In these schemes, how to implement authorization and how to search for the authorization are the key problems to be solved.

In this paper, facing with a shared big XML document in the cloud, we proposed a new authorization and trusted query method to finish the query for big XML data, which uses index vector to represent the authorization of content and use the triangular matrix to indicate the structure. It is a good trusted query method.

3 Preliminaries

Definition 1: *XML tree.* An XML document [16] is a rooted, labeled tree, represented as a tuple $t = (r_d, V_d, E_d, \Phi_{E_d})$ whose individual components have the following meaning:

- r_d is the root node of XML document d, i.e. the only node with no entering edges;
- V_d is a set of nodes;
- $E_d \subseteq V_d * V_d$ is the set of edges, catching the parent-child relationships between nodes of t;
- $\Phi_{E_d} : E_d \rightarrow$ *label* Label is an alphabet of node tags; Φ_{E_d} is a node labeling function.

Definition 2: *Main Structure tree.* A main structure tree is a data structure that is a compact representation of XML document. It is concise, accurate and convenient summary of the structure. Main structure tree describes every unique label path exactly once, no matter how many times it appears in the XML document.

Definition 3: *Authorization Index Vector.* The index vector $a = (x_1, x_2, x_3, \dots, x_n)$ is used to represent authorization information for XML document, the dimension of vector is the number n of leaf nodes in main structure tree, every vector's subcomponent represents the authorization of each leaf node. For XML document, the content of leaf node is the core information, so the authorization of leaf node can well represent the authorization of the whole XML document.

4 XML Trusted Query Method

In the literatures on XML search, most of them make the semi-structured XML document change into linear or geometric representation, and then come down to the mathematical problem to deal with it. In this scheme, we are also inspired by this idea, and make XML's authorization change into index vector, make XML's structure into triangular matrix, make the search request change into query vector. Therefore, the secure queries of XML document are finally transformed into the combination of matrix and index vector. The detailed trusted query process is shown below.

4.1 Extracting Main Structure Information

In most cases, there is much different information with same repetitive structure in an XML document. For example, the electronic health records in the hospital contain thousands of patients' information and the electronic book records include thousands of authors' information. In the process of XML query request, we are more concerned with the content of XML document than its structure. That is to say, for the user, he is more concerned with the specific content. Therefore, the authorization of leaf node is the core.

In order to obtain a concise summary of the structure, here we extract the main structure of XML document. Figure 1a is an XML document tree, and Fig. 1b is its main structure tree. Node C and H are the repeated nodes with same subtree, we label them with C* and H* in Fig. 1b.

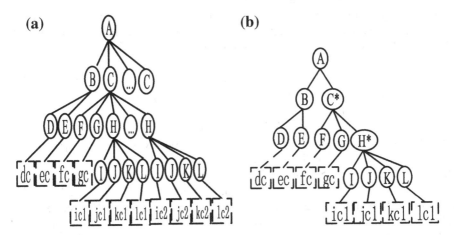

Fig. 1. a. An XML document tree, b. The main structure tree to Fig. 1a

4.2 Creating the Triangular Matrix

After extracting main structure tree, a triangular matrix is used to represent main structure tree [17, 18]. The dimension of matrix is decided by the number of leaf nodes in main structure tree.

The rule of creation and storage is as follows:

(1) To the leaf node: the leaf nodes are saved in the diagonal sequentially in the matrix.
(2) To the intermediate node: every intermediate node will be saved in the lower left corner of all its children position, and whose storage position is decided by all its children' position together in matrix. We choose the maximum value among its children nodes' abscissa values as its abscissa value, its ordinate value is the minimum value among its children nodes' ordinate values.

We assume that any node a saved in [i, j] of matrix, and its abscissa value is i, its ordinate value is j, and then the calculation formula about i and j are shown in formula (1) and (2):

$$i = \begin{cases} k & if \quad node\ a \in leaf\ node \\ \max(i_1, i_2, \ldots i_m) & if \quad node\ a \in int\ ermediate\ node \end{cases} \tag{1}$$

$$j = \begin{cases} k & if \quad node\ a \in leaf\ node \\ \min(j_1, j_2, \ldots j_m) & if \quad node\ a \in int\ ermediate\ node \end{cases} \tag{2}$$

Here, k is the sequence of leaf node a in all the leaf nodes. According to the storage rule, all the leaf nodes are stored sequentially in the diagonal from left to right. So $k = 0, 1, 2, \cdots$. $i_1, i_2, \ldots i_m$ are the children' abscissa value of node a sequentially. $j_1, j_2, \ldots j_m$ are the children' ordinate value of node a sequentially.

For example, in Fig. 1b, the number of leaf nodes is 8, so the dimension of matrix is 8*8. All the leaf nodes are stored sequentially in the diagonal from left to right. The first leaf node 'D' is saved in [0, 0], the second leaf node 'E' is saved in [1, 1]..., the last leaf node 'L' is saved in [7, 7].

Example 1: in Fig. 1b, node 'B' has two children node 'D' and node 'E'. Node 'D' is in [0, 0], node 'E' is in [1, 1], so node 'B' is save in [x, y], that is x = max(0,1) = 1, y = min(0,1) = 0. So node 'D' is in [1, 0].

Example 2: in Fig. 1b, node 'H' has four children, they are nodes 'I', 'J', 'K', 'L'. Node 'I' is saved in [4, 4], node 'J' is saved in [5, 5], node 'K' is saved in [6, 6], node 'L' is saved in [7, 7], assume that the storage position of node 'H' is [x, y], x = max (4,5,6,7) = 7, y = min(4,5,6,7) = 4, so node 'H' is saved in [7, 4] in matrix.

Example 3: Node 'C' has three children, they are nodes 'F', 'G', 'H'. Node 'F' is saved in [2, 2], node 'G' is saved in [3, 3], node 'H' is saved in [7, 4], assume that the storage position of node 'C' is [x, y], x = max(2,3,7) = 7, y = min(2,3,4) = 2, so node 'C' is saved in [7, 2]. By this way the main structure tree of XML document is saved in a matrix. Further, it can be converted to a numerical matrix, if the value in the matrix is 1, it is a real node, and value 0 indicates that there is no node in this location. They are showed in Fig. 2.

(a)   **(b)**

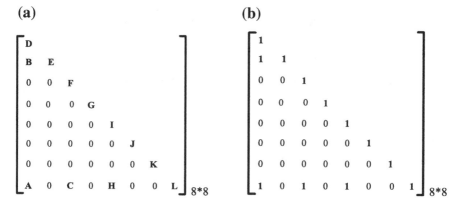

Fig. 2. a. The storage matrix to Fig. 1b, b. The numerical matrix to Fig. 2a

4.3   Creating Authorization Index Vector

After creating the triangular matrix, structure information of XML document is changed into a matrix. For a legitimate user, who wants to get the useful information? Taking electronic health records as an example, every personal user wants to get his personal therapy information; as to a pathological researcher, he wants to get some pathological information of patients; as to the pharmaceutical companies, they are concerned about medical information. So the content information is the core, that's to say: the leaf nodes' authorization is the core of authorization. Here, authorization index vector is proposed to represent leaf node's authorization. In the index vector, value 1 indicates that the leaf node is authorized to access, and value 0 means that the leaf node is not allowed access. Corresponding to Fig. 1b, authorization index vector of leaf node is in displayed below Fig. 3.

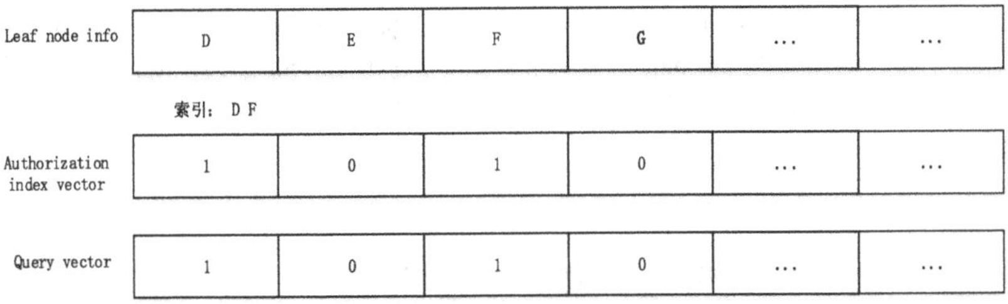

Fig. 3. The index vector

In order to speed up the query, the user query request is also converted into vector, and the creation of query vector is also based on the information of leaf nodes. For the user, he first chooses every node what he wants to get and then through the filter of authorization index vector. The steps of trusted query are listed as follows:

- Create structure matrix M:{ }
- Leaf node information x_1(D, E, F, G..........)
- Query vector x_2 (1, 0, 1, 0......)
- Authorization index vector x_3 (1, 0, 1, 0 ......)
- $x_2 = Digit(x_1)$;
- $x_4 = x_3$ & x_2;
- $A^* \leftarrow x_4$ @ M;
- result = A^*‖EncInfo.

In above, Digit() is a function, which can make $x1$ digitize; Symbol '&' represents 'and' operation, which is a filter of query request through the authorization index vector; '@' is a combination operation, the query request after authorization filter combines with structure matrix, the temporary query result is A^*; "‖" is a link operation, that means A^* must obtain encoding information about the leaf node to get the final query result.

The detailed process is shown in Fig. 4.

Algorithm : Trusted Query Procedure

Input: ID, QueryRequest   **Output:** result

1.	variant SearchProc( )	// Running in the server
2.	{ Matrix M, A*;	
3.	Vector x_1, x_2, x_3, x_4;	
4.	string req;	//the user's search request
5.	variant result;	//the search result
6.	x_3=AuthorizationIndexVector(ID);	
7.	A=ChangeStrucMatrix( );	//Change main structure to matrix
8.	While listening ()	// listening the user's request
9.	{	
10.	x_1=CreateRequestVector(req);	//Create vector for the user's request
11.	x_2=Digit (x_1);	
12.	x_4= x_3 & x_2;	//filter request by the authorization index
13.	A*=Combine(x_4, M);	//the validate request and strucure A*
14.	result=A* ‖ EncInfo;	//by the Encoding to get result
15.	return result;	
16.	}	
17.	}	

Fig. 4. The process of trusted query

5   Experiments and Results

To assess the validity of the proposal approach, we design a simulation software to implement the trusted query for shared XML document. It uses Visual C++ 6.0 as visual software development tool, and with the DOM technology to obtain the element and leaf node information in XML document [19, 20]. This software includes two parts: the server and the client.

In Fig. 5, it is main frame in server, left area displays main structure tree about the shared XML document, and right area is the function area. For the server, it is a monitor program, which includes user information management (registration, modification information, logout, etc.), nodes' authorization of different users, nodes' encoding and loading of shared XML document. In the normal working state, the server can monitor and listen all kinds of query request, registration or logout requests from the client and then respond to them.

For the client, it includes connect module, query request module and display module.

(1) Connect module: the user must fill in the user and password information to verify his identity. At the same time, he need fill in the server's information including IP address and port number.

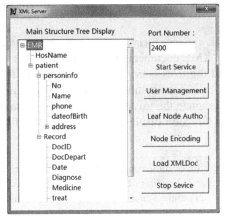
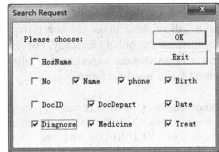

Fig. 5. The display of server   **Fig. 6.** The query request in client

(2) Query request module: after connection the user can send query request by the 'SearchRequest' module, its detailed information is shown in Fig. 6. In this part, the user can choose what he wants to get. In Fig. 6, every check button corresponds to a leaf node of XML main structure tree.

(3) Display module is used to display current search's structure, and the user can choose whether to display the structure or not.

In client, after sending the query request it will get the detailed result and display in the list area. Further, in this area, we can get the query time of this query and display in middle area. The example is shown in Fig. 7. From the display result and acquired data we know that it has a good performance in trusted query.

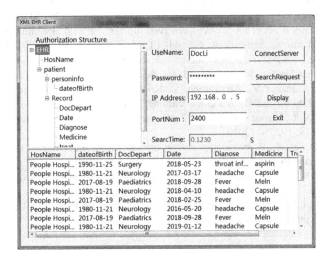

Fig. 7. The main frame in client

6   Conclusion

In this paper, we have proposed a new XML trusted query method, which uses the triangular matrix to save the main structure of XML document, uses the index vector to represent the authorization of leaf nodes, and digitizes query request to speed up the search. All of these make the query request be a combination calculation, which not only increase the query efficiency, but also complete the trusted query. The simulation software provides the experiment results and function display, which shows that this method has a good performance.

Acknowledgment. This work was supported by the Innovation Funding of Nanjing Institute of Technology (No. CKJB201704), the Scientific Research Funding of Nanjing Institute of Technology (No. ZKJ201612), and the National Natural Science Foundation of China (No. 61701221).

References

1. Hwang, J.H., Ryu, K.H.: A weighted common structure based clustering technique for XML documents. J. Syst. Softw. **83**(7), 1267–1274 (2010)
2. Hristidis, V., Koudas, N., Papakonstantinou, Y., Srivastava, D.: Keyword proximity search in XML trees. IEEE Trans. Knowl. Data Eng. **18**(4), 525–539 (2006)
3. Tekli, J., Chbeir, R., Yetongnon, K.: An overview on XML similarity: background, current trends and future directions. Comput. Sci. Rev. **3**(3), 151–173 (2009)
4. Lee, J.-G., Whang, K.-Y., et al.: The dynamic predicate: integrating access control with query processing in XML databases. VLDB J. **16**(3), 371–387 (2007)
5. Tan, Z., Zhang, L., Wang, W., Shi, B.: XML data exchange with target constraints. Inf. Process. Manag. **49**(2), 465–483 (2013)
6. Yin, H., Qin, Z., et al.: Secure conjunctive multi-keyword ranked search over encrypted cloud data for multiple data owners. Future Gener. Comput. Syst. **100**, 689–700 (2019)
7. Smithamol, M.B., Sridhar, R.: PECS: privacy enhanced conjunctive search over encrypted data in the cloud supporting parallel search. Comput. Commun. **126**, 50–63 (2018)
8. Song, W., Wang, B., et al.: A privacy-preserved full-text retrieval algorithm over encrypted data for cloud storage applications. J. Parallel Distrib. Comput. **99**, 14–27 (2017)
9. Li, S., Xu, C., Zhang, Y.: CSED: client-side encrypted deduplication scheme based on proofs of ownership for cloud storage. J. Inf. Secur. Appl. **46**, 250–258 (2019)
10. Kalpana, G., Kumar, P.V., Aljawarneh, S., Krishnaiah, R.V.: Shifted adaption homomorphism encryption for mobile and cloud learning. Comput. Electr. Eng. **65**, 178–195 (2018)
11. Ullah, S., Li, X.Y., Hussain, M.T., Lan, Z.: Kernel homomorphic encryption protocol. J. Inf. Secur. Appl. **48**, 102366 (2019)
12. Alloghani, M., et al.: A systematic review on the status and progress of homomorphic encryption technologies. J. Inf. Secur. Appl. **48**, 102362 (2019)
13. An, D., Park, S.: Efficient access control labeling scheme for secure XML query processing. Comput. Stand. Interf. **33**(5), 439–447 (2011)
14. Chebotko, A., Chang, S., Lu, S., Fotouhi, F.: Secure XML querying based on authorization graphs. Inf. Syst. Front. **14**(3), 617–632 (2012)

15. Sun, L., Wang, H., Jururajin, R., Sriprakash, S.: A purpose based access control in XML databases system. In: Proceedings of 4th International Conference on Network and System Security, pp. 486–493 (2010)
16. Wu, H., Tang, Z.: Automatic classification method for XML documents. Int. J. Digit. Content Technol. Appl. **5**(12), 153–161 (2011)
17. Guo, L., Wang, J., Wu, H., Du, H.: eXtensible markup language access control model with filtering privacy based on matrix storage. IET Commun. **8**(11), 1919–1927 (2014)
18. Guo, L., Wang, J., Du, H.: XML privacy protection model based on cloud storage. Comput. Stand. Interf. **36**(3), 454–464 (2014)
19. XML DOM Tutorial. http://www.w3schools.com/dom
20. Mirabi, M., Ibrahim, H., Udzir, N.I., Mamat, A.: An encoding scheme based on fractional number for querying and updating XML data. J. Syst. Softw. **85**(8), 1831–1851(2012)

Microservice Architecture Design for Big Data in Tactical Cloud

Liyuan Tang[1(✉)], Haoren Hu[2], Zhonghua Wang[1], Jiansheng Wang[1], and Yahui Li[1]

[1] Aeronautics Computing Technique Research Institute, Xi'an 710065, China
1140614393@qq.com
[2] School of Computer Science and Technology, Xidian University, Xi'an 710071, China

Abstract. With the rapid development of emerging technologies such as big data and cloud computing, the research on the "Tactical Cloud" with resource awareness, real-time data sharing and collaborative operations is driven. The tactical cloud is to autonomously complete the intelligent process from task delivery to execution, which is related to situational awareness, dynamic programming, load scheduling, and data synchronization. However, monolithic architecture is used to complete various customization functions on the traditional airborne computers, which results in the problems such as low collaboration and inability to share data in time, especially the requirements of big data. In order to solve the above problems, this paper presents the microservice architecture firstly. Besides, based on the bounded context method for microservice decomposition, the design ideas and implementation schemes for resource scheduling and monitoring and data synchronization in the tactical cloud are proposed to provide efficient and fast collaborative combat capabilities. Briefly, resource scheduling and monitoring provide load scheduling and fault warning for microservices, and data synchronization make functions decomposed into microservices to share various tactical data between aircraft nodes in time.

Keywords: Tactical cloud · Microservice · Resource scheduling · Data synchronization

1 Introduction

During recent years, with the rapid development of emerging technologies such as new sensors, cloud computing, and artificial intelligence, information technology is widely used in all walks of life. That being the case, aeronautics computing technique is undergoing a spiraling upswing, as well. In order to meet the future needs of air fight, the goal to achieve no casualties, intelligent weapons, and superior combat performance has become a development trend. Nevertheless, there are several key issues such as insufficient interoperability between combat units and the inability to share the situation. Therefore, With the core concept of cross-domain collaboration at land, sea,

© Springer Nature Singapore Pte Ltd. 2020
Y. Tian et al. (Eds.): ICBDS 2019, CCIS 1210, pp. 402–416, 2020.
https://doi.org/10.1007/978-981-15-7530-3_31

air, space and network, the US military put forward the idea called "combat cloud" in 2013 [1].

The tactical cloud is derived from combat cloud. It builds remote combat nodes based on aircraft formation. The key is to abstract all the perceptible resources in the aircraft formation, and to manage and schedule them in a unified manner. This makes the aircraft formation capable of super-computing, dynamic storage and efficient task execution [2]. Traditional airborne computers perform various customization functions in Monolithic, which causes the following problems [3]:

1. Unbalanced loads result in varying levels of utilization.
2. The efficiency of the services is insufficient with the unstable speed of task execution.
3. Over-coupling of functions is not conducive to develop, reuse or redeploy the programs.
4. The synergy is not enough to achieve the cooperation between the aircrafts.
5. It only performs tasks based on native data and cannot synchronize information to other combat devices.

Monolithic architecture is clearly not suitable for collaborative task required by tactical cloud in the context of big data. It is necessary to introduce a suitable distributed architecture. Johnu George et al. [4] of Texas A&M University combined Hadoop MapReduce with Mobile Distributed File System (MDFS) by enabling Hadoop MapReduce on mobile devices that replaced its default filesystem with MDFS. MDFS provides strong consistency guarantee for reads, but data is written primarily by creating or appending files. Grace Lewis et al. [5] made forward-deployed, discoverable, virtual-machine-based tactical cloudlets hosted on vehicles or other platforms to provide infrastructure to offload computation. They present experimentation results for five different cloudlet provisioning mechanisms. It is mentioned that the pre-provisioned-VM-based solution can discover more powerful or less-loaded cloudlets. As for data synchronization between mobile devices and central servers, this paper didn't give a specific solution.

In response to the tactical cloud, many domestic scholars and research institutions have also carried out related work. Gao Xiaoguang et al. [6] proposed a new concept named "tactical cloud" based on the anti-stealth antagonizing and cloud computing. What's more, they represent a new networking anti-stealth fire control technology, and described its design ideas. Based on cloud computing technologies such as multi-cloud and edge computing, Tang Suchun et al. [7] proposed a "cloud-edge-end" three-tier organization structure and the information resource service system of naval tactical cloud. Zhang Yunzhi et al. [8] proposed the tactical cloud for air defense and antimissile interceptors, with future demand of anti-missile cooperative combat. Compared with foreign studies, most of the domestic research on tactical cloud is still in conceptual design. It can be concluded from the above that the main problem of research now is the lack of detailed design and implementation of key technologies, especially task coordination, resource scheduling, and data sharing. Therefore, a microservice architecture suitable for tactical cloud in the context of big data is described. We present the design ideas and implementation solutions of the two key technologies, which are resource scheduling and monitoring, and data synchronization.

2 Background

2.1 Tactical Cloud

Due to the lack of interoperability between combat units, the situation is hard to be shared and the coordination efficiency is insufficient. Therefore, the emerging technologies such as new sensors, cloud computing, and Internet of Things have been applied. Gradually, the combat cloud, which is based on the depth perception of the battlefield environment, real-time data sharing and distributed collaborative operations, has emerged. It aggregates the computing power of all server clusters and is able to quickly collect and analyze data from any source on the network. That's why it can gather the forces of various combat systems. The tactical cloud is derived from combat cloud, which is a part of the combat cloud. And the relationship between "Combat Cloud" and "Tactical Cloud" is shown in the Fig. 1. We study the aerial tactical cloud in this paper.

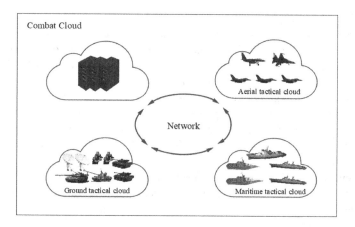

Fig. 1. Relationship between "Combat Cloud" and "Tactical Cloud"

As shown in Fig. 2, the tactical cloud consists of two roles, which are the central node and member nodes. The central node is responsible for planning task intelligence, decomposing tasks, evaluating resource performance, and scheduling resources. And member nodes provide services on various resources to complete the tasks assigned by the central node.

2.2 Microservice

Currently, most information systems are still in monolithic architecture. That is, all functions are integrated into one application and run as a whole [9]. The monolithic architecture has been mature, not only simple to implement, but also easy to test. However, with the increase of scale and the change of demand, the system becomes increasingly complex. There are also problems such as increased maintenance costs,

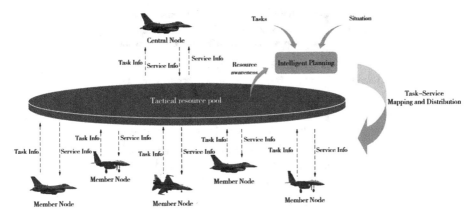

Fig. 2. Physical structure of the "Tactical Cloud"

limited functional expansion, and limited technology upgrades [10]. The microservice architecture is an emerging style compared to the traditional monolithic architecture. Its core idea is to decompose the application into a set of different services around business functions. Each of these services is a separate software unit that can be deployed and run separately. Lightweight communications are used between services for data transfer and mutual invocation [11]. Microservice not only can make rational use of resources, but also facilitate deployment and maintenance. It also has high scalability, good fault tolerance, and is able to work over heterogeneous systems. Therefore, it can better adapt to the airborne environment, solving the problem of heterogeneous systems and resource shortages in cloud.

3 System Design

3.1 Technical Framework

In tactical cloud, all the resources are generally divided into embedded devices and general-purpose computers. On general-purpose computers, the operating systems are generally VxWorks, CentOS, Ubuntu, and Windows. As shown in Fig. 3, the resources on different systems are virtualized in different ways. Microservices usually run on virtual machines of general-purpose computers or directly on embedded systems. However, the core components of microservices generally run on virtual machines of general-purpose computers. The core components provide microservice loading, service registration and discovery, service monitoring, data synchronization, logging, and data persistence. This ensures stable operation of the microservices architecture, providing real-time and efficient task collaboration. The following describes the two components in the architecture.

Zookeeper was a research project by Yahoo to solve the distributed coordination of their internal systems. It was later applied to Apache Hadoop as a subproject to solve distributed problems such as load balancing, cluster management, state synchronization, and application configuration [12]. Zookeeper's data model is similar to Unix's

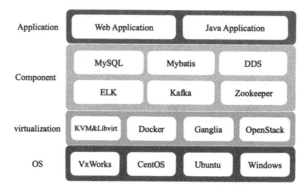

Fig. 3. Technical architecture diagram

file system, and its node management and monitoring notification work well. Therefore, it is often used as a registry in the Dubbo to implement dynamic management of services [13].

DDS (Data Distribution Service) is a network communication middleware for distributed applications, which defines a "data-centric" publish-subscribe communication model, first used in the US Navy [14]. It can establish communication channels between heterogeneous nodes, ignoring differences in the hardware, operating system, network and even language. DDS builds a global data space around topics, and the behavior of data transmission is specified by its QoS Policy to achieve customized data transmission [15].

3.2 System Architecture

The system architecture of tactical cloud is shown in Fig. 4. The underlying basic resources consist of airborne computers, database, combat weapons, sensors, and so on. After abstraction, the basic resources can be regarded as three major categories. They are computing resources, data resources, and load resources, which constitute a resource pool. In addition, these resources will be further virtualized. They can be packaged into a specific service pool, including data sharing, resource situational awareness, task scheduling and management, and combat actions. Based on the service pool, we define and implement microservices, which are made up of consumers, providers and registry. And the RESTful [16] (Representational State Transfer) API provides an entry for service invocations that respond to requests of task processing.

3.3 Granularity Evaluation

The service pool mainly includes data sharing, situation awareness, task scheduling and management, and operational actions. There are various options when they are decomposed into microservices, which influence the performance. Scenario requirements are an important consideration. For example, in our paper, tactical cloud has high requirements for response delays. So, the communication between microservices

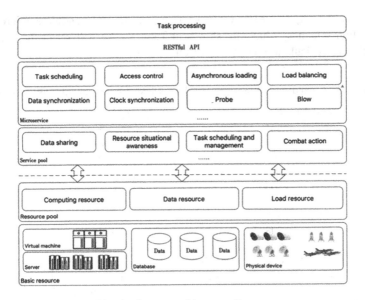

Fig. 4. System architecture diagram

cannot be too dense. In addition, due to the low functional relevance, the requirement for the cohesion of the tactical cloud is not important.

We adopt a granularity evaluation approach of microservices based on bounded context [17] to choose the best solution. We take the system of the load scheduling and monitoring as an example. Use cases and domain entities are listed in Table 1.

Table 1. Use cases and domain entities for load scheduling and monitoring systems

No.	Use cases	Read Entities	Write Entities
Task1	SelectAddr	ReqContext(Req)	ServAddr(SA)
Task2	WeighLoad	AddList(AL) ReqContext(Req)	ServAddr(SA)
Task3	ReadAddrList	ReqContext(Req)	AddrList(AL)
Task4	ApplyForServi	Service(Serv) ReqContext(Req)	ServAddr(SA)
Task5	UpdateAddrList	–	AddrList(AL)
Task6	MonitorLoad	AddrsList(AL)	LoadData(LD)
Task7	MonitorDevFail	Device(Dev) FaultLog(FL)	–
Task8	MonitorServFail	Service(Serv) FaultLog(FL)	–
Task9	GetServState	AddrList(AL)	ServStateList(SSL)
Task10	ControlDev	Device(Dev)	–

Based on the requirements, we have designed several candidate microservices decomposition schemes, which are shown in Table 2. We will select the appropriate solution through calculation and comparison.

Table 2. Candidate microservices for load scheduling and monitoring systems

Candidate	Services	Use cases	Entities
SC0	S01	Task1	Req, SA
	S02	Task2	AL, Req, SA
	S03	Task3	Req, AL
	S04	Task4	Serv, Req, SA
	S05	Task5	AL
	S06	Task6	AL, LD
	S07	Task7	Dev, FL
	S08	Task8	Serv, FL
	S09	Task9	AL, SSL
	S10	Task10	Dev
SC1	S11	Task1–10	Req, SA, AL, LD, Dev, Serv, FL, SSL
SC2	S21	Task1, Task4	Req, SA, Serv
	S22	Task2	AL, Req, SA
	S23	Task3, Task5	Req, AL
	S24	Task6	AL, LD
	S25	Task7, Tak8	Dev, Serv, FL
	S26	Task9	AL, SSL
	S27	Task10	Dev
SC3	S31	Task1, Task4	Req, SA, Serv
	S32	Task2, Task3, Task5	AL, Req, SA
	S33	Task6, Task9	AL, LD, SSL
	S34	Task7, Tak8, Task10	Dev, Serv, FL

The candidate microservices from SC0 to SC3 are decomposed according to four indexes: service cohesion, service coupling, use case convergence, and domain entity convergence. SC0 has the greatest cohesion, and each service is only used as a use case. SC1 has the least coupling, which consists of only one service. There is no problem of interaction between services. SC2 is decomposed based on use case convergence, and SC3 is decomposed based on domain entity convergence. What's more, SC3 further merges the use cases of the same domain entities on the basis of SC2.

The indicators of the above four decomposition schemes are calculated based on bounded context:

1. We calculated its indicators separately for each candidate microservice, and got the matrix named W. Each row of W corresponds to the indexes of candidate microservice from SC0 to SC4. And from left to right, each column respectively represents microservices' service cohesion, service coupling, use case convergence, and entity convergence.

$$W = \begin{bmatrix} 1.0 & 524.0 & 2.0 & 4.5 \\ 0.52 & 0.0 & 11.0 & 9.0 \\ 0.71 & 748.57 & 2.43 & 4.29 \\ 0.35 & 1360.0 & 3.5 & 4.5 \end{bmatrix}$$

Wherein, for the first column, the larger the value, the higher the cohesion. For the second column, the smaller the value, the lower the coupling. For the third and fourth column, the smaller the value, the better the convergence.

2. We normalized the matrix named W and got the matrix named W'.

$$W' = \begin{bmatrix} 0.39 & 0.21 & 0.74 & 0.96 \\ 0.20 & 1.0 & 0.0 & 0.0 \\ 0.28 & 0.45 & 0.95 & 1.0 \\ 0.14 & 0.0 & 0.83 & 0.96 \end{bmatrix}$$

3. Finally, W' was weighted and summed according to the priority weight vector $\eta = [0.2, 0.3, 0.2, 0.3]$. So, we got the final comprehensive indicator $Q = [0.577, 0.34, 0.681, 0.482]$, which indicates that SC2 is the best.

4 Key Technologies

4.1 Service Registration and Discovery

In the microservice architecture for tactical cloud, the key issue is how to manage services, that is, efficient registration and discovery of services. Nowadays, the mainstream management framework for microservice is Dubbo and Spring Cloud. We chose Dubbo and expanded it accordingly.

Dubbo is a high-performance framework for microservice. Figure 5 is a classic structure description of Dubbo on its official website. It is mainly composed of three parts, which are registry, provider and consumer. The monitor is an optional part. Following is the process [18].

1. Registry starts first, followed by the container which loads the providers. provider registers its services to the registry with their addresses and names. Registry will record and monitor after receiving it.
2. When consumer starts, it subscribes to registry and requests a list of addresses for the required services. Once registry detects changes to the service provider, it immediately notifies its consumers to delete or update the corresponding information;
3. Consumer uses its own load balancing to select a service;
4. Consumer calls the corresponding service;
5. Monitor counts and records the service invocations and other information.

Due to the limitations of language, Dubbo's functional modules need to be implemented using Java. In the airborne environment, there are various heterogeneous problems, especially embedded devices are mostly developed in C language.

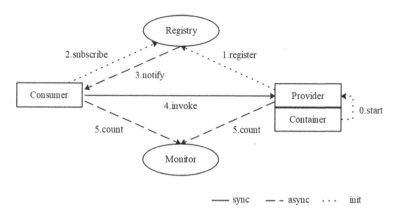

Fig. 5. Dubbo structure diagram

Therefore, Dubbo cannot be used directly to reach functional requirements. So, we have made some extensions to Dubbo, adding service support for other languages, and the principles of service registration and discovery remain unchanged.

For other language, we use RESTful API and Web Service to provide services. And the data is in JSON or XML format. Both RESTful API and Web Service are based on the HTTP protocol. The mainstream development language has support for RESTful API or Web Service, which can work over the heterogeneous systems. As shown in Fig. 6, the task processing is accessed by calling a unified RESTful API. The RESTful API will call the function provided by the consumer. The consumer then invokes the provider to response and returns the data to the task processing module. What's more, consumer uses load balancing to select a provider and invoke its services. The monitor will monitor the load of all providers and servers.

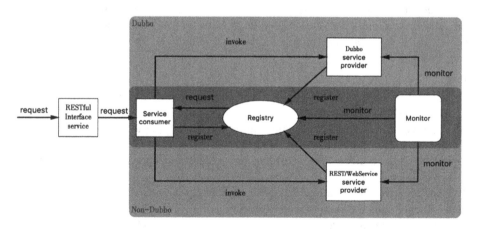

Fig. 6. Service registration and discovery architecture diagram

4.2 Resource Scheduling and Monitoring

Tactical cloud contains central node and member nodes. Member nodes provide services, while the central node is used for load balancing and resource scheduling, as shown in Fig. 7.

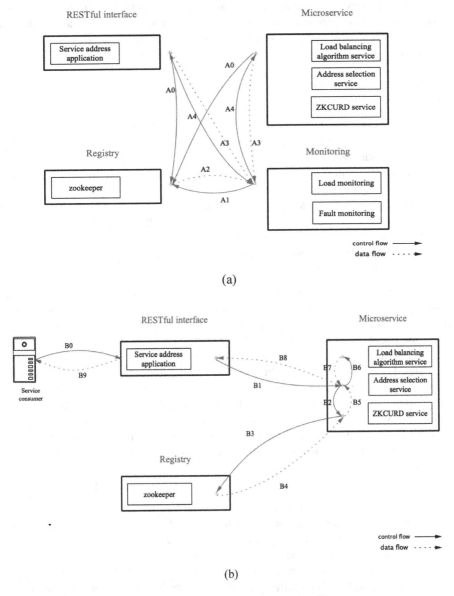

Fig. 7. Scheduling and monitoring operation diagram

The design of load balancing and resource scheduling is related to the balance of the system. Unbalanced load and unreasonable scheduling will reduce the responsiveness of service and the performance of overall system. In order to make this function reliable and usable, we have adopted a microservice architecture to design system, without deploying a complete scheduling system on the central node. Functions can be decomposed into microservices and deployed on different nodes, which can improve processing efficiency and reliability. In the tactical cloud, each node is a standby central node. Once the central node fails, it quickly switches to the standby node, which improves the fault tolerance of the system. The monitoring service is the same as load balancing and resource scheduling, and uses the microservice architecture, as well.

As shown in Fig. 7(a), the specific processing of the monitoring module is as follows:

A0. All services in the tactical cloud are registered in the registry.

A1. The monitoring initiates a request to the registry to obtain a list of registered service addresses.

A2. The registry returns the address list to the monitoring, and the monitoring will start the listener of zookeeper.

A3. The monitoring collects status information according to the address list, and runs load monitoring and fault monitoring according to the status information.

A4. The monitoring manages the device and dynamically adjusts the service deployment according to the load situation to make the server or service reach a stable load.

It is important to note that Dubbo integrates Zookeeper's client operations and implements service registration through configuration files and proxy mechanisms. However, non-Dubbo services cannot be registered directly. So, for non-Dubbo services, the client needs to call the RESTful registration interface at startup.

Load balancing and resource scheduling are mainly based on load balancing strategies. For Dubbo and non-Dubbo services, the load balancing strategy is different. Dubbo uses a client-based load balancing strategy. It calculates the service address based on the address list obtained from the registry and the configured load balancing algorithm. But non-Dubbo service consumer nodes cannot use the class libraries and configurations integrated by Dubbo. It needs to add middleware to complete the operation of the load balancing algorithm. As shown in Fig. 7(b), the main process is as follows.

B0. Consumer invokes the interface of service address application.

B1. Service address application calls address selection service.

B2. The address selection service calls the ZKCURD (Zookeeper Create, Update, Retrieve, Delete) service to obtain the service address list.

B3. ZKCURD service requests address list by using class library of the ZKClient.

B4. The Zookeeper Registry returns the address list to the ZKCURD service.

B5. The ZKCURD service returns an address list to the address selection service.

B6. The address selection service invokes the load balancing algorithm service, and transmits the request and the address list of the service address application as parameters to the load balancing algorithm service.

B7. The load balancing algorithm service calculates and returns the service address.

B8. The address selection service returns the result to the service address application.

B9. Service address application returns the response.

The above process seems complicated, but not all steps are required for each request. The process takes all the steps on the first call. After that, the address selection service will cache the address list to the local. Then the above operation steps are simplified into six processes such as B0, B1, B6, B7, B8, and B9.

4.3   Data Synchronization

The essence of tactical cloud is the collaborative processing of tasks based on deep fusion of multidimensional data. How to synchronize data across aircraft nodes in an efficient way is the basis of data fusion. In addition, tactical cloud has heterogeneous characteristics between nodes, as well as the need to share resources across nodes. To deal with these problems, we build a global data space through DDS middleware and adopt a microservice architecture [3] to achieve data synchronization in time. The structure of data synchronization is shown in Fig. 8. When the underlying resource data changes, the load scheduling module in Sect. 4.2 selects a suitable node for data processing and then initiates a synchronization request. The core process includes inter-node communication and service invocation. Inter-node communication refers to the data communication process between the aircraft nodes, which is implemented with DDS. Service invocation include basic services and service combinations. The basic services layer provides atomic microservices, and the service combination layer refers to the combination and invocation of the basic services according to business logic.

Inter-node Communication. We use the data distribution service (DDS) for communication between nodes. The request-reply model is used to implement the distribution of synchronization information and feedback of results. DDS defines a "data-centric" publish-subscribe communication model. Publishers send data, and subscribers receive the published data which they subscribe to. It uses the topic that identifies the shared data to associate the publisher with the subscriber. Thus, a global data space is formed for all nodes. The publisher sends data of a particular topic to all subscribers of that topic, and the subscriber receives data of the particular topic from all publishers of that topic [15, 19]. However, the common publish-subscribe mode does not return detailed confirmation information after data processing. Therefore, based on the request-reply model of RTI DDS, we design a communication method with feedback of synchronization results.

We implement remote process control through the request-reply model. The requester and replier are interrelated by a specified service name. As with the publish-subscribe model, a topic identifies the type of shared data. There are two roles in the request-reply model, which are request topic and reply topic. The request topic is used to identify the request data from the requester, and the reply topic is used to identify the reply data from the replier [20]. As shown in Fig. 9, the synchronization information is

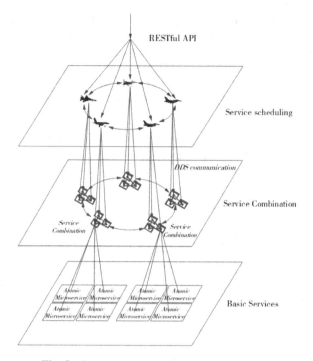

Fig. 8. Data synchronization hierarchy diagram

packaged in requester's data request for distribution. In other words, a request with the synchronization information will be distributed to any replier who need. After receiving and operating, the other nodes encapsulate the feedback information in the replier's data reply, and then return it to the node who sends the request. In this way, the node who originates the request will receive the feedback from other nodes in the cloud. In addition, it is able to locate nodes who failed to sync and get detailed error messages. In tactical cloud, each valid node is peer-to-peer, both as a requester or as a replier.

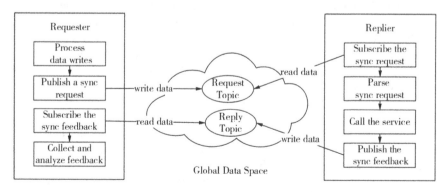

Fig. 9. Request/Reply synchronization model

Service Invocation. Data synchronization module is decomposed into the microservices. We encapsulate the basic operations into atomic microservices, which will be combined and called for data operations according to the task requirements.

The following is an example of the crash of a warplane node. When a crash occurs, all resources and tasks on that node will be invalidated. Under this condition, the underlying resource data information changes. A failure warning will be issued after the monitor detects it. And then, the load scheduling module selects a suitable node for data preprocessing and initiates a data synchronization request. Each node will call the functions provided by the combined service layer on its own node and try to delete this part of the data from the database while receiving the request. The service combination layer calls the atomic services in combination according to the requirements, and then returns the results. The services involved are: ① Data Query, ② Platform Data deletion, ③ Load Data Deletion, ④ Computing Data Deletion, ⑤ Inter-node Communication. The detailed process of the node which initiates the synchronization request is as Algorithm 1.

```
Algorithm 1 Algorithm for deleting a failure node
Input: Platform ID(platformId), Operation(OP_DELETE)
Output: Result(ack {status, detailed info})
1. Call the Data Query to extract the related data which
need to delete according to platformId;
2. if no data need to delete then
3.   Return Success and detailed info;
4. Call each related data modification service according
to the requirement separately, including Platform Data
deletion, Load Data Deletion, and Computing Data Del-
etion. These services can be called at the same time and
will return the result.
5. if failed to delete, then
6.   Rollback Step4;
7.   Return Failed and detailed error message;
8. Call the Inter-node Communication to package the com-
mand into the data modification request and share it
across the aircraft nodes. The service will also analysis
other nodes' sync feedback;
9. Return Success and detailed info.
```

5 Conclusion

Based on the application scenarios and requirements of the tactical cloud, this paper introduces the microservice architecture and gives the detailed description. We propose the design ideas and implementation schemes for resource scheduling and monitoring and data synchronization in the tactical cloud. The design of scheduling and monitoring is to load scheduling and fault warning for microservices. Data synchronization between nodes is realized by using DDS to build a global data space between heterogeneous systems and adopting a microservice architecture for service calls. In the future, we will introduce microservices to realize technical problems such as task intelligent decision-making and task combination in the tactical cloud. Furthermore, we will try to optimize the logical design and deployment of the microservice architecture.

References

1. Zhang, J.: USAF combat cloud concept under the perspective of intelligence fusion. J. Intell. **36**(11), 1–7, 27 (2017)
2. Hu, Y.: Air force "Combat Cloud" development and prospect. Mod. Navig. **01**, 74–78 (2017)
3. Xin, Y.: Survey of implementation framework for microservices architecture. Comput. Eng. Appl. **54**(19), 10–17 (2018)
4. George, J., Chen, C.-A.: Hadoop MapReduce for tactical clouds. In: IEEE 3rd International Conference on Cloud Networking. LNCS, pp. 320–326 (2014)
5. Lewis, G., Echeverría, S.: Tactical cloudlets: moving cloud computing to the edge. In: IEEE Military Communications Conference. LNCS, pp. 1440–1446 (2014)
6. Gao, X.: Design of networking anti-stealth fire control system based on cloud cooperating technology. Syst. Eng. Electron. **35**(11), 2320–2328 (2013)
7. Tang, S.: Design of information resource service architecture for naval tactical cloud. Ship Electron. Eng. **39**(2), 103–109 (2019)
8. Zhang, Y.: Research on distributed combat system of air defense anti-missile based on tactical cloud. Aerodyn. Missile J. **03**, 55–60 (2018)
9. Jiang, Y.: Design of infrastructure based on micro-services architecture. Comput. Eng. Softw. **37**(05), 93–97 (2016)
10. Li, C.: Unified application development platform based on micro-service architecture. Comput. Syst. Appl. **26**(04), 43–48 (2017)
11. Hao, T.: Elastic resource provisioning approach for container in micro-service architecture. J. Comput. Res. Dev. **54**(03), 597–608 (2017)
12. Huang, Y.: Design and Implement Distributed Coordination Framework based on Zookeeper. Zhejiang University (2012)
13. Xie, L.: Design and implementation of distributed service architecture based on dubbox. Softw. Guide **15**(05), 13–15 (2016)
14. Zhou, J.: Application of data distribution service in command and control system. Syst. Constr. **27**(002), 44–50 (2018)
15. Zou, G.: Automatic discovery technology of real-time data distribution service. Comput. Technol. Dev. **27**(1), 25–29 (2017)
16. Han, L.: Java RESTful Web Service in Action, 2nd edn. China Machine Press, Beijing (2016)
17. Zhong, C.: Evaluating granularity of microservices-oriented system based on bounded context. J. Software **30**(10), 3227–3241 (2019)
18. Apache Dubbo. http://dubbo.apache.org/en-us/. Accessed 19 Nov 2019
19. Wang, P.D.: Cross-domain data synchronization based on DDS. Commun. Technol. **48**(4), 447–452 (2015)
20. Lv, G.Z.: Design and implementation of request and reply model based on DDS. Inf. Commun. **1**, 86–88 (2018)

Using GitHub Open Sources and Database Methods Designed to Auto-Generate Chinese Tang Dynasty Poetry

Hai Yu[1]([⊠]), Zi-Xuan Li[2], and Yu-Yan Jiang[2]

[1] Faculty of Computer Center, The Department of Information Science and Engineering, Jinling College, Nanjing University, Nanjing 210089, China
billhaitsyu_2014@163.com
[2] School of Information Engineering, Jinling College, Nanjing University, Nanjing 210089, China
linuxzi@outlook.com, jiangyuyancite@163.com

Abstract. Writing a Tang-Dynasty poetry in Chinese is very popular and useful in the tradition Chinese culture education field, In this paper we use GitHub open sources "jieba" Algorithm for text segmentation of Chinese Tang Dynasty poetry and database methods to auto-generate Chinese old Tang-Dynasty poetry, focus on AI for education field and poetry making project, through Chinese word semantic matching, short sentence combination and verse rhyme pattern rules.

Keywords: GitHub · AI algorithm · jieba · Database · Tang-dynasty poetry · Verse rhyme · Java

1 Tang-Dynasty Poetry Introduction

In the long cultural history in China, Tang Dynasty was the summit for writing old-style poetry, a lot of famous poets like Li Bai, Du Fu, as world known poets, whose works reflected social life in the Tang Dynasty and related issues, like natural scene descriptions, emotions, friendship between poems, the throes of war and so on.

The Tang Dynasty had been the mature stage and the most prosperous period of Chinese poetry. During this period, a large number of outstanding poets emerged, such as Li Bai, Du Fu, and other famous poets. The famous poets were more than 2300. Their works are also preserved in the poems of the whole Tang Dynasty. We focus on whole Tang Dynasty resources. The total number of Tang poems surpasses forty thousand. Tang poetry has covered a wide range of subjects. Some revealed the dark side of society, some praised the just war and some expressed patriotism, some depicted the beautiful and charming motherland, others poems expressed personal aspirations and the love of children and the sorrow and joy of friendship and life. Our project will focus on the auto generation of Tang Poetry for education and entertainment purposes, just for the trial of using Github jieba [1] and tradition database methods to realize it.

© Springer Nature Singapore Pte Ltd. 2020
Y. Tian et al. (Eds.): ICBDS 2019, CCIS 1210, pp. 417–428, 2020.
https://doi.org/10.1007/978-981-15-7530-3_32

The difficulty of auto-generating Tang Dynasty poems is how to handle tonal pattern, In this paper, we only focus on quatrain. A quatrain is a poem consisting of four lines, each of which can have five or seven characters. Structural constraints are required on the quatrain [2]. This paper we presents a novel approach to generating Chinese classical poetry exemplified using Li Bai, a well-known Tang Dynasty poet. By calling corresponding Github jieba sentence cut Algorithm [1], jieba support the text segmentation smoothly. We use Github pinyin [3] verse detect method to confirm the verse rhythm rule. The poetry auto generated by our programming will select words that can handle Tonal rhythm patterns and structural constraints. In the last part of this paper we will present auto-generating quatrain. The generated quatrains is easy to understand and meet the requirements of sentence rhythm by Github pinyin method.

2   About Tang Dynasty Poetry Elements and Basic Principles

Tang Dynasty Poetry is rich in beauty and full of rhythm, for example the famous Tang Dynasty poetry by Wang Zhihuan, Whose famous poem climbing the Huang Que Tower is translated as follows:

The day time is becoming shorter with the mountain close the sun

The Yellow River flows into the sea at the end of the day

You can enjoy one thousand mile sight by climbing to a greater height

Here, we put the Chinese version of above-mentioned poem as follows:

登鹳雀楼　(climbing the Huang Que Tower)

唐 王之涣 (Wang Zhihuan Tang Dynasty Poet)

白日移山尽,黄河入海流.

欲穷千里目,更上一层楼.

In above poem, this work will consist of four sentences, each of which has five characters or seven characters, and considering the twenty-eight style metrics of level and oblique tones, the composition of Tang Dynasty poems should be in accordance with the rules and forms of classical poetic composition. These rules we only discuss quatrain sentences that consist of five characters poetry elements and its principles.

The current poetry thematic characters used in the generation of quatrains come from the book Poetics "Poetry Essence" written by Liu Wenwei, a scholar of the Qing

Dynasty, which contains two-level classifications. Three reference books, namely "Enlightenment of Voice and Rhyme", "Xun Meng Poetry Sentence", "Li Weng rhyming characters", are collected to match the skills of duality and the rhythm of sound and rhythm. They contain several themes, such as Astronomy, Climate, Season, Preface, Temple, Human relationship, Literature, Tour and Scenic spot, Flowers, Bamboo, Birds, Animals and so on. With the above topics we have a good coverage of common ancient poetry and scenarios, writers can choose themes in the process of poetry writing.

3 Tang Dynasty Poetry Auto Generating Related Field Development

On the web, we can do research by way of Tang Dynasty Sentences, an automatic poetry writing system developed by the Natural Language Computing Group of Microsoft Asia Research Institute. Firstly, when the user has selected some key words, the system generates the first sentence according to the key words determined by the user. The users can choose the first sentence manually or input it by themselves.

Next, the user clicks on the input box of the second sentence, and the system automatically generates the second sentence according to the first sentence. Similarly, the generation of the third and fourth sentences are also relevant to the information of the previous sentences [7]. By comparing our system and Microsoft poetry system for the auto-generating output results, we think our auto-generation poetry is easy to be understood and full of tone rhyming.

4 Tang Dynasty Poetry Works Characters Data Set Database Entities Designing and Characters Processing Matching and Generating

In this paper, we use Mysql database as our Tang Dynasty database, using Mysql SQL to load the Li Bai dynasty poetry into the database, before this we need jieba to cut poetry sentences into the element characters, then put these well-known characters of poetry into the database. For example, we name what we have stored in a Mysql database Chunks table. The table definition as following SQL [9]:

CREATE SCHEMA IF NOT EXISTS mydb DEFAULT CHARACTER SET utf8;

USE mydb;

--   Table mydb.Chunks

CREATE TABLE IF NOT EXISTS mydb.Chunks (

C_Id   INT NOT NULL AUTO_INCREMENT,

C_Chinese   VARCHAR(10) NULL,

C_Character   VARCHAR(32) NULL,

C_Word_Feature   VARCHAR(4) NULL,

PRIMARY KEY (C_Id),

UNIQUE INDEX idtable1_UNIQUE (C_Id ASC) VISIBLE)

ENGINE = InnoDB;

In above table Chunks, the column C_Chinese is for short words, including two or three words and the column C_Character is for poet imagery scenarios like season, emotion, location, description etc. C_Word_Feature column contain values: 'N' stands for noun, 'A' stands for adverb, 'V' stands for Verb.

An example is given by citing a sentence from Tang Dynasty as follows:

'闲敲棋子落灯花' (Translation as follows)

Playing chess in rainy night and seeing the snuff from oil lamp (Author waiting a visiting friend).

The above line is divided into 闲敲 (press or knock lightly) 棋子 (chess) 落灯花 (snuff from oil lamp) words respectively by AI Algorithm Jieba [6]. By using Java

Table 1. The Chunk tables attributes and its values.

C_Id	C_Chinese	C_Character	C_Word_Feature
0	闲敲(press or knock lightly)	Emotion('乐',here mean happy)	Verb
1	棋子(chess)	N/A	Noun
2	落灯花(snuff from oil lamp)	N/A	Verb

language we can call this Algorithm and insert into the above Chunk table database, the column values listed in Table 1:

The other table Combine is for character matching in poetry which is defined as follows:

```
----------------------------------------------------------

-- Table mydb.Combine

----------------------------------------------------------

CREATE TABLE IF NOT EXISTS mydb.Combine (

  Co_Id   INT NOT NULL AUTO_INCREMENT,

  Co_First_Id   INT NULL,

  Co_Second_Id   INT NULL,

  PRIMARY KEY (Co_Id),

  UNIQUE INDEX Co_Id_UNIQUE (Co_Id ASC) VISIBLE,

  INDEX C_Id_idx (Co_Second_Id   ASC) VISIBLE,

  CONSTRAINT C_Id1

  FOREIGN KEY (Co_First_Id)

  REFERENCES mydb.Chunks (C_Id)

  ON DELETE NO ACTION

  ON UPDATE NO ACTION,

  CONSTRAINT C_Id2

  FOREIGN KEY (Co_Second_Id)

  REFERENCES mydb.Chunks(C_Id)

  ON DELETE NO ACTION

  ON UPDATE NO ACTION)

ENGINE = InnoDB;
```

For example, the data have been stored in Table 2:

Table 2. The combine database table attributes and its values

Co_Id	Co_First_Id	Co_Second_Id
0	0[闲敲](press or knock lightly)	1[棋子] (chess)

e.g. We just let two Chunk words Co_First_Id and Co_Second_Id become a combination based on the best matching patterns. After the expansion of our database, we will be accessible to more useful word pairs in this pattern.

If the above lines are divided into single words or words are adopted in a manual way, it will take a lot of time to finish the classification of well-known poetic works. As a result, In here we call jieba java Algorithm. It should be regarded as a leader in the field of word segmentation. The jieba Algorithm we can use the following three ways:

(1) Search engine mode: on the basis of precise pattern, long words are segmented again.
(2) Precise mode: try to cut the sentence to the most precise, which is suitable for text analysis.
(3) Full mode: scan all the words that can be used in a sentence, which is very fast, but can not solve ambiguity.

Based on the above three methods, we use precise mode. Now we need load Tang Dynasty poetic works (cut lines into characters) into the text file by calling Jieba Algorithm; then use Mysql database, and Load data tools as follows:

```
LOAD DATA LOCAL INFILE 'C:\poetry_name.txt'

    [REPLACE | IGNORE]

    INTO TABLE potery_name

    [CHARACTER SET   'utf8']

    [FIELDS

        [TERMINATED BY ',']

        [[OPTIONALLY] ENCLOSED BY 'char']

        [ESCAPED BY 'char']

    ]

    [LINES

        [STARTING BY 'string']

        [TERMINATED BY 'string']

    ]

    [IGNORE number LINES]

    [(col_name_or_user_var,...)]

    [SET col_name = expr,...]
```

In here we need to look up the on-line whole Tang-dynasty poetry and its relevant materials, the volume is text file about 10 Mb size. After finishing the loading job, now we focus on word processing matching, this part will take use of the following software programming chart to implement it, In this procedure, we can see the detail information from Fig. 1. Show the word processing and matching method, Also including Tang Dynasty generating procedures.

It is important to analyze the rhyming words for the matching of the rhyming of the verse. This can use GitHub pinying to test the rhyming words, The detail information can be seen as the Fig. 1.

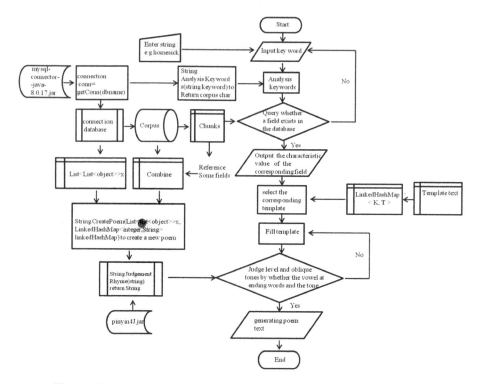

Fig. 1. The word matching and auto-tang dynasty poetry generating diagram

5   Related Work on Tang-Dynasty Auto-Generating and Result Discussion

Clean the corpus table and make a structural analysis of the poem with Jing Ye Si (静夜思).

All corpus we need to clean fall into three types: Noun, Verb, Adverb.

床前/明月光,疑是/地上霜.

A A /N N N,V V /N N N.

举头/望明月,低头/思故乡.

V V / V V V, V N/V V V.

The poem may be translated as follows:

The bright moon in front of the bed.

Suspected to be frost on the ground.

Raising my head, I see the moon so bright.

Down my eyes, nostalgia comes around me.

After 60 poems by Li bai of the Tang Dynasty have been input, we finally use Java programming to implement the rhyming and get the following auto-generating output: Auto generation one as follows (To distinguish from rhyming)

相看/君山好，肠断/柳条青

V V / N N N,   V V / N N N

泪添/见我去(qù)，伴羞/知别苦(kǔ).

V V / V V V,   V V / V V V

Auto generation two as follows:

炉火伴紫烟，劳劳泪痕湿(shī)

N N / A A A, A A / V V V

庭前挂石壁(bì)，举头远行役(yì)

A A / V V V,   V V / V V V

Above auto-generating poem one may be translated as following:

Standing on the YueYang Tower,

Remember the scene of willow on the Jun Mountain which make my heart broken.

With endless tears from my eyes, shyness and misery intertwined.

Couldn't do nothing more but bid farewell to him.

Above auto-generating poem is a good poet that using Li bai style (The characters directly adopted from Li bai sixty poems). Poem two is also auto-generative, it may be translated as:

Incense smoke rise gradually from the censer

bathed despondently in tears again.

gazing after people severing in army.

who had disappeared in the distance.

I stand lonely in the yard.

So far, Our auto-generating system works well. The auto-generated poet has a good sense to write complicated scenarios and beautiful rhythmic lines. The reason is we adopt the following check: by importing external packet pinyin4J.jar. This jar contains a word-phonetic converter, so we can use the function (public String[] toHanyuPinyinStringArray(char ch)) to translate each word to Chinese phonetic alphabet. For example as following:

In Poem 1,we can get (qù) from"去"，(kǔ) from"苦".

In Poem 2,we can get(bì) from"壁"，(shī) from"湿"，(yì) from"役".

All the results of each group share the final syllable rhymes. This is key for writing Tong Dynasty poems. From this, we can testify every lines and make sure that they follow the rule of poetry of the Tang Dynasty.

6   Future Work on Tang-Dynasty Auto-Generating

Now system only focus on poetry auto-generating, future work will provide the poetry parameter, the main ideal is we input the parameter like Who, When, Where, Why, What input options, for example, I want to visit Canada Algonquin Park, Algonquin park has beautiful landscapes, to seek greater understanding of Canada precious and its heritage, so system input the parameter as following:

'Algonquin'→ 阿刚昆(Chinese name) → 刚昆 (this part for where parameter)
'Autumn'→ 秋天(Chinese name) → 秋色 (this part is for when parameter)
'visiting'→旅游地特色(place) → 枫叶、自然风光 (this part is for what parameter, here cite the maple leaf and natural scene)
'emotion'→ enjoy →欢快(Chinese) → 引用著名诗句 (this part is for emotion parameter, cited the famous poem in the history)

Above if I want to write a Tang Dynasty describe the feeling of the visiting Algonquin park will might be like as following in Chinese

刚昆一路秋色浓, 满眼风光不与同.
枫叶迎风递真情, 一片冰心在玉壶.

Translation version as following:

Algonquin autumn look like more colors (where and when)

Landscapes will different from other places (where related)

A leaf of Maple delivery deep feeling (emotion)

My heart like a white ice in a jade pot (cited part)

Last poetry sentence cited from Tang well-known poet Wang Chong Ling, like this manual to write a poetry is good way and have more sense style. The future work also want to provide the corresponding image related auto-generating poetry scene, this is useful for better understanding the poetry main topic when the Four-Sentence poem is generated, the user can click on "Write Poetry Title Scenarios" to enter the title and name of the poem, and then the poem can be painted and saved or shared according to the content of the poem.

7 Conclusion

Since several years, writing traditional Chinese poetry is encouraged in school education, also is becoming more attractive choice for all level Chinese student and media audience, Young Student often feel tough, because it is difficult to write a traditional tang dynasty poem, so we focus on using Artificial Intelligent Software to create tang poems for Chinese culture education field. Due to the system complicated and word semantic analysis problem, this will be a challenging task system, Future further study will be continued to improve the quality of auto generating tang dynasty poetry, including using GitHub open source and latest AI studying result or related issues, the references list involved AI technology will be applied to our future further studying work, specially use RNN to make the Chinese classical auto generating Chinese poems project more intelligent and meaningful. We will concern related studying methods in the poetry generation fields, including RNN encoder-decoder [4] or related [10, 13–17]. Mutual Reinforcement Learning [5], salient-clue mechanism [6], Statistical MT Approach [8], Statistical machine translation models [12], framework under constrained optimization [11] etc.

In the following study procedure, we will make a better annotation scheme, and build static and dynamic scenarios separately. At the same time we focus on the use of structural, rhythmical and tonal patterns jointly, without utilizing any constraint templates. In this paper we use the limited resources to get the experimental results, as shown that our system auto-generation poetry is easy to be understood and full of tone rhyming, this will encourage our team to continue to study it.

References

1. GitHub Jieba. https://GitHub.com/fxsjy/jieba. Accessed 20 Oct 2019
2. Wang, L.: A Summary of Rhyming Constraints of Chinese Poems. Beijing Press, Beijing (2002)
3. GitHub Pinyin. https://GitHub.com/hotoo/pinyin. Accessed 4 Oct 2019
4. Yi, X., Li, R., Sun, M.: Generating Chinese classical poems with RNN encoder-decoder. In: Sun, M., Wang, X., Chang, B., Xiong, D. (eds.) CCL/NLP-NABD -2017. LNCS (LNAI), vol. 10565, pp. 211–223. Springer, Cham (2017). https://doi.org/10.1007/978-3-319-69005-6_18
5. Yi, X., Sun, M., Li, R., Li, W.: Automatic poetry generation with mutual reinforcement learning, pp. 3143–3153 (2018). https://doi.org/10.18653/v1/d18-1353
6. Yi, X., Li, R., Sun, M.: Chinese poetry generation with a salient-clue mechanism (2018)
7. Microsoft Asia Research Institute Duilian. http://duilian.msra.cn/jueju/intro.html

8. Jiang, L., Zhou, M.: Generating Chinese couplets using a statistical MT approach. In: The 22nd International Conference on Computational Linguistics, Manchester, England (2008)
9. Hai, Y.: Database Basic Principles and Applications Development Tutorials. Nanjing University Press, Nanjing (2017)
10. Luo, Y., Huang, Y.: Text steganography with high embedding rate: using recurrent neural networks to generate Chinese classic poetry, pp. 99–104 (2017). https://doi.org/10.1145/3082031.3083240
11. Yan, R., Jiang, H., Lapata, M.: Poet: automatic Chinese poetry composition through a generative summarization framework under constrained optimization. In: Proceedings of IJCAI (2013)
12. He, J., Zhou, M., Jiang, L.: Generating Chinese classical poems with statistical machine translation models. In: Proceedings of the 26 AAAI Conference on Artificial Intelligence (2012)
13. Zhang, X., Lapata, M.: Chinese poetry generation with recurrent neural networks. In: Proceedings of the 2014 Conference on Empirical Methods in Natural Language Processing (EMNLP), pp. 670–680 (2014)
14. Wang, Q., Luo, T., Wang, D., et al.: Chinese song iambics generation with neural attention based model. CoRR.abs/1604.06274 (2016)
15. Wang, Z., He, W., Wu, H., et al.: Chinese poetry generation with planning based neural network. arXiv preprint arXiv:1610.09889 (2016)
16. Yan, R., Li, C.T., Hu, X., et al.: Chinese couplet generation with neural network structures. In: Proceedings of Meeting of the Association for Computational Linguistics (2016)
17. Wei, W., Huang, W., Wang, J., Deng, Z.: Chinese classical poetry and couplet generation based on multi-task learning. J. Chin. Inf. Process. 33(11), 115–124 (2019)

Distributed Image Retrieval Base on LSH Indexing on Spark

Zelei Hou[1], Chao Huang[1], Jiagao Wu[1,2($\boxtimes$)], and Linfeng Liu[1,2]

[1] School of Computer, Nanjing University of Posts and Telecommunications,
Nanjing 210023, Jiangsu, China
zlhou191@163.com, h13281645190@163.com, {jgwu,liulf}@njupt.edu.cn
[2] Jiangsu Key Laboratory of Big Data Security and Intelligent Processing,
Nanjing 210023, Jiangsu, China

Abstract. With the advent of the era of big data, how to process massive image, video and other multimedia data timely and accurately has become a new challenge in related fields. Aiming at the computational bottleneck and inefficiency of traditional image content retrieval system, in this paper, a distributed image retrieval framework base on Location Sensitive Hash (LSH) indexing is proposed on Spark, which combines with the distributed storage and computing characteristics of Spark big data platform. Then, distributed K-means based Bag of Visual Word (BoVW) algorithm and LSH algorithm are proposed to build LSH index vectors on Spark in parallel. The experiment shows that the retrieval time of our framework can be reduced significantly, and both retrieval recall and precision are high compared with the traditional retrieval method.

Keywords: Image retrieval · BoVW · LSH · Spark · Algorithm

1 Introduction

With the rapid development of image acquisition and storage technology and the gradually improve of Internet multimedia, massive image big data is being produced all the time, and the Internet industry has put forward higher requirements for image processing. These increasing image data for efficient storage and fast retrieval have become the biggest problem we face.

The traditional image retrieval adopts centralized operation, which has computational bottleneck, cannot provide fast retrieval and satisfy the storage of mass data. The traditional storage mode stores the data on a single server, the cost of storage will be greatly increased, and the later maintenance will be difficult. As a result, distributed system with its excellent computing performance and the ability to store large amounts of data stand out in data retrieval.

Supported by National Natural Science Foundation of China under Grants Nos. 41571389 and 61872191, TIADMP of Chongqing under Grant No. cstc2018jszx-cyztzxX0015.

Apache Spark, a fast and versatile computing engine designed for large-scale data processing, provides a new Ideas for solving high-dimensional image big data retrieval problems with suitable for massive data operations, high reliability and high scalability. The problem of image retrieval can be attributed to the approximate search of high-dimensional vector. Many researchers have studied the content-based retrieval algorithm. These algorithms include index tree algorithms based on spatial partition, such as R-tree, KD-Tree, etc. These algorithms are all accurate search, but in the high-dimensional data space, the efficiency is not ideal, in the face of high-dimensional data, there will be dimension disaster problem. So Location Sensitive Hashing (LSH) algorithm [1,2] is introduced, which is an approximate nearest neighbor query algorithm. LSH solves dimension disaster problem, and works well when dealing with high-dimensional data.

In this paper, we present a framework for massive image retrieval on Spark, and build the LSH index in parallel. In this framework, we optimize the problem that the K-means algorithm is too time-consuming in constructing Bag of Visual Word (BoVW) [3–5] vector, and construct LSH index of image in parallel with Resilient Distributed Datasets (RDD).

The main work of this paper includes the following aspects:

(1) A distributed image retrieval framework base on LSH indexing is proposed on Spark, which combines with the distributed storage and computing characteristics of Spark big data platform.
(2) K-means-based BoVW distributed algorithm is proposed by extracting SIFT feature data point sets combined with Spark computing framework.
(3) Parallel BoVW and LSH algorithms are proposed to build LSH index vectors and retrieval based on constructed LSH index on Spark.

The rest of this paper is organized as follows. We first discuss related work in Sect. 2, and then the framework is given in Sect. 3. We introduce the proposed algorithms in Sect. 4. Experimental evaluation is discussed in Sect. 5. Finally, we conclude our work in Sect. 6.

2   Related Work

2.1   BoVW

Bag of words model (BoW) first appeared in the fields of neuro-linguistic programming (NLP) and information retrieval (IR). This model ignores the syntax and a word order of text and uses a sequence of word frequencies to express a text or a document. In recent years, BoW model has been widely used in computer vision. In analogy with the BoW applied in text, the local feature of the image is treated as word. Using a set of word frequency vectors to represent images is helpful for large-scale image retrieval. Some people abbreviate it as Bag of Feature model or Bag of Visual Word.

The basic principle of BoVW is that the number of local features of the same kind is used instead of the number of different local features to represent the image. Other local feature vectors are divided by the distance to the centers of the clusters, so that an image is represented by a k-dimensional vector whose elements are the number of local vectors belonging to that class.

SIFT Feature. SIFT feature is a widely used image descriptor with good performance. It is robust to scale and affine changes. Each SIFT vector is 128 dimensional, and an image usually contains hundreds or thousands of SIFT vectors. The scale invariance of SIFT feature means that the SIFT feature does not change much when the image is rotated, scaled, the brightness of the image is adjusted and the observer's perspective is changed. In this paper, We use the Feature Detector in OpenCV to find the SIFT feature vector and save it in the node storage space as a txt file read by spark to complete the initialization of RDD, complete the construction of the picture expression.

K-Means Clustering Algorithm. For a given sample set, the sample set is divided into K clusters according to the distance between the samples. Let the points in the cluster be connected as closely as possible, and make the distance between the clusters as large as possible. In this paper, We use the KmeansMode in Spark MILB to train the clustering center [6].

2.2 LSH

The LSH algorithm is an approximate nearest neighbor query algorithm, which returns some points that are closest to the query point.

LSH is a Hash index algorithm for high-dimensional vectors. Unlike KD-Tree, R-Tree and other tree index algorithms, LSH algorithm has a good effect on high-dimensional vector.

Hash Function. Define a Hash function h, h is a mapping of Euclidean distance to Hash encoding space U. $B(q,r)$ represents a space in which the Euclidean distance to q is less than r. For the data to be queried point p, $h(p)$ indicates that p is mapped by the hash function, and Pr represents the probability. If both of the following conditions are met, the Hash function satisfies the (r_1, r_2, p_1, p_2)-sensitive.

If $p \in B(q,r_1)$, then $Pr_H\{h(p) = h(q)\} \geq p_1$.
If $p \notin B(q,r_1)$, then $Pr_H\{h(p) = h(q)\} \leq p_2$.
The key idea of LSH algorithm is that vectors generate one-dimensional index values through a locality-sensitive function h, which is stored in the index table. And look it up in the index to the same item with index value as the result of the query. The resulting point is assumed to be similar to the input vector.

$$h_{a,b}(v) = \left\lfloor \frac{a \cdot v + b}{r} \right\rfloor \tag{1}$$

where v is a vector point between high dimensional features, a is a high dimensional vector based on normal distribution, r is a positive integer, and b is an integer between $[0, r]$. The parameters r and b are adjustments for the reduced dimension of the high-dimensional vector. Based on the selection of projection vector a of p-stable distribution (normal distribution is a special stable distribution), two similar points in high-dimensional space can be mapped to get the same or similar index values.

Hash Family. We amplify the gap between the high probability p_1 and low probability p_2 by concatenating several functions.

Define a function family $g = \{h_1, h_2, ..., h_K\}$, where h_i is a function satisfing the (r_1, r_2, p_1, p_2)-sensitive.

We choose L functions $g_1, g_2, ..., g_L$ independently and uniformly at random. During preprocessing, we store each v in the bucket $g_j(v)$, for $j = 1, ..., L$. Since the total number of buckets may be large, we retain only the non-empty buckets by resorting to hashing.

To process a query q, we search all buckets $g_1(q), g_2(q), ..., g_L(q)$. We can define $g(v) = g(q)$, for each g, If there exist $h_i(v) = h_i(q)$ for some $i = 1, ..., K$, and the total number of i no less than 2. If there exist $g_j(v) = g_j(q)$ for some $j = 1, ..., L$, and the total number of j no less than a threshold value, we think of v are similar to q.

2.3   Apache Spark

Eventually, we use the Apache Spark for generating cluster centers and building indexes in parallel.

Apache Spark is a fast and versatile computing engine designed for large-scale data processing. Spark is an open-source, Hadoop-like, universal parallel framework for MapReduce at UC Berkeley AMP lab. Spark MapReduce has the advantages of Hadoop, but unlike MapReduce, intermediate job output can be stored in memory. This eliminates the need to read and write HDFS, so Spark can be better suited to iterative MapReduce algorithms such as data mining and machine learning. Spark is an open source clustered computing environment similar to Hadoop, but there are some useful differences between the two that make Spark better at performing certain workloads, in other words, spark enables memory-distributed datasets to optimize iterative workloads in addition to providing interactive queries. Although Spark was created to support iterative jobs on distributed data sets, it is actually a complement to Hadoop and runs in parallel on the Hadoop file system. This behavior is supported through a third-party clustering framework called MESOS. Spark was developed by the Algorithms, Machines, and People Lab at the University of California, Berkeley, to build large, low-latency data analysis applications [7–10].

3   Framwork

Figure 1 is our distributed image retrieval framework, which is composed of three parts, the first is the BoVW model, which is an image content representation of

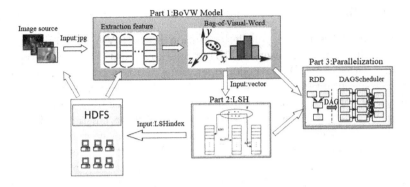

Fig. 1. Distributed image retrieval framwork on spark.

BoVW, the second is LSH, which is an approximate nearest neighbor search algorithm, and the third part is Parallelization, which is a combination of BoVW and LSH algorithms and an implementation of parallelization of index and retrieval.

3.1 BoVW Model

In BoVW, the local features of the images in the image set are extracted and the feature vectors are calculated. Then the calculated feature vectors will be divided into several classes by clustering method, and the center of each class need to be recorded. The classification of the feature vector depends on its Euclidean distance from the center of the class. Thus, many local feature vectors can be classified and images are represented by a class of high-dimensional Vectors. Each dimension value represents the number of local features that belong to this category, so it can be approximated that the similarity of two high-dimensional vectors means the local feature of the images represented are similar in the category and number. The image content was transformed from hundreds of SIFT dimension vectors to a uniform dimension high-dimensional vector to simplify the expression of image content and the computation of retrieval.

3.2 LSH Indexing

Locality-Sensitive Hashing (LSH) is the algorithm we used to solve the problem of finding the approximate high-dimensional vector in our framework. In this part, the high-dimensional vector obtained by BoVW is mapped to the low dimensional vector without changing the similarity through a set of special hash function, so LSH can simplify the computational complexity and improve the retrieval efficiency. In order to strike a balance between accuracy and computation, k hash functions and L buckets are selected in LSH. Finally, the index of LSH is stored in HDFS.

3.3 Parallelization

Parallelization refers to the parallel operation both BoVW and LSH. We use the resilient distributed datasets (RDD) of Spark to parallelize the operation by designing a series of RDD conversion operations and related data structures.

The massive input data set is saved in HDFS. After the Spark loads the input data set, which will be split and transmitted to the nodes to generate PairRDD in the nodes, we use the KMeansModel in the Mllib to clustering. By setting the number of cluster centers and iterations, then cluster centers generated are recorded in each node. Then the original PairRDD and the generated clustering center are used to construct the word bag vector of each image, Based on the BoVW vector, we generate LSH parameters, including the gauss Vector, which are serialized and then passed to the remote executor node, which needs to deserialize the parameters to execute BoVWRDD uses the mapValues function to multiply each vector by a gauss vector plus a modified value. Each element will be assigned to the same bucket as its nearest neighbor, so it will get up to $L \times K$ Bucket numbers Then, during the retrieval phase, we will use the bucket number as our index [11].

4   Algorithms

4.1 K-Means Based BoVW

K-Means of BoVW. Let an image set $D = \{I_0, I_1, I_2, ..., I_{maxD}\}$, where I_i is the i-th image and $maxD$ is the total number of images. For any image $I = \{S_0, S_1, S_2,..., S_{max}\}$, where S_i is the i-th SIFT vector of the image and max is the total number of the SIFT vectors of the image.

For SIFT vector $S_i = (v_0, v_1, v_2, ..., v_{128})$, where $0 \leq v_j \leq 255$. Thus, the spatial range of SIFT vector is in 256^{128}. We use a K-means clustering method to find the representative SIFT vector, which becomes the standard of SIFT classification. We classify the image features according to the Euclidean Distance, in which K-means clustering analysis is used, and searching for the representative SIFT among the magnanimous SIFT features means finding the cluster center vector of clustering analysis.

K-means algorithm is an unsupervised clustering algorithm. For a given set of samples, according to the distance between samples, the samples are divided into c clusters, so that the points in the clusters are connected together as closely as possible, and the distance between clusters is as large as possible.

$$c - center = \{u_i | i \in [1, c], u_i \in R^{128}\} \qquad (2)$$

Then, the K-mean of BoVW algorithmic can be described as:

Step1. Give each cluster center an appropriate initial value.

Step2. Classify all the samples $\{S_0, S_1, S_2, ..., S_{max}\}$ to corresponding cluster C_j labels according to $\{u_1, u_2, u_3, ..., u_c\}$, that is

$$j^* = argmin||S_i - u_j||, S_i \in C_{j^*} \tag{3}$$

Step.3. Update cluster centers $\{u_1, u_2, u_3, ..., u_c\}$.

$$u_i = \frac{1}{|C_i|} \sum_{S_j \in C_i} S_j \tag{4}$$

Step.4. Repeat 2–3 until c-center is convergent or until the maximum number of iterations n_{max} is reached.

The BoVW Vector of image I_i can be defined as $V_i = (v_0, v_1, v_2, ..., v_c)$, where v_i represents the number of SIFT features that belong to this cluster center. That is,

$$v_i = \sum_{S_j \in C_i and S_j \in I_i} f(S_j, u_i) \tag{5}$$

where

$$f(S_j, u_i) = \begin{cases} 1, & S_j \in C_i \\ 0, & S_j \notin C_i \end{cases}$$

According to $f(S_j, u_i)$, if S_j is the closest to C_i in all cluster centers, the function value is 1, otherwise 0.

Parallel BoVW Algorithm. The input data set is an image data set D with SIFT feature text file stored on HDFS, then read in with textFile in spark, and generate initial RDD, then transform to integer by data type conversion, and cluster all SIFT vectors with KMeansModel function in milb. The cluster center is saved as a text file and the BoVW vector of the same image is obtained by cluster analysis of SIFT features.

The pseudo code of the parallel BoVW algorithm in Apache Spark is follows:

Algorithm 1: Parallel BoVW algorithm

Input: Image dataset D, the number of clusters c, the maximum number of iterations n_{max}.

Output: BoVW vector set BoVWRDD $= V_i(v_0,v_1,v_2,...,v_c)$.

val sc =new SparkContext(conf) /*Create SparkContext*/

val iniRDD = sc.textFile(D). /*Read in text file with SIFT feature.*/

val numRDD= iniRDD.map(.toInt)

/*Converts a character variable to an integer variable.*/

KMeansModel clusters = KMeans.train(numRDD.rdd(),c,n_{max});

/*Clustering data sets using K-means.*/

val BoVWRDD = numRDD.mapValues(

    val V[c];

    /*An array of c dimensions, the value of which represents the number of SIFT features of Type c.*/

    for each element{

        i=Min(element, clusters);

        /*The cluster center is the closest to the i-th center in all clusters.*/

        vector [i]++; })

        /*The record value of the number of SIFT features belonging to class i-th is plus one.*/

4.2   Parallel LSH

LSH. The input to the LSH Algorithm is the BoVW vector V for each image. From Eq. (1) we can know that a is a vector in the same dimension as the input, it follows the Gaussian Distribution, b is the correction parameter, the manual setting makes most of the similar images be divided into a bucket, r is the bucket width, if the bucket width is set too large, then a large number of V will be divided into the same bucket. Increase the amount of retrieval data while reducing the precision rate. If the bucket width is too small, the similar V can not be divided into a bucket, which reduces the recall rate.

Define the Hash function family as follows: $H_{L,K} = \{h_{a,b,r} \mid a \in A,\ b \in B,\ r \in R\}$ $A = \{a_1,a_2,...,a_K\}$, $B = \{b_1,b_2\ ,...\ b_{L*K}\}$, $R = \{r_1,r_2,...,r_L\}$. Then, we have

$$h_{a_l,b_{l,k},r_l}(V) = \left\lfloor \frac{a_l \cdot V + b_{l,k}}{r_l} \right\rfloor \qquad (6)$$

From this we get the bucket number $h_{a,b,r}(V_i)$ of each V.

Parallel LSH Algorithm. Algorithm 2 illustrates the parallelization of the LSH algorithm. It takes five steps to describe the process. First, we generate the basic parameters of the LSH Algorithm, including the gauss distribution vector, the correction factor, the width of the bucket. And the second step, we serialize the generated instances of the LSH class. In Step 3, we upload the LSH arguments to Spark, BoVWRDD takes the LSH arguments to and from $L \times K$, and in step 4, we take all the LSH elements based on their bucket numbers Put together elements that have the same bucket number, and when looking up, the input element goes directly to the bucket that has the same bucket number as it.

Algorithm 2: Parallel LSH algorithm

Input: BoVW vector set BoVWRDD. the parameters of LSH: K, L, a, b, r.

Output: LSH index is a container that contains a number of
$V_i(v_0,v_1,v_2,...,v_c)$.
(class)LSH LSH = LSH_shell.ini();
/*Initializes the parameters of the LSH algorithm */
SerializeLSH();
/*The LSH parameter is serialized so that it can be passed between nodes */
val LSHRDD =BoVWRDD. mapValues(
List bucket;
For each $V \in$ BoVWRDD
for $i = 1, 2, \cdots, L$ **do**
    for $j = 1, 2, \cdots, K$ **do**　.
        bucketTemp=$(V \cdot a+ b) / r$;
        /* LSH indexes are generated for each BoVW vector.*/
        bucket.add(bucketTemp);
    end
end
return bucket;)
LSH index = LSHRDD. groupBy(each bucket);
/*Polymerizing element according to bucket number.*/

---

5   Experimental Results

The experimental data set used in this paper is from the ANRRAFFUT project, which is supported by the French National Research Institute and co-sponsored by INRIA and a private French company, the Advestigo Company. The data set is classical. The project provides a Bigann dataset evaluation for evaluating approximate nearest neighbor query algorithms and an INRIA Holidays dataset for evaluating image retrieval.

The number of images is 696, and the image dataset is 5.18 GB in size. Through our research, we select L = 5, K = 25 as LSH algorithm parameters.

Example of retrieval result:

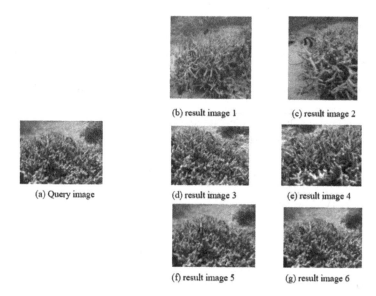

(a) Query image

(b) result image 1

(c) result image 2

(d) result image 3

(e) result image 4

(f) result image 5

(g) result image 6

Fig. 2. Query results.

Figure 2 shows the results of our search. Figure 2(a) is our query image and the other 6 images are the results of our search. And we can see that Fig. 2(b), (d) are not similar enough, but some still have similarities. Figure 2(d), (e), (f), (g) are the most similar to the image to be queried in our dataset.

Figure 3 shows the effect of the number of nodes on the retrieval efficiency. We can see that when the number of nodes is small, the increase of the number of nodes has a great effect on the efficiency, but after 3 nodes, the improvement of the efficiency does not change much This is because when the number of nodes is relatively small, the tasks of each node are mainly concentrated in the computation and retrieval, and the increase of the number of nodes will make the computation and retrieval tasks scattered to each node and executed concurrently so that time drops, but at the same time, the node task allocation and communication occupy time gradually increase, and eventually make the overall time reduction is relatively slow.

We took a sample of 50 images. Figure 4 shows a recall ratio of no less than 60% for 34 of the 50 samples in the search results. The peak value of Fig. 4 indicates that the recall ratio of 16 images in the sample is about 80% (5 images in the dataset are similar to the query image, 3 similar images are retrieved, and 5 images are retrieved).

Figure 5 shows that the precision of 32 images in 50 samples is not less than 60% , and the peak value of Fig. 5 indicates that the precision of 21 images in the sample is about 60% (3 of 5 images are similar to the query image) . The efficiency and effectiveness of the system are considerable.

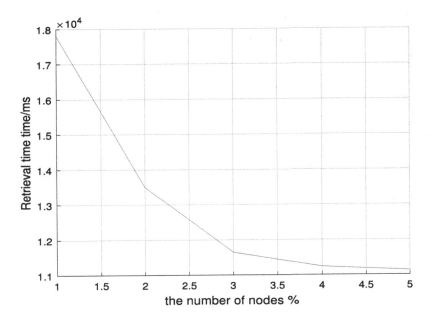

Fig. 3. The retrieve time vs. the number of nodes on Spark.

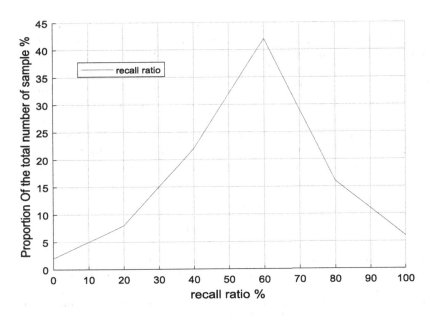

Fig. 4. The distribution of sample precision ratio.

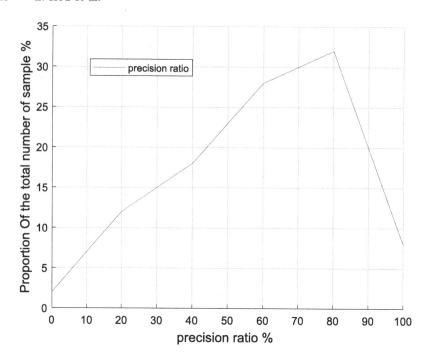

Fig. 5. The distribution of sample recall ratio.

6   Conclusions

In our research, we propose a kind of content-based massive image retrieval, we use the distributed computing platform Spark, after combining the BoVW model for representing image content with the nearest neighbor retrieval algorithm LSH. Compared with the traditional method, the retrieval time of the framework is greatly shortened, and the recall and precision of the retrieval are improved.

The future direction of improvement lies in the construction of BoVW model. It takes more than 95% time in the process of constructing index, and the effect of clustering is very uncertain. If we select the representative value of SIFT feature vector more effectively, it will further improve the accuracy of our framework.

References

1. Datar, M., Immorlica, N., Indyk, P., Mirrokni, V.S.: Locality-sensitive hashing scheme based on P-stable distributions. In: Proceedings of the Twentieth Annual Symposium on Computational Geometry, pp. 253–262. ACM (2004)
2. Gionis, A., Indyk, P., Motwani, R., et al.: Similarity search in high dimensions via hashing. In: Vldb, vol. 99, pp. 518–529 (1999)
3. Ren, R., Collomosse, J., Jose, J.: A BOVW based query generative model. In: Lee, K.-T., Tsai, W.-H., Liao, H.-Y.M., Chen, T., Hsieh, J.-W., Tseng, C.-C. (eds.) MMM 2011. LNCS, vol. 6523, pp. 118–128. Springer, Heidelberg (2011). https:// doi.org/10.1007/978-3-642-17832-0_12

4. Battiato, S., Farinella, G.M., Messina, E., Puglisi, G.: Understanding geometric manipulations of images through BOVW-based hashing. In: 2011 IEEE International Conference on Multimedia and Expo, pp. 1–6. IEEE (2011)
5. Kumar, M.D., Babaie, M., Zhu, S., Kalra, S., Tizhoosh, H.R.: A comparative study of CNN, BOVW and LBP for classification of histopathological images. In: 2017 IEEE Symposium Series on Computational Intelligence (SSCI), pp. 1–7. IEEE (2017)
6. Alham, N.K., Li, M., Liu, Y., Hammoud, S.: A mapreduce-based distributed svm algorithm for automatic image annotation. Comput. Math. Appl. **62**(7), 2801–2811 (2011)
7. Yin, D., Liu, D.: Content-based image retrial based on Hadoop. Math. Probl. Eng. (2013)
8. Jai-Andaloussi, S., Elabdouli, A., Chaffai, A., Madrane, N., Sekkaki, A.: Medical content based image retrieval by using the Hadoop framework. In: ICT 2013, pp. 1–5. IEEE (2013)
9. Hare, J.S., Samangooei, S., Lewis, P.H.: Practical scalable image analysis and indexing using Hadoop. Multimed. Tools Appl. **71**(3), 1215–1248 (2014)
10. Mezzoudj, S., Seghir, R., Saadna, Y., et al.: A parallel content-based image retrieval system using spark and tachyon frameworks. J. King Saud Univ. Comput. Inf. Sci. (2019)
11. Zhang, W., Li, D., Xu, Y., Zhang, Y.: Shuffle-efficient distributed locality sensitive hashing on spark. In: 2016 IEEE Conference on Computer Communications Workshops (INFOCOM WKSHPS), pp. 766–767. IEEE (2016)

Blockchain and Internet of Things

A Blockchain Based Terminal Security of IoT

Dawei Li[1,2(✉)] and Xue Gao[3]

[1] School of Computing Engineering,
Nanjing Institute of Technology, Nanjing 211167, China
lidw@njit.edu.cn
[2] Energy Research Institute,
Nanjing Institute of Technology, Nanjing 211167, China
[3] State Grid Electric Power Research Institute, Nanjing 211106, China
gaoxue@sgepri.sgcc.com.cn

Abstract. With the rapid development of the IoTs, the distributed access of a large number of terminals poses a serious challenge to the credibility of the system. To solve the above problems, based on the decentralized block chain technology, a terminal authentication scheme suitable for the IoT is proposed. The scheme uses block chain node to record information of terminals, the consensus mechanism is improved through key sharing algorithm, and efficient distributed authentication is realized. The simulation results show that the proposed scheme is feasible.

Keywords: Block chain · Security · Access authentication

1 Introduction

Nowadays Internet of Things (IOT) has played an important role in the application of all aspets. However, with the increase of mobile smart terminals and ubiquitous access services, the impact of security such as the credibility of terminals is increasing.

In traditional systems, the security of access terminals mainly depends on centralized key management, which requires a lot of time and management costs. Once the key system is vulnerable, it will lead to the security crisis of the whole system. With the continuous development of IoTs, the requirements of frequency, complexity and timeliness of information interaction among agents are getting higher and higher, and the type, number and processing capacity of intelligent terminals are also greatly improved. Centralized means of information exchange have been unable to meet the trust needs of multi-participated business systems.

Block chain is a distributed digital ledger technology, which has the characteristics of subject peer-to-peer, open and transparent, secure communication, difficult to tamper with and multi-party consensus. Block chain is becoming a new technology which will have a significant impact on the future after big data, cloud computing, artificial intelligence, virtual reality and other technologies. It is also increasingly widely used in information systems. Block chain technology provides good technical support for distributed trust relationship of Internet of Things terminals, and is an effective way to build safe Internet of Things.

© Springer Nature Singapore Pte Ltd. 2020
Y. Tian et al. (Eds.): ICBDS 2019, CCIS 1210, pp. 445–454, 2020.
https://doi.org/10.1007/978-981-15-7530-3_34

Based on block chain technology, this paper studies the trustworthiness strategies and schemes for terminals in IoT. Through decentralized trustworthiness information maintenance, distributed authentication mechanism is realized, the dependence of authentication center nodes in traditional Internet of Things security protocols is improved, and group access authentication is realized. On the premise of ensuring security, the response speed of concurrent access of a large number of nodes in IoT is improved.

2   Related Work

IoT refers to the infrastructure that links things, people, systems, information resources and intelligent services in the information system, and realizes the functions of intelligent identification, location, tracking, control, monitoring and management. The security trusted scheme first needs to solve the trustworthiness threat brought by wide-area deployment of networked terminals, especially to avoid node replication and man-in-the-middle attack.

In the research of terminal trustworthiness in the ubiquitous Internet of Things, the common method is centralized authentication based on public key certificates [1–5]. That is to say, the certificate management public key is used to bind the user's public key and the user's ID through the third party's trusted CA, and generate the certificate used to verify the identity of the terminal. This authentication method requires a centralized authentication server to manage the user's digital certificate or identity token trustfully. Owing to the wide coverage and large data volume of IoT, centralized authentication will reduce the efficiency and security of authentication, so distributed authentication is more suitable for IoT.

Secondly, due to the limitation of computing power and battery power of IoT terminals, the security research of Internet of Things terminals mostly focuses on reducing the computational complexity, storage complexity and communication overhead of the algorithm. For example, Chang Qing et al. [6] proposed a wireless sensor node authentication protocol based on elliptic curve encryption algorithm, and Zou Changzhong et al. [7] proposed a node ID verification-based anti-DoS attack. Node authentication protocol reduces the time cost of authentication and the communication load of network on the premise of guaranteeing good attack defensiveness. For decentralized distributed authentication, some researchers have proposed a distributed node authentication mechanism based on the concept of secret sharing [8]. The purpose of secure authentication is achieved by generating session key using node ID or using digital signature algorithm.

The application of block chain technology in trusted security algorithm is mainly to establish distributed PKI, Conner and others use public general ledger to record user certificates, associate user ID with public key certificates in a public way, and realize distributed PKI system [9]. Mastsumoto proposes a PKI framework IKP [10] based on ETF incentive strategy to improve the security of authentication CA. However, due to the different application scenarios of these studies, it is difficult to be used in the IoT business in terms of operational efficiency and complexity.

3 Security Framework

The key of Trustworthy Computing in IoT system is terminal trustworthiness. Access authentication is a method and mechanism to confirm whether an entity has access rights to certain resources or services in computer system by cryptographic means. In this paper, the terminal access authentication mechanism based on block chain is constructed to ensure the terminal trustworthiness in IoT.

3.1 Overall Framework

The IoT terminal trustworthiness framework consists of three parts: membership authentication and authorization service, block chain service engine and intelligent contract service editing service. It realizes the functions of IoT terminal identity validity authentication, IoT terminal trustworthiness storage, IoT authentication parameters and protocol configuration. As shown in Fig. 1.

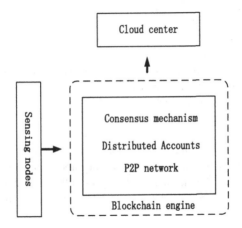

Fig. 1. Trusted management framework.

The core function of the system runs in the trusted access gateway (hereinafter referred to as gateway) which is ubiquitous in the IoT. Ubiquitous in the IoT terminal authentication to the gateway, gateway inquiry block chain module authentication information to verify the identity of the terminal. Authenticated terminals act as trusted terminals to gain access to business networks and resources. For terminals that cannot be verified, they are blacklisted as untrusted terminals.

The Block Chain Service Engine is responsible for maintaining distributed accounts of terminal access behavior in the ubiquitous Internet of Things, storing digital signatures of each legitimate node in the Block Chain, and the behavior and status of terminal access service network. For newly registered nodes, block chain service module generates new authentication blocks through consensus algorithm. Business editing module achieves authentication parameters and protocol configuration of IoT through intelligent contract of block chain, and realizes terminal initialization according to different requirements of IoT system.

3.2   Authentication Steps

IoT terminal before entering the network, first of all, the key management system generates the unique key corresponding to the terminal identification of the IoT terminal. Common uniqueness identifiers are generated by hardware serial number, MAC address, production batch number and so on. With uniqueness identifier as the generating parameter, the authentication private key is obtained by cryptographic algorithm, which is widely used in the terminal of IoT.

All ubiquitous terminals of the Internet of Things can compute the public key corresponding to any identification locally. The key management system stores the certificate information of the IoT terminal in the block chain, each block stores the certificate of one terminal, and the block chain runs in the gateway node.

In order to exchange information with distributed authentication members in the process of authentication, it is necessary to contact the gateway to obtain access privileges of Intranet before the ubiquitous terminals of the Internet of Things access the service network. After the terminal acquires the communication privileges of the intranet, the gateway selects eligible legal terminals from the terminals included in the application scenario to form an authentication group. By retrieving the data recorded in the block chain, the gateway chooses the nodes with the same business type, close geographical location, sufficient electricity and high activity to form an authentication group. The number of authentication group terminals is conFig.d according to the actual requirements of the ubiquitous business scenario of the Internet of Things. Through the business process and specifications of the IoT, the terminal authentication group node votes for the admission of the new entry node, gains 51% of the nodes after passing the authentication block chain accounting authority, generates the credibility endorsement of the new node as the terminal, thus realizing the access of the IoT terminal.

3.3   Algorithm Description

In the initial stage of ubiquitous electric IoT, the system selects two large prime number p and q, constructs a q-order finite field F_q, selects hash function $H_1(x) : \{0, 1\}^* \rightarrow Z_q^*$, $H_1(x) : \{0, 1\}^* \rightarrow Z_q^*$, sets up the membership set of authentication group $U = \{u_i | i = 1, \ldots, n\}$, and calculates $x_i = H_1(PID_i)$.

Generating Group Signature Key Pairs in IoT Gateway (P_k, S_k). The number of members of authentication group meeting the security requirements of IoT is t, Gateway randomly selects $t - 1$ elements $a_1, \ldots, a_{t-1} \in Z_p^*$, let $f(x) = S_k + a_1 x + a_2 x^2 + \ldots + a_{t-1} x^{t-1}$ calculates $y_i = f(x_i)$, $1 \leq i \leq t \leq n$. As a share of authority, it is sent to all legitimate and active business terminals recorded in the block chain.

When authenticating, the gateway sends the request information M of the terminal to be authenticated in the IoT to the authentication group node, agrees that the node accessed by the terminal signs M according to its share of authority, generates the ballot $\sigma_i = H_2(y_i)||M$, and sends (σ_i, y_i, M) as the authentication criterion to the gateway.

After receiving the message σ_i from the node, the gateway first calculates the value of $H_2(y_i)||M$ through the existing information to determine the validity of the authentication criterion sent by the node. After receiving t valid sub-authentication criteria, t pairs of points can be obtained: $(x_1, y_1), \ldots, (x_t, y_t)$. The Lagrange secret sharing algorithm is used to calculate:

$$S_k = \sum_{j=i}^{t} y_j \prod_{1 < l < t, l \neq j} \frac{x_l}{x_l - x_j} \tag{1}$$

The group key S_k is obtained, which indicates that the number of legitimate terminals meeting the threshold has been confirmed to authenticate the new incoming terminals. The gateway submits authentication information to the accounting node, generates new blocks, and at the same time, encrypts tokens with S_k, and sends the results to the gateway. The gateway decrypts the token with the public key P_k and sends it to the IoT terminal requesting access to the network. The authentication ends.

4 Simulation Analysis

At present, the mainstream block chain system can be divided into three types: public chain, alliance chain and private chain. The alliance chain refers to the block chain managed by the alliance or several organizations in the industry. The data in the alliance chain only allows the organizations in the system to read, read, modify and access activities. The security of the system is guaranteed by establishing access quasi-test and access rights. The consensus process in the alliance chain is controlled by pre-selected nodes. In addition to the advantages of block chains, it also has the advantages of strong controllability, data default is not open, fast transaction speed, customizable access control strategy and so on.

These characteristics of the alliance chain are particularly suitable for the industry ecology of the IoT. The typical development platform of alliance chain is Hyperledger Fabric project, which is a super account project sponsored by Linux Foundation and contributed by Digital Asset and IBM. It is a very popular implementation scheme of modular block chain network framework. Hyperledger Fabric supports plug-and-play and customized development of authentication, consensus and intelligent contract modules, and adapts to the complexity and high accuracy of the entire economic ecosystem. Hyperledger Fabric uses docker container technology to run an intelligent contract called Chaincode, providing a modular framework to implement node, chain code (intelligent contract) execution and configurable consensus and member services.

This research uses HyperLedger Fabric alliance chain to build the experimental environment. The experimental environment is a computing cluster consisting of five workstations. Each workstation is equipped with Intel i7-7700HQ CPU, main frequency 2.80 GHz, 16 GB DDRIII memory and 256 GB SSD hard disk. The operating system is CentOS 7. The system runs Docker container-level virtualization system to simulate P2P block chain network. The container layout tool is kubernetes 1.9. One of the five workstations is cluster manager and four are computing nodes.

The Internet of Things terminal consists of raspberry pie and tablet computer. Among them, the raspberry pie adopts 3b version, which is conFig.d as BCM2837B0 SOC, integrates 4-core ARM Cortex-A53 64-bit CPU, main frequency is 1.4 GHz, 1 GB LPDDR2 SDRAM. Huawei M5 platform is adopted in the flat intelligent terminal, which is equipped with Siqilin 960 ARM architecture chip. It integrates four main frequency 2.4 G processing cores, 4 GB memory and 64 GB memory.

The simulation system consists of client software, gateway software and trusted configuration software, which run in the terminal of IoT. The simulation system architecture is shown in Fig. 2 and Fig. 3. Among them, IoT gateway is deployed in computing cluster, IoT terminal is connected with business network and authentication server cluster through network controller.

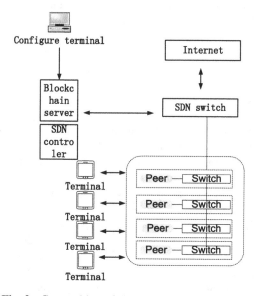

Fig. 2. Composition of simulation platform in logic.

The core algorithm is shown in the Fig. 4.

Figure 5 shows the time cost of trusted access from application to completion for IoT terminals. Contrast curve is the time cost of traditional key center centralized management. All data were averaged for 10 trials. From the data results, it can be seen that under the traditional centralized access authentication scheme, the computing and network overhead of the authentication center increases with the increase of the number of terminals in the Internet of Things, resulting in the reduction of authentication efficiency, which is directly reflected in the rapid growth of authentication time. In the block-chain-based distributed authentication scheme, when the number of terminal nodes in the Internet of Things is small, the authentication efficiency is lower than that

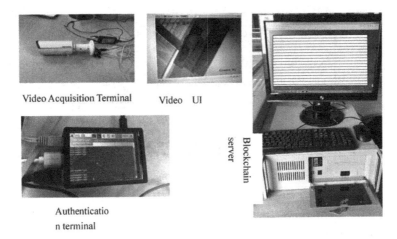

Video Acquisition Terminal   Video   UI

Authenticatio
n terminal

Blockchain
server

Fig. 3. Composition of simulation platform in physical.

```
Do  User.Transaction.send(LocalNode)          // user sent transaction
If     User.Right==false          // account has no authority
Then      User.Transaction.send(LocalNode)=false   // transaction deny
   Do User.Right.ApplyForAuthorized()       // apply
Elseif User.Right==true                    // have the permission
Then      User.Transaction.send(LocalNode)=true    // apply scucess
Do     Transaction=LocalNode.Receive(data)       // receive transaction
Do     LocalNode.Broadcast(Transaction)         //broadcast information
Do     Block=ServerNode.Block.Unpack(Transaction) // generate block
Do     ServerNode.Broadcast(Block)          // broadcast block information
Do     Block=LocalNode.Receive(data)     // receive block information
Do     Contract=LocalNode.getContract(Block)     // get information
If     Contract.Transaction.ReturnValue==True   // transaction ok
Then      ServerDevice.Execute(Contract.Transaction)       // execute
Elseif    Contract.ReturnValue==true         // return false
Ser   verDevice.Refuse(Contract.Transaction)  // deny transaction
```

Fig. 4. The core algorithm.

of centralized authentication. This is because the cost of running distributed authentication protocol in the block-chain scheme is larger when the network scale is small. When the scale of the Internet of Things increases, the authentication efficiency is obviously improved.

Figure 6 shows the increase of CPU load of single node with the number of nodes in concurrent access. Because of the flexible scheduling algorithm of kubernetes, the increase of CPU is within the acceptable range. Figure 7 shows the comparison of authentication time under different thresholds of authentication group nodes under the

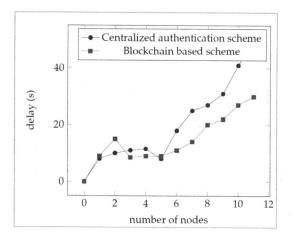

Fig. 5. Curve of authentication efficiency.

same size of Internet of Things nodes. According to Byzantine fault-tolerant principle, the increase in the number of authentication group nodes will bring about an increase in security, but the increase in the number of information exchanges will increase the authentication time correspondingly and reduce the authentication efficiency.

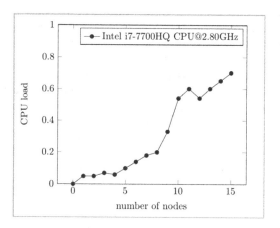

Fig. 6. CPU performance in concurrent requests.

In the application of block chain, concurrent quantity is an important index. Figure 8 shows the relationship between the generation time of new blocks and the scale of existing block chains in this system. The analysis of simulation data shows that the generation time of new blocks increases with the increase of the length of block chains, but the overall performance decreases slightly. Therefore, the scheme proposed in this paper is suitable for the situation of large number of concurrent access terminals in the IoT.

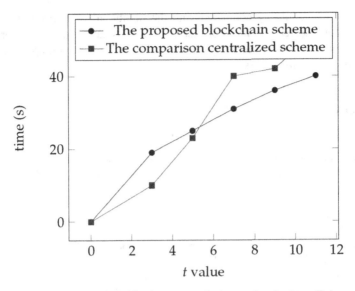

Fig. 7. The impact of certification group size on authentication efficiency.

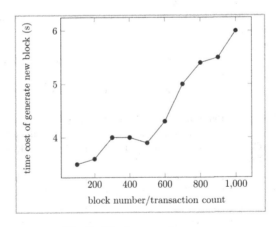

Fig. 8. Block generation curve.

5   Conclusion

With the wide application of the IoT in all kinds of business of information system, the credibility of the terminals of the IoT has become a key factor restricting the security and reliability of information system. In this paper, the decentralized distributed trust of block chains is applied to the research of terminal trustworthiness in IoT. A practical scheme is proposed. Compared with the traditional centralized key scheme, this scheme is based on the verifiability of block chains and avoids the system overhead caused by running decryption algorithm during authentication. The simulation experiment based on hyperledger platform shows that the proposed scheme has significantly improved the authentication efficiency compared with the traditional centralized authentication scheme. Further research will focus on testing the access authentication performance of the system in the actual business application scenario through pilot application under the condition of massive access.

References

1. Kan, L., Wei, Y., Hafiz Muhammad, A., Siyuan, W., Linchao, G., Kai, H.: A multiple blockchains architecture on inter-blockchain communication. In: 2018 IEEE International Conference on Software Quality, Reliability and Security Companion (QRS-C), Lisbon, Portugal, pp. 139–145 (2018)
2. Li, H.G., Tian, H.B., Zhang, F.G., He, J.J.: Blockchain-based searchable symmetric encryption scheme. Comput. Electr. Eng. **73**, 32–45 (2019)
3. Andoni, M., Robu, V., Flynn, D., Abram, S., Geach, D., Jenkins, D., McCallum, P., Peacock, A.: Blockchain technology in the energy sector: a systematic review of challenges and opportunities. Renew. Sustain. Energy Rev. **100**, 143–174 (2019)
4. Sun, J., Yan, J., Zhang, K.Z.K.: Blockchain-based sharing services: what blockchain technology can contribute to smart cities. Financ. Innov. **2**(1), 1–9 (2016). https://doi.org/10.1186/s40854-016-0040-y
5. Lou, J., Zhang, Q., Qi, Z., Lei, K.: A blockchain-based key management scheme for named data networking. In: 2018 1st IEEE International Conference on Hot Information-Centric Networking (HotICN), Shenzhen, China, pp. 141–146 (2018)
6. Chang, Q., Zhang, Y.G., Qin, L.L.: A node authentication protocol based on ECC in WSN. In: International Conference on Computer Design and Applications, ICCDA 2010, vol. 2, pp. 606–609. IEEE Computer Society, Piscataway (2010)
7. Zou, C.Z.: Based on node ID confirmation defend DoS attacks in wireless sensor networks. J. Chin. Comput. Syst. **33**(3), 486–491 (2012)
8. Haimabati, D., Raja, D.: Monitoring threshold cryptography based wireless sensor networks with projective plane. In: 5th International Conference on Computers and Devices for Communication (CO-DEC), Kanyakumari, India, pp. 1–4. IEEE Computer Society, Washington DC (2012)
9. Fromknecht, C., Velicanu, D.: CertCoin: a NameCoin based decentralized authentication system. Technical Report, 6.857 Class Project, Massachusetts Institute of Technology (2014)
10. Matsumoto, S., Reischuk, R.M.: IKP: turning a PKI around with decentralized automated incentives. In: Security and Privacy, pp. 410–426 (2017). https://doi.org/10.1109/sp.2017.57

Key Factors Affecting Blockchain Adoption in Organizations

Abubakar Mohammed[1(✉)], Vidyasagar Potdar[1], and Li Yang[2]

[1] Blockchain R&D Lab, School of Management, Faculty of Business and Law,
Curtin University, Perth, Australia
abubakar.mohammed@postgrad.curtin.edu.au,
v.potdar@curtin.edu.au
[2] Institute of Automation, Qilu University of Technology
(Shandong Academy of Sciences), Jinan, China
liyang@sdas.org

Abstract. Blockchain is a decentralized network with a distributed ledger designed to store data permanently, thus offering immutability, trust, transparency, and security. It is a disruptive technological innovation beneficial to many industries. Even with such useful features, blockchain is still finding its roots in the industry. Blockchain adoption has been slower than expected. Hence, understanding the critical reasons for such delayed adoption becomes a very crucial issue. In this paper, we attempt to answer a straightforward research question "How to sell blockchain to a C-level executive?" We believe that this is the fundamental research question that needs to be answered to understand what decision-makers think of blockchain. To answer this question, we adopted a non-participant form of netnography research methodology, and we did a targeted search of social media platforms (LinkedIn, Facebook, and Twitter) to find opinions shared by experts on this topic. We gathered 98 comments posted on social platforms as secondary data for our study. Data screening was conducted to determine the relevant comments, meaning that some comments (or posts) were not related to the research question, and were omitted from the study. We selected 44 comments and categorized all the comments to identify five key factors that influence blockchain adoption in organizations, and these factors are cost, trust, awareness, efficiency, and storytelling. This research work will contribute to the body of knowledge because it will provide an insightful message to the organization towards blockchain adoption as well as give the industries an unbiased direction to build their blockchain strategy.

Keywords: Blockchain · Adoption · Factors · Cost · Trust · Awareness · Efficiency · Storytelling

1 Introduction

In 2008, the concept of blockchain was proposed by Satoshi Nakamoto [1] and implemented as an open-source project in 2009. Bitcoin was the first real-world application of blockchain technology [1]. Bitcoin is a decentralized peer-to-peer network for cryptocurrency and is one of the well-known use cases of blockchain technology [1–3].

As defined by [4], "A blockchain is a distributed database, which is shared among and agreed upon a peer-to-peer network. It consists of a linked sequence of blocks, holding timestamped transactions that are secured by public-key cryptography and verified by the network community. Once an element is appended to the blockchain, it cannot be altered, turning a blockchain into a permanent record of past activity."

Blockchain is a distributed technology [5, 6] that stores data in immutable forms [7–9], whereby there is no need for a central authority to manage the transactions [10]. Blockchain provides a trust model dependent on a group consensus, which approves transactions and permits the addition to the chain. Each record in the public blockchain is verified by its users who hold a full copy of the blockchain. Blockchain provides a decentralized environment [11], with immutability, trust, transparency, and security [12, 13], which has made it a disruptive technology [14]. The essential features of blockchain technology are cryptography, (i.e., public key infrastructure, hashing), decentralized consensus algorithms (i.e., proof of stake, proof of work, and practical byzantine fault tolerance), and distributed computation [15].

These features have made blockchain as a unique technology among other systems, and that is why it has drawn significant attention from several industries such as supply chain, education, healthcare, mining, agriculture, government, and finance.

1.1 Characteristics of Blockchain

Blockchain technology has key characteristics, which include decentralization, anonymity, immutability, and transparency [16, 17].

Decentralization: The nature of decentralization in blockchain technology, it means that technology has no central database or authority to manage the network. Every participant in the network has the right to interact with the system and verify the transactions. For instance, in Bitcoin and Ethereum platforms, users submit transactions for miners to sequence into blocks. Participants in the network can verify this transaction without the help of intermediaries.

Anonymity: Anonymity is a key component of the public blockchain, which allows a user to interact with another user in a public blockchain network without disclosing each other's identity. The user can only be identified by public keys, which is the key component of the cryptosystems [18]. In a public blockchain, transactions show up on an open system, where others can see all transactions. The transactions show up as a series of numbers, which is why no one can identify who the real user is.

Immutability: Immutability is another important characteristic of blockchain technology, which means that once a record (data or transactions) is added to a block, it permanently remains and cannot be changed. In each block, the transactional history contains a cryptographic hash of the original data. This hash is unique, and any attempt to change the block content is prevented [19].

Transparency: Blockchain has the potential to add transparency not only to financial transactions but also to business processes. For instance, in supply chain management, blockchain can allow tracking of a product across the supply chain, which provides customers with details on the source of origin to ensure its authenticity [20].

1.2 Types of Blockchain

Blockchain types can be categorized into three types: public blockchain, private blockchain, and consortium blockchain [21–23].

Public Blockchain: All transactions that happen on public blockchains are fully transparent to the participants in the network, anybody can join the system, and can verify the transactions. A public blockchain is mainly used for cryptocurrencies (e.g., Bitcoin, Ethereum, and Litecoin), and no one has complete control over the network [23].

A Private Blockchain is also known as permissioned blockchain (e.g., Hyperledger and R3 Corda), this is managed by a centralized entity. It only permits verified users to be part of the system, and only these users can check or add information to the blockchain. This is primarily used in private enterprises that do not want their sensitive information to be known by the public [22].

Consortium Blockchain is like a hybrid of the public and the private blockchain [22]. Consortium blockchains are often used in scenarios where there are multiple organizations involved in business activity, e.g., supply chain network comprising of different companies, including manufacturer, distributor, transporter, etc.

Since blockchain is in the development stage, there is a need for further research to explore the factors that would influence the adoption of blockchain in organizations [24]. However, the existing literature on blockchain covers technical challenges such as scalability, latency, security, privacy and also includes other application-driven research areas such as use cases for different businesses (e.g., supply chain, banking, etc.) [25–27]. However, what is missing in these studies is the investigation of blockchain adoption in organizations. Therefore, understanding the key factors that influence an organization to adopt blockchain is a significant research gap. Thus, this paper aims to identify key factors that would affect the adoption of blockchain in organizations.

The paper is organized as follows. The next section provides the state of blockchain adoption and statistics from top consulting agencies around the world. Section 3 describes the research problem. Section 4 explains the methodology adopted for data collection and analysis. Section 5 provides the findings of the research, and lastly, Sect. 6 presents the conclusion and future.

2 State of Blockchain Adoption

According to a 2019 report, Gartner predicts that the market for blockchain technology would be more than $176 billion by 2025 and $3.1 trillion by 2030 [28]. This shows that the market is growing rapidly. This report also states that "many CIOs overestimate the capabilities and short-term benefits of blockchain as a technology to help them achieve their business goals." [28]. This is a very critical statement, which points out that organizations should utilize the potential benefit of blockchain to improve their business operations.

A recent PwC report [29], indicates that of the "600 executives from 15 territories, 84% say their organizations have at least some involvement with blockchain technology". Their findings show that financial service is still the leading industry in adopting blockchain, and also found that blockchain has potential in other industries like energy, utilities as well as the healthcare sector. These findings also show that the US is the most advanced country in developing blockchain; however, it is expected China to lead soon [29]. A recent statement by Chinese President supporting blockchain technology has dramatically stirred the blockchain industry around the world [30].

Another report by Wintergreen [31] found that the worldwide blockchain market was valued at $708 million in 2017 and is estimated to reach $60.7 billion by 2024. A similar report from Tractica [32] states that the growing adoption of blockchain will drive the worldwide market size from $4.6 billion in 2018 to $20.3 billion by 2025.

International Data Corporation (IDC), estimates that blockchain technology will slowly grow to reach $11.7 billion by 2022 [33]. IDC reports [34] that the global blockchain expenditure is estimated to be almost $2.9 billion in 2019 that is an 88.7% growth from the $1.5 billion spent in 2018. IDC also expects global blockchain spending to see agile development from 2018 to 2022, with a five-year compound annual growth rate (CAGR) of 76%, and total global expenditure will add up to $12.4 billion in 2022 [34].

As for the investment sector, the financial industry, such as banking, securities, investment services, and insurance services, are estimated to invest more than $1.1 billion in 2019. While, manufacturing, professional services industries, and distribution services are also expected to see spending on blockchain to a total of $653 million and $642 million, respectively, in 2019 [34]. In terms of use cases, trade finance, cross border payments, and settlements are expected to receive the maximum investment ($453 million and $285 million) [34]. However, in terms of country's wise spending on blockchain in 2019, U.S. will be the leading with $1.1 billion, followed by Western Europe with $674 million and China $319 million [34].

Overall, what we observe from the research reported by top consulting agencies is that there is going to be a huge market going forward and a pressing need to understand how adoption will happen across different sectors. These reports clearly show that huge investments in blockchain shortly.

3   Research Problem

Blockchain adoption in organizations is still in its early phase, and there is limited research available in this space [24, 35]. Blockchain, with its unique and useful features, is still finding its roots in the industry [36]. Adoption of any emerging technology (like blockchain) depends on various factors. These factors are very crucial for decision-makers when choosing new technology for their respective organization. The decision-maker needs to consider not only the positive impacts of the blockchain adoption but also the right factors to be considered. Hence, identifying the key factors becomes a very vital issue. This paper investigates this problem by attempting to identify the key factors that decision-makers would value when considering blockchain technology for their organization.

4   Research Methodology

4.1   Netnography Research Method

Netnography is a method designed to study online cultures and communities [37]. This method allows the use of available online resources to get a public viewpoint on a specific topic or idea. The internet is filled up with a lot of information on various areas. It is a channel for individuals to share their thoughts and opinions on different topics [38]. With the increasing relevance of the use of social networks, online spaces are exceptional and productive for research. In [39], states that "netnography is an excellent resource for the seasoned qualitative researcher and a useful entry point for the newcomer to qualitative research." In this paper, we adopted a non-participant form of netnography to understand expert's opinions on blockchain adoption by qualitatively analyzing social media posts from Facebook, Twitter, and LinkedIn.

4.2   Social Media Data Collection Process

Qualitative data were collected via comments posted on social media platforms. We gathered 98 comments that discussed ideas relating to blockchain adoption. We used these posts as secondary data in our study. We conducted a content analysis by categorizing all the comments into different themes to identify important factors that influence blockchain adoption in an organization. We used Nvivo software data analysis.

Data screening was conducted to determine the relevant posts, meaning that some posts (or comments) were not related to the research question, and were omitted from the study. Among 98 comments, we selected 44 comments, and we also categorized all the comments to identify five key factors that influence blockchain adoption in organizations, and these factors are cost, trust, awareness, efficiency, and storytelling. The following section discusses the findings of this research.

5   Data Analysis and Findings

This section presents the research findings. Based on the evaluation conducted by all the authors, we categorized the data into different themes to identify the important factors that answer the research question. We analyzed and identified five relevant factors that will lead to blockchain adoption. Table 1 lists the identified key factors.

Table 1. Key factors

Factors
Cost
Trust
Awareness
Efficiency
Storytelling

5.1 Cost

Cost is the first factor; we can categorize cost into two aspects direct cost and indirect cost. The direct cost is related to obtaining or implementing blockchain technology, i.e., the capital expenditure, while indirect costs refer to maintaining, upgrading, and using the technology, i.e., the operational expenditure. The cost has come out as a significant factor in the adoption of blockchain [40].

In our research, we gathered ten comments, we have shown five comments here (C001-C005) that addressed cost as a key factor. These comments came from experts like CTOs, CEOs, and academic leaders like professors.

Observation 1. Experts mentioned that if blockchain can improve RoI (Return on Investment), which is what most of the organizations want in their business. Experts also highlighted that it is better to sell a solution rather than technology. The solution may use blockchain as an underlying technology, but the idea is to provide a cost-effective solution that addresses business problems. As the expert (C001) stated that *"...Why not sell solutions rather than blockchain? Do the folks care if you are implementing blockchain or only about how you can save them 20% or more. If you can't do the latter, will they ever buy what you are selling? Business and sales 101"*, While (C002) added that *"First we need to understand their current workflow. Then can analyze how their system can be beneficial with blockchain. We need to provide them real data that how it can improve their customer base and can increase margins..."* The most important thing is to save costs. As said by (C003), *there are two ways to make a business emotional. You either help them make money or save money"*.

Observation 2. Risk is a cost for an organization; hence, any approach that can mitigate risk or reduce risk will be valued by organizations. If blockchain technology can help an organization to manage risks better, then they would consider it, otherwise no. Because organizations are looking for technology that would make them reduce risks and increase RoI. The following statements from the expert indicate that cost is an essential factor to be considered *"...You don't sell blockchain any more than selling databases or backup archives. These are tools. You sell how to reduce risk or increase ROI. Follow the money"* (C004).

Observation 3. Cost plays a significant role as a motivator of blockchain adoption in any industry that is looking for blockchain implementation. It is understood that blockchain will reduce operational costs [41, 42] at the same time, it can provide risk management. *"....If you are manipulating risk perceptions you are selling fear. If you are claiming to improve ROI, you are selling greed. If you can make an evidence-based case that competitors can outperform you in market share with blockchain LMK"* (C005).

Inference 1. Our findings align with [41–43], which has shown that cost plays a critical role in the adoption of new and disruptive technology.

5.2 Trust

Trust is an essential factor that affects technology adoption [8, 44]. We know that people buy from who they "trust." For a business that offers a "digital trust machine," i.e., *blockchain, you first need to build your trust as an individual and an organization.*

In our research, we gathered ten comments, we have shown five comments here (T001-T005) that addressed trust as a critical factor. These comments came from experts like blockchain developers, blockchain consultants, digital marketing managers, and marketing consultants. The supporting statements from experts also recap the same argument.

"Sell them the power and trust of blockchain + tell them but that they can change the world. Confidence and experience will play an important role. Note: Blockchain is not the answer to every question" (T001).
"One's approach depends on factors like relationships, trust, client openness, etc. However key thing is to take an incremental approach, take it slow, don't try to suggest complete flipping of legacy, but augmenting legacy systems to modernize and make them more robust and secure" (T002).

To me *"...I would tell them that using a blockchain means having a mechanism that enables and "structure" the trust between the parties: each relevant participants keeps its own copy, always updated, of the "ledger" of the transactions"* (T003), but as (T004) states *"..What you sell is an application using Blockchain tech. Also building the trust, don't make them feel they need to change or feeling stupid are important I think".*

Observation 4. Most people do not care about what technology goes behind. What they usually care about is how it solves their problem and makes their lives better. In (T005) opinion *"...Give them basic examples than explain to them how they can use blockchain to grow their business and they don't have to trust middle-man to run their business".*

Inference 2. Our findings also align with [45–48] study stated that trust is a vital component that influences innovation adoption.

5.3 Awareness

Awareness has been identified as a significant factor in technology adoption. Blockchain awareness among individuals and organizations is an important factor [49]. Because if we make people understand what blockchain is and how it works, i.e.

increase their overall knowledge of the technology, they are more likely to understand the benefit of blockchain, which will help to increase the adoption.

In our study, we gathered nine comments, we have shown four comments here (A001–A004) that addressed awareness as a key factor. These comments came from experts like a consultant, chairman and managing director, co-founder and managing partner, and digital marketing manager. These are the people who have significant experience in technology diffusion.

Observation 5. Another thing to consider is by providing workshops with real business use cases and examples because many people only see one use case of blockchain as cryptocurrency. This perception needs to be changed. For instance, in the supply chain, blockchain is a perfect solution for customers who are facing transparency problems. As stated by (A001) *"Explain it simple in 1 sentence that even a child would understand. Follow up with use cases"*.

Observation 6. Creating awareness among individuals and organizations is essential to educate people about blockchain solutions and its potential benefit to industries.

> *"Make it easy to understand. Break it down into pieces of the puzzle that is simpler to comprehend. Focus on identifying pain areas and highlighting how the use of Blockchain technology can solve those critical issues for them in the most efficient & full proof manner. You will see a more favourable response and reaction" (A002).*

> *"Don't talk about blockchain. It's just a new layer of a boring tech stack that the c suite already knows nothing about. Talk about what problem you're solving" (A003).*

Observation 7. Once individuals and organizations realized what blockchain is capable of doing and how it can help in growing businesses. Perhaps, they will adopt it. Otherwise, they will be skeptical.

> *"You cannot sell something to people that do not understand its benefits. So, first of all, you have to put your time and energy to educate the business leaders. Blockchain is here. We are already witnessing the potential benefit to many industries" (A004).*

Inference 3. Our findings also align with [50–52] research mentioned awareness as an influential factor for technology adoption.

5.4 Efficiency

Efficiency (or business efficiency) is identified as another important factor for technology adoption. Organizations normally consider technology that would add value to their business and make their business more efficient and accurate [53].

In our study, we gathered seven comments, we have shown two comments here (E001-E002) that addressed efficiency as a key factor. These comments came from experts like CEO, system analyst, founder, and director. The findings recommended that efficiency as one of the key adoption drivers. The expert supports the following statements:

> *"Like any sale, sell them the benefits as they apply to them, not the underlying tech. find the pain that their current solution is creating and tell them how the new one solves it" (E001).*

Observation 8. It is better to sell a solution that will improve business efficiency rather than selling blockchain. As supported by (E002) *"...Customers demand trust, transparency, and efficiency. That's what you sell. Blockchain is just the name of the technology"*

Inference 4. Our findings align with [54] study stated efficiency is an essential factor for the adoption of technology.

5.5   Storytelling

We identified storytelling as a fifth factor leading to blockchain adoption [55, 56]. Storytelling helps customers relate to technology and understand how technology can solve their business problems. When you take a customer through a storytelling journey, you can relate their problems clearly and show when and where technology can resolve these problems and the resulting benefits due to technology adoption.

In our study, we gathered eight comments, we have shown two comments here (S001-S002) that addressed storytelling as a key factor. These comments came from experts like directors and senior managers. The expert supports the following statements:

"Outline a specific pain/risk-mitigating scenario in their world and don't mention the word blockchain until they have bought into it as a viable solution. It's great to then say, "what if I told you that what I just explained is possible using blockchain technology?" (S001).

Observation 9. Storytelling works by giving some examples that can relate to people's mindsets and business models.

"Focus on their existing challenges and offer blockchain solutions that cannot be attained with their current systems. Important to emphasize the integration point of blockchain tech and their legacy systems. Blockchain may only solve a fraction of the problem, and that's ok. Blockchain purists may argue that this approach defeats the point of implementing blockchain technology altogether, but for the aforementioned enterprise executives, a gradual transition is the best way forward" (S002).

Inference 5. Our findings align with [57] the study stated storytelling as a key factor for the adoption of technology.

6   Conclusion and Future Work

The findings from this study identified some key relevant factors that would influence the adoption of blockchain technology in an organization. This study will contribute to the body of knowledge because it will provide insight into the organization towards the adoption of blockchain technology as well as give the industries an unbiased direction to build their blockchain strategy. This study also provides an understanding and awareness of blockchain technology adoption. This study will be further extended to test the identified factors using a quantitative approach, as well as more interviews (face to face interviews) will be conducted with blockchain experts to get more insights towards the adoption of blockchain technology in organizations. This study could also be extended by considering the impact, challenges as well as the consequences of blockchain adoption in organizations.

Acknowledgments. The authors would like to acknowledge the contribution of an Australian Government Research Training Program Scholarship and Food Agility CRC Scholarship in supporting this research. This research is conducted within the Blockchain Research & Development Lab at Curtin University's Faculty of Business & Law.

References

1. Nakamoto, S.: Bitcoin: a peer-to-peer electronic cash system (2008)
2. Crosby, M., Pattanayak, P., Verma, S., Kalyanaraman, V.: Blockchain technology: beyond bitcoin. Appl. Innov. **2**(6–10), 71 (2016)
3. Fahmy, S.F.: Blockchain and its uses. Semantic Scholar (2018)
4. Seebacher, S., Schüritz, R.: Blockchain technology as an enabler of service systems: a structured literature review. In: Za, S., Drăgoicea, M., Cavallari, M. (eds.) IESS 2017. LNBIP, vol. 279, pp. 12–23. Springer, Cham (2017). https://doi.org/10.1007/978-3-319-56925-3_2
5. Ahram, T., Sargolzaei, A., Sargolzaei, S., Daniels, J., Amaba, B.: Blockchain technology innovations. In: 2017 IEEE Technology & Engineering Management Conference, pp. 137–141. IEEE, Santa Clara (2017)
6. Wang, H., Chen, K., Xu, D.: A maturity model for blockchain adoption. Finan. Innov. **2**(1), 12 (2016). https://doi.org/10.1186/s40854-016-0031-z
7. Lindman, J., Tuunainen, V.K., Rossi, M.: Opportunities and risks of blockchain technologies–a research agenda. In: Proceedings of the 50th Hawaii International Conference on System Sciences, HICSS, Hilton Waikoloa Village, US, pp. 1533–1542 (2017)
8. Mendling, J., et al.: Blockchains for business process management-challenges and opportunities. ACM Trans. Manag. Inf. Syst. **9**(1), 4 (2018)
9. Risius, M., Spohrer, K.: A blockchain research framework. Bus. Inf. Syst. Eng. **59**(6), 385–409 (2017). https://doi.org/10.1007/s12599-017-0506-0
10. Wörner, D., Von Bomhard, T., Schreier, Y.-P., Bilgeri, D.: The Bitcoin ecosystem: disruption beyond financial services. In: Twenty-Fourth European Conference on Information Systems (ECIS), pp. 1–16. Research Platform Alexandria, İstanbul (2016)
11. Yli-Huumo, J., Ko, D., Choi, S., Park, S., Smolander, K.: Where is current research on blockchain technology?—a systematic review. PLoS ONE **11**(10), e0163477 (2016)
12. Kharitonov, A.: A framework for strategic intra-and inter-organizational adoption of the blockchain technology. SSRN 3005343 (2017)
13. Tapscott, D., Tapscott, A.: The impact of the blockchain goes beyond financial services. Harvard Bus. Rev. **10**, 2–5 (2016)
14. Trautman, L.J.: Is disruptive blockchain technology the future of financial services. SSRN (2016)
15. Salviotti, G., De Rossi, L.M., Abbatemarco, N.: A structured framework to assess the business application landscape of blockchain technologies. In: Proceedings of the 51st Hawaii International Conference on System Sciences, pp. 3467–3476. Curran Associates, Waikoloa Village (2018)
16. Francisco, K., Swanson, D.: The supply chain has no clothes: technology adoption of blockchain for supply chain transparency. Logistics **2**(1), 2 (2018)

17. Kim, S.-S., Jang, W.-J., Phuong, H.-T., Gim, G.-Y.: A comparative study on the intention of using blockchain technology in Korea and Vietnam. Adv. Sci. Technol. Lett. **150**, 214–216 (2018)
18. Clohessy, T., Acton, T., Rogers, N.: Blockchain adoption: technological, organisational and environmental considerations. In: Treiblmaier, H., Beck, R. (eds.) Business Transformation through Blockchain, pp. 47–76. Springer, Cham (2019). https://doi.org/10.1007/978-3-319-98911-2_2
19. Srivastav, K.: A guide to blockchain immutability and challenges. https://dzone.com/articles/a-guide-to-blockchain-immutability-and-chief-chall. Accessed 30 July 2019
20. Lisk: Blockchain transparency explained. https://lisk.io/academy/blockchain-basics/benefits-of-blockchain/blockchain-transparency-explained. Accessed 30 July 2019
21. Buterin, V.: On public and private blockchains. https://blog.ethereum.org/2015/08/07/on-public-and-private-blockchains/. Accessed 31 July 2019
22. Dragonchain: What different types of blockchains are there? https://dragonchain.com/blog/differences-between-public-private-blockchains. Accessed 31 July 2019
23. Hiremath, O.S.: Different types of blockchain and why we need them. https://www.edureka.co/blog/types-of-blockchain/#DifferenttypesofBlockchain. Accessed 30 July 2019
24. Iansiti, M., Lakhani, K.R.: The truth about blockchain. Harv. Bus. Rev. **95**(1), 118–127 (2017)
25. Gräther, W., Kolvenbach, S., Ruland, R., Schütte, J., Torres, C., Wendland, F.: Blockchain for education: lifelong learning passport. In: Proceedings of 1st ERCIM Blockchain Workshop. European Society for Socially Embedded Technologies, Amsterdam (2018)
26. Mannaro, K., Pinna, A., Marchesi, M.: Crypto-trading: Blockchain-oriented energy market. In: 2017 AEIT International Annual Conference, pp. 1–5. IEEE, Cagliari (2017)
27. Tian, F.: An agri-food supply chain traceability system for China based on RFID & blockchain technology. In: 13th International Conference on Service Systems and Service Management (ICSSSM), pp. 1–6. IEEE, Kunming (2016)
28. Gartner: Gartner predicts 90% of current enterprise blockchain platform implementations will require replacement by 2021. https://www.gartner.com/en/newsroom/press-releases/2019-07-03-gartner-predicts-90-of-current-enterprise-blockchain. Accessed 30 July 2019
29. PwC: PwC's Global Blockchain survey 2018, Blockchain is here. What's your next move. https://www.pwc.com/gx/en/issues/blockchain/blockchain-in-business.html. Accessed 30 July 2019
30. Wood, C.: China goes bullish on blockchain. https://www.businessinsider.com.au/china-bullish-on-blockchain-xi-jinping-2019-10. Accessed 15 Nov 2019
31. WinterGreen: Blockchain: market shares, strategies, and forecasts, worldwide, 2018 to 2024. https://www.wintergreenresearch.com/blockchain. Accessed 31 July 2019
32. Tractica: Enterprise blockchain revenue to surpass $20 Billion by 2025. https://www.tractica.com/newsroom/press-releases/enterprise-blockchain-revenue-to-surpass-20-billion-by-2025/. Accessed 30 July 2019
33. IDC: Worldwide spending on blockchain forecast to reach $11.7 billion in 2022, According to New IDC Spending Guide. https://www.idc.com/getdoc.jsp?containerId=prUS44150518. Accessed 08 Sept 2018
34. IDC: Worldwide blockchain spending forecast to reach $2.9 billion in 2019, According to New IDC Spending Guide. https://www.idc.com/getdoc.jsp?containerId=prUS44898819. Accessed 14 June 2019
35. Gammelgaard, B., Welling, H.S., Nielsen, P.B.M.: Blockchain technology for supply chains: a guidebook, 27 (2019)

36. Chen, S., Yan, J., Tan, B., Liu, X., Li, Y.: Processes and challenges for the adoption of blockchain technology in food supply chains: a thematic analysis. In: IConference, pp. 1–4. iSchools (2019)

37. Kozinets, R.V.: The field behind the screen: using netnography for marketing research in online communities. J. Mark. Res. **39**(1), 61–72 (2002)

38. Kaya, S., Argan, M., Yetim, G.: From experience to summit or vice versa? Netnography study on a virtual community of mountaineering. Univ. J. Educ. Res. **5**(7), 1117–1126 (2017)

39. Bowler Jr., G.M.: Netnography: a method specifically designed to study cultures and communities online. Qual. Rep. **15**(5), 1270–1275 (2010)

40. Tornatzky, L.G., Klein, K.J.: Innovation characteristics and innovation adoption-implementation: a meta-analysis of findings. IEEE Trans. Eng. Manag. **1**, 28–45 (1982)

41. Nagy, D., Schuessler, J., Dubinsky, A.: Defining and identifying disruptive innovations. Ind. Mark. Manag. **57**, 119–126 (2016)

42. Shen, Y.-C., Huang, C.-Y., Chu, C.-H., Hsu, C.-T.: A benefit–cost perspective of the consumer adoption of the mobile banking system. Behav. Inf. Technol. **29**(5), 497–511 (2010)

43. Walsh, S.T., Kirchhoff, B.A., Newbert, S.: Differentiating market strategies for disruptive technologies. IEEE Trans. Eng. Manag. **49**(4), 341–351 (2002)

44. AlAwadhi, S.: A proposed model of trust factors for e-government adoption and civic engagement. In: Proceedings of the 52nd Hawaii International Conference on System Sciences, HICSS, Grand Wailea, Maui, pp. 3161–3170 (2019)

45. Alzahrani, L., Al-Karaghouli, W., Weerakkody, V.: Analysing the critical factors influencing trust in e-government adoption from citizens' perspective: a systematic review and a conceptual framework. Int. Bus. Rev. **26**(1), 164–175 (2017)

46. Gao, L., Waechter, K.A.: Examining the role of initial trust in user adoption of mobile payment services: an empirical investigation. Inf. Syst. Front. **19**(3), 525–548 (2015). https://doi.org/10.1007/s10796-015-9611-0

47. Lippert, S.K., Davis, M.: A conceptual model integrating trust into planned change activities to enhance technology adoption behavior. J. Inf. Sci. **32**, 434–448 (2006)

48. Rouibah, K., Lowry, P.B., Hwang, Y.: The effects of perceived enjoyment and perceived risks on trust formation and intentions to use online payment systems: new perspectives from an Arab country. Electron. Commer. Res. Appl. **19**, 33–43 (2016)

49. Lee, R.L., Blouin, M.C.: Factors affecting web disclosure adoption in the nonprofit sector. J. Comput. Inf. Syst. **59**(4), 363–372 (2019)

50. Quaddus, M., Hofmeyer, G.: An investigation into the factors influencing the adoption of B2B trading exchanges in small businesses. Eur. J. Inf. Syst. **16**, 202–215 (2007)

51. Sabah, N.M.: Exploring students' awareness and perceptions: influencing factors and individual differences driving m-learning adoption. Comput. Hum. Behav. **65**, 522–533 (2016)

52. Safeena, R., Date, H., Kammani, A., Hundewale, N.: Technology adoption and Indian consumers: study on mobile banking. Int. J. Comput. Theory Eng. **4**(6), 1020 (2012)

53. Akroush, M.N., Zuriekat, M.I., Al Jabali, H.I., Asfour, N.A.: Determinants of purchasing intentions of energy-efficient products: the roles of energy awareness and perceived benefits. Int. J. Energy Sect. Manag. **13**(1), 128–148 (2019)

54. Galang, R.M.N.: Government efficiency and international technology adoption: the spread of electronic ticketing among airlines. J. Int. Bus. Stud. **43**(7), 631–654 (2012). https://doi.org/10.1057/jibs.2012.20

55. Ch'ng, E., Cai, S., Leow, F.-T., Zhang, T.E.: Adoption and use of emerging cultural technologies in China's museums. J. Cult. Herit. **37**, 170–180 (2019)

56. Revythi, A., Tselios, N.: Extension of technology acceptance model by using system usability scale to assess behavioral intention to use e-learning. Educ. Inf. Technol. **24**(4), 2341–2355 (2019). https://doi.org/10.1007/s10639-019-09869-4

57. Akgün, A.E., Keskin, H., Ayar, H., Erdoğan, E.: The influence of storytelling approach in travel writings on readers' empathy and travel intentions. Procedia-Soc. Behav. Sci. **207**, 577–586 (2015)

An IoT-Based Congestion-Aware Emergency Evacuation Approach

Najla Al-nabhan[(✉)]

Computer Science Department, King Saud University, Riyadh, Saudi Arabia
nalnabhan@ksu.edu.sa

Abstract. Internet of Things (IoT) is one of the promising technologies for tackling issues of modern cities by creating a massive world-wide network of interconnected physical objects embedded with electronics, software, sensors, and network connectivity. IoT-Enabled Smart City Buildings today vulnerable to several types of hazards. As IoT and its enabling technologies allow sustainable development of smart cities, one of important IoT applications in modern cities is providing emergency management. Today, there are quite view emergency evacuation systems have been developed to reduce loss of people and increase survival rate during any hazard. However, during the process of evacuation, avoiding people congestion along paths and emergency exits is crucial. This paper proposes an IoT-based Congestion-Avoidance Emergency Evacuation Approach that can be easily integrated into smart buildings. It relays on three types of nodes to perform different evacuation tasks. Simulation shows the proposed approach avoids congestion by evacuating evacuees through less-congested paths.

Keywords: Internet of things · Smart cities · Smart infrastructure · Smart buildings · IoT-Enabled smart city · Emergency evacuation and management · Congestion-awareness

1 Introduction

The Smart Cities allow the integration of data and digital technologies into a strategic approach to achieve sustainability, citizen well-being, and economic development. Applications of Internet of Things-Enabled Smart City (IES-City) inspire a vision of a city where the key components of infrastructure and services can be integrated in a way that new features and applications can easily be combined with whatever capability existed before. The most important services that are targeted by IES-City development are environmental, emergency response, traffic and energy management capabilities [1–5].

As achieving IES-City vision necessitates moving beyond many current implementations that allow limited degree of integration, this paper proposes an IoT-based Congestion-Avoidance Emergency Evacuation (ICAEE) Approach that can be easily integrated into smart buildings. Generally speaking, most of organizations are vulnerable to many kinds of emergencies that might cause loss of lives and resources. The magnitude of human suffering resulted by such incidents is huge. Furthermore, many

© Springer Nature Singapore Pte Ltd. 2020
Y. Tian et al. (Eds.): ICBDS 2019, CCIS 1210, pp. 468–478, 2020.
https://doi.org/10.1007/978-981-15-7530-3_36

life aspects might be affected including health, housing, safety, access to clean water, and other life-saving commodities. Therefore, it is importance for all organizations to implement appropriate emergency management system to save lives and mitigate the impact on these important aspects [1–5].

Developing an effective Emergency Management System (EMS) helps organization to launch a coordinated response as effectively as possible when disasters or other crises strike. Moreover, as it's important to develop low-cost EMS that utilizes and suits the existing facilities. An efficient EMS should only require smooth additions of functions as opposed to wholesale replacement or retrofitting. By performing such continuous integration and improvement, IES-cities can integrate new capabilities by simply acquiring and adding them to the existing infrastructure with minimal cost and amount of changes [1–5].

Our proposed ICAEE approach relies on low-cost sensors and actuators that are widely used and deployed in almost all buildings today such as cameras, digital screens, and gateways to detect and response to hazards. EMS can include functions that are responsible for creating a framework that saves lives and reduces suffering from hazards and disasters. It can be described in terms of four phases as shown in Fig. 1. In emergency evacuation context, EMS targets to avoid congestion, minimize fatalities and reduce evacuation time.

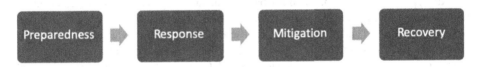

Fig. 1. The different phases of emergency management.

Nowadays, employing IoT for emergency management is quite practical for several reasons. Many buildings, such as malls, hospitals, schools and companies in private and public sectors, are equipped with sensors that detect fire and many types of hazards. They also equipped with actuators such as microphones and screens that can guide evacuees during hazards. Moreover, most of these buildings have gateways that can provide high speed internet connection required for remote response and upper-layer services [6, 7]. A general architecture for IES-City that suits our ICAEE approach is presented below in Fig. 2.

The presented ICAEE approach in this work targets to prevent congestion by acting previously to balance the load of the evacuees among the different available paths of the evacuation area. It integrates the deployed IoT network and cloud capabilities to calculate evacuation paths when congestion is either predicted or detected. Congestion detection and prediction is done by the mean of different types of sensor nodes that are deployed in the underlying area. Our approach is intended to be adaptive, in order to function in real time, and to avoid congestion in calculating evacuation path capacity.

The rest of this paper is organized as follows, Sect. 2 reviews some recent most relevant approaches. Section 3 presents the design of our approach. Section 4 shows our performance results. Finally, Sect. 5 concludes this paper with future work.

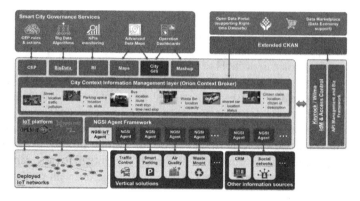

Fig. 2. Smart cities reference architecture powered by FIWARE [1].

2 Related Work

As IoT-based information technology systems are powering new business models and innovative cloud-supported solutions addressing many issues in different industries, this section reviews some of the recent IoT-based emergency evacuation approaches.

An opportunistic-communications-based evacuation system (OCES) and an intelligent evacuation system (IES) were proposed in [8]. They used sensors nodes (SNs) to observe the hazard intensity. The proposed systems were evaluated using their developed DBES simulator to measure their effectiveness. For IES, increasing SNs range improves the overall performance. For OCES, its performance was enhanced when number of pedestrians in the evacuation area is increased as a result of improving connectivity. In [9], a multi-path routing algorithm to conclude the best path for evacuees with respect to their health conditions and capabilities has been proposed. The algorithm utilized the deployed SNs and decision nodes (DNs) in the evacuation area. SNs are used to sense the hazards, then they send alerts to a DN. The DNs make evacuation decisions based on the exchanged Smart Packets (SPs) and then provides evacuees with the best available path. Simulation indicates that to achieve higher evacuation performance, DN should increase the range of information related to spatial characteristics of the hazard.

Reference [10], presented an efficient Wireless Sensor and Actuator Network (WSAN), which is a combines Wireless Sensor Nodes (WSNs) and Radio-frequency identification (RFID) technologies. A Global Positioning System (GPS) was used to determine pilgrims' locations. Two mobile actuators were deployed, which were authorities' vehicles and pilgrims' group leaders. Mobile vehicles managed the segmentation of the network into co-centric rings, while each leader carried a portable RFID reader to transmit data to their phones. This assisted in reducing the communication cost and node failure and enhancing the network accessibility. Their findings revealed that the rings' communication overlay acts a crucial function in improving the evacuation from crowded areas through a smoother and complete process. In [11], an indoor distributed, flow-based guiding approach was proposed to quickly evacuate people to a safe exit using a WSN. In [12], researchers presented a distributed emergency guiding algorithm with a load-balancing framework. It consisted of a load-balancing guiding schema to guide evacuees through safe and short paths to the nearest exists. It relies on calculations done by an analytical model that computes the estimated evacuation time while taking into account the exit capacity, path capacity and length, real-time pedestrians' movements, and people distribution.

We differentiate our ICAEE approach from the existing approaches as follows. Our approach includes two types of SNs: exit sensor and normal sensor. When a hazard occurs, the altitude value is higher in the normal sensor, which re-computes by using the link reversal schema in a Temporally Ordered Routing Algorithm (TORA), which represents the analytical model, and people are then guided to a safe exit as an emergency guiding that represents load-balancing guiding schema. Results indicated that the proposed model can minimize the total evacuation time.

3   The Proposed Approach

The following subsections explain our approach. We first explain our assumptions on the underlying area then we present the implemented algorithms on each key component of our system.

3.1   Modeling the Underlying Area

The underlying area (or building) is modelled as follows. It has three main technological components including: sensors, gateways and cloud servers. Sensors are classified into 3 types: basic sensor nodes (SNs), master nodes (MNs), and exit nodes (ExNs). Basic sensors are deployed in fixed locations within the evacuation area. They are used to sense congestion in the path and detect the presence of evacuees within their surrounding area. Master nodes are deployed also in fixed locations within a confined area but with less density. They are responsible for various sensing, computation, and evacuation tasks. Instead, ExNs are deployed near to the exits to monitor the areas nearby exits in order to avoid dangerous congestion in these areas. They also used for evacuees' guidance. Communication with cloud is exclusive to MNs.

Moreover, our model includes A getaway which acts as an interface between the local Things or SNs and cloud servers that handle critical evacuation decisions that require central processing and higher computation capabilities than offered by local sensors.

3.2   Main Algorithms

Master Nodes Algorithm. MNs estimates number of evacuees from neighbouring SNs in order to compute Path Congestion Indicator (PCI). They also receive congestion-related data from other nearby MNs and ExNs in order to collectively detect congestion. Every MN can make evacuation decisions locally when its nearby areas are either not congested or its congestion level is considered to be controllable based on a pre-determined threshold. Furthermore, MNs receive evacuation decisions from the cloud servers in some situations in order to appropriately guide evacuees.

Figure 3 shows the flowchart of the implemented algorithm at MNs. It main steps are described as follows: At a given time (t), each MN estimates number of evacuees in its nearby paths based on data received from its nearby SNs. Then, each MN calculates PCI metric for each nearby path and compares the computed value to a predefined threshold. If the computed PCI value does not exceed the given threshold, evacuation paths are computed locally by MNs and nearby path signs are adjusted. Otherwise, congestion is detected and reported to the cloud and nearby MNs and ExNs.

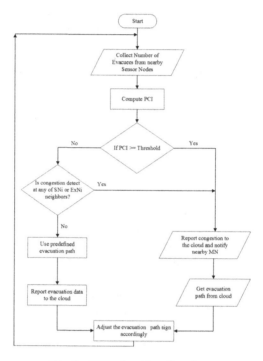

Fig. 3. MNs algorithm flowchart.

Exit Node Algorithm. Exit nodes are responsible for many functions in our ICAEE approach. ExNs are responsible for cooperatively estimating number of evacuees in all paths nearby exits. They also responsible for exits signs and all nearby signs accordingly. The presented flowchart in Fig. 4 illustrates ExNs algorithm. The main steps of ExNs algorithm are as follows: Each ExN estimates number of evacuees (NEs) within the areas nearby a specific exit. Then, for each nearby path, it computes the product of exit congestion factor (ECF) and capacity. Then, an ExN compare the estimated NEs with the computed product for each exit path. When NEs exceeds the computed product, congestion is detected at that and its sign is turned OFF. Moreover, the exit sign is also turned OFF and congestion when congestion detected in all paths leading to it. Nearby MNs are alerted whenever congestion is detected by ExNs.

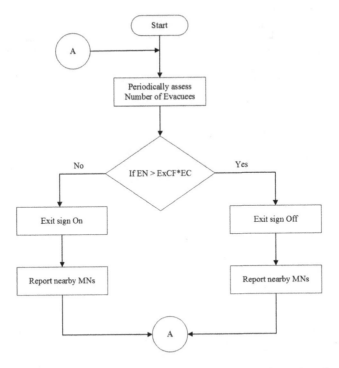

Fig. 4. Flowchart illustrating the algorithm implemented at exit nodes.

Cloud Algorithm. Cloud server(s) receives the collected data from all MNs and computes the least congested paths in centralized fashion. Then, the computed paths are communicated to MNs in order to adjust the signs of their nearby paths and guide evacuees. Figure 5(a) shows the flowchart illustrating the logic implemented at cloud servers. The main steps are as follows: the cloud computing receives data from all MNs concerning their congested paths and nearby exits. The cloud computes the least congested path using the algorithm presented in Fig. 5(b). Then, the cloud updates all MNs concerning the least congested path.

4   Performance Evaluation

In this section we discuss the performance evaluation of the proposed approach. We first present our performance factors, then scenarios and results are discussed. We used MATLAB 2019 to implement our simulator.

4.1   Performance Factors

The main performance factors that are considered in evaluating the performance of our approach are as follows: 1) number of survivals (or survival rate), 2) number of

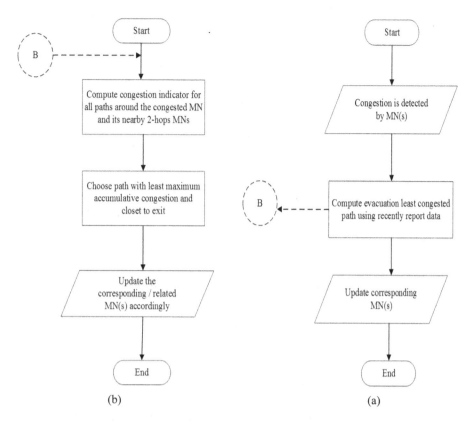

Fig. 5. Flowchart illustrating the logic implemented at cloud servers.

fatalities, 3) Evacuation time, and number of congestion points, which represents the number of detected congestion points during the evacuation process.

4.2 Simulation Setup and Results

We divided the underlying area into 9 × 9 cells. Each cell has 4 MNs installed at its corners. It also includes 4 exits with 4 ExNs installed near to each exit. SNs are installed on the edges of each cell to monitor the paths. We performed two experiments to measure the system efficiency. Each experiment was repeated 20 times in order to get averaged results.

In the first experiment, we assumed fixed number of congestion points (2 points). These congestion points in turn are located randomly in each simulation run. We changed number of evacuees to be: 80, 110, 140, 170 and 200, as assumed in [13]. In the second experiment, we fixed number of evacuees to be 90, while changing the number of congestion point to be 1, 2, 3, and 4 points.

For the results of experiment 1, Fig. 6 shows the impact of changing number of evacuees over average number of survivals. Survival rate also varies between 97% and 89% as a result of congestion. As number of evacuees varies between 60 and 180, the crowd varies between normal, up normal and dangerous crowd which indicates that our proposed ICAEE approach has significantly tolerated the increase in number of evacuees and that it balances the load of evacuees among paths based on guiding them to the less-congested paths. Figure 7, shows the impact of increasing number of evacuees over evacuation time in terms. As the figure shows, the average evacuation time has been increased as a result of guide evacuees to farther but less-congested paths regardless their presence to near but more-congested exit(s).

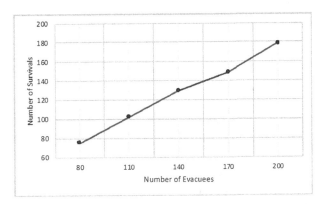

Fig. 6. ICAEE performance results for variable number of evacuees.

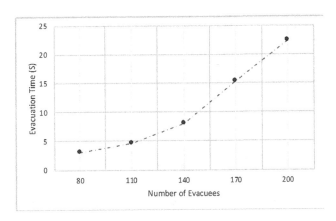

Fig. 7. Evacuation time when number of evacuees varies between 80 and 200.

For experiment 2, Fig. 8 and Fig. 9 show the impact of varying number of congestion points between 1 and 4 when number of evacuees is fixed to 90. Figure 8) shows the impact of maximizing number of congestion points on average number of survivals which varies between 75 and 85 evacuees. The corresponding survivals rate is 93%, 92%, 86%, 85%. On the other hand, creating more congestion points during evacuation also maximizes evacuation time as shown in Fig. 9 which is expected to guide evacuees to the exist through safe and less-congested paths.

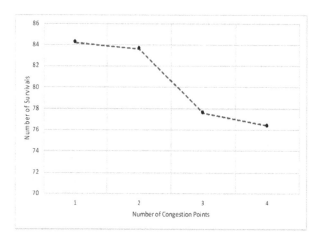

Fig. 8. ICAEE performance when number of congestion points varies between 1 and 4.

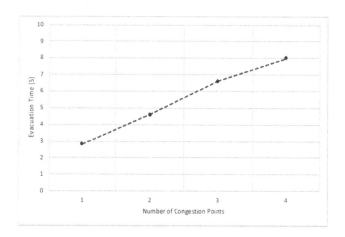

Fig. 9. ICAEE evacuation time when number of congestion points varies between 1 and 4.

5   Conclusion

In this paper, we propose an IoT-based Congestion-Avoidance Emergency Evacuation Approach that can be easily integrated into smart buildings to perform real time evacuation when congestion is considered as significant risk. It aims to utilize the facilities that exist in most of the organizations today to provide congestion avoidance during evacuation. Our proposed approach is aware if congestion especially near to exists. It relays on three types of sensors to perform different monitoring, computation, communication tasks. It also utilizes the computation power offered by cloud to perform path calculation when congestion exceeds a certain threshold.

We studied the performance of the proposed approach using simulation. Simulation shows that ICAEE can avoid and resolve congestion issues for different number of evacuees, and congestion points. Simulation also show an increase in evacuation time when number of evacuees or congestion points are increased as a normal result for guiding people through longer but less-congested paths. In Future, we plan to extend this research by employing ICAEE for different building models and different congestion scenarios.

References

1. Jin, J., Gubbi, J., Marusic, S., Palaniswami, M.: An information framework for creating a smart city through internet of things. IEEE Internet Things J. **1**(2), 112–121 (2014). https://doi.org/10.1109/JIOT.2013.2296516
2. International Technical Working Group on IoT-Enabled Smart City Framework: The IES-City framework, national institute of standards and technologies, US department of commerce, vol. 1, no. 1 (2018)
3. Chen, F.C., Chang, R.Y., Lin, W.Y., Chen, S.H., Chen, Y.C., Li, C.N.: Disaster and emergency management system. In: 2012 15th International Symposium on Wireless Personal Multimedia Communications (WPMC), pp. 363–368 (2012)
4. Mehmood, Y., Ahmad, F., Yaqoob, I., Adnane, A., Imran, M., Guizani, S.: Internet-of-things-based smart cities: recent advances and challenges. Commun. Mag. IEEE **55**(9), 16–24 (2017)
5. Alavi, A.H., Jiao, P.C., Buttlar, W.G., Lajnef, N.: Internet of things-enabled smart cities: state-of-the-art and future trends **129**, 589–606 (2018)
6. Desmet, A., Gelenbe, E.: Reactive and proactive congestion management for emergency building evacuation. In: 38th Annual IEEE Conference on Local Computer Networks, pp. 727–730 (2013)
7. Akinwande, O.J., Bi, H., Gelenbe, E.: Managing crowds in hazards with dynamic grouping. IEEE Access **3**, 1060–1070 (2015)
8. Filippoupolitis, A., Gorbil, G., Gelenbe, E.: Autonomous navigation systems for emergency management in buildings. In: 2011 IEEE GLOBECOM Workshops (GC Wkshps), pp. 1056–1061 (2011)
9. Filippoupolitis, A., Gorbil, G., Gelenbe, E.: Spatial computers for emergency management. In: 2011 Fifth IEEE Conference on Self-Adaptive and Self-Organizing Systems Workshops (SASOW), pp. 61–66 (2011)
10. Bi, H., Akinwande, O.: Multi-path routing in emergency with health-aware classification. In: 2015 2nd International Conference on Information and Communication Technologies for Disaster Management (ICT-DM), pp. 109–115 (2015)
11. Hashish, S., Ahmed, M.: Efficient wireless sensor network rings overlay for crowd management in Arafat area of Makkah. IEEE International Conference in Signal Processing, Informatics, Communication and Energy Systems (SPICES), pp. 1–6 (2015)
12. Chen, P.Y., Kao, Z.F., Chen, W.T., Lin, C.H.: A distributed flow-based guiding protocol in wireless sensor networks. In: International Conference on Parallel Processing, pp. 105–114 (2011)

13. Chen, L.W., Cheng, J.H., Tseng, Y.C.: Distributed emergency guiding with evacuation time optimization based on wireless sensor networks. IEEE Trans. Parallel Distrib. Syst. **27**, 419–427 (2016)
14. Bi, H., Gelenbe, E.: Routing diverse evacuees with cognitive packets. In: 2014 IEEE International Conference on Pervasive Computing and Communications Workshops (PERCOM Workshops), pp. 291–296 (2014)

Directional Virtual Coordinate Approach for 3-D IoT Systems in Smart Cities

Najla Al-nabhan[1(✉)], Aseel Bin Othman[1], Anura Jayasumana[2], and Mahindre Gunjan[2]

[1] Computer Science Department, King Saud University, Riyadh, Saudi Arabia
nalnabhan@ksu.edu.sa
[2] Department of Electrical and Computer Engineering,
Colorado State University, Fort Collins, CO, USA

Abstract. Internet of Things (IoT) and its enabling technologies are major components of future smart cities. With the growing number of devices connecting to the Internet, it has become necessary for the IoT network infrastructure to enhance its capabilities and capture such scalability. Understanding the IoT infrastructure is the first step in influencing its performance. A network topology is usually mapped by retrieving physical location of devices. For large-scale and heterogeneous networks, such as IoT, topology mapping using connectivity information has been proven more effective than mapping using physical distances. However, connectivity information alone will lead to a loss of a sense of directionality in the network nodes. In this paper, we propose a 3D-directional virtual coordinates topology mapping approach which preserves the physical network characteristics, models connectivity-, and regains directionality of the network. Simulation results show an improved accuracy and efficiency of our proposed approach compared to the existing approaches.

Keywords: Internet of things · Smart cities · 3-D directional virtual coordinates · Topology preserving maps · Virtual coordinate system

1 Introduction

The future of computing technologies will exceed the traditional use of desktop computers as number of physical objects connected to the Internet is growing immensely. These objects or devices embed sensors, actuators, and software, enabling them to connect and communicate together through a unique addressing scheme without the need for a human interface. The growth of these devices in a communication-actuation network forms what is known as the Internet of Things (IoT).

Smart cities are viewed as the future of urban living as they promise to boost efficiency of city services and improve quality of life for citizens while helping to improve safety, adapt to the rapid growth and cost of aging infrastructures. Accordingly, smart cities must weave IoT and interconnected devices into the existing infrastructure to bring entire communities online easily and effectively. In IoT, devices blend seamlessly into our surrounding environment creating a network in which information transmits between devices through the Internet. IoT devices are applicable

© Springer Nature Singapore Pte Ltd. 2020
Y. Tian et al. (Eds.): ICBDS 2019, CCIS 1210, pp. 479–498, 2020.
https://doi.org/10.1007/978-981-15-7530-3_37

in many domains, spanning from environmental monitoring, transportation and logistics, and healthcare to smart living and industrial settings, where IoT performs a significant role in monitoring and controlling [1, 2].

The main characteristic shared by IoT devices is heterogeneity, which requires the IoT infrastructure to be able to support this heterogeneity. Additionally, number of devices in IoT networks grow extensively, and expected to reach 70 billion devices by 2020 [3]. IoT infrastructure and capabilities are expanding to capture such scalability and modularity challenges. In addition to scalability aspects, the heterogeneity of devices adds to the challenges of the network infrastructure. Understanding the IoT network is the first step in influencing its performance. Further, to understand the network strongly, we need to understand its structure or topology.

Network topological features for two-dimensional (2-D) or three-dimensional (3-D) networks are usually mapped by retrieving the physical location information of devices (or nodes), where the distance between nodes is measured using Euclidean distance. Locating the node in Physical Coordinate Systems (PCSs) is done using many techniques, such as Received Signal Strength Indicator (RSSI) and Global Positioning System (GPS) [4]. For a large-scale sensor network such as IoT, the use of such a localization technique inappropriate, impractical or inaccurate. These techniques are affected by noise and signal fading. GPS is inapplicable for indoor IoT networks. It is also not practical in large-scale network of inexpensive devices as it increases hardware requirements, as well as cost [5].

Relying on PCS is not a feasible option for large-scale networks such as IoT and smart cities applications, and social networks [6], especially when there is no sense of physical coordinates or when nodes are unable to identify their physical positions. Instead, we can rely on the connectivity information between IoT devices to identify the distance between nodes as the number of hops, rather than the Euclidean distance. This alternative is more realistic and feasible than physical coordinates in large-scale networks.

The idea is similar to the idea of a metro system, where the metro map shows how the stations are connected and number of stops (hops) between stations rather than the exact distance information between the stations. Such a connectivity-based map is more practical, as it has smaller size. Virtual Coordinate Systems (VCSs) provide an appropriate alternative to physical coordinates for the routing, self-organization, and mapping of large-scale networks. Traditionally, a VCS characterizes each node by a vector of the smallest hop distance from the node to a set of nodes, called anchors.

A transformation is applied to transfer the VCS to a system with node directionality information named the Directional Virtual Coordinate System (DVCS) [8]. This novel technique regains directionality information to complement the connectivity information in VCS. With the recovery of directionality information, DVCS solves the issues of identical node coordinates and local minima related to VCS. Moreover, there is no increase in cost for implementing the DVCS technique, as each node calculates its directionality information locally with the help of existing anchor nodes. Topology mapping can be extracted effectively from DVCS for 2-D networks [11].

In this research, we propose a topology-preserving mapping technique for 3-D IoT networks. We use VCS to extract physical hop-based connectivity information. We also applied DVCS concepts that regain directionality information from VCS. The underlying 3-D IoT network is modelled as a graph considering the X, Y, and Z planes. Our approach utilizes selected anchor nodes to generate a virtual topology map. This map will contain the characteristics of the physical network, such as the layout, connectivity, and directionality information. The proposed DVCS-based technique will be simulated using MATLAB, and its accuracy will be assessed in comparison to the actual network in a physical coordinates system.

The remainder of this paper is organized as follows. Section 2 presents the background of VCSs, directionality in VCSs, and network topology mapping. Section 3 focuses on reviewing the existing most relevant topological mapping techniques using both virtual and directional coordinate systems. Section 4 presents the proposed approach for extracting the topology-preserving map for 3-D IoT networks. Section 5 we discuss evaluate the performance of our approach. Finally, in Sect. 6, we conclude this report.

2 Background

2.1 Transforming Direction-Less Virtual Coordinate System to Directional Virtual Coordinate System

Considering a 3-D network with N nodes, a VCS is a system in which each node n_i is characterized by its VC, which measures the minimum hop distance in a subset of nodes called anchors denoted by the set M. Anchors in a VCS are similar to other nodes in the network with no additional capabilities. The process of selecting anchors in a VCS is done either randomly or using a specific anchor placement procedure. Moreover, anchors will flood the network so nodes can calculate the minimum hop distance to each of these anchors in the network. Hence, each node n_i will be characterized by a vector (VC) of anchor distances that is represented as $n_i = [h_{n_iA_1}, h_{n_iA_2}, \ldots h_{n_iA_M}]$, here $h_{n_iA_j} \geq 0$ the minimum hop distance from node n_i anchor A_j. herefore, a VCS is represented as a combination of these vectors into a matrix P. Let P be a matrix of size $N \times M$ representing all VCs of all nodes in the network. The i th row is the vector of length M of the node, and the j th column corresponds to the virtual ordinate of all nodes in the network in closest hop distance to the j th anchor.

$$P[N \times M] = \begin{matrix} h_{n1A1} & h_{n1A2}\ldots & h_{n1A_M} \\ h_{n2A1} & h_{n2A2}\ldots & h_{n1AM} \\ \vdots & \vdots & \vdots \\ h_{n_NA1} & h_{n_NA2} & h_{n_NA_M} \end{matrix}$$

As the VCS includes hop distances measurements from nodes to anchors in the network, the DVCS includes directionality information by computing the direction from a node to each pair of anchors in the network. It recovers directions using a transformation function that measures the distance from each node in the network [8]. Considering a 1-D network, which included two anchors A_j and A_K with VCs calculated from each node to both anchors. Figure 1 shows the nodes' VCs are represented as (hop distance to A_j, hop distance to A_k). It is shown from the VCs that the two anchors are three hops apart, and the nodes propagate radially from the anchors, thus losing directionality.

To gain directionality, transformation from VCS to DVCS is made through a number of steps [8, 11], these steps are described as follows: 1) Multiplying the results of the calculated difference $(h_{niAj} - h_{niAk})$ and sum $(h_{niAj} + h_{niAk})$ of the VC of each node to both anchors: $(h_{niAj} - h_{niAk}) \times (h_{niAj} + h_{niAk})$ which results in a direction denoted in Fig. 2 as a black line. 2) Nonetheless, the direction must be normalized, so it is calculated by Eq. (1) [8], which results in the green line in Fig. 2 as a final direction of the nodes with respect to the anchors in the network.

$$f(h_{niAj}, h_{niAk}) = 1/2h_{A_jA_k}(h_{niAj} - h_{n_iA_k}) \times (h_{niAj} + h_{n_iA_k}) \tag{1}$$

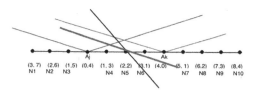

Fig. 1. Representation of direction of a 1-D network with respect to two anchor nodes A_j and A_k

2.2 An Illustrating Example of Transforming VCS to DVCS in 1-D Network Using Two Anchors

Considering the same network in Fig. 1, Table 1 shows into steps how VCS-to-DVCS transformation function is calculated. Now, we apply the transformation function systematically in a table to simplify it. When adding hop distance of a node to both anchors, we can see that the value between the anchors is constant at 4. On the other hand, when subtracting the hop distances, constant values are constant on the outer areas of the anchors. Applying the normalization generates directionality, and the mid-point is determined between the anchors while the values propagate away from the mid-point to create a direction similar to the represented direction in Fig. 1.

Table 1. Steps of transforming VC to DVC in a 1-D network

Node ID	N1	N2	N3	A_j	N4	N5	N6	A_k	N7	N8	N9	N10
h_{niAj}	3	2	1	0	1	2	3	4	5	6	7	8
h_{niAk}	7	6	5	4	3	2	1	0	1	2	3	4
$(h_{niAj} + h_{niAk})$	10	8	6	4	4	4	4	4	6	8	10	12
$(h_{niAj} - h_{niAk})$	−4	−4	−4	−4	−2	0	2	4	4	4	4	4
$1/2h_{AjAk}$	1/8	1/8	1/8	1/8	1/8	1/8	1/8	1/8	1/8	1/8	1/8	1/8
$f(h_{niAj}, h_{niAk})$	−5	−4	−3	−2	−1	0	1	2	3	4	5	6

The DVCS transformation function can be applied to a 2-D network with multiple anchor nodes. In a 2-D network where four anchors are placed, each node will calculate locally the transformation function for $f(h_{n_iA1}, h_{n_iA2}), f(h_{n_iA1}, h_{n_iA3}), f(h_{n_iA1}, h_{n_iA4}),$ $f(h_{n_iA2}, h_{n_iA3}), f(h_{n_iA2}, h_{n_iA4}),$ and $f(h_{n_iA3}, h_{n_iA4}),$ and $f(h_{n_iA3}, h_{n_iA4})$. Furthermore, the evaluation of this function produces positive- and negative-signed nodes depending on the direction of that node to the anchors. Based on the number of anchors, the number of signs combination differs, producing more sectors. If four anchors are used, 2^4 different sign combinations are possible at max [8, 11].

2.3 ENS Anchor Selection Mechanism

Anchors in the network can be selected randomly. However, a technique called Extreme Node Search (ENS) was proposed for anchor selection for VCS [11]. ENS aims to assign nodes furthest apart as anchor nodes. In ENS, each node determines whether it can be an anchor node by evaluating its local minima/maxima in DVCs within its h-hop neighborhood. The ENS logic is explained in [9, 11].

The ENS algorithm will change the initial anchor location to be placed on the borders of the network. Additionally, ENS increases the number of anchors, hence enhancing performance [9]. In Fig. 2, the initially selected anchors are shown as black squares, and the extreme nodes identified by ENS are shown as red dots. The extreme nodes will then become the network anchors replacing the initially selected anchors.

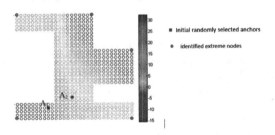

Fig. 2. A 2D application of ENS algorithm [9]. (Color figure online)

3   Related Work

This section reviews the existing work most relevant to our proposed directional virtual topology-mapping scheme.

Geographical routing using VCs has better reachability compared to Euclidean distance measurements. However, the main issue with VCS is associated with the lack of a unique identifier for nodes. Aksa in [13] proposed a solution to this problem by developing a greedy protocol based on a VCS named Billiardo. A Bypassing Void Routing Protocol based on Virtual Coordinate Mapping (BVR-VCM) was proposed by Zhang et al. in [14] to solve the sensor network void problem. BVR-VCM is divided into three phases: in the first phase, the void is detected and void edge information, such as geographic coordinates and node labels, is collected. The second phase is responsible for mapping the void to VCs. The VCs form a path around the void edges to create a circle. The final phase is responsible for dividing the void into three regions where different routing approaches are applied. Simulation results show that the protocol advances the transmission delay and average delivery ratio while reducing overhead and energy consumption.

VCs are also applied in the field of Web service discovery. Shah et al. [15] argues that the use of traditional search techniques in the Web is not suitable for IoT.

Shukla et al. [16] proposed a novel approach by assigning VCs using graph theoretical dominating sets.

As VCS lacks physical network information; network voids, boundaries, and node position in X, Y, (Z) directions. A novel technique was proposed by Dulanjalie et al. [12] that acquires sensor network TPM from VCs. The topology map is able to preserve the network features, such as boundaries and voids. Furthermore, the authors obtained the topology map coordinates for both 2-D and 3-D networks using Singular Value Decomposition (SVD).

VCs lose directionality of the nodes in the network. Therefore, two methodologies were proposed by Dhanapala et al. [8] to help recuperate the information loss in VCs. The first methodology proposes generating TPMs using the Topology Coordinates (TCs) of the nodes. This is proven to preserve the network information, such as network boundary, shape, and voids, without the need for the exact coordinates of the nodes. The second methodology proposes a transformation of VCs to DVCs. This is done by viewing each node as a vector space and defining a unit vector in the anchor direction and naming it in the virtual direction. Both methods were applied in 1-D and 2-D network models. As a result, the DVCS was utilized in routing and successfully outperformed existing VCS routing schemes.

In this paper, we focus on extending the use of DVCS for 3-D IoT networks. Our approach obtains the DVCS, and it uses SVD for TPM extraction. A detailed design of our methodology is presented in the next section.

4   3-D DVCS Approach for IoT

In this work, we propose a TPM approach for IoT networks represented in a 3-D environment. The mapping scheme aims to transform physical IoT networks into a virtual representation of that network. It also aims to map the network in a simple and precise manner. The proposed scheme will preserve vital characteristics of the physical network, including connectivity and directionality information.

4.1   Modelling IoT in 3-D

In this work, the underlying IoT network is represented in a 3-D coordinate system, where each IoT device is represented as a node in a 3-D graph. Each node has X, Y, and Z coordinates: the first number represents the projection of the point on the X-axis, the second represents the projection on the Y-axis, and the third is the projection on the Z-axis.

We assume our IoT network is static or mobile in a way that does not affect its connectivity. We also assume that our 3-D IoT network is modeled using an undirected graph, which means there is a link between nodes A and B if and only if they are within the communication range of each other, i.e., there is a link from A to B and vice versa. These assumptions are important for modelling the underlying network and mapping the topology in VCs.

4.2 Anchor Selection Mechanisms

Number of anchors and their placement play an important role in the performance of any VCS and DVCS-based algorithm [9, 11, 20]. Having a large number of nodes and a large number of anchors increases the computation cost of VCs [10]. On the other hand, if the network is large and number of anchors is very small, the previously described local minima and identical nodes problem would occur [8]. Therefore, in our approach, number of anchors will be determined to be the smallest number that avoids local minima and identical node IDs.

To achieve a high performance, we will follow two approaches for anchor selection mechanisms. First, we will use random anchor selection as recommended by the authors in [5–7, 10, 15, 17, 19]. Second, we will upgrade the ENS algorithm [9] for 3-D networks and implement it as an anchor selection mechanism.

4.3 Calculating Virtual Coordinates in 3D

After selecting anchors in the given network, virtual coordinates are calculated for all nodes in the network with respect to the anchors. We will use algorithm proposed in the literature [4–9]. The algorithm will measure the shortest hop-distance of each node in the network to the selected anchors. We will apply the Dijkstra algorithm to measure the node-to-anchor distances. Each node will be characterized by a distance vector represented as $n_i = [h_{n_i A_1}, h_{n_i A_2}, \ldots h_{n_i A_M}]$, where $h_{n_i A_j} \geq 0$ is the minimum hop distance from node n_i to anchor A_j. The VCS is a combination of these vectors in a matrix P of size $N \times M$ representing all VCs of all nodes in the network.

4.4 Extracting Directional Virtual Coordinates in 3D

DVCS regains the directionality information lost in VCS by computing the direction from a node to each pair of anchors in the network. For a 3-D network, we will use Eq. (1) described in Sect. 2. The function calculates the VCs from a node to a pair of anchors.

4.5 Generating a Directionality-Based Topology-Preserving Map in 3D

Topology mapping is the act of obtaining the representation of an extracted DVCS. Topology preserving maps resemble the IoT network's characteristics in terms of connectivity and directionality. We extracted a representation of the network by computing the Singular Value Decomposition (SVD) for the 3-D directional coordinates. This approach is widely used by authors in [5–7, 9, 16, 18, 21]. The SVD will produce three matrices U, S, and V of sizes N × N, N × M, and M × M, respectively. We will then calculate the Principle Components (PCs) by $P_{SVD} = U \times S$. As the columns of this new P_{SVD} are arranged in descending order of the original coordinate set, we will use only the second, third, and fourth PCs of that matrix. This will generate the TCs that will aid in plotting the map. The TC matrix is denoted by: $[X_T Y_T Z_T] = [P_{SVD}^2, P_{SVD}^3, P_{SVD}^4]$.

5 Performance Evaluation

5.1 Performance Factors

Our approach generates TPMs based on DVCS. To measure the accuracy of the extracted topology map, we will compare it to the physical network by measuring the "out of order" nodes. This measure attempts to ensure that nodes connectivity has not been changed during the mapping process in DVCS.

In order to compare the accuracy of our approach to the existing approaches, we will use a similar approach to the error rate measure which was used by [7, 11, 12]. The error function in previous work calculates the percentage of out-of-order nodes in a 2-D network. The out-of-order nodes are compared to the physical network. An indicator function $I_{i,j}$ is defined to indicate whether the node i in the physical network is out of order to node j, where:

$$I_{i,j} = \begin{cases} 1 & \text{if } i \text{ and } j \text{ are out of order} \\ 0 & \text{if } i \text{ and } j \text{ are in order or } i = j \end{cases}$$

The topology preserving error function was defined in [7, 11, 12] as:

$$E_{TP} = \% \frac{\sum I_{i,j}}{\text{total number of possible pairs in the network } (P_2^N)}$$

We extended the error function to be used in 3-D networks. Let us assume one of the three axis is fixed, the remaining two axis will form a 2-D plane. We will select this 2-D plane and apply the error function to it. Then, we can move up the fixed axis and calculate error for all planes and the sum of all errors is calculated for the fixed axis. This is implemented on all three axes of the 3-D network. At the end, we sum up all the out of order nodes in all three axis and return the final error percentage using the equation.

5.2 Simulation Variables

The effectiveness of the 3-D DVCS is evaluated using four illustrative examples of diverse network shapes; a cube shaped network with 511 nodes, an hourglass shaped network with 1639 nodes, a cylindrical shaped network with 2313 nodes, and finally a buildings and bridge shaped network having 2973 nodes. These networks have been chosen to replicate a variety of network structures. For example, we used networks with many corners and edges, a network with a large void in the middle, a network with no sides or corners and finally a large complex shape network. Furthermore, we created networks that outline a shape to allow is to visually compare our resulting TPMs with the original maps.

Communication range of the networks are equal to the shortest distance that will allow node to communicate to the neighbor node. In our case, the communication range for the first two networks are equal to 1 while the communication range of the last two networks are equal to 3.5. We use hop distance h = 5 * communication range for selecting extreme nodes in ENS to assist the algorithm in reaching the network borders.

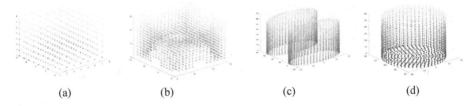

(a)   (b)   (c)   (d)

Fig. 3. 3-D networks: (a) Cube network (b) Hourglass network (c) Building network (d) Cylindrical

5.3 Simulation Setup

To achieve the objectives of this project, we implemented a MATLAB simulator to simulate the proposed approach and measure its efficiency. We designed 5 simulation experiments that are used to analyze and discuss the performance our proposed approach. Experiments were simulated in MATLAB R2017b. The presented simulation results represent an average of 50 runs per experiment.

The effectiveness and accuracy of our proposed 3-D DVCS approach in mapping the topology of 3-D network was evaluated using four illustrative examples of diverse network shapes including: 1) a cube-shaped network with 511 nodes, 2) an hourglass shaped network with 1639 nodes, 3) a cylindrical shaped network with 2313 nodes, and finally 4) a buildings and bridge shaped network having 2973 nodes. The networks are presented in Fig. 3. These networks have been chosen to replicate a variety of network structures. For example, we used networks with many corners and edges, a network with a large void in the center, a network with no sides or corners and finally a large complex shape network.

Each network is modelled as 3-D Graph $G(N, E)$, where N represents set of nodes located in 3-D plane and E represents the links between these nodes. In each network, a communication range R is used to define links between neighboring nodes. R represents the maximum distance which defines a region such that a node can communicate with any nodes located in this region. In designed experiments, the communication range equals 1 m in the first two networks, while range it equals 3.5 m in the other two experiments. We use hop distance $h = 5 * R$ for selecting extreme nodes in ENS in order to allow the algorithm to reach network borders.

The networks are visualized using 3-D graphs with each node projecting its value on X, Y and Z axis. As shown in Fig. 3 above, node color varies depending on the value of the Z-axis in the physical network. This helps to better visualize the node placement in the physical network and how it is mapped into the generated topology maps using our proposed 3-D DVCS approach. Each node placed in a unique Z value has a different color. So, the number of colors equal the number of Z unique values. Also, for better visualization, the anchor nodes are represented as red dots (.) in all figures.

Ranges of the X, Y and Z axes are dynamic and change depending on the X, Y and Z results generated by the corresponding TPMs. The calculation of SVD in both VCS and DVCS generates X, Y and Z values that differs from their values in the original network. Therefore, the axes values change depending on the network original range and the calculations of the TPMs.

We performed simulation on two different experiments. In the first experiment, we used a random anchor generation mechanism to select random nodes. In the second experiment, we generated anchors using ENS algorithm presented in Sect. 2.3.

5.4   Simulation Result

5.4.1   EXPERIMENT-I: Random Anchor Generation Mechanism

In this section, we generate a random number of anchors and place them randomly in the network. The TPM is extracted using on VCS, presented in Sect. 2.1, and our proposed 3-D DVCS approach. The number of anchors randomly generated is related to the total number of network nodes. In [1, 2], they used 1%. In this experiment, we select 1% of network nodes as anchors. The cube-shaped network has 5 anchors (1% of network nodes) chosen out of the total number of nodes which equals 511. A sample of a resulted TPMs of the corresponding physical topologies using both VCS and our DVCS approach is shown in Fig. 4. As a general observation, generating anchors randomly creates different TPMs depending on the anchor location. Based on the 50 generated TPMs using 3-D DVCS in this experiment, they all share a common characteristic which is that they are all slightly distorted from the original physical network. In the DVCS TPM, the network is more distorted and lost its shape. The TPM generated is not flipped or rotated from the physical network. We can see the color series are the same as the physical network. However, what makes the DVCS unique is the

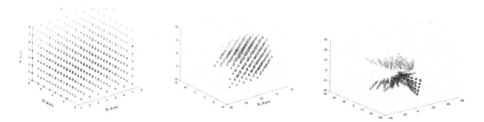

Fig. 4. TPM based on VCS and DVCS with random anchor generation mechanism, (a) cube physical map with anchor nodes in red (b) cube TPM based on VCS, (c) cube TPM based on DVCS (Color figure online)

directions of the nodes. The propagation of nodes in DVCS varies depending on the anchor placement unlike the nodes in VCS which has no direction. This shows that our approach has preserved the directionality information that was lost in VCS.

The presented topology mapping in used for visualization purposes. However, in 3D topology mapping, error function is used to evaluate the accuracy of the topology mapping approach. The average error rate for the cube-shaped network is shown in Table 2. The TPM generated from our approach has a lower average error rate than that of TPM using VCS. The error rates show that for a cube-shaped network, which represents a simply shaped network, our approach can achieve better topology mapping that preserves directionality information lost in VCS using a small set of randomly selected anchors.

For the **Hourglass network**, it has 16 anchors (1% of network nodes) chosen out of the total number of nodes. A sample of some of the resulting TPMs of the corresponding physical topologies using both VCS and our DVCS approach are shown in Fig. 5. Hourglass-shaped networks are considered to be complex networks for topology mapping. For the majority of simulation runs, VCS TPM of the hourglass-shaped network shows high distortion with random anchors placement. The corners of the network are mapped closer to each other and the middle area of the network is mapped outwards. The generated map is also rotated to one side of the network due to the SVD computation. The average error rate, minimum and maximum errors, for the hourglass network is shown in Table 2.

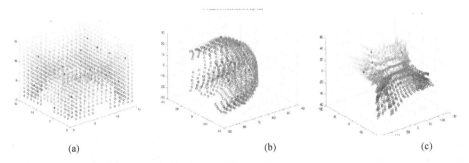

(a)   (b)   (c)

Fig. 5. TPM based on VCS and DVCS with random anchor generation mechanism, (a) hourglass physical map with anchor nodes in red (b) hourglass TPM based on VCS, (c) hourglass TPM based on DVCS (Color figure online)

For Cylinder network, we consider a network of has 21 anchors (1% of network nodes) chosen out of the total number of nodes. A sample of some of the resulting TPMs of the corresponding physical topologies using both VCS and our DVCS approach are shown in Fig. 6. Figure 6(a) shows the physical map with anchor nodes colored in red. The TPM generated based on VCS are shown in Fig. 6(b). Moreover, the TPM generated based on our approach is represented in Fig. 6(c).

The VCS TPMs, similar to the previous shapes, show a distortion, rotation and tilted backwards. As we can see from the node colors, the yellow nodes originally located at the top is now rotated to the side and also tilted to the back while the purple colored nodes have come forward. As for our approach, the TPM generated is twisted creating a bow shape. We can see half of the map is within the color ranges as the physical network while the other half is the opposite. However, the propagation of nodes in DVCS varies depending on the anchor placement unlike the nodes in VCS which has no clear direction.

The average error rate, minimum and maximum errors for the Cylinder network are shown in Table 2. The TPM generated from our approach has a lower average error rate than that of TPM using VCS. The average error rate for our approach is 1.563 and using VCS the average is slightly higher at 1.940. Furthermore, our approach achieves a maximum error of 3.168 and a minimum error of 0.244. Also, the maximum error using VCS is equal to DVCS maximum error whereas the minimum is 0.233.

The Cylinder network has a large number of anchors. We have established that the number of anchors affect the resulting map and error rate percentage. Subsequently, we are using a considerably large number of anchors in the Cylinder network that are randomly placed all around the network. We are getting good results for both VCS and DVCS. Moreover, our approach shows we can achieve a good resulting topology map for a circular network with no angels that contains a large number of nodes.

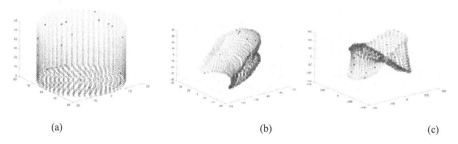

(a)   (b)   (c)

Fig. 6. TPM based on VCS and DVCS with random anchor generation mechanism, (a) cylinder physical map with anchor nodes in red (b) cylinder TPM based on VCS, (c) cylinder TPM based on DVCS (Color figure online)

For Buildings and bridge network, we consider networks that have 30 anchors (1% of network nodes) chosen out of the total number of nodes. A sample of some of the resulting TPMs of the corresponding physical topologies using both VCS and our DVCS approach are shown in Fig. 7. Figure 7(a) shows the physical map with anchor nodes colored in red. The TPM generated based on VCS are shown in Fig. 7(b). Moreover, the TPM generated based on our approach is represented in Fig. 7(c).

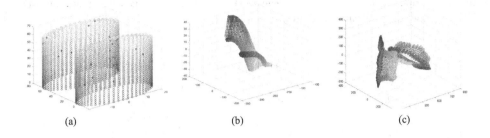

(a)   (b)   (c)

Fig. 7. TPM based on VCS and DVCS with random anchor generation mechanism, (a) Buildings physical map with anchor nodes in red (b) Buildings TPM based on VCS, (c) Buildings TPM based on DVCS (Color figure online)

For random anchor generation mechanism, the TPMs generated from the 50 simulation runs are different. However, for the majority of the runs, there are similarities in the resulting TPMs. The VCS TPMs, similar to the previous shapes, show a distortion and a rotation. The yellow nodes originally located at the top is tilted to the side while the purple colored nodes have moved upward. The general shape is still preserved, and the nodes are mapped much closer together.

In regard to our approach, the TPM generated is twisted also, similar to the Hourglass network. Each building is rotated at a different angle than the other, this is clearly visible by the node colors. Since DVCS is concerned about creating direction while preserving characteristics of the VCS. The resulting map of DVCS show a propagation of nodes that vary depending on the anchor placement. The average error rate, minimum and maximum errors for the Buildings network are shown in Table 2. The TPM generated from our approach has a lower average error rate than that of TPM using VCS. The average error rate for our approach is 6.035 and using VCS the average is slightly higher at 6.598. Furthermore, our approach achieves a maximum error of 7.023 and a minimum error of 3.772. Also, the maximum error using VCS is equal to 6.773 whereas the minimum is 2.966. The Buildings network has a large number of nodes and anchors. As we are using a large number of anchors in the network, it is likely the anchors will be randomly distributed all around the network which leads to good results.

To conclude EXPERIMENT-I, the TPM generated based on VCS show a very similar representation of the physical network with a distortion. The reason is that VCS considers only the hop distances between all nodes and anchors and the resulting map is based on SVD computation. SVD creates a minor distortion in the resulting map while still preserving connectivity and general structure. The TPM generated by using our 3-D DVCS approach has resulted in very close and even slightly better results than VCS. Our approach preserves significant features, such as the physical voids and boundaries of the physical network while also adding directionality information the is lost in VCS. In this experiment, the distribution of anchors is random and provided good results. However, we can't completely rely on random anchor generation as the results are unexpected. Therefore, in our next experiment we will investigate the 3-D ENS anchor selection and generation mechanism.

Table 2. Summary of TPM error rates in EXPERIMENT-I

Shape	No. of nodes	No. of anchors	Coordinate system	Avg. error rate (E_{TP} %)	Max. error rate (E_{TP} %)	Min. error rate (E_{TP} %)
Cube	511	5	VCS	3.192	5.370	1.196
			DVCS	**2.328**	**3.454**	**1.089**
Hourglass	1639	16	VCS	1.944	2.941	0.751
			DVCS	**1.015**	**2.577**	**0.335**
Cylinder	2131	21	VCS	1.940	3.168	0.233
			DVCS	**1.563**	**3.168**	**0.244**
Buildings and Bridge	2973	30	VCS	6.598	6.773	2.966
			DVCS	**6.035**	**7.023**	**3.772**

5.4.2   EXPERIMENT-II: 3-D ENS Anchor Selection and Generation Mechanism

This simulation will be focused on extracting the TPMs based on VCS and our proposed 3-D DVCS approach using anchors generated by the 3-D ENS algorithm. The ENS algorithm is run 10 times and the smallest anchor number generated was used in this experiment.

For cube-shaped network, we consider a network of 6 anchors generated by the 3-D ENS algorithm. The resulting TPMs of the corresponding physical topologies using both VCS and our DVCS approach are shown in Fig. 8. The ENS algorithm has selected the nodes in the network corners as anchors. These nodes are the nodes that are furthest apart in the network. By using these nodes as anchors, we can see that the resulting TPMs have a more defined topology where corners and edges are more visible. The resulting TPM based on VCS show no distortion but a complete flip to the side. Further, this can be visualized by the node colors, all the node colors match the physical network but are flipped to the right due to SVD computation. The resulting TPM based on our approach has generated a pincushion distortion with a slight rotation in the network that is also due to the SVD computation function. However, directions resulting from anchors are clearly represented. Error rates calculated for the VCS maps have resulted in 0% error while in our approach it is slightly higher with a value of 0.2616. Error rates are shown in Table 3.

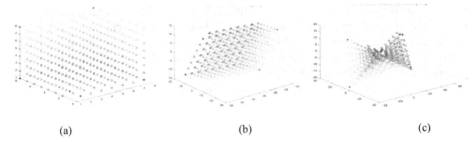

(a)   (b)   (c)

Fig. 8. TPM based on VCS and DVCS with ENS anchor generation mechanism, (a) Cube physical map with anchor nodes in red (b) Cube TPM based on VCS, (c) Cube TPM based on DVCS (Color figure online)

The **hourglass network** has 7 anchors generated by the 3-D ENS algorithm. The resulting TPMs of the corresponding physical topologies using both VCS and our DVCS approach are shown in Fig. 9. The ENS algorithm has chosen the anchor nodes in some of the network corners and allocated anchors in the void edges. By using these nodes as anchors, we can see that the resulting TPMs have a more defined topology where corners and edges are more visible. The resulting TPM using VCS shows no distortion however the map is upside down due to SVD function. Further, this can be visualized by the node colors. The resulting TPM based on our approach has generated a map that represents the physical network structure and void however the map is flipped on the right side due to SVD functionality. Nevertheless, the calculated directions resulting from anchors are clearly represented. Error rates in Table 3 for the VCS maps have resulted in 0.0854 percent error while in our approach it is higher with a value of 0.416.

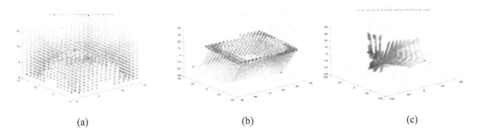

(a)   (b)   (c)

Fig. 9. TPM based on VCS and DVCS with ENS anchor generation mechanism, (a) Cube physical map with anchor nodes in red (b) Cube TPM based on VCS, (c) Cube TPM based on DVCS (Color figure online)

The **Cylinder network** has 6 anchors generated by the 3-D ENS algorithm. The resulting TPMs of the corresponding physical topologies using both VCS and our DVCS approach are shown Fig. 10. Since the Cylinder network has no corners or sides, the ENS algorithm has chosen the anchors in the network to be placed all around the cylinder. By using these anchors, we can see that the resulting TPM using VCS created corners and edges for the network. The VCS works very well with networks that have corners, since the Cylinder has no corners, the VCS will create corners and edges. The map is flipped to the side, due to SVD function, this can be visualized by the node colors. The resulting TPM based on our approach has generated a map with no clear structure. However, the propagation of directions resulting from anchors are clearly represented. Error rates in Table 3 show that for the VCS maps have resulted in 0.2861 error while in our approach it is higher with a value of 0.9006.

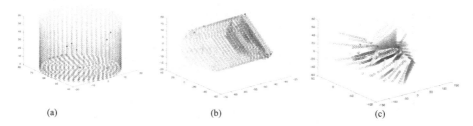

(a)   (b)   (c)

Fig. 10. TPM based on VCS and DVCS with ENS anchor generation mechanism, (a) Cylinder physical map with anchor nodes in red (b) Cylinder TPM based on VCS, (c) Cylinder TPM based on DVCS (Color figure online)

The 3-D ENS algorithm for this network generated 8 anchors. The resulting TPMs of the corresponding physical topologies using both VCS and our DVCS approach are shown in Fig. 11. Figure 11(a) shows the physical map of the 3-D networks with nodes colored in red representing the local minima/maxima of the network within its h-hop neighborhood nodes. The TPM generated based on VCS are shown in Fig. 11(b). Moreover, the TPM generated based on our approach is represented in Fig. 11(c). Similar to the Cylinder network, the Buildings and Bridge network has no corners. The ENS algorithm has chosen the anchors in the network to be placed around the floor edges of the buildings. By using these anchors, we can see that the resulting TPM using VCS created corners and edges for the network similar to the Cylinder network. Also, the VCS has mapped the two buildings to be narrower and closer to each other. The resulting TPM based on our approach has generated a map with no clear structure. However, the propagation of directions resulting from anchors are clearly represented.

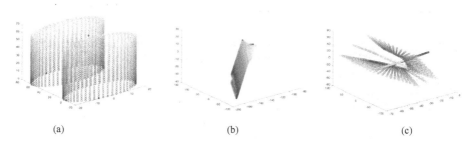

(a)   (b)   (c)

Fig. 11. TPM based on VCS and DVCS with ENS anchor generation mechanism, (a) Cylinder physical map with anchor nodes in red (b) Cylinder TPM based on VCS, (c) Cylinder TPM based on DVCS (Color figure online)

Error rates in Table 3 show that the VCS maps have resulted in 6.7734 error while in our approach it is higher with a value of 6.5955.

Table 3. Simulation runs of ENS anchor generation mechanism with error rate

Shape	No. of nodes	No. of anchors	Coordinate system	Avg. error rate (E_{TP} %)
Cube	511	6	VCS	0
			DVCS	**0.2616**
Hourglass	1639	7	VCS	0.0854
			DVCS	**0.416**
Cylinder	2131	6	VCS	0.2861
			DVCS	**0.9006**
Buildings and Bridge	2973	8	VCS	6.7734
			DVCS	**6.5955**

The resulting TPMs using ENS anchors show a visible difference compared to using random anchors. A smaller number of anchor nodes which are placed in the local minima and maxima show a significantly better topology with minimum error. The resulting topology maps are more angular with a clear structure. Angularity is due to the placement of ENS anchors as they are located at the network corners and edges.

The ENS algorithm works well with networks that have a visible local minima and maxima like in the cube and hourglass network. As for cylindrical shaped network, its more challenging to generate a map close to the physical network as ENS forcefully creates corners and edges. Nonetheless ENS has proved to obtain overall error rates less than 1% for 3 out of 4 networks. Using ENS, the TPM based on VCS show a better error rate than TPM based on DVCS. The VCS works very well with networks that have corners. Strategically placing anchors in the corners of the network provides an efficient VCS based TPM. On the other hand, the 3-D DVCS algorithm focuses on creating directionality which is clearly represented in the TPMs above. The DVCS TPMs nodes propagate in the direction of the anchors. Since the anchor number is very small, the number of directions is also small. Therefore, the DVCS algorithm creates a smaller number of directions with different arrangement of nodes in the network. Nonetheless, ENS has clearly demonstrate the effectiveness of the proposed method in generating 3-D TPM with a very small error rate and a small number of anchor nodes. In the next experiment we will be exploring the effectiveness of combining both benefits of random and ENS anchor generation mechanisms.

6 Conclusion and Future Work

The Internet of Things (IoT) is a massively growing technology. enormous number of IoT devices are being connected to the internet. To enhance the performance of a large-scale network, it is necessary to understand the IoT topology. Mapping and visualizing the network topology provides critical information such as the network structure, layout, neighborhood information, and an understanding of how these devices are connected. The physical structure of the IoT network can be mapped using the node physical location and physical distances. However, for large-scale networks, like IoT, topology mapping using connectivity information has been proven more effective than mapping using physical distances. Topology preserving maps (TPM) are an efficient way to map a physical network to a virtual network while preserving its physical characteristics. TPMs can be generated using connectivity information. Although, using only connectivity information will map the network nodes and its connections, but there is no sense of directionality in the network.

Virtual Coordinate Systems (VCS) provides an alternative for physical node locations. It assigns each node in the network with a virtual coordinate VC. This VC is represented by the distance between node and anchor nodes in the network. VCS is a simple yet affective approach in mapping large-scale networks. However, there are many limitations to using this approach. The VCS may lead to identical coordinates that lead to inconsistent results. Also, the VCS may create a local minima problem. The local minima problem occurs when a node cannot discover which of its neighbors is closer to the target node than it is. It occurs due to the lack of directionality information of the nodes in a VCS.

In this project, we proposed a novel 3-D directional topology mapping approach that preserves directionality and network connectivity information of the physical network. The proposed 3-D Directional Virtual Coordinate System (DVCS) solves the limitations of the VCS while also introducing directionality in a virtual network. Our approach was able to generate efficient topology maps for 3-D IoT networks with acceptable error. Since IoT networks can be deployed in various ways, we studied the effectiveness of our approach on various deterministic and non-deterministic networks. To evaluate the accuracy of our proposed approach, we propose an error calculation function that is an extension for the previously existing error calculation function in the literature. It efficiently evaluates 3-D TPM generated from our approach.

Our approach utilizes two anchor selection mechanisms; random and ENS. These selection mechanisms' affect was studied separately and combined on various networks. Random generation is cost-effective but is not always reliable. On the other hand, ENS has a higher computational cost but provides efficient topology mapping results.

With use of anchors, we calculated the VCS which as well as the proposed 3-D DVCS. We studied the results of topology maps using both VCS and DVCS. We implemented a MATLAB simulator to simulate the proposed approach and measure its efficiency. We designed two different experiments to analyze the performance of our proposed approach. We used four networks; cube-shaped network, hourglass network, cylinder network and a building network. In the first experiment we generated a random number of anchors and placed them randomly in four different networks. The resulting TPMs generated based on VCS and DVCS presented distortions due to SVD computation. Although, our 3-D DVCS presented acceptable error percentage than VCS. Our approach preserves significant features, such as the physical voids and boundaries of the physical network while also adding directionality information that is lost in VCS.

In the second experiment, we generated anchors using ENS algorithm. We have found that the ENS algorithm works well with networks that have a visible local minima and maxima like in the cube and hourglass network. As for cylindrical shaped network, its more challenging to generate a map close to the physical network as ENS forcefully creates corners and edges. ENS uses a very small number of anchors that are strategically placed to generate TPM. The results show a significantly better topology mapping with minimum error. ENS has clearly demonstrate the effectiveness of the proposed method in generating 3-D TPM with a very small error rate using a small number of anchor nodes. IoT networks are employed in variety of applications. We based our project on non-mobile IoT networks. Since our approach has proven to generate efficient TPMs with a small percentage of anchors in various network sizes and densities, we plan to extend this project to study the approach on mobile networks. We can employ the mobility of anchors to better map the topology.

References

1. Gubbi, J., Buyya, R., Marusic, S., Palaniswami, M.: Internet of Things (IoT): A vision, architectural elements, and future directions. Future Gener. Comput. Syst. **29**(7), 1645–1660 (2013)
2. Li, S., Xu, L.D., Zhao, S.: The internet of things: a survey. Inf. Syst. Front. **17**(2), 243–259 (2015)
3. IoT: Number of connected devices worldwide 2012-2025. Statista. https://www.statista.com/statistics/471264/iot-number-of-connected-devices-worldwide/. Accessed 11 Apr 2018
4. Bachrach, J., Taylor, C.: Localization in sensor networks. In: Handbook of Sensor Networks: Algorithms and Architectures. Wiley (2005)
5. Jayasumana, A.P., Paffenroth, R., Ramasamy, S.: Topology maps and distance-free localization from partial virtual coordinates for IoT networks. In: 2016 IEEE International Conference on Communications, ICC 2016 (2016)
6. Jayasumana, A.P., Paffenroth, R., Ramasamy, S.: Network topology mapping from partial virtual coordinates and graph geodesics, December 2017
7. Galka, M.: Twisted tracks: watch metro maps transform to real-life geography. The Guardian, 27 June 2017
8. Dhanapala, D.C., Jayasumana, A.P.: Topology preserving maps-extracting layout maps of wireless sensor networks from virtual coordinates. IEEE/ACM Trans. Netw. **22**, 784–797 (2014)
9. Dhanapala, D.C., Jayasumana, A.P.: Directional virtual coordinate systems for wireless sensor networks. In: IEEE International Conference on Communication, no. June, pp. 2–7 (2011)
10. Jiang, Y., Jayasumana, A.P.: Anchor selection and geo-logical routing in 3D wireless sensor networks. In: Proceedings of Conference on Local Computing Network, LCN, pp. 502–505 (2014)
11. Buoud, A.F., Jayasumana, A.P.: Topology preserving map to physical map - a thin-plate spline based transform. In: 2016 IEEE 41st Conference on Local Computer Networks (LCN), pp. 262–270 (2016)
12. Dhanapala, D.C., Jayasumana, A.P.: Anchor selection and topology preserving maps in WSNs - A directional virtual coordinate based approach. In: Proceedings of Conference Local Computing Network, LCN, pp. 571–579 (2011)

13. Dulanjalie, C.D., Anura, P.J.: Topology preserving maps from virtual coordinates for wireless sensor networks, pp. 136–143 (2010)
14. Aksa, K.: Billiardo: a novel virtual coordinates routing protocol based on multiple sinks for wireless sensor network. Wirel. Pers. Commun. **94**(3), 1147–1164 (2017). https://doi.org/10. 1007/s11277-016-3675-0
15. Zhang, D., Dong, E.: A virtual coordinate-based bypassing void routing for wireless sensor networks. IEEE Sens. J. **15**(7), 3853–3862 (2015)
16. Shah, M., Sardana, A.: Searching in internet of things using VCS. In: Proceedings of First International Conference on Security of Internet of Things - Security 2012, pp. 63–67 (2012)
17. Shukla, S., Misra, R., Agarwal, A.: Virtual coordinate system using dominating set for GPS-free adhoc networks. Ann. Telecommun. Telecommun. **72**(3–4), 199–208 (2017). https:// doi.org/10.1007/s12243-017-0563-x
18. Beckery, S., Seibert, J., Zage, D., Nita-Rotaru, C., Statey, R.: Applying game theory to analyze attacks and defenses in virtual coordinate systems. In: 2011 IEEE/IFIP 41st International Conference on Dependable Systems & Networks (DSN), Hong Kong, China, pp. 133–144 (2011)
19. Ma, Z., Jia, W., Wang, G.: Routing with virtual region coordinates in wireless sensor networks. In: 2011 IEEE 10th International Conference on Trust, Security and Privacy in Computing and Communications, Changsha, China, pp. 1657–1661 (2011)
20. Dhanapala, D.C., Jayasumana, A.P., Mehta, S.: On boundary detection of 2-D and 3-D wireless sensor networks. In: 2011 IEEE Global Telecommunication Conference - GLOBECOM 2011, pp. 1–5 (2011)
21. Dhanapala, D.C., Jayasumana, A.P.: Clueless nodes to network-cognizant smart nodes: achieving network awareness in wireless sensor networks. In: 2012 IEEE Consumer Communication Network Conference CCNC2012, no. Vc, pp. 174–179 (2012)
22. Gunathillake, A., Savkin, A.V., Jayasumana, A.P.: Topology mapping algorithm for 2D and 3D wireless sensor networks based on maximum likelihood estimation. Comput. Netw. **130**, 1–15 (2018)

Security in Cloud and Fog Computing

Privacy Preservation of Future Trajectory Using Dummy Rotation Algorithm in Fog Computing

Shadan AlHamed[1], Mznah AlRodhaan[1], and Yuan Tian[2(✉)]

[1] King Saud University, Riyadh, Kingdom of Saudi Arabia
437203604@student.ksu.edu.sa, rodhaan@KSU.EDU.SA
[2] Nanjing Institute of Technology, Nanjing, China
ytian@njit.edu.cn

Abstract. Fog computing has been introduced for extending cloud computing to the edge of the network, which brings features and services closer to end-users. Despite all the benefits provided, fog computing still suffers from security and privacy issues. Location privacy has a critical issue since fog nodes collect sensitive data. The users continuously send queries to the Location-based service (LBS) server, which may cause vulnerabilities where an attacker may track users. Subsequently, location privacy is not adequate to preserve privacy and attackers can still deduce the movement pattern of the user. Therefore, trajectory privacy has been used to provide better protection for the whole trajectory of the user. Meanwhile, most of the existing researches did not protect the future location of the user, while attackers may predict or estimate the users' next position if the geographical environment constraints are not considered and the historical data of the user not protected. To resolve the addressed issues and provide better privacy, we developed an approach for preserving the user's future trajectory privacy by predicting the future location of the user using Extended Mobility Markov Chain (n-MMC) and then generating dummy trajectories by Dummy Rotation Algorithm. The results show that the system can achieve privacy preservation of the future trajectory of the user with an average accuracy of 60%.

Keywords: Fog computing · Location Privacy · Trajectory Privacy · Extended Mobility Markov Chain · Dummy Rotation Algorithm

1 Introduction

Cloud computing is becoming an essential part of most of the systems and applications, such as providing reliable services, distributed resources, management, and computational power. In contrast with the rapid growth of the number of devices, cloud computing may not be capable of handling this growth, which leads to undesirable possession of computing resources, storage space and becomes a cause of network congestion in the clouds [1]. Consequently, fog computing was presented by Cisco in 2012 to address these challenges [2]. Fog computing extends a part of cloud computing to the edge of the network, where computational power and resources are closer to the

© Springer Nature Singapore Pte Ltd. 2020
Y. Tian et al. (Eds.): ICBDS 2019, CCIS 1210, pp. 501–513, 2020.
https://doi.org/10.1007/978-981-15-7530-3_38

user achieving a better performance. Also, it supports devices' mobility, location awareness, and geographic distribution and real-time applications.

In contrast, fog computing has challenges and issues to be resolved such as network bandwidth constraints, resource-constrained devices, and security and privacy issues [3]. One of the most important challenges in security and privacy is location privacy in fog nodes since they have high mobility and distributed in large areas. Several Location Privacy techniques have been proposed to solve this issue, such as obfuscation-based techniques, anonymity-based techniques and dummy-based techniques [4]. However, location privacy is not capable of providing enough protection to the user since the background information of the user should be protected from attackers or advertisers. Trajectory Privacy has been introduced to protect the correlations between locations of the user and background information or the user's historical information. Most of location privacy techniques have been applied for the trajectory of the user to protect all positions for better preservation of privacy [5]. Although, there is an issue regarding the future or next location of the user where attackers may predict the next location of the user since most of the researches did not consider the real geographical environment. Consequently, the attacker could also distinguish between real and fake positions.

In this paper, we proposed a system that preserves the privacy of the user future trajectory by predicting the future location of the user using Extended Mobility Markov Chain (n-MMC) and then, generating dummy trajectories, using Dummy Rotation Algorithm by rotating the real trajectory of the user. The remainder of this paper is organized as follows. Section 2 reviews related work where Sect. 3 presents the system model, preliminaries and algorithms. Results and evaluation are discussed in Sect. 4, and at the end Sect. 5 concludes the paper.

2 Related Work

The system is mainly composed of two approaches which are location prediction and trajectory privacy. In this chapter, several studies for location prediction that are based on Markov Model are discussed. Then, trajectory privacy techniques studies are presented in the second section.

2.1 Location Prediction

Location Prediction has become an important and challenging problem especially with the increasing number of mobile devices. Moreover, location prediction could be used for several applications including location-based services, resource allocation, weather forecasting, and others [6]. Markov Models is the most widely used application for location prediction because of its reliability to predict and show results with different parameters for the system. Moreover, there are several Markov Models that have been developed to be adapted to different systems and purposes, such as Markov chain, the Hidden Markov model, and other models [7]. The following studies are location prediction systems that are based on different Markov Models.

First, Qiao et al. [8, 9] proposed two Markov models one is based on the Hidden Markov Model and the other is a hybrid Markov-based model. In [8], they showed a trajectory prediction algorithm using Hidden Markov Model. The system is able to self-adaptively select important parameters which are necessary for real-world scenarios. On the other hand, in [9], they presented a hybrid Markov-based model to predict users' future movements. The model considers the spatiotemporal characteristics of real human mobility data by using real human trajectories extracted from data traffic of an LTE network.

Du et al., [10] proposed a model composed of a Continuous-Time Series Markov Model (CTS-MM) to enhance the Hidden Markov Model (HMM) to consider the time information in location prediction. The Gaussian Mixed Model (GMM) is used for modeling the posterior probability of the location with a continuous time series. Then, the discrete-time sequence of the HMM is simulated to the continuous sequence, which enables the model to predict the location in different real-time.

Similarly, Chen et al., [11] explained a system for predicting the next location where three models are used for moving objects. First, Global Markov Model (GMM) was used to discover global behaviors of the moving objects. Then, Personal Markov Model (PMM) mines the individual patterns of each moving object using past trajectories. In the end, Regional Markov Model (RMM) considers the geographic similarity between and clusters the trajectories to mine the movement patterns.

Moreover, Gambs et al., [12] extended a previously proposed Mobility Markov Chain (MMC) to n-Mobility Markov Chain (n-MMC). The n-MMC model considered the previous n visited locations to provide a better prediction process. Also, the states of the model are ranked by decreasing order of importance and observing the next location based on locations that the user visited.

In our system, Extended Mobility Markov Chain (n-MMC) is used since it considers the previous n visited locations which increase the accuracy of the prediction and protect the right future position of the user.

2.2 Trajectory Privacy

In recent years, trajectory privacy preservation gained attractive attention, since a lot of applications are based on location-based services (LBSs). Although, location privacy is not enough to satisfy privacy requirements where attackers may expose sensitive information of the user. Several location privacy techniques have been modified to cover all positions on the user's trajectory such as Obfuscation techniques, mix-zones, anonymity techniques, and dummy generation techniques [5]. Some of these studies are described as followed.

Hwang et al., [13] have been used obfuscation technique to send randomly queries on different trajectories for breaking query issuing time to confuse attackers. Also, the system forms the cloaking region based on the user's privacy profile where malicious LBS will not be able to reconstruct the user's trajectory. In mix-zones, Memon et al., [14] applied mix-zones on the road network for designing the physical environment for vehicles. Multiple mix-zones are used to cover the road network which was assigned a pseudonym in each zone for the user.

For anonymity or clocking techniques Liao et al., [15] explained the K-anonymity trajectory algorithm that selects (K − 1) dummy locations through Sliding Window. Furthermore, it introduces a trajectory selection mechanism into an algorithm to resist attacks in continuous queries. In addition, Gao et al., [16] proposed a personalized anonymization model to balance the trajectory privacy and data utility. The model selects a k-anonymity trajectory, then construct an anonymity region based on trajectory distance and used the trajectory angle to evaluate trajectory similarity and direction.in advance, Peng et al., [17] presented the collaborative trajectory privacy-preserving (CTPP) which consists of two algorithms that are multi-hop caching-aware cloaking (MCC) algorithm to share the desired data received from multi-hop peers with which the user can construct a cloaking area and locally obtain the results for future queries. Also, a collaborative privacy-preserving querying (CPPQ) algorithm, which enables the user to issue a fake query using obfuscating strategy to prevent the adversary from reconstructing a user's actual trajectory from continuous queries. Dummy Generation Techniques are based on generating dummies (fake) points or trajectories where the user's real trajectory is used to generate multiple dummy trajectories that prevent LBS attackers from obtaining user's information [4]. Niu et al., [18] showed the trajectory privacy protection scheme DUMMY-T to protect user privacy in continuous LBS. DUMMY-T is based on spatial cloaking and dummy based techniques where it generates a set of dummy locations with considering the minimum cloaking region and background information. After the generation of dummies, Dummy Paths Constructing (DPC) algorithm connected dummy locations into dummy paths by considering the location reachability property. Furthermore, Wang et al., [19] discussed the model which is based on fog structure, which stores mobile users' partial important information in a fog server to ensure physical control. Fog server is responsible for generating dummy trajectories to hide the real trajectory of the user. For ensuring data security, an encryption algorithm is used to encrypts users' data and then send it to the LBS server. Additionally, Hayashida et al., [20] explored a way to remove the unrealistic assumptions in maps by using a set of visiting points and uses this set to estimate the next estimated location. After that dummy generation algorithm to generate the trajectories of dummies where attackers cannot distinguish the user from dummies.

However, most trajectory privacy techniques did not consider protecting the future position of the user while attackers could infer the next location of the user using historical positions of the user or movement patterns of the user. In our system, the whole trajectory of the user which contains current position, previous positions and predicted position (Future position) will be protected from attackers.

3   System Model

The system developed to protect the user's future trajectory from being predicted and attacked by attackers. When the user starts to move, the system predicts the future location that the user may visit it using the Extended Mobility Markov Chain (n-MMC) [12]. After predicting the location, the trajectory of the user including the predicted location is used to generate dummy trajectories using Dummy Rotation Algorithm by rotating the real trajectory of the user to confuse the attackers from identifying the real trajectory of the user. The preliminaries, system model and algorithms are shown in detail as follows.

3.1   Preliminaries

In Table 1, there are some symbols listed for more clarification.

Table 1. Symbols list with a description.

Symbol	Description
L_i	Locations (latitude, longitude)
k_i	A cluster
c_i	Centroid of k_i cluster
m	Mobility trace
P_i	probability for next position
T_r	Real trajectory
T_D	Dummy trajectories
D	Number of dummy trajectories
θ	Rotation angle
n	The number of previously visited positions and one current position as the level of Markov model

In Fig. 1, let T_r be the real trajectory of the user where it composed of previously visited positions n − 1 and current position. When the user starts to move, Extended Mobility Markov Chain (n-MMC) will predict the next position of the user based on previously visited positions. n-MMC will predict the next position with the highest probability P_i and adding it to the trajectory T_r. Then, the Dummy Rotation Algorithm will generate dummy trajectories T_D by rotating real trajectory T_r with a specified Rotation angle θ and number of dummy trajectories D.

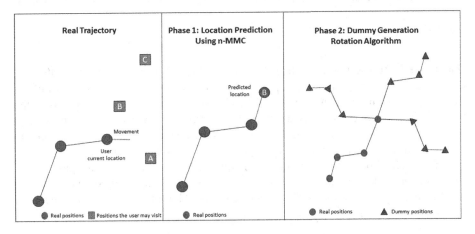

Fig. 1. Phases of the system.

3.2   System Model

The system model in Fig. 2 consists of the user, the fog server at the user side, and the LBS server to provide services. The steps of the system model are as following:

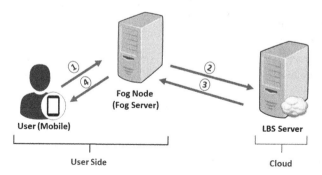

Fig. 2. System model of trajectory privacy preservation system.

1. When the user starts to move, the current position uploaded to the fog server for predicting and protecting the future location the user may visit.
2. At the fog server, it starts the phase of predicting of the future location using Extended Mobility Markov Chain (n-MMC).
3. After the prediction phase, the system generates dummy trajectories based on previous, current and predicted future locations. For more data-security, the data may be encrypted using an encryption algorithm.
4. The LBS server obtains the query services, decrypts the data and sends it to the user.
5. The fog server receives the information from the LBS server and sends it to the user.

3.3   Algorithms

Location Clustering Using k-Mean Clustering Algorithm (Preprocessing Stage).
k-means is one of the simplest unsupervised learning algorithms that solve most of the clustering problem where the number of the clusters k should be specified based on the type of data. Each cluster has a centroid that represents the center of the cluster obtained as the mean of the distance. Data points are assigned to the nearest cluster and the centroids are computed as the average of all data points in each cluster. For our system, each Location L_i contains latitudes and longitudes as pairs $L_i = (\text{latitude}, \text{longitude})$ where each L_i will be assigned to a cluster k based on the shortest distance between L_i and the centroids c_i of clusters. Algorithm 1 shows the process of the k-mean Algorithm.

Algorithm 1: K-mean Clustering

Inputs:	K : number of clusters, L_i: Locations (latitude, longitude)
Output:	K_i clusters in which each cluster has a centroid C_i

Assume L_i locations and randomly selected centroids C_i of K clusters.

For each L_i

Find the distance between L_1 and all centroids C_i of K clusters

Allocate the location L_1 to the centroid C_i of cluster K_i with minimum distance.

Find the new centroid C_i of the K_i the cluster which is the mean value of the cluster.

Repeat Reallocation until all locations L_i assigned to clusters and centroids are calculated.

End for

Label each cluster K_i with its centroid C_i.

Location Prediction Using Extended Mobility Markov Chain (n-MMC). Extended Mobility Markov Chain (n-MMC) developed [12] to incorporate previously visited positions. n-MMC provides advantages to be used in several applications such as in geo-privacy mechanisms, LBSs to estimate the next movement of a user and location-aware proactive resource migration [12]. In the same way, n-MMC has been used in our system for preserving the privacy of the future trajectory of the user. In Algorithm 2, n-MMC consists of a set of states S_i and a set of transitions P_i. The MMC will create a state S_i for each cluster and count the occurrence of mobility traces between clusters to compute the probability for each mobility trace. For the transition matrix, each row presents the current state and the columns represent the destination states where the state with the highest probability is the next predicted state. In n-MMC, n indicates how many pervious positions will be considered in predicting the next state. For example, if $n = 2$ it means one pervious position and the current position as pair considered for prediction. The following algorithm showed the process in detail.

Algorithm 2: n-MMC

Inputs:	K_l clusters
Output:	Transition matrix M of an n-MMC
	For each K_l cluster
	Create the corresponding state S_i
	End For
	For each mobility Trace m
	Label trace m within n-1 previous positions and current position.
	End For
	Squash all mobility traces sharing the same label into a single occurrence.
	Compute all the transition probabilities P_i between states.
	Return the transition matrix M of Mobility Markov chain

Dummy Rotation Algorithm. Dummy generation techniques are the most known and used techniques for trajectory privacy [19] because of their ability to confuse attackers by adding multiple fake positions or trajectories 'dummies'. Dummy Rotation Algorithm is one of the dummy generation techniques that generate fake trajectories by rotating the real trajectories with a specified angle. Algorithm 3 explains the Dummy Rotation Algorithm.

Algorithm 3: Dummy Rotation Algorithm

Inputs:	T_r: real trajectory, D: number of dummy trajectories, θ: Rotation angle.

Output:	Dummy trajectories T_D

Set T_r as current trajectory T_c , $T_c = T_r$

For $i = 1:1:D$ do

    Select a rotation point in T_c randomly

    Rotate T_c by θ to generate a new trajectory.

    Set T_i as the current trajectory, $T_c = T_i$

End for

4   Evaluation and Results

For Evaluating the system, we have used the GeoLife dataset which contains data from 182 users and 17,621 trajectories created by Microsoft Research Asia. We have measures location prediction and trajectory privacy as followed.

4.1   Location Prediction

For evaluating the efficiency of n-MMC, the metric accuracy of prediction is used as the ratio between the number of correct predictions over the total number of predictions about 60% for all users in the Geolife dataset.

$$Accuracy = \frac{correct\,predictions}{Total\,predictions} \tag{1}$$

Moreover, Fig. 3 shows the results obtained for Three users with n ranging from 1 to 5. The overall accuracy of n-MMC for n from 1 to 5 is

Figure 3 shows that accuracy improves as n increases but when n > 2 the accuracy seems stable or even decreases slightly. Finally, the results show that the accuracy is the best when n = 2 for most of the cases.

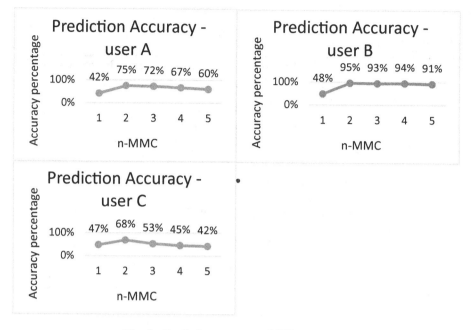

Fig. 3. Prediction accuracy of different users.

4.2   Trajectory Privacy

For trajectory privacy, we aim to balance between Trajectory Disclosure Probability (TDP) and Position Disclosure Probability (PDP). TDP and PDP are defined as the following:

Trajectory Disclosure Probability (TDP). Trajectory Disclosure Probability is the probability of identifying the real trajectory of the user among all possible trajectories including real and dummy trajectories [19]. More intersections correspond to a lower TDP as the number of possible paths is increased.

Disclosure Probability (PDP). Position Disclosure Probability is described as the probability of inferring each reallocation in the real trajectory. PDP [19, 5] determined as

$$PDP = \frac{n+1}{n+D+1} \tag{2}$$

Where $n+1$ are the number of real positions and D are the number of dummy positions.

Figure 4 shows the generation of dummy trajectories of a user at 2-MMC, where the number of dummies $D = 2$ (red dashed line) and $\theta = 120$ between trajectories. For PDP the number of real positions is 3 (n = 2 and one predicted position) and PDP = 0.13. on the other hand, from the figure we deduced that there are no intersections between the real path and dummy trajectories, so the number of all possible paths is 3 and TDP = 0.33.

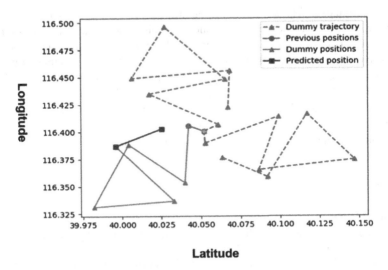

Fig. 4. Dummy rotation generation algorithm of trajectory of the user. (Color figure online)

With the increasing number of dummy trajectories, PDP decreases as the number of dummy positions increases. On the other hand, more intersections mean a higher PDP and a smaller TDP. Thus, there should be a balance between PDP and TDP. Results shown in Fig. 5 presents the results of PDP and TDP with a different number of dummies (2, 4, 6)

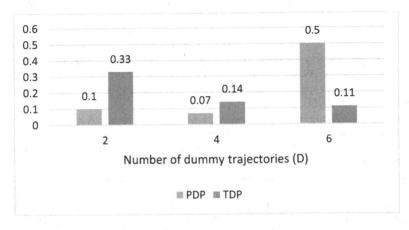

Fig. 5. PDP and TDP comparison.

for a user using 2-MMC. It shows that PDP increases with more intersections at $D = 6$ where TDP decreases. TDP and PDP achieved the balance at $D = 4$.

5 Conclusion

With all techniques and approaches developed to preserve the privacy of the trajectory of the user, still there are several issues and constraints did not take into account. One of these issues is to protect the future location of the user, while attackers may predict or estimate the users' next position. In this paper, we developed a system that preserves the privacy of the user future trajectory by predicting the future location of the user using Extended Mobility Markov Chain (n-MMC) and then, generating dummy trajectories, using Dummy Rotation Algorithm by rotating the real trajectory of the user. The system shows that it could achieve privacy preservation with an average accuracy of 60% and provide Trajectory privacy to the whole trajectory of the user.

References

1. Hong, H.J.: From cloud computing to fog computing: unleash the power of edge and end devices. In: Proceedings of the International Conference on Cloud Computing Technology and Science, CloudCom, vol. 2017, pp. 331–334 (2017)
2. Stojmenovic, I., Wen, S., Huang, X., Luan, H.: An overview of Fog computing and its security issues. Concurr. Comput. Pract. Exp. **28**(10), 2991–3005 (2016)
3. Mukherjee, M., et al.: Security and privacy in fog computing: challenges. IEEE Access **5**, 19293–19304 (2017)
4. Wernke, M., Skvortsov, P., Dürr, F., Rothermel, K.: A classification of location privacy attacks and approaches. Pers. Ubiquitous Comput. **18**(1), 163–175 (2012). https://doi.org/10.1007/s00779-012-0633-z
5. Chow, C.Y., Mokbel, M.F.: Trajectory privacy in location-based services and data publication. ACM SIGKDD Explor. Newsl. **13**(1), 19 (2011)
6. Wu, R., Luo, G., Shao, J., Tian, L., Peng, C.: Location prediction on trajectory data: a review. Big Data Min. Anal. **1**(2), 108–127 (2018)
7. Petzold, J., Bagci, F., Trumler, W., Ungerer, T.: Comparison of different methods for next location prediction. In: Nagel, W.E., Walter, W.V., Lehner, W. (eds.) Euro-Par 2006. LNCS, vol. 4128, pp. 909–918. Springer, Heidelberg (2006). https://doi.org/10.1007/11823285_96
8. Qiao, S., Shen, D., Wang, X., Han, N., Zhu, W.: A self-adaptive parameter selection trajectory prediction approach via hidden Markov models. IEEE Trans. Intell. Transp. Syst. **16**(1), 284–296 (2015)
9. Qiao, Y., Si, Z., Zhang, Y., Ben Abdesslem, F., Zhang, X., Yang, J.: A hybrid Markov-based model for human mobility prediction. Neurocomputing **278**, 99–109 (2018)
10. Du, Y., Wang, C., Qiao, Y., Zhao, D., Guo, W.: A geographical location prediction method based on continuous time series Markov model. PLoS One **13**(11), e0207063 (2018)
11. Chen, M., Yu, X., Liu, Y.: Mining moving patterns for predicting next location. Inf. Syst. **54**, 156–168 (2015)
12. Gambs, S., Killijian, M.O., Del Prado Cortez, M.N.: Next place prediction using mobility Markov chains. In: Proceedings of the First Workshop on Measurement, Privacy, and Mobility - MPM 2012, pp. 1–6 (2012)

13. Hwang, R.H., Hsueh, Y.L., Chung, H.W.: A novel time-obfuscated algorithm for trajectory privacy protection. IEEE Trans. Serv. Comput. 7(2), 126–139 (2014)
14. Memon, I., Chen, L., Arain, Q.A., Memon, H., Chen, G.: Pseudonym changing strategy with multiple mix zones for trajectory privacy protection in road networks. Int. J. Commun Syst 31(1), e3437 (2018)
15. Liao, D., Li, H., Sun, G., Anand, V.: Protecting user trajectory in location-based services. In: 2015 IEEE Global Communications Conference (GLOBECOM), pp. 1–6 (2015)
16. Gao, S., Ma, J., Sun, C., Li, X.: Balancing trajectory privacy and data utility using a personalized anonymization model. J. Netw. Comput. Appl. 38, 125–134 (2014)
17. Peng, T., Liu, Q., Meng, D., Wang, G.: Collaborative trajectory privacy preserving scheme in location-based services. Inf. Sci. (Ny) 387, 165–179 (2017)
18. Niu, B., Gao, S., Li, F., Li, H., Lu, Z.: Protection of location privacy in continuous LBSs against adversaries with background information. In: 2016 International Conference on Computing, Networking and Communications (ICNC), pp. 1–6 (2016)
19. Wang, T., et al.: Trajectory privacy preservation based on a fog structure for cloud location services. IEEE Access 5, 7692–7701 (2017)
20. Hayashida, S., Amagata, D., Hara, T., Xie, X.: Dummy generation based on user-movement estimation for location privacy protection. IEEE Access 6, 22958–22969 (2018)

Enabling Secure and Efficient Data Sharing and Integrity Auditing for Cloud-Assisted Industrial Control System

Yuanfei Tu[1,2(✉)], Qingjian Su[1], and Yang Geng[2]

[1] Nanjing Tech University, Nanjing 211800, China
yuanfeitu@163.com
[2] Nanjing University of Post and Telecommunication, Nanjing 21003, China

Abstract. With the development of Cloud Computing, which is applying to Industrial Internet of Things, the security of industrial data is confronting enormous risk. Unfortunately, existing data sharing schemes are not suitable for the industry control system because of the heavy computation operations, latency-sensitive service, and resource-limited devices. Also, since the data is stored on the cloud, the data integrity are crucial issues related to privacy and trust. In order to protect the confidentiality and integrity of data in such an environment, we propose a secure and efficient data sharing scheme by employing Ciphertext-Policy Attribute Based Encryption (CP-ABE), which integrates data encryption, access control, decryption outsourcing and data integrity verification. Moreover, the length of ciphertext is fixed. The scheme is analyzed in detail from security, efficiency and computation cost.

Keywords: Industrial control system · Confidentiality · Decryption outsourcing · Constant ciphertext length · Integrity

1 Introduction

With the integration of IT into the ICS, the independent and closed industrial control system begin to use cloud computing, big data and other technologies for storing and analyzing data [1]. Industrial control system is facing with multiple threats from external networks in this process, such as malicious intrusions, computer viruses, cyber attacks, etc. The most well-known is the 2010 "Stuxnet" virus incident in Iran [2]. In the traditional industrial control system, data is transmitted in plaintext. If the plaintext data is sent and stored directly on the cloud platform, the ICS mat be exposed to threats such as leakage and tampering, and resulting in irreparable damage [3, 4]. In recent years, countries around the world have put forward very valuable indicators and guidelines for safety practice, such as the "Network Security Law" promulgated by china. The law proposes to strengthen the security protection of key information infrastructure and maintain national network security [5].

In order to protect the confidentiality of industrial data, cryptography is an effective solution. Halas [6] simulated the 3DES and AES algorithms in the PLC respectively, the results show that the AES algorithm has better performance and meets the real-time

© Springer Nature Singapore Pte Ltd. 2020
Y. Tian et al. (Eds.): ICBDS 2019, CCIS 1210, pp. 514–528, 2020.
https://doi.org/10.1007/978-981-15-7530-3_39

requirements, but the key distribution and management has not been well solved. After that, to achieve higher security, two semi-homomorphic encryption algorithms are used and improved by Li [7, 8]. They are applied to PLC to implement the function of the encryption controller, the results show that the computation cost on PLC is large and cannot satisfy the real-time requirement for the control system. Due to the particularity of the industrial control system, the cryptography tool cannot be simply applied to industrial control system. The cryptography not only protecting the confidentiality of the data, but also ensuring the real-time and availability of the system at the same time [9]. In addition, these "one-to-one" encryption methods cannot achieve the flexible access control function of the data in the cloud computing environment, and are not sufficient to satisfy the change of the user identity.

To adapt to the fine-grained control strategy and the security requirements in an open network environment, an Attribute-Based Encryption (ABE) algorithm has been proposed [10]. The ABE is derived from distributed computing, which uses a one-to-many encryption method to provide users with flexible access methods, unlike traditional one-to-one encryption algorithms. Sahai [11] proposed a Ciphertxt-policy attribute-based encryption (CP-ABE) algorithm, that embeds the access control policy in the ciphertext, only users who meet the access policy can decrypt successfully, thus achieving fine-grained access control.

On the basis, Ruj [12] first introduced the CP-ABE scheme to the smart grids to realize an access control mechanism. They presented a specific algorithm and evaluated the computation cost on encryption and decryption. Similarly, Das [13] adopted the CP-ABE Scheme and built an access control model from the top layer of the Cyber-Physical Systems. The model uses time, location, identity and other attributes to build a secure information sharing framework for IoT devices. Rajat [14] also designed a communication model for an IIoT environment, and utilized an CP-ABE algorithm to secure the data communication. However, in the above schemes, the computation cost is high because ABE require many pairing-based operations. In some resource limited applications, such as IoT, ICS, it may become a bottleneck. To deal with this challenging issue, Guan [15] presented a CP-ABE scheme to secure the data acquisition for the Cloud-Supported Internet of Things in Smart Grid. They partitioned the acquired data into several blocks, then encrypted and transmitted the data blocks in parallel according to the Bethencourt's CP-ABE scheme [16]. It reduces the response time overhead compared to Bethencourt's scheme, but the pairing-based operations on data receiver are not reduced. Furthermore, in current CP-ABE schemes, the computation cost (the pairing operations) and the ciphertext length both grow with the size of the access structure or the number of attributes. Therefore, it causes the increasing decryption overhead and storage space. To this end, Doshi [17] proposed a constant-ciphertext CP-ABE algorithm from the perspective of ciphertext length, which reduces the user's storage and decryption overhead.

In addition, some scholars adopted the method of outsourcing computation to reduce the decryption overhead on user side. Qin [18] designed a CP-ABE scheme which outsourcing most of the decryption operations to a third party, thus reducing the decryption overhead on the user side. The scheme also supports verifying the integrity of the data by calculating the hash value after merging the ciphertext and the key. Similar to Qin, Yang [20] also applied this idea to the medical IoT environment and build a lightweight data sharing system based on CP-ABE. However, neither of the schemes [18, 19] achieved a constant ciphertext length.

In this paper, we propose an encryption scheme based on CP-ABE, which effectively controls user's access to resources and protects data integrity in the cloud assisted ICS. The scheme adopts the hybrid encryption method, the industrial data is encrypted by the AES algorithm, and the AES key is encrypted by the CP-ABE algorithm, thereby obtaining a shorter encryption time and higher security. In addition, the scheme achieves high efficiency and low storage on the user side, because the length of ciphertext and the number of bilinear pairing evaluations are fixed to a constant, and most of the decryption are outsourced to the cloud. At the same time, in order to cope with the occurrence of storage data corruption, tampering and rollback attacks, the scheme also supports verifing data integrity and key correctness. Finally, the paper analyzes the correctness, security and performance of the algorithm and adds the simulation experiment of the scheme.

2 Preliminaries and System Model

2.1 Access Structure

Definition 1. Let $P = \{P_1, P_2, \cdots, P_n\}$ be a set of parties. A collection $A \subseteq 2^P$ is monotone, if $\forall B, C{:}B \in A$ and $B \subseteq C$ then $C \subseteq A$. Access structure A is a non-empty subsets of 2^P, i.e. $A \subseteq 2^{\{P_1, \cdots, P_n\}} \setminus \varnothing$.

2.2 Bilinear Paring

Let G_1, G_2 be two multiplicative cyclic groups of prime order p. Let g be a generator of G_1, and e a bilinear map, $e : G_1 \times G_1 \rightarrow G_2$ with the following properties:

1) Bilinearity: for all $a, b \in Z_p$, we have $e(g^a, g^b) = e(g, g)^{ab}$.
2) Non-degenerate: $e(g, g) \neq 1$.
3) Computability: $\forall (u, v) \in G_1$, there is a polynomial time method to calculated $e(u, v)$.

2.3 System Model

The system model constructed in this paper is shown in Fig. 1. The system model consists of five entities: Key Generation Center (KGC), Industrial Control System (ICS), Private Cloud (PrC), Public cloud (PuC), and Data User (DU). The main functions of each entity are summarized as follows:

1) Key Generation Center (KGC): KGC is an independent and trusted organization with the ability to authorize the users, evaluate their attributes and generate their secrete keys accordingly. In the initialization phase, KGC mainly calculates the system public parameters and the master key, then, retains the master private key,

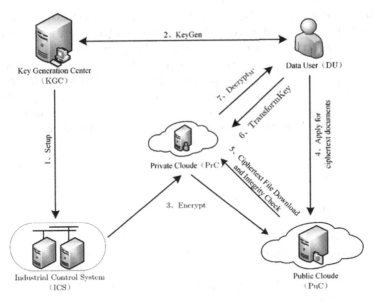

Fig. 1. System model.

and sends the system master public key to the ICS. In the private key generation phase, KGC mainly calculates attribute private key sk_L, and send sk_L to DU.

2) Data User (DU): DU is a staff member who wants to read field data in an enterprise (including managers, engineers, operators). To protect data security, a new user needs to contact the KGC for registration and obtains a legal GID. Then the KGC generates a secret key for each of the attributes the DU claims to have. When a DU requests a file stored on the PuC, the PuC transmits the file to the PrC, then the DU downloads the encrypted file via the PrC. The DU will receive a partially decrypted file from the PrC if he has the required attributes, and then he can obtain the plaintext by his secret key.

3) Private Cloud (PrC): PrC is a cloud platform built by an enterprise for its own use. It is a proprietary resource of an enterprise. Enterprises deploying applications on private clouds can get the most effective control over data security, and quality of service, but not large-scale data storage. In this scheme, the data requested by the DU will be sent to the PrC from the PuC. Then the PrC decrypts the encrypted data and generates a partially decrypted ciphertext M'. Lastly, the M' will be transferred to DU to finish the final decryption process. In addition, the solution also deploys a real-time data integrity check service on the private cloud. The private cloud periodically checks the data integrity stored on the public cloud in a challenge response process.

4) Public cloud (PuC): PuC is an information product provided by a third party for enterprises. Enterprises can perform data storage and resource custody services on PuC. In this model, PuC is a semi-trusted party and the data stored on it are encrypted. It retrieves the data requested by the DU, then sends the ciphertext to the PrC to generate the partially decrypted ciphertext.

5) Industrial Control System (ICS): ICS is a system that monitors field devices and collects field data (including equipment status parameters, process parameters, site environmental data, etc.) within the enterprise. In this model, ICS first encrypts the data set with a symmetric encryption algorithm (AES) to form a data ciphertext, and then encrypts the symmetric key with the CP-ABE algorithm to form a key ciphertext. Finally, the data ciphertext and the key ciphertext are uploaded to the public cloud storage according to a certain format. To protect the security of ICS, ICS cannot directly connect to the public cloud of the external network.

3 Our Construction

3.1 Framework

In order to solve the problem of secure and fine-grained data sharing, our scheme adopts an encrypting algorithm in [17], and applies the idea of outsourcing decryption to the proposed scheme. The scheme mainly consists of six algorithms: *Setup*, *Encrypt*, *KeyGen*, *TransformKey*, *Decrypt$_{M'}$* and *Decrypt*, and the function of each algorithm is briefly described as follows.

1) $Setup(\lambda) \rightarrow \{PP, mpk, msk\}$: The Setup algorithm is run by the KGC. The Setup algorithm takes security parameters λ, and output system public parameters PP, and system master key pair (mpk, msk).

2) $KeyGen(msk, L) \rightarrow \{sk_L\}$: The KeyGen algorithm is run by the KGC. The Key-Gen algorithm takes as inputs the public parameters PP, system master private key msk, user attribute list L, and output the user's attribute private key sk_L.

3) $Encrypt(M, mpk, W) \rightarrow \{CT\}$: The Encrypt algorithm is run by the ICS. The Encrypt algorithm takes as symmetric encryption key M, system master public key mpk, an access structure W, and output key ciphertext CT.

4) $TransformKey(sk_L, GID) \rightarrow \{tk_{GID}\}$: The TransformKey algorithm is run by the DU. The TransformKey algorithm takes as inputs user attribute private key sk_L, global identifier GID, and output conversion key pair $tk_{GID} = (tpk_{i,j}, tsk_{GID})_{i\in[1,n],j\in[1,n_i]}$.

5) $Decrypt_{M'}(tpk_{i,j}, L) \rightarrow \{M'\}$: The Decrypt$_{M'}$ algorithm is run by the PrC. If the secret key of the user satisfies the access structure defined by the ICS, the PrC is able to execute the Decrypt$_{M'}$ algorithm correctly, and the user will obtain a partially decrypted ciphertext M' from the PrC.

6) $Decrypt(M', tsk_{GID}) \rightarrow \{M\}$: The Decrypt algorithm is run by the DU. The Decrypt algorithm takes as inputs part decrypts ciphertext M', user convert private key tsk_{GID}, and output symmetric key M.

3.2 Algorithm Descriptions

Assume $U = \{att_1, att_2, \cdots, att_n\}$ is a set of attributes, $S_i = \{v_{i,1}, v_{i,2}, \cdots v_{i,n_i}\}$ is the set of all possible values for att_i, where n_i is the maximum number of attribute values, $L = \{L_1, L_2, \cdots L_n\}$ is a set of attributes of the user, $W = \{W_1, W_2, \cdots W_k\}$ is the access structure. The detailed construction process of the scheme is described as follows:

1) $Setup(\lambda) \rightarrow \{PP, mpk, msk\}$: KGC selects a large prime number p, a bilinear group (G_1, G_T) with order p. Here $e : G_1 \times G_1 \rightarrow G_T$ is a pair of bilinear map, and $H : \{0,1\}^* \rightarrow G_1$ and $H_1 : \{0,1\}^* \rightarrow Z_p$ are two anti-collision hash functions, the KGC selects a generator $g, u \in G_1$, and calculates public parameters are

$$PP = \{G_1, G_T, H, e, g, u\} \tag{1}$$

Then, the KGC calculates the pair of system master key (mpk, msk). The KGC assigns a unique global identifier GID to users with permissions, and adds GID to list T_{GID}. Then, the KGC selects $\alpha_{i,j} \in Z_{P(i \in [1,n], j \in [1,n_i])}$ and $t \in Z_P$, calculate $Y = e(g, g)^t$ and $T_{i,j} = g^{-\alpha_{i,j}}$, and generates the system master key (mpk, msk) are

$$\begin{cases} msk = (t, \alpha_{i,j}(i \in [1, n], j \in [1, n_i])) \\ mpk = (Y, T_{i,j}(i \in [1, n], j \in [1, n_i])) \end{cases} \tag{2}$$

2) $KeyGen(msk, L) \rightarrow \{sk_L\}$: When a data user contacts the KGC to obtain the private key corresponding to the attributes L he claims to have, the KGC first check wether the user's GID is valid. If the user owns a valid GID, then the KGC performs the KeyGen algorithm to generate the private key for the user. The algorithm takes as inputs the system master key msk, the user's attributes L, then outputs the private key sk_L are

$$\begin{cases} sk_1 = g^{\alpha_{i,j}} H(GID)^{\alpha_{i,j}}\big|_{v_{i,j} \in L} \\ sk_2 = g^t \left(\prod_{v_{i,j} \in L} g^{\alpha_{i,j}}\big|_{v_{i,j} \in L} \right) \end{cases} \tag{3}$$
$$sk_L = \{sk_1, sk_2\}$$

3) $Encrypt(M, mpk, W) \rightarrow \{CT\}$: After the ICS encrypts the field data by AES, the ICS performs the CP-ABE algorithm to encrypt the AES key. Given a public key mpk, user access structure W, and the AES key, the ICS selects a random value $s \in Z_P$ encrypt the AES key $M(M \in Z_P)$, and outputs the ciphertext is

$$\begin{cases} C_0 = MY^s \\ C_1 = \left(\prod_{v_{i,j} \in W} T_{i,j} \right)^s \\ C_2 = g^s \end{cases} \tag{4}$$

The ICS also calculates the verification ciphertext for key M is $V = H_1(u^M)$. Lastly, the ICS sends the encrypted data $CT = \{C_0, C_1, C_2, V\}$ and $AES(M, DATA)$ to the public cloud.

In the industrial field, there is amount of field data that needs to be encrypted. CP-ABE encryption is not suitable for encrypting large files, because of its slow encryption speed, long time, and poor real-time performance. Symmetric encryption is suitable for encrypting large files, however the algorithm key delivery is a problem that must be considered. Therefore, this scheme uses hybrid encryption to improve the efficiency in the scheme. The file transfer format defined in the hybrid encryption scheme is shown in Fig. 2. M is a AES key, and CT is the ciphertext of M by our CP-ABE algorithm.

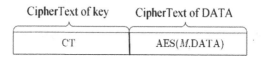

Fig. 2. File transfer format.

4) *TransformKey*(sk_L, *GID*) → $\{tk_{GID}\}$: The DU performs the *TransformKey* algorithm to transform his private key sk_L to a conversion key tk_{GID}. The DU chooses a random value $z \in Z_P$, then outputs the conversion key tk_{GID} are

$$\begin{cases} tpk_{i,j} = \left(sk_1^{\frac{1}{z}}, sk_2^{\frac{1}{z}}, H(GID)^{\frac{1}{z}} \right)_{v_{i,j} \in L} \\ tsk_{GID} = z \end{cases}$$

$$tk_{GID} = \left(tpk_{i,j}, tsk_{GID} \right)_{v_{i,j} \in L} \tag{5}$$

5) *Decrypt*$_{M'}$ $\left(tpk_{i,j}, L \right)$ → $\{M'\}$: When a user is interested in a shared file, it sends a request to the cloud. Once the cloud receives a user's request, it responds to transmit the requested file CT and AES (M, DATA) to the private cloud. Then the PrC tries to decrypt the CT partially. If the attribute list L meet ciphertext access strategies W (which is $L|=W$), the PrC can finish the partial decryption successfully and outputs the transformed ciphertext M'

$$M' = \frac{e\left(C_2, sk_2^{\frac{1}{z}}\right)}{e\left(C_2, \prod_{v_{i,j} \in L} sk_1^{\frac{1}{z}}\right) e\left(C_1, H(GID)^{\frac{1}{z}}\right)} = e(g, g)^{\frac{st}{z}} \tag{6}$$

Instead, the decryption fails and outputs.

Finally, the PrC will return M' and $AES(M, DATA)$ to the DU.

6) $Decrypt(M', tsk_{GID}) \rightarrow \{M\}$: After the DU received the M' from the PrC, the DU only needs to perform a simple exponential operation to obtain the symmetric encryption key M. The decryption of the AES key M is:

$$M = \frac{C_0}{(M')^{tsk_{GID}}} \tag{7}$$

Then the DU verifies whether the AES key is intact or not. The DU checks whether or not $H_1(u^M) = V$ holds, if the equation is true, the obtained M is valid.

Finally, the DU utilizes the key M to decrypt the ciphertext $AES(M, DATA)$ and gets the field data.

3.3   Data Integrity Verification

Encryption can protect the confidentiality of data stored on the public cloud, however it cannot guarantee the file stored on cloud are not modified by unauthorized parties or corrupted due to software bugs or configuration errors. In this subsection, we expand our scheme and apply it on the PrC to verify the integrity of the file stored on the PuC. The PrC supplies an auditing scheme to check the integrity of shared file on the PuC, ensuring the file the DU received is intact. Through a challenge-response technique, the PrC periodically challenges the PuC and authenticates the PuC's respond to the challenge. Our approach is divided into two phases: Setup Phase and Challenge-Response Phase. The detailed procedures are described in the following.

Initialization Phase

Step 1: The private cloud randomly chooses $\alpha \in Z_P$, then generates the key pair $\{g^\alpha, \alpha\}$.

Step 2: The private cloud first splits the ciphertext F into blocks and divides it into $F = \{f_1, f_2, \cdots, f_n\}$, then random chooses $r_i \in Z_P$, and calculates the corresponding set of authentication elements for all data blocks $\Psi = \{\lambda_1, \lambda_2, \cdots, \lambda_n\}$, in the formula $\lambda_i = (H(i) \cdot u^{r_i})^\alpha$, $H(i)$ is a hash operation.

Step 3: The private cloud sends $\{r_i, \lambda_i\}$ alongside with its received encrypted file to the public cloud.

Challenge stage

Step 1: The private cloud acts as a verifier and initiates periodic integrity verification to public cloud. First, selecting t pieces of data blocks from $F = \{f_1, f_2, \cdots, f_n\}$, and select a random number $v_i \in Z_P$ for each file number, then combine the number and the random number to form a challenge request $\{i, v_i\}_{i \in [1,n]}$ and send to public cloud.

Step 2: Public cloud utilization v_i to make the following calculate:

$$\eta = \sum_{i=i_1}^{i_t} v_i \cdot r_i, \quad \lambda = \prod_{i=i_1}^{i_t} \lambda_i^{v_i} \tag{8}$$

Then it sends $\{\eta, \lambda\}$ as a response message to the private cloud.

Step 3: After receiving the $\{\eta, \lambda\}$, the private cloud judges whether the following equation is established. If the equation is established, the data stored in the public cloud is complete and usable.

$$e(\lambda, g) = e\left(\prod_{i=i_1}^{i_t} H(i)^{v_i} \cdot u^{\eta}, g^{\alpha}\right) \tag{9}$$

4   System Scheme Analysis

4.1   Confidentiality Analysis

Our scheme adopts a hybrid encryption method, that encrypts industrial data using a symmetric encryption algorithm (AES), then encrypts the symmetric key M with the CP-ABE algorithm. It can be seen that the confidentiality of the industrial data depends on the symmetric encryption algorithm (AES), and the confidentiality of the AES key mainly depends on the security of the CP-ABE. We adopt and improve the CP-ABE algorithm in [17] to encrypt the key M, and the algorithm [17] has proven to be CPA secure under the decisional q-parallel BDHE assumption. We add a set of components for outsourcing decryption on the algorithm [17] and the secret key's random value z is embedded in the public key $tpk_{i,j}$. Thus unauthorized users (such as the attackers) are unable to separate the value z in a polynomial time and obtain symmetric key M through the correct decryption, because they don't have the attributes that satisfy the access policy.

4.2   Anti-collusion Attack

Our CP-ABE scheme is secure against the collusion attack for any number of users. When a user colludes with other malicious users, they have to calculating the value of st, g, z correctly before they can successfully decrypt the ciphertext. However, in our algorithm, random values s is embedded in ciphertext, random values t is embedded in the private key, the collaborators cannot separate the component s and t, even if it obtains the ciphertext and private key components. In addition, They need $H(GID)$ in Bilinear pairing operation, however every GID is unique, and their hash value $H(GID)$ is unique. Therefore, unauthorized users cannot calculate the value of $e(g,g)^{\frac{st}{z}}$ by collusion.

4.3   Data Integrity

In our construction, the integrity of the shared file on the PuC can be verified by employing the bilinear map function. We ensure the shared file possession and recoverability on the cloud by the way of file partition, encoding and checking random subset of the file. To alleviate the data owner's burden, the cumbersome auditing task is delegated to PrC. The PrC is able to perform an infinite number of verifications without leaking any content of the file.

To ensure a symmetric key M is available correctly, the user must calculate the key's verification code through exponential operation and hash value $H_1(u^M)$. Then, the method of equality verification is used to verify the correctness of the key verification code.

The data integrity check method in our paper is compared with the traditional method of decrypting and re-verifying by the user in [19], our algorithm can implement on the data file in a sustainable manner, and reduce the calculated overhead on the side of client, the file content can be guaranteed cannot be leaked at the sametime.

5   Performance Analysis

In this subsection, we analyze and compare our scheme with the schemes [17, 18] and [19] from the aspects of scheme performance, computational overhead, and communication ciphertext length. Then, we make a quantitative analysis of the communication consumption and add a simulation experiment of the scheme. Let $|G_1|$, $|G_T|$ and $|Z_P|$ denote the length of each element in G_1, G_T and Z_P respectively. Let E_1, E_T denote the exponential operation in G_1 and G_T respectively. Let P representing pairing operations. Let n denoting the number of user attributes.

5.1   Capability Analysis

As shown in Table 1, our scheme supports outsourced decryption and constant ciphertext length, it also supports the function of verifying the correctness of the key and the integrity of the data.

Table 1. Comparison of program performance.

Scheme	Decryption outsourcing	Constant ciphertext length	Verifiable
[17]	No	Yes	No
[18]	Yes	No	Symmetric key
[19]	Yes	No	Data
Our scheme	Yes	Yes	Symmetric key/data

5.2   Storage Overhead

The ICS generates the full ciphertext, stores it and sends it to the PrC periodically. As the same, the PrC will stores the received ciphertext and forward it to the PuC. Since the cloud storage space is large and can be extended easily, the storage overhead on the resource limited ICS is crucially important. On the other hand, the storage overhead on the data user is another essential issue to be considered. Thus, we pick up some schemes to compare with ours in terms of storage overhead on the ICS and the Data User, and eventually show the results in Table 2. The symmetric encryption ciphertext length is not considered here.

Table 2. Comparison of storage overhead.

Scheme	Storage on ICS	Storage on DU
[17]	–	$4|G_1|$
[18]	$(n+2)|G_1| + |G_T|$	$(n+2)|G_1|$
[19]	$3|G_1| + |G_T| + 2n|Z_p|$	$2|G_T|$
Our scheme	$2|G_1| + |G_T|$	$|G_T|$

Our scheme outsources the decryption to the private cloud which is also used in the article [17], so that, the ciphertext length required to be stored on the user side is only $|G_T|$ better than $4|G_1|$ in [17]. The schemes [18] and [19] adopts the method of computational outsourcing, the lengths of the ciphertexts are related to the number of attributes, especially in the [19], the ciphertext length of the client are increasesed with the number of attributes. Since the size of ciphertext in our scheme is a constant value, the storage consumption required by the ICS or the user is minimal, that is a constant value.

5.3   Energy Consumption on Communication

The energy consumption of communication in our scheme mainly includes two parts. The first part is communication between the ICS and the private cloud, and the second part is communication between the user and the private cloud. Since the length of ciphertext is directly related to the energy consumption on communication, we start with quantizing the ciphertext Length. Then using the method proposed by [20], we evaluate the energy consumption of communication in our scheme.

Quantizing Ciphertext Length. In our scheme, the Tate pair is defined in a finite field F_P on the elliptic curve, the order p of G_1 and G_T is a 20 *Byte* prime. If G_T is a p-order subgroup of multiplicative group of the finite field F_{p^2}, F_{p^3} and F_{p^6}, in order to meet the security level of 1024-bit RSA, the length of prime p on finite field F_{p^2}, F_{p^3} and F_{p^6} is 64 *Byte*, 42.5 *Byte* and 20 *Byte* respectively.

In our scheme, the bilinear e employs the Tate pairing. The Tate pairing is defined in a finite field F_P on the elliptic curve, the order p of G_1 and G_T is a 20 Byte prime. In order to deliver a level of security equivalent to that of 1024-bit RSA, the length of prime p on finite field F_P^2, F_P^3 and F_P^6 is 64 Byte, 42.5 Byte and 20 Byte respectively, if G_T is a p-order subgroup of the multiplicative group of the finite field F_{p^2}, F_{p^3}, F_{p^6} respectively. Through the above analysis, the length of the communication ciphertext between the ICS and the private cloud is $Size_M = 2|G_1| + |G_T| = 3|p|(Byte)$, which is also the storage overhead on the ICS.

According to the same analysis method, the length of the communication ciphertext between the user and the private cloud is $Size_{M'} = |G_T| = |p|(Byte)$, which is also the storage overhead on the data user.

We also compare quantitatively the storage overhead on the ICS of our scheme with [17, 18] and [19]. The results are shown in Fig. 3.

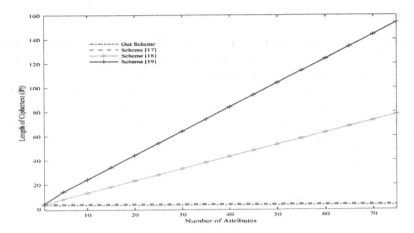

Fig. 3. Length of ciphertext.

From Fig. 3, we can conclude that the storage overhead of the scheme [18, 19] are linear increasing with attributes, which is not suitable for the ICS, because the storage capacity of the ICS is fixed and small.

In contrary, due to the constant ciphertext length, our scheme has the smallest storage overhead on the ICS. If we adopts the AES-128bit to encrypt the field data, the full ciphertext stored on the ICS is only 3 * 64 + 16 = 208 byte.

Evaluating the Energy Consumption. According to [20], we suppose that a Chipcon CC1100 radio is used as the communication module, and the energy consumption is 28.6 µJ and 59.2 µJ to transmit and receive 1 Byte respectively. The energy consumption caused by each communication between the ICS and the private cloud is

$$(3|p|) \times (28.6 + 59.2) = 263.4|p|_{(\mu J)} \tag{10}$$

According to the same analysis method, the energy consumption generated by the private cloud and the user is

$$(|p|) \times (28.6 + 59.2) = 87.8|p|_{(\mu J)} \tag{11}$$

When $|p|$ is prime numbers of 20 *Byte*, 42.5 *Byte* and 64 *Byte*, energy consumption at each communication stage is shown in Table 3.

Table 3. Communication energy consumption.

Communication phase	$|p| = 20\,Byte$	$|p| = 42.5\,Byte$	$|p| = 64\,Byte$
ICS-PrC communication energy loss (mJ)	5.27	11.19	16.86
PrC - DU communication energy loss (mJ)	1.76	3.73	5.62

5.4   Decryption Cost

We compare the computation cost of our scheme with the schemes, and the results are shown in Table 4. Since we fix the size of ciphertext to a constant value, the computation of decryption is constant. However the computation cost in [18, 19] are linearly related to the number of attributes. Especially, the computation cost on the user side in our scheme is minimum. It is because the decryption is outsourced to the private cloud, and the ciphertext sent to the user is transformed into a short and constant length ciphertext. The data user only need a small and constant consumption and then get the plaintext.

Table 4. Comparison of computation cost.

Scheme	Decryption cost on PrC	Decryption cost on DU
[17]	–	$3P + nE_1$
[18]	$(n + 2)P + 2nE_T$	E_T
[19]	$3P + 2nE_1$	$7E_1$
Our scheme	$3P$	E_T

5.5   Experimental Simulation

In this subsection, we verifies the computational consumption of the above theoretical analysis results. The experiment uses the bilinear pair cryptographic library (PBC Library), the elliptic curve uses Type A: $y^2 = x^3 + x$, the emulation hardware is Inter (R) Core (TM) i5-3470 3.2 GHz CPU, 4.00 GB memory, Windows7 32 bit system, and the symmetric encryption algorithm uses 128 bit AES algorithm.

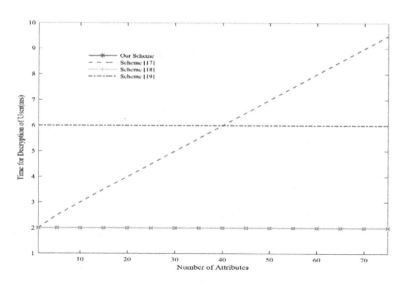

Fig. 4. Time for decryption of user.

We simulate the computation time incurred in decryption on data user in Fig. 4. From Fig. 4, it can be seen that the decryption time of the scheme [17] is linear increasing with attributes. Our scheme and scheme [18, 19] have a lower time, due to the decryption outsourcing. Although the decryption time of scheme [18] is as same as ours, our scheme's ciphertext length is vastly superior to [18].

6 Conclusion

In this paper, we propose a secure data sharing scheme in cloud-assisted ICS based on CP-ABE, which allows the shared file to be accessed if the user's attributes satisfy the access policy embedded in ciphertext. Our scheme fixes the ciphertext length to a constant value and delegates the decryption to the private cloud thus achieving high efficiency, small and constant local storage, especially suits the resource-constrained devices. Furthermore, our scheme supports verifying the encrypted file stored on the public cloud. Especially, the auditing task is performed by the private cloud, hence reducing the computation overhead on the ICS. Finally, we analyze the security properties and evaluate the performance of our scheme in theoretical and experimental aspects. The results show that the scheme achieves security, integrity and efficiency.

Foundation Items. National Natural Science Foundation of China (61572263, 61272084, 61972209). The Natural Science Foundation of the Jiangsu Higher Education Institutions of China (11KJA520002).

References

1. Agrawal, S., Boneh, D., Boyen, X.: Efficient lattice (H)IBE in the standard model. In: Gilbert, H. (ed.) EUROCRYPT 2010. LNCS, vol. 6110, pp. 553–572. Springer, Heidelberg (2010). https://doi.org/10.1007/978-3-642-13190-5_28
2. Trautman, L.J.: Industrial Cyber Vulnerabilities: Lessons from Stuxnet and the Internet of Things. Social Science Electronic Publishing (2017)
3. Babu, B., Ijyas, T., Muneer, P., et al.: Security issues in SCADA based industrial control systems. In: International Conference on Anti-Cyber Crimes, pp. 47–51. IEEE, Saudi Arabia (2017)
4. Kriaa, S., Pietre-Cambacedes, L., Bouissou, M., et al.: A survey of approaches combining safety and security for industrial control systems. Reliab. Eng. Syst. Saf. **139**, 156–178 (2015)
5. Zhou, X.F., Chen, X.Z.: Gray analytical hierarchical assessment model for industry control system security. Netinfo Secur. **1**, 15–20 (2014)
6. Halas, M., Bestak, I., Kovac, M.: Performance measurement of encryption algorithms and their effect on real running in PLC networks. In: International Conference on Telecommunications and Signal Processing, pp. 161–164. IEEE, Prague (2012)
7. Li, X., Liu, M., Zhang, R., et al.: Demo abstract: an industrial control system testbed for the encrypted controller. In: 2018 ACM/IEEE 9th International Conference on Cyber-Physical Systems (ICCPS), pp. 343–344. IEEE, Porto (2018)
8. Li, X.: Research on experimental platform and method of industrial control system encryption controller. Zhejiang University, Monster (2018)

9. Cheminod, M., Durante, L., Valenzano, A.: Review of security issues in industrial networks. IEEE Trans. Ind. Inform. **9**(1), 277–293 (2013)

10. Sahai, A., Waters, B.: Fuzzy identity-based encryption. In: Cramer, R. (ed.) EUROCRYPT 2005. LNCS, vol. 3494, pp. 457–473. Springer, Heidelberg (2005). https://doi.org/10.1007/11426639_27

11. Bethencourt, J., Sahai, A., Waters, B.: Ciphertext-policy attribute-based encryption. In: IEEE Symposium on Security and Privacy, pp. 321–334. IEEE, Oakland (2007)

12. Ruj, S., Nayak, A., Stojmenovic, I.: A security architecture for data aggregation and access control in smart grids. IEEE Trans. Smart Grid **4**(1), 196–205 (2013)

13. Das, P.K., Narayanan, S., Sharma, N.K., et al.: Context-sensitive policy based security in Internet of Things. In: IEEE International Conference on Smart Computing, pp. 1–6. IEEE, Louis (2016)

14. Aujla, G.S., Chaudhary, R., Garg, S., et al.: SDN-enabled multi-attribute-based secure communication for smart grid in IIoT environment. IEEE Trans. Indu. Inform. **14**(6), 2629–2640 (2018)

15. Guan, Z., Jing, L., Wu, L., et al.: Achieving efficient and secure data acquisition for cloud-supported Internet of Things in smart grid. IEEE Internet Things J. **4**(6), 1934–1944 (2017)

16. Bethencourt, J., Sahai, A., Waters, B.: Ciphertext-policy attribute based encryption. In: 2007 IEEE Symposium on Security and Privacy, pp. 321–334. IEEE, Oakland (2007)

17. Doshi, N., Jinwala, D.: Constant Ciphertext Length in CP-ABE. https://eprint.iacr.org/2012/500.pdf. Accessed 29 Aug 2012

18. Qin, B., Deng, R.H., Liu, S., et al.: Attribute-based encryption with efficient verifiable outsourced decryption. IEEE Trans. Inf. Forensics Secur. **10**(7), 1384–1393 (2015)

19. Yang, Y., Liu, X., Deng, R.H.: Lightweight break-glass access control system for healthcare Internet-of-Things. IEEE Trans. Indu. Inform. **14**(8), 3610–3617 (2017)

20. Ren, K., Zeng, K., Lou, W., Moran, P.J.: On broadcast authentication in wireless sensor networks. In: Cheng, X., Li, W., Znati, T. (eds.) Wireless Algorithms Systems and Applications WASA 2006. LNCS, vol. 4138, pp. 502–514. Springer, Heidelberg (2006). https://doi.org/10.1007/11814856_48

An Evolutionary Task Offloading Schema for Edge Computing

Pei Sun[1(✉)], Baojing Chen[1], Shaocong Han[2], Huizhong Shi[2],
Zhenwei Yang[1], and Xing Li[1]

[1] State Grid Gansu Electric Power Information $ Communication Company,
Lanzhou, China
xtsunpei@163.com

[2] Nanjing Nari Information & Communication Technology Co. Ltd., Nanjing,
China

Abstract. Edge computing allows users to access to applications with high-bandwidth and low-latency. The advantages include fast data transmission and task migration between mobile devices and edge cloud. In this work, we propose a novel task migration model with cached data to reduce service response time and energy consumption. An evolutionary task offloading schema is then developed to optimize the migration strategy on the edge cloud. As a result, our schema is able to minimize the aforementioned objective function while satisfying the resource constraints. We have conducted simulations to prove the effectiveness of our schema in energy-saving, during task migration.

Keywords: Task offloading · Edge computing · Genetic algorithm

1 Introduction

In recent years, the rapid development of cloud computing (CC), big data, Internet of Things (IoT), and upgrading of intelligent mobile terminals [1–11] have brought opportunities and challenges for emerging services. Users are increasingly demanding better quality of services, including lower response time, better energy efficiency, easier service access and etc. To meet user requirements, a new paradigm named multi-access edge computing (MEC) has been proposed. MEC attracts the attention of academics and industry since it provides content providers and application developers cloud-computing utility and an optimized service environment at the edge of the network. This paradigm is characterized by ultra-low latency and high bandwidth as well as real-time access.

To give a brief introduction on MEC, operators control Radio Access Network (RAN) edge to allow participants to provide applications and services to users in a flexibly and rapidly manner. For better energy consumption and latency of service, computing tasks and data have been migrated from cloud to edge nodes, resulting in improved user experience. Meanwhile, mobile nodes also take advantage of the edge cloud by adopting the appropriate decision-making process for task offloading. However, it is still noticeable that edge nodes have limited resource in the context of the rapidly increasing number of mobile devices and services. When both mobile and cloud

© Springer Nature Singapore Pte Ltd. 2020
Y. Tian et al. (Eds.): ICBDS 2019, CCIS 1210, pp. 529–540, 2020.
https://doi.org/10.1007/978-981-15-7530-3_40

tasks are migrated to edge node, the usage of computing and storage capabilities should be optimized. This problem is addressed by optimizing task offloading schema.

The research of task offloading focuses on the sending of tasks to edge servers, often a small data center near to the users. To be more specific, the tasks running on edge server has less than one-millisecond standard latency when 5G facilitate the usage of cloud resources so can effectively support low-delay application. Connected with nearest users, edge servers perform more efficiently than a cloud in the sending and receiving of application data. Task offloading in MEC is an essential technique to allow users to access computational capabilities at the network edge. Each user can decide to offload a computational task instead of running it locally. Since the primary purpose of offloading is to reduce the energy consumption and execution time, most previous works have considered these two parameters [12–27].

In existing solutions, edge caching technique has been proposed to improve efficiency, but the computing capabilities of the edge node is often neglected. When considering task migration, the scenarios of complex dependencies among tasks have not been well-studies. Most of the existing work aim at solving coarse-grained migration problem with simple dependencies. In this paper, we propose an optimized schema of task caching and offloading. During the optimization, the considered aspects include: edge caching, joint optimization, complex dependencies, energy consumption and user requirements. To the best of our knowledge, this work is the pioneer in attempting to tackle the problems of computation and storage consumption, energy efficiency, task dependency and many other realistic constraints in multi-access edge computing environment. An evolutionary task offloading schema is used to meet the all requirements. The proposed schema will minimize the price and improve the utility of the edge service while meeting its deadline.

The rest of the paper is organized as follows. Section 2 provides literature review on MEC task offloading. Section 3 defines the problem and provides solutions, i.e., our proposed evolutionary task offloading schema. In Sect. 4, we describe our simulation settings, present the results and discuss our findings. Finally, Sect. 5 concludes the paper.

2   Related Work

Edge computing stands for a cloud-based IT service environment running at the edge of a network. The goal of edge computing and MEC is to offer low-latency, high-bandwidth, real-time access to latency-sensitive applications distributed at the edge of the network. The primary target of edge computing is to control network congestion and improve quality of service by executing related task processing closer to the end user, thus improving the delivery of content to them. A large number of applications that have already been realized include augmented reality (AR), virtual reality (VR), connected cars, IoT applications and so on [1].

Large public venues and enterprise organizations also benefit from edge computing. Enterprises are increasingly motivated to use small cell networks to transmit data at sizable locations such as offices, campuses, or stadiums. Edge computing lets operators host content and applications close to the edge of the network. It also brings new levels of performance and access to mobile, wireless, and wired networks. The technology is routinely mentioned in conversations about the infrastructure of 5G networks and Network Function Virtualization (NFV) technology, particularly for handling the huge number of IoT devices (commercial and industrial) that are constantly connected to the network [2].

Currently, task migration and task offloading algorithms are key research topics in MEC or mobile cloud computing. Some studies have presented task migration and task offloading strategies in term of minimizing delay, minimizing energy consumption or minimizing both of these at the same time [3] An approach for minimizing delay was proposed in [4]; this adopted a Markov decision process approach to handle transmission decisions, which include where the computation tasks are scheduled based on the queueing state of the task buffer, the execution state of the local processing unit, and the state of the transmission unit. In [5], Liu et al. studied the task offloading problem from a matching perspective and aimed to optimize the total network delay. They proposed a pricing-based one-to-one matching algorithm and pricing-based one-to-many matching algorithms for the task offloading. Chen et al. investigated the task offloading problem in ultra-dense network aiming to minimize the delay while saving the battery life of user's equipment, and formulated the task offloading problem as a mixed integer nonlinear program [6]. A control-theoretic approach and a two-level resource allocation and admission control mechanism for a cluster of edge servers in the MEC environment is presented in [7].

In terms of minimizing energy consumption, Kwak et al. considered network traffic, cloud workloads and also the ability of CPU frequency scaling and network interface selection between WiFi and cellular to minimize energy when offloading tasks [8]. Cao et al. proposed an energy-optimal offloading algorithm of mobile computing to achieve the maximum saving energy based on combinatorial optimization method [9]. Jiang et al. discussed the tradeo_ between energy optimization applications running in mobile devices [10]. In [11], Wang et al. proposed an energy-efficient and deadline-aware task offloading strategy based on the channel constraint, with the goal of minimizing the energy consumption of mobile devices while satisfying the deadline constraints of mobile cloud workflows. They employed an adaptive inertia weight-based particle swarm optimization to solve the optimization problem.

To minimize the latency of all devices under limited communication and computation resource constraints, Ren et al. designed a multi-user video compression offloading. They studied and compared three models: local compression, edge cloud compression, and partial compression offloading. For the local compression model, a convex optimization problem was formulated to minimize the weighted-sum delay of all devices under the communication resource constraint. They considered that massive online monitoring data should be transmitted and analyzed by a central unit. For the edge cloud compression model, this work analyzed the task completion process by modeling a joint resource allocation problem with the constraints of both communication and computation resources. For the partial compression offloading model, they first devised a piecewise optimization problem and then derived an optimal data segmentation strategy in a piecewise structure. Finally, numerical results demonstrated that the partial compression offloading can more efficiently reduce end-to-end latency 6 in comparison with the two other models [28]. A centralized computational offloading model may be challenging to run when massive offloading information is received in real time. As errors during the data gathering step may produce inefficient results, the local mode is more reliable and accurate than centralized solutions. Therefore, in many cases, the results of distributed approaches are more robust than those of centralized solutions. Due to the computational complexity of the scenario and numerous data from independent MDs, computation offloading for multi-user and multi-MEC systems poses a great challenge in a centralized environment [29].

In addition, several studies have considered the caching problem in MEC, for example, caching content in small cell base stations [30, 31] or mmWave-cellular networks [32] have been proposed to enhance the quality of the experience and minimize delay. However, we rarely see research on both task caching and migration. The genetic algorithm is a method for solving both constrained and unconstrained optimization problems that is based on natural selection, the process that drives biological evolution. It has been widely used in scheduling optimization problems. For task migration problems, several strategies have been proposed based on GA, such as in [33] and [34]. Shi et al. proposed the mobility-aware computing offloading strategy of distributed mobile cloud called MAGA, and an integer encoding based adaptive genetic algorithm is implemented for offloading decisions [33]. Deng et al. considered the complex dependencies between service components and introduced a mobility model and a trade-off fault-tolerance mechanism for the offloading system, which provides robust offloading decisions for mobile services and effectively optimizes the time and energy consumption of these services [34]. However, neither of these two papers addressed the issue of edge caching in their offloading strategies, which is considered in our paper.

3   Problem Statement

For the goal of minimizing the total cost while satisfying user requirement, we first introduce a task topology model, then we discuss a caching algorithm based on the task model.

3.1   Task Topology

Two main task partitioning models are often seen in MEC: coarse-grained vs. fine-grained. Coarse-grained tasks assume that the whole service as an object, thus they do not divide it into several subtasks, and the entire task is considered when migrating it to the edge cloud. On the other hand, fine-grained task migration takes that the application contains multiple subtasks, and these subtasks have dependencies and execution sequence which can be then denoted as a directed acyclic graph (DAG). We argue that both topology models have their drawbacks when describing the real tasks in edge MEC scenario. The coarse-grained model cannot make full use of the advantage of the edge cloud. The fine-grained one over-simplifies the complex relationship between subtasks. Consequently, we introduce a new task topology model to address the aforementioned problems. Our offloading decision for the tasks of an application has to be made based on the following concern: the organization of subtasks that can be shown as a workflow with clear dependencies. Each subtask in the application can be either executed remotely (offloaded) to the edge cloud or locally on mobile devices. Due to the dependencies, once a subtask is offloaded, all of its following subtasks running on local device cannot start until the result is returned back to local side, though the local resources are free. This is the difference between previous independent offloading services and our new model. Before, this problem was understood as multiple services simultaneously executed or offloaded, locally or remotely.

Given that M mobile requests exist in the service range of a MEC system, we assume that there are N computation tasks. Different requests may contain the same task. To be more specific, we use the following notations to model the computing task.

Let $R_{m,n} = \{x_n, d_n, t_m\}$ denote that the request m containing task n, where x_n is the required computing resources, d_n denotes the required data size and t_m is the required completion time specified in request m. Assume that the edge node can keep the result of task n in the cache sized C_{edge}. We use $s_n = 1$ and $s_n = 0$ to denote the cases that task n is cached or not, respectively.

For each complex task n, we use $n = \{n_1, n_2, \ldots, n_v\}$ to represent the subtasks after fine-grained partitioning. According to our topology model, we have shown an example in Fig. 1. In graph $G_n = (V_n, E_n)$, the set of subtasks are denoted as $V_n = \{n_1, n_2, \ldots, n_v\}$ and the dependencies between subtasks are denoted as the set of directed edges E_n. To be more specific in dependency definition, let e_{ij}^n be the data transfer information from the subtask i to the subtask j. Subtask j can be started only if the predecessor subtask i has been completed and the data transmission has finished.

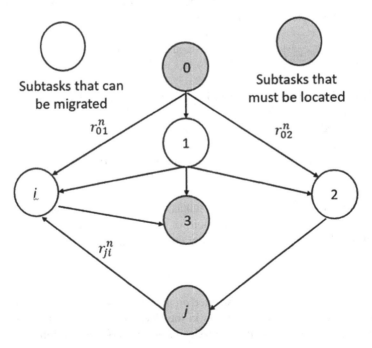

Fig. 1. Task topology: white nodes are migratable tasks; gray nodes are local tasks

As shown in Fig. 1, there are two type of subtasks, i.e., the one that must be executed locally and the one that can be migrated to the cloud. We use V_L to denote the set of subtasks running locally, such as subtask 0, subtask u, and subtask v. On the other hand, subtask 1, subtask 2, and subtask m belong to the group V_M that can be migrated, but none of these subtasks must be executed remotely. Our proposed evolutionary schema will make the decision on migration according to many factors. The dependencies between subtasks are denoted by using a binary variable $r_{ij}^n \in \{0, 1\}$ where $r_{ij}^n = 1$ indicates that the subtask i is a predecessor of the subtask j, otherwise $r_{ij}^n = 1$. It is important to notice that having subtask i as the predecessor of the subtask j does not mean $e_{i,j}^n$ must be greater than 0.

3.2   Time and Energy Consumption

The objective of the task offloading optimization based on task caching is to minimize the cost of migration, while meet the task completion time requirement. Before offloading, the algorithm must consider the time and energy consumption on mobile devices and the edge cloud. Thus, we first create a task energy model and a completion time model to describe the aforementioned factors.

We use $n_i \in V_L$ to denote the situation where the subtask i of the task n is executed on the mobile device. Regarding task completion time t_i^n, we assume that it is either a constant value C_i^n or relevant to the task size w_i^n and the CPU capacity of the mobile device CPU_l. The memory and I/O intensive tasks belong to the first type while CPU intensive ones are in the second group. Then the execution time t_i^n of the subtask i of the task n can be expressed as follows:

$$t_i^n = \begin{cases} C_i^n & \text{Constant Execution Time} \\ w_i^n / CPU_l & \text{Otherwise} \end{cases} \tag{1}$$

Similarly, the subtask i of the task n executed on the edge cloud may have a constant completion time $d_i^n = C_i^n$ or d_i^n is determined by the task size w_i^n and the CPU capacity of the edge cloud CPU_e. We denote it as follows:

$$d_i^n = \begin{cases} C_i^n & \text{Constant Execution Time} \\ w_i^n / CPU_e & \text{Otherwise} \end{cases} \tag{2}$$

The mobile device is working if the subtask i of the task n is being executed on it. In this case, the local energy consumption for execution g_i^n is determined by its execution time t_i^n and the energy consumption coefficient α_i^n:

$$g_i^n = t_i^n \alpha_i^n \tag{3}$$

If the subtask i of the task n is executed on the edge cloud, the mobile device is in a sleep state, and the energy consumption in the sleep state of the mobile device is p_l. Thus, the local energy consumption for sleep state h_i^n is defined as follows:

$$h_i^n = d_i^n p_l \tag{3}$$

Given $r_{i,j}^n = 1$, we know that the subtask i is a predecessor of the subtask j. When both subtasks i and j are executed locally, no data transmission overhead occurs on the internet, and it is same for the case where both subtasks running on edge cloud. In both cases, we have $t_{ij}^n = 0$ and $g_{ij}^n = 0$ for the aforementioned situations. If the locations where subtasks i and j are executed locally are executed are different (one is on the edge cloud and the other is on the device), data transmission delay t_{ij}^n is be calculated by Eq. (4), which depends on the result data amount e_{ij}^n and the transmission rate B_{ij}^n.

$$t_{ij}^n = e_{ij}^n / B_{ij}^n \tag{4}$$

Besides, the energy consumption g_{ij}^n for transmitting the result data is shown as follows:

$$g_{ij}^n = t_{ij}^n \alpha_{ij}^n \tag{5}$$

where α_{ij}^n is the energy consumption coefficient.

The ultimate goal of offloading schema is to reduce the energy consumption of devices using edge caching and fine-grained task migration. Meanwhile, our schema will try to meet the task delay time requirement. If subtask i of the task n is executed on the edge cloud, we define $D_i^n = 1$. The transmission time t_n^x of the task n depends on the total data size s_i^n transferred between the device and the edge cloud and the execution decision D_i^n of the subtasks, which is calculated as the following:

$$t_n^x = \sum_{i=1}^{v} D_i^n \left(s_i^n / B_{ij}^n \right) \tag{6}$$

The execution time T_n^x of the subtask i of the task n is related to the execution location and it can be calculated according to the following equation:

$$T_i^n = (1 - D_i^n)t_i^n + D_i^n d_i^n \tag{7}$$

The start time of subtask i in task n is calculated based on the completion time of its predecessors and the result data transmission delay between them. The following equation defines it:

$$S_i^n = \max_{j \in V_n} r_{ij}^n (F_j^n + |D_i^n - D_j^n| t_{ij}^n) \tag{8}$$

Then, the time when the subtask i is completed can be calculated from S_i^n and T_i^n as follows:

$$F_i^n = S_j^n + T_j^n \tag{9}$$

We use $c_n \in \{0, 1\}$ to denote whether task n is cached on the edge node or not. The completion time of task n is the time when the last subtask is completed plus the data transmission time of task n. The execution time of task n is presented in the following equation:

$$T_n = c_n F_j^n + (1 - c_n)(F_j^n + t_n^x) \tag{10}$$

The execution energy consumption of the subtask i is related to the execution location D_i^n, and it is presented as follows:

$$X_i^n = (1 - D_i^n)g_i^n + D_i^n h_i^n \tag{11}$$

Therefore, the energy consumption of the mobile device when the entire task n is executed is shown as follows:

$$E_n = (1 - c_n)t_n^x \alpha_i^n + \sum_{i=1}^{v} X_i^n + \sum_{i,j \in V_n} |D_i^n - D_j^n|g_{ij}^n \tag{12}$$

According to the aforementioned analysis, the mathematical model of energy optimization under the task completion time constraints is presented as follows:

$$\begin{aligned} \min : &\sum_{i=1}^{m} E_i \\ s.t. : &\sum_{k=1}^{K} c_k d_k \le C_{edge} \\ &F_i^n \le t_m \end{aligned} \tag{13}$$

4 Evolutionary Approach and Simulations

In this paper, we design a genetic algorithm to finish the optimization task for minimizing energy consumption. The basic components of genetic algorithm contain: a fitness function for optimization, a population of chromosomes, selection of which chromosomes will reproduce, crossover to produce.

The fitness value is the measurement of adaptability of the natural population to the environment. The fitness function is used to evaluate the performance of the individual. In this paper, we define the fitness function using the total energy consumption of mobile devices, which is shown as follows:

$$1/\sum_{i=1}^{m} E_i \tag{14}$$

In the initialization phase, the population size is set to be 100, the crossover probability is 0.8, the mutation probability is 0.2, The algorithm stops when the population is iteratively evolved up to 500 times, or the most adaptive chromosome individual in the continuous five generations of population does not vary more than 1%.

In the selection phase, the probability of occurrence of each individual in the offspring is calculated according to the fitness value of the individual. The crossover operation exchange genes of two parents to produce new individuals, and their excellent quality is retained in the new population with certain probabilities. The mutation operation replaces certain gene values in the chromosome coding string with other gene values according to the mutation probability, thereby forming a new individual, which is a supplementary method for generating new individuals, and enhances the local search ability of the genetic algorithm. Table 1 shows some parameter settings.

Table 1. Simulation parameters.

Parameter	Value
CPU_l	1000 MIPS
CPU_e	8000 MIPS
B_{ij}^n	100 Mbps
α_i^n	0.4
α_{ij}^n	0.02
p_l	0.005

The simulation was implemented using C++. The values of user number m and task type N were 10 and 3, respectively. Each user submitted one task at each time. The maximum cache capacity of the edge cloud is set to be 2 GB, and the total size of data transferred by all subtasks is generated randomly. In order to observe computational efficiency, we report that the running time was around 5 s in a Linux System running on a computer of 8 GB memory and Intel Core i7 CPU. In order to analyze the impact of the task cache on task execution performance, we present the task completion time and energy consumption with and without a cache. The results can be found in Fig. 2 and Fig. 3.

It can be seen that the task execution time remains same when the number of iterations increases. The main optimization goal, energy consumption, reduces significantly as more generations are produced in GA. The results converge after 150 iterations. The caching strategy has shown its impact on task execution time and energy consumption since it significantly reduces the time and energy consumption required

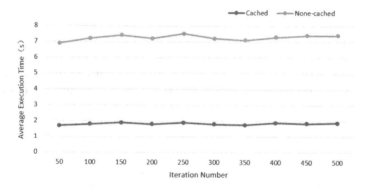

Fig. 2. Evolution of average task execution time: cached vs. none-cached

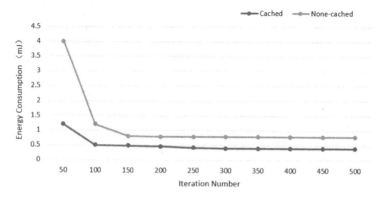

Fig. 3. Energy consumption: cached vs. none-cached

for task data transmission. As compare to other strategies where all tasks being executed in the edge cloud or mobile devices, our schema can make offloading decision more precisely and efficiently.

5   Conclusions

In this work, we design a fine-grained task topology model to describe the realist tasks in edge computing. An evolutionary task offloading schema is then developed to optimize the migration strategy on the edge cloud. As a result, our schema is able to minimize the aforementioned objective function while satisfying the resource and completion time constraints. Our simulation results have proved the effectiveness of our schema. In future work, we will consider more network environment parameters and predict the mobile task execution and data transmission more precisely.

References

1. Peng, K., Lin, R., Huang, B., Zou, H., Yang, F.: Link importance evaluation of data center network based on maximum flow. J. Internet Technol. **18**(1), 23–31 (2017)
2. Quan, W., Liu, Y., Zhang, H., Yu, S.: Enhancing crowd collaborations for software defined vehicular networks. IEEE Commun. Mag. **55**(8), 80–86 (2017)
3. Qi, L., Dou, W., Zhou, Y., Yu, J., Hu, C.: A context-aware service evaluation approach over big data for cloud applications. IEEE Trans. Cloud Comput. **1**, 1 (2015)
4. Li, W., Xia, Y., Zhou, M., Sun, X., Zhu, Q.: Fluctuation-aware and predictive workflow scheduling in cost-effective Infrastructure-as-a-Service clouds. IEEE Access (2018)
5. Xu, X., Zhao, X., Ruan, F., et al.: Data placement for privacy-aware applications over big data in hybrid clouds. Secur. Commun. Netw. **2017**, 1–15 (2017)
6. Qi, L., Xu, X., Zhang, X., et al.: Structural balance theory-based e-commerce recommendation over big rating data. IEEE Trans. Big Data (2016)
7. Peng, K., Zou, H., Lin, R., Yang, F.: Small business-oriented index construction of cloud data. In: Xiang, Y., Stojmenovic, I., Apduhan, B.O., Wang, G., Nakano, K., Zomaya, A. (eds.) ICA3PP 2012. LNCS, vol. 7440, pp. 156–165. Springer, Heidelberg (2012). https://doi.org/10.1007/978-3-642-33065-0_17
8. Wang, T., Bhuiyan, M.Z.A., Wang, G., Rahman, M.A., Wu, J., Cao, J.: Big data reduction for a smart citys critical infrastructural health monitoring. IEEE Commun. Mag. **56**(3), 128–133 (2018)
9. Xiang, H., Xu, X., Zheng, H., et al.: An adaptive cloudlet placement method for mobile applications over GPS big data. In: Proceedings of the Global Communications Conference (GLOBECOM, 2016), pp. 1–6. IEEE (2016)
10. Zhou, H., Leung, V.C.M., Zhu, C., Xu, S., Fan, J.: Predicting temporal social contact patterns for data forwarding in opportunistic mobile networks. IEEE Trans. Veh. Technol. **66**(11), 10372–10383 (2017)
11. Peng, K., Leung, V.C.M., Huang, Q.: Clustering approach based on mini batch Kmeans for intrusion detection system over big data. IEEE Access **6**, 11897–11906 (2018)
12. Zhang, K., et al.: Energy-efficient offloading for mobile edge computing in 5G heterogeneous networks. IEEE Access **4**(c), 5896–5907 (2016)
13. Zhao, P., Tian, H., Qin, C., Nie, G.: Energy-saving offloading by jointly allocating radio and computational resources for mobile edge computing. IEEE Access **5**, 11255–11268 (2017)
14. Zhang, J., et al.: Energy-latency trade-off for energy-aware offloading in mobile edge computing networks. IEEE Internet Things J. **4662**(c), 1–13 (2017)
15. Hao, Y., Chen, M., Hu, L., Hossain, M.S., Ghoneim, A.: Energy efficient task caching and offloading for mobile edge computing. IEEE Access **6**(March), 11365–11373 (2018)
16. Zhang, G., Zhang, W., Cao, Y., Li, D., Wang, L.: Energy-delay tradeoff for dynamic offloading in mobile-edge computing system with energy harvesting devices. IEEE Trans. Ind. Inform. **3203**(c), 1 (2018)
17. You, C., Huang, K., Chae, H., Kim, B.H.: Energy-efficient resource allocation for mobile-edge computation offloading. IEEE Trans. Wirel. Commun. **16**(3), 1397–1411 (2017)
18. Li, S., Zhang, Z., Zhang, P., Qin, X., Tao, Y., Liu, L.: Energy-aware mobile edge computation offloading for IoT over heterogenous networks. IEEE Access **7**, 1 (2019)
19. Fan, W., Liu, Y., Tang, B., Wu, F., Wang, Z.: Computation offloading based on cooperations of mobile edge computing-enabled base stations. IEEE Access **6**(X), 22622–22633 (2017)
20. Guo, F., Zhang, H., Ji, H., Li, X., Leung, V.C.: An efficient computation offloading management scheme in the densely deployed small cell networks with mobile edge computing. IEEE/ACM Trans. Netw. 1–14 (2018)

21. Dai, Y., Xu, D., Maharjan, S., Zhang, Y.: Joint computation offloading and user association in multi-task mobile edge computing. IEEE Trans. Veh. Technol. **9545**(c), 1–13 (2018)

22. Tran, T.X., Pompili, D.: Joint task offloading and resource allocation for multi-server mobile-edge computing networks. IEEE Access **5**, 3302–3312 (2017)

23. Dinh, T.Q., Tang, J., La, Q.D., Quek, T.Q.: Offloading in mobile edge computing: task allocation and computational frequency scaling. IEEE Trans. Commun. **65**(8), 3571–3584 (2017)

24. Chen, M., Hao, Y.: Task offloading for mobile edge computing in software defined ultra-dense network. IEEE J. Sel. Areas Commun. **36**(3), 587–597 (2018)

25. Ugwuanyi, E.E., Ghosh, S., Iqbal, M., Dagiuklas, T.: Reliable resource provisioning using bankers' deadlock avoidance algorithm in MEC for industrial IoT. IEEE Access **6**, 43327–43335 (2018)

26. Huang, L., Feng, X., Zhang, L., Qian, L., Wu, Y.: Multi-server multi-user multi-task computation offloading for mobile edge computing networks. Sensors **19**(6), 1446 (2019)

27. Li, K.: Computation offloading strategy optimization with multiple heterogeneous servers in mobile edge computing. IEEE Trans. Sustain. Comput. **XX**, 1 (2019)

28. Ren, J., Yu, G., Cai, Y., He, Y.: Latency optimization for resource allocation in mobile-edge computation offloading. IEEE Trans. Wirel. Commun. **17**(8), 5506–5519 (2018)

29. Han, Z., Gu, Y., Saad, W.: Matching Theory for Wireless Networks. Springer, Heidelberg (2017). https://doi.org/10.1007/978-3-319-56252-0

30. Bastug, E.; Bennis, M.; Kountouris, M. Cache-enabled small cell networks: modeling and tradeoffs. In: Proceedings of the 2014 11th International Symposium on Wireless Communications Systems (ISWCS), Barcelona, Spain, 26–29 August 2014

31. Blasco, P., Gunduz, D.: Learning-based optimization of cache content in a small cell base station. In: Proceedings of the 2014 IEEE International Conference on Communications (ICC), Sydney, Australia, 10–14 July 2014, pp. 1897–1903 (2014)

32. Giatsoglou, N., Ntontin, K., Kartsakli, E., Antonopoulos, A., Verikoukis, C.V.: D2D-aware device caching in MmWave-cellular networks. IEEE J. Sel. Area. Commun. **35**, 2025–2037 (2017)

33. Shi, Y., Chen, S., Xu, X.: MAGA: a mobility-aware computation offloading decision for distributed mobile cloud computing. IEEE Internet Things J. **5**, 164–174 (2018)

34. Deng, S., Huang, L., Taheri, J., Zomaya, A.Y.: Computation offloading for service workflow in mobile cloud computing. IEEE Trans. Parallel Distrib. Syst. **26**, 3317–3329 (2015)

Data Leakage Prevention System
for Smart Grid

Chengzhi Jiang[1] and Song Deng[2(✉)]

[1] Nanjing Institute of Technology, Nanjing, China
`jiangchengzhi_epri@163.com`
[2] Nanjing University of Posts and Telecommunications, Nanjing, China
`dengsong@njupt.edu.cn`

Abstract. With the large-scale application of advanced information and communication technologies such as wireless communication and Internet of Things in the smart grid, the threat of viruses, Trojans and hackers from the Internet is becoming more and more serious. Compared with the traditional power grid, the more complex access environment, flexible access methods and a large number of access terminals in smart grid bring new challenges to data security protection. Existing data encryption and access control schemes are difficult to meet the actual needs of data leakage prevention in all aspects of smart grid. This paper proposes a smart grid data leakage prevention system architecture based on label and strategy, focusing on the design and implementation of data leakage prevention system for smart grid from the perspective of unified data management platform, terminal and network data leakage prevention. The system design architecture and scheme proposed in this paper can help solve the data security protection of smart grid data from transmission to storage, and has important practical reference value.

Keywords: Data leakage prevention · Data label · Policy expression · Smart grid

1 Introduction

With the construction of strong smart grid [13], the use of a large number of intelligent collection and intelligent terminal equipment, and the wide use of 3G/WIFI and other wireless communication technologies, the number of ways in which sensitive data can be compromised and leaked increases. Sensitive data protection is the basis of safe and stable operation of business systems in smart grid generation, transmission, transformation, distribution and utilization. At the same time, with the construction of the three data centers of China State Grid Corporation, the data of various business systems are centralized for storage increasingly, and the reliable storage and protection of sensitive data become

Supported by the National Natural Science Foundation of China (No. 51977113, 51507084).

more and more important. Sensitive data of each business system of smart power grid needs to be controlled in the whole life cycle to prevent leakage of sensitive data of each business system in smart power grid and provide guarantee for the safe and stable operation of strong smart grid [7].

At the same time, state grid corporation of China is building a comprehensive unstructured data center (unstructured data mainly includes documents, pictures, voice and video data) to support the management and utilization requirements of unstructured data for the whole SG-ERP business. The whole unstructured data runs through all links of generation, transmission, transformation, distribution, utilization and dispatch, and almost exists in all business applications of power grid. Therefore, the controllable, auditable and leak-free of the whole unstructured data content is crucial to the construction of SG-ERP of state grid corporation of China. Due to the lack of comprehensive preventive measures, there are still a large number of leakage risks in the storage, transmission and use of sensitive unstructured data, mainly as follows: (1) Failure to store sensitive unstructured data encrypted can easily lead to leakage of sensitive unstructured data in the process of transmission and use; (2) Failure to implement corresponding security management measures for offline sensitive unstructured data can easily lead to leakage of sensitive unstructured data offline; (3) Unstructured data cannot be effectively monitored without auditing offline content such as browsing, printing and duplication of unstructured data; The protection against leakage of unstructured data needs to be strengthened.

With the implementation of SG-ERP informationization and its further development, more and more business application systems (safety production, marketing management, material management, etc.) will widely use mobile intelligent terminal access and power information intranet for real-time and non-real-time data communication and data exchange. At the same time, with the construction of a strong smart grid featuring "informationization, digitalization, automation and interaction", there is an increasing demand for interaction between various kinds of smart grid service information systems and the network (GRPS/CDMA/3G, etc.). As a result, there will be more business needs to use mobile communication technology, which put forward higher requirements for the establishment of a strong information security protection system. However, as an open mobile intelligent terminal operating platform, how to ensure that confidential data in mobile intelligent terminal will not be leaked in the whole life cycle of generation, transmission, storage and destruction has become an urgent need and need to be considered in the process of company information construction.

The remainder of this paper is organized as follows. Section 2 discusses the related works. Section 3 focuses design and implementation of data leakage prevention system for smart grid from architecture, unified management platform, data leakage prevention for terminal and network. Finally, conclusions are given in Sect. 4.

2   Related Works

Li et al. [11] investigated privacy leakage under privacy control in online social network, investigate the effectiveness of privacy control mechanisms against privacy leakage from the perspective of information flow. Guevara et al. [8] proposed a novel algorithm to detect anomalous user behavior in computer sessions, the activities classified as possible anomalies are double-checked by applying Markov chains. Cai et al. [3] proposed a framework that can effectively prevent information leakage in mobile messaging system, realized the end-to-end communication encryption and prevents the communication information from being intercepted by the third party. Prakash et al. [15] proposed a personalized anonymization approach, which preserves the privacy while the sensitive data is published. Katz et al. [10] proposed a new context based model (CoBAn), which can deal with accidental and intentional data leakage via an organizations monitored channels of communication. Alneyadi et al. [2] clearly defined DLPS and classified the active research directions in the field, and conducted a comprehensive survey of the current DLPS mechanism. Peneti et al. [14] proposed an algorithm for data leakage prevention with time stamp. Documents with complete confidential or non-confidential content are 100% detected by this method. Lu et al. [12] proposed a Collaborative graph-based mechanism for Distributed big data Leakage Detection (CoDLD), which can transfer the problem of data detection into graph matching problem by converting documents into weighted graphs. Hauer et al. [9] proposed a concept for establishing DLP and ILP within the scope of IS. Establish certain IS measures to reduce the risk of technology-based data breaches. Zhu et al. [17] proposed an effective data loss prevention framework, analyzes the data protection requirements in IC foundries, and combines current DLP (data leakage prevention) methods to protect IC field sensitive data security. Fan et al. [6] proposed a file distribution model designed to prevent data leakage. The model can choose the file distribution plan with the least overlap between the set of user files obtained, so that the source of the leak can be easily identified. Alneyadi et al. [1] proposed a statistical data leakage prevention (DLP) model used statistical data analysis to detect confidential data semantics and classify data according to semantics. Trieu et al. [16] classified document sensitivity in real time through semantic and content analysis, and proposed a method to classify the sensitivity of a document for data leakage prevention. Canbay et al. [4] proposed a cascaded Data Leakage Prevention (DLP) system for Turkish language, solve data leakage by detecting modified attacks on sensitive words.

3   Design and Implementation of Data Leakage Prevention System for Smart Grid

3.1   Architecture

At present, data leakage prevention mainly has two kinds of architectures, one is a data leakage prevention system widely used in China using traditional encryption and decryption methods; the other is a data leakage prevention system [5] which adopts data label and policy expression used by some foreign manufacturers. (1) Data leakage prevention system based on transparent encryption and decryption. This architecture uses file filtering driver to protect sensitive data with access control and security policies, as shown in Fig. 1.

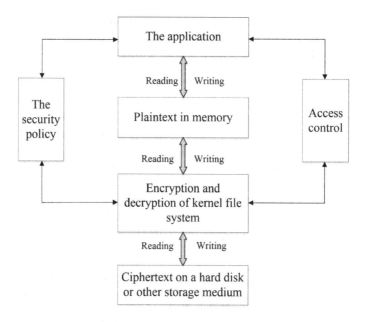

Fig. 1. Data leakage prevention system based on transparent encryption and decryption.

Under this architecture, users can use the application file to encrypt and decrypt the file system through the kernel file system. To complete, users use the sensitive data files as usual and normal operation of these files. Sensitive data files are processed by the kernel driver and file system, and the files stored on the disk are encrypted files. The user's access to sensitive data on the disk is handled by the access control module. Different users have different roles and permissions and can only access sensitive data permitted by their permissions. The security policy specifies the encryption policy used by the file filtering driver, including the encryption algorithm and the key; the security policy also specifies the operations allowed after the user reads the decrypted sensitive data file from the memory, such as copy, edit, and send permissions, so as to ensure that the use of sensitive data can also be protected. Under this architecture, since the driver belongs to the kernel program and is protected by the operating system, the security and execution efficiency of the sensitive data protection is high, and since the driver works at the bottom of the system, it is not necessary for the user to change the habit of using it and also can complete the transparent encryption and decryption of sensitive data. At the same time, the architecture is a low-level development technology that is difficult to implement and error-prone, and the data leakage prevention technology using encryption also has the risk of decryption failure. (2) Data leakage prevention system based on marking and strategy technology. This system uses sensitive data tagging, different tags with different data anti-leakage strategies, and protection against sensitive data by developing comprehensive and flexible tags and policies. The architecture based on label and policy is shown in Fig. 2.

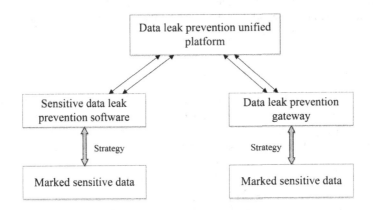

Fig. 2. Data leakage prevention system based on label and policy.

The data leakage prevention scheme under the architecture is composed of a data leakage prevention management platform, sensitive data leakage prevention software and a leak prevention gateway. The data leakage prevention unified management platform completes the policy management and sensitivity to data leakage prevention. Data classification, sensitive data tag management, alarm management, and log auditing; data leakage prevention software can be directly installed on servers, various types of intelligent mobile terminals or various internal and external network terminal devices, and protects the marked sensitive data according to policies. The data leakage prevention gateway is used to collect data transmitted in the network in real time, analyze the collected network data, discover the marked sensitive data from it, and implement blocking according to the strategy. This data leakage prevention system based on tagging and policy technology can implement different anti-leakage policies for different levels of sensitive data, which is more flexible than the transparent encryption and decryption system, and can be marked to the data center, network and terminal. All aspects of the implementation of sensitive data protection, and because the system uses data markers to identify and monitor sensitive data, can prevent data loss caused by decryption failure, and has higher reliability than the first architecture. We also tend to adopt the first architecture in the company's data leakage prevention design.

3.2   Data Leakage Prevention Unified Management Platform

In the above data leakage prevention system based on label and policy technology, the data leakage prevention unified management platform mainly provides management functions, and is responsible for the creation of sensitive data label in the unified management system, the classification of sensitive data, the setting of sensitive data protection strategies, and permissions and log management, etc. The labels and policies set in the unified management platform will be delivered and synchronized to the data leakage prevention software on the terminal, and the log information returned by the data leakage prevention software on the terminal will be collected and analyzed.

3.3   Data Leakage Prevention for Terminal

The data leak-proof software on the terminal data leakage receives the marking and protection strategy information issued by the unified management platform. Its sensitive data protection will mainly include marking, sensitive data discovery, sensitive data blocking, transparent encryption and decryption of sensitive data and destruction of sensitive data. The marking of sensitive data on the terminal is completed by the file creator and stored in the embedded database on PCs and terminal devices. When the client uses sensitive data, it generates its Hash value in real time, and judges whether the data operated by the user is sensitive to sensitive data by matching the tag in the database. On the basis of sensitive data discovery, the policy table is used to identify the user's operation behavior on sensitive data, and the corresponding blocking measures are performed according to the corresponding policy parameters in the policy table; on the other hand, it completes sensitive data by character coverage method for those sensitive data that are not allowed to be saved.

The process of protecting terminal data from leakage is shown in Fig. 3. Firstly, the data leak-proof software receives the strategy issued by the unified management platform, and marks the sensitive data manually by the document creator on the terminal. When users operate sensitive data on the terminal, they match the markers by generating Hash to identify whether or not. If it is not sensitive data, the protection process is terminated, if it is sensitive data, its use is monitored, the operation violating the policy is blocked, and if the network transmits sensitive data, it needs to be encrypted.

Data leak prevention on the terminal mainly combines marking, strategy, various blocking measures and transparent encryption and decryption technology to implement protection. The strategy is issued by the unified data leak prevention management platform. The leak prevention software on the terminal polls the management platform for the latest strategy in the online state.

3.4   Data Leakage Prevention for Network

Network data leakage prevention is mainly completed through the leakage prevention gateway, including network data collection, network data analysis, and

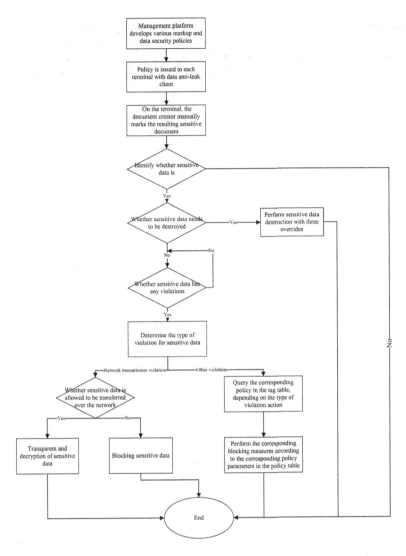

Fig. 3. The flow of data leakage prevention for terminal.

sensitive data discovery and blocking of sensitive data. Network data collection is connected to the network by means of mirror image, and network traffic is collected through open source packet capture tools such as Libpcap or Tcpdump. Through protocol analysis and packet analysis, the MAC address, usage mode, destination and corresponding data mark of the sender of sensitive data in the collected network data are obtained. Sensitive data discovery: the sensitive data stored in the network can be found through data marking and combined with the marking of sensitive data, and the specific location of sensitive data storage (IP address, sensitive data storage path, etc.) can be returned. Sensitive data blocking the transmission of unencrypted marked sensitive data on the network. The leakage prevention and design process of network data are shown in Fig. 4, mainly including network data collection, analysis and discovery. The leakage prevention gateway collects network data through the mirror port to analyze the network data set and find its storage location.

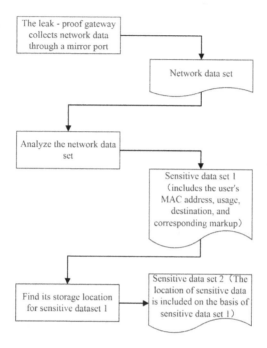

Fig. 4. The flow of data leakage prevention for network.

4   Conclusions

To better solve the continuous development of information and intelligence in smart grid, various types of business data are likely to cause leakage in terminal interaction, transmission and storage. Based on the analysis of the research status of data leakage protection at home and abroad, combined with the actual needs of informationization, intelligence and interactive development for smart grid, this paper introduces the design and implementation of data leakage prevention system for smart grid from the architecture, unified management platform, data leakage prevention for terminal and network.

References

1. Alneyadi, S., Sithirasenan, E., Muthukkumarasamy, V.: Detecting data semantic: a data leakage prevention approach. In: 2015 IEEE Trustcom/BigDataSE/ISPA, vol. 1, pp. 910–917. IEEE (2015)

2. Alneyadi, S., Sithirasenan, E., Muthukkumarasamy, V.: A survey on data leakage prevention systems. J. Netw. Comput. Appl. **62**, 137–152 (2016)
3. Cai, Y., Wu, F.: Data security framework for electric company mobile apps to prevent information leakage. Proc. Comput. Sci. **139**, 280–286 (2018)
4. Canbay, Y., Yazici, H., Sagiroglu, S.: A Turkish language based data leakage prevention system. In: 2017 5th International Symposium on Digital Forensic and Security (ISDFS), pp. 1–6. IEEE (2017)
5. Deng, S., Yue, D., Zhou, A., Fu, X., Yang, L., Xue, Y.: Distributed content filtering algorithm based on data label and policy expression in active distribution networks. Neurocomputing **270**, 159–169 (2017)
6. Fan, Y., Rongwei, Y., Lina, W., Xiaoyan, M.: A distribution model for data leakage prevention. In: Proceedings 2013 International Conference on Mechatronic Sciences, Electric Engineering and Computer (MEC), pp. 2617–2620. IEEE (2013)
7. Fang, X., Misra, S., Xue, G., Yang, D.: Smart grid—the new and improved power grid: a survey. IEEE Commun. Surv. Tut. **14**(4), 944–980 (2011)
8. Guevara, C., Santos, M., Lopez, V.: Data leakage detection algorithm based on task sequences and probabilities. Knowl.-Based Syst. **120**, 236–246 (2017)
9. Hauer, B.: Data and information leakage prevention within the scope of information security. IEEE Access **3**, 2554–2565 (2015)
10. Katz, G., Elovici, Y., Shapira, B.: CoBAn: a context based model for data leakage prevention. Inf. Sci. **262**, 137–158 (2014)
11. Li, Y., Li, Y., Yan, Q., Deng, R.H.: Privacy leakage analysis in online social networks. Comput. Sec. **49**, 239–254 (2015)
12. Lu, Y., Huang, X., Li, D., Zhang, Y.: Collaborative graph-based mechanism for distributed big data leakage prevention. In: 2018 IEEE Global Communications Conference (GLOBECOM), pp. 1–7. IEEE (2018)
13. Moslehi, K., Kumar, R., et al.: A reliability perspective of the smart grid. IEEE Trans. Smart Grid **1**(1), 57–64 (2010)
14. Peneti, S., Rani, B.P.: Data leakage prevention system with time stamp. In: 2016 International Conference on Information Communication and Embedded Systems (ICICES), pp. 1–4. IEEE (2016)
15. Prakash, M., Singaravel, G.: An approach for prevention of privacy breach and information leakage in sensitive data mining. Comput. Elect. Eng. **45**, 134–140 (2015)
16. Trieu, L.Q., Tran, T.N., Tran, M.K., Tran, M.T.: Document sensitivity classification for data leakage prevention with twitter-based document embedding and query expansion. In: 2017 13th International Conference on Computational Intelligence and Security (CIS), pp. 537–542. IEEE (2017)
17. Zhu, S., Guo, E., Lu, M., Yue, A.: An efficient data leakage prevention framework for semiconductor industry. In: 2016 IEEE International Conference on Industrial Engineering and Engineering Management (IEEM), pp. 1866–1869. IEEE (2016)

Artificial Intelligence/Machine Learning Security

Optimizing the Efficiency of Machine Learning Techniques

Anwar Ullah[1], Muhammad Zubair Asghar[1], Anam Habib[1],
Saiqa Aleem[2], Fazal Masud Kundi[1], and Asad Masood Khattak[2(✉)]

[1] Institute of Computing and Information Technology, Gomal University,
Dera Ismail Khan, Pakistan
anwarullah151@gmail.com, anamhabib19@gmail.com,
fmkundi@gmail.com, zubair@gu.edu.pk
[2] College of Technological Innovation, Zayed University, Abu Dhabi, UAE
{Saiqa.Aleem, Asad.Khattak}@zu.ac.ae

Abstract. The prediction of judicial decisions based on historical datasets in the legal domain is a challenging task. To answer the question about how the court will render a decision in a particular case has remained an important issue. Prior studies conducted on the prediction of judicial case decisions have datasets with limited size by experimenting less efficient set of predictors variables applied to different machine learning classifiers. In this work, we investigate and apply more efficient sets of predictors variables with a machine learning classifier over a large size legal dataset for court judgment prediction. Experimental results are encouraging and depict that incorporation of feature selection technique has significantly improved the performance of predictive classifier.

Keywords: Judicial case decisions · Machine learning · Random forest · Feature selection · Statistical test

1 Introduction

Machine learning is an emerging scientific study of algorithms and statistical models and is the part of Artificial Intelligence that makes the system capable of learning automatically and to improve from experience using from and test data [1]. Machine learning has diverse applications such as disease prediction [2], stock trend prediction [3], judicial decision prediction [4] and others [5].

Like others domains, applying machine learning techniques in the legal domain has received considerable attention from researchers for developing practical applications that could assist judicial experts in predicting judicial case decisions efficiently [6].

The existing studies [4, 7–9] on judicial case decision prediction in legal documents have several limitations such as:

(i) Limited availability of reliable dataset in the legal domain, (ii) poor selection of predictors variables for judicial case prediction, and (iii) less focus on predicting multiple classes of judicial case decisions, which proceeds in performance degradation of machine learning classifiers. The work performed by Katz et al. [9] on judicial case predictions aimed at predicting lower court decisions using machine learning classifier,

© Springer Nature Singapore Pte Ltd. 2020
Y. Tian et al. (Eds.): ICBDS 2019, CCIS 1210, pp. 553–567, 2020.
https://doi.org/10.1007/978-981-15-7530-3_42

namely decision tree. The major limitations of the work include the limited size of the dataset predicting only three classes of judicial case decisions and low performance of the classifier due to poor selection of predictors variables.

To overcome the aforementioned issues, we proposed advancement in the baseline work accomplished by Katz et al. [9] by making following contributions:

(i) Extending the benchmark dataset in the legal domain, the acquired dataset contains four centuries of high quality expertly coded data concerning each case decided by the supreme court between the terms of 1791 and 2017. The dataset contains as many as two hundred and forty variables. Many of these variables are categorical, taking multiple possible values, and these variables form the basis of both our feature and target variables. (ii) Extending the prediction classes for judicial case decisions from 3 to 12 such as affirmed, reversed, stay/petition/motion granted, vacated, no disposition etc. [10], and (iii) applying proper statistical tests such as chi-square [11] which calculates normal distribution variation considering that feature instance is unrelated to the value of class & Principal Component Analysis that perform conversion of data at individual node to a new space while calculating the optimal split on that node. Furthermore, PCA is applied to perform dimensionality reduction [4]. Lastly, Principal Component Analysis is applied for efficient selection of predictor variables for gaining improved performance w.r.t efficient prediction of judicial case decisions by the machine learning classifier, namely Random forest.

1.1   Problem Statement

The sentiment analysis in legal documents is a challenging task, aiming at the prediction of judicial decisions based on historical datasets in the legal domain.

Finding an answer to a question that how will the judiciary decision in particular circumstances of case, has remained an important subject matter in law reviews, newspapers, journals, magazines and television talk shows. Previously few studies are conducted on the prediction of judicial decisions, using datasets with limited size by experimenting less efficient set of predictors variables applied on different machine learning classifiers [9, 12]. Therefore, it is required to investigate and apply more efficient sets of predictors variables with a machine learning classifier on a large size legal dataset for court judgment prediction.

1.2   Research Questions

The following research questions will be addressed: RQ.1: How to apply the machine learning technique (Random forest) for the efficient prediction of supreme court decisions? RQ.2: What are the predictors (variables) which are significant for the case judgment prediction in supreme court decisions?

1.3   Significance of the Study

To perform prediction of supreme court decisions using machine learning techniques applied on legal documents(datasets), we have preferred a baseline work performed by Katz et al. [9] and our proposed study has significant benefits on the following grounds.

(i). Selection of revised predictor variables by applying different statistical techniques such as chi-square test and principle component analysis(PCA) for efficient prediction of supreme court decisions, (ii). Applying machine learning classifier namely, Random forest for judgment prediction, (iii). Judgment prediction in term of 12 decision classes, and (iv). The efficiency of the proposed work is

Performance evaluation for the proposed technique as compared with other machine learning classifiers and baseline studies.

2   Related Work

This section presents a review of associated studies based on sentiment analysis on legal documents.

Any kind of legal instruction is mainly recorded in natural, however relatively in a certain language. This unstructured legal big data needs to be processed using some natural language processing techniques include machine learning techniques specifically supervised machine learning techniques [7], and deep learning based techniques [13]. In the field of supervised machine learning techniques variant studies have been conducted. For instance, Katz et al. [6] proposed a generalized model for the prediction of U.S Supreme Court case decisions. The proposed technique is based on Decision Tree model. The dataset contains case decisions from year 1953 to 2013, taken from U.S Supreme Court database. The system attained an accuracy of 69.7% for the court's whole confirm/reverse judgments, while individual justice's system attains 70.9% of the votes. However, more efficient results can be achieved, if size of legal dataset is increased, and by selecting more efficient predictors variables, which can enhance the prediction accuracy of multiple machine learning techniques. Another related study in predicting attitudes of the US Supreme Court in out of sample perspective, conducted by Katz et al. [9] proposed a generalized supervised machine learning model. The proposed model is based on Random Forest algorithm together with particular feature engineering. The system achieves acceptable accuracy results at both case level decisions and justice vote level. The dataset contains decision cases from year (1816–2015) taken from U.S supreme court database. Likewise, Katz et al. [6] work, this study also has a drawback of limited dataset size and lack of efficient predictors. Another relevant work, Sivakumar [12] investigates a comparable analysis of different ML algorithms to predict future case decisions of U.S Supreme Court. Different supervised ML techniques are tested and good results are attained. The dataset contains 567 cases decisions of a single judge. Experiments are conducted on very small legal dataset. Work can be improved by experimenting other ML techniques on larger legal dataset, which should contain the judgment decisions of different judges. Following the subject of predicting the relevant court rulings, Liu and Chen [4] proposed approach is based on text mining methods for feature extraction from previous cases and supervised machine learning classifier SVM is used to predict judgments consequently from historic criminal cases. Proposed studies could precisely forecast a ruling class attained hit rate accuracy of 80.62% and 77.23% for the top 7 & 9 articles. Similar to the prior work of [6, 9, 12] it has very limited dataset used for the experiment conduction with only criminal cases are considered. Datasets can be extended by adding a variety of cases and other information retrieval models like BM25 and LDA can be applied on large datasets to check the efficiency of the proposed model. In another related work within the field of supervised machine learning, Martin et al. [14] conduct a comparative study specially to compare the combined case predictive accuracy of the whole group of human legal experts with the outcomes of their statistical forecasting model, namely Classification Tree, which predicts the case outcome, grounded on information retrieve from the historical supreme decisions. Tree Model was applied on 628 cases' decisions, which are taken from the natural court available at Washington University website. Overall Statistical model outperformed Legal experts. Although, for attaining more efficient outcomes, the work can be enhanced by increasing the size of the legal dataset as well as model can be trained on more reliable dataset. The work of Aletras et al. [8] proposed a supervised machine learning technique to forecast judicial judgments, i.e. whether there is negligence or non-negligence with respect to an explicit Article of the agreement of the ECtHR judgments. The dataset contains Cases, which were retrieved from the publically available electronic database of the HUDOC ECHR. The SVM model predicts the promising results with a 79% accuracy on average. Dataset is limited to cases which contain only article 3,6 and 8. Despite more proficient results can be attained by applying the other popular ML methods on larger datasets which contains variety of cases. To predict what will be the case decision and estimate the date of judgments of cases decided by French Supreme Court, Sulea et al. [15] proposed a novel method by using Machine learning model, namely SVM. The model was trained on bag of words with bigram features. The results are evaluated by applying 10-fold cross-validation. The prediction is limited, as it works at word-level and there is need to extend it to the sentence-level by considering those sentence which is most effective in predicting the ruling. Some related studies focusing on predicting the decisions of supreme court cases.

From the context of deep learning, research scientist has conducted different studies for the prediction of judicial case decisions. For example, the Attention-based neural network model was proposed by Luo et al. [13], which can predict the charge and extract the appropriate article for a given case. The proposed system is based on SVM and neural network (NN) models with a combination of different mechanisms like Stochastic gradient descent, POS tagging, and Bi-GRU. Satisfactory results are achieved. However, the model can't handle multiple defendant cases, so it can be enhanced to handle such cases for further improvements. In other work, Landthaler et al. [16] proposed a novel scheme for text searching in Legal documents to find the exact and semantically related matches. The proposed system is based on Mikolovs word2vec model for word Embeddings. Experiments are performed on two datasets acquired from European Union Data Protection Directive (EU-DPD) Act and 10 German rental contract templates available on the internet. The system attained overall good results but the major limitation is that if the dataset size increases, it results in slow performance, however proposed system can be enhanced by applying other major Natural language preprocessing steps in combinations with word Embeddings. Similarly, in another notable study reacted to legal documents, Ye et al. [17] proposed a system to perform automatic legal document generation and to create the court opinions from fact descriptions in legal cases. The proposed method is based on Seq 2Seq model, which consists of LSTM as an encoder and decoder. Dataset is taken from published legal documents in China's judgments online. The system attained satisfactory results. The scope of this study is limited in terms as it only focusses those cases, which have one defendant and one charge by excluding the complex cases with multiple defendant and multiple charges, as well as it only produces rationales (summary of the specific legal reasons given by the court in support of its decision) in court views by neglecting charge prediction. However, system efficiency can be improved by using more advanced technologies like reinforcement learning. Some of the recent studies also investigate the Judicial judgement cases such as Long et al. [18] explore the task of predicting judgments of civil cases. In this work, they proposed Legal Reading Comprehension (LRC) framework to manage complex and multiple text inputs. Furthermore, a novel AutoJudge neural model is introduced to integrate the law articles. Experimental results depict that proposed approach outperforms with an accuracy of 82.2% than all the baselines. In future, a more general and larger dataset will benefit the research on judgment prediction. Similarly, to predict criminal punishment in judicial system Das et al. [19] proposed a combinational system with Artificial Intelligence and Human. They exploit several machine learning algorithms like Naive Bayes, Support Vector Classifier, Decision Tree, Random Forest, Logistic Regression, Multiple Linear Regression, ANN Classifier, and ANN Regression to observe which algorithm perform best. The results demonstrate that with the assistance of the human, machine intelligence will become more accurate. However, more additional work is required to properly leverage the hybrid model framework.

3 Proposed Methodology

The proposed system is comprised of the following modules. (i) Data Acquisition and Preparation, (ii) Applying statistical tests for efficient predictors/variable selection, (iii) Prediction using machine learning based classification.

3.1 Data Acquisition and Preparation

The bench mark dataset in the legal domain is acquired to conduct experiments [20]. Judicial case decision prediction is a challenging task while applying machine learning techniques. To conduct the experiments for the judicial case decisions prediction, we have collected the dataset from the supreme court database [21], it is a valuable resource of judicial cases, receiving considerable attention of researchers.

3.2 Feature Engineering for Case Judgment Prediction

The Supreme Court legal cases decisions dataset contains a wide range of potential features and the majority of these variables are categorical variables, therefore we begin to prepare the legal dataset by choosing those variables which help in judicial case decision prediction from such features [9].

After the removal of noisy and irrelevant data by rescaling and subtracting from the given dataset as mentioned in section[(n)we prepared our legal supreme court case decisions dataset for the experimentation. Our legal dataset contains 31 categorical predictor variables.

Feature Selection. Feature Selection (FS) is one of the most important steps in any machine learning problem solving to eliminate the irrelevant features from the dataset by selecting the most efficient attributes, because, during the training phase, relevant features have a huge influence on the performance of model, yielding to higher accuracy. Whereas, irrelevant features negatively impact the model's performance. The Supreme Court legal cases decisions dataset contains a wide range of potential features and the majority of these variables are categorical variables, therefore we begin to prepare the legal dataset by choosing those variables which help in judicial case decision prediction from such features [9].

Feature Selection Techniques. There are several commonly used FS techniques for efficient feature selection from a given dataset, which results in dimensionality reduction, yielding improvement in the model's performance These are listed as follows: (i) Principal Component Analysis [22], (ii) Information Gain [23], (iii) Extra Tree Classifier [24], Recursive Feature Elimination [25] and (v) Chi-Square Test.

FS and Judicial Case Decision Prediction. As reported in the literature [14], the selection of efficient predictors (features) for judicial case decision prediction is a challenging task due to availability of large number of categorical variables. Therefore, to address this challenge we apply Chi-square test [11] for choosing optimal set of predictors variables, which could assist in efficient prediction of judicial (supreme court) case decisions.

Applying a Chi-Square Test for Efficient Selection of Features (Predictors/ Variables). The selection of Chi-Square test for feature selection in our work is motivated by the prior studies conducted in this context. Tehseen and Kumar (2017) [11] used Chi-Square test for feature selection and obtained improved results with respect to implementation of SVM classifier.

The mathematical model (Eq. 1) of the Chi-Square test is given as follows:

$$X^2 = \frac{(Observer\,frequency - Expected\,frequecy)^2}{Expected\,frequency} \tag{1}$$

Where observed frequency = no. of observations of class, expected frequency = no. of expected observation of class, if there was no relationship between the feature and the target, and x^2 is used for the best feature selection.

We have applied a Chi-Square test to select the desired number of features with best chi-scores. Those features which have high chi-score indicate, that feature has more association with target class. We have experimented Chi-square test by using sklearn library in python with the integration SelectKBest function in order to select the desired number a relevant feature which have high relationship with the multi class target variables.

Detail Analysis of Chi-Square Test: It is a mathematical test that performed the computation of expected distribution variation assuming feature instance independent from the class number. The metrics used for Chi-Square calculation are named as: false positives (f_{+ve}), true positives (t_{+ve}), false negatives (f_{-ve}), and true negatives (t_{-ve}), positive case probability (P_{+ve}), negative case probability (P_{-ve}) (Eq. 2).

$$
\begin{aligned}
Chi-square_{metric} &= t\left(t_{+ve}, (t_{+ve}+f_{+ve})P_{+ve}\right) + t\left(f_{-ve}, (f_{-ve}+t_{-ve})P_{+ve}\right) \\
&+ t\left(f_{+ve}, (t_{+ve}+f_{+ve})P_{-ve}\right) + t\left(t_{-ve}, (f_{-ve}+t_{;-ve})P_{-ve}\right)
\end{aligned}
\tag{2}
$$

while the description of "t" is represented in Eq. 1.

The chi-square test involved different steps: (i) hypothesis identification, (ii) investigation scheme designing, (iii) sample data analysis, and (iv) results in inference. The advantage of using chi-square test is that it chooses a fusion of discrete and continuous features.

3.3   Prediction Using Machine Learning Based Classification

The Random Forest classifier has shown promising prediction results in different domains, such as business, politics, stock trend prediction and others [1, 3]. Therefore, we choose to apply Random Forest Machine Learning Classifier with the optimal set of predictor variables, already selected in the previous phase (Sect. 3.2).

The mathematical formulation (see Eq. 3) of RF is given as under.

$$
D = \{(x_i, y_i)\}_{i=1}^{n}
\tag{3}
$$

The above equation represents as follows:

D represents the training data, where xi indicates input vector and yi are the outcomes associated with xi.

$$
h = \{h_1(x), h_2(x), h_3(x), \ldots\ldots\ldots\ldots\ldots h_k(x)\}
\tag{4}
$$

In Eq. 4, h is a set of predictions of kth classifiers (Decision Trees) which constructs the Random Forest.

$$
Prediction = Mode(h)
\tag{5}
$$

Where mode returns the highest voted target labels predicted by Random Forest in Eq. 5.

In order to perform the prediction via the trained random forest algorithm, it is necessary to pass the test features over the rules of each randomly generated trees. We will model 100(n) random decision trees to form the random forest. So each random forest will perform prediction of different targets(outcomes) for a similar test feature. After that each predicted target votes will be considered and calculated.

In order to further elaborate the working of the RF algorithm, we suppose that there are 100 random decision trees, predicting nearly 12 unique targets (outcomes), i.e. t1, t2, ... t12. The final prediction is based on the majority voting scheme, i.e. the target (t_i) with maximum votes is deemed the winner.

A random forest is an approach that uses ensemble method. In ensemble learning the aim is to link variant learned models results to generate an optimal model. Random forest is considered as a simple algorithm, but regardless of that it can generate up-to-date classification results.

A Random forest algorithm has the following pseudocode (Algorithm 1) to represent it's working.

Algorithm 1. Generic Working of Random Forest algorithm

Input: X=Train data, R=Overall Features, r=members of features, T=Amount of tress
Output: Input data bagged class tag
Begin
1. while a single tree in Forest T:
    i. Choose a bootstrap sample M with size N out of training data.
    ii. Build the tree Bt through iteratively repeating the different steps regarding tree individual node.
        a. Select randomly r from R
        b. Choose the optimal between f.
        c. Divide the node.
2. When the creation of T trees is performed, examples of Test data will be sent to individual tree and the allocation of class tag on the basis of majority votes will be executed
End

An overview of the working of Random forest Classifier for judicial case prediction is presented in Fig. 1.

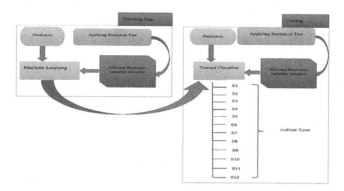

Fig. 1. Proposed system.

4   Results and Discussion

In this section, we discuss the results obtained from experiments performed in response to answering posed research questions.

4.1   Answer to RQ.1: How to Apply Machine Learning Techniques (Random Forest) for the Efficient Prediction of Supreme Court Decisions?

To answer RQ1 we applied RF classifier for efficient prediction of supreme court decisions, the detailed working mechanism of this experiment is presented in Sect. 3.3 (proposed methodology). To determine the optimized Random Forest Classifier, we have to tune its parameter values. The parameter values that give best performance of the proposed RF classifier, is presented in Table 1.

4.2   Answer to RQ.2: What Are the Predictors (Variables) Which Are Significant for the Case Judgment Prediction of Supreme Court Decisions?

To answer this research question, we perform two experiments: (i) Applying RF classifier for Case Judgment Prediction without Feature Selection, and (ii) Applying RF classifier for Case Judgment Prediction with Feature Selection. The detail of each experiment is presented in the following sections.

Applying RF Classifier for Case Judgment Prediction Without Feature Selection
The Random Forest is based on an ensemble method, which combines several machine learning techniques into one model to reduce variance and bias. We choose Random Forest because it performs better in prediction problems. After splitting the dataset into train and test modules with a ratio of 80%(train) and 20%(test), we applied the Supervised Machine Learning Algorithm, namely Random Forest classifier, to investigate the performance for judicial case decision prediction in the legal domain. The results obtained from the experiment (Table 2), depicts an accuracy of 64%, precision (73%), recall (85%), and F-score (76%), which are not satisfactory.

Therefore, it can be concluded that without feature selection, the results obtained from the implementation of RF, are not very satisfactory and it needs to be improvement by implementing some effective feature selection techniques.

Applying RF Classifier for Case Judgment Prediction with Feature Selection
Before applying the RF classifier for Case Judgment Prediction on the acquired dataset, we applied feature selection technique for selecting appropriate features from the acquired dataset. This assists in improving the performance of classifier in terms better prediction results. Firstly, we applied feature section, described as follows:

Feature Selection. The legal dataset of Supreme Court case decisions is the raw form contains noisy data, therefore feature set compilation becomes mandatory task to specify the relevant feature set. For this purpose, we rescale the data by removing null columns and by removing null values from the rows by applying using Pandas

Table 1. Parameter setting for random forest classifier.

Parameter name	Description
n_estimators = '100'	The number of trees in the forest
Criterion = 'gini'	The function to measure the quality of a split. Supported criteria are "gini" for the Gini impurity and "entropy" for the information gain. Note: this parameter is tree-specific
max_features = 'auto'	The number of features to consider when looking for the best split
max_depth = 'none'	The maximum depth of the tree. If None, then nodes are expanded until all leaves are pure or until all leaves contain less than min_samples_split samples
min_samples_split = '2'	The minimum number of samples required to split an internal node
min_samples_leaf = '1'	A split point at any depth will only be considered if it leaves at least min_samples_leaf training samples in each of the left and right branches. This may have the effect of smoothing the model, especially in regression
min_weight_fraction_leaf = '0'	The minimum weighted fraction of the sum total of weights (of all the input samples) required to be at a leaf node. Samples have equal weight when sample_weight is not provided
max_leaf_nodes = 'none'	Grow trees with max_leaf_nodes in best-first fashion. Best nodes are defined as relative reduction in impurity. If None then unlimited number of leaf nodes
min_impurity_decrease = '0'	A node will be split if this split induces a decrease of the impurity greater than or equal to this value
Bootstrap = 'true'	Whether bootstrap samples are used when building trees. If False, the whole datset is used to build each tree
oob_score = 'true'	Whether to use out-of-bag samples to estimate the generalization accuracy
n_jobs = 'none'	The number of jobs to run in parallel for both fits and predict. None means 1 unless in a joblib.parallel_backend context. -1 means using all processors. See Glossary for more details.
random_state = 'none'	random_state is the random number generator; If None, the random number generator is the RandomState instance used by np.random
Verbose = '0'	Controls the verbosity when fitting and predicting
warm_start = 'false'	When set to True, reuse the solution of the previous call to fit and add more estimators to the ensemble, otherwise, just fit a whole new forest
class_weight = 'none'	Weights associated with classes in the form {class_label: weight}. If not given, all classes are supposed to have weight one

Table 2. Performance evaluation results for applying RF classifiers on the raw dataset (without feature selection).

Labels	Precision	Recall	F1-Score
1	0.73	0.14	0.24
2	0.68	0.85	0.76
3	0.56	0.56	0.56
4	0.35	0.13	0.19
5	0.39	0.20	0.27
6	0.35	0.13	0.19
7	0.33	0.07	0.12
8	0.45	0.34	0.39
9	0.54	0.33	0.41
10	0.44	0.21	0.28
11	0.30	0.05	0.08
12	0.51	0.26	0.35
Accuracy	64%		

technique [9]. After noise removal, we applied Chi-Square test for the efficient selection of predictors (variables) from the legal dataset [9]. After applying the Chi-Square Test by using pandas library with the integration of sklearn feature selection method named SelectKBest function, the Chi-Square relevancy score is assigned to the predictors (variables) dependent upon feature relationship and dependency with the multiple target classes.

After assigning the Chi-Square relevancy score to predictor variables, Chi-Square-based relevancy scores are arranged in the descending order with the higher relevancy score predictors (variables) appearing at the top. For this purpose, we applied the SelectKBest function (available in SKlearn library) on the features dataset and selected the top 8 predictor variables for judicial case judgment prediction, which are most efficient and depend upon the multiple target classes.

Applying RF Classifier. After predicting the top 8 most efficient predictor variables from 31 variables by applying the Chi-Square test, we again apply the RF classifier in order to investigate whether the 8 efficient predictors(variables) have efficient relationships and dependency with the multiple target classes? and whether the model's performance and accuracy can be increased? For this purpose, we split the data into train and test sets in the ratio of 80%(train) and 20%(test). After this, we have applied the Supervised Machine Learning Algorithm, namely Random Forest, to investigate its performance and Accuracy when applying it on the dataset with top 8 selected feature-set. The Experimental results are evaluated in terms of accuracy, precision, recall, and F-score. The experimental results presented in Table 3 show that the RF achieved surprisingly improvement results with high accuracy of (98%), precision (98%), recall (98%) and F-score (99%), depicting that. these 8 predictor variables have significant relation with the multiple target classes.

Table 3. Applying RF classifier on the selected feature set for cases judgment prediction.

Labels	Precision	Recall	F1-Score
1	1.00	0.95	0.97
2	0.99	0.99	0.99
3	0.99	0.99	0.99
4	0.98	1.00	0.98
5	0.98	0.99	0.99
6	0.99	0.98	0.99
7	1.00	0.98	0.99
8	0.99	0.98	0.98
9	0.97	0.98	0.98
10	0.92	0.98	0.95
11	0.98	0.98	0.98
12	0.98	0.98	0.98

4.3   Answer to RQ.3: How to Investigate the Performance of the Proposed Model W.R.T Baseline Studies?

To answer to RQ3, we conducted experiments and compared the performance of the proposed RF classifier with other machine learning algorithms and baseline methods. Detail of these experiments is given as under.

Comparison with Other Machine Learning Classifiers. In order to investigate the performance of other well-known machine learning classifiers as compared to the proposed model, we conducted a series of experiments by applying other ML classifiers such as Logistic Regression, Multinomial NB and K-nearest neighbor.

Applying the Logistic Regression Model. We applied Logistic Regression model on improved feature selection dataset and its performance is measured in term of precision (0.33), Recall (0.50), F1-Score (0.36), and accuracy (50%), which is very low as compared to our proposed model having accuracy of 98%, 0.99% precision 0.99% recall and 0.99%, F-Score. Experimental results are reported in Table 4.

Table 4. Comparison with other machine learning classifiers.

Classifier	Precision	Recall	F1-Score	Accuracy
Logistic regression	0.33	0.50	0.36	50%
Multinomial NB	0.43	0.25	0.29	25%
K-nearest neighbour	0.60	0.63	0.60	63%
Random forest (proposed) with improved feature selection	0.99	0.99	0.99	98%

Applying the Multinomial NB Model. We applied Multinomial NB model on improved feature selection dataset and its performance is measured in terms of precision (0.43%), recall (0.25%), F-Score (0.29%) and accuracy (25%), which is very low as compared to our proposed model having accuracy of 98%, 0.99%, precision 0.99% recall and 0.99%. F-Score. Experimental results are reported in Table 4.

Applying K-nearest Neighbor. We applied K-nearest neighbor model on improved feature selection dataset and its performance is measured in terms of precision (0.60%), recall (0.63%), F-Score (0.60%) and accuracy (63%), which is very low as compared to our proposed model having accuracy of 98%, 0.99% precision 0.99% recall and 0.99% F-Score. Experimental results are reported in Table 4.

Summary. From above discussion, it is evident that the proposed *Random Forest classifier with* improved feature selection outperformed other machine learning algorithms (Logistic Regression, Multinomial NB, KNN) in legal domain applied.r.t different evaluation metrics, and achieved promising results in terms of improved accuracy (98%), precision (99%), recall (98%), and F-score (99%). Experimental results are reported in Table 4.

5   Conclusion and Future Work

The objective of this work is to perform the task of judicial case decision prediction using machine learning technique with feature selection. The proposed research study covers following modules: i) Data Acquisition and Preparation, (ii) Applying statistical tests for efficient predictors/variable selection, and (iii) Prediction using machine learning based classification.

The proposed study aims to predict the judicial case decisions into 12 decisions classes by using revised predictor variables (DecisionType, Term, Petitioner, Respondent, and caseOrigin, etc.) that are selected by implementing a statistical technique namely chi-square test, and lastly, Random Forest classifier is used to classify the judicial case decisions into 12 decisions classes. The obtained results reveal that the performance of the proposed method is efficient in terms of accuracy (98%), precision (0.99), recall (0.99), and f1-score (0.99) with respect to the comparing baseline studies. The proposed architecture predicts the decisions related to supreme case database.

The proposed study has the following limitations: (i). insufficient usage of predictor variables limited to certain domain, (ii) techniques applied for the selection of predictor variables is limited to chi-square, (iii) the proposed framework applied limited machine learning techniques for judicial case predictions, (iv) dataset size is small related to only supreme court database that needs to be increased for obtaining more robust results, (v) experiments are conducted using traditional machine learning approaches, however other approaches like deep learning models can be applied for the performance upgradation of the proposed framework.

Future guidelines are as follows: (i). exploiting advanced predictor variables regarding multiple domains, (ii). enhancing the approaches used for predictor variable selection, (iii). extending the work by using further machine learning models on an increased legal dataset that contain enhanced decision classes, and (iv) applying deep learning models for efficient prediction of judicial case decisions.

Acknowledgement. This research work was supported by Zayed University Provost Research Fellowship Award R18114.

References

1. Singh, A., Thakur, N., Sharma, A.: A review of supervised machine learning algorithms. In: Hoda, M.N. (ed.) 3rd International Conference on Computing for Sustainable Global Development (INDIACom) 2016, pp. 1310–1315. IEEE (2016)
2. Kourou, K., Exarchos, T.P., Exarchos, K.P., Karamouzis, M.V., Fotiadis, D.I.: Machine learning applications in cancer prognosis and prediction. Comput. Struct. Biotechnol. J. **13**, 8–17 (2015)
3. Asghar, M.Z., Rahman, F., Kundi, F.M., Ahmad, S.: Development of stock market trend prediction system using multiple regression. Comput. Math. Organ. Theory **25**(3), 271–301 (2019). https://doi.org/10.1007/s10588-019-09292-7
4. Liu, Y.H., Chen, Y.L.: A two-phase sentiment analysis approach for judgement prediction. J. Inf. Sci. **44**(5), 504–607 (2018)
5. Habib, A., Akbar, S., Asghar, M.Z., Khattak, A.M., Ali, R., Batool, U.: Rumor detection in business reviews using supervised machine learning. In: 2018 5th International Conference on Behavioral, Economic, and Socio-Cultural Computing (BESC), pp. 233–237. IEEE, Taiwan (2018)
6. Katz, D.M., Bommarito, I.I., Michael, J., Blackman, J.: Predicting the behavior of the supreme court of the united states: A general approach. arXiv preprint arXiv:1407.6333 (2014)
7. Medvedeva, M., Vols, M., Wieling, M.: Judicial decisions of the European court of human rights: looking into the crystal ball. In: Proceedings of the Conference on Empirical Legal Studies. Michigan (2018)
8. Aletras, N., Tsarapatsanis, D., Preoţiuc-Pietro, D., Lampos, V.: Predicting judicial decisions of the European court of human rights: a natural language processing perspective. PeerJ Comput. Sci. **2**, e93 (2016)
9. Katz, D.M., Bommarito II, M.J., Blackman, J.: A general approach for predicting the behavior of the Supreme Court of the United States. PLoS ONE **12**(4), e0174698 (2017)
10. The Supreme Court Database. http://scdb.wustl.edu/documentation.php?var=caseDispo sition,last. Accessed 24 Nov 2019
11. Thaseen, I.S., Kumar, C.A.: Intrusion detection model using fusion of chi-square feature selection and multi class SVM. J. King Saud Univ.-Comput. Inf. Sci. **29**(4), 462–472 (2017)
12. Sivakumar, S.: Predicting US Supreme Court Decision Making (2015). http://srisai85. github.io/courts/courts.html. Accessed 21 Oct 2019
13. Luo, B., Feng, Y., Xu, J., Zhang, X., Zhao, D.: Learning to predict charges for criminal cases with a legal basis. arXiv preprint arXiv:1707.09168 (2017)
14. Martin, A.D., Quinn, K.M., Ruger, T.W., Kim, P.T.: Competing approaches to predicting supreme court decision making. Perspect. Polit. **2**(4), 761–767 (2004)
15. Sulea, O.M., Zampieri, M., Vela, M., van Genabith, J.: Predicting the law area and decisions of French supreme court cases. arXiv preprint arXiv:1708.01681 (2017)
16. Landthaler, J., Waltl, B., Holl, P., Matthes, F.: Extending full text search for legal document collections using word embeddings. In: JURIX, pp. 73–82 (2016)

17. Ye, H., Jiang, X., Luo, Z., Chao, W.: Interpretable charge predictions for criminal cases: Learning to generate court views from fact descriptions. arXiv preprint arXiv:1802.08504 (2018)
18. Long, S., Tu, C., Liu, Z., Sun, M.: Automatic judgment prediction via legal reading comprehension. In: Sun, M., Huang, X., Ji, H., Liu, Z., Liu, Y. (eds.) CCL 2019. LNCS (LNAI), vol. 11856, pp. 558–572. Springer, Cham (2019). https://doi.org/10.1007/978-3-030-32381-3_45
19. Das, A.K., Ashrafi, A., Ahmmad, M.: Joint Cognition of Both Human and Machine for Predicting Criminal Punishment in Judicial System, pp. 36–40. IEEE (2019)
20. Spaeth, H.: The Supreme Court Database (2018). http://scdb.wustl.edu/index.php. Accessed 1 Nov 2019
21. Spaeth, H.: The Supreme Court Database. http://supremecourtdatabase.org/. Accessed 5 Nov 2019
22. Li, Y., Yan, C., Liu, W., Li, M.: A principle component analysis-based random forest with the potential nearest neighbor method for automobile insurance fraud identification. Appl. Soft Comput. **70**, 1000–1009 (2018)
23. Uğuz, H.: A two-stage feature selection method for text categorization by using information gain, principal component analysis and genetic algorithm. Knowl.-Based Syst. **24**(7), 1024–1032 (2011)
24. Brownlee, J.: https://machinelearningmastery.com/feature-selection-machine-learning-python/ (2016). Accessed 15 Sept 2019
25. Lahoti, S.: Packt. https://hub.packtpub.com/4-ways-implement-feature-selection-python-machine-learning. Accessed 19 Sept 2019

Community Detection Based on DeepWalk in Large Scale Networks

Yunfang Chen[1], Li Wang[1], Dehao Qi[1], and Wei Zhang[1,2(✉)]

[1] Nanjing University of Posts and Telecommunications, Nanjing 210023, Jiangsu, China
zhangw@njupt.edu.cn
[2] Jiangsu Key Laboratory of Big Data Security and Intelligent Processing, Nanjing University of Posts and Telecommunications, Nanjing 210023, Jiangsu, China

Abstract. The large scale and complex structure of real networks bring enormous challenges to traditional community detection methods. In order to detect community structure in large scale networks more accurately and efficiently, we propose a community detection algorithm based on network embedding representation method. This algorithm first selects the DeepWalk network embedding method to represent the vertices in the network graph as low-dimensional vector representations which reflect the topology in the network. Then this algorithm treats each vertex as a sample, and each dimension of the vector representation as a feature. Finally, the sample data are input into the variational Gaussian mixture clustering model to obtain the clusters in the network. Experimental results on the DBLP dataset show that the model method of this paper can more effectively discover the communities in large scale networks. Through further analysis of the excavated community structure, the organizational characteristics within the community are better revealed.

Keywords: DeepWalk · Community detection · Network representation learning · Variational Gaussian mixture clustering

1 Introduction

Many complex systems take the form of networks, such as social networks, biological networks, and information networks. With the increasing scale of network data, there are more and more vertices in complex network graphs, and the relationships between these vertices are more and more complicated. It is desirable to be able to identify a subset of the vertices in a network graph such that the connections of the vertices within the subset are more intensive than the subset with the rest of the graph. These subsets are called communities, and the method of partitioning subsets is called community detection. Community detection has been applied to a variety of fields, such as social network analysis, communication and traffic design, biological networks [1, 2, 3, 4].

In order to detect community structures on complex networks, researchers are constantly exploring and researching community detection methods of networks.

Y. Tian et al. (Eds.): ICBDS 2019, CCIS 1210, pp. 568–583, 2020.
https://doi.org/10.1007/978-981-15-7530-3_43

Existing community detection approaches can be broadly classified into two categories [5]: Topology-based and topic-based approaches. Topic-based approaches consider the text content attribute of the vertex in the network. On the other hand, topology-based community detection approaches consider the connection among the vertices in the network. Since the goal of our method is to detect communities that are formed into network topologies, we will review topology-based approach to community detection in this section.

The traditional topology-based community detection algorithms mainly include graph partitioning [6, 7], GN [8] algorithm, random walk algorithm [9], modularity-based algorithm [10] and so on. Graph partitioning partition the vertices in the graph into different subsets, and the number of edges between the subsets are guaranteed to be the least, such as the Kernighan–Lin (KL) algorithm [6] and the spectral bisection method based on Laplace matrix [7]. The K-L algorithm is based on greedy features and uses the principles of optimizing the edges within and between communities to partition complex networks into communities. However, this method is difficult to apply to actual application because the algorithm needs to know the size of the community in advance.

The spectral algorithm is to use the eigenvectors of the adjacency matrix or the Laplacian matrix to project the vertices into a new space and cluster them in a new space using traditional clustering methods (such as k-means). The drawback of this method is that the network can only be partitioned into two parts at a time, and multiple iterations of the partitioned sub-communities are required to finally partition the network into several sub-communities. The Girvan-Newman (GN) [11] algorithm is a hierarchical clustering algorithm based on edge betweenness partitioning. The algorithm continuously deletes the edge with the largest edge betweenness in the network, and then recalculates the edge betweenness of each edge in the network. This loop until all the edges in the network are deleted, and finally a hierarchical clustering tree is established. However, the algorithm requires repeated calculations and high complexity, which is not suitable for processing large-scale network.

The basic idea of the random walk [12] strategy method is that a "random walker" will always spend a long time in a community because the community structure is relatively close and highly connected. Therefore, starting from a specified vertex, a "random walker" will complete all the vertices within a community in a relatively short time. Therefore, we define some similarity between vertices to implement community detection. The method based on modularity improvement uses modularity as the objective function. Meanwhile, it takes the Simulate Anneal Arithmetic (SAA) as the local search method, which improves its accuracy. But due to the lack of prior knowledge, the algorithm has great limitations.

These traditional topology-based network representation in community detection usually directly uses the observed adjacency matrix, which may contain noise or redundant information. The embedding representation first aims to learn the dense and continuous representations of vertices in a low-dimensional space, so that the noise or redundant information can be reduced and the intrinsic structure information can be preserved [13]. As each vertex is represented by a vector containing its information of interest, many iterative or combinatorial problems in network analysis can be tackled by computing mapping functions, distance metrics or operations on the embedding vectors, and thus avoid high complexity. As the vertices are not coupling any more, it is convenient to apply main-stream parallel computing solutions for large-scale network analysis. DeepWalk [14] is a representative deep learning-based model for network embedding, which generalizes recent advancements in language modeling and unsupervised feature learning (or deep learning) from sequences of words to graphs. And it uses local information obtained from truncated random walks to learn latent representations by treating walks as the equivalent of sentences. As an online algorithm, DeepWalk is also scalable, which builds useful incremental results, and is trivially to parallelizable. These qualities make it suitable for a broad class of real-world applications such as network classification, and anomaly detection.

Therefore, we propose a topology-based community detection method which uses DeepWalk embedding representation. Firstly, considering the high-dimensional sparsity of the network, we use the network embedding method of DeepWalk to represent the vertices in the network graph as low-dimensional vectors. Then the machine learning clustering algorithm is used to further detect the community based on the low-dimensional vector representation. The DeepWalk algorithm takes the network graph as input and generates a series of short random walk sequences starting from each vertex. It learns the vector representation of vertices in a network graph by modeling a short random walk sequence. This process can be understood as embedding the topology in the network into a low-dimensional vector space. The low-dimensional vector representation of each vertex reflects the connection of the vertex in the network to some extent. Then, the vertex vector representation matrix of the entire network graph is input into the variational Bayesian Gaussian mixture model (VBGMM) to obtain vertices clustering results based on network topology.

Our primary contributions can be summarized as follows:

(1) Combine the method of DeepWalk network representation learning with the variational Bayesian Gaussian mixture model for community detection.
(2) Embed high-dimensional networks into low-dimensional vector spaces while maintaining relationships between vertices, which is imported for community detection.
(3) Partition the community without specifying the number of communities in advance.

2   Background

2.1   Community Detection

The community can be regarded as a special subgraph in the network graph, which is a deep feature common in complex networks. Community detection refers to the process of partitioning a network into several communities according to the specific relationship among vertices in a network graph [15, 16].

Considering the network graph $G(V, E)$. Assume the vertices' sets $C_1, \cdots C_k$ meet the following conditions:

$$C_1 \cup C_2 \cup \cdots \cup C_k = G$$

$$C_i \cap C_j = \emptyset, \forall i \neq j$$

$$Pr(V_{C_i}, V_{C_i}) > Pr(V_{C_i}, V_{C_i}), \forall i \neq j$$

Then, $C = \{C_1, \cdots C_k\}$ is a partition of network G. Each set C_i represents a community in the network. $Pr(V_{C_i}, V_{C_i})$ indicates the probability that two vertices inside C_i have edges. $Pr(V_{C_i}, V_{C_i})$ indicates the probability that there exist edges between C_i and C_j.

2.2 DeepWalk

DeepWalk is a representative deep learning-based model for network embedding. The model focuses on embedding each vertex in a network to a low-dimensional vector space. In fact, it uses a vector to represent a vertex in the network. Using DeepWalk algorithm, the process of representing vertices as vectors in networks can be divided into two parts (as Fig. 1): Firstly, generating sequences of vertices in networks graph by random walk; secondly, inputting sequence of vertices into skip-gram language model. Through continuous training of the skip-gram model, the vector representation matrix $\Phi \in \mathbb{R}^{|V| \times d}$ of each vertex in the network is finally obtained.

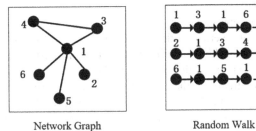
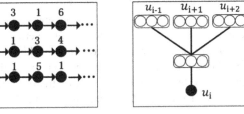

| Network Graph | Random Walk | Skip-Gram |

Fig. 1. DeepWalk model

2.3 Gaussian Mixture Model

After using DeepWalk to represent the vertices in the network as low-dimensional vectors, it is necessary to cluster the vertices. Variational Bayesian Gaussian mixture model (VBGMM) is selected as clustering algorithm in this paper. Since VBGMM is an extension of the basic Gaussian mixture model, this section introduces the principle of the Gaussian mixture model.

The Gaussian Mixture Model (GMM) is a classical clustering algorithm [17]. It uses a Gaussian distribution as a parametric model, assuming that the data obey a mixed Gaussian distribution and estimate the parameters using the Expectation Maximization (EM) algorithm.

With a random variable X, the expression of its mixed Gaussian model is:

$$p(x) = \sum_{i=1}^{K} \alpha_i p(x|\mu_i, \Sigma_i) \tag{1}$$

As can be seen from the above formula, the distribution consists of K "mixed components", each of which corresponds to a Gaussian distribution. α_i means "mixing coefficient", where $0 \leq \alpha_i \leq 1$ and $\sum_{i=1}^{K} \alpha_i = 1$. $p(x|\mu_i, \Sigma_i)$ is the distribution of the i-th Gaussian component, where μ_i and Σ_i are the parameters of the i-th Gaussian mixed component.

3 Proposed Algorithm

3.1 Algorithm Description

The algorithm in this paper is based on the network structure for community detection. Its input is a network graph $G(V,E)$, and the adjacency matrix $A \in \mathbb{R}^{|V| \times |V|}$ of the graph. Correspondingly, $V = \{v_1, v_2, \cdots, v_n\}$ represents the vertex set and $E = \{e_{ij}|i,j \in V, i \neq j\}$ refers to the edge set with m numbers. In this work, we only considered the undirected and unweighted network, which can be described by the adjacency matrix A. In addition, the input parameters include the embedding size d, the window size w, the random walk sequence length t, and the number of random walk sequences γ. The algorithm first uses a random walk to generate a series of vertex sequences in the network graph, and then inputs the vertex sequence into the skip-gram model for training to obtain the vector representation matrix $\Phi \in \mathbb{R}^{|V| \times d}$, where a row represents a vector representation of one vertex in the matrix, and the vector representation can reflect the structural relationship of the original vertex in the network graph. Considering the i-th column of Φ as x_i, Φ is treated as $D = \{x_1, x_2, \cdots, x_n\}$. Finally, the vertex vector representation matrix of the entire network graph is input into the variational Bayesian Gaussian mixture model to obtain the clustering result of the network graph. Here we consider each cluster as a community, and each vertex in the cluster is a community member. The overview of the proposed algorithm in this paper is illustrated in Fig. 2.

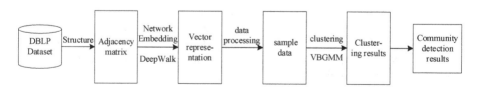

Fig. 2. The flowchart of proposed algorithm.

3.2 Vector Representation

DeepWalk algorithm consists of two main parts: a random walk generator and an update procedure. Firstly, the random walk generator randomly and uniformly selects network vertices, and then generates a fixed-length random walk sequence W_{v_i} with v_i as the root. For each vertex, the generator generates γ random walk sequence of length t. Usually, the length of the random walk sequence depends on the number of vertices or the size of the graph. If the number of vertices in the graph is relatively large, the length of the walk can be relatively long, so as to better address the relationship among vertices in the graph.

Line 3 in the Algorithm 1 specifies that each vertex needs to generate γ random walk sequences. In each loop of the process of generating a random walk sequence, the algorithm first shuffles all the vertices in the network graph G, and then traverses each vertex in the set V and generate a random walk sequence $|W_{v_i}| = t$ for each vertex v_i. Finally, the walk sequence W_{v_i}, the vertex representation matrix Φ, and the window size w are input into the Skip-Gram algorithm (Line 7).

Algorithm 1: Vector Representation Process of Vertex

Input: G(V, E), w, d, γ, t
Output: matrix of vertex representations $\Phi \in \mathbb{R}^{|V| \times d}$
1: Initialize Φ
2: Build a binary Tree T from V
3: for i=0 to γ do
4:   $O = \mathbf{shuffle}(V)$
5:   for each $v_i \in O$ do
6:     $W_{v_i} = \text{RandomWalk}(G, v_i, t)$
7:     $\mathbf{SkipGram}(\Phi, W_{v_i}, w)$
8:   end
9: end

The Skip-Gram model is actually divided into two steps. The first is to build the model, and the second is to obtain the vector representation of the vertex through the model. The modeling process of Skip-Gram is actually very similar to that of the self-encoder, i.e., constructing a neural network based on the training data. When the model is trained, we don't need to use this model to deal with new tasks, but rather the parameters we need to get in the training model, such as the weight matrix of the hidden layer - these weights are the vector of words we really need. In this paper, the weight matrix is the vector representation matrix of the vertices.

In line 3 of Algorithm 2, the loss function is defined as the conditional probability of the output vertex, usually in logarithmic form, i.e., $J(\Phi) = -\log Pr(u_k|\Phi(v_j))$. The next step is to derive the loss function. By this way, we get the update rule of the vector representation matrix: $\Phi = \Phi - \alpha \frac{\partial J}{\partial \Phi}$. From this update rule, we can see that the computational complexity is very high for a large corpus. In order to speed up the training process, the algorithm uses the Hierarchical Softmax method.

Hierarchical Softmax decomposes the conditional probability by assigning each vertex to the leaf vertex of the binary tree and encoding the vertex using the Huffman code. If the vertex appears relatively frequently, its path will be set to be shorter. Suppose the path from the root vertex b_0 to another vertex u_k is a sequence of tree vertices $(b_0, b_1, \cdots, b_{[log|V|]})$, where $b_{[log|V|]}$ indicates the vertex u_k, so there is:

$$Pr\left(u_k|\Phi\left(v_j\right)\right) = \prod_{l=1}^{[log|V|]} Pr\left(b_l|\Phi\left(v_j\right)\right) \tag{2}$$

$$Pr\left(b_l|\Phi\left(v_j\right)\right) = 1/\left(1 + e^{-\Phi\left(v_j\right)\cdot\Psi(b_l)}\right) \tag{3}$$

Where, $\Psi(b_l)$ is the latent representation of the parent vertex of b_l.

Algorithm 2: The updating process of Φ

Input: Φ, W_{v_i}, w
Output: the updated Φ
1: for each $v_j \in W_{v_i}$ do
2: for each $u_k \in W_{v_i}[j - w : j + w]$ do
3:    $J(\Phi) = -\log Pr\left(u_k|\Phi(v_j)\right)$
4:    $\Phi = \Phi - \alpha\frac{\partial J}{\partial\Phi}$
5: end
6: end

3.3   Vertex Clustering

The ultimate goal of this section is to cluster the vertices in the network. In the previous section, we have obtained the vector representation matrix Φ for the network. In the matrix Φ, we consider each vertex as a sample, and the vector representation of the vertex is treated as a sample feature. So Φ can be treated as a sample set $D = \{x_1, x_2, \cdots, x_n\}$, where each element x_i^T in set D is a column vector of dimension d, and $D \in \mathbb{R}^{|V|\times d}$.

In this section, we treat the variational Bayesian Gaussian mixture model (VBGMM) as a clustering model for sample data. The VBGMM that we used is based on the GMM (Sect. 2.3). The difference is that the VBGMM adopts the variational inference algorithm [18] to train the model parameters. The VBGMM model assumes that the sample generation process is given by a mixed Gaussian distribution: First, the corresponding Gaussian mixture component $p(x|\mu_i, \Sigma_i)$ is selected by the "mixing coefficient" $\alpha_1, \alpha_2, \cdots, \alpha_k$, where α_i is the probability that the i-th mixed component is selected; then, the sampling is performed according to the probability density function $p(x|\mu_i, \Sigma_i)$ of the selected mixed component, thereby generating corresponding sample data.

If the sample set $D = \{x_1, x_2, \cdots, x_n\}$ is generated by the above process, and the random variable $z_j \in \{1, 2, \cdots, k\}$ represents the Gaussian mixture component of samples generated by the set D. Here, the values of z_j are unknown. Obviously, the prior probability $P(z_j = i)$ of z_j corresponds to $\alpha_i (i = 1, 2, \cdots, k)$. According to Bayesian theorem, the posterior probability distribution of z_j is shown as:

$$p(z_j = i | x_j) = \frac{P(z_j = i) \cdot p(x_j | z_j = i)}{p(x_j)} = \frac{\alpha_i p(x_j | \mu_i, \Sigma_i)}{\sum_{l=1}^{K} \alpha_l p(x_j | \mu_l, \Sigma_l)} \tag{4}$$

$p(z_j = i | x_j)$ gives the posterior probability of the i-th Gaussian mixture component to generate x_j. In other words, in clustering, this equation indicates the probability that the sample belongs to the category z_j. For convenience of description, we abbreviate $p(z_j = i | x_j)$ into $\gamma_{ji} (i = 1, 2, 3, \cdots, k)$, where γ_{ji} denotes the probability of sample x_j in the i-th cluster. Usually, we choose the most probable mixture component as the final cluster result of sample data points.

After the Gaussian mixture distribution is known, the Gaussian mixture model partition the set D into k mixed components (clusters) $C = \{C_1, C_2, \cdots, C_k\}$, each mixed component (cluster) λ_j of the sample data x_j is determined as follows:

$$\lambda_j = \underset{i \in \{1, 2, \cdots, k\}}{\arg\max} \gamma_{ji} \tag{5}$$

In fact, the Gaussian mixture model used for clustering needs to determine a probability model (Gaussian distribution) in advance, and then initialize its parameters. By continuously iterating and updating the parameters, the clusters can be obtained. For this model, in order to determine the Gaussian distribution, the parameters we need to solve are $\{\alpha_i, \mu_i, \Sigma_i | 1 \leq i \leq k\}$. In this paper, we use a variational inference algorithm to estimate the parameters.

Gaussian mixture model based on variational inference algorithm includes two weight distribution prior methods in the acquisition of parameters: One is the finite mixing model of Dirichlet distribution, the other is the infinite mixing model of Dirichlet process [19]. In this experiment, we choose the latter method to estimate the parameters of the model. When the concentration parameter (weight_concentration_prior) is set small enough and the mixed component parameter is larger than the number of virtual mixed components, the result of the variational Bayesian Gaussian mixture model can make mixed weights approach 0. By this way, the model can automatically select the appropriate number of virtual components. The overall flow of the variational Bayesian Gaussian mixture clustering algorithm is as follow:

Algorithm 3: Gaussian mixture clustering

Input: sample data set $D = \{x_1, x_2, \cdots, x_n\}$;
    the maximum number of mixed components k_{max};
    concentration parameter weight_concentration_prior and other parameters
Output: cluster partition $C = \{C_1, C_2, \cdots, C_k\}$
1: Initializing the parameters $\{(\alpha_i, \mu_i, \Sigma_i) | 1 \leq i \leq k_{max}\}$
2: while the maximum number of iterations is not reached do
3:   for j=1: n do
4:      $\gamma_{ji} = p(z_j = i | x_j)(1 \leq i \leq k_{max})$
5:   end
6:   for i=1: k_{max} do
7:      Calculate the new μ_i', Σ_i' and α_i'
8:   end
9:   update $\{(\alpha_i, \mu_i, \Sigma_i) | 1 \leq i \leq k_{max}\}$ to $\{(\alpha_i', \mu_i', \Sigma_i') | 1 \leq i \leq k_{max}\}$
10: end
11: $C_i = \phi\{1 \leq i \leq k\}$
12: for j=1: n do
13:   Calculate λ_j for sample data point x_j
14:   $C_{\lambda_j} = C_{\lambda_j} \cup \{x_j\}$
15: end

Line 2 to line 10 are based on the Dirichlet process algorithm to infer the model parameters, and iteratively update. When the parameter estimation algorithm stop condition (the maximum number of iterations is reached) is satisfied, the cluster partition of the sample data points is determined according to the Gaussian mixture distribution. It should be noted that the parameter k_{max} of the model only indicates the maximum number of mixed components that may be used. In fact, the number of mixed components required by the model is often less than k_{max} in actual operation, and is depending on the specific quantity of sample data.

4 Experiments

This paper uses a subset of the DBLP literatures dataset covering four research areas: database (SIGMOD, ICDE, VLDB, EDBT, PODS, ICDT, DASFAA, SSDBM, CIKM), data mining (KDD, ICDM, SDM, PKDD, PAKDD), artificial intelligent (IJCAI, AAAI, NIPS, ICML, ECML, ACML, IJCNN, UAI, ECAI, COLT, ACL, KR) and computer vision (CVPR, ICCV, ECCV, ACCV, MM, ICPR, ICIP, ICME), which amount to 30422 articles. Considering each article as a vertex, 30422 articles constitute a network graph of 30422 vertices.

The experiment uses F-measure as a comprehensive evaluation metric, which is the harmonic mean of the precision and the recall. Calculated as follows:

$$F = \frac{(\alpha^2 + 1)P \times R}{\alpha^2(P + R)} \tag{6}$$

Where, P represents precision, which is the ratio of the number of related literatures retrieved to the total literatures retrieved. R is recall, which is the ratio of the number of related literatures retrieved to the related literatures in the literature library. When $\alpha = 1$, it becomes the most common F1-measure, $F1 = \frac{2P \times R}{P + R}$, which is used in our paper. Generally, the higher the F1-measure, the better the algorithm performance.

4.1 Algorithm Comparison

Because the DBLP dataset used in this paper has relatively many vertices, it is said that the vector has a large dimension and cannot display the Gaussian clustering effect intuitively. Therefore, this experiment extracts a small dataset from DBLP for vector representation and gives an example of community partitioning. There are 272 vertices in the dataset, which can be partitioned into two communities. In the experiment, we represent it as a two-dimensional vector space, and then cluster the sample sets by Gaussian mixture clustering model and variational Gaussian mixture model respectively. For comparison, in both of two models, we set the number k of the initial clusters to be 5. In Table 1, we present the cluster labels corresponding to the sample data in the two models.

Table 1. Cluster label.

model	cluster label
GMM	0 1 0 3 0 3 0 0 1 0 1 0 2 1 2 3 1 2 1 2 1 1 0 4 2 0 1 2 0 2 2 2 4 0 4 1 1 2 1 0 2 1 0 1 2 0 4 3 2 1 2 0 1 2 1 2 4 1 2 2 3 0 1 2 1 0 2 2 3 2 0 1 2 4 3 2 3 2 0 0 2 2 4 3 4 0 2 2 3 0 3 0 1 2 1 2 0 0 1 2 3 0 3 2 0 1 2 1 0 0 2 3 0 2 1 2 3 0 1 0 3 4 2 1 0 0 1 2 3 0 1 0 3 0 1 2 1 0 1 0 2 3 2 2 2 1 2 1 0 1 2 2 3 2 4 4 2 0 1 0 3 0 1 0 4 2 3 0 1 0 1 3 2 4 0 2 2 3 0 2 1 2 0 0 1 2 0 1 2 3 2 1 2 0 2 2 0 2 3 2 3 2 0 1 2 1 2 0 1 2 3 2 1 0 4 2 3 0 1 2 1 0 1 2 2 2 2 4 2 4 3 0 3 0 1 1 2 0 3 2 3 0 4 0 0 3 2 3 2 3 2 4 2 0 0 4 2 1 2 2 0 1 0 1 3 2 0 3 0 1 2
VBGMM	1 0 1 0 1 0 1 1 0 1 0 1 1 0 1 0 0 1 0 1 0 0 1 1 1 1 0 1 1 1 1 1 1 1 1 0 0 1 0 1 1 0 1 0 1 1 1 0 1 0 1 1 0 1 0 1 0 1 1 0 1 1 0 1 0 1 0 1 1 1 0 1 1 0 1 1 0 1 0 1 1 1 1 1 0 1 1 1 1 0 1 0 1 0 1 0 1 1 1 0 1 0 1 0 1 1 0 1 0 1 1 1 0 1 1 0 1 0 1 0 1 0 1 1 0 1 1 0 1 0 1 0 1 0 1 0 1 0 1 0 1 1 0 1 1 1 0 1 0 1 0 1 1 0 1 1 1 1 1 0 1 0 1 0 1 1 1 0 1 0 1 0 0 1 1 1 1 1 0 1 1 0 1 1 1 0 1 1 0 1 0 1 0 1 1 1 1 1 1 0 1 0 1 1 0 1 0 1 1 0 1 0 1 0 1 1 1 0 1 0 1 0 1 0 1 1 1 1 1 1 1 1 0 1 0 1 0 0 1 1 0 1 0 1 0 1 1 0 1 0 1 0 1 1 1 1 1 1 0 1 1 1 0 1 0 0 1 1 0 1 0 1

Figure 3 is a cluster figure based on the model prediction results in Table 1.

GMM

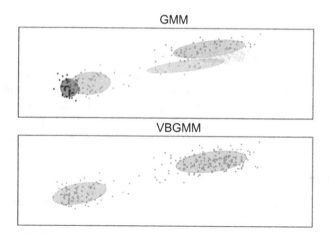

VBGMM

Fig. 3. The clustering figure of the sample data.

Table 1 shows the clusters' labels of the sample data using the two models respectively, and the clustering result of the sample data is shown in Fig. 3. It can be observed in the table and the figure that GMM partitions the sample data into five categories (0, 1, 2, 3, 4), while the VBGMM partitions five categories (0 and 1). The number of clusters of VBGMM is exactly equal to the real number of communities. Obviously, it can be seen that the GMM can only partition the samples based on the given parameter k, while the VBGMM is able to cluster according to the number of actual communities in the sample data. That is the advantage of choosing VBGMM model for clustering.

4.2 Parameters Analysis

The experiment in this section consists of two stages. First, our algorithm represents the vertices in the network as vectors. This stage mainly uses the DeepWalk network embedding algorithm. And there are four parameters involved, including the walk sequences length t, the walks γ per vertex, the dimension d of the vertex vectors representation space, and the size w of the window. The second stage, our algorithm clusters the vector representations of the vertices and then analyzes the community structure in the clustering results. In this stage, the variational Bayesian Gaussian mixture model is used. The parameters mainly include the cluster number k and the concentration parameter weight_concentration_prior.

Parameters during Network Embedding. In order to evaluate the impact of the above four parameters on the performance of the model, we adjust the parameters one by one. We fixed three parameters at a time and set different values of another parameter. By this way, we recorded the results of vertex vector representation. Then, clustering is performed, and the clustering effect is measured by the F1-measure.

In Fig. 4, we fix the walking length t, the dimension D of vertices vector representation, and the window size w, and change the number of walks to get F1-measure.

Then by changing the window size, F1 curve can be obtained. From this figure, we can see that the learning algorithm achieves the best clustering effect and gradually becomes stable when the number of walks γ reaches 60. Moreover, when the window size w is equivalent to 15, the F1-measure of clustering results is obviously larger than that in other window sizes. Therefore, in this paper's experiment, in order to achieve a more accurate community partitioning result, we set the window w to 15, and the number of vertex's walks γ to 60. In the experiment, we did not take a larger number of walks in view of the model runtime.

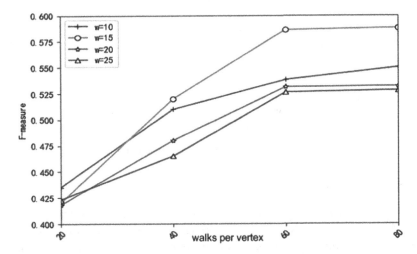

Fig. 4. The F1-measure by changing walks and window size.

In Fig. 5, we set different dimensions of vector representation and different length of the walk, and calculate the corresponding F1-measure. Obviously, the F1 curve is the highest when the walk length t is 60, and the curve is the lowest when the walk length is 20, which means that when the walk length is small, the vertex's walk sequence may not have traversed all the vertices associated with the starting vertex. Also, when the vertex vector representation dimension d is less than 128, the F1-measure is positively correlated with d. But when the dimension is greater than 128, the four F1 curves have a downward trend. Therefore, in this experiment, we set the walk sequence length to 60 and the dimension of vector representation to 128.

Parameters during Clustering. Considering the variational Bayesian Gaussian mixture model for clustering, the concentration parameter is mainly adjusted in this experiment. Because when the value of the concentration parameter is small enough, just need to set the number of clusters k > k_{real} (k_{real} is the real number of communities), and the model will automatically adjust the k to fit the actual number of clusters. In this experiment, we set the concentration parameter weight_concentration_ prior = 0.001.

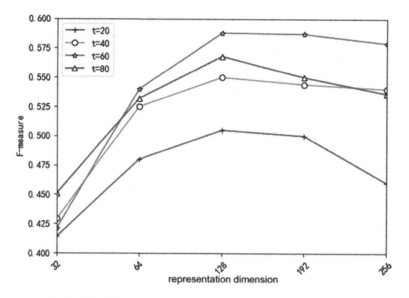

Fig. 5. The F1-measure by changing dimension and walk length.

4.3   Result Analysis

In Sect. 4.2, we have analyzed the effect of the main parameters on the experimental results of the model. In this section, the experiment is performed according to the above parameter settings. First, the vertices in the network are represented as low-dimensional vectors. Then the low-dimensional vectors of vertices are clustered to obtain the cluster label of each vertex in the network. In this result, we consider each cluster as a community. Finally, based on the clustering results, we partition the network into 11 communities. Figure 6 is the distribution of the number of vertices in each community.

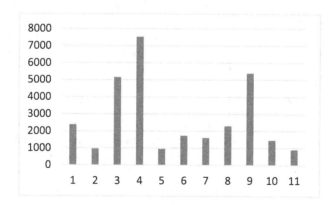

Fig. 6. Distribution of the number of vertices in the community.

Figure 7 is a two-dimensional space community figure drawn according to the distribution of vertices in the network.

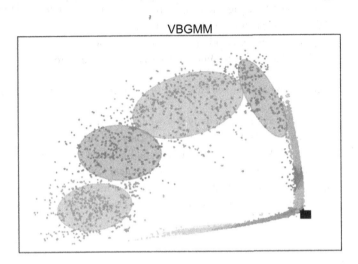

Fig. 7. The distribution of vertices in the network.

From Fig. 6, we can get the distribution of vertices in the entire network: Community 3, 4, and 9 have relatively many vertices and are called large communities. We suspect that these larger communities may be core communities. Among these communities, community 4 is the largest, with more than 7,000 vertices, accounting for 25% of the total number of vertices in the network. Community 2, 5, and 11 have the fewest number of vertices, and these communities are small communities. The size of the community 1, 6, 7, 8, 10 is relatively moderate.

The size of each community in Fig. 7 is clear. There are 11 colors in the figure, each of which represents a community. In Table 2, we list all 11 communities and the title of literature in each community.

In the Table 2, we analyze the internal characteristics of the community. One representative vertex (literature) title is selected from each community, and the category information of the community is known by analyzing the title theme. It can be seen from the table that community C1 mainly studies clustering algorithms; community C2 is mainly about image retrieval; community C3 is the study of classification algorithms; C4 is mainly about optimization algorithm; C5 mainly involves videos and images; the research content of community C6 includes feature selection, feature vector and other issues; community C7 mainly involves the performance and management of database; community C8 mainly involves the collection and analysis of web-based data; community C9 mainly involves knowledge system and reasoning system; community C10 mainly involves various query problems in the database field; community C11 mainly studies Bayesian networks, social networks etc.

Table 2. The title information of community vertex.

Community	Title of literature
C1	Document Clustering and Cluster Topic Extraction in Multilingual Corpora
C2	PBIR—Perception-Based Image Retrieval
C3	A parallel learning algorithm for text classification
C4	Optimal Algorithms for Finding User Access Sessions from Very Large Web Logs
C5	Recognizing Multitasked Activities from Video Using Stochastic Context-Free Grammar
C6	Feature Selection for Activity Recognition in Multi-Robot Domains
C7	Analyzing the Performance of Pattern Database Heuristics
C8	Mining the Web for Answers to Natural Language Questions
C9	UPML: A Framework for Knowledge System Reuse
C10	Query optimization in xml-based information integration
C11	Real-Time Semi-Automatic Segmentation Using a Bayesian Network

5 Conclusion

We propose a topology-based community detection method for large-scale networks, which applies the network representation learning and clustering algorithms. Finally, the above methods are used to mine the community from the DBLP literature dataset. The experimental results demonstrate that our method improves the accuracy of community detection. Through further analysis of the excavated community structure, the organizational characteristics within the community are better revealed. Using the feature information in the directed graph and the weight information of the edges to discover community is our future research direction.

References

1. Rani, S., Mehrotra, M.: Community detection in social networks: literature review. J. Inf. Knowl. Manag. **18**(02), 1–84 (2019)
2. Girdhar, N., Bharadwaj, K.K.: Community detection in signed social networks using multiobjective genetic algorithm. J. Assoc. Inf. Sci. Technol. **70**(08), 788–804 (2019)
3. Emilsson, V., Ilkov, M., Lamb, J.R., et al.: Co-regulatory networks of human serum proteins link genetics to disease. Science **361**(6404), 769–773 (2018)
4. Atay, Y., Koc, I., Babaoglu, I., et al.: Community detection from biological and social networks: a comparative analysis of metaheuristic algorithms. Appl. Soft Comput. **50**, 194–211 (2017)
5. Fani, H., Zarrinkalam, F., Bagheri, E., Du, W.: Time-sensitive topic-based communities on twitter. In: Khoury, R., Drummond, C. (eds.) AI 2016. LNCS (LNAI), vol. 9673, pp. 192–204. Springer, Cham (2016). https://doi.org/10.1007/978-3-319-34111-8_25
6. Kernighan, B.W., Lin, S.: An efficient heuristic procedure for partitioning graphs. Bell Syst. Tech. J. **49**(2), 291–307 (1970)

7. Fiedler, M.: Algebraic connectivity of graphs. Czech. Math. J. **23**(98), 298–305 (1973)

8. Grivan, M., Newman, M.E.J.: Community structure in social and biological networks. Proc. Nat. Acad. Sci. U.S.A. **99**(12), 7821–7826 (2001)

9. Pons, P., Latapy, M.: Computing communities in large networks using random walks. J. Graph Algorithms Appl. **10**(2), 191–218 (2006)

10. Shang, R.H., Bai, J., Jiao, L.C., et al.: Community detection based on modularity and an improved genetic algorithm. Phys. A Stat. Mech. Appl. **392**(5), 1215–1231 (2013)

11. Despalatović, L., Vojković, T., Vukicevic, D.: Community structure in networks: Girvan-Newman algorithm improvement. In: 37th International Convention on Information and Communication Technology, Electronics and Microelectronics (MIPRO), pp. 997–1002. IEEE, Opatija (2014)

12. Katzir, L., Hardiman, S.J.: Estimating clustering coefficients and size of social networks via random walk. ACM Trans. Web **9**(4) (2015). Article no. 19

13. Cui, P., Wang, X., Pei, J., et al.: A survey on network embedding. IEEE Trans. Knowl. Data Eng. **31**(5), 833–852 (2019)

14. Perozzi, B., Al-Rfou, R., Skiena, S.: Deepwalk: online learning of social representations. In: Proceedings of the 20th ACM SIGKDD International Conference on Knowledge Discovery and Data Mining, pp. 701–710. ACM, NY, USA (2014)

15. Fortunato, S.: Community detection in graphs. Phys. Rep. **486**(3–5), 75–174 (2010)

16. Porter, M.A., Onnela, J.P., Mucha, P.J.: Communities in networks. Not. Ams **56**(9), 4294–4303 (2009)

17. Bilmes, J.A.: A gentle tutorial of the EM algorithm and its application to parameter estimation for Gaussian mixture and hidden Markov models. Int. Comput. Sci. Inst. **4**(510), 1–126 (1998)

18. Nasios, N., Bors, A.G.: Variational learning for Gaussian mixture models. IEEE Trans. Syst. Man Cybern. Part B (Cybern.) **36**(4), 849–862 (2006)

19. Blei, D.M., Jordan, M.I.: Variational inference for Dirichlet process mixtures. Bayesian Anal. **1**(1), 121–143 (2006)

A Systematic Review of Artificial Intelligence and Machine Learning Techniques for Cyber Security

Rahman Ali[1]([⊠]), Asmat Ali[2], Farkhund Iqbal[3],
Asad Masood Khattak[3], and Saiqa Aleem[3]

[1] Quaid-e-Azam College of Commerce, University of Peshawar, Peshawar,
Pakistan
`rehmanali@uop.edu.pk`
[2] Department of Computer Science, University of Peshawar, Peshawar, Pakistan
`aasmat76@gmail.com`
[3] College of Technological Innovation, Zyed University, Abu Dhabi, UAE
`{Farkhund.Iqbal,asad.khattak,saiqa.aleem}@zu.ac.ae`

Abstract. The use of technologies, procedures, and practices, designed to protect networks, programs, and data from attacks, damages, or unauthorized access, are called cyber security. Research community has applied different methods in the area of detection of cyber security attacks. However, literature lacks a systematic literature review (SLR) to summarize the use of Artificial Intelligence (AI) and Machine Learning (ML) methods, specifically the use of classifiers, in the detection of cyber security attacks. To cover the vacuum, this paper presents a systematic literature review of existing classification algorithms, applied to the area of detection of cyber security attacks. Relevant literature, qualifying specialized search criteria, is retrieved and extracted from the online libraries of Science Direct and Google Scholar. Total 63 research articles were found in these libraries, which are further filtered and refined to 21 articles. These 21 articles are critically reviewed and the following information are extracted: method used, classifier used, problem solved and domain selected. From the extracted information, a detailed taxonomy is prepared and presented to help beginners in the area to understand the problem. As a result of meta-level analysis, it is concluded that Support Vector Machine (SVM), Random Forest (RF), Decision Tree (DT) and Artificial Neural Network (ANN) are the most frequently used classifiers in the area of detection of cyber security.

Keywords: Cyber security · Cyber analytics · Machine learning · Classification algorithms · Taxonomy

1 Introduction

Cyber security refers to the set of policies, techniques, technologies, and processes, which work together to protect the confidentiality, integrity, and availability of computing resources, networks, software programs, and data from attacks [1]. Cyber security can be implemented at different levels, such as application, network, devices,

© Springer Nature Singapore Pte Ltd. 2020
Y. Tian et al. (Eds.): ICBDS 2019, CCIS 1210, pp. 584–593, 2020.
https://doi.org/10.1007/978-981-15-7530-3_44

host, and data. For the implementation of cyber security, a large number of application tools and procedures are available, such as firewalls, antivirus software, intrusion detection systems (IDSs), and intrusion protection systems (IPSs). These tools solely work to prevent cyber-attacks and detect security cracks. With the growth in internet-based technologies and solutions for real-world problems, chances of cyber-attacks have increased. Furthermore, with the passage of time, new kinds of cyber-attacks are encounters by the organizations, for which they shall remain vigilant to monitor the situation, detect the attacks and cure them before they affect the network or data. These cyber-attacks can be either internal or external. The tools and applications designed must also watch against the internal threats and attacks which come from individuals or entities within the organization. In internal threats, individuals misuse their authoritative roles of accessing or denying data, devices and/or networks.

1.1 Existing Research

To identify and prevent cyber threats, the tools, algorithms and procedures designed must have to monitor indicators and factors which are significant signs of cyber-attacks. Find these indicators and factors is a challenging task. The use of Artificial Intelligence (AI) techniques [2] in the area of cyber security has been discussed in literature, which has focused on the use of Machine Learning (ML) [3, 4], Deep Learning (DL) [5–7], Data Mining (DM) [3, 8], Data Science (DS) [9] and many others [10, 11]. These methods associate the indicators with types of attacks, learn frequently used patterns of the data, and predict future threats for abnormal futuristic behaviors of the intruders and attackers. The review articles published so far, using ML methods, have overlooked the approach of systematic literature review, therefore this paper is focused on discovering the methods of detecting cyber security attacks using a systematic literature review (SLR).

1.2 Research Objectives

This paper is aimed for readers who wish to begin research in the field of ML methods, specifically classification algorithms, for cyber security. As classifiers is a subset of ML algorithms, which is further a subset of AI, a great emphasis is placed on systematic review of these classifiers' application to cyber security. To make the work more focused, the research objectives are presented in Table 1 in the form of research questions.

1.3 Research Contributions and Paper Structure

This SLR is corresponding to existing studies and provides the following contributions, for the readers having interest in the area of use of ML classifiers in cyber security:

- Initially, 63 primary studies, related to ML classifiers, dealing cyber security, are retrieved from online libraries. The researchers who are new in the area can use the list of these studies for further research in this area.

Table 1. Research objectives.

Research questions (RQ)	Description of the research questions
RQ1	Which Machine Learning (ML) algorithms are used for detection of cyber security attacks?
RQ2	How ML is used to improve cyber security?
RQ3	Which classification algorithms are available to predict a security attack?
RQ4	Which classifiers are used for what type of security threat handling?
RQ5	Which application areas are covered by classifiers to implement cyber security?

- Finally, 21 primary studies are selected on the basis of inclusion exclusion criteria for onward consideration, which provide benchmarks to the community for comparative analysis of their future works.
- The research identifies the most frequently used classifiers in the area of detection of cyber security attacks.
- The research analyzes state-of-the-art classifiers, in the selected 21 studies, and expresses the research ideas of the studies concerned in the field of detection of cyber security attacks.
- The research presents a detailed taxonomy of the use of classifiers for detection of cyber security attacks.

The rest of paper is structured as follows: Section 2 describes research methodology, which further explains the process of selecting primary research articles and defines inclusion exclusion criteria etc. Section 3 performs meta-level analysis of the selected papers and presents a comprehensive taxonomy of the classifiers used in detection of cyber security attacks. Section 4 concludes the work done and recommendation future research directions.

2 Research Methodology

To meet the research objectives and answer the research questions, the proposed SLR is presented using guidelines of Kitchenham and Charters research [12].

2.1 Selection of Primary Studies

Special focus is placed on journal articles due to the use of popular techniques in their methodologies. Primary studies are selected based on combination of the following keywords, decided by the experts' group, using Boolean operators AND and OR. The search strings used is: ("machine learning classifier" OR "machine learning-based classifier" OR "ML classifier" OR "ML-based classifier" OR "classification algorithm" OR "classification methods" OR "classifier") AND ("cyber security" OR "cyber-security" OR "cybersecurity")

The search query is executed over the following two libraries, shown in Table 2, which has returned total 63 articles.

Table 2. List of online libraries and the number of articles retrieved.

S.No	Library	URL	Number of studies
1	ScienceDirect	https://www.sciencedirect.com/	19
2	Google Scholar	https://scholar.google.com/	44
TOTAL Articles Retrieved			**63**

The search is run against title, keywords and abstract of the research papers published since January 2017 till October 18, 2019. All the retrieved articles are stored in a separate EndNote library for further meta-level analysis and required information extraction.

2.2 Inclusion and Exclusion Criteria

To further refine the searched results and extract the most relevant studies, inclusion and exclusion criteria, shown in Table 3, are applied.

Table 3. Inclusion and exclusion criteria for filtering primary studies.

Inclusion Criteria	
IC1	The paper must contain information related to ML classifiers applied in the area of cyber security
IC2	The paper published in a peer reviewed journal
IC3	The paper published during January 2017 till October 18, 2019
Exclusion Criteria	
EC1	Papers focusing economic, business or legal impacts of cyber security and machine learning
EC2	Grey literature such as blogs, technical report and government documents
EC3	Non-English papers
EC4	Survey papers
EC5	Duplicate papers
EC6	Papers not published in any scholarly journal
EC7	The study did not focus on cyber attacks

2.3 Selection and Filtering Results

During the search process, using the search query over the selected libraries, total 63 studies are identified. This number is condensed to 21 by applying inclusion/exclusion criteria. Summary of the filtration process is shown in Table 4.

Table 4. Summary of literature after inclusion/exclusion criteria.

S. No	Library	Details of excluded papers	Final number of studies
1	ScienceDirect	Duplicate = 1; Survey = 2; NOT Journal = 1; Irrelevant = 5	19 − 09 = 10
2	Google Scholar	Duplicate = 1; Survey = 10; NOT Journal = 8; Book section = 7; Irrelevant = 7	44 − 33 = 11
TOTAL Articles			**21**

2.4   Meta-level Data Extraction

To perform a meta-level analysis of the selected relevant literature on cyber security treated using machine learning classifiers, each paper is critically reviewed the following information are extracted, such as: Method used, Machine Learning (ML) classifier, Problem solved and domain to which the method is applied. Meta-level analysis is shown in Table 5.

Table 5. Meta-level analysis of the selected relevant literature on cyber security using machine learning (ML) classifiers

S. No	References	Method used	ML classifier used	Problem solved	Domain selected
1	Patel et al. [13]	Combination of machine-learning, ontology and fuzzy logic are used in a distributed management structure	Support Vector Machine (SVM)	Intrusion Detection and Prevention (IDP)	Smart Grid ecosystems
2	Cohen et al. [14]	General descriptive features, extracted from email components (header, body, and attachments) are used	Random Forest (RF)	Detection of malicious email	E-mail
3	Guerrero-Higuera et al. [15]	Artificial Neural Network (ANN) classifiers are used for a number of cyber security attacks	Multi-Layer Perceptron (MLP)	Detecting Denial of Service & Spoofing on Real Time Location Systems for autonomous robots	Indoor real time localization systems for autonomous robots
4	Jaint et al. [16]	Detection of smishing SMS using rule-based classifiers	Rule-based classifiers [DT, RIPPER, PRISM]	Detection of Smishing Messages in Mobile Environment	Mobile Environment
5	Katzir et al. [17]	Studying the adversarial resilience of cyber security detection systems using supervised ML	Ensemble algorithms	Studying adversarial resilience of cyber security detection systems	General
6	Giang Nguyena et al. [18]	Incremental learning framework from mobile device log history	SVM, Logistic Regression, ANN	Mobile malware detection system	Mobile

(continued)

Table 5. (*continued*)

S. No	References	Method used	ML classifier used	Problem solved	Domain selected
7	Arivudainambi et al. [19]	Hybrid approach of Principal Component Analysis (PCA) and ANN for classifying malicious traffic	PCA and ANN	Malware traffic classification	Malicious traffic classification
8	Martin et al. [20]	Malware detection on the basis of fusion of static and dynamic features through ensemble classifiers	Ensemble classifiers	Malware detection	Android devices
9	Noor et al. [21]	Automate cyber threat attribution (total 36 threats) using different classifiers	NB, KNN, DTree, RF and Deep Learning-based NN	Detection of 36 well-known threats	General
10	Sahingoes et al. [22]	Random Forest applied over NLP based features	Random Forest	Phishing detection from URLs	Electronic commerce
11	Al-Khateeb et al. [23]	Recursive Bayesian estimation technique	Bayesian Network (BN)	Detection of hijacking autonomous cars	Autonomous cars
12	Moore et al. [24]	A hybrid of feature extraction and selection with ANN	ANN	Detection of no-threats and severity of threats in network	Networks
13	Sharma et al. [25]	Distributed framework architecture	Genetic programming, CART, SVM and Dynamic Bayesian game model	Detection of Advanced persistent threats (APTs)	Internet of things (IoT) devices
14	Azmoodeh et al. [26]	Detection of ransomware based on energy consumption footprint	KNN, Neural Network, SVM and RF	Detecting crypto-ransomware	Android devices
15	Jianwen et al. [27]	RGB-colored images and global features extraction techniques from images	RF, KNN, SVM	Malware Visualization	Malware Visualization
16	Ghaneam et al. [28]	Hybridization of an Artificial Bee Colony and Monarch Butterfly Optimization	ANN	Detecting intrusions into network systems	Network systems
17	Yongjun et al. [29]	Instruction2vec- an improved static binary analysis technique using machine learning	Deep learning - Convolutional neural networks (CNNs)	Automated vulnerability detection	Software Engineering
18	Nissim et al. [30]	Protecting Scholarly Digital Libraries from Infected Papers	Active Machine Learning	Detecting Infected Papers	Research online libraries
19	Thamilarasu et al. [31]	Deep-Learning-based Intrusion Detection for the Internet of Things	Deep-Learning	Internet of Things	Internet of Things
20	Vinayakumar et al. [32]	Robust Intelligent Malware Detection Using Deep Learning	Deep-Learning	Intelligent Malware Detection	Intelligent Malware Detection
21	Toledo et al. [33]	Supervised Machine Learning Algorithms	DT, KNN, SVM, NB	Encrypted DNP3 Traffic Classification	Traffic Classification

From the data extraction and summary, it is evident that Probabilistic, Decision Tree-, Deep Learning, Artificial Neural Network, Instance-based Learning, Active Machine Learning, Rule-based Learning, Kernel Function-based Classifier, Logistic Regression, Ensemble Classifiers and Genetic Programming are the widely used ML-classifiers which have extensively been used in cyber security domain for detection of cyber attacks and dealing with them.

3 Meta-data Analysis and Results Generation

The relevant literature in the area of cyber security attacks is thoroughly analyzed and meta-level information are extracted which are presented in the form of a taxonomy. The subsequent sections explain the details.

3.1 Detection of Cyber Security in Different Application Areas

During analysis of the literature, it was identified that detection of cyber security attacks has been studied in various application domains (see last column of Table 5). A few applications areas are enlisted as follows: smart grid ecosystems, indoor real time localization systems for autonomous robots systems, mobile environment (detect smishing SMS), mobile malware detection system, malicious traffic classification, android malware detection, electronic commerce, autonomous driving of connected cars, network traffic data, internet of things (IoT) devices, android devices, malware visualization, detecting intrusions into network systems, software engineering, research online libraries, intelligent malware detection and encrypted DNP3 traffic classification.

3.2 ML-Classifiers and the Types of Cyber Security

There is a wide range of use of ML-classifiers in the area of cyber security (see problem solved column of Table 5). The classifiers have been used for: intrusion detection and prevention (IDP), detection of malicious email, detecting denial of service & spoofing on real time location systems, detection of smishing messages in mobile environment, malware traffic detection, phishing detection from URLs, detection of hijacking autonomous cars, detection of no-threats and severity of threats, detection of advanced persistent threats (APTs), detecting crypto-ransomware, malware visualization, detecting intrusions into network systems, automated vulnerability detection, detecting Infected research papers in digital library, detection of cyber threats in Internet of Things (IoT), intelligent malware detection and encrypted DNP3 traffic classification.

3.3 Classifiers Used - Taxonomy of ML-Classifier for Cyber Security

A taxonomy, shown in Fig. 1, is drawn on the basis of SLR of the 21 papers, reviewed. As depicted, the use of ML-classifiers in the area of detection of cyber security is dominated by the use of decision tree-based classifiers. Other most commonly used classifiers are enlisted as follows: artificial neural network-based classifiers, k-nearest neighbor-based classifiers, deep learning-based classifiers and support vector machine-

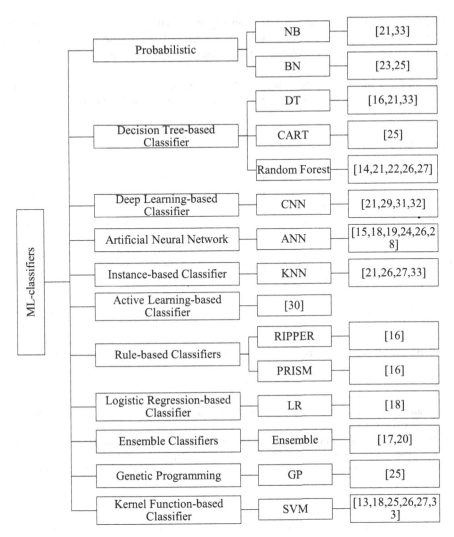

Fig. 1. Taxonomy of ML-classifiers for cyber security.

based classifiers. Apart from these families of the classifiers, other classifiers have also been used in cyber security detection.

4   Conclusion and Future Work

In this paper, a systematic literature review of the machine learning classifiers, applied to the area of detection of cyber security attack, is performed. The articles have been reviewed from from the perspectives of method used, ML-classifiers used, and problem solved. A taxonomy is presented which shows that ANN, SVM and Random Forest (RF) are the best classifiers to solve the problem of malware detection in the problem in-hand. Ensemble classifiers are also widely used with good performance. Further research work could be directed towards the use of deep learning and ensemble learning for improving the accuracy of detection of cyber security attacks.

Acknowledgement. This study is supported by Research Incentive Funds (# R18055) and Research Cluster award (# R17082), Zayed University, United Arab Emirates.

References

1. Vacca, J.R.: Computer and Information Security Handbook. Newnes, Oxford (2012)
2. Wu, S.X., Banzhaf, W.: The use of computational intelligence in intrusion detection systems: a review. Appl. Soft Comput. **10**(1), 1–35 (2010)
3. Bučzak, A.L., Guven, E.: A survey of data mining and machine learning methods for cyber security intrusion detection. IEEE Commun. Surv. Tutor. **18**(2), 1153–1176 (2015)
4. Torres, J.M., Comesaña, C.I., García-Nieto, P.J.: Machine learning techniques applied to cybersecurity. Int. J. Mach. Learn. Cybern. **10**(10), 2823–2836 (2019)
5. Xin, Y., et al.: Machine learning and deep learning methods for cybersecurity. IEEE Access **6**, 35365–35381 (2018)
6. Wickramasinghe, C.S., et al.: Generalization of deep learning for cyber-physical system security: a survey. In: IECON 2018-44th Annual Conference of the IEEE Industrial Electronics Society. IEEE (2018)
7. Berman, D.S., et al.: A survey of deep learning methods for cyber security. Information **10**(4), 122 (2019)
8. Thuraisingham, B., et al.: Data mining for security applications. In: 2008 IEEE/IFIP International Conference on Embedded and Ubiquitous Computing. IEEE (2018)
9. Adams, N., et al.: Data Analysis for Network Cyber-Security. World Scientific Publishing Co. Inc., River Edge (2014)
10. Garcia-Teodoro, P., et al.: Anomaly-based network intrusion detection: techniques, systems and challenges. Comput. Secur. **28**(1–2), 18–28 (2009)
11. Sperotto, A., et al.: An overview of IP flow-based intrusion detection. IEEE Commun. Surv. Tutor. **12**(3), 343–356 (2010)
12. Keele, S.: Guidelines for performing systematic literature reviews in software engineering, Technical report, Ver. 2.3 EBSE Technical Report. EBSE (2007)
13. Patel, A., et al.: A nifty collaborative intrusion detection and prevention architecture for Smart Grid ecosystems. Comput. Secur. **64**, 92–109 (2017)
14. Cohen, A., Nissim, N., Elovici, Y.: Novel set of general descriptive features for enhanced detection of malicious emails using machine learning methods. Expert Syst. Appl. **110**, 143–169 (2018)
15. Guerrero-Higueras, Á.M., DeCastro-García, N., Matellán, V.: Detection of Cyber-attacks to indoor real time localization systems for autonomous robots. Robot. Auton. Syst. **99**, 75–83 (2018)
16. Jain, A.K., Gupta, B.B.: Rule-based framework for detection of smishing messages in mobile environment. Procedia Comput. Sci. **125**, 617–623 (2018)
17. Katzir, Z., Elovici, Y.: Quantifying the resilience of machine learning classifiers used for cyber security. Expert Syst. Appl. **92**, 419–429 (2018)
18. Nguyen, G., et al.: A heuristics approach to mine behavioural data logs in mobile malware detection system. Data Knowl. Eng. **115**, 129–151 (2018)

19. Arivudainambi, D., et al.: Malware traffic classification using principal component analysis and artificial neural network for extreme surveillance. Comput. Commun. **147**, 50–57 (2019)
20. Martín, A., Lara-Cabrera, R., Camacho, D.: Android malware detection through hybrid features fusion and ensemble classifiers: the AndroPyTool framework and the OmniDroid dataset. Inf. Fusion **52**, 128–142 (2019)
21. Noor, U., et al.: A machine learning-based FinTech cyber threat attribution framework using high-level indicators of compromise. Future Gener. Comput. Syst. **96**, 227–242 (2019)
22. Sahingoz, O.K., et al.: Machine learning based phishing detection from URLs. Expert Syst. Appl. **117**, 345–357 (2019)
23. Al-Khateeb, H., et al.: Proactive threat detection for connected cars using recursive Bayesian estimation. IEEE Sens. J. **18**(12), 4822–4831 (2017)
24. Moore, K.L., et al.: Feature extraction and feature selection for classifying cyber traffic threats. J. Defense Model. Simul. Appl. Methodol. Technol. JDMS **14**(3), 217–231 (2017)
25. Sharma, P.K., Moon, S.Y., Moon, D., Park, J.H.: DFA-AD: a distributed framework architecture for the detection of advanced persistent threats. Cluster Comput. **20**(1), 597–609 (2016). https://doi.org/10.1007/s10586-016-0716-0
26. Azmoodeh, A., Dehghantanha, A., Conti, M., Choo, K.-K.R.: Detecting crypto-ransomware in IoT networks based on energy consumption footprint. J. Ambient Intell. Human. Comput. **9**(4), 1141–1152 (2017). https://doi.org/10.1007/s12652-017-0558-5
27. Fu, J., et al.: Malware visualization for fine-grained classification. IEEE Access **6**, 14510–14523 (2018)
28. Ghanem, W.A., Jantan, A.: Training a neural network for cyberattack classification applications using hybridization of an artificial bee colony and monarch butterfly optimization. Neural Process. Lett. **51**, 1–42 (2019)
29. Lee, Y., et al.: Instruction2vec: efficient preprocessor of assembly code to detect software weakness with CNN. Appl. Sci. **9**(19), 4086 (2019)
30. Nissim, N., et al.: Sec-Lib: protecting scholarly digital libraries from infected papers using active machine learning framework. IEEE Access **7**, 110050–110073 (2019)
31. Thamilarasu, G., Chawla, S.: Towards deep-learning-driven intrusion detection for the internet of things. Sensors **19**(9), 1977 (2019)
32. Vinayakumar, R., et al.: Robust intelligent malware detection using deep learning. IEEE Access **7**, 46717–46738 (2019)
33. De Toledo, T.R., Torrisi, N.M.: Encrypted DNP3 traffic classification using supervised machine learning algorithms. Mach. Learn. Knowl. Extr. **1**(1), 384–399 (2019)

Study on Indicator Recognition Method of Water Meter Based on Convolution Neural Network

Shuaicheng Pan, Lei Han[(⊠)], Yi Tao, and Qingyu Liu

Nanjing Institute of Technology, Nanjing 211167, China
psc351@foxmail.com, hanl@njit.edu.cn

Abstract. In order to improve the accuracy of water meter character recognition, this paper proposes a character recognition method based on deep convolutional neural network. Traditional identification methods need to build a large number of templates, which requires a lot of work, and are easy to be interfered by external light and sundries, so the identification accuracy is low. The object of the experiment is the water meter dial with the character of word wheel and the corresponding data set is established. A character recognition method based on deep convolutional neural network is proposed to solve the problem of half-character on water meter. First to pretreatment of data set, the main data set is rotating images and augmentation, and then according to the classical convolution neural network structure, construct a can identify characters at the same time and dial the convolutional neural network model, training on the data set tests, the experimental results show that the method effectively improves the water meter word wheel character recognition accuracy.

Keywords: Convolutional neural network · Intelligent table recognition · Image recognition · Character recognition · Halfword recognition

1 Introduction

Intelligent meter investment and operation and maintenance cost is low, fast, high efficiency, wide application prospects. The camera reading table mainly includes character positioning, character segmentation and character recognition. The method based on area aggregation runs faster, but is easily affected by low image resolution and noise [1]. The target recognition algorithm matches feature vectors through improved feature matching algorithm, which improves the accuracy but decreases the recognition speed. Template matching based on euler number groups the template images and matches the target image with the template with the same euler number. At the same time, the above methods are easily affected by environmental factors and are not robust.

To improve the performances of classification, several fusion methods have been developed by combining different feature extraction and classification methods. CNN-ELM classifier has been proposed by Zeng, Y. et al. [6] for traffic sign recognition and achieved human level accuracy. Guo, L. et al. [7] have proposed Hybrid CNN-ELM with improved accuracy and validate its performance on MNIST

© Springer Nature Singapore Pte Ltd. 2020
Y. Tian et al. (Eds.): ICBDS 2019, CCIS 1210, pp. 594–602, 2020.
https://doi.org/10.1007/978-981-15-7530-3_45

dataset. Gurpinar, F. et al. [8] have replaced ELM to Kernel ELM for classification that minimizes the mean absolute error. Face features have been extracted from a pre-trained deep convolutional network. Kernel extreme learning machines are used for classification. Yoo, Y. et al. [9] proposed a novel fast learning architecture of CNN-ELM. Their core architecture is based on a local image (local receptive field) version of the ELM adopting random feature learning. Weng, Q. et al. [10] combines ELM classifier with the CNN-learned features instead of the fully connected layers of CNN to land-use classification.

The method proposed in this paper combines the characteristics of the classical network structure to build a new type of convolution neural network M_CNN (Modified_CNN) suitable for water meter image recognition. The experiment shows that it can not only recognize the word wheel figure of water meter but also recognize the digital image. And not easily affected by environmental factors. The rest of the paper is organized as follows: Sect. 2 describes the classical neural network used in this paper, Sect. 3 describes the network structure, Sect. 4 is the experiment, and finally the conclusion.

2 Related Work

The classical neural network based on CNN includes LeNet5, AlexNet, GoogLeNet, etc. As an early CNN, LeNet5 adopted ReLU activation function, added Dropout layer and expanded the amount of training data. However, AlexNet has only eight layers. The first five layers are convolution layer, and the last three layers are full connection layer. The network depth is not deep enough, and the discarding pool layer is prone to over-fitting.

GoogLeNet injected the modularization idea into CNN and used the convolution of 1×1 to carry out the elevating dimension. Its sparse connection structure improved the adaptability of the network to a variety of complex images, but it took too long to apply it to the calculation of character recognition.

The first four layers of M_CNN proposed in this paper can be regarded as a module. In the future, the structure of the module remains unchanged and only some parameters such as convolution kernel are changed. M_CNN is a convolutional neural network specially constructed for water meter characters, which USES the character-istics and ideas of classic CNN for reference, and more suitable for the use of camera meter reading scene.

M_CNN is improved on the basis of CNN_ON_MNIST [1, 6] and CNN_ON_-CIFAR [3] to build a model that can recognize both the number and the small wheel. CNN_ON_CIFAR can effectively identify images in the cifar-105 dataset, which is built for 10 common objects in nature. This network can be used to identify the word wheel image of water meter. CNN_ON_MNIST can effectively recognize handwritten digits, this network can effectively recognize water meter character image.

By combining the two models, a new neural network M_CNN is constructed, which can recognize the word wheel image and character image of water meter at the same time. By using the self-built water meter training set and test set, the training, testing and generalization ability is better.

3   Proposed Model

As shown in Fig. 1, M_CNN draw lessons from the modular design idea, the two convolution layer, one of the biggest pooling layer, a dropout as a module, the network use a total of three such module, the first module number convolution kernels is 32, the second module has 64 convolution kernels, the third module has 128 convolution kernels, the convolution kernel module size is 3 × 3, pooling nucleus is 2 × 2, drouput ratio is 0.25, finally after a flattening all connections, regularization operation again suppress a layer of neurons activate prevent fitting, Finally complete connection layer can output a 128 - dimensional vector, softmax layer will this vector as input, and then calculate the test images respectively belong to the probability distribution of the 10 class, softmax using cross entropy loss function (cross-entro-py) to calculate each forecast loss value size, commonly used loss value calculation function and hinge loss [4], but the hinge loss calculation value is without calibration, it is difficult to decide on all the classes. However, the value of cross-en-tropy can be used to determine all classes, which will give the prediction probability of each class and finally output the prediction result.

4   Experiment Results

4.1   Experimental Setup

This experimental platform is Intel i7-8700 processor, 16G of memory, GTX1080 graphics card, 4G video memory dell workstation, using Tensorflow as the back-end Keras platform to build M_CNN, and training and verification on the data set.

Character acquisition is completed through raspberry PI and macro camera, and character samples are shown in Fig. 2. USB HD macro camera is adopted with 8 million pixels and the maximum resolution is 640 × 480. The word wheel sample is shown in Fig. 3. The image segmentation is processed by OpenCV, and five spinner code plates and four decimal dial are cut out.

The collected digital and pointer samples are divided into 10 categories from 0 to 9. The training set and test set are divided according to 4:1, and are independent of each other without intersection.

For the half-word problem of numeric characters, as shown in Fig. 3, the number shown in the upper part is 0, that is, the number that has been displayed completely recently is read according to the scroll direction of the word wheel, and the specific reading is read out in combination with the reading of the dial pointer. For the roulette half-word problem, according to the empirical table reading method, it is classified into the number of the last time, and then read more accurate Numbers according to the following X0.1, X0.01 and X0.001 dial. This is done for each dial. The last dial is almost always a pointer to an integer because it is the smallest unit indicator.

M_CNN model parameters include activation function, pooling method, pooled core size, discard ratio, classifier, loss function, optimizer, etc. See Table 2 for specific parameters.

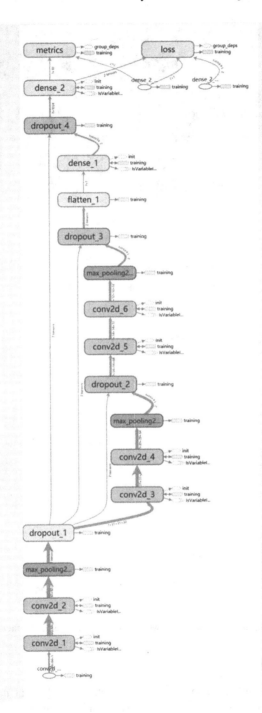

Fig. 1. Architecture of M_CNN.

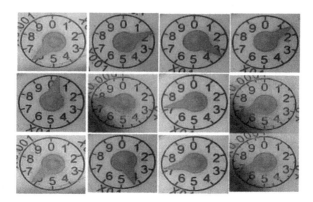

Fig. 2. Sample images.

Table 1. Data set specification.

The total number of sheets	9 200
Number of training sets	8 280
Number of test sets	920
Figure (height × width) (pixels)	136 × 136

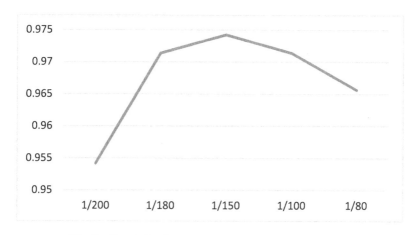

Fig. 3. Correlation between accuracy and rescaling factor.

4.2 Results and Analysis

Based on the self-built data set and training set, the traditional neural network and M_CNN were used for training test respectively, and the results were shown in Table 3 and Table 4. The loss changes and accuracy changes of CNN_ON_MNIST training are shown in Fig. 4. The loss value increases in the test set, indicating that the network

Table 2. Parameters specification.

Training parameters	Value
activation function	ReLu
Pooling method	Max pool
Pool Size	(2, 2)
Dropout	0.25
classifier	Softmax
Loss function	Categorical_crossentropy
optimizer	Adadelta
Rescaling factor	1/255

basically has no fitting and cannot be effectively identified. The change when CNN_ON_CIFAR is used is shown in Fig. 5. The loss fluctuation on the test set is large, indicating that the trained network cannot be well fitted. Overall, M_CNN showed better performance in terms of loss and accuracy.

Table 3. Comparison of accuracy between traditional neural network and M_CNN.

Network name	Recognition accuracy/%
CNN_ON_MNIST	85.67
CNN_ON_CIFAR	91.97
M_CNN	97.13
ResNet v1	94.84
ResNet v2	63.61

Table 4. Comparison of loss between traditional neural network and M_CNN.

Network name	Loss value
CNN_ON_MNIST	0.62
CNN_ON_CIFAR	0.21
M_CNN	0.19
ResNet v1	0.27
ResNet v2	1.76

Accuracy and loss values are compared as follows, respectively showing the accuracy and loss values of CNN_ON_MNIST, CNN_ON_CIFAR, ResNet and M_CNN. By comparison, M_CNN has better performance in accuracy and loss values. Although ResNet is a classic classification network, it does not perform well when both the word wheel and the character image are needed, and the training time is much longer than M_CNN.

4.3   Experimental Comparison

In order to solve the imbalance between sample data, the method of data expansion was proposed. It was found from the actual data collection that not every sample had the same number, which would interfere with the learning process.In order to balance the number of samples and avoid too few samples in the training process and poor fitting, re-scaling factor was added in the sample pretreatment.The experiment shows that when the rescaling factor is set as 1/150, the accuracy rate is the highest (See Fig. 4).

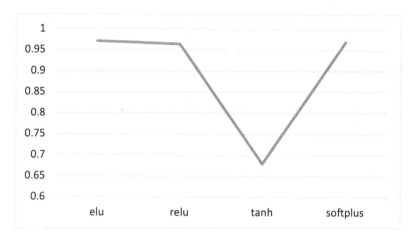

Fig. 4. Correlation between accuracy and activation function.

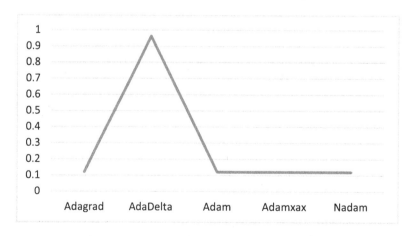

Fig. 5. Correlation between accuracy and optimizer.

Activation function is actually the function relation between the output of upper node and the input of lower node. The common activation function includes Sigmoid, tanh, ReLU, elu and softplus function. The Sigmoid function in deep neural network causes the gradient to disappear when the gradient reverse transmission, which has been less used. Use a different activation function in the penultimate full connection layer. The last full connection layer is a classifier, all other things being equal. In order to avoid chance, each activation function was repeated three times, and the accuracy rate was averaged. It is found that the activation function of elu is slightly better than that of relu.

The optimizer is used to minimize the loss function, for example, SGD, RMSprop, Adagrad, AdaDelta, Adam. When SGD randomly selects the gradient, noise will be introduced, so that the direction of weight updating is not necessarily correct, and the problem of local optimal solution is not solved. RMSprop is often used to train circular neural networks. The effects of Adagrad, AdaDelta and Adam on the model were compared. Experimental results show that the AdaDelta optimizer is more accurate than others. Adadelta is an extended version with greater robustness. Instead of accumulating all the past gradients, it adjusts the learning rate according to the updated movement window. So despite many updates, Adadelta continues to learn.

5 Conclusion

Based on the classic CNN_ON_MNIST and CNN_ON_CIFAR, this paper proposes MC_CNN which can identify water meters. Based on the raspberry PI platform, it can be read and identified by external hardware and software, without the need to transform the inside of the water meter. Compared with the traditional magnetic induction reading can effectively avoid the problem of magnetic disappearance. Compared with pattern matching, it can reduce the complexity of image preprocessing and the error of manual parameter selection. Compared with other neural networks, accuracy and loss values are also better. The optimal rescaling factor, optimizer and activation function were found by experiments. Mature development can be further extended to the identification of electricity meters, heating meters.

Acknowledgment. This work was supported by the Natural Science Foundation of Jiangsu Higher Education Institutions of China (No. 17KJB520010), and Research foundation of Nanjing Institute of Technology (No. CKJB201804), and Practice and innovation training program for college students in jiangsu province (No. 213345214301801).

References

1. Zhang, Y., Wang, S., Dong, Z.: Classification of Alzheimer disease based on structural magnetic resonance imaging by kernel support vector machine decision tree. Prog. Electromagn. Res. **144**, 171–184 (2014)
2. Chaplot, S., Patnaik, L.M., Jagannathan, N.R.: Classification of magnetic resonance brain images using wavelets as input to support vector machine and neural network. Biomed. Sign. Process. Control **1**, 86–92 (2006)

3. Maitra, M., Chatterjee, A.: A Slantlet transform based intelligent system for magnetic resonance brain image classification. Biomed. Sign. Process. Control **1**, 299–306 (2006)
4. El-Dahshan, E.S.A., Hosny, T., Salem, A.B.M.: Hybrid intelligent techniques for MRI brain images classification. Digit. Sign. Process. **1**, 299–306 (2006)
5. Zhang, Y., Wu, L., Wang, S.: Magnetic resonance brain image classification by an improved artificial bee colony algorithm. Prog. Electromagn. Res. **116**, 65–79 (2011)
6. Zeng, Y., Xu, X., Fang, Y., Zhao, K.: Traffic sign recognition using deep convolutional networks and extreme learning machine. In: He, X., Gao, X., Zhang, Y., Zhou, Z.-H., Liu, Z.-Y., Fu, B., Hu, F., Zhang, Z. (eds.) IScIDE 2015. LNCS, vol. 9242, pp. 272–280. Springer, Cham (2015). https://doi.org/10.1007/978-3-319-23989-7_28
7. Guo, L., Ding, S.: A hybrid deep learning cnn-elm model and its application in handwritten numeral recognition. J. Comput. Inf. Syst. **11**(7), 2673–2680 (2015)
8. Gurpinar, F., Kaya, H., Dibeklioglu, H., Salah, A.: Kernel ELM and CNN based facial age estimation. In: Proceedings of the IEEE Conference on Computer Vision and Pattern Recognition Workshops, pp. 80–86 (2016)
9. Youngwoo, Y., Oh, S. Y.: Fast training of convolutional neural network classifiers through extreme learning machines. In: 2016 International Joint Conference on Neural Networks (IJCNN). IEEE (2016)
10. Weng, Q., Mao, Z., Lin, J., Guo, W.: Land-use classification via extreme learning classifier based on deep convolutional features. IEEE Geosci. Remote Sens. Lett. **14**, 704–708 (2017)

A Deep Learning Approach for Anomaly-Based Network Intrusion Detection

Najwa Altwaijry⬤, Ameerah ALQahtani⬤, and Isra AlTuraiki[(✉)]⬤

College of Computer and Information Sciences, King Saud University,
Riyadh, Saudi Arabia
{ntwaijry,ialturaiki}@ksu.edu.sa, 438204059@student.ksu.edu.sa

Abstract. Cybersecurity threats have increased dramatically in recent years, and the techniques used by the attackers continue to evolve and become more ingenious. These attacks harm organizations on many levels, such as economic, reputational, and legal. Therefore, an Anomaly Detection Based Network Intrusion Detection System (ADNIDS) is an essential component of any standard security framework in computer networks. In this paper, we propose two deep learning-based models, BDNN and MDNN, for binary and multiclass classification of network attacks, respectively. We evaluate the performance of our proposed models on the well-known NSL-KDD dataset and compare our results with similar deep-learning approaches and state-of-the-art classification models. Experimental results show that our models achieve good performance in terms of accuracy and recall.

Keywords: Deep learning · Cybersecurity · Anomaly detection · network intrusion detection system · NSL-KDD

1 Introduction

Network intrusion detection systems (NIDS) are currently the standard security requirement for computer networks. They help in detecting attacks and malicious activities inside the network. NIDS monitor and assess network traffic that passes between devices within an organization. If any potential intrusion is detected, an alert issued [11]. NIDS are used along with traditional security tools, such as firewalls, access control systems, and antivirus software, to protect information and communication systems against attack [5].

NIDS can be classified into: *Signature-based* (SNIDS) and *Anomaly detection-based* (ADNIDS) [2]. In SNIDS, network traffic is monitored against pre-defined attack signatures in order to identify a potential attacks. They are widely regarded as the most effective methods of detecting known attacks and have less false-alarm rates than ADNIDS [2]. However, they are not as effective at detecting new attacks as they lack the appropriate attack signature to do so.[2].

© Springer Nature Singapore Pte Ltd. 2020
Y. Tian et al. (Eds.): ICBDS 2019, CCIS 1210, pp. 603–615, 2020.
https://doi.org/10.1007/978-981-15-7530-3_46

In ADNIDS, unusual traffic, which potentially deviates from the expected traffic pattern is detected. ADNIDS are more effective in detecting attacks that have not previously been observed. While these systems have a higher false-positive rate than SNIDS, they have gained wide acceptance in the research community on the grounds that they are theoretically capable of detecting new forms of attack [2].

In general, network intrusion detection can be formulated as a classification problem. NIDS should be able to distinguish between authorized traffic and potential attacks. ADNIDS have been developed using a range of machine learning techniques, including: *random forests* (RF), *self-organized maps* (SOM), *support vector machines* (SVM), and *artificial neural networks* (ANN). However, the majority of the established machine learning techniques operate on shallow learning principles and are unable to deal with the massive intrusion data classification issues associated with a real network application environment [11].

Researchers have effectively employed deep learning-based methods in a range of applications, including image, audio, and speech-based systems [9]. The contemporary approaches seek to identify an effective feature representation within a enormous amount of unlabeled data and consequently apply the features that have been learned to a limited amount of labeled data within a supervised classification [2]. This can be effective because deep learning methods can identify more effective representations from the data to generate more effective models than shallow-based approaches. As such, this research aims to develop a deep learning-based approach for ADNIDS with the objective of classifying novel attacks by examining the structures of normal behavior in network traffic. An intrusion is defined as any traffic that diverges from a normal traffic pattern.

As datasets become larger, systems will be required to perform more and more classification tasks and this will result in a reduced level of accuracy [11].

The paper is organized as follows: Sect. 2 covers the previous studies in the area of anomaly detection using deep learning and machine learning techniques. In the Sect. 3, an overview of our proposed model for anomaly detection-based Network intrusion detection system (ADNIDS) is presented. In Sect. 4, experimental settings, and performance measures are outlined, then we present our performance evaluation. Our conclusions and planning for future works are provided in Sect. 5.

2   Related Work

Various machine learning approaches have been used to detect abnormal traffic, anomalies and attacks in network traffic. Panda et al. [15] used *naïve Bayes* to build a model for anomaly based network intrusion detection. Experiments applied over 10% KD'99 [19] dataset showed a detection rate of 95%. Wang et al. [21] presented a model for intrusion detection using Artificial Neural Networks and fuzzy clustering, (FC-ANN). Fuzzy c-means clustering was used to produce six training subsets, on which six ANNs are trained, with one hidden layer and mean absolute error as the error function. ANN results were aggregated using another ANN to aggregate different ANN's result and reduce detection errors. They tested the model on the KDD'99 dataset, reporting an accuracy of 96.71%, greater than BPNN and naïve Bayes.

Ingre et al. [8] constructed an ANN-based model to detect anomaly intrusion. In the proposed ANN architecture, twenty-nine neurons were used in the input layer and twenty-one neurons in the hidden layer. The model was based on tansig transfer function, Levenberg-Marquardt and BFGS quasi-Newton Backpropagation (BFG) algorithm for updating weight and bias. The model was applied to NSL-KDD dataset [7,19]. Training and testing applied on dataset with 41 full features and with reduced features.The detection rate of the model was 81.2% in 2-class classification and 79.9% for five-class classification.

Mukkamala et al. [14] built an intrusion detection models using SVM and ANN. The SVM model was trained using the radial bias function. For the ANN, A multi-layer, feedforward network was trained using the scaled conjugate gradient decent algorithm. Experiments were conducted using 41 and 13 feature subsets. The experimental evaluation using KDD'99 datasets showed that SVM performed better than neural networks, in terms of training time and accuracy of intrusion detection. It was also noticed that models produced using training with the 41 features outperformed that trained with the 13 features.

Machine learning techniques have been widely utilized to recognize different types of attacks and most of them belong to shallow learning and require feature engineering and selection [16]. It assumes the availability of handcrafted features [16]. However, with the availability of massive data, shallow learning may not be suitable to solve the problem of classification in real world environments [16,22]. This is due to the need for high level of human expert involvement in data preparation. In addition, these techniques are subject to high probability of detection error [22].

To handle the above limitations, recently deep learning has achieved real successes in automatically finding a correlation in the data [22]. It can be used for deeper analysis of network data and quick identification of anomalies.

Tang et al. [18], presented a Deep Neural Network (DNN) model for anomaly detection in software defined networking context. The simple deep neural network consisted of an input layer, three hidden layers, and an output layer. The model was evaluated using the NSL-KDD dataset, with an accuracy of 75.75% in the binary classification problem using six basic features.

Javaid et al. [9] presented a self-taught learning (STL) a deep learning approach for network intrusion detection. The proposed approach consisted of two phases: unsupervised feature learning and classification. In the unsupervised feature learning phase, sparse autoencoder is used to obtain feature representation from large group of unlabeled data. Then, in the classification phase, soft-max regression is applied. Using NSL-KDD dataset, the model obtained accuracy values of 88.39% and 79.10% for 2-class and 5-class classification problems, respectively.

Yin et al. [22] proposed a model for intrusion detection using *Recurrent Neural Networks*. The model consists of forward and back propagation stages. Forward propagation calculates the output values, whereas back propagation passes residuals accumulated to update the weights. The training model consist of 20 hidden nodes, the learning rate was set to 0.1, the number of epochs to 50, sigmoid was used as the activation function, and SoftMax was used as the classification function. Experimental results using NSL-KDD dataset showed the accuracy values were 83.28% and 81.29% for binary and multiple classification, respectively.

Deep learning can be combined with shallow learning for a more effective intrusion detection capability. Al-Qatf et al. [1] proposed an STL based intrusion detection system. The model combines sparse autoencoder and SVM. They used sparse autoencoder to reconstruct and learn the input training dataset. A SVM was then trained using the new training dataset to construct a model for the prediction of the intrusion attacks. The evaluation results using NSL-KDD dataset showed that the model accelerated SVM training and testing times. The obtained accuracy values were 84.96% and 80.48% for binary and multiple classification, respectively. These results outperform the performance of traditional methods such as: J48, naïve Bayesian, random forest, and SVM.

Shone et al. [17] used Non-Symmetric Deep Auto-Encoder (NDAE) along with Random Forest classification algorithm. NDAE is non-symmetric deep auto encoder (NDAE) and used for unsupervised feature learning The proposed model uses two NDAEs arranged in a stack. Each NDAE has three hidden layers, with each hidden layer using the same number of neurons as that of features. Experimental results using the KDD Cup 99 dataset showed an accuracy of 97.85% for 5-class classification.

It is observed that the majority of ADNIDS models using machine learning or deep learning techniques achieve high accuracy in the binary classification problem (normal, anomaly) when applied on KDD'99 [19]. As KDD'99 has inherent bias in its training and testing sets [13,19], results reported for models trained on this dataset are biased, and report higher than expected accuracy values. The literature also shows that the performance of ADNIDS machine learning models for binary classification is better than it is for multiclass classification. Thus, network intrusion detection binary and multiclass classification remains an open problem.

3   Methodology

3.1   Dataset Description

This research will be carried out over the NSL-KDD dataset. The NSL-KDD dataset is an improved and reduced version of the KDD'99 dataset [19], which was used as a benchmark dataset to assess intrusion detection systems. The biggest disadvantage of the KDD'99 dataset is that it contains a large number of redundant records in both training and test data [19], which causes learning classifiers to be biased towards the more frequent records during training, as well as increasing classification accuracy whenever these same records appear in the test set. The NSL-KDD overcomes the above limitations and provides better evaluation of classifiers by removing redundant data [7,19]. The training set KDDTrain$^+$ contains 125,973 records, and the testing set KDDTest$^+$ contains 22,544 records [19]. In addition, the KDDTest^{-21} contains 11,850 records, where these records were not classified correctly by all 21 classifiers in [19]. The dataset simulates the following types of attacks:

1. Denial of Service (DoS): where an attacker attempts to make some resource too busy to handle valid requests or denies legal users access to a machine.
2. Probing Attack: in which an attacker attempts to collect data on a network of computers to find a way around an obstacle to violate the network's security controls.
3. User to Root Attack (U2R) is an attack in which an attacker gains access as a normal user account on the system, then searches to find any vulnerability to exploit and gain root access to the system.
4. Remote to Local Attack (R2L) send packets to a machine via a network, where the attacker does not have an account on that machine, in order to exploit some breaches to earn local access as a user of that machine.

The dataset has 5 classes that are normal, and 4 types of attacks: DoS, Probe, R2L, and U2R. The number of instances and attribute names of different attack classes in the NSL-KDD dataset are shown in Table 1. The testing set has some specific attack types that are not in the training set, thereby allowing realistic intrusion detection system evaluation. Such attacks are highlighted in the table [19].

Each record in the NSL-KDD dataset has 41 features, divided into three groups. *Basic features* are derived from TCP-IP connections, *traffic features* are collected from window intervals or the number of connections, and *content features* are taken from the application layer data of connections. The details of the 41 attributes are shown in Table 2.

3.2   Data Preprocessing

The NSL-KDD dataset, in its original format, cannot be directly processed. An ordinal encoding is used for conversion of non-numeric features to numeric features prior to the application of the model.

Categorical features in the NSL-KDD dataset are first converted into numerical values. For example, 'protocol_type' has three types of attributes: 'tcp', 'udp', and 'icmp'. We use ordinal encoding to convert the categorical values into numerical values, e.g. $1, 2, 3$. This is repeated for all categorical features (Protocol Type, Service and Flag), thus mapping the 41-dimensional feature map with textual categorical features into a 41-dimensional feature map with numerical categorical features.

Next, we scale all samples in KDDTrain$^+$ and KDDTest$^+$, as the NSL-KDD dataset's features have an extremely large gap between minimum and maximum

Table 1. Distribution of the NSL-KDD dataset

Attack class	Training set	Attribute name in training set	Testing set	Attribute name in Testing set
DOS	45927	back,land, teardrop, neptune, pod, smurf	7458	back,land, teardrop, neptune, pod, smurf, **udpstorm, apache2, processtable, worm, mailbomb**
Probing	11656	ipsweep, nmap, portsweep, satan	2421	ipsweep,nmap, portsweep, satan, **mscan, saint**
User to Root Attack (U2R)	52	loadmodule, buffer-overflow, perl, rootkit	200	buffer-overflow,loadmodule, perl,rootkit, **sqlattack, xterm, ps**
Remote to Local Attack (R2L)	995	fpt-write, guess-passwd, imap, multihop, phf, spy, warezclient, warezmaster	2754	fpt-write, guess-passwd, imap, multihop, phf, spy, warezmaster, **xlock, xsnoop, snmpguess, snmpgetattack, httptun-nel,sendmail, named**

Table 2. Details of the 41 attributes in the NSL-KDD dataset. Con: Continuous, Sym: Symbolic

Feat.	No.	Feature Name	Types	Feat.	No.	Feature name	Types
Basic features	1	Duration	Con	Traffic features	23	count	Con
	2	Protocol_type	Sym		24	Srv_count	Con
	3	Service	Sym		25	Serror_rate	Con
	4	Flag	Sym		26	Srv_scrror_rate	Con
	5	Src_bytes	Con		27	Rcrror_rate	Con
	6	Dst_bytes	Con		28	Srv_rcrror_rate	Con
	7	Land	Sym		29	Same_srv_rate	Con
	8	wrong_fragment	Con		30	diff_srv_rate	Con
	9	Urgent	Con		31	Srv_diff_host_rate	Con
	10	Bot	Con		32	Dst_host_count	Con
Content features	11	Num_failed_logins	Con		33	Dst_host_srv_count	Con
	12	Logged_in	Sym		34	Dst_host_same_srv_rate	Con
	13	Num_compromised	Con		35	Dst_host_diif_srv_rate	Con
	14	Root_shell	Con		36	dst_bost_same_src_port_rate	Con
	15	Su_attempted	Con		37	Dst_host_srv_diff_host_rate	Con
	16	Num_root	Con		38	Dst_host_serror_rate	Con
	17	Num_file_creations	Con		39	Dst_bost_srv_scrror_rate	Con
	18	Num_shells	Con		40	Dst_host_rcrror_rate	Con
	19	Num_access_files	Con		41	Dst_host_srv_rerror_rate	Con
	20	Num_outbound_cmds	Con				
	21	Is_host_login	Sym				
	22	is_guesl_login	Sym				

values. Samples are scaled into a distribution with mean equal to 0 and standard deviation equal to 1.

3.3 Deep Neural Network (DNN)

In this study, we propose two fully connected neural network models: BDDN and MDDN, where the first model (BDNN) is used for binary classification, and the second model (MDNN) is used for multiclass classification of network attacks. Both models consist of 4 hidden fully connected layers. The numbers of neurons in each hidden layer are 1024, 768, 512 and 256, respectively. The architecture of BDDN is shown in Figure 1.

The hidden layers employ the ReLU [6] nonlinearity function, defined as shown in Eq. 1:

$$ReLU(x) = max(0, x) \tag{1}$$

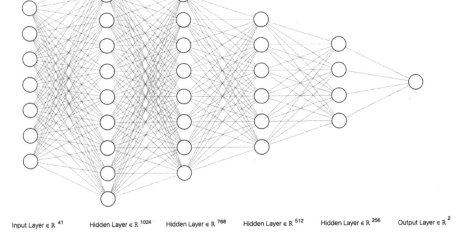

Input Layer ∈ R ^{41} Hidden Layer ∈ R ^{1024} Hidden Layer ∈ R ^{768} Hidden Layer ∈ R ^{512} Hidden Layer ∈ R ^{256} Output Layer ∈ R ^{2}

Fig. 1. Proposed Deep Neural Network model for binary classification (normal, anomaly)

A loss function is then employed in order to estimate the loss (error), and to make comparisons and measurements of the accuracy of the prediction result compared with the correct result. For BDNN, loss is calculated using **cross-entropy** or **log loss** as shown in Eq. 2:

$$H_p(q) = -\frac{1}{N} \sum_{i=1}^{N} y_i \cdot \log\left(p\left(y_i\right)\right) + \left(1 - y_i\right) \cdot \log\left(1 - p\left(y_i\right)\right) \tag{2}$$

where y_i is the label (1 for normal traffic and 0 for anomalous traffic) and $p(y_i)$ is the predicted probability of the point being normal traffic for all N points.

For multi-class classification in MDNN, we use **Categorical cross-entropy loss**, defined as shown below in Eq. 3:

$$H_p(q) = -\frac{1}{N} \sum_{i=1}^{N} y_i \cdot \log\left(p\left(y_i\right)\right) \tag{3}$$

where y_i is the label (0: normal, 1: Denial of service (DOS), 2: probing (Probe), 3: user to root (U2R) and 4: root to local (R2L)), and N denotes the number of classes.

We train both our neural networks for 100 epochs, using a batch size of 32, and the Adam [12] optimizer to minimize the loss of Binary cross–entropy and Categorical cross–entropy.

Batch Normalization and Regularization: We employ dropout and batch normalization between the fully connected layers. Dropout removes neurons with their connections randomly. We implement dropout (with a probability of 0.5) in all hidden fully connected layers. In addition, we use L2 regularization, with $\lambda = 0.0005$. The DNNs could easily overfit the training data without regularization and dropout, even when trained on a large number of samples. Regularization and dropout obviate overfitting and speedup the BDNN and MDNN models' training.

Classification: The last layer is a fully connected layer, which outputs the class of the input. For Binary classification, we use the Sigmoid activation function as shown in Eq. 4. Unlike linear functions, the output of the Sigmoid activation function is always in the range $[0, 1]$.

$$sigmoid = \frac{1}{1 + e^{-x}} \tag{4}$$

For Multi-class classification, we use the Softmax activation function, which outputs the probabilities of each class, where the largest class probability is selected as the output class, as shown in Eq. 5.

$$softmax\left(x_i\right) = \frac{e^{x_i}}{\sum_{j=1}^{n} e^{x_j}} \tag{5}$$

where x_i defines an input.

4   Experimental Results

4.1   Experimental Settings

The proposed frameworks were implemented using Tensorflow [20], an open source machine learning library, utilising Keras [10]. Experiments were carried out using GPUs running on the Google Colab [3] environment in order to minimize training time.

4.2   Performance Measures

For the evaluation of the proposed frameworks, we consider the most important performance indicators for intrusion detection systems. The following performance measures are calculated: accuracy, precision, detection rate, and F-measure.

Accuracy is the percentage of records classified correctly and it is calculated as follows:

$$Accuracy = \frac{TP + TN}{TP + TN + FP + FN} \tag{6}$$

Precision (P) is the percentage of records correctly classified as anomaly out of the total number of records classified as anomaly. Precision is calculated as follows:

$$P = \frac{TP}{TP + FP} \tag{7}$$

Detection Rate (DR): also *True Positive Rate* or *Recall*, the percentage of records correctly classified as anomaly out of the total number of anomaly records. The detection rate can be calculated as follows:

$$DR = \frac{TP}{TP + FN} \tag{8}$$

F-measure (F) is a measure that combines both precision and detection rate and it is calculated as follows:

$$F = \frac{2 * P * DR}{P + DR} \tag{9}$$

where TP (true positive) indicates the number of anomaly records that are identified as anomaly. FP (False positive) is the number of normal records that are identified as anomaly. TN (true Negative) is the number of normal records that are identified as normal. FN (false negative) is the number of anomaly records that are identified as normal.

4.3   Performance Evaluation

Our experiments are designed and conducted to study the efficiency and effectiveness of our proposed models. We evaluate the performance of BDNN and MDNN using the NSL-KDD dataset. The obtained results are compared with (1) the results of similar approaches in the literature and (2) results of various state-of-the-art classification algorithms. In particular, we compare BDNN with naïve Bayes, J48, Random Forest, Bagging, and Adaboost implemented in *Waikato Environment for Knowledge Analysis* (WEKA) [4]. All models were trained on KDDTrain$^+$ and tested on KDDTest$^+$. BDNN is designed for binary classification of network traffic into: normal or anomaly. MDNN deals with multiclass classification into five labels: normal, DOS, R2L, U2R and Probe.

Binary Classification Results. In this section, we present the classification results of BDNN on KDDTest$^+$ after training using KDDTrain$^+$. Table 3 shows the performance measures of BDNN compared to similar approaches in the literature. In terms of classification accuracy, BDNN performs better than ANN [8], SDN-DNN [18], and RNN-IDS [22] achieving an accuracy value of 84.70%. The results also shows that BDNN is able to detect 84.70% of all attacks, outperforming STL-IDS [1] and SDN-DDN [18]. The last row in Table 3 presents our training accuracy.

Table 3. Performance comparison with several related literature approaches for binary classification

Model	Accuracy	Precision	Recall	F-measure	Training datasets	Testing datasets
STL-IDS [1]	84.96%	96.23%	76.57%	85.28%	KDDTrain$^+$	KDDTest$^+$
ANN [8]	81.20%	N/A	N/A	N/A	KDDTrain$^+$	KDDTest$^+$
DNN [9]	88.39%	85.44%	95.95%	90.40%	KDDTrain$^+$	KDDTest$^+$
SDN-DDN [18]	75.75%	83.00%	75.00%	74.00%	KDDTrain$^+$ (6 features)	KDDTest$^+$
RNN-IDS [22]	83.28%	N/A	97.09%	N/A	KDDTrain$^+$	KDDTest$^+$
BDNN	84.70%	79.45%	87.00%	83.05%	KDDTrain$^+$	KDDTest$^+$
BDNN	99.50%	99.45%	99.69%	99.57%	80% of KDDTrain$^+$	20% of KDDTrain$^+$

Next, we compare our work with various state-of-the-art classification algorithms, as shown in Table 4. BDNN achieves the highest accuracy among all models. Its detection rate outperforms all other models by a large margin, where it is able to detect 87.00% of all attacks, with an F-measure of 83.05%. The best precision value is obtained by J48.

Table 4. Performance comparison with state-of-the-art approaches for binary classification

Model	Accuracy	Precision	Recall	F-measure
BDNN	**84.70%**	79.45%	**87.00%**	83.05%
naïve Bayes [4]	76.12%	92.38%	63.27%	75.10%
J48 [4]	81.53%	**97.14%**	69.61%	81.10%
Random Forest [4]	80.45%	97.05%	67.72%	79.77%
Bagging [4]	82.63%	91.87%	76.23%	**83.32%**
Adaboost [4]	78.44%	95.28%	65.37%	77.54%

Multiclass Classification Results. In this section, we present classification results on KDDTest$^+$ after training on KDDTrain$^+$. Table 5 presents our results compared with various models from the literature. It should be noted that Shone et al. [17] report training and not testing results, thereby improving their various performance measures values. The last row in Table 5 presents our training accuracy.

MDNN is able to correctly classify only 77.55% of the traffic records. However, MDNN is able to detect 77.55% of all attacks, outperforming STL-IDS [1] and DNN [9]. The results show that the classification accuracy of MDNN is lower than BDNN. MDNN outperforms NDAE [17] in terms of accuracy when tested using KDDTrain+.

Table 5. Performance comparisons with several related literature approaches for multiclass classification.

Model	Accuracy	Precision	Recall	F-measure	Training datasets	Testing datasets
STL-IDS [1]	80.48%	93.92%	68.28%	79.078 %	KDDTrain+	KDDTest+
ANN [8]	79.9%	N/A	N/A	N/A	KDDTrain+	KDDTest+
DNN [9]	79.10%	83%	68%	75.76%	KDDTrain+	KDDTest+
NDAE [17]	85.42%	100.00%	85.42%	87.37%	KDDTrain+	10% of KDDTrain+
RNN-IDS [22]	81.29%	N/A	97.09%	N/A	KDDTrain+	KDDTest+
MDNN	77.55%	81.23%	77.55%	75.43%	KDDTrain+	KDDTest+
MDNN	99.5%	99.53%	99.5%	99.51%	80% of KDDTrain+	20% of KDDTrain+

Table 6 presents the comparison of MDNN with state-of-the-art classification algorithms. MDNN achieves the best results in terms of accuracy, recall, and F-measure outperforming all the evaluated models.

Table 6. Performance comparison with state-of-the-art approaches for multi-class classification

Model	Accuracy	Precision	Recall	F-measure
MDNN	**77.55%**	81.23%	**77.55%**	**75.43%**
naïve Bayes [4]	72.73%	76.1%	72.7%	72.6%
J48 [4]	74.99%	79.6%	75.0%	71.1%
Random Forest [4]	76.45%	**82.1%**	76.4%	72.5%
Bagging [4]	74.83%	78.3%	74.8%	71.6%
Adaboost [4]	66.43%	N/A	66.0%	N/A

5   Conclusion

Network intrusion detection systems are important tools for monitoring network traffic. They are designed to detect abnormal and malicious network activity. In this paper, we presented two network intrusion detection models based on deep learning. Our models, BDNN and MDNN, are designed for binary and multi-class classification, respectively.

Our models were able to achieve excellent performance compared to state-of-the-art classification algorithms. In particular, BDNN and MDNN outperform naïve Bayes, J48, Random Forest, Bagging, and Adaboost in terms of accuracy and recall. In addition, they achieved excellent results compared to similar approaches. We observed that the classification accuracy of MDNN is lower than that of BDNN.

The proposed models can be used to detect unusual events, such as new attacks and violations inside an organization's network. In the future, the proposed models can be improved by increasing the number of hidden layers and neurons, or adding some convolutional layers, using different optimizers and trying new values for the learning rate.

Acknowledgment. This research project was supported by a grant from the *Research Center of the Female Scientific and Medical Colleges*, the Deanship of Scientific Research, King Saud University.

References

1. Al-Qatf, M., Lasheng, Y., Al-Habib, M., Al-Sabahi, K.: Deep learning approach combining sparse autoencoder with SVM for network intrusion detection. IEEE Access **6**, 52843–52856 (2018)
2. Aminanto, E., Kim, K.: Deep learning in intrusion detection system: an overview. In: 2016 International Research Conference on Engineering and Technology (2016 IRCET). Higher Education Forum (2016)
3. Welcome To Colaboratory - Colaboratory. https://colab.research.google.com/notebooks/welcome.ipynb
4. Frank, E., Hall, M.A., Witten, I.H.: The WEKA Workbench. Morgan Kaufmann, Burlington (2016)
5. Garcia-Teodoro, P., Diaz-Verdejo, J., Maciá-Fernández, G., Vázquez, E.: Anomaly-based network intrusion detection: techniques, systems and challenges. Comput. Secur. **28**(1–2), 18–28 (2009)
6. Glorot, X., Bordes, A., Bengio, Y.: Deep sparse rectifier neural networks. In: Proceedings of the Fourteenth International Conference on Artificial Intelligence and Statistics, pp. 315–323 (2011)
7. Hamid, Y., Balasaraswathi, V.R., Journaux, L., Sugumaran, M.: Benchmark datasets for network intrusion detection: a review. IJ Netw. Secur. **20**(4), 645–654 (2018)
8. Ingre, B., Yadav, A.: Performance analysis of NSL-KDD dataset using ANN. In: 2015 International Conference on Signal Processing and Communication Engineering Systems, pp. 92–96. IEEE (2015)
9. Javaid, A., Niyaz, Q., Sun, W., Alam, M.: A deep learning approach for network intrusion detection system. In: Proceedings of the 9th EAI International Conference on Bio-inspired Information and Communications Technologies (formerly BIONETICS), pp. 21–26. ICST (Institute for Computer Sciences, Social-Informatics and ...) (2016)
10. Home - Keras Documentation. https://keras.io/
11. Kim, K., Aminanto, M.E.: Deep learning in intrusion detection perspective: overview and further challenges. In: 2017 International Workshop on Big Data and Information Security (IWBIS), pp. 5–10. IEEE (2017)
12. Kingma, D.P., Ba, J.: Adam: a method for stochastic optimization. arXiv preprint arXiv:1412.6980 (2014)
13. Lee, B., Amaresh, S., Green, C., Engels, D.: Comparative study of deep learning models for network intrusion detection. SMU Data Sci. Rev. **1**(1), 8 (2018)

14. Mukkamala, S., Janoski, G., Sung, A.: Intrusion detection using neural networks and support vector machines. In: Proceedings of the 2002 International Joint Conference on Neural Networks. IJCNN 2002 (Cat. No. 02CH37290), vol. 2, pp. 1702–1707. IEEE (2002)
15. Panda, M., Patra, M.R.: Network intrusion detection using Naive Bayes. Int. J. Comput. Sci. Netw. Secur. **7**(12), 258–263 (2007)
16. Pasupa, K., Sunhem, W.: A comparison between shallow and deep architecture classifiers on small dataset. In: 2016 8th International Conference on Information Technology and Electrical Engineering (ICITEE), pp. 1–6. IEEE (2016)
17. Shone, N., Ngoc, T.N., Phai, V.D., Shi, Q.: A deep learning approach to network intrusion detection. IEEE Trans. Emerg. Top. Comput. Intell. **2**(1), 41–50 (2018)
18. Tang, T.A., Mhamdi, L., McLernon, D., Zaidi, S.A.R., Ghogho, M.: Deep learning approach for network intrusion detection in software defined networking. In: 2016 International Conference on Wireless Networks and Mobile Communications (WINCOM), pp. 258–263. IEEE (2016)
19. Tavallaee, M., Bagheri, E., Lu, W., Ghorbani, A.A.: A detailed analysis of the KDD CUP 99 data set. In: 2009 IEEE Symposium on Computational Intelligence for Security and Defense Applications, pp. 1–6. IEEE (2009)
20. TensorFlow. https://www.tensorflow.org/
21. Wang, G., Hao, J., Ma, J., Huang, L.: A new approach to intrusion detection using artificial neural networks and fuzzy clustering. Expert Syst. Appl. **37**(9), 6225–6232 (2010)
22. Yin, C., Zhu, Y., Fei, J., He, X.: A deep learning approach for intrusion detection using recurrent neural networks. IEEE Access **5**, 21954–21961 (2017)

Over-Sampling Multi-classification Method Based on Centroid Space

Haiyong Wang[1], Weizheng Guan[2($\boxtimes$)], and Kaixin Zhang[2]

[1] School of Computer, Nanjing University of Posts and Telecommunications, Nanjing 210003, Jiangsu, China
[2] School of Internet of Things, Nanjing University of Posts and Telecommunications, Nanjing 210003, Jiangsu, China
1240205380@qq.com

Abstract. The problem of unbalanced data generally exists in various application fields of large data and machine learning, such as medical diagnosis, anomaly detection and so on. Researchers have proposed or adopted a variety of methods to learn unbalanced data. For example, SMOTE algorithm in data sampling, or EasyEnsemble method in ensemble learning. Oversampling method in data sampling may have some problems, such as low accuracy of over-fitting classification, while under-sampling method may lead to under-fitting. In this paper, an up-sampling method based on centroid space (CSUP) is proposed, which mainly aims at multi-classification problems. The proposed method solves the problem of data set imbalance well. Firstly, the initial centroid is obtained by solving the Euclidean distance between samples, and then the total distance is obtained by summing up the Euclidean distance of each centroid. By dividing the Euclidean distance of a single centroid by the total Euclidean distance, the sample points need to be increased can be obtained. The weight is multiplied by the number of sample points needed to be balanced, which makes the unbalanced data set more balanced in distribution and effectively improves the classification effect of the classifier. The experimental results show that the classification accuracy of CSUP is significantly higher than that of other algorithms, suvch as SMOTE. Adaboost etc.

Keywords: Up-sampling · SMOTE algorithm · Ensemble learning · Unbalanced data · Centroid

1 Introduction

Unbalanced data widely exists in people's actual production and life, and the learning of unbalanced data usually faces great challenges [1]. Traditional machine learning [2] classification algorithms usually assume that the proportion of different classes of data is balanced, treat different classes of samples equally, and aim at improving the overall classification accuracy. However, this kind of algorithm does not take data distribution into account. When the number of one class of data is much larger than that of other classes, it will cause classifiers to lean towards most classes, making the classification accuracy of most classes higher while that of minority classes lower. In the worst case, minority classes will be regarded as most classes. The outliers are ignored and all

© Springer Nature Singapore Pte Ltd. 2020
Y. Tian et al. (Eds.): ICBDS 2019, CCIS 1210, pp. 616–632, 2020.
https://doi.org/10.1007/978-981-15-7530-3_47

samples are classified into most classes. In this case, the model learnt is obviously wrong and may cause serious consequences [3]. For example, in the field of medical diagnosis, if a patient with cancer is misjudged as normal, it may cost his life. For example, in bank fraud detection, generally speaking, most of the customers are trading normally, but the behavior of individual customers may be fraudulent. Although the number of such actions is very small, the losses caused are huge. Traditional machine learning classification methods have great limitations in unbalanced data sets. We must take some measures to ensure that we can learn important information from these few samples. Therefore, it is of great significance to study such problems [4].

At present, many effective technologies have been used to alleviate the problem of unbalanced data learning, such as data sampling and ensemble learning [5]. Data sampling generally balances data distribution by adding or reducing samples. It is mainly divided into two ways: over-sampling and under-sampling. The simplest way is to resample the original data randomly [6]. Random oversampling is to extract samples from a few samples randomly and repeatedly and add them to the original samples. Random undersampling is to extract samples from most samples randomly and repeatedly and delete them from the original samples. By setting the appropriate sampling proportion, different samples can eventually achieve balance. Both random oversampling and random undersampling have some defects. Random over-sampling is easy to cause over-fitting because it simply duplicates samples, while random under-sampling may lose some useful information because it reduces most kinds of samples.

Integrated learning is a method to accomplish learning tasks by building and combining multiple learners. By combining multiple learners, it can often achieve better generalization performance than a single learner. According to the generation method of integrated individual learners, integrated learning can be divided into two main categories: (1) Bagging, as see in Fig. 1, there is no strong dependency and parallel method [7]; and (2) Boosting, as see in Fig. 2, there is strong dependency and serialization method [8]. Bagging uses boostraping (random sampling with return) technology to sample the original sample back. After obtaining a series of sub-samples, Bagging trains each sub-sample to get multiple learners, and then integrates them. Random forest is a variant of Bagging. Boosting iteratively trains the original samples. Each iteration modifies the distribution of the original samples according to the training results of the previous iteration, and then integrates them after obtaining different learners. The classical Boosting method is Adaboost.

Bagging and Boosting, two algorithms of ensemble learning, increase the weight of misclassified samples and decrease the weight of correct classified samples in the same proportion for the problem of unbalanced data distribution, but the classification effect is not good. Scholar Jin Xu proposed an under-sampling method for unbalanced data based on centroid space [9]. This algorithm is based on the principle of under-sampling, proposed to reduce the number of multi-class samples, so that the sample data can be balanced, and trained with support vector machine to get the model [10], and then validated the test set. For the algorithm proposed by scholar Jin Xu, the accuracy of classification has been improved to some extent, but there are many improvements in the selection of algorithm and final training model. In this paper, under-sampling algorithm is selected to process unbalanced data, which is prone to inadequate training and low learning ability, which is commonly called under-fitting.

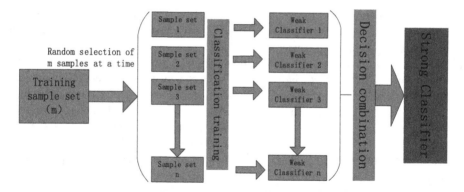

Fig. 1. Bagging algorithm flow chart.

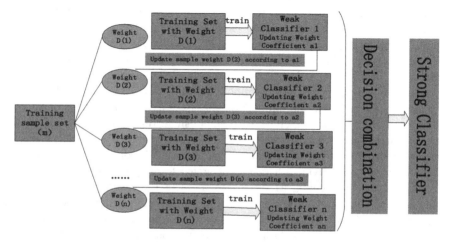

Fig. 2. Boosting algorithm flow chart.

Support Vector Machine (SVM) is used to train the model. The classification effect of SVM is obvious for binary classification problems with small sample set and simple sample set, but it is not good for multi-classification problems with large sample set [11].

On the basis of over-sampling technology, Bagging and Boosting integrated learning idea, this paper proposes a new hybrid integrated sampling algorithm, which is based on the multi-classification algorithm of up-sampling in centroid space. The core of this algorithm is to do up-sampling on the basis of centroid space to deal with multi-classification problems. Firstly, small classes are found. The initial centroid of this paper is then clustered using k-means algorithm, and K clusters are finally obtained. Choose the sample with the greatest similarity to its centroid in each cluster to form the final sample set of small class samples [12]. This method guarantees the attribute of information content in samples to the greatest extent, while following the premise of increasing the number of small samples. The main process of obtaining the initial centroid is as follows: Firstly, the sum of Euclidean distances between each sample in the sample set and other samples is calculated separately, then the sample with the minimum distance is taken as the first initial cluster centroid, then the sample with the largest centroid distance of the first initial cluster is taken as the second initial centroid, and finally the sample with the largest centroid distance of the first initial cluster is taken as the second initial centroid. The maximum sample of the distance between the first and the second centroid is the third initial centroid; by analogy, the initial centroid set of the k-means algorithm will be obtained. The first initial centroid is obtained by solving, not by random selection, because the randomly selected samples may not represent the attributes of the small class of feature samples, which is prone to large generalization errors. The core of this method is to get the Euclidean distance between each centroid on the basis of the centroid, sum all the Euclidean distances of the centroid, and get a total Euclidean distance. Then divide the single Euclidean distance of each centroid by the total Euclidean distance separately, we can get that each small class of centroid samples need to increase the number of samples. Increase weight. By multiplying the weight by the total number of samples that need to be increased, the number of samples with each centroid can be increased, and the final data distribution balanced sample set can be obtained, which can improve the classification effect of the classifier. The experimental results show that the classification accuracy of the proposed method is better than that of other methods.

Section 2 presents the related research, and introduces sampling technology and typical methods in sampling technology in detail: SMOTE algorithm, random sampling, Adaboost algorithm, SVM algorithm; Sect. 3 introduces the method proposed in detail; Sect. 4 introduces the comparative experiments and the data sets used, mainly using the classification accuracy as the performance evaluation index to analyze and summarize the full text.

2 Related Work

At present, there are many methods to alleviate the imbalance problem through data sampling and ensemble learning. In data sampling technology, there are mainly two ways: oversampling and undersampling. SMOTE (Synthetic Minority Oversampling) is an effective method for over-sampling. Its basic idea is to synthesize new samples according to the feature space similarity of a few samples. Random under-sampling is a typical method in under-sampling. Its main idea is to delete some samples randomly from a large sample set until the number of small samples is balanced. Of course, in the process of dealing with imbalance problems, it is often applied to the method of integrated university. Here we introduce a widely used method of integrated learning, AdaBoost algorithm. AdaBoost algorithm is a classical boosting algorithm, which achieves better prediction effect by combining weak classifiers. These algorithms are described below.

2.1   SMOTE Algorithm

Chawla et al. proposed a method of over-sampling a few classes by creating synthetic samples. It is called SMOTE (Synthetic Minority Over-sampling Technology) [13]. It is an improvement of random over-sampling technology and can avoid the problem of over-fitting model to a certain extent. Here's how to synthesize new samples.

If the number of samples of a minority class in the training set is T, then SMOTE algorithm will synthesize NT new samples for this minority class. This requires that N must be a positive integer. If given N < 1, the algorithm will "think" that the sample number of a few classes is T = NT, and will force N = 1.

Consider a sample i of this minority class, whose eigenvectors are X_i, $i \in \{1, ..., T\}$:

1) Firstly, K nearest neighbors (e.g. Euclidean distance) of sample X_i are found from all T samples of this minority class, which are denoted as X_i (near), near $\in \{1, ..., k\}$.
2) Then, a sample X_i (nn) is randomly selected from the K neighbors and regenerated into a random number $\zeta 1$ between 0 and 1 to synthesize a new sample X_{i1}:

$$X_{i1} = X_I + \zeta 1 \times (X_I(nn) - X_I) \qquad (1)$$

3) Repeat step 2 NN times to synthesize NN new samples: $X_i new \in 1, ..., N$. Then, NT new samples can be synthesized for all T minority samples by the above operations.

If the feature dimension of the sample is 2 dimensional space, then each sample can be represented by a point on the two-dimensional plane. A new sample X_{i1} synthesized by SMOTE algorithm is equivalent to a point on the line segment between the point representing the sample X_i and the point representing the present X_i (nn). So the algorithm is based on "interpolation" to synthesize new samples. SMOTE algorithm improves the problem of unbalanced data sets and improves the accuracy of classification and prediction of samples. However, random under-sampling method will lose many samples' information, and SMOTE over-sampling method will make a few classes of sample data set over-fitting [14].

2.2   Random Sampling Algorithm

Simple random sampling is that the probability of each sample unit being sampled is equal, each sample unit is completely independent, and there is no certain correlation and exclusion between them. There are two forms of random sampling, random up-sampling and random down-sampling. The main idea of random up-sampling is to increase the number of samples in small classes until the number of samples in large classes is balanced. The main idea of random down-sampling is to delete some samples randomly from large classes of samples until the number of samples in small classes is flat. Heng. These two methods alleviate the problem of data inequality to a certain extent, but whether they increase the number of small samples or reduce the number of large samples, they will result in the loss of important information and the introduction of irrelevant feature attributes, and may delete some samples which have a greater positive impact on classification and increase the complexity of data. Those noise samples or those that have no effect on classification remain in the large sample set, which affects the accuracy of classification [15].

2.3 Adaboost Algorithm

Adaboost algorithm is a classical boosting algorithm, which achieves better prediction effect by combining weak classifiers [16]. The basic process is as follows: Firstly, each sample is given the same weight, for example, the number of samples is m, the weight of each sample is set to 1/m, and a weak classifier is trained based on the sample distribution. Each iteration of Adaboost adjusts the weight distribution of the samples, especially for the wrong samples, which greatly increases the weight, so that more attention will be paid to the wrong samples in the next iteration training. According to the results of classification, the weight of samples is updated, and the weight of samples with wrong classification is increased, while the weight of samples with wrong classification is reduced. At the same time, the weight of the weak classifier is obtained. According to the new distribution of samples, a new round of training is carried out to update the weight of samples, and new weak classifiers and their weights are obtained. Through T iteration cycles, T weak classifiers and their weights are obtained. Finally, T weak classifiers Sm and their weights are linearly combined to obtain the final strong classifier.

The training process of the algorithm is as follows:

Input: Training sample set $\{(X_1, Y_1), (X_2, Y_2)... (X_i, Y_i)\}$, i = 1, 2, 3,... n, $Y_i \in \{1,0\}$, iteration times T, base classifier f.

Output : $H(X) = \text{sign}[\sum_{i=1}^{T} \sigma_t f_t(X)]$

1) Initialization of Sample Distribution Weight $D_t(i) = \frac{1}{n}$, i = 1,2,3,...,n
2) For t = 1 to T :

2.1) Training weak classifier f_t: X →Y based on sample distribution D_t

2.2) Calculating the classification error rate et = $\sum_{i=1}^{n} D_t(i)I(f_t(X_i) \neq Y_i)$, I is the indicator function.

2.3) Calculating the Weight of Weak Classifier $\sigma_t = \frac{1}{2}\ln\frac{1-e_t}{e_t}$

2.4) Updating Sample Weights $Dt + 1(i) = \frac{D_t(i)}{Z_t}\exp(-\sigma_t Y_i f_t(X_i))$, $i = 1, 2,$

3,..., n, $Zt = \sum_{i=1}^{n} D_t(i)\exp(-\sigma_t Y_i f_t(X_i))$ is a normalization factor

3) End For
4) $H(X) = \text{sign}[\sum_{i=1}^{T} \sigma_t f_t(X)]$
5) Return H(X)

2.4 SVM Algorithm

The purpose of SVM is to find an optimal classification surface that maximizes the classification interval of all kinds of samples. Taking two classifications as an example, the training set T is assumed to be m d-dimensional samples, T = {(x₁, y₁), (x₂, y₂),... (xₘ, yₘ)}, where $X_i \in R_m$, $Y_i \in (-1,1)$ is the class label of the training sample, and R_m is the feature space of the input sample. In the case of nonlinearity, the definition $\varphi(x)$ maps the sample to the high-dimensional space [17]. The training process of SVM is to find an optimal classification surface, so that two kinds of samples can be classified through the classification surface, and the error is minimum. SVM is proposed by Boser et al. based on structural risk minimization to meet the maximum classification interval between two types of samples. SVM is to solve the following quadratic programming problems. Its core content is: For the non-linear separable problem in the input space, a suitable mapping is selected to map the sample points in the input space to a high-dimensional feature space, and the corresponding sample points are linearly separable in the space. Moreover, through the in-depth study of the kernel function, the calculation in the process of finding the decision function is still in the original space, which greatly reduces the computational complexity. Computing complexity of high-dimensional feature space after mapping. The algorithm steps are as follows:

1) Known training set, T = {(x₁,y₁), (x₂,y₂),...,(xₘ,yₘ)}, where $x_i \in R_m, y_i \in (-1,1)$, i = 1, 2,...,M.
2) In this paper, the kernel function to be selected is Radial Basis Function, i.e. K(x, x') = exp[−σ| x−xi|2]and the appropriate penalty parameter C is chosen. Construct and solve optimization problems such as formula (2) and formula (3), and find the optimal solution a* = (a1*, a2*,... (aM*) T.

$$\max Q(a) = \sum\nolimits_{i=1}^{M} a_i - \frac{1}{2}\sum\nolimits_{i=1}^{M} a_i a_j y_i y_j H\left(x_i, x_j\right) \tag{2}$$

$$\sum\nolimits_{i=1}^{M} a_i y_i = 0;\ i = 1, 2, \ldots, M. \tag{3}$$

3) In a* = (a1*, a2*,..., aM*)T. The positive component a_j^*, which is less than C, is selected and b*, which is calculated.
4) Finding Decision Function y = sign[$\sum\limits_{I=1}^{M} a_i^* y_i H\left(x_i, x_j\right) + b^*$]

3 Up-Sampling Multi-classification Method Based on Centroid Space

3.1 Up-Sampling Algorithm Based on Centroid Space

The main idea of this algorithm is to use k-means algorithm to cluster small sample sets, so that the number of samples in large sample sets is approximately equal to that in small sample sets. That is to say, over-sampling is used in small sample sets, which basically solves the problem of uneven distribution of data. Finally, the processed data sets are processed. Machine learning algorithm is used for model learning to complete classification.

In this paper, the upper sampling algorithm based on centroid space is mainly based on K-means algorithm for small sample set, and K-means algorithm is used to solve the centroid and get centroid clusters of samples. The process of solving the centroid is as follows: Suppose the data set is D = {(x1, y1), (x2, y2),... (xN, yN)}, where N is the number of data objects and K is the number of clusters, the initial centroid set of K clusters is found to be C = {c1, c2,... Ck}. The process of solving the center of mass is as follows:

1) Calculate the Euclidean distance between each sample and other samples in data set D:

$$\text{Dist}\left(x_i, x_j\right) = \sqrt{\left(a_{i1} - a_{j1}\right)^2 + \left(a_{i2} - a_{j2}\right)^2 + \ldots + \left(a_{ik} - a_{jk}\right)^2} \qquad (4)$$

2) From the above formula, the sum of the Euclidean distances between each sample and other samples in data set D is:

$$\text{sumDist}(xi, xj) = \sum_{i,j \in D} \text{Dist}(xi, xj) \qquad (5)$$

3) According to the above formula, the initial center of mass xFirst = $\underbrace{argmin}_{x_i \in D}$(sumDist (xi,xj)) is obtained, and the initial center of mass C1 is obtained by using this formula. The initial centroid obtained by this method is based on the minimum sum of the Euclidean distance between the sample and other samples, so it does not produce noise between samples. The precondition for the initial centroid is that the sample must belong to a small cluster of samples.

4) For the remaining k−1 centroids, take the sample with the largest distance from the first initial cluster centroid as the second initial centroid, and xSecond = $\underbrace{argmin}_{x_i \in D}$(-sumDist(xi, xj)), so as to get the second centroid C2, and then take the sample with the largest distance from the first and second centroids as the sample The third initial center of mass, and $\underbrace{argmax}_{x_i \in (D-(X_{First} \cup Xsecond))}$ (Dist(x$_i$, x$_{First}$) + Dist(x$_i$, x$_{Secend}$), then get the third centroid C3, and by analogy, The centroid set of K-means algorithm will be obtained {C1, C2, C3, ..., Ck}. The first initial centroid is obtained by solving, not by random selection, because the randomly selected samples may not represent the attributes of the small class of feature samples, which is prone to large generalization errors. The proposed algorithm is based on the centroid space up-sampling algorithm. Assuming data set D, positive class (large class) sample set is $X^+ = \{(x_1^+, y_1^+), \ldots, (x_m^+, y_m^+)\}$, negative class (subclass) sample set is $X^- = \{(x_1^-, y_1^-), \ldots, (x_n^-, y_n^-)\}$, for the data sets of these two types of samples satisfying m >> n, we use the up-sampling algorithm here, mainly for negative sample

sets to cluster by K-means to get centroid clusters, and then according to the distribution of centroid clusters to increase negative samples, so that the number of positive samples and negative samples can reach a balance. And finally reach n ≈ m.

The introduction of the similarity calculation formulas of samples and centroids in k-means algorithm is assumed that each sample is expressed as xi = $(a_{i1}, a_{i2}, \ldots, a_{ik})$ each center of mass is expressed as $C_j = (b_{j1}, b_{j2}, \ldots, b_{jk},)$, then the similarity between sample x_i and each centroid C_j is also measured by Euclidean distance. The smaller the distance, the greater the similarity. The calculation formula is as follows:

$$\text{Sim}(x_i, c_j) = \frac{xi * c_j}{||xi|| * ||c_j||} = \frac{\sum_{h=1}^{k} a_{ih} * b_{jh}}{\sqrt{\sum_{h=1}^{k} a_{ih}^2} * \sqrt{\sum_{h=1}^{k} C_{jh}^2}} \tag{6}$$

5) For the samples with the greatest similarity in each cluster, the similarity is measured according to the Euclidean distance. The closer the distance is, the higher the similarity is. For the clusters with negative classes, the upper sampling method is used to increase the number of negative classes according to the weight of the Euclidean distance in the total distance, and new samples are always obtained. This set $X^- = \{(x_1^-, y_1^-),\ldots,(x_m^-, y_m^-)\}$ The balanced data set is obtained, and then classified by using other multi-classification models. Finally, the training model is tested and validated by the test set.

The specific algorithm described in this paper based on the centroid space upsampling algorithm is as follows:

Up-sampling algorithm based on centroid space:

Input : Data set D = $\{(x_1,y_1),(x_2,y_2),\ldots, (x_{n+m},y_{n+m})\}$ = $X^+ \cup X^-$, positive class (large class) sample set is $X^+ = \{(x_1^+, y_1^+),\ldots, (x_m^+, y_m^+)\}$, negative class (subclass) sample set is $X^- = \{(x_1^-, y_1^-),\ldots,(x_n^-, y_n^-)\}$, for these two types of samples, the data set satisfies m > > n.

Output : Balanced data set D*.

1) Using the centroid algorithm mentioned above, K initial cluster centers {C1,C2,... Ck}.

2) For data set D, there are positive class samples X^+ and negative class samples X^-. The number of samples needed to be balanced is obtained by subtracting the number of positive samples from the number of negative samples, and $X^+ - X^-$ = G. At the same time, the unbalance degree of the sample set is b = $\frac{X^+}{X^-}$, then b ∈ (0,1).

3) For each example $x_i \in X^-$, i = 1,2,...,n

4) According to the above similarity formula and cluster update formula, a new centroid set { $c_1', c_2', \cdots, c_k'$ }, the new centroid cluster has the highest similarity and the smallest generalization error.

5) Based on the new centroid cluster, there is a first centroid X1. For solving the Euclidean distance corresponding to the first centroid is L1, for solving the second

centroid is L2, and for solving the Euclidean distance corresponding to the second centroid is L2. By analogy, for solving the K centroid, the corresponding Euclidean distance is Lk.

6) Ltotal = sum (L1, L2,...,Lk).
7) Calculate the proportion of the Euclidean distance of each centroid cluster in the total Euclidean distance and $Pi = \frac{Li}{Ltotal}$
8) According to the weight of the Euclidean distance occupied by each centroid cluster, the number of samples needed to increase for each centroid cluster and $gi = Pi \times G$ can be obtained.

This algorithm improves the classification imbalance problem obviously. We introduce the concept of centroid space, use centroid-based up-sampling method for negative samples, and solve centroid clusters based on K-mean algorithm. This algorithm can make the added samples more aggregated, thus reducing the generalization error. For the eventual balanced sample set, we use centroid-based up sampling method to solve centroid clusters. We use multi-classification method to train and get the model. Finally, we use the test set to test and verify. Here we use cross-validation method to test and verify.

3.2   A Multi-classification Method Based on the Above Algorithms

The first chapter is mainly about the processing algorithm of unbalanced data sets, while this chapter is mainly about the introduction of classification algorithm. In order to solve the simple binary classification problem, Vapnik et al. put forward a general and efficient machine learning method SVM (Support Vector Machine). SVM has good accuracy and generalization ability in dealing with binary classification problems, but it is incomplete in dealing with multi-classification problems. It is necessary for the original SVM algorithm to carry out classification. Improvement. This chapter proposes an improved algorithm based on SVM.

The characteristic of multi-classification problem is that there is one attribute with the highest weight for each category in the sample set, but there are common data domains among these attributes. The improved algorithm based on SVM proposed in this chapter aims at such multi-classification problem, grouping each data in the data set. As a binary classification problem, the improved SVM algorithm can be used to treat the multi-classification problem as multiple binary classification problems. According to the idea of multi-classification problem, the decision models of multiple attributes should be similar, keeping the local optimum of each training sub-model while minimizing the global differences among the models. For each binary classification problem, the decision function f_r can be expressed as the sum of a common decision function g0 and a modified function g_r:

$$f_r = g0 + g_r \tag{7}$$

Specifically, its decision function f_r can be written as follows:

$$f_r(x) = w \times \varphi(x) + b + w_r \times \varphi_r(x) + b_r, \text{ where } r = 1, 2, 3 \ldots \qquad (8)$$

For the above formulas, the common decision function is $g0 = w \times \varphi(x) + b$, and the correction function for each category is $g_r = w_r \times \varphi(x) + b_r$.

The objective function of the improved SVM-based algorithm proposed in this paper is as follows:

$$\min_{\substack{w_1, w_2 \ldots, w_r}} \frac{1}{2}(w \cdot w) + \frac{\gamma}{2}\sum_{r=1}^{r}(w_r \cdot w_r) +$$

$$p_1, p_2, \ldots p_r,$$

$$d_1, d_2, \ldots d_r,$$

$$\sum_{r=1}^{r}\left(\frac{1}{v_r^+ m_r^+}\sum \zeta_i^r\right)$$

s.t.

$$w \cdot \varphi(x_i) + b + w_r \cdot \varphi_r(x_r) + d_r \geq 1 - \zeta_i^r, (w \cdot \varphi(x_i) + b + w_r\varphi_r(x_r) + d_r) \geq 1 + p_r^2 - \zeta_j^r,$$

$$\zeta_i^r \geq 0, \ \zeta_j^r \geq 0, \quad i \in X^+, j \in X^-, r = 1, 2, 3, \ldots$$

$$(9)$$

For the above formulas m_r^+ and m_r^- respectively represent the number of samples of minority and majority classes in the r-th category. For each class, the number of relevant sample points is different. The regularization constants of v_r^+ and v_r^- correspond to the minority and majority classes in the r-th category respectively, and the constants are the decisive ones. The weights between the policy function and the correlation correction function are expressed as relaxation variables in the first category of r for the ζ_i^r and ζ_j^r, respectively.

Based on the principle of structural risk and empirical risk minimization, in order to better optimize the above objective functions, we need to give the following explanations and explanations:

1) Firstly, the improved SVM-based algorithm needs to consider the similarity and consistency of classification among the r categories while ensuring the optimal classification of each category sample, so as to obtain useful inductive information among different categories. For the $\sum_{r=1}^{r}(w_r \cdot w_r)$ in the objective function, the difference between different categories is expressed. The larger the value is, the greater the difference between different categories is. On the contrary, the smaller the value is, the smaller the difference between different categories is, and the degree of punishment can be adjusted by γ.

2) The kernels used in the common decision function and the correction function may be the same or different. In this experiment, we will use two kinds of kernels, linear kernels and Gauss kernels.

3) The improved algorithm based on SVM, as SVM, classifies the attributes of samples, uses these specific attributes to construct models, and improves the generalization ability of models by mining hidden information between samples.

4) In the original SVM model, the relaxation variable represents the correction function. Since the relaxation variable must not be less than 0, the correction function must also be greater than or equal to 0. In the improved algorithm, the correction function represents the degree of difference between tasks, so the correction function need not be set to be greater than 0.

By introducing Lagrangian vectors α and β, the Lagrangian function corresponding to the objective function of the improved SVM based algorithm can be written as follows:

$$L(w, w_1, w_2, \ldots, w_r, p_1, p_2, \ldots p_r, d_1, d_2, \ldots d_r, , \alpha, \beta)$$

$$= (w \cdot w) \frac{\gamma}{2} \sum_{r=1}^r (w_r \cdot w_r)$$

$$+ \sum_{r=1}^r \left(\frac{1}{v_r^+ m_r^+} \sum \zeta_i^r \right) + \sum_{r=1}^r \left(\frac{1}{v_r^- m_r^-} \sum \zeta_j^r \right) - \sum_{r=1}^r \left(\sum_{i=1}^i \alpha_i (w \cdot \varphi(x_i) + b + w_r \cdot \varphi_r(x_i) + d_r - 1 + \zeta_i^r) \right)$$

$$+ \sum^i \alpha_j (w \cdot \varphi(x_j) + b + w_r \cdot \varphi_r(x_j) + d_r + 1 + p_r^2 - \zeta_j^r)) -$$

$$\sum_{r=1}^r \sum_{r=1}^i \beta_i \zeta_i^r - \sum_{r=1}^r \sum_{r=1}^i \beta_j \zeta_j^r - v \sum_{r=1}^r p_r^2$$

$$(10)$$

According to KKT condition, we can get:

$$\frac{\partial L}{\partial W} = 0 \Rightarrow w = \sum_{i=1}^r \alpha_i y_i \varphi(x_i) \tag{11}$$

$$\frac{\partial L}{\partial w_r} = 0 \Rightarrow w_r = \frac{1}{r} \sum_{i=1}^r \alpha_i y_i \varphi_r(x_i) \tag{12}$$

$$\frac{\partial L}{\partial b} = 0 \Rightarrow \sum_{i=1}^r \alpha_i - \sum_{i=1}^r \alpha_j = 0, \, r = 1, 2, \ldots, t \tag{13}$$

$$\frac{\partial L}{\partial p_r} = 0 \Rightarrow \sum_{i=1}^r \alpha_j = v, \, r = 1, 2, \ldots, t \tag{14}$$

$$\frac{\partial L}{\partial \zeta_i^r} = 0 \Rightarrow \alpha_i + \beta_i = \frac{1}{v_r^+ m_r^+}, \, i \in T_r^+, \, r = 1, \ldots, t \tag{15}$$

$$\frac{\partial L}{\partial \zeta_j^r} = 0 \Rightarrow \alpha_i + \beta_i = \frac{1}{v_r^- m_r^-}, \, j \in T_r^-, \, r = 1, \ldots, t \tag{16}$$

By introducing the above equation into the objective function of the improved SVM-based algorithm, the dual equation can be obtained:

$$\min \sum_{i=1}^{r} \sum_{j=1}^{r} \alpha_i \alpha_j y_i y_j (\varphi(x_i) \cdot \varphi(x_j)) + \frac{1}{r} \sum_{i=1}^{r} \sum_{j=1}^{r} \alpha_i \alpha_j y_i y_j (\varphi(x_i) \cdot \varphi(x_j))$$

$$\text{s.t} \quad \sum_{i=1}^{r} \alpha_i y_i = 0, \quad r = 1, 2, \ldots, t$$

$$\sum \alpha_i = v, \sum \alpha_j = v, r = 1, 2, \ldots, t$$

$$0 \le \alpha_i \le \frac{1}{V_r^+ m_r^+}, i \in T_r^+, r = 1, \ldots, t$$

$$0 \le \alpha_j \le \frac{1}{V_r^- m_r^-}, j \in T_r^-, r = 1, \ldots, t$$

$$\alpha_i \ge 0, i = 1, \ldots, r$$

$$(17)$$

From the above formulas, the time complexity of the dual form of the objective function of the improved SVM-based algorithm is $O(N^3)$

4   Design of Experiment and Analysis of Experiment Results

4.1   Experimental Performance Evaluation Indicators

For the learning of unbalanced data, the general evaluation method of overall accuracy is obviously not applicable. Therefore, this paper adopts four different indicators to evaluate the performance of the model, including Precision, Recall, F-Measure and G-mean. The confusion matrix is shown in the Table 1. These indicators are defined as follows:

$$\text{Precision} = \frac{TP}{TP + FP}, \text{Recall} = \frac{TP}{TP + FN}$$

$$\text{F—Measure} = \frac{(1 + \beta^2) \cdot Precision \cdot Recall}{\beta^2 \cdot Precision + Recall}$$ Among them, β is a relatively important factor to regulate Precision and Recall.

Table 1. Confusion matrix.

	Positive	Negative
True	True Positive (TP)	True Nagative (TN)
False	False Positive (FP)	False Negative (FN)

$$\text{G—mean} = \sqrt{\frac{TP}{TP + FN} \times \frac{TN}{TN + FP}} = \sqrt{TPRTNR}$$

In many classification applications, we always hope to identify all the few samples as far as possible. For example, in the field of anomaly detection, we hope to detect all the outliers as far as possible so as not to cause great losses. This requirement is reflected in the performance evaluation index, which pays more attention to Recall index, expecting it to approach 1 as close as possible (if higher Precision can be obtained, it will be more perfect). Therefore, our goal is to improve Recall as much as possible, allowing a slight sacrifice of Precision, so that F-measure or G-measure can be integrated as a whole. Standard performance remains stable or improved.

Experimental environment: The experimental environment adopted in this paper is mainly based on the performance of the author's laptop. The processor: intel (R) Core (TM) i7-8550U CPU@1.80 GHz 2.00 GHz, RAM 8.00 GB, Anaconda3.

4.2 Experimental Design

In order to reduce the deviation caused by random partitioning of data sets, all experiments in this paper adopt the method of 10-fold cross-validation, which divides the whole data set into 10 parts, nine of them are selected for training each time, the remaining one is used for testing, and the final evaluation index takes the average of 10 training times.

The data set used in the experiment is from UCI database, and the classifier for identifying tutors and students is trained through the data of scientific research papers and other items. Table 2 lists the basic information of these unbalanced data sets, including the name of the data set, the number of samples, the number of a few samples and the degree of unbalance (d = a few samples/a majority of samples).

Table 2. Basic information of unbalanced data sets.

Name	Sample size	Few samples	Non-equilibrium degree (d)
Liver1	12500	481	0.04
Liver2	12500	926	0.08
Liver3	12500	1339	0.12
Liver4	12500	1724	0.16

This paper mainly uses precision, G-means as evaluation measure.

4.3 Analysis and Summary of Experimental Results

The experiment is implemented on Anaconda platform. The proposed algorithm is based on the centroid space up-sampling (CSUP) algorithm, compared with SMOTE algorithm, random down-sampling (RDS) algorithm and Adaboost algorithm in the same data set. Table 3 is the comparison of the experimental results.

The information in Table 3 is shown in Fig. 3 and Fig. 4. The results are more intuitive and easy to compare.

According to Fig. 3, when precision is used as an evaluation index, The precision value of CSUP proposed in this paper is higher than that of other algorithms. Although the imbalance rate increases and the precision value decreases, the precision value of the algorithms proposed in this paper increases by an average of 2% compared with

Table 3. Comparison of experimental results of various algorithms on dataset Liver.

d	0.04		0.08		0.12		0.16	
	Precision	G-mean	Precision	G-mean	Precision	G-mean	Precision	G-mean
CSUP	**0.8731**	**0.9074**	**0.8432**	**0.8456**	**0.8193**	0.7812	0.7742	0.7526
SMOTE	0.6932	0.8461	0.7116	0.8137	0.7485	0.8044	0.7653	0.7754
Adaboost	0.8346	0.8567	0.8191	0.8291	0.8012	**0.8103**	**0.7832**	**0.7865**
RDS	0.7954	0.8101	0.7632	0.7724	0.7311	0.7427	0.6945	0.7159

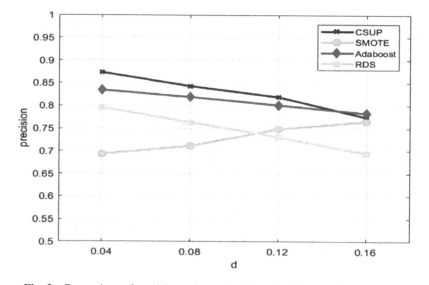

Fig. 3. Comparison of precision values of various algorithms on liver data set.

that of the other algorithms. With the improvement of the balance rate, the precision value of other algorithms decreases, but the overall performance of the up-sampling algorithm based on centroid space in this paper is not affected, and it has good practicability.

According to the results shown in Fig. 4, when G-means is used as the evaluation index, CSUP has better effect than SMOTE algorithm, Adaboost algorithm and RDS. Compared with Adaboost algorithm, the average improvement of RDS is 2% to 3%. Compared with SMOTE algorithm and RDS, the algorithm proposed in this paper improves more, and the accuracy of sample classification is higher than that of upper sampling. For this data set, with the increase of the unbalance rate, the G-mean evaluation index of each algorithm has decreased, so our research focus in the later period can be focused on the process of increasing the unevenness rate, and the G-mean and other indicators have also improved.

In addition, CSUP is proposed. If the multi-classification problem is simply divided into two categories, the time complexity of the algorithm is $O(N^{n-1})$, while the time

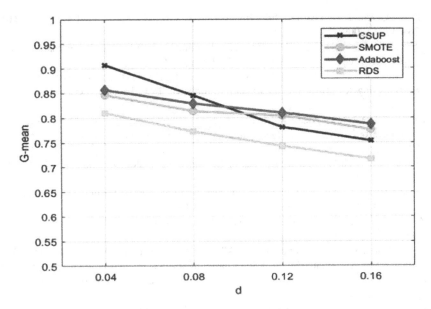

Fig. 4. Comparisons of G-mean values of algorithms on liver data set.

complexity of the improved SVM algorithm based on multi-classification is $O(N^3)$. For the research of multi-classification problem, the CSUP algorithm in this paper can be used for reference in future research, aiming at solving the problem of data set imbalance. the overall performance index precision and G-mean are both better, and the multi-classification problem is also solved to a certain extent. Help, the algorithm proposed in this paper must be improved in the future, that is, in the process of increasing the unbalance rate, the performance of each index will decline to a certain extent, although other algorithms will also appear in this situation, so the performance change in the process of improving the unbalance degree is also our future calculation. The main work of law research.

Acknowledgments. This research is supported by Jiangsu Province Education Information Research funded topic (20172105), Nanjing University of Posts and Telecommunications Teaching Reform Project (JG06717JX66) and CERNET Innovation Project (NGII20180620). The authors thank the sponsors for their support and the reviewers for helpful comments.

References

1. Zhai, Y., Yang, B.R., Qu, W.: Overview of imbalanced data mining. Comput. Sci. **37**(10), 27–32 (2010)
2. Zhou, Z.H.: Machine Learning. Tsinghua University Press, Beijing (2016)
3. Zhao, N., Zhang, X. F., Zhang, L. Y.: Overview of imbalanced data classification. Comput. Sci. **45**(S1), 22–27 + 57 (2018)

4. He, H., Garcia, E.A.: Learning from imbalanced data. IEEE Trans. Knowl. Data Eng. **21**(9), 1263–1284 (2009)
5. Chen, S.L., Shen, S.Q., Li, D.S.: Ensemble learning method for imbalanced data based on sample weight updating. Comput. Sci. **45**(07), 31–37 (2018)
6. Ng, W.W.Y., Hu, J., Yeung, D.S., Yin, S., Roli, F.: Diversified sensitivity-based undersampling for imbalance classification problems. IEEE Trans. Cybern. **45**(11), 2402–2412 (2015)
7. Huang, F., Xie, G., Xiao, R.: Research on ensemble learning. In: 2009 International Conference on Artificial Intelligence and Computational Intelligence, Shanghai, pp. 249–252 (2009)
8. Wang, S.X., Pan, P., Chen, D., Lu, Y.S.: Adaptive multiclass boosting classification algorithm. Comput. Sci. **44**(07), 185–190 (2017)
9. Jin, X., Wang, L., Sun, G.X., Li, H.K.: Under-sampling method for unbalanced data based on centroid space. Comput. Sci. **46**(02), 50–55 (2019)
10. Zhang, S., Shang, X.Y., Wang, W., Huang, X.L.: Optimizing the classification accuracy of imbalanced dataset based on SVM. In: 2010 International Conference on Computer Application and System Modeling (ICCASM 2010), Taiyuan, pp. V4-338-V4-341 (2010)
11. Tran, B., Xue, B., Zhang, M. J.: A PSO based hybrid feature selection algorithm for high-dimensional classification. In: Proceedings of IEEE Congress on Evolutionary Computation, pp. 3801–3808 (2016)
12. Babbar, R., Partalas, I., Gaussier, E., Amini, M.R., Amblard, C.: Learning taxonomy adaptation in large-scale classification. J. Mach. Learn. Res. **17**(1), 3350–3386 (2016)
13. Chawla, N.V., Bowyer, K.W., Hall, L.O., et al.: SMOTE: synthetic minority over sampling technique. J. Artif. Intell. Res. **16**(1), 321–357 (2002)
14. Lv, D., Ma, Z.C., Yang, S.B., Li, X.B., Ma, Z.X., Jiang, F.: The application of SMOTE algorithm for unbalanced data. In: Proceedings of the 2018 International Conference on Artificial Intelligence and Virtual Reality (AIVR 2018). ACM, New York, pp. 10–13 (2018)
15. Barua, S., Islam, M.M., Yao, X., Murase, K.: MWMOTE–majority weighted minority oversampling technique for imbalanced data set learning. IEEE Trans. Knowl. Data Eng. **26** (2), 405–425 (2014)
16. Hsu, K.W.: Heterogeneous AdaBoost with stochastic algorithm selection. In: Proceedings of the 11th International Conference on Ubiquitous Information Management and Communication (IMCOM 2017). ACM, New York, Article 40, 8 p. (2017)
17. Deepa, T., Punlthavalli, M.A.: New sampling technique and SVM classification for feature selection in high-dimensional imbalanced dataset. In: 3rd International Conference on Electronics Computer Technology (ICECT), Kanyakumari, India, pp. 395–398. IEEE (2011)

A Blockchain-Based IoT Workflow Management Approach

Ming Jin[1(✉)], Chenchen Dou[1], Peichun Pan[2], Ming Wan[2], Biying Sun[1], and Wenxuan Zhang[1]

[1] State Grid Gansu Electric Power Information and Communication Company, Beijing, China
17789632366@163.com
[2] Nanjing Nari Information and Communication Technology Co. Ltd., Nanjing, China

Abstract. The centralized authority of workflow management has low transparency in data sharing among third party entities. Blockchain technique provides new solution to manage assets in a distributed manner. In this paper, we aim at designing a decentralized IoT workflow management solution where the rules to control data transmission and access are governed using blockchain. We adopt a secure execution technique to store the encrypted dataset and save only the hash map information in the blockchain. As a result, our solution offers flexible data access control and better data sharing transparency to the vast amount of data generated by IoT devices. The simulation results showed that efficiency and throughput can be greatly improved in managing IoT workflow.

Keywords: IoT · Workflow · Blockchain

1 Introduction

Thanks to the technology advancement of IoT, more devices are now equipped with embedded hardware to communicate, compute and complete data processing and transmission tasks [1, 2]. For example, our appliances have been retrofitted with ability to connect to the WiFi and Cellular network [3]. To name a few of them, smart phones, health monitors, smart TVs, smart ovens, smart air-conditioner, and smart door locks are becoming more and more popular in our daily life. The aforementioned devices collect and transmit large amount sensitive data over internet [4]. Typically, IoT devices such as surveillance cameras and health monitoring devices [5] detect privacy information about the users. However, these devices only have limited computational resources, thus are not capable of analyze the data locally [6, 7]. Consequently, the sensitive user data is delivered to third party server for further processing and storage, which means the third party services have to be trusted and secure. Unfortunately, violations of data privacy for unauthorized purposes have been reported against the service providers [8]. This undue advantage by service providers is caused by centralized management where a third party system is trusted as a top authority to control user data. In order to resolve the data access policy enforcement problem between users

© Springer Nature Singapore Pte Ltd. 2020
Y. Tian et al. (Eds.): ICBDS 2019, CCIS 1210, pp. 633–644, 2020.
https://doi.org/10.1007/978-981-15-7530-3_48

and service providers, using decentralized workflow management for IoT data asset based on Blockchain [9] and smart contract technology [10] shows its potential.

The most successful application with the advance of blockchain technique appears to be the Bitcoin [9], which allows decentralized asset management in finance sector. The transactions of electronic fund are enabled and recorded without a centralized banking system. Users transfer money globally with secured digital evidence kept by many participants of blockchain. Due to the initial success of blockchain technology, several of applications have been proposed such as insurance automation, supply chain management, file storage for commercial purpose [11]. Regarding IoT device, Slock It [12] provides a platform that allows devices like smart locks to be controlled by authorized users.

In this paper, we are inspired by the aforementioned decentralized solutions, and aim at limiting the authority of centralized IoT workflow management systems. Blockchain technology [9] and smart contracts [10] allow decentralized management of workflow among untrusted participants. The integrity of transaction state is guaranteed by distributed consensus among those untrusted participants in Blockchain. The mechanism is to enforce that each current block generated by the participants must contain a hash of the previous block in the chain, making the unexpected modification of the previous transactions in Blockchain identifiable.

On the other hand, smart contracts [13] are autonomous applications embedded in the blockchain. To enforce the rules that govern interaction among participants, we leverage the autonomous smart contracts in the blockchain network without need of centralized trust. Users are able to control how their data is accessed and used with the capability of smart contract providing them workflow management privilege. Moreover, we put smart contract computations on separated virtual machines. With this design, participants cannot change application results. As a result, we can offer secured data access control with capability of track workflow distribution among the participants, yielding appropriate accountability.

All workflow on the blockchain has to be accessed publicly for the participants to be able to verify transactions [14]. Our proposed system addresses this issue by keeping the hash of the encrypted data in the blockchain, while the raw information is secured using trusted computing. Due to this improvement, we can easily verify the integrity within the scope of our data storage. With the equipped trusted execution environment, the protection of user data is achieved by process isolation enclaves on memory, and then securing the enclave's memory pages with CPU [15].

We summarize the contribution of this paper as follows.

- We propose to use blockchain platform for decentralized IoT workflow management.
- We adopt smart contracts to offer data access control among IoT users and IoT service providers.
- We implement data storage using trusted execution environment to enhance data storage security.
- We create a prototype platform on real and test the effectiveness of proposed solution.

The rest of the paper is organized as follows. Section 2 provides literature review on Blockchain, trusted execution environment and IoT. Section 3 discusses the scope, case for distributed workflow management system. Section 4 provides the architecture design of proposed system. In Section 4, we describe our implementation details and Section 5 provides the experimental results. Finally, Section 6 concludes the paper.

2 Related Work

In this section, we provide literature review on blockchain, and IoT system.

2.1 Blockchain

Blockchain is designed to work in a distributed manner where the history of transactions is stored by a distributed consensus among untrusted participants without a centralized authority. The participants bundle proved transaction in blocks by calculating a hash of previous block included in the current block. These tasks require computational resources, and stop the blockchain from being attacked. With the development of blockchain technology, many researchers have suggested different application scenarios where blockchain can be applied. Zyskind et al. [13] proposed a blockchain based solution to decentralize storage of data. Dorri et al. [22] used blockchain to manage IoT network. By providing a light weight blockchain consensus system, devices with low processing power can run blockchain independently. Various works exist on how to improve the performance of blockchain technology as seen in [23].

The data storage and computations in blockchain can be undertaken by these decentralized participants to determine the current blockchain state autonomously. Smart contract is used to name such autonomous. By using smart contracts, decentralized data access policy control can be enforced without the need of a third party entity. As a result, it has great potential to ensure continuous service delivery for users.

The Ethereum [10] smart contract is a typical Turing complete computation implementation of smart contract. The Ethereum smart contract is based on blockchain and can be managed by the participants to determine the state of integrity of the contract program autonomously. The protocol contains incentive mechanism, asking the contract owner to pay Ethereum gas to the participants. The higher the gas paid, the faster the speed of contract execution and confirmation in the system. The contract owners also need to pay for the storage on the blockchain. Storing only the hash of data on blockchain will reduce the storage resource consumption. The interaction between participants and smart contract is achieved by giving a unique address in the blockchain for each smart contract. The participants use it to get the contract and the API of the contract. Through the smart contract API, the smart contract can be executed.

2.2 Internet of Things

The term internet of things (IoT) was first used in RFID research suggesting the improvement of chain logistics with internet connectivity [25]. Upon the growth of usage of the term, Ashton [25] sees that IoT is more appropriate to describe physical objects which can record, generate, and act upon information on the internet. These tasks were mainly performed by people, therefore suffering from drawbacks of limited capability, attention, and accuracy to be effective at capturing data about the real world for decision-making.

The evolution of digital devices grant new capabilities to sense and task actions in the real world with the help of sensors and actuators. The advancement in computation, communication and device miniaturization enables IoT systems which typically include IoT devices, sensors, actuators, IoT Hubs, IoT Gateway and cloud service provider. IoT devices are capable of sensing and collecting data. The data is then transmitted over network for further storage and processing. IoT hub is responsible for having different devices with disparate communication protocol like zigbee or bluetooth connected to the IoT network. IoT gateway works in IoT networks, helping data aggregation on the client network. At the end, cloud services offer ultimate storage and computation solution for all the data collected in IoT system.

With regards to IoT integrated industry application, Manyika [26] reports that IoT could potentially improve worksite operations in the construction, oil and gas, and mining industries to the tune of $470 Billion. The applications can offer predictive maintenance of equipment and optimize supply chains. From the review that was performed, it has been proved that the IoT techniques has great potential in improving the methods that are employed in construction significantly.

Although the IoT system and applications have been widely deployed, there are evidences showing that even the most well-known commercial products are not safe. In the work of Earlence et al. [1], an experiment have revealed security drawback of a smart lock, which can be compromised by attacking the Samsung Smart Application. The attackers have gained full control of unlocking in a condition when their privilege is limited to lock action only. Vijay et al. [24] show how they capture non encrypted network traffic from Wemo device to perform a replay attack on the device.

3   System Overview

Our proposed system works on decentralization of workflow management using blockchain and trusted execution environment. The trust between IoT service provider and the users is established based on smart contract. Our workflow management system gives users full control to data execution, storage and sharing. With smart contracts, users enforce data access rules autonomously over untrusted participants on blockchain. In our system, all data has been encrypted before transmission with asymmetric cryptographic protocols [20] for key exchanging.

3.1   Assumptions

In this paper, we assume that the IoT workflow management service providers is untrusted since they fully control user data in data usage and sharing. Meanwhile, we consider all third party users who request access to data to be untrusted. We assume all non-data owner may leak data or use it for unauthorized purposes such as user's email for direct marketing.

We consider adversaries that seek to compromise the data storage cloud services by obtaining root privilege access to low level system resources such as memory, hard drives and Input/Output systems. These attackers employ techniques that compromise highly privilege applications such as Operating System and hyper-visors. In this paper we do not consider replay attacks and denial of service attacks.

Users are assumed to be knowledgeable of the importance of data privacy and the consequences of privacy disclosure. Thus, users demand control and acknowledgement over the data usage in IoT workflow. With the help of blockchain, IoT vendors and service providers can provide trusted services where the workflow management is accomplished via publicly verifiable smart contracts program running on blockchain. The immutable data access history of users' data has been recorded and provided in the blockchain system. The chain structure makes it difficult for the malicious attackers to modify the entries.

3.2 Smart Contract

Smart contracts allow individual participants carrying different interest to announce rules that satisfy multiple participants' interest. The rules will be encoded into smart contracts and later enforced by the participants. The state of the contract can be verified independently. For instance, if a user want to manage the data access policy in centralized management system such Smartthings [1, 21], the service provide has to be trusted to undertake and enforce the policy. With smart contracts, the users participates in how the policy is enforced due to the fact that the policy enforcement is achieved by the participants in blockchain.

As shown in Fig. 1, the Smart contract provides three major functions to enable decentralized access control policy to user data. Due to the limited data storage and high expense required to store data in blockchain, we only stores the hash information in smart contract. The actual IoT data is encrypted and stored on cloud server using trusted execution environment. The three major functions of smart contract consist of user and device registration, data I/O and access control.

User registration utilize the user registration mechanism on Ethereum network. When joining the Ethereum network, a public private key pair is generated for each new user as the identification. By using the private key, user can perform further other functions in the smart contract system.

Every registered user is allowed to register their IoT components by providing valid and identifiable information for the device. In our design, a hash map is used to link the devices and the owner address on the blockchain.

To write data in the blockchain, owner's information should be provided together with device id and data. The owner's information and the device ID will be combined to generate the key in hash map. This settings allows all devices' data to be stored uniquely with the distinctive hash values. The smart contract first check the owner's information and the device ID, and then allows data to be written to the contract if registration information matched.

Pseudo-code of Smart Contract

Functions :

HashMap Registration(key:ownerInfo,value:List[DeviceIds])

HashMap DataI/O(key:(ownerInfo,deviceId), value:List[DataHash])

HashMap AccessControl(key:(ownerInfo,accessInfo,deviceId),value: bool isAllowed)

1: start

   REGISTERUSER(ownerInfo)

     InsertToHashMap(userRegistry)

  end

  start

   REGISTERDEVICE(ownerInfo,deviceID)

     InsertToHashMap(deviceRegistry)

  end

2: start

   WRITEDATA(ownerInfo,deviceID,Data)

    if(owner == ownerInfo)

       deviceData[owner,deviceID].List.InsertData(hash(Data))

  end

  start

   READDATA(ownerInfo,accessInfo,deviceID)

    if(DataAccessRegistry(accessInfo))== true

       return deviceData[hash(accessInfo,deviceID])

  end

3: start

   GRANTACCESS(ownerInfo,accessInfo,deviceID)

    if(owner == ownerInfo)

     DataAccessRegistry[hash(ownerInfo,accessInfo,deviceID)] =true

  end

  start

   DENYACCESS(ownerInfo,accessInfo,deviceID)

    if(owner == ownerInfo)

     DataAccessRegistry[hash(ownerInfo,accessInfo,deviceID)]=false

  end

Fig. 1. Smart contract algorithm design: registration, data I/O and access control

When any participant wants to access to IoT data from a different owner, a permission need to be granted first. The requesting user must provide the owner information o, the device ID and the information of requestor. The data owner grants access permission by using a hash map in smart contract containing owner information and device ID as key and the list of the access consent values. To revoke a permitted access, simply remove the requestor's information from the list. Every data access attempt must go through the validation process where the hash map is checked to ensure only permitted requesting user can access the IoT data.

4   Detailed Workflow Management and Implementation

In Fig. 2, we show a detailed diagram of workflow management. For a device to participate, first, the device registers itself in the blockchain via the IoT gateway. The IoT gateway communicates the trusted execution environment and performs remote attestation as shown in the figure.

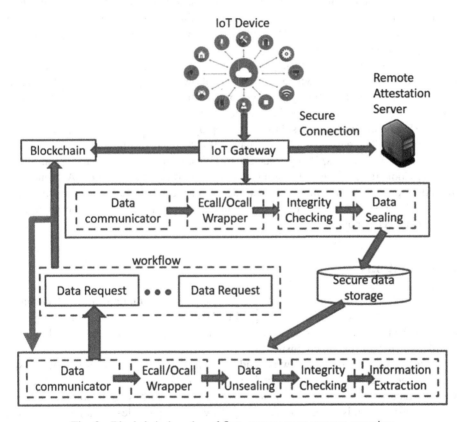

Fig. 2. Blockchain based workflow management system: overview

The gateway in the system takes certain amount of computational work including retrieving the smart contract, encrypting and hashing the data. The hashed data going into the blockchain through the use of WRITEDATA function of smart contract. Meanwhile, the actual IoT data is encrypted and sent to the trust execution environment. The trust execution environment examines the hash-based message authentication code (HMAC) of the data and appends the HMAC of the data before the data is sealed and written to disk. The communication between IoT gateway and trusted environment is done by the Ecall/Ocall wrapper.

To read data, the access permission must be granted in the smart contract by specifying the identity information of requestor. The GRANTACCESSS function must be invoked first. If the data owner would like to withdraw any access consent, DENYACCESS function will be used for that purpose. The data requestor will have to get the smart contract for the hash map information. The smart contract verifies the access permission in the READDATA function, and then returns the hash of data if the validation is successful. With the hash information, the requestor can now communicates with the secure storage system to request the actual IoT data. The application of trusted execution environment again checks with the smart-contract determine whether the requestor is authorized to the data hash identifier. If successful, the application loads the data from its storage. The following step involves data unsealing, integrity checking, and data extraction.

As the workflow management involves a group of read and write operations, all access control permissions will be examined following the sequence of tasks. When any step reports an error, the system will notify all responsible participants to reconsider the workflow design or modify the access policies.

To implement and test our solution, we deploy 10 IoT devices with sensors and 2 mobile phones. The devices includes Huawei Band 2 Pro All-in-One Activity Tracker Smart Fitness Wristbands, Philips Hue Smart Hubs, CHEF iQ Multi-Functional Smart Pressure Cookers and heart rate monitor application on mobile devices. All functions are coded to retrieve the smart contract address in the blockchain and perform operations such register devices, write data, read data, write and read access policy update and revoke access policy.

5 Simulations

In Fig. 3, we verify the efficiency of storage resource consumption in the blockchain. The two alternative solutions are saving all IoT data in the blockchain and saving only the hash data in the blockchain. By considering 4 types of devices, we show the cumulative storage resource consumption over 100 s.

Device 1 denotes the smart wristband recording user activity information. As we can see from the figure, a considerable amount of data storage has been consumed when all data is stored in the blockchain. As we switch to hash data storage, 90% of storage consumption is saved approximately. Device 2 requires less storage space when saving all data in the blockchain, but the hash data storage still shows significant effect in reducing the overhead of blockchain system. Device 3 and device 4 are design with single data sensing purpose, thus do not generate much data during the testing duration.

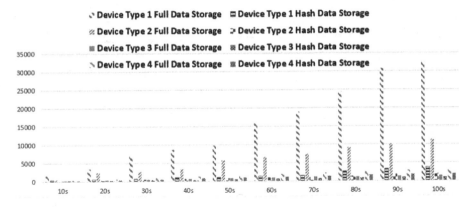

Fig. 3. Storage resource consumption in the blockchain: full data storage vs. hash data storage

Consequently, a reduction of 40% storage consumption can be observed in the simulation results. We can see that saving only the hash data will benefit all types of devices where the devices generating more data get more reduction of storage consumption.

In Fig. 4, we show the impact of increasing data write operations in the workflow. The system performance is measured with transaction throughput over an increasing amount of data write operations between 1000 requests to 3000 requests. The results show that the throughput decreases slightly as the total number of WRITEDATA operation increases with or without hashing. The throughput without hashing is higher due to the fact that hashing function takes processing time but only stores very limited amount of data. Without hashing, the write transaction throughput is 14.26 writes per second for 1000 WRITEDATA operations. With hashing, the number is 12.18 for the same settings. At 3000 WRITEDATA operations, the transaction throughput results are 13.41 and 10.93 writes per second for full data storage and hashing data storage, respectively.

In Fig. 5, we examine the computational resource consumption for sealing and unsealing operations in the secured execution environment. The x-axis denotes the block size and the y-axis shows the computing cost. When the block size of 512 bytes, the average sealing time for a single record sized of 2.0 MB is 423 ms compared to 1202 ms when using 64 bytes block size. When the block size increases, the sealing and unsealing time drop down significantly. The reduction in the frequency of operations of data blocks results in the aforementioned impact.

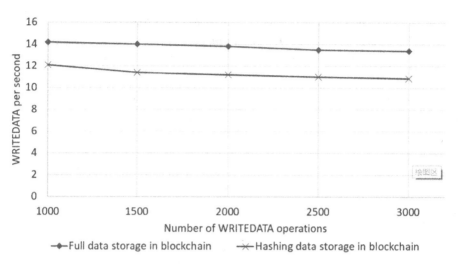

Fig. 4. Throughput examination: full data storage vs. hash data storage

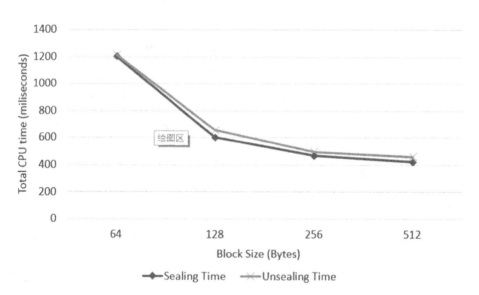

Fig. 5. Computational resource consumption: sealing vs.unsealing

6 Conclusions

With the advancement of IoT device, the urgent need of data privacy management including data access control and data usage transparency is observable. To manage the vast amount of data generated by IoT devices in a centralized way appears to be improper. In this paper, we propose a decentralized IoT workflow management solution where the rules to control data transmission and access are governed using blockchain. We adopt a secure execution technique to store the encrypted dataset and save only the hash map information in the blockchain. As a result, our solution offers flexible data access control and better data sharing transparency to the vast amount of data generated by IoT devices. We have implemented our design and tested the system with real world device and data. The simulation results are positive in regards of resource consumptions while our system offers better flexibilities. Our future work plan aims at accelerating the WRITEDATA operations with better storage hardware and improved access control mechanism.

References

1. Fernandes, E., Jung, J., Prakash, A.: Security analysis of emerging smart home applications. In: Proceedings of the 37th IEEE Symposium on Security and Privacy (2016)
2. Jia, Y.J., Chen, Q.A., Wang, S., Rahmati, A., Fernandes, E., Mao, Z.M., Prakash, A.: ContexIoT: Towards providing contextual integrity to appified IoT platforms. In: Proceedings of the 21st Network and Distributed System Security Symposium (NDSS 2017), San Diego, CA (2017)
3. Gubbi, J., Buyya, R., Marusic, S., Palaniswami, M.: Internet of things (iot): A vision, architectural elements, and future directions. Future Gener. Comput. Syst. **29**(7), 1645–1660 (2013)
4. Bertino, E.: Data privacy for iot systems: Concepts, approaches, and research directions. In: 2016 IEEE International Conference on Big Data (Big Data), pp. 3645–3647. IEEE (2016)
5. Williams, P.A.H., McCauley, V.: Always connected: The security challenges of the healthcare internet of things. In: 2016 IEEE 3rd World Forum on Internet of Things (WFIoT), pp. 30–35 (2016)
6. Gonzalez, N.M., Goya, W.A., de Fatima Pereira, R., Langona, K., Silva, E.A., de Brito Carvalho, T.C.M., Miers, C.C., Mngs, J.E., Sefidcon, A.: Fog computing: Data analytics and cloud distributed processing on the network edges. In: 2016 35th International Conference of the Chilean Computer Science Society (SCCC), pp. 1–9 (2016)
7. Masud, M.M., Khan, L., Thuraisingham, B.: A scalable multi-level feature extraction technique to detect malicious executables. Inf. Syst. Front. **10**(1), 33–45 (2008). http://dx.doi.org/10.1007/s10796-007-9054-3
8. Hu, H., Ahn, G.-J., Jorgensen, J.: Detecting and resolving privacy conflicts for collaborative data sharing in online social networks. In: Proceedings of the 27th Annual Computer Security Applications Conference, ser. ACSAC 2011, pp. 103–112. ACM, New York (2011). http://doi.acm.org/10.1145/2076732.2076747
9. Nakamoto, S.: A peer-to-peer electronic cash system. bitcoin.org, (2009) Accessed 08 Sept 2017
10. Foundation, E.: Ethereums white paper. https://github.com/ethereum/wiki/wiki/White-Paper (2014). Accessed 08 Sept 2017

11. Filecoin: Filecoin: A decentralized storage network. https://filecoin.io/filecoin.pdf (2017). Accessed 08 Sept 2017
12. Slock: Initial coin offering market. https://slock.it/ (2017). Accessed 08 Sept 2017
13. Zyskind, G., Nathan, O., et al.: Decentralizing privacy: Using blockchain to protect personal data. In: Security and Privacy Workshops (SPW), pp. 180–184. IEEE (2015)
14. Kosba, A., Miller, A., Shi, E., Wen, Z., Papamanthou, C.: Hawk: The blockchain model of cryptography and privacy preserving smart contracts. In: 2016 IEEE Symposium on Security and Privacy (SP), pp. 839–858. IEEE (2016)
15. Costan, V., Devadas, S.: Intel SGX explained. IACR Cryptology ePrint Archive, vol. 2016, p. 86 (2016). http://eprint.iacr.org/2016/086
16. Crosby, M., Pattanayak, P., Verma, S.: Blockchain technology: Beyond bitcoin (2016)
17. Santos, N., Raj, H., Saroiu, S., Wolman, A.: Using arm trustzone to build a trusted language runtime for mobile applications. In: ACM SIGARCH Computer Architecture News 42(1), pp. 67–80. ACM (2014)
18. Van Doorn, L.: Hardware virtualization trends. In: ACM/Usenix International Conference On Virtual Execution Environments: Proceedings of the 2 nd International Conference on Virtual Execution Environments, vol. 14, no. 16, p. 45 (2006)
19. Karande, V., Bauman, E., Lin, Z., Khan, L.: Sgxlog: Securing system logs with sgx. In: Proceedings of the 2017 ACM on Asia Conference on Computer and Communications Security, ser. ASIA CCS 2017, pp. 19–30. ACM, New York (2017). http://doi.acm.org/10.1145/3052973.3053034
20. Rivest, R.L., Shamir, A., Adleman, L.: A method for obtaining digital signatures and public-key cryptosystems. Commun. ACM 21(2), 120–126 (1978). http://doi.acm.org/10.1145/359340.359342
21. Hue, P.: Philip hue iot portal. http://www2.meethue.com/en-us/ (2017). Accessed 08 Sept 2017
22. Dorri, A., Kanhere, S.S., Jurdak, R.: Towards an optimized blockchain for iot. In: Proceedings of the Second International Conference on Internet-of-Things Design and Implementation, ser. IoTDI 2017, pp. 173–178. ACM, New York (2017). http://doi.acm.org/10.1145/3054977.3055003
23. Eyal, I., Gencer, A.E., Sirer, E.G., Van Renesse, R.: Bitcoin-ng: A scalable blockchain protocol. In: NSDI 2016, pp. 45–59 (2016)
24. Sivaraman, V., Chan, D., Earl, D., Boreli, R.: Smartphones attacking smart-homes. In: Proceedings of the 9th ACM Conference on Security & Privacy in Wireless and Mobile Networks, ser. WiSec 2016, pp. 195–200. ACM, New York (2016). http://doi.acm.org/10.1145/2939918.2939925
25. Ashton, K.: That 'internet of things' thing in the real world, things matter more than ideas. RFID J. 22(7), 97–114 (2009) http://www.rfidjournal.com/article/print/4986. Accessed 23 March 2018
26. Manyika, J: The Internet of Things: Mapping the Value Beyond the Hype. McKinsey Global Institute (2015)

Research on Identity-Based Cryptograph and Its Application in Power IoT

Xiaogang Wei[✉] and Yongbing Lian

Nari Group Corporation/State Grid Electric Power Research Institute,
Nanjing 210003, Jiangsu, China
weixiaogang@sgepri.sgcc.com.cn

Abstract. With the development of the power IoT in China, Various kinds of business terminals emerge endlessly. And the low computing power makes it difficult to run PKI authentication measures based on digital certificates, which brings opportunities for attackers and seriously threatens the security of business systems. This paper firstly introduces the security risks of the sensing terminals access to power IoT, secondly researches the user authentication technology, and then designs and implements a lightweight authentication protocol based on appropriate technology, considering that the PKI improves the difficulty of terminal authentication in large-scale IoT and the CPK reduces the security of terminal access authentication, and finally evaluates the advantage of the protocol based on attack testing and application data. The results show that the lightweight authentication protocol has a high reference value for terminal authentication, data transmission security and even the overall security protection of the perception layer in power IoT. And the lightweight authentication protocol can be used for preventing terminal counterfeiting and data leakage.

Keywords: Identity-Based cryptograph · Combined public key · Secure access · Power IoT

1 Introduction

The Internet of things (IoT), is the penetration, expansion and extension of the Internet into the physical world to realize the connection between things, things and people, and people. In order to cope with the changes in the form of power grid and meet the needs of social development, in early 2019, China's State Grid formally proposed to build an all-round power IoT. Power IoT connects power users and their equipment, power grid enterprises and their equipment, power generation enterprises and their equipment, suppliers and their equipment, as well as people and things, generating shared data so as to serve users, power grid enterprises, power generation enterprises, suppliers, government and society.

With the development of the power Internet of Things, edge computing is gradually applied to all kinds of business. The horizontal interaction demand of business is prominent and the scope of security boundary is expanding and difficult to define. Thus, the existing protection system mainly based on isolation cannot meet the extensive interconnection demand between things. Traditional authentication measures

Y. Tian et al. (Eds.): ICBDS 2019, CCIS 1210, pp. 645–654, 2020.
https://doi.org/10.1007/978-981-15-7530-3_49

based on digital certificates are difficult to implement in massive sensing terminals with limited computing, storage, bandwidth resources. Only through simple IP, MAC binding and other means of protection, the sensing terminal has the risk of being counterfeited. Attackers can use counterfeit sensing terminals to illegally acquire or tamper with power business data and launch network attacks on the business station. Therefore, it is necessary to research a secure access mode of sensing terminals and implement an effective authentication protocol.

2 Research on Authentication Technology

There are three kinds of commonly used identity authentication technologies: password-based authentication, cryptographic authentication and biometric or equipment feature authentication. Among them, password-based authentication is simple and easy to use. It is also a commonly used authentication method. However, HTTP, SMTP, TELNET and other application layer protocols use plaintext mode to transmit passwords, which is easy to be eavesdropped by attackers, and through dictionary and exhaustive attacks, attackers can easily obtain passwords, which directly leads to the failure of this authentication method. There are PKI, CPK and IBC for cryptographic authentication methods and the authentication methods based on biometric or device feature identify biology or equipment by unique features such as fingerprints and iris.

Therefore, password-based authentication is not suitable for the access of massive sensing terminals in the power IoT and fingerprints of devices are difficult to obtain in a simple way, then the acquisition of fingerprints of devices is too complex and difficult to implement for massive sensing terminals. So it is appropriate to use cryptographic authentication for the authentication of massive sensing terminals.

2.1 Public Key Infrastructure

PKI (Public Key Infrastructure) [1, 2] provides a complete, mature and reliable solution for network communication confidentiality, integrity and non-repudiation through the key management system and cryptographic services such as data encryption and digital signature. Key management is accomplished by a trusted digital certificate authority (CA). The user digital certificate issued by CA based on the user certificate request file is the carrier of the user's public key and identity information, which is presented publicly in the form of X.509.

2.2 Combined Public Key

CPK (Combined Public Key) technology combines key production with key management, realizes digital signature and key exchange, and meets the needs of entity identification and data confidentiality in large-scale information network and non-information network. Based on ECC elliptic curve cryptography technology, CPK can generate almost infinite public keys with a small number of seeds and simplify key management. Users can apply for key pairs through Key Management Center (KMC) [3].

2.3   Identity-Based Cryptograph

User identity information such as name, IP address, e-mail address, mobile phone number and so on can be used by IBC (Identity-Based Cryptograph) as user public key [4]. The user's private key is calculated by the key generation center (KGC) based on the system parameter and user identification information, and distributed to the user through a secure method. Public keys are determined directly by identity information and do not require third parties to participate in the generation. That is the main feature of IBC.

2.4   Comparison of Three Authentication Methods

The comparative analysis of PKI, CPK and IBC is shown in the following Table 1.

Table 1. Technology and cost comparison of three authentication methods

Item	PKI	CPK	IBC
Use of digital certificates	Yes	No	No
Acquisition of public key	Content of digital certificate	Generated by KMC	User identity information
The way of public key management	Digital certificate	Maintenance of public key matrix	No need
Acquisition of private key	Generated by user	Generated by KMC	Generated by KGC
Distribution of private keys	Stored safely by user	Additional security access is required	Safe Online Distribution is supported
Data volume in network transmission	Large	Middle	Small
Operational efficiency	Low	High	Middle
Security	High	Low	Middle
Cost of implementation	High	Low	Low
Management cost	High	Low	Low

Table 1 shows that PKI authentication is feasible in small-scale IoT applications, but PKI authentication will reduce the access efficiency of sensing terminals, while the maintenance of digital certificates of massive terminals will increase the management cost in a large-scale IoT application. Therefore, the appropriate authentication method of sensing terminals should be chosen from CPK and IBC. The high operational efficiency of CPK is at the expense of security [5, 6], and IBC has absolute advantages in private key distribution [7, 8], network data transmission, public key management and security. SM9, as a standard of IBC system, has been issued by the National Cryptographic Administration and will be used widely in IoT scenario.

In summary, the lightweight authentication mechanism in this paper is based on IBC authentication method.

3   Authentication Protocol Design

3.1   Prototype Analysis

There are two application scenarios of IBC identity authentication system [9–11], one is encryption-decryption, the other is signature-verification. The following two application scenarios are analyzed and explained.

The process of encryption and decryption is shown in Fig. 1. In the encryption-decryption application scenario, user B encrypts the data by using the system parameters of KGC and the public key of user A. User A can decrypt the ciphertext data sent by user B by inputting the system parameters and the private key applied from KGC, thus ensuring the security of data transmission. Unlike traditional PKI authentication system, user A does not need to obtain digital certificate from CA through certificate request file, and then extract public key from digital certificate, but directly uses its ID as public key.

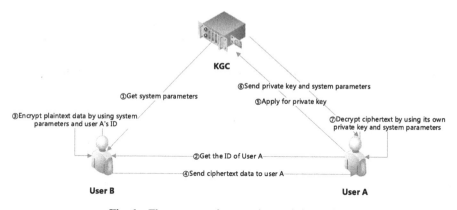

Fig. 1. The process of encryption and decryption

The process of signature and verification is shown in Fig. 2. In the signature-verification application scenario, user B sign hash value of plaintext data by using system parameters and the private key applied from KGC. User A can verify the signature and plaintext data of user B by using the system parameters of KGC and the public key of user B, thus verifying the identity of user B. Unlike traditional PKI authentication system, user B does not need to obtain digital certificate from CA through certificate request file, and then extract public key from digital certificate, but directly uses its ID as public key.

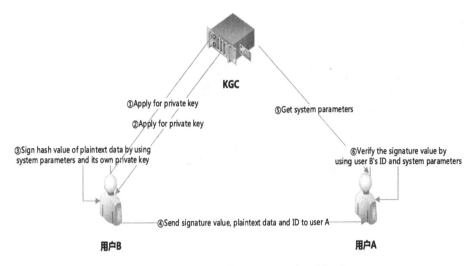

Fig. 2. The process of signature and verification

3.2 Protocol Design

Considering the actual application, IoT could be divided into four layers: the perceptual layer, the network layer, the platform layer and the application layer, as shown in Fig. 3. In this paper, the lightweight authentication is designed between sensing terminals and the edge for the perceptual layer.

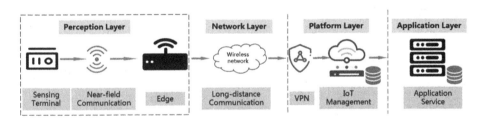

Fig. 3. The overall architecture of the IoT

Lightweight authentication is mainly based on the two prototypes mentioned above. Take SM9 issued by the National Cryptographic Administration as an example, the terminal must obtain the parameters of SM9 system from KGC when connecting for the first time, and then steps for the secure access based on two-way authentication are as follows and Fig. 4 shows the overall process of the terminal access.

Step 1: Equipment Registration. The terminal or the edge send the unique ID (as public key), random number, application time of key and validity period of key to the KGC. In addition to the unique ID, other information needs to be encrypted by the public key of the KGC. The KGC receives the ciphertext data and decrypts it with the

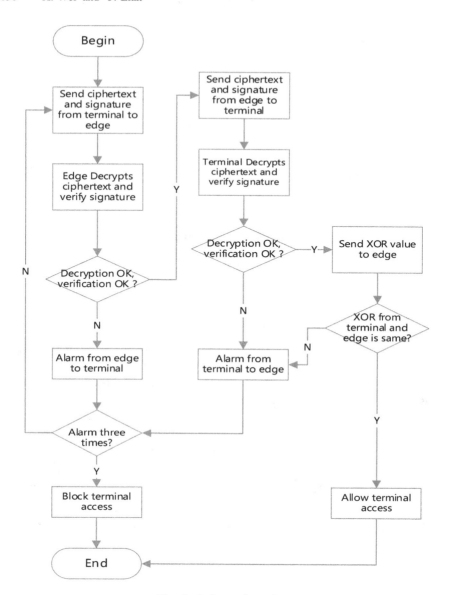

Fig. 4. Software flow chart

private key to obtain the registration correlation, then give the terminal or the edge feedback on registration results.

Step 2: Application and Distribution of Private Key. The terminal or the edge calculate the relevant parameters and apply for the private key to the KGC. And, the KGC calculates the parameters sent by the terminal or the edge with the primary private keys, and sends the calculated results (intermediate results) to the terminal or the edge.

Then, the terminal or the edge computes the private key for signature and the encryption respectively.

Step 3: Identity Authentication. First, the terminal generates a random number, encrypts the random number with the public key of the edge, and signs the hash value of the random number with its own private key, then sends the ciphertext data and signature value to the edge. Second, The edge decrypts the ciphertext data of the terminal with its own private key, obtains the random number of the terminal, and uses the public key of the terminal to verify the signature value. And then, The process of sending ciphertext data and signature value to the terminal to decrypt and verify is similar to that mentioned above, and it is not discussed here. Finally, The terminal and the edge respectively perform XOR operations on their own and the other party's random numbers, and compare the XOR values of the two parties. The two-way authentication between the terminal and the edge passes only if the edge passes the signature verification of the terminal, the terminal passes the signature verification of the edge and both XOR values are identical.

Step 4: Encrypted Communication. Based on SM4 symmetrical encryption algorithm issued by the National Cryptographic Administration and using the XOR operation value above as the key, the transmission data between the terminal and the edge is encrypted, which includes data encryption and decryption from the terminal to the edge, and data encryption and decryption from the edge to the terminal.

4   Authentication Protocol Implementation

This paper mainly describes the implementation of authentication process. And, to facilitate the process elaboration, we first define the relevant symbols, as shown in Table 2.

Table 2. Symbol Definition table

Symbol	Definition
rt and re	Random numbers produced by the terminal and the edge respectively
DKt and DKe	Session keys synthesized by the terminal and the edge respectively
IDt and IDe	ID (as public key) for the terminal and the edge respectively
$PriKeyt$ and $PriKeye$	Private key for the terminal and the edge respectively
$H(r)$	Hash value for r parameter
$Encrypt(p1,p2,p3)$	Encryption of p2 by input p1 and p3
$Decrypt(p1,p2,p3)$	Decryption of P2 by input P1 and P3
$Sign(p1,p2,p3)$	Input P1 and P3 to sign P2
$Verify(p1,p2,p3)$	Input P1 and P3 to Verify P2
$\parallel$	Connector

Terminal Sends Authentication Request. The terminal generates random number rt for encryption and signature operation.

$$A1 = Encrypt(params, rt, IDe) \tag{1}$$

$$A2 = Sign(params, H(rt), PriKeyt) \tag{2}$$

$$A = A1\|A2 \tag{3}$$

Terminal Authentication. The edge decrypts the ciphertext data and verifies the signature of the terminal.

$$rt = Decrypt(params, A1, PriKeye) \tag{4}$$

$$Verify(params, A2, IDt) = H(rt) \tag{5}$$

Edge Sends Authentication Request. The edge generates random number re for encryption and signature operation, then synthesize the session key.

$$B1 = Encrypt(params, re, IDt) \tag{6}$$

$$B2 = Sign(params, H(re), PriKeye) \tag{7}$$

$$B = B1\|B2 \tag{8}$$

$$DKe = re \oplus rt \tag{9}$$

Edge Authentication. The terminal decrypts the ciphertext data and verifies the signature of the edge, then synthesize the session key.

$$re = Decrypt(params, B1, PriKeyt) \tag{10}$$

$$Verify(params, B2, IDe) = H(re) \tag{11}$$

$$DKt = rt \oplus re \tag{12}$$

Key Agreement and Authentication Confirmation. The terminal hashes the session key and sends the operation result C to the edge. And, the edge hashes the session key and compares whether C and D are the same.

$$C = H(DKt) \tag{13}$$

$$D = H(DKe) \tag{14}$$

If the formula (4) (5) (10) (11) is right and C and D are equal, the one party verify the identity of the other party and two parties hold the same session key for the subsequent encrypted communication based on SM4. Otherwise, the edge gives the warning of negotiation failure in order to notify the terminal to initiate the negotiation again.

5 Application and Evaluation

The lightweight authentication protocol designed in this paper has been applied in the secure access process of the sensing terminals in power IoT. It realizes the identification and block of the illegal terminal in the perception layer of the power IoT, preventing the attacker from attacking the business system through the terminal device. Now, The advantage of this protocol is evaluated in terms of security and network resource consumption.

Security. All users in this protocol need to register with the KGC first. Only registered users can apply for the private key corresponding to their ID. This can prevent users from counterfeiting attacks, and the KGC only transmits the intermediate results of private key calculation to users. Users need to calculate the final private key by themselves. So the private key security is ensured. In addition, session key is used for encrypted communication only when both sides agree. If an attacker tampers with the session key, the session key will not be used. Also, the session key is updated regularly to prevent it from leaking.

Network Resource Consumption. In the PKI authentication system, both sides need to exchange digital certificates (size is about 1 K Bytes) after the start of a new connections of network. Assuming that each terminal start 100 connections a day, in the IoT, a network service with 100,000 terminals provided by one station will consume about 9.5 GB network traffic. This protocol does not need to use digital certificates for two-way authentication, which greatly reduces network bandwidth and network traffic consumption.

6 Conclusion

Considering that the PKI improves the difficulty of terminal authentication in large-scale IoT and the CPK reduces the security of terminal access authentication, this paper designs a lightweight authentication protocol and encrypted communication method for the sensing terminal in power IoT through in-depth research of IBC authentication system. Also, the implementation process of the core functions is elaborated in detail. Based on the attack test and application data, the advantage evaluation of the protocol in terms of security and network resource consumption is given. The results show that the lightweight authentication protocol has a high reference value for terminal authentication, data transmission security and even the overall security protection of the perception layer in power IoT.

Acknowledgments. This work is supported by the science and technology project of State Grid Corporation of China: "Research on Fundamental Protection Architecture and Terminal Layer

Security Monitoring and Protection Technology of SG-eIoT" (Grand No. SGGR0000X TJS1900274).

References

1. Diffie, W., Hellman, M.E.: New directions in cryptography. IEEE Trans. Inf. Theor. **22**(6), 644–654 (1976)
2. Hu, X.-D., Wei, Q.-fang.: Applied Cryptography Course. Publishing House of Electronics Industry, Beijing (2005)
3. Nan, X.,-H., Chen., Z.: Summary of Network Security Technology. National Defense Industry Press, Beijing (2003)
4. Shamir, A.: Identity-based cryptosystems and signature schemes. In: Blakley, G.R., Chaum, D. (eds.) CRYPTO 1984. LNCS, vol. 196, pp. 47–53. Springer, Heidelberg (1985). https://doi.org/10.1007/3-540-39568-7_5
5. Guan, H.: Performance analysis of CPK and PKI. Netw. Comput. Secur. **8**, 17–18 (2003)
6. Zhou, J.-F., Ma, T.: Comparison and analysis of PKI, CPK and IBC. J. Inf. Eng. Univ. **6**(3), 26–31 (2005)
7. Xu, S.-W., Li, X.-Y.: A new solution to the IBC key escrow problem. Comput. Appl. Softw. **35**(9), 307–310 (2018)
8. Zhou, J.-F.: Research on Key Escrow Problem of Identity-Based Cryptography. Information Engineering University (2006)
9. Xu, L.-J.: RESEARCH and Application on Identity-Based Cryptosystem. Shandong University (2007)
10. Xu, A., Liu, G.: Security protection technology of smart substation based on SM9 identity-based cryptographic. Autom. Panorama **2**, 65–71 (2018)
11. Guo, M.-W.: Discussion on identity authentication solution of IoT. Guangdong Commun. Technol. **39**(2), 24–28 (2019)

Author Index

Printed in the United States
By Bookmasters